D1454754

Novell® NetWare® 386:
The Complete Reference

Tom Sheldon

Osborne **McGraw-Hill**

Berkeley New York St. Louis San Francisco
Auckland Bogatá Hamburg London Madrid
Mexico City Milan Montreal New Delhi Panama City
Paris São Paulo Singapore Sydney
Tokyo Toronto

Osborne **McGraw-Hill**
2600 Tenth Street
Berkeley, California 94710
U.S.A.

For information on translations or book distributors outside of the U.S.A., please write to Osborne **McGraw-Hill** at the above address.

Novell Netware 386 Complete Reference

890 DOC 99876543

ISBN 0-07-881665-3

C
O
N
T
E
N
T
S

A
T

A

G
L
A
N
C
E

CONTENTS

PART TWO   **Networking with NetWare 386, Advanced Concepts**

SEVEN   **Network Architecture and NetWare Open Systems**

PART FOUR Installing Netware

PART SEVEN Appendixes

Special thanks to Tony Selyum for technical editing. His broad knowledge of computers and the computer industry helped keep this book on course. Now that this is done, we can play 18 holes. Thanks also to Alexandra, my wife and project manager on the home front. Her high standards and copy editing skills gave the book its final touch.

Additional thanks to the following: Pattie Heiser of Novell, who was instrumental in providing important and timely information about NetWare 386. Deni Conner and Thomas Conrad Corporation for supplying network equipment and technical support as needed. Last but not least, Jeff Pepper, Jill Pisoni, and the staff at Osborne McGraw-Hill for all their help and support.

ACKNOWLEDGMENTS

Novell NetWare is a network operating system that allows computer users to connect their systems together and share resources, files, and programs. In addition, because the network forms a communications system that could be compared to a telephone system, users can exchange electronic mail and messages. At the same time, a computer network can provide a platform to accommodate emerging computer technologies. Both hardware and software vendors now see the cabling system as an attachment point for many types of computing systems.

The term *interoperability* is used to refer to the ability of diverse hardware and software systems to connect and communicate. These systems may use different operating systems (DOS, Macintosh, Unix, IBM, DEC, etc.) and are usually connected to the same network cabling system. In such a scheme, any network resource, whether it be a mainframe or personal computer, can be accessed by any user in the same way with the same interface. Files created on one system can be used on any other system without alteration. At this writing, interoperability is still in its early stages, but the acceptance of important international network standards by most vendors is an indication of its future potential and should be a consideration of anyone planning a network. The topics and discussions in this book encompass these new standards.

There is an increasing need for computer networks and information about them. Because most organizations already have a number of personal computers in place, networks are a logical growth step. This complete reference for Novell NetWare 386 is designed to fill the information gap for readers who need to know more about networks and NetWare.

About This Book

There is a wide range of information that must be gathered and studied by anyone who is planning, installing, managing, or using a Novell NetWare 386 network. This book attempts to provide as much of this information as possible. With any book of this size, a balance must be made between topics of interest to a few readers and topics of interest to many readers. Although some topics are only covered briefly, enough information is provided to help readers understand the concepts and refer to additional information in industry publications and journals. In some cases, information on leading edge products can only be obtained from the vendors of such products. Appendix D provides a list of publications and vendors.

While much of the information covered in this book is also covered in the Novell NetWare manual set, many readers will find this book useful as a tutorial or single source reference. Those familiar with NetWare know it comes with a number of manuals that may not be readily accessible, or are too cumbersome to use. In addition, the topics are arranged for reference and not as a tutorial. This book provides both a tutorial and desktop reference.

A step-by-step approach is used to introduce unfamiliar readers to networks and NetWare concepts. While the book can be opened to any page and used as a reference, each chapter is designed to build on concepts learned in previous chapters. This approach differs from the Novell NetWare manuals, which are mainly designed for reference. The Novell manuals are arranged in alphabetical order with the assumption you know exactly what you are looking for. This book attempts to place commands and other topics under headings that relate to the tasks you might be attempting to perform. For example, the numerous commands and instructions for handling files are located under a single chapter heading related to files.

This book was also written for those who are planning or installing a NetWare 386 network. Every attempt is made to provide as much information as possible to help you with your endeavor, however, it should be understood that no two network installations are alike. It is highly recommended that your final plans be reviewed by a local vendor or consultant who has experience in similar installations. This book is designed to help you arm yourself with the concepts, terms, and product knowledge you will need to talk intelligently with these experts about your particular needs.

How This Book Is Organized

This book is designed to help readers become familiar with Novell NetWare 386 and the equipment required to establish a computer network under this operating system. The following readers are addressed:

- Planners
- Installers
- Managers
- Everyday users

As mentioned previously, this book is organized to follow the procedures a system planner might use when establishing a network. Part I introduces basic network concepts and the features of Novell NetWare 386. In addition, a history of the industry and its terminology are introduced.

Part II expands on the network concepts to describe how networks operate both behind the scenes at the operating system level and at the user level. A range of networks is discussed, from those used by a small office to those used by large international organizations that span the globe. The methods and equipment used to build such networks are introduced.

Part III then covers the evaluation, planning, and purchase of a network. The first chapter in this part presents general information and points to consider. The next chapter then evaluates server hardware and the final chapter evaluates network topologies and hardware.

Part IV covers the installation of the network and NetWare 386. Installers are introduced to the installation steps and given information they will need to prepare for the installation. The installation of the server and the installation of workstations are covered in separate chapters.

Part V covers NetWare 386 commands and management techniques. Post-installation procedures that need to be performed before any user signs on are covered first. These steps include the creation of user accounts and the assignment of login restrictions and passwords. The creation of directories and the installation of applications software are also covered. Other topics include file commands, login scripts, printing, menu systems, backup procedures, and the accounting system.

Part VI covers the ongoing monitoring and maintenance of the NetWare 386 system. Managers are introduced to console commands used to track the performance of the server and network and to make adjustments to the performance. Hardware monitoring and software monitoring are covered in separate chapters. Keep in mind that the information in these chapters is presented for easy reference when a particular task needs to be performed. Unlike the Novell manuals, commands to perform specific tasks are grouped together, rather than in alphabetical order.

Conventions

You should find this book easy reading. Each chapter is split into several main topics that are listed at the beginning of each chapter. These topics are then divided into further sections. While a glossary is not provided, an extensive index will assist readers who need help with terms.

Various exercises and examples are presented throughout the book. Commands you are to type are set off from the normal text in bold. Listings from the computer are shown in a courier type that closely matches the screen display. Many illustrations are actual screen images from a NetWare 386 workstation or server. Keyboard keys are presented in small capitals, as in ENTER.

Additional Information

Writing this "complete reference" has been an attempt to present everything to everyone without becoming too vague for lack of space. Any reader who requires additional information is welcome to write me at the address below. In addition, I am interested in critiques and comments for future editions. If you would like to see other information, please let me know.

Tom Sheldon
1729 Roscoe Place
Cambria, CA 93428

This book has been written to fill the need for a single source of information on the Novell NetWare 386 operating system. You'll become familiar with the terminology and concepts of networks and how they relate to NetWare 386.

This book is of particular interest to the following:

- *Network planners.* If you are planning and designing a NetWare installation, this book will lead you through discussions of concepts, hardware components, management issues, NetWare features, and NetWare commands.

- *Network integrators and installers.* Those involved in network and NetWare installation procedures will benefit from the step-by-step instructions for getting NetWare up and running.

- *Network managers.* Network managers will benefit from topics that cover the planning, design, installation, and management of a NetWare system. This book is also a handy reference for day-to-day tasks.

- *Everyday users.* Users will find this book useful for day-to-day tasks, especially when considering that NetWare comes with only one set of manuals that are typically in demand by every user on the network.

WHY THIS BOOK IS FOR YOU

Introduction to Networking

Networking Overview

O
N
E

In the 1980s, the microcomputer caused an immense change in business and industry by giving users access to previously unavailable computing resources and information. The longstanding typewriter was practically replaced after over 100 years of service by these systems, which were appropriately dubbed "personal computers."

In the 1960s and 1970s, the computing resources and information for an entire company were often handled by a single centralized mainframe computer system. These systems were tightly controlled by an information systems department that divided its workload as it or higher-level management saw fit. The price of storage and processing was high, so many users simply never benefited from the systems. But this changed when minicomputers became available, which allowed individual departments to have their own computer systems at a fraction of the cost of mainframe systems.

Eventually personal computers caused a similar shift to the individual user's desktop. However, the information in personal computers is not easily shared and may be hard to access. In addition, useful information may be spread out among many computers, rather than integrated in a central location. So, a trend back to centralized information storage oc-

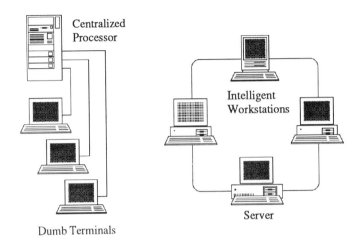

Centralized
Processor

Intelligent
Workstations

Server

Dumb Terminals

Figure 1-1.   Centralized systems (left) and network computing systems (right)

curred in the mid 1980s. Personal computers were wired together into *networks* of computers, and files were stored on centralized file systems that could be accessed by other users, as seen in Figure 1-1.

One feature stands out when you compare networks to centralized minicomputer and mainframe systems. A network consists of many computers that access files and resources from a central *server,* but each computer performs its own processing. A minicomputer or mainframe system centralizes its processing—dumb terminals rely almost completely on the central system for processing, file access, and other activities. Networks are known as *distributed processing systems* because each system can load and run programs in its own memory. Since the file server is not burdened by the need to provide processing to individual workstations, it can be optimized to provide file and network services.

Individual computers in distributed systems, called *nodes* or *workstations,* do not burden a central system because they can perform simple

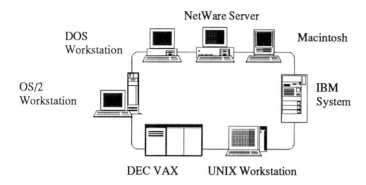

Figure 1-2. Computer networks are becoming modular platforms for the inter-connection of many different devices

to complex tasks on their own. The server is used exclusively to handle file storage and retrieval, network management tasks, user management, and security. Each individual PC logs onto the server to access programs, files, and other network services such as electronic mail.

While networks provide a better solution to the computing needs of a business, traditional minicomputers and mainframe systems are not becoming obsolete. Instead, their power is being used for intensive computing tasks by users who connect to them through the network. In fact, networks are now seen as company-wide computing *platforms* that provide the modular connectivity for different types of computing systems, as shown in Figure 1-2. Many vendors are designing and building hardware around a standard developed by the International Standards Organization (ISO) that will eventually allow any type of system to be connected to the network platform. The ISO standards are discussed in Chapter 7 for those who need to plan networks in this way.

This and the next few chapters explore exactly what a computer network is. You will learn about the basic concepts and terminology used in the world of *network computing.* Those already familiar with the basics may want to jump ahead to Chapter 4, which discusses Novell's networking strategy, and Chapter 5, which discusses Novell NetWare 386.

Why Establish a Computer Network?

What is a network? Why would a network be established? What benefits are derived from their use. This section starts with those basic questions and helps you build a better understanding of networks over the next few chapters.

A network is first a communications system that links computers and computer resources in the same way that a phone system links telephones. One of the goals of network computing is to make it as easy to connect with another network resource as it is to call another person over the phone, whether that resource is in the same building or on the other side of the globe. The resource may be a printer, plotter, or storage device. Networks minimize distance and communications problems and give users access to information anywhere on the network.

In most cases an organization already has personal computers, mini-computers, mainframes, and peripherals in place. Networks provide a convenient way to tie the systems together into a combined communications system. Advances in computer networking hardware and software technology are even allowing unrelated systems to work together. But keep in mind that a link to a network does not reduce a PC's capabilities; instead, they are enhanced when connected to a network.

The most common reasons for establishing a computer network are listed here and outlined in the following sections:

- Program and file sharing

- Network resource sharing

- Economical expansion of the PC base

- Ability to use network software

- Electronic mail

- Creation of work groups

- Centralized management

- Security

- Access to other operating systems

- Enhancement of the corporate structure

Program and file sharing   Networkable versions of many popular software packages can be purchased at considerable cost savings when compared to buying individually licensed copies. The program and its data files can be stored on the file server for access by any network user. While users can save files in personal directories, they may also save them in public directories where other users can read or edit them. A database program is an ideal application for a network. A single database file can be accessed by multiple users simultaneously. However, a feature called *record-locking* ensures that no two users edit the same record in the file simultaneously. This prevents overwriting of data if two users attempted to make changes at the same time.

Network resource sharing   Network resources include printers, plotters, storage devices, and even other computing systems such as minicomputers and mainframes. These resources are easily shared through networks.

Economical expansion of the PC base   Networks provide an economical way to expand the number of computers in an organization by using inexpensive diskless workstations that use the server's filing system instead of a built-in filing system. Through resource sharing, printers and other devices can be used by several users instead of only the user at the attached computer.

Ability to use network software   Database management software is most commonly used on networks; however, electronic mail is also important. A new class of *groupware* is becoming available. Groupware is designed for groups of users who have a need to interact with each other over the network.

Electronic mail   Electronic mail is used to send messages or documents to users or groups of users on the network. Users can more easily communicate with one another. Messages are dropped in "mailboxes" for the recipient to read at a convenient time; alarms can inform users when they have mail. Meetings can be arranged and schedules can be managed. Some electronic mail and scheduling packages can track the schedules of an entire company, allowing users to schedule their activities around those of others.

Creation of work groups   Groups of users may work in a department or be assigned to a special project. NetWare allows groups of users to be assigned special directories and resources not accessible by other users. Messages and electronic mail can be sent to each member of the group by referencing the group name.

Centralized management   Because most of the resources of a network are centered around the server, management becomes easy. Backups and file system optimization can be handled in one location.

Security   NetWare has advanced security features to ensure files are protected from unauthorized users. Diskless workstations can be used to prevent sensitive data from being downloaded to disk. Managers can prevent users from working outside their own assigned directories, and login restrictions can be applied. For example, a manager can assign a specific workstation to a user for a specific period of time. This prevents the user from logging on in an unsupervised area during an unauthorized time period.

Access to other operating systems   Novell NetWare 386 allows workstations to connect with computing systems that use different operating systems. Apple Macintosh and OS/2 users can connect to a NetWare 386 server and share files and resources in the same way as DOS users. In addition, IBM and other host systems can be connected to the network.

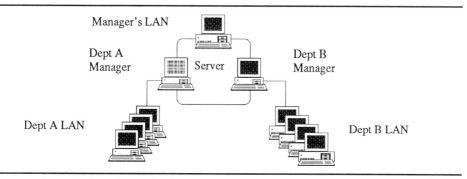

Figure 1-3.   Networks closely parallel the structure of a company

Enhancement of the corporate structure   Networks can bring about a change in the essential management structure of an organization by stimulating work group structures in which departments exist only logically within the computer management and directory structure. The actual distribution of managers, groups, and other employees is arranged to promote peer-to-peer relationships. Department managers might be grouped together outside their respective departments, while special project groups might be scattered throughout the building so members can take advantage of various company resources. In this organization the computer network links managers to their staff or groups to their leaders, as shown in Figure 1-3.

Components of a Network

A computer network consists of both hardware and software. This book covers NetWare 386 and the hardware associated with it. Each of the basic components required to build a network are discussed here and in the next two chapters. Chapters 4 and 5 discuss the features of NetWare 386.

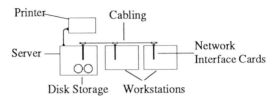

Figure 1-4.   The components of a network

A basic network is made up of the following hardware, as illustrated in Figure 1-4.

- Server

- Workstations

- Network interface cards

- Cabling system

- Shared resources and peripherals

The following sections describe each network component.

Server   The server runs the network operating system and offers network services to workstations. These services include file storage, user management, security, common network commands, system manager commands, and much more. A NetWare 386 file server must be a high-performance system that uses an 80386 or 80486 microprocessor, high-capacity disk drives, and large amounts of memory. Chapter 13 provides a complete discussion of file server systems for NetWare 386.

Workstations   When a computer is attached to a network, it becomes a node on the network and is referred to as a workstation. Workstations can be DOS-based personal computers, Apple Macintosh systems, systems running OS/2, and diskless workstations. Diskless workstations do not have floppy disk drives or hard drives. Instead, they boot directly from the server using a special boot routine on the network interface card. They are inexpensive and provide security because users cannot download files to disk.

Network interface cards (NICs)   Each computer to be attached to the network requires an interface. While an interface may be built in, in most cases it must be added as an optional item. The interface card must match the type of network being used, as discussed in the next chapter. The network cable attaches to the back of the NIC.

Cabling system   The network cabling system is the wire used to connect the server and nodes together. Cable may be coaxial cable, similar to that used for cable television, or twisted pair, like that used for a phone system. Expensive, high-speed fiber optic cable is also available, but it is most often used to connect several networks over long distances or in special high-traffic situations.

Shared resources and peripherals   Shared resources include the storage devices attached to the server, optical disk drives, printers, plotters, and other equipment that can be used by anyone on the network. NetWare 386 includes commands to share printers attached not only to the server but to workstations as well.

How Network Connections Are Made

While most organizations already have personal computers and peripherals in place, the equipment required to make connections to other systems usually must be purchased. Network connections are made to the network interface cards in each PC and server over the cable or media. The architecture of a network is defined by the cabling system, as well as the rules and method used to access that cable as discussed below.

Network Interface Cards (NICs)

Network interface cards are available from a variety of manufacturers. You can choose from several different types, depending on how you want to configure and wire your network. The three most popular network types are ARCNET, Ethernet, and Token Ring. In the old days of network computing (two or three years ago), cabling was more standardized— ARCNET and Ethernet used coaxial cable, and Token Ring used twisted pair. Today network cards can be purchased that support a range of media, which makes network planning and configuration much easier. Decisions are now based on cost, cabling distance, and topology. Topology is related to how you would draw a map of the cable through a building. A topology may include linear, circular, or star-like cable runs, as discussed later. Network cards and their topology are discussed in the next chapter.

Network Media

Network media is the cable used to connect a network. Coaxial cable was one of the first types to be used, but twisted pair has been gaining in popularity. Fiber optic cable is just coming into use for microcomputer networks. As processing requirements and network traffic increases, fiber optic cable will no doubt be used more and more:

Cables are rated for network use in several ways:

- The transmission speed or the rate it will transfer information

- Maximum cable length before a signal booster is required

- Shielding requirements

- Price

Network Architecture

The *architecture* of a network defines the layout of the cabling system and workstations attached to it, as well as the rules used to transfer signals from one network station to another. The physical layout of the cable system is known as the topology of the network. Before any station can use this cable system, it must first establish a communications session with another node on the network. This session involves the use of communication protocols to establish the session and cable access methods to send signals over the cable.

Topology

The *topology* of a network is a description of how the cable is layed out from one node to another. It is best seen as the "map" of the cabling system. Cable may be linear, running from one end of a building to another with two distinct ends like a snake, or it may be strung in a ring so it loops back on itself. Another topology is a star, in which cable branches from a central box or *concentrator*. Figure 1-5 shows each of these topologies, which are often just general descriptions. In reality, a linear cable may zig-zag through a building in all but linear fashion. A ring may do the same, but it must eventually loop back on itself.

Your most important consideration with any cable system is how it transmits signals and the method used by workstations to gain access to the cable, as discussed next.

Cable Access Method

The *cable access method* describes how a node gains access to the cable system. Linear cable systems may use a carrier sensing method, while ring and star systems may use a token passing method. When the card gains access to the cable, it begins sending packets of information to other nodes. When a network interface card is purchased, it is purchased for use with a specific topology using a specific cable access method.

The two access methods are described in the following sections.

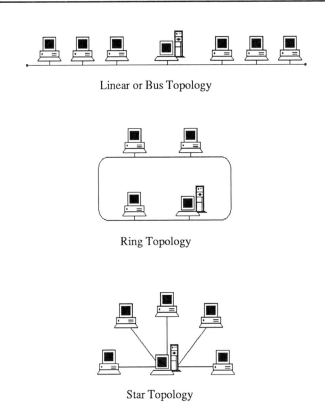

Linear or Bus Topology

Ring Topology

Star Topology

Figure 1-5.   Network topologies

Carrier sensing   The *carrier sensing method* is used mainly on linear cable systems. A node checks to see if the cable is in use before it begins transmitting. Its transmission is like a radio broadcast across the entire cable; every other node hears it and then determines whether the transmission is for it. If not, it rejects the broadcast. If two nodes broadcast at the same time, a collision occurs and both back off, wait for a random amount of time, and try again. Performance degrades when network traffic is heavy because collisions occur that require retransmission. However, published tests have shown this slowdown to be minimal unless hundreds of nodes are attached. The most common carrier sensing method is CSMA (Carrier Sense Multiple Access).

Token passing   The *token passing method* is normally used on ring networks, or networks that behave like a ring. The concept of a "token" is used to define how a node can access the cable. When a station is ready to transmit, it must wait for an available token and then take possession of the token. This prevents two machines from using the cable simultaneously. When the station has a token, it can package and address information for another station on the network. After the transmission, the token is released. Token passing systems send packets in a relay fashion. Each station examines a packet's address to determine if it is the recipient. If not, it passes the packet on to its neighbor or the next station in line. Of course, hundreds or thousands of packets may be transmitted every second.

Communications Protocols

Communications protocols are the rules and procedures used on a network to establish communications between nodes. Protocols define different levels of communications. High-level rules define how applications communicate, while low-level rules define how signals are transmitted over a cable. Communications protocols can be compared to diplomatic protocols, in which the activities of each corps member are defined by rules at his or her level. When network protocols are defined and published, vendors can easily design and manufacture network products that work on multivendor systems.

NetWare uses a form of a protocol designed by Xerox, but is moving toward the Open System Interconnection (OSI) protocol model as defined by the International Standards Organization (ISO). This model is coming into widespread use with networks and is referred to often in this book to explain how network systems connect and communicate.

When a user sends a message to another user over the network, the rules at each level of the protocol stack transform the message. As the message is prepared for transmission, an address is attached and, if the message is long, it may be split into smaller packets. The lower protocol rules make sure the other station is ready to receive the message, and then define how the transmission should be monitored by each station as it passes over the cable. At the receiving station the protocol stack defines how to reassemble and unpack the message, and then how to present it on the user's screen.

The Range of Networks

Networks come in all sizes. While a single PC attached to a printer is not considered a network, cabling two PCs to a single printer using a switchbox is, technically, a network. Most networks, however, provide many types of shared devices, services, and security for their users. Such networks may exist within a single office, throughout a building, span several buildings, or span cities and countries. The following sections describe the three levels of networking, as illustrated in Figure 1-6. Chapter 3 further describes network and internetwork connections.

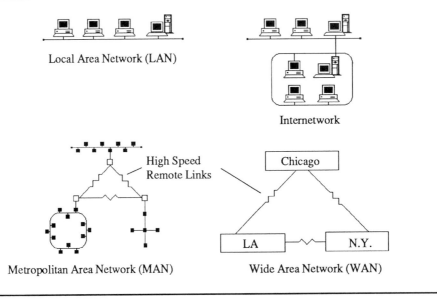

Figure 1-6.   The range of networks

Local area network (LAN)   A small network (3 to 50 nodes) usually located within a single building or group of buildings belonging to an organization.

Interconnected networks (Internetwork)   Two or more networks may be connected together to form a company-wide network system. A large network may also be split into several smaller networks in this way to optimize performance or management.

Metropolitan area network (MAN)   This is an interconnected set of LANs within a specific area, such as a campus, industrial park, or city. Special high-speed backbone cables or connection services such as the phone company may be used to connect the LANs into an internetwork.

Wide area network (WAN)   This is a network that spans countries and the globe. The airline reservations system is a good example. Large corporations that have regional or worldwide offices may interconnect their local area networks into wide area networks. WANs are typically characterized by some form of remote communications, such as high-speed phone lines, microwave dishes, or satellites.

Network Operating System Features

Early network operating systems provided simple file services and some security features. But user demands have increased, and modern network operating systems offer a wide range of services. NetWare has a reputation for being the most secure network operating system on the market and offers features normally found only in larger host systems. Hundreds of personal computers that use different operating systems may be interconnected. Although NetWare 386 is more expensive, its features are in demand by system administrators and information systems departments.

The following sections outline important and necessary features of advanced network operating systems.

File and directory services   In a network, users gain access to programs and files on a central file server. Because users have entrusted their files to this server and its managers, a high level of reliability, backup, and security must be maintained. An advanced operating system like NetWare 386 provides these features in software and supports important hardware features like system fault tolerance (SFT), as described next.

System fault tolerance   Advanced network operating systems must provide a way to ensure network survivability if components fail. With NetWare's System Fault Tolerance (SFT) feature, the server's hard drive can be mirrored by a second hard drive, thus providing continuous real-time backup. The mirrored drive can be on the same controller or a second duplexed controller. A future version of NetWare 386 will allow the entire server to be duplexed. However, recent trends in hardware design integrate mirroring and duplexing functions in the server rather than the network operating system software. The Compaq SystemPro is an example. Service on fault tolerant components can be performed by technicians who have little knowledge of the operating system.

Disk caching   Disk caching improves hard disk performance by using some system memory as a holding area for blocks from disk that may need to be accessed again. Pulling this information from memory is much faster than getting it from the hard drive.

Transaction tracking system (TTS)   A *transaction* is a change in a record or set of records in a database file. A NetWare method, *transaction tracking*, is used to protect database files from corruption should a workstation or server fail, such as during a power outage. If a complete transaction is not finished, the TTS system backs out of any changes made during the transaction and restores the database to its former state.

Security   Networks allow users to store their files in a central location, rather than in their personal hard drives or floppy disks. Because of this, the security of the filing system becomes a major consideration that must be dealt with in the network operating system. Novell NetWare provides a sophisticated and reliable password security system that can lock or limit user access to directories and files. In addition, users can be prevented from logging into workstations other than those to which they are assigned. Time restrictions can be placed on a user's session so that, for example, no user can log in after 5:00.

Resource sharing   A resource is a printer, plotter, backup system, or other device that many users need to use. A network operating system must allow access to these devices over the network so that any user can theoretically use any device elsewhere on the network.

Remote access   Networks may need to connect with workstations or other LANs at remote locations. However, using third-party communications systems may expose the network to intruders. A network must have adequate security features to ensure that only authorized users can gain access.

Bridges   Bridges allow networks to interconnect with other networks. With NetWare, bridges can be installed directly in the server by simply adding additional network interface cards. Bridges can also be located elsewhere on the network.

Gateways   Gateways allow systems with different protocols to interconnect. For example, a gateway allows a NetWare network to interconnect with an IBM mainframe system. Users on the network can then access the IBM through the gateway.

Interoperability   *Interoperability* is a movement in the networking industry that allows many types of operating systems and vendor products to share the same network cabling system. NetWare 386 provides an interim method of interoperability until the more standardized protocols defined by the OSI protocol model come into use. With NetWare 386, systems and products from a wide range of vendors can easily attach to the network.

Special servers   A network operating system should allow for special servers, such as those dedicated to handling a database or printing.

Software management tools   Software management tools are essential as networks grow in size. It may be impossible to track the activities and performance of MANs and WANs without them. One solution is to centralize managers and then give them tools to manage servers and workstations remotely.

A Behind-the-Scenes
Look at Networking

Network Computing: How It Works
Cabling the Network
Types of Networks

The network cabling system is attached to a network interface card on each workstation to provide a communications link between workstations. The workstations in turn must load a small program that defines the protocols and access methods used by the card and cable. In addition, each workstation loads a special shell that directs NetWare commands to the server and DOS commands to the local operating system.

This chapter takes a behind-the-scenes look at the protocols and access methods used by workstations as they communicate with other workstations or the NetWare file server. A basic understanding of these protocols is important for those who are developing network strategies and purchasing equipment. Many decisions are based on the protocols used by the network and the equipment attached to it.

Network Computing: How It Works

Most users are unaware of the routines that go on behind the user interface of an application. The interface hides the underlying processes with menus and screen prompts. Looking just below this layer we find the program code and routines that make it all happen. Normally this is the domain of programmers and technicians, but a quick look at the methods programmers and developers use to create applications and operating systems can shed some light on how networks work.

Protocols

All network communications are based on *protocols,* or rules. These rules define how a message to be sent is prepared, how a communications channel is established, and how the communications are managed once underway. Protocols are generally published standards defined by committees. NetWare uses an implementation of a protocol originally defined by Xerox.

In an ideal world only one set of protocols would exist, and every computer system would be able to talk with every other computer system. In reality many protocol standards exist, and computers that use these different standards cannot easily be connected together. In recent years the Open Systems Interconnection (OSI) model developed by the International Standards Organization (ISO) has come into wide acceptance. As an international standard, the OSI model promotes the development of products that can work together in a multivendor networking environment. Novell plans to implement the OSI model throughout its product line.

The OSI model defines network protocols in layers as shown in Figure 2-1. Each level contains rules and procedures that correspond to each step in the communications process. These rules are used on both sides of the connection, but in reverse order. The sender packages the information and sends it over the cable using rules starting at the top and going to the bottom of the stack. The receiver then unpacks the information and displays it on the screen using the same rules in the reverse order. These rules are described here:

- Rules at the top level determine how information in an application can be sent over a network and used by an application running on another system.

- The middle levels determine how connections are established and how packages of information, or *packets,* are sent.

Application
Presentation
Session
Transport
Network
Data Link
Physical

Figure 2-1.   The OSI protocol model

- At the bottom level are rules that define the actual transmission process through the cable.

Keep in mind that protocols are only rules that define how network communications take place. Software and hardware vendors use these rules to create products that work with other vendors' products. When programs are designed around the higher level protocol rules, an actual translation of data can take place when data is transferred between unlike systems. When only low-level rules are used, data transported over the network may be recognizable only by a specific system.

Up and Down the Protocol Ladder

Network protocols are like ladders. Information being sent passes down through the ladder on its way to the cable, while information being received climbs the ladder. The following analogy explains how a message is sent from one user to another; however, keep in mind that not all network communications are between two network users. In most cases network traffic is headed for storage on the file server or from the server file back to a workstation's memory. When a session is established between two stations, it is known as a connection-oriented session. A connectionless seesion simply sends packets without an expected response.

Almost everyone has had the opportunity to send or receive an overnight express-mail package. While the process may seem simple enough, there are underlying procedures and rules that must be followed to schedule and route packages for proper, on-time delivery. The following compares the steps in the express delivery to the seven-layer OSI protocol stack. Assume a computer user creates a document and stores it on a disk to be sent to a person in another town. The analogy is helpful in explaining the process.

1. The sender prepares the message using a word processor and labels it with the recipient's name and address.

   This step relates to the OSI level 7 application layer. Text is typed at a workstation using an application that provides a user interface. The application may be an electronic mail package that requests the name and address of the recipient.

2. The sender saves the file to disk as an ASCII (text-only) file, which is a file that can be read by any other word processor.

   This step relates to the OSI level 6 presentation rules, which are concerned with the presentation of characters, numbers, and other information. You may need to do some conversion if the data is to be used by a different type of computer or application.

3. The sender calls the express service to inform them of a package to pick up. The express service then begins coordinating the pick-up and delivery of the package. A number designates the delivery session.

   This step relates to the OSI level 5 session rules. On a network, both sending and receiving stations must use the same communications parameters. The session layer coordinates and synchronizes the two systems and maintains the communications session.

4. The sender does not need to be concerned with the activities of the delivery service, because it handles all other details of delivery. The service determines how to get the package from one place to another and in what amount of time. The sender may specify a certain level of service, such as next day or second day.

   This step relates to the OSI level 4 transport rules. The transport layer insulates higher layers from the details of networking. In some cases, an application is free to perform other tasks while data is transferred in the background.

5. The delivery service may map out the exact route the package must take to get to its destination. If the package is delivered in the same city, no intercity services are required. If the package is going across the country, the route it takes through various airport terminals is determined.

   This step relates to the OSI level 3 network rules. It is this level that defines how network information passes from one workstation to another. If an internetwork exists, packets may need to be "routed" through special devices that separate one network from another.

6. The express service arrives to pick up the package. An invoice is completed and last minute confirmations are made.

   This correlates to the transmission or data-link layer 2 of the OSI model. Data packets are prepared for delivery over the network. This level has a direct link to the network interface card and its connection to the network.

7. The package is transported by vehicle and airplane to its destination.

   This relates to the OSI level 1 physical layer, which is the cable system.

When the package arrives at the destination, the process reverses as the package is delivered to the user. The user opens the package, places the disk in a computer system, and opens the file, which is presented on the screen using an applications program.

Media Access Methods

The methods used when data packets are transferred from a workstation's memory to the physical network cable are referred to as the *media access methods*. If we can explain the delivery of packets over a network in terms of an overnight delivery service, the media access rules are like the rules of the road for the express service driver. Picture the driver pulling out of your parking lot. The driver first stops at the street and then looks both ways before proceeding.

A similar process occurs when packets are ready to move out on the network cable. The carrier sensing (CSMA) or token passing access method may be used, depending on the type of network interface card installed in the workstation and the topology of the network cable system. Both are described below:

- *Carrier sensing or CSMA (Carrier Sense Multiple Access)* A node checks to see if the cable is in use before transmitting. Also referred to as the collision detection method.

- *Token passing* A node waits for a "token" to become available, which means it can transmit its packets. This assures that no other network is transmitting.

If the express service driver were using the collision detection method, he could simply pull out on the street without looking. If a car is headed towards him, he must back up and try again later (assuming he does not get hit). The token passing method is more controlled because cable access is only given when a token arrives at a workstation. In the case of the express service driver, assume a stop light exists at the parking lot exit.

- The collision detection method usually provides higher throughput on a cable system because a workstation can simply gain access to the cable whenever required. As long as network traffic is not heavy, collisions are unlikely to occur and the network operates at a high speed.

- Token passing networks tend to be extremely reliable and maintain a constant speed, but that speed is often slower than networks using collision detection methods. The constant speed is due to the fact that only one station can use the token at once. In addition, a station cannot overuse the token, which would deprive other stations from accessing the cable.

For those who will be evaluating and purchasing network interface cards and cabling, the access method is an important consideration. If speed is the main requirement, a system using the collision detection method such as Ethernet may be appropriate. If reliability is important, a token passing scheme may be preferable.

Addressing Schemes

Each node on a network is given a special address. This address may be hard-wired by the manufacturer or selected by the user when changing switches on the card. In addition, each network has a specific address, so if two or more networks are bridged together, a node's complete address consists of its network address plus its node address, as shown in Figure 2-2. You can think of a network address as a street and a node address as a house number.

Packets

Information sent between nodes is "packaged" according to the protocol rules. At each level, information is added to packets in the form of headers and trailers. This information may include the source and destination address, communications parameters, and synchronization information. Packets usually contain 512 bytes of data plus the header and trailer information.

Newer network cards allow larger packet sizes, which increases network performance. If a message is broken into many small packets, they must be reassembled at the receiving station, which degrades performance. If packets are large, less packets are sent. Packet size on NetWare 386 may be as high as 4202 bytes.

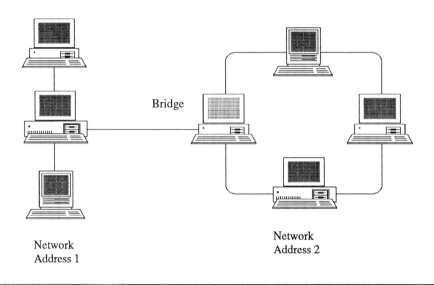

Figure 2-2.   Network addressing schemes

Cabling the Network

The cable used to connect networks is often referred to as the network *media.* You can classify the types of cable in terms of the following factors:

- Transmission speed

- Maximum length

- Shielding against interference

The three most popular cable types are copper twisted pair, copper coaxial, and optical fiber. Each type is discussed in the following sections.

Twisted Pair

Twisted pair wire is exactly that—two insulated strands of copper wire braided together and, in most cases, wrapped in a protective shield. The twisting reduces the electrical interference. Most telephone wiring is twisted pair, and it has recently been put to use as a connection media for networks. While twisted pair wire has a slow transmission rate and limited length for networks, you should consider it for the following reasons:

- Twisted pair is already installed in many buildings as telephone cable. A bundle of these wires usually contains unused pairs that can be used for network cabling. Most important, the cable usually branches from a centralized wiring closet and runs to the location of workstations. This wiring closet can become the network wiring center.

- While transmission speed of twisted pair has been slow, recent advances in network card technology have allowed manufacturers to boost this speed, thus making twisted pair a viable solution for networking.

- Twisted pair is easily combined with other cable types to form extended networks. For example, the wiring closets for two separate departments could be interconnected with a long coaxial cable, thus forming two linked networks.

Coaxial Cable

Coaxial cable is commonly used in cable television networks. It consists of a copper core surrounded by insulation. This in turn is surrounded by a braided metal sleeve that helps block interference. The entire cable is then wrapped in a protective cover. Some building codes require that this cable be fire safe when used in plenum spaces. When burned, cable of this type does not produce toxic gases that might pass through the air supply of buildings.

There are several types of coaxial cable that may be either thick or thin. Long network trunks can be designed with thick cable; however, it is more expensive than thin cable which has a shorter potential distance. The transmission speed of coaxial cable, can be high, but the higher this rate is, the less the potential distance. While ARCNET cabling has a slow transmission speed, it has a greater distance than Ethernet.

Fiber Optic Cable

Fiber optic cable transmits data signals with light. The modulated light passes through a glass core, which is surrounded by a reflective cladding. This assembly is in turn surrounded by a protective covering. Transmission rates for networks are usually in the range of 100M bits-per-second, but rates as high as 500M bits-per-second are used in some special applications. Fiber optic cable is not affected by interference and cannot be monitored, which is useful in high-security situations.

Types of Networks

Network planners and managers who are purchasing network equipment and cabling must evaluate the type of network they will use. A combination of features, including the access methods, cable type, and topology, must be considered before purchasing network interface cards. Three of the most popular network types, Ethernet, ARCNET, and Token Ring are discussed in this section.

Network interface cards and cabling systems are usually designed around the specifications of the Institute of Electrical and Electronics Engineers (IEEE). The IEEE Project 802 consists of a set of committees that defines several methods of controlling access to the physical transmission medium, four of which are listed here:

- The 802.3 committee defines a family of carrier sensing standards such as CSMA/CD for Ethernet.

- The 802.4 committee defines a token passing standard over a bus topology.

- The 802.5 committee defines a token passing standard over a ring topology such as IBM Token Ring.

- The 802.6 committee defines high-speed fiber optic networks for campus-wide or metropolitan areas.

Many vendors now offer twisted pair network cards for networks that traditionally support coaxial cable. The 802.3 committee is in the process of defining a new network standard for twisted pair Ethernet called 10BASE-T that should be complete by the time you read this.

Ethernet Networks

An Ethernet LAN uses a linear (bus) topology that typically consists of a single trunk of coaxial cable. A carrier sensing access method with collision detection (CSMA/CD) is used. Ethernet has a transmission rate of 10M bits-per-second.

There are two types of coaxial cable used in Ethernet: thick and thin. While thin cable is cheaper than thick cable, its maximum length is 185 meters (607 feet). Thick cable permits longer cable runs of 500 meters (1640 feet). This section discusses thin Ethernet cable, which is more commonly used in small LANs. Thick cable is often used as a *backbone* to connect multiple networks over wide distances.

Thin Ethernet cable is wired in cable segments from one workstation to the next to form a single linear trunk. The ends of each cable segment are fitted with a BNC-type twist-on connector, which plugs into a T-connector on the back of the network interface card, as shown in Figure 2-3. The farthest ends of the trunk are fitted with terminators, one of which is grounded.

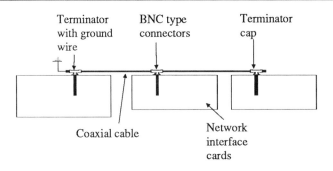

Figure 2-3. An Ethernet thin wire configuration

Ethernet networks also can be built using twisted pair and fiber optic cable. Additionally, combinations of cable may be used. For example, fiber optic cable may be used to join two distant Ethernet networks wired with thin coaxial cable.

ARCNET Networks

ARCNET networks commonly use coaxial cable, but most interface card vendors now support the use of twisted pair, which is a more practical solution for short distances. ARCNET networks are token passing with a bus topology, but hubs are used to distribute workstations in a star-like configuration as seen in Figure 2-4. As with Ethernet coaxial cable, ARCNET segments are attached to cards and hubs using BNC-type twist-on connectors.

Both passive and active hubs are used to distribute workstations from a central point. Nodes can be connected up to 609 meters (2000 feet) from an active hub and up to 30 meters (100 feet) from a passive hub. Passive hubs usually have four ports; active hubs usually have eight ports. The hub concept provides a unique way to distribute workstations. For example, active hubs can be used to distribute workstations within a single department. Each department's active hub then can be connected to a linear "backbone" segment to create an extended network, as shown in Figure 2-5.

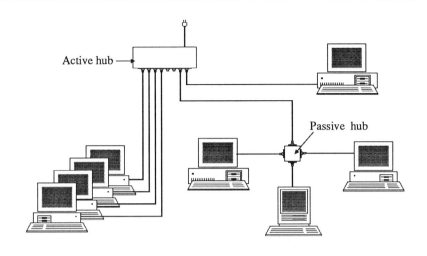

Figure 2-4.   An ARCNET configuration

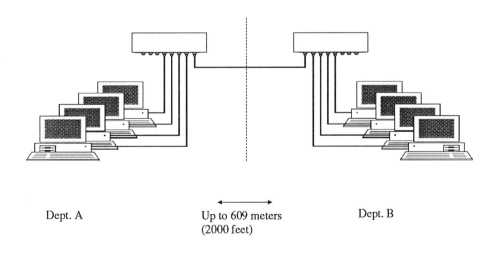

Figure 2-5.   ARCNET allows for the flexible distribution of workstations throughout a building

ARCNET workstations use a token passing scheme to access the network. However, the token does not travel in a physical ring but a logical one. Each workstation is assigned a number and the token passes to each workstation in the correct numeric order, even if the stations are not physically connected in that order.

Token Ring Networks

Token Ring networks are exactly what their name implies: A token passing access scheme is used on a ring topology. However, Token Ring can take on the appearance of a star topology since stations can branch from a central hub, or multistation access unit (MAU) as IBM calls it. Special shielded cable is normally used, but unshielded telephone-type twisted pair is also supported. Existing telephone wire makes an excellent media for Token Ring.

Token Ring as it comes from IBM is rated at 4M bits-per-second or 16M bits-per-second. The equipment required to run the faster Token Ring

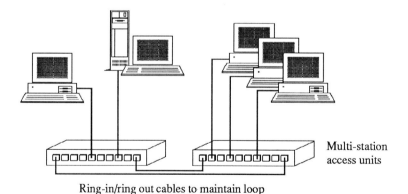

Multi-station access units

Ring-in/ring out cables to maintain loop

Figure 2-6. A Token Ring configuration

network is more expensive, and unshielded twisted pair wire cannot be used. The total length of the entire ring cannot exceed 366 meters (1200 feet) and the maximum distance a station can be placed from a MAU is 100 meters (330 feet) using shielded twisted pair wire.

A typical Token Ring configuration is shown in Figure 2-6. Two MAU units are connected together. Up to eight workstations may then be attached to each MAU. Since the logical ring must always be maintained for token passing, the two MAUs are connected together using special ring-in and ring-out ports.

Expanding the Network

Expanding and Interconnecting LANS
Making Remote Connections

A local area network (LAN) is usually contained within a single building and built on one type of network card and cable. Expanding the network is often a simple matter of adding workstations. However, a LAN has limits to the length of its cable and the number of attached workstations. Performance can degrade if too many workstations are attached.

Such limitations call for an expansion of the LAN, which can be done in several ways. A *repeater* can extend the distance of a LAN by boosting its signals to accommodate longer distances. A *bridge* may interconnect two LANs or divide an overloaded LAN into two separate trunks. A *router* is a bridge-like device that interconnects several LANs and provides the best possible routes for packets to follow when traversing the interconnection.

Other requirements may call for the connection to a LAN in a distant part of the same building. While this can be done with a repeater, long-distance fiber optic links may be preferable. When you need to connect with workstations or LANs located on the other side of a campus or city, you can establish a metropolitan area network (MAN) using *remote connections,* such as telephone, microwave, or satellite connections. Similarly, *Wide area networks* (WANs) that are regional, national, or global in size may be connected using similar remote connection methods.

Connections can be made to a minicomputer, mainframe, or other systems that use different operating systems and protocols, thus forming a *gateway.*

This chapter discusses these connections in two sections. The first section describes network interconnection methods for the local environment. The second section describes remote connections.

Expanding and Interconnecting LANs

This section explains the use of repeaters, bridges, routers, and gateways. The basic concepts of each are covered here, and Chapter 9 contains a more complete discussion.

Repeaters

As mentioned earlier, a repeater boosts the signal of a cable to allow the LAN to extend beyond its normal limits. The unit is usually a small box with a cable-in and cable-out connection. Typically used on Ethernet networks, repeaters are available for ARCNET and Token Ring networks as well.

Bridges

A bridge allows two or more separate and distinct LANs to be connected. Bridges can also split a large LAN into two separate LANs to increase performance. In NetWare a bridge is formed by simply adding two or more network interface cards in the server, as shown in Figure 3-1. Other bridge features are listed here:

- Bridges can connect different types of networks. Figure 3-2 illustrates the bridging of three separate networks, two of which are Ethernet and one Token Ring.

- Bridges located in NetWare servers are referred to as *internal bridges,* while *external bridges* are established in separate workstations on the LAN.

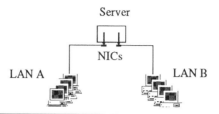

Figure 3-1.   A bridge can split a large LAN into two separate LANs to increase performance and database

- Bridges are also widely available from non-Novell sources. They can provide sophisticated functions managers may require when building large internetworks. For example, up to 80% of network traffic is usually meant for a local LAN. Bridges can provide filtering techniques to keep specific network traffic within certain boundaries, thus reducing bottlenecks.

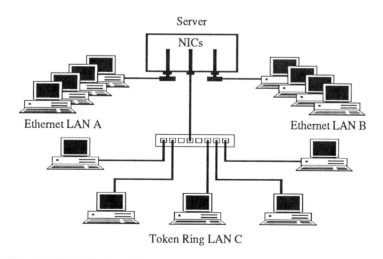

Figure 3-2.   A bridge interconnects different types of networks

Note that bridged connections use the data link layer of a protocol stack like the OSI stack discussed in Chapter 2. Higher- level protocols are not involved, so bridges can pass any type of network traffic at high speeds, including packets from systems that use different protocol stacks.

Backbones

Backbones are special high-performance connections used to link servers in an internetwork, as shown in Figure 3-3. The most important characteristics of backbones are as follows:

- Backbones are high-performance links such as fiber optic or coaxial cables.

- A backbone cable is connected to an interface card that is separate from the one used to connect workstations.

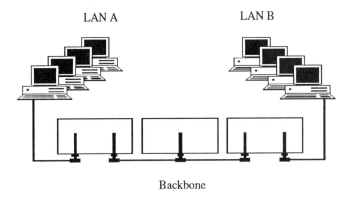

Figure 3-3. Backbones link servers in an internetwork

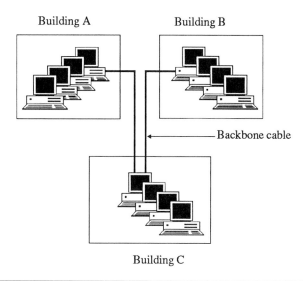

Building A   Building B

Backbone cable

Building C

Figure 3-4.   Backbones can provide long-distance, high-speed links between servers

- Workstations are never attached to the backbone segment.

- Backbones can be short lengths of cable used to connect servers that are grouped at a single location for management reasons.

- Backbones can provide long-distance connections that provide high-speed links between servers, as shown in Figure 3-4.

Modular Systems

Modular units for the interconnection of a wide range of computer networks are available from various manufacturers. These units centralize the connection of networks and in most cases provide network management software that can monitor and filter network traffic. The units provide a built-in backbone in the form of a data bus with plug-in slots. The units can also be connected with similar units at other locations with a backbone cable.

Routers

There are both advantages and disadvantages to expanding a network. More resources become available to network users, and communication between users can increase on a city, regional, national, or global scale. But managing such a large network can be a problem. Management becomes easier if the large interconnected LAN is logically divided into smaller domains. For example, one group of users may be prohibited from accessing the internetwork, while another group may be allowed to access only one other segment besides their local LAN.

Routers can help to logically divide LANs in this way. In addition, routers can be used to direct network traffic along the best possible routes or to divide traffic along two separate routes. Large LANs use redundant links to ensure interconnections of the LANs. If one link goes down, the other can take over. But dual links can cause loopbacks in the traffic that degrade or even stop the flow of network traffic. Routers can cut off traffic in one link until needed, such as when the other fails.

A router configuration for three separate LANs is shown in Figure 3-5. The routers connect each network to the other two networks and block traffic that may attempt to loop back through the triangular configuration. If one of the links, such as router A to router C, fails, traffic between A and C can be rerouted through the middle router B.

Routers can be used for both local, metropolitan, or wide area networks. Routers work at the network layer of a protocol stack, which means that the addressing information of packets can be monitored and used to manage the network.

Gateways

A gateway is a connection point and translator between two different types of protocols. The connection of a NetWare LAN to an IBM or DEC minicomputer or mainframe is a good example. When a system is connected through a gateway to a LAN, users at any workstation can access the system.

A gateway to an IBM SNA host system from an IBM Token Ring LAN is shown in Figure 3-6.

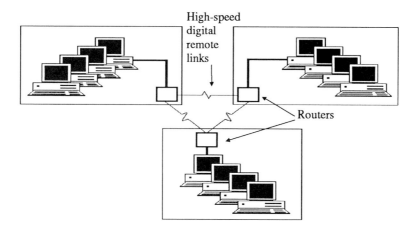

Figure 3-5.   Routers can be used to manage packet transmission between multiple interconnected networks

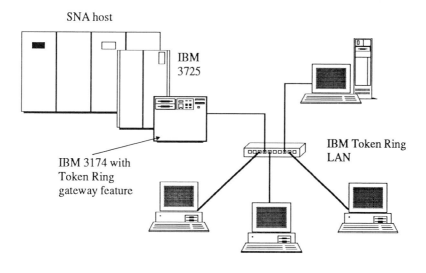

Figure 3-6.   Gateways provide links between systems that use different operating systems and communications protocols

Making Remote Connections

A remote connection is defined in this chapter as one requiring a connection other than a direct-connect cable. Remote connections may be established through the phone system or with microwave dishes and satellites. Connections range in size from a single user who needs to access the LAN from home to an entire LAN. This section describes the range of connections and some of the techniques used to make the connections.

The following methods can be used to establish remote connections:

- Point-to-point voice-grade telephone lines.

- Public data networks like Tymnet and Telenet with packet-switching techniques that use X.25 protocols.

- High-speed lines like Digital Data Service (DDS) and T1.

The last two methods may use a combination of circuit-switching lines, microwave communications, or satellite.

Connecting Remote Workstations

A single user or a group of users may need to access the LAN from a remote site. Traveling salesmen or users who need to do work from home can make simple workstation-to-LAN connections using modems and standard telephone lines, as shown in Figure 3-7.

Both the security and transmission speed of such connections must be considered. NetWare provides security through login restrictions for remote users, similar to those for local users. Novell communications software also calls back a remote user after an initiating call to ensure that the remote site is the one that has been authorized to log in. Regarding the communications rate, high speed modems should be used whenever possible. In addition, packages such as Norton-Lambert Close-Up or PC-Any-Ware allow remote workstations to access the network as if they were

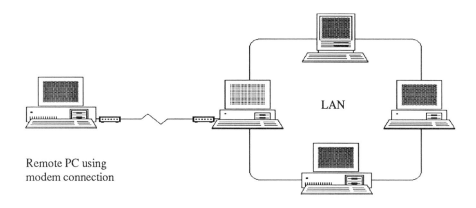

Figure 3-7.   A modem can allow a single user to connect with a LAN from a remote site

attached locally. Only screen information and keyboard commands are transmitted over the connection, thus improving access. These packages do require that a local machine be dedicated to handle the processing tasks of the remote user.

LAN to LAN Remote Connections

Wide area connections are made between LANs at remote locations so files can be shared and electronic mail can be sent to users at the remote sites. When a remote LAN-to-LAN connection is made, a workstation on each LAN is usually dedicated as a remote bridge. The remote connection software is then run exclusively in the bridge. This configuration is shown in Figure 3-8.

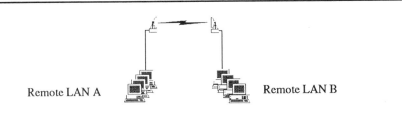

Figure 3-8.   High-performance connections can be used to link LANs with LANs

When LANs are connected to other LANs, more than one user will most likely need to use the bridge at the same time. Therefore, it is important that the right level of communications be determined so the appropriate equipment, software, and connections can be made. Decisions are based on the following:

- Number of users who need to access the connection.

- Type of applications and file access.

- Will files be transferred?

- Will electronic mail be used?

If it is determined that the remote connection will have a lot of activity, high-speed lines are essential. Periodic activity may allow the use of lower-speed, less expensive lines. Each is discussed below.

Types of Connections

The line speed of the connection usually determines what type of connection is used. Standard modems transmit at speeds of 2400 and 9600 baud, which is usually inadequate for LAN-to-LAN connections. Several other methods are described in the following sections.

Packet-Switched Networks

Just as a network allows many users to attach to and use a common cabling system, public data networks allow users to call into a worldwide communications network that provides high-speed, relatively inexpensive voice and data transmission capabilities. Call-in nodes are located in most major cities. Such networks are operated by the government in many countries but are privately operated in the United States. The operator leases time on the networks. The services use existing telephone lines, microwaves, and satellite equipment.

A method called *packet switching* is used to transmit information, as opposed to *circuit switching*. A circuit-switched line is like the dedicated voice line you would use to call a friend in the same town. These lines remain open to service a single call until the callers hang up. The lines may then be used to create another connection. Packet switching, on the other hand, shares connections between nodes with multiple users to optimize the line and reduce the rate. Voice and data are divided into packets that are transmitted constantly over the network. Packets from many different calls may be intermixed as they traverse the lines, but this assures that there is no idle time on the connection. The receiving end must sort, reassemble, and distribute the packets to the appropriate callers.

System designers can use packet-switched data services to form internetwork connections. An international standard called X.25 is used to access packet-switched networks. Because packet-switched lines are nondedicated, they can be accessed and used only when necessary. Charges are often made according to the number of packets sent. New, faster asynchronous modems that use new encoding methods are competing with X.25, however. Speeds can be as high as 64K bits-per-second.

Direct Digital Service Lines (DDS)

Direct digital service lines operate at speeds up to 56K bits-per-second in the United States and 64K bits-per- second in Europe. DDS lines are highly reliable, using a synchronous protocol. They generally cost more to implement than X.25 methods; however, the increased speed may be necessary when LANs must transfer files or provide direct file access.

T1 and T3 Links

T1 and T3 links are high-speed digital lines used when high performance is required between remote sites. T1 transfer speeds of up to 1.544M bits-per-second are available in the United States, and up to 2.048M bits-per-second are available in Europe. T1 can be used when immediate access to the most current information is required. T1 lines can also be subdivided into multiple channels that support voice, video, and data.

Newer T3 links can provide rates up to 44.736 M bits-per-second. T3 rates are appropriate for corporations who need to centralize their data processing facilities for mission-critical applications. Remote users need high-speed links to maintain a reasonable level of performance.

Novell Networking Strategies

Adapted from the *Netware Buyer's Guide*

F
O
U
R

History of NetWare
Strategies for the 1990s

Novell was founded in 1983 with the primary goal of developing products that could be used to network personal computers. From this beginning, the company's products have grown to become industry standards. Important advances in NetWare allowed networks to grow from departmental systems to company-wide internetworks. This chapter discusses Novell's networking strategies and trends in the network industry.

Novell has adopted a *network computing* strategy for the 1990s. This strategy aims to expand networking to the corporate-wide level by allowing non-DOS systems such as the Apple Macintosh, OS/2, Unix workstations, and others to be connected as a unified network. Systems on the network will be able to share resources and files without regard to the type of operating system running on the workstation. Minicomputers and mainframes from DEC and IBM also will be part of the network computing platform, sharing their resources and computing power.

Part of Novell's strategy is to see the network itself, not just a server, as a modular platform for development and expansion. In this way data and services can be distributed anywhere in the network for access by any user. For example, a user at a DOS workstation on a NetWare network using IPX protocols could access files on a Unix system attached to a network running TCP/IP protocols. The network itself is seen as a sort of "plug-and- play" device to which any type of computer running any type of operating system can be attached.

This type of platform provides an ideal environment for *distributed applications* in which several computers on the network share a processing task. For example, imagine a complex simulator program distributing parts of its processing load to idle workstations. This is in sharp contrast to old centralized processing systems where the central computer performed the processing for all the terminals. Eventually the combined computing power of a network platform running the right application could exceed the processing power of most minicomputers and mainframes.

Future distributed applications will take advantage of idle computing systems so there is no waste of processing power. Complex tasks will not be confined to a single machine; instead, any system on the network might take part in a processing task. Of course, this type of processing will require advanced software that is not yet available, but protocols and standards are being defined now to make such applications possible. Program-to-program communications and interaction across machine and operating system boundaries will be essential. This is the future of Novell NetWare.

History of NetWare

Novell NetWare was announced in 1983, the same year IBM announced its XT personal computer and IBM PC DOS 2.0. Each of these products set new standards. The IBM XT was the first personal computer from IBM to include a hard drive, while IBM PC DOS 2.0 was the first PC operating system to support hard drives without the need for special patches. The XT and DOS 2.0 created an environment for the development of sophisticated PC-based applications and products. NetWare was to become the network operating system of choice for these systems.

Novell originally developed NetWare to run on a Motorola MC68000 microprocessor-based server using the Novell S-Net network configuration. When DOS 2.0 and the IBM XT were announced, many companies including Novell saw the opportunity for product development. Since NetWare was written in C, a so-called "portable" programming language, Novell was able to easily port some of the code from its existing NetWare to the new system.

However, the DOS/Intel 8088 environment is not the best environment to run multiuser applications, especially a multiuser operating system like NetWare. The BIOS (Basic Input/Output System) was designed for the original PC (and required for DOS) as a single-user system. Novell made an important decision to bypass the I/O system altogether and create an operating system that would run more effectively in multi-user mode. Because of this, NetWare was written for the hardware of 8088-based systems, bypassing DOS and its I/O system. This strategy has been Novell's good fortune ever since. Other companies that wrote their network operating systems to run under DOS have been plagued by its limitations.

The trade-off for Novell was the need to write and consistently update drivers to give users DOS compatibility. These problems were quickly overcome with the use of DOS *shells* at the workstations. Shells allow users to run DOS in the normal way but issue NetWare commands as well. The shell intercepts network commands and directs them to the server. Almost all DOS applications can be run under the NetWare operating system through the DOS shell. In addition, security features and redundancy features, which are impossible to design into the DOS file structure, have become a mark of excellence for NetWare.

In the meantime Novell improved NetWare as hardware technology improved. NetWare 286 runs in the more efficient protected mode on the 80286 processor. In 1989 Novell announced NetWare 386, the first operating system to take full advantage of the Intel 80386 microprocessor. The 80386 is especially adaptable to multiuser environments like networks. Novell has placed the new 386 operating system at the top of its product line, not only because it is the most powerful network operating system, but also because the 80386 processor (and the 80486) is an ideal platform for network operating system development.

Strategies for the 1990s

Novell's strategy has always been to accelerate the growth of networking. In the past it developed hardware products to encourage growth in important areas of networking, and then left the manufacturing of those products to other vendors. Some of these vendors soon became important suppliers of products in the expanding network marketplace.

Novell's strategy for the 1990s revolves around network computing. This section explores software, hardware, and network management technology that Novell and other companies will develop over the next few years. Because Novell is a major force in the network industry, their corporate strategy can be considered an important indicator of the direction the entire industry is taking. Recent surveys and estimates indicate that Novell NetWare is used at approximately 60% of the existing network installation sites. The remaining 40% are shared by products such as 3COM's 3+Open and 3+Share, Banyan Vines, IBM PC LAN, and others.

The driving force behind Novell's network computing strategy is an architecture known as *NetWare Open Systems.* NetWare Open Systems dictates the following:

- Make the services provided by NetWare available on expanding platforms

- Make NetWare protocol independent by supporting important industry standards such as TCP/IP and the OSI protocol stack

- Provide integrated routing and wide area networking

- Keep the architecture open and provide development tools that can be used to create applications that operate in a distributed, network computing environment.

Novell plans to implement this strategy by providing or supporting server platforms, open architecture, open protocol technology, and NetWare services. *NetWare services* refers to the NetWare operating system itself, which is available as NetWare 386 or Portable NetWare. NetWare 386 operates on Intel 80386 and 80486 based systems, while Portable NetWare allows NetWare services to be implemented under operating systems such as Unix, VMS, and OS/2.

Network Computing

Because NetWare has become established in many organizations as a platform for integrating personal computer systems, a logical step is to use this same platform to expand an entire organization's computing power. A wide variety of computers may exist, including host systems from IBM and DEC, as well as desktop systems like the Macintosh or personal computers running DOS and OS/2. With network computing, these systems can be interconnected to allow data, applications, and processing power to be shared by any machine connected to the network.

The goal of network computing is to provide transparent access to the data and resources of any computing system from any other system. The key is to use the existing network as the platform to build these new integrated services. Transparency is made difficult by conflicting hardware and software standards, different media and protocol standards, as well as unique operating systems. Since it is unlikely that only one networking or operating system will become an industry standard, only operating systems that allow users to integrate multiple standards can provide network computing solutions.

Novell NetWare achieved part of this goal early in its development by supporting media independence and a strategy it calls *open protocol technology* (OPT). Media independence allows NetWare to run over 30 different types of networks on more than 100 different network adapters. Open protocol technology allows NetWare to support DOS, OS/2, and Macintosh computers on the same network with future plans for Unix workstations. OPT also provides a smooth migration to industry standard protocols such as TCP/IP and OSI.

NetWare Server Operating Systems

Because businesses have different needs, no one type of computer system can be expected to fit them all. Large departmentalized businesses may have different computing needs within each department. Some may even wish to convert their existing minicomputers into servers to maximize the performance of a network. As a result, Novell makes the NetWare operating system available in several forms, as described in the next sections.

NetWare 386

Novell NetWare 386 is a completely rewritten version of NetWare designed to take advantage of the Intel 80386 and 80486 environments. Performance is increased two to three times over previous versions of the operating system. Future versions will expand on the network computing concept and provide an optimized environment for distributed applications development. NetWare 386 is optimized for network use and future growth and will no doubt set new standards.

Portable NetWare

Portable NetWare is a C version of the NetWare services that runs on a host operating system, unlike NetWare 386, which runs on Intel 80386 and 80486 processors. Portable NetWare can run on a variety of general-purpose operating systems, including Unix-based minicomputers and OS/2-based application servers. Portable NetWare is a licensed product. It is ported to a system and sold by the system manufacturers through their own distribution channels.

NetWare for VMS

NetWare for VMS, which was announced in 1988, allows NetWare services to run on the DEC VAX/VMS platform. Users can log into VAX servers, access VMS data transparently, and use VMS applications through terminal emulation.

Open Protocol Technology

Novell's open protocol technology (OPT) provides a way to use multiple protocols on a network. This is an important consideration when there is a need to interconnect network components that normally operate under different operating systems. OPT also provides a migration path to future protocol standards such as the Open Systems Interconnection (OSI) model developed by the International Standards Organization (ISO). When the OSI model is fully adopted, network hardware and software from a multitude of vendors will be able to connect into a network.

Novell's OPT provides a unique solution to the problem of integrating multiple standards now and as the OSI model evolves into industry-wide acceptance. The OPT strategy seeks to provide independence from the network media, transport protocols, client- server protocols, and operating systems. This independence is discussed in the following sections.

Media Independence

Novell introduced the concept of media independence in 1983 by allowing NetWare to recognize network adapters made by different manufacturers. This strategy allowed NetWare to run on a variety of network hardware, so NetWare quickly became a major network operating system. Today more than 100 network adapter drivers are certified to work with NetWare, and many of these drivers are included with the software.

Early versions of NetWare also provided internetwork bridging. A bridge allows two or more separate networks to be joined into one internetwork. In this way, users on an Ethernet network, for example, could transparently connect with users on a Token Ring network.

Transport Protocol Independence

Transport protocols define the rules for "transporting" packets of information from one workstation to another. They include the media access protocols discussed in previous chapters. Transport protocols are a form of peer-to-peer communications between two systems. Novell's transport protocol is the Internetwork Packet Exchange (IPX), but other protocols that may need to be taken into consideration when establishing a multi-vendor internetwork are

- Apple Computers AppleTalk

- IBM's NetBEUI/DLC

- IBM's Systems Network Architecture (SNA)

- Industry standard TCP/IP

- The emerging Open Systems Interconnection (OSI) protocols

Protocol independence is an important step in the development of NetWare and is as important in scope as the introduction of media independence. It allows a NetWare 386 network to use more than one communications protocol on the same adapter and provides increased flexibility when designing a network. NetWare 386 will become protocol independent with version 3.1. The two components of NetWare's architecture that make this possible are open data-link interface and NetWare Streams, as described in the following sections. For additional information refer to Chapter 7.

Open Data-Link Interface   This specification is designed to allow NetWare to send and receive multiple protocols on the same adapter. It is an interim solution that provides a migration path to OSI. As an example, an adapter might support IPX/SPX, TCP/IP, and AppleTalk concurrently. At the bottom level are network interface cards that receive or send different protocol packets using a multiple link interface driver (MLID) which is written by the vendor of the interface card. The MLID then passes the information in the packet to the link support layer (LSL). The LSL is like a switchboard—it routes the packet information to the appropriate protocol stack. In Figure 4-1, an IPX and TCP/IP protocol stack exists. The

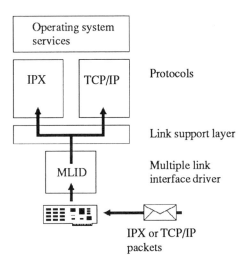

Figure 4-1.   Open protocol technology allows several protocols to exist on a NetWare network

packet information passes through and is interpreted by the protocol stack in the normal way. At the top, the information is given to the NetWare operating system.

NetWare Streams   NetWare Streams provides the same set of interfaces as the open data-link interface, but at a higher level that supports interprocess communications (IP) for server-based applications. NetBIOS, Named Pipes, and AT&T's Transport Library Interface (TLI) are examples of protocol-dependent mechanisms that allow the remote processes of distributed applications to communicate. Novell provides support for these IPC mechanisms within the Streams environment, thus allowing applications written to them to run in the protocol-independent environment of NetWare.

Planned Support for Industry Standards

Novell supports TCP/IP and OSI as part of its protocol independence strategy. Under TCP/IP, NetWare will include support for Telnet, FTP, SMTP, the R series utilities, and other recognized TCP/IP applications. In the OSI environment, Novell will support the most popular OSI applications protocols, such as X.400.

Novell also plans to support IBM's Systems Applications Architecture (SAA) which defines standards for application interfaces, user interfaces, and communications protocols between IBM computing systems. Chapter 7 provides additional information.

Client-Server Protocol Independence

The NetWare Core Protocol is a client-server model that delivers NetWare services (see "NetWare Services" below) to DOS and OS/2 users. Client-server protocols define the rules that apply when a workstation (the client) makes a request from the server. Clients make requests and servers fill them.

Other client-server protocols exist, such as the Apple's AppleTalk Filing Protocol (AFP) for Macintosh systems and Sun Microsystem's Network File System (NFS) for Unix clients. Novell will support these and other client-server protocols in future releases of NetWare to ensure that the operating system running at a workstation can access the services of a NetWare server. This strategy gives network designers flexibility to maintain or add stations that use operating systems other than DOS.

NetWare Services

NetWare services are the core of a NetWare Open Systems network. They include file, print, and security services among others, as described in the following sections.

File and Print Services

NetWare's file system allows multiple users to access shared files on a NetWare server. Clients can be DOS, OS/2, and Macintosh workstations. In addition, support for Unix workstations is planned. The file system can provide up to 32 terabytes of disk storage on volumes that can span multiple physical disk drives. In addition, NetWare's system fault tolerance (SFT) feature increases system reliability. SFT allows disks to be mirrored or an entire physical disk and controller to be duplexed, as discussed in Chapter 5. Future versions of NetWare will allow an entire server to be mirrored.

Novell print services allow workstations to use printers attached to the server or attached to individual workstations. A workstation can become a print server and service print jobs from other workstations. In this way printer management can be distributed and print jobs can take place at printers closer to the users that initiate them.

Communications Services

Novell provides a complete set of communications services for network users. These services are available as add-on packages in most cases. Through LAN-to-host links, workstations can go over the network to access a minicomputer or mainframe system. Through LAN-to-LAN links, wide area networks can be constructed to allow users to communicate with other users, file servers, and resources on other networks. Remote links allow users to connect into a network from a workstation at a remote site.

Database Services

Part of Novell's network computing solution is to provide back-end database services that run on the server. The following products are available:

- NetWare Btrieve is a key-indexed record manager that supports high-performance data handling for several data management applications.

- SQL provides back-end database services for many front-end applications, including Lotus 1-2-3 version 3.0 and others. A NetWare loadable module (NLM) for NetWare 386 is planned.

Store-and-Forward Services

When direct connections are established between LANs, messages can usually be sent from a workstation on one LAN to a workstation on another in real time. However, it may not be feasible to maintain a constant real-time connection between LANs. In this case *store-and-forward messaging* can collect messages and distribute them to users during an established communications session.

The NetWare message handling service (MHS) collects and delivers messages to like and unlike systems on local and wide area networks. In the future Novell will provide a gateway to enable PC LAN-based message products to communicate with OSI-compatible mail systems. These products are discussed further in Chapter 11.

Management Services

Management services allow users on large internetworks to access the services of any server. In addition, network managers can manage servers and workstations through the network. Management Services are described in the following sections.

Distributed Directory Services

A distributed directory service keeps track of all network users, servers, and resources on large internetworks. This information is kept in a "global" database. By accessing the database, users can determine which services they need and quickly access them, without regard to their location. All NetWare Open Systems products will adhere to the distributed directory service.

Distributed directory service is designed with large internetworks in mind. It provides centralized management of the entire network directory with a common naming service. A directory database is updated at regular intervals. The service is based on the OSI X.500 protocol standards, but provides gateways to other directory services, including Apple Name Binding Protocol, Sun Microsystems' Yellow Pages (NFS support), the TCP/IP Domain Name Service, and the current NetWare directory service. These products are discussed further in Chapter 11.

System Management

Under NetWare Open Systems, Novell plans to integrate network management functions with directory services to provide full network management capabilities. Management can be distributed so that each network platform is managed on its own, or management can be centralized so it can be handled by a single management staff.

Novell will provide management products that enable network managers to manage all the NetWare services. Centralized bidirectional management will be provided by a gateway between NetWare management services and IBM's NetView or systems based on OSI, such as DEC's Enterprise Management Architecture and AT&T's Universal Network Management Architecture.

Security Management

As networks expand to include many corporate-wide resources, security becomes an issue. Novell NetWare has always provided a high level of security; however, with NetWare 386, security is expanded even further with the following improvements.

Encryption   Passwords are encrypted before crossing the cable to prevent unauthorized cable taps from determining a user's password.

Authentication   When a user logs into a NetWare 386 system, an identification key is assigned to the account. These keys are assigned dynamically for each login session and allow NetWare to confirm a user's identity each time a service or access to data is requested.

Authorization   An authorization process must be completed before a user is granted services or data.

   User authentication and service authorization capabilities will be built into directory services. The global database of users will contain information about the related access rights to ensure that resources are only granted to those with proper authorization.

Open Architecture

A computing system with an open architecture is one that encourages the development of third-party applications. Novell supports third-party development through NetWare Open Systems. While this section is of interest mostly to program designers, managers who are evaluating the use of NetWare should take note of Novell's willingness to promote applications development with an open strategy. This strategy ensures that a variety of useful and productive software is available to take advantage of NetWare and network computing.

   Novell addresses five areas in its open architecture strategy, as outlined in the following sections.

Open Server Platforms

Distributed applications will be a major area of discussion and development in the 1990s. As processing power increases at the server, software vendors become more interested in using part of that processing power. NetWare 386 and Portable NetWare allow applications such as database management programs to run at the server where they can more easily take advantage of network services to increase performance.

Typically, when a workstation runs an application from the server, it retrieves the entire application plus the data file from the server; then it runs the program in its own memory. While this is an important aspect of networking, it is often inefficient to transfer an entire program or data file to the workstation. A more efficient method is to deliver only the portions of the program and file the workstation actually needs.

A distributed application can split its workload between the file server and workstations. The "front end" of this arrangement is the workstation, where screen and keyboard activities are handled. At the "back end" is the server, where shared tasks such as disk input and output are handled. As the processing power of the server increases, the function of the backend processing at the server can increase.

Open APIs

To encourage the development of software for a particular system, applications programming interfaces (APIs) must be available. APIs provide the "hooks" programmers can tie into to take advantage of a particular NetWare service. NetWare 386 includes a well-defined set of interfaces that software developers can use to port or develop applications to work in the distributed environment of a network. The following are available:

- A C library interface module that links to the operating system and provides an ANSI-C-compatible interface. Developers can use standard function calls to access NetWare resources.

- A set of extended function calls that make NetWare-specific features available to server-based applications. These extended functions are used to access security, accounting, queue management, and transaction tracking features.

- A C library interface to NetWare's support of industry standard interprocess communications (IPC) mechanisms for server- based applications, including NetBIOS, Unix Transport Library Interface (TLI), Named Pipes, and SPX.

- NetWare Btrieve, NetWare SQL, and NetWare mail handling service (MHS) provide important programming interfaces that can be used to create distributed applications.

Support for Industry Standard Interfaces

Novell supports industry standard interfaces such as the Macintosh and OS/2. NetWare for Macintosh supports the AppleTalk Filing Protocol (AFP), which defines file and print services in the Macintosh environment. The NetWare Requester provides for the connection of OS/2 workstations and adds support for the standard OS/2 APIs.

NetWare 386 and Portable NetWare support NetBIOS, Unix Transport Library Interface, and Named Pipes for distributed applications.

Application Portability

When industry standard APIs are used, third-party software applications can be ported to other environments as well. Novell supports industry standard APIs, so developers can port the applications they develop to other environments as well, thus increasing their return on investment.

Development Tools

Novell makes a complete set of development tools and support services available to developers. The Professional Developer Series includes API documentation, programming libraries, technical assistance, and an annual developer's conference. Two important tools are described here.

NetWare 386 Programmer's Workbench   A set of tools developers need to create complete distributed applications for NetWare 386. A developer's version of NetWare 386 is included, along with a 386 C network

compiler, a C network compiler for DOS and OS/2, and a full set of API documentation.

NetWare Remote Procedure Calls (RPC)   A set of tools designed to assist developers in creating code necessary to extend application procedure calls across the network to a server or client. The code can be created in several environments such as NetWare 386, DOS, OS/2, Unix, and VMS. Macintosh support is planned. RPC also provides an interface to protocols such as NetWare's Sequenced Packet Exchange (SPX), while interfaces to NetBIOS, Named Pipes, and TCP/IP Sockets are available from NetWise, the original developer of the NetWare RPC technology.

NetWare 386 Features

Features of NetWare 386
NetWare Administrative and Service Features
Differences Between NetWare 286
  And NetWare 386 Commands

NetWare 386 is a true server operating system designed specifically for the Intel 80386 microprocessor. It is also designed to take advantage of the Intel 80486. Unlike previous versions, NetWare 386 has been completely rewritten to take advantage of the processor's sophisticated features.

NetWare 386 initially was shipped in early 1989. Version 3.0 provided the basic operating system, which served as the platform for all subsequent improvements to the product. Version 3.1, shipped in July of 1990, expanded upon the earlier platform. Since Novell offered free and automatic upgrades of version 3.1 for those who purchased version 3.0, this book covers only version 3.1 of the operating system.

Features of NetWare 386

NetWare 386 is designed to be a network operating system for today and the future. Its open and modular design allows the concept of network computing as described in Chapter 4 to take place. The following provides a quick overview of its technical specifications and features.

Logical users supported per server	250
Concurrent open files per server	100,000
Concurrent TTS transactions	25,000
Volumes per file server	64
Logical drives per volume	32
Directory entries per volume	2,097,152
Maximum file size	4 GB[*]
Maximum theoretical storage capacity	32 TB[*]
Maximum theoretical RAM memory	4 GB[*]
Cache buffers	Dynamic

[*] GB (billion bytes) = 1000 MB
TB (trillion bytes) = 1000 GB

Table 5-1.   NetWare 386 Specifications

Technical Overview

NetWare 386 specifications, shown in Table 5-1, are based on a theoretical maximum for the Novell NetWare file system. Keep in mind that, due to current limitations of microcomputer technology, some of these maximums cannot be reached. More detail is provided on some features later in the chapter.

Note: Future versions of NetWare will support up to 1000 users.

Hardware Requirements

NetWare 386 requires a network server system, workstations, network interface cards, and connecting cable. The server must be an Intel 80386- or 80486-based system with a minimum of 2MB of RAM, but more memory will probably be required, depending on the number of users and other network requirements. If you use more than 70MB of disk space, start with 4MB. One advantage of NetWare is that it warns supervisors when memory should be added to improve the server's performance. If more memory is required, the message appears after the system is used for a brief period. A discussion of servers and server evaluation methods is covered in Chapter 13.

Workstations can be MS DOS-compatible systems, OS/2 systems, and Apple Macintosh systems. The type of network cards used depends on the cabling system, topology, and cable access method. A complete discussion starts in Chapter 2 and continues in Chapter 8. Methods used to evaluate possible network systems are covered in Chapter 14.

Recommended Hardware

Servers should be high-performance systems using advanced bus technology such as IBM's Micro Channel Architecture (MCA) or the Extended Industry Standard Architecture (EISA). EISA is used in Compaq systems as well as many other non-IBM systems. MCA and EISA systems can use 32-bit network interface cards and disk controller boards to significantly improve the performance of the server. Most bottlenecks occur in these components as network traffic increases.

Bottlenecks also occur at the disk drive and controller when large amounts of input/output are requested by LAN users. One way to increase performance is to install additional hard drives and then span volumes over multiple drives. The server then can read or write a file at several locations simultaneously. More details on this feature are covered later. In addition you can use Novell disk coprocessor boards to further optimize disk performance.

NetWare 386 Architecture

The *System Executive* is the main component of NetWare 386. It allocates memory, grants access to files, and schedules tasks. The System Executive is a full 32-bit operating system. Unlike previous versions of NetWare, NetWare 386 automatically allocates memory to network services as they are needed. The *Dynamic Resource Configuration* feature ensures that every major network operation is allocated the correct amount of memory within the memory limitations of the system. You need not bring down the server to change these options.

Note: Downing the server is a process of logging out all users, closing all data and program files, and turning the system off or returning to DOS.

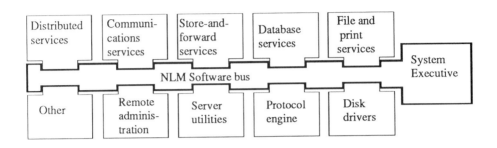

Figure 5-1. The NetWare 386 operating system uses a modular design that allows applications and utilities to be loaded and unloaded

Expandability

NetWare 386 has an expandable architecture that allows additional software modules to be added to the network, even while the network server is running. As shown in Figure 5-1, third-party products such as applications, drivers, and utilities become a part of the network operating system. These modules are known as *NetWare loadable modules* (NLM). Because they are located in the server along with the operating system, they become tightly coupled with the entire system and have instant access to services. Typical server-based applications might include a database or communications module.

Modular architecture design makes it easy to install the operating system and change its configuration. An installation utility is included that greatly improves the setup time over previous versions of NetWare. Network adapters, disk drivers, and other peripherals are *linked* to the operating system when it is started, which means that the startup configuration can be altered easily without going through a lengthy reconfiguration process. New link commands can be executed while the operating system is running.

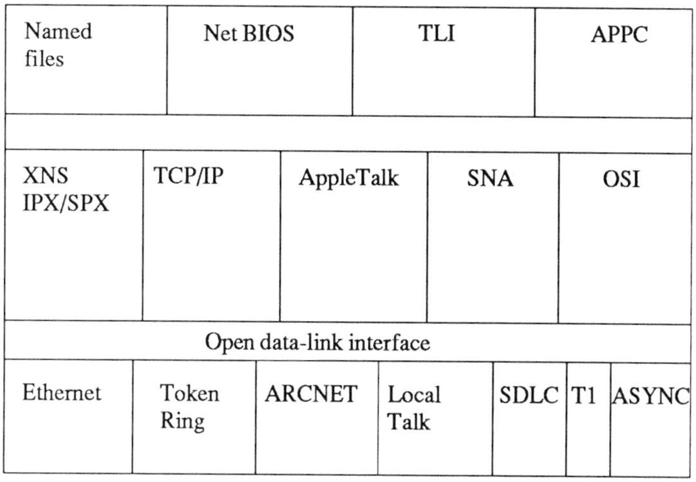

Named files	Net BIOS		TLI		APPC
XNS IPX/SPX	TCP/IP	AppleTalk	SNA		OSI
Open data-link interface					
Ethernet	Token Ring	ARCNET	Local Talk	SDLC	T1	ASYNC

Figure 5-2.   The open data-link interface

Protocol Independence

Current and future versions of NetWare include a protocol independent structure known as the open data-link interface that allows different protocols such as IPX/SPX, AppleTalk, TCP/IP, SNA, and the OSI stack to be loaded and unloaded on the network server as needed.

The complete protocol engine is shown in Figure 5-2. Many varied network interface cards are allowed, as shown at the bottom of the figure. A link layer allows the drivers of these cards to attach to one or more protocol stacks, as shown in the middle. At the top of the figure, you can see services available from several different industry standard inter-process control mechanisms. This scheme allows a NetWare network to become a platform for network computing, as described in Chapter 4.

Internetworking

A NetWare 386 network can be integrated into a multivendor network with ease due to its protocol independence. Operating systems and hardware from many different vendors may now share the NetWare network. Net-Ware 386 also provides an internal router feature that allows a NetWare server to connect with up to 16 different networks, making them appear as one logical network, as discussed in Chapter 3. A bridge to other networks can be established internally in the server or in an external bridge.

Workstation Support

NetWare 386 supports a wide variety of workstations, including DOS machines, OS/2 systems, and the Apple Macintosh. Windows 3.0 is also supported in DOS workstations. Future versions of NetWare will support workstations such as those running the Unix operating system. For DOS workstations you can place the NetWare shell in expanded or extended mem-ory, thus freeing up memory for applications.

The NetWare file system supports other operating systems by allow-ing multiple types of files to be stored on the server. Since each operating system supported by NetWare uses a different filenaming convention, the methods used to store those files must be taken into consideration. For example, Macintosh files require two entries in the file table. To allow all workstation operating systems to store files using their familiar naming schemes, NetWare supports files that require multiple name spaces.

NetWare File System Features

The storage capacity of NetWare 386 has increased vastly. Up to 32 trillion bytes of disk storage is possible. Volumes, once limited to a single disk, can now span multiple disk drives, which means that large databases and applications, such as those previously stored on minicomputers and main-frames, can now be stored on the file server. Access to files stored on multiple disks is much faster since simultaneous input/output can be handled by each drive. This is shown here:

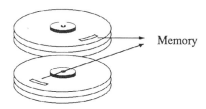

The file system prevents wasted space by allocating to files only the amount of disk space they need, rather than writing a file to a predefined disk space and filling unused space with null characters. Deleted files are easier to salvage, and an optional feature allows the file system to retain deleted files until deliberately purged by the system manager. Supervisors can allocate disk space to users as required.

NetWare optimizes the performance of a server's storage devices using directory hashing, elevator seeking, and disk caching. These are covered in the following sections.

Directory Hashing

Directory hashing reduces file scanning time by mapping a given file to an index and then searching the index instead of the entire directory. NetWare creates two tables for each volume's directory and keeps them in memory. The first table is a *hash table,* which mathematically groups directories and filenames. Hash table searches are not sequential, and because they do not start at the top and scan through the entire list, they are much faster. If a file is requested using the so-called *wildcard search* method, in which only part of the filename is given, the second table is used. This table groups filenames so that wildcard searches are optimized.

Elevator Seeking

Elevator seeking is a technique used to optimize how files are read from the disk. NetWare assembles its current requests for disks in an order of priority based on the current position of the disk head. In this way the head does not jump around the disk to service requests. It reads the next available request as the head moves over the disk surface, even if the request is not in the specified order.

Disk Caching

Disk caching is a common technique used to increase the performance of a disk system by minimizing disk access. A block of data placed in memory is easier to read than one on disk, so a system with a read request reads additional data beyond the request in anticipation that it might be requested later. The extra data is stored in the cache memory.

During a disk write, the system places data to be written to disk in a cache and holds it there until the cache is full, or until there is a lull in disk activity. Data is then written according to disk location to optimize the write procedures further.

System Fault Tolerance Features

Failure of a server and its hard disk can be an especially serious problem on a LAN. An uninterruptible power supply (UPS) can provide protection from power failures. Failure of a hard drive can be disastrous, so backups must be made daily and in some cases continuously in real time using disk mirroring techniques or dedicated backup servers. A drive may fail suddenly, or it may begin to lose the integrity of its magnetic surface over time, resulting in lost data.

NetWare has several levels of protection to guard against hard disk problems. For example, files are read after they are written to ensure data integrity. Other features are discussed in the following sections.

Duplicate Directory
And File Allocation Table

The location and size of files is kept in the file allocation table (FAT) of a hard drive. This table is usually located in one place on most hard drives.

If data is lost in the file allocation table area of the disk, you could lose entire files.

Under NetWare, duplicate copies of the FAT are stored in different locations on the physical disk. If one of the FATs is corrupted, the other copy temporarily takes over. The corrupted table is repaired using a copy of the secondary file allocation table. Defective blocks are marked as unusable, and new blocks with the correct FAT data are rebuilt elsewhere on the disk. All reallocation is handled by NetWare; however, managers periodically must monitor the amount of hard disk space that is being reallocated, since it may be indicative of a failing drive.

Hot Fix Redirection Area

NetWare does a read-after-write verification in which a block of data is written to a hard disk; then the data is immediately read back from the disk and compared to the original data, which is still in memory. If the data from disk matches the data in memory, the write operation is considered successful. The data in memory is released and the next write operation proceeds. If the data does not match, the disk surface may be defective. The Hot Fix feature then takes over to correct it.

Hot Fix enables a hard disk to maintain the same data integrity that it had when first tested and installed. The Hot Fix feature sets aside a small portion of the disk's storage area as the Hot Fix redirection area. This area receives data blocks that are redirected from faulty blocks or blocks that the operating system has determined will go bad.

Disk Mirroring

If a hard disk suffers a complete mechanical failure, all data is lost. Restoration can be made from backups, but the system down time may not be acceptable.

NetWare 386 provides a *disk mirroring* option that allows simultaneous duplication of the data on one drive to another. With disk mirroring, two drives on the same channel are paired together, as shown here:

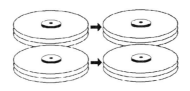

Primary drives   Mirroring drives

Blocks of data written to the primary drive are duplicated on the secondary drive. The disks operate in tandem as files are updated. If one disk fails, the other disk can continue to operate without data loss or interruption of services. NetWare sends a warning message that a disk failure has taken place so that repairs can take place and mirroring can be reestablished.

Duplexing

Disk duplexing takes disk mirroring one step further by protecting against the failure of not only the disk drives, but also the channel between the disk and the file server. This channel includes the controller and interface cable.

One advantage that comes from disk duplexing besides protection is known as *split seeks*. During a read request, the operating system sends a request to whichever drive can respond the fastest, and then reads from that drive.

Future versions of NetWare will include system fault tolerance (SFT) level III, which will allow the entire server to be mirrored to another server. If one server should fail, the other server immediately takes over the management of the LAN.

Transaction Tracking System

The transaction tracking system (TTS) prevents database corruption if the system fails while data is being written to disk. The resulting file may be incompletely written, corrupting the database and possibly making it inaccessible. Database corruption of this sort may go unnoticed, until it's too late in some cases.

When TTS is enabled, an entire sequence of transactions to a database is viewed as a single event that must be completed or backed out of. If the changes are not completed and the system goes down, NetWare restores the database to its previous state before the changes were begun. The lost transactions must be reentered, but the database will remain intact.

NetWare Administrative And Service Features

The following administration features and services are available with NetWare. The security and work group-manager features are built into the operating system. Other features may need to be installed separately but are included with NetWare.

Security Features

Security in NetWare is based on *user profiles*. The network supervisor establishes a person as an authorized user on the network and grants various rights for use of network resources. Resources include the file system, applications, printers, and other peripherals.

NetWare login security allows the system supervisor to prevent access to the system by unauthorized users. A password system can prevent or control logins. Users can be forced to log in at specific workstations or only during specific times. Accounts can also be closed or temporarily disabled for security reasons. NetWare 386 encrypts passwords as they are typed to prevent would-be intruders from "listening" to the password transmission on the cable using various monitoring devices.

A network user's privileges to the directories and files of the NetWare file system are granted with *rights*. These rights allow supervisors or managers to control who can list files in a directory, read a file, change a file, or create a new file. Users can also be given the Delete right, if necessary. The rights can apply to an entire directory, or to specific files. For a list of rights, refer to "NetWare File and Directory Rights" later in this chapter.

Directories and files can be given specific attributes by the supervisor or a manager. Attributes are important because they cannot be overridden, even by users who might be granted the right to perform a task in a directory. For example, files can be given the Delete Inhibit attribute, which prevents them from being erased. Even if users have the Delete right in a directory, they cannot remove the file (unless they are also given the Access Control right).

NetWare security features allow a system supervisor to

- Disable a user's account

- Specify an account expiration date

- Require a user to have a password

- Specify the minimum length of a password

- Force a user to change passwords periodically

- Forbid users from changing to a recently used password

- Restrict the times when a user can log in

- Restrict the physical station from which a user can log in

- Restrict the number of concurrent connections for each user

- Restrict the amount of disk space a user can have

- Keep an audit trail of all LOGIN and LOGOUT requests

- Keep an audit trail of account lockouts

- Monitor intruder detection and account lockout

- Check for security holes in the network

NetWare makes half-hour security checks to ensure that each user has the right to remain logged on the system. Warnings are given to log out five minutes ahead of an automatic logout.

NetWare File and Directory Rights

Tables 5-2 and 5-3 describe the differences between file and directory rights in NetWare 286 and NetWare 386. Those who are familiar with NetWare 286 must know how the rights have changed for NetWare 386.

NetWare 286	NetWare 386	Changes
	Supervisor	A new right that grants all rights in a directory to a user. It cannot be revoked in a subdirectory.
Open		Removed in NetWare 386. Now granted with Read, Write, or Create rights.
Search	File Scan	Right to search to root of directory granted automatically when any right is granted.
Parental	Access Control	Rights granted to users with this right can be revoked at subdirectory and file level. No longer grants right to create or rename subdirectories.
Delete	Erase	None
Create, Open	Create	Allows users to create subdirectories without need for Access Control right.
Modify	Modify	Access Control is not required to rename directories and files.
Read, Open	Read	A separate Open right is no longer required.
Write, Open	Write	A separate Open right is no longer required.

Table 5-2.   New and Modified Rights

NetWare 286	NetWare 386	Changes
S (Shareable)	S	No change.
NS (Nonshareable)		Files are defaulted to Nonshareable with no attribute designated.
RW (Read Write)	RW	No change.
RO (Read Only)	RO	Also assigns Delete Inhibit and Rename Inhibit.
Execute Only	X	No change.
Hidden	H	No change. Note: may be applied to directory.
System	Sy	Now Sy, not S. May be applied to directory.
I (Index)	I	Automatically assigned to all files with more than 64 FAT entries.
T (Transactional)	T	No change.
Modified	A	Now referred to as Archive Needed.
	D (Delete Inhibit)	File or directory cannot be erased.
	P (Purge)	Purges file or directory upon deletion.
	R (Rename Inhibit)	File or directory cannot be renamed.
	RA (Read Audit)	Tracks file reads.
	WA (Write Audit)	Tracks write audits.
	C (Copy Inhibit)	Restricts Macintosh users from copying.

Table 5-3.   New and Modified File and Directory Attributes

Work Group and User Management

All NetWare networks consist of a supervisor and users. Under NetWare 386 a new hierarchy of users can be implemented by supervisors who want to share their management tasks, out of necessity, or to match the management structure of an organization.

Work group managers are created to manage users and groups. The supervisor grants a work group manager supervisory control over users and the resources associated with them. In most cases work group managers are users who are already department managers in an organization. Work group managers can create or remove users. Another level of managers, called *user account managers*, cannot create new users but have most of the same power as work group managers. User account managers can be created to assist work group managers.

Work group and user account managers are usually given rights to manage a specific directory and its subdirectories, as well as the users who have access to them.

Resource Accounting

Government agencies, schools, and work groups within large corporations may need to track the time and usage of their server and network resources. For example, a firm doing government research may need to account for the time users spend on special projects, or a school may need to track accounts for student users. Another reason to track system usage is to gather performance data that can substantiate the need to purchase additional equipment such as disk storage or memory.

NetWare's resource accounting features allow supervisors to monitor network usage and bill user accounts accordingly. The features of the system include the ability to set up a credit limit for each user, monitor the account balances of each user, and generate an audit trail of system usage.

Accounts can be charged for network usage based on the following:

- Connection time to the server

- Blocks read from disk

- Blocks written to disk

- Requests received from a workstation

- Amount of disk storage used

System supervisors can set up user accounts and account balances for some or all users on the network. The use of print servers and database servers can also be charged.

NetWare Name Service

The NetWare name service (NNS) is a new Novell feature that can provide simplified network administration on extended networks that have many resources and more than one server. NNS enables NetWare users to access multiple servers and resources with a single login command. For network supervisors NNS simplifies the task of maintaining a consistent user environment.

NetWare name service can be used to define a logical group of servers, called a *domain*. Users then log into the domain and have access to the resources in the domain, depending on their access rights. According to Novell, NNS advances NetWare beyond a *server-based* network operating system to a *services-based* operating system.

Message and Mail Handling System

In the past Novell offered a message handling system utility that routed and transferred files from one location to another usually remote location. The application used a store-and-forward technology that delivered the messages and files at a convenient or predefined time. Store-and-forward is an alternative to expensive real-time connections between LANs or other systems. In a store-and-forward system, a connection is made and files are transmitted to the remote system. Message files on the remote system are then received and the connection is terminated.

In early 1990 Novell announced plans to develop a new utility, called the mail handling system (MHS), that is compliant with X.400 specifications, which are accepted as world-wide mail handling standards. A development agreement with Retix, a company based in Santa Monica, CA, creates an X.400 gateway to allow NetWare networks to interface with X.400-based systems like TeleMail 400 and MCI.

Print Services

NetWare 386 includes a print server utility that allows network users to share up to 16 printers. Up to 5 printers can be attached to the server, and the remaining printers can be attached to workstations. A print server can also be established in a dedicated workstation. Other print servers can be added to add more that 16 printers to the network.

The printing services include the following:

- A print server NetWare loadable module used to install the print server in the file server.

- A command to install a print server in a dedicated workstation, if necessary.

- A terminate-and-stay-resident utility for workstations that support shareable printers. The shared printers are managed by the printer server or the local user.

Network Monitoring and Management

NetWare 386 offers the following six features that make management of the server and network easier.

Virtual console services   With this feature, network supervisors can administer the network without leaving their workstations. Any command that can be given at the server console can be given at the management workstation. The NetWare remote management facility (RMF) can be used to add additional remote management. It enables network supervisors to execute console commands over asynchronous lines or through third-party bridges and routers.

Resource management   Resource management features in NetWare 386 can be used to track and manage system resources.

Added	Modified	Unchanged	Deleted
ALLOW	ATOTAL	BRGEN	HIDEFILE
CHKDIR	ATTACH	CASTOFF	HOLDON
DSPACE	BINDFIX	CASTON	HOLDOFF
NBACKUP	BINDREST	COLORPAL	LARCHIVE
PSC	CAPTURE	DOSGEN	LRESTORE
UPGRADE	CHKVOL	ENDCAP	MACBACK
RPRINTER	FCONSOLE	LOGOUT	MAIL
PSERVER	FILER	MENU	NARCHIVE
	FLAG	NPRINT	NRESTORE
	FLAGDIR	PAUDIT	PSTAT
	GRANT	PRINTDEF	SHOWFILE
	LISTDIR	SESSION	
	LOGIN	SETPASS	
	MAKEUSER	SETTS	
	MAP	SYSTIME	
	NCOPY	USERLIST	
	NDIR	VERSION	
	NVER	WHOAMI	
	PCONSOLE		
	PRINTCON		
	PURGE		
	REMOVE		
	RENDIR		
	REVOKE		
	RIGHTS		
	SALVAGE		
	SECURITY		
	SEND		
	SHGEN		
	SLIST		
	SMODE		
	SYSCON		
	TLIST		
	USERDEF		
	VOLINFO		

Table 5-4. Comparison of NetWare 386 commands to NetWare 286 commands

Management agent loadable module   An operating system management agent enables network services and server resources, such as LAN and disk subsystems, to be monitored and controlled by any network management system.

Memory management   NetWare 386 manages and tracks all system memory and allocates it dynamically.

NLM autoload facility   This feature simplifies the process of loading server-based application loadable modules by ensuring all prerequisite NLMs are loaded automatically in the right order.

Server-Based Applications

NetWare 386 is optimized to support back-end server applications. For example, a database "engine" can be added to the server as a NetWare loadable module. Database requests are processed as back-end processes rather than being sent out over the line to a workstation for processing. This reduces traffic, increases performance, and provides security, because the entire database is not sent over the line where it could be tapped by intruders using cable monitoring systems.

Differences Between NetWare 286 And NetWare 386 Commands

Table 5-4 is for readers who have some familiarity with previous versions of NetWare. Besides the differences described earlier such as increased memory and file system capacity, NetWare loadable modules, and protocol independence, the commands listed in the table have been added, modified, or removed.

The NetWare Networking Environment

The System Supervisor
Users, Groups, and Access Rights
Tasks of a Network Manager
Hardware and Software Support
Planning System Security

This chapter provides information for those unfamiliar with a NetWare networking environment. You will learn about the organization of users and their activities, as well as the management tasks required to maintain an effective network environment. Making the transition to a LAN is an important process that should be well thought out and documented. This chapter provides the concepts and information you need to do that.

The System Supervisor

The network supervisor is responsible for all aspects of managing one or more servers in a network system. Each server can have its own supervisor, or a single supervisor may be used for all servers. Supervisor access to the server is controlled with login password security, just as it is for all other users. The tasks of a supervisor begin with the installation of the server, but in some cases the supervisor is given control of a server after it has already been installed.

The supervisor has the highest level of access to the server and can perform any task in any directory. A supervisor's security rights start at the root directory and are not blocked in any subdirectory. A supervisor may designate another user as a supervisor, but this is not recommended. Instead, a user can be designated a manager of a directory and the users who have access to that directory, but the manager's extended rights should be limited to that directory and its subdirectories.

The tasks of a supervisor are listed here, but keep in mind that many of these tasks can be delegated to an alternate manager who has been granted the security rights to do so.

- Install the server

- Create the initial supervisor password

- Change the supervisor password and user passwords as required for system security

- Administer the security system

- Create directory structures for programs and data

- Install applications

- Create and delete users

- Designate users as managers with special rights

- Monitor the performance of the system

- Ensure that data is properly protected with backup procedures and other techniques

One of the first steps in planning for a LAN is to determine who will manage it. In many organizations, the system supervisor is the person who suggested installing a LAN in the first place. A supervisor may also be a technically oriented in-house person who is familiar with computer systems. He or she may rely on a staff of technicians who implement their directives based on company policies and organization. An alternative is to use an outside consulting service that can supply management services, as well as hardware service and support. Consulting services may also have a stock of replacement parts and diagnostic equipment.

Technically, the supervisor is the person logged in with the SUPER-VISOR name who has complete system access. But this person should also have a normal login name used when they need to access the network for nonsupervisory duties. This is important for security reasons since it is not advisable for the person logged in as SUPERVISOR to ever leave his or her workstation unattended. Another user could walk up to the station and gain complete access to the network.

The supervisor's password is the master key to the system. It should be written down and placed in a locked safe or given to a person of authority. Another suggestion is to create a two- or three-word password, and then give a portion of the password to two or three different users. These users must then confer if there is ever a need to access the server when the supervisor is not around.

Users, Groups, and Access Rights

Below the supervisor is a hierarchy of managers and users who have different levels of access to the system. Access to a server is controlled by the NetWare login security system, while access to directories and files is controlled by a set of rights that can be granted or revoked.

Users

The network supervisor creates new users or delegates the task to a work group manager, as discussed later. This task involves assigning passwords and login scripts to users, as well as creating their personal directories. Rights are then granted to each user as required, but this can also be done by making the user a member of a group that already has the rights required by the user, as discussed under "Groups."

The supervisor may need to assign users certain login restrictions. For example, the time a user logs in can be restricted to between 9:00 am and 5:00 pm, or users can be prevented from logging in at workstations other than their own.

Groups

Groups are collections of users created to make network management easier. They also make electronic mail and message delivery easier. When a group of users exists, the supervisor or a network manager can assign login restrictions or rights to the group, rather than one-by-one for each user in the group. Groups are referred to by name. For example, all users are automatically made members of the EVERYONE group. If a message is sent to the group EVERYONE, all users will receive it. If EVERYONE is granted the right to use a program in a directory, all users will automatically be granted rights to that directory.

Groups can be patterned after the organizational structure of a business. For example, groups called MANAGERS or CLERKS can be created. Supervisors can then grant these groups rights or send messages to them. A supervisor usually adds users to a group and then grants rights to the group. The exception is when a new user is granted rights to his or her personal directory.

Managers

Managers are created to relieve the supervisor from some management tasks. Managers are given control of one or more users or groups and the directories they work in. Managers may have full supervisory rights over the groups and directories they control, but have normal rights outside that domain. For example, a sales department manager is granted control of the SALES group and given full supervisory rights in a directory called SALES.

Managers can create or remove users, create new subdirectories, add programs, and perform other supervisory tasks. In addition, the manager can create other managers to assist in certain tasks, but these "assistant" managers are restricted to the same domain assigned to the manager.

Access Rights

Security is important in a multiuser environment such as a local area network to prevent users from destroying or corrupting important data files, and to allow users to maintain privacy or security with their own files and directories. Login restrictions prevent unauthorized users from gaining access to the server and can also be used to restrict how authorized users gain entry to the system.

Access to files and directories on a NetWare server is granted or restricted using a set of *rights*. These rights allow a user to perform a specific task, such as create a file, edit a file, or delete a file. Each right must be granted individually. For example, a user might be granted the right to create and edit a file, but not to delete it. Rights are usually granted to a user for a particular directory, but rights can also be applied to files. In this way a user may have rights to work in a directory, but may be restricted on how they can work with a specific file in that directory.

Security is managed on a NetWare system on four levels, as described in the following sections.

Login/Password Security

All users must have an account, which is usually named after the user. The account is then assigned a confidential password that must be typed every time the user logs in. Account restrictions can be applied to any user's account. For example, users can be restricted to logging in at only their personal workstations, or they can be prevented from logging into other workstations simultaneously. This prevents users from working in unsupervised areas where they might access sensitive data or download the company's valuable files to disk and remove them from the building.

Trustee Security

Trustee rights are the rights granted to users in directories. Each user must be assigned these rights on an individual basis, unless they are part of a group. Users are allowed to perform tasks when they are granted rights and prevented from performing tasks when those rights are revoked. The rights are listed in Table 6-1.

Directory Security

When a user is granted rights in a directory, the rights are also granted in any subdirectories. A feature called the *inherited rights mask* can be used

A (Access Control)	Grants a user complete control within a single directory. This right can be given to group managers.
C (Create)	Grants a user the right to create files.
E (Erase)	Grants a user the right to erase files.
F (File Scan)	Grants users the right to list files in a directory.
M (Modify)	Users with this right can change the name and attributes of a directory and its subdirectories.
R (Read)	Users with this right can open and read files in a directory.
S (Supervisor)	Gives a user complete control in a directory and its subdirectories. A user with Supervisor status in a directory controls its subdirectories without limitations. This right can be granted to work group managers.
W (Write)	Users with this right can open and write to files in directories.

Table 6-1.   Trustee Rights

by supervisors or managers to block the rights that users might inherit in a subdirectory from the parent directory. The inherited rights mask is applied to each subdirectory individually.

A user's rights in a subdirectory become a combination of rights inherited from the parent directory and those blocked by an inherited rights mask. These rights are known as a user's *effective rights.*

File and Directory Attributes

Files and directories can be marked with various attributes by supervisors, or managers who have Supervisor, Access Control, or Modify rights in a directory. Files can be marked to prevent them from being altered or erased, even by users who may have such rights in a directory. Directory

D (Delete Inhibit)	Prevents users from erasing a directory.
R (Rename Inhibit)	Prevents a directory from being renamed.
P (Purge)	Causes files in the directory to be purged immediately if they are deleted.
H (Hidden)	Hides directories and prevents their deletion.
S or Sy (System)	Indicates the directory is used by the system and will not appear in a directory listing.
V (Visible)	This attribute applies only to Macintosh directories and relates to gray folders.

Table 6-2.   Directory Attributes

attributes are briefly described in Table 6-2, and file attributes are listed in Table 6-3. A complete discussion continues in Chapter 21.

Tasks of a Network Manager

Some of the more important tasks of a network manager are discussed in the following sections. Many are required before the installation and should be made a part of the installation plan. Other tasks are performed after installation, but most are performed on an ongoing basis.

Managing the Transition to a LAN

The transition to a LAN requires planning, setup, and training. New procedures must be implemented, and it is necessary to work with personnel managers and department managers to establish how the system will be used by each department and its users. Installation procedures should be planned around the schedules of employees. In some cases these schedules may be hard to change, and it may be necessary to perform the installation after hours.

A (Archive Needed)	Automatically applied to modified files and indicates they need to be backed up.
C (Copy Inhibit)	Restricts the copy rights of users logged in at a Macintosh workstation, even if the user has Read and File Scan trustee rights in the directory.
D (Delete Inhibit)	Prevents users from deleting a file, even if the user has Erase trustee rights in the directory.
E (Execute Only)	Prevents EXE and COM files from being altered or copied and can be used to prevent virus infections.
H (Hidden)	Files with this attribute do not appear in DOS DIR listings and cannot be deleted or copied.
I (Indexed)	Indexes the FAT (File Allocation Table) entry of large files to improve access from the hard drive.
P (Purge)	When the Purge attribute is assigned to a file, the file is automatically purged from the system when deleted. The SALVAGE command cannot be used to recover the file.
Ra (Read Audit)	Creates an audit trail of file reads.
Ro/Rw (Read Only/ Read Write)	Files with the Read Only attribute cannot be edited, only read. Files with the Read Write attribute can be edited.
R (Rename Inhibit)	Prevents files from being renamed.
S (Shareable)	Allows database files to be used by several users.
Sy (System File)	Marks files as system files and prevents them from being copied or deleted.
T (Transactional)	Indicates that the file will be protected by the transactional tracking system.
W (Write Audit)	Creates an audit trail of file writes.

Table 6-3.   File Attributes

Once the LAN is installed, training is important, but the transition of users to the new environment can be eased by providing batch files and helpful menus. In fact users can be totally insulated from the network environment with menus. Clerks who use a single data entry application, for example, can be placed directly in the application they work with. This is done by identifying a user by login name and executing a set of commands based on that name. The commands also may be based on the groups the user belongs to. For example, when a member of the CLERKS group logs in, the system login script can be made to execute commands to start the application clerks work with.

An early part of planning is to categorize users according to the applications and data files they must use. Users can be assigned access to the specific directory where an application or its data files are located and prevented from working outside these directories. Access may be granted to individual users or to groups, such as a group of clerks or a group of managers. Groups are important in NetWare because they make management tasks easier. For example, it is easier to assign directory rights to all the users in a group rather than each user individually. Groups can be created that follow the organizational chart of the company. They also can be created for groups of users working on special projects or according to the applications that need to be accessed.

Users must understand that access to the system is limited according to their access rights, which are often determined by personnel or department managers, as well as the supervisor. Managers are interested in the files to which their employees have access.

Documentation

Log sheets should be kept for the entire network system, including logs for all the hardware, software, and users on the network. Logs help avoid confusion and provide a smooth transition when new managers take over the system. Managers can use the software and user logs as guidelines for creating directory structures and an effective login security system. Technicians can use hardware logs to determine the service history of hardware and to establish preventive maintenance schedules.

Examples of log sheets you will need during the planning, installation, and ongoing maintenance of the network are listed here. Chapter 12 provides guidelines for creating log worksheets. Planners who are designing a network may want to refer to those guidelines now in order to begin collecting information about existing hardware and the needs of users.

- Users and user-needs worksheet

- Software-needs assessment sheet

- Directory structure planning sheet

- Management structure planning sheet

- Worksheet to plan the system security, including directory and file access rights for users

- Master log for existing equipment

- Log of existing PCs that will become workstations

- Workstation configuration logs, including board types and board settings

- File server planning and configuration sheets

- Worksheet to plan and log the installation parameters

- Log to track all problems and their solutions for future reference

A computer database can be used to track network information. A computerized database is superior to a paper system because the information can be indexed and searched and reports can be easily generated.

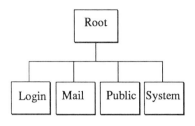

Figure 6-1.   Directories created during NetWare installation

Managing the NetWare File System

Once the NetWare server and its system files have been installed, the task of building the directory structure, installing applications, creating users, assigning user rights, and generally managing the system can begin.

Initially, NetWare creates the following directories on the main system volume, as shown in Figure 6-1:

ROOT	The NetWare file system has a ROOT directory similar to the DOS environment. All directories branch from the ROOT. No user should ever have rights in the ROOT directory.
SYSTEM	This directory contains NetWare supervisory and diagnostic programs that should only be used by the supervisor; therefore, the supervisor is the only user who should have access rights to the SYSTEM directory. The directory also holds important data files such as resource accounting information that should not be available to other users.

LOGIN	This directory contains commands for logging into the system. Users switch to this directory to log into the NetWare server.
MAIL	The MAIL directory is used by various mail systems to store messages and other information. A subdirectory for each user is created in this directory to hold personal login scripts.
PUBLIC	The PUBLIC directory holds the programs and command utilities for NetWare. Each user created on the server is automatically granted access rights to run the programs in this directory.

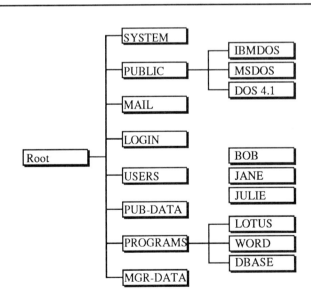

Figure 6-2.   Example of a NetWare directories structure

Other Directories

There are many ways to build a directory structure on the server. It may be designed to match the management structure of the company or the applications used. In Figure 6-2, applications branch from the PRO-GRAMS directory and users' personal directories branch from the USERS directory. Users can be granted full access rights in their personal directories, which means they can create subdirectories and store their personal files in them. Users cannot see or work with files in other users' personal directories unless they have been given specific access rights to do so.

Figure 6-2 also shows a MGR-DATA directory and a PUB-DATA directory. These directories illustrate how directories can be designed to store files that need to be accessed by other users. For example, while the PUB-DATA directory is available to all users, the MGR-DATA directory is only accessible to a group of managers.

Search Drive Mappings

Notice in Figure 6-2 that applications programs such as Lotus 1-2-3 and Microsoft Word are located in their own directories. Users should always run these programs while logged into their personal directories or one of the public directories. This prevents users from storing files in the program directory. One reason for this is to keep the file system organized; another has to do with the way directory access rights are granted. Users should be granted only the right to run programs in the PROGRAMS subdirectories; however, they can be granted file creation and editing rights in the PUB-DATA directory or their personal directories.

NetWare uses a feature called *search drive mapping* that allows programs to be run from other directories, much like the DOS PATH command. A search drive specifies the order directories should be searched when a user executes a command or utility not located in the current directory. Managers are responsible for granting users rights in program directories and setting up search drives to those directories.

Preparing the Printers

When printers are attached to the network server, print jobs from work-stations are placed in queues before they begin printing. Since many users may send jobs to printers, queues store the jobs and send them to the printer in the order received and as the printer becomes available. In addition, several printers may be attached to a single queue, so queues can be used to distribute print jobs among them.

An operator can be assigned to manage print queues and keep the printers in operation by changing paper or forms when necessary. Print queue operators can change the order of the jobs in the queues, giving some jobs priority over others, or they can remove jobs from the queue.

Preparing for Emergencies

A plan of action must be developed in the event the file server or the network becomes inoperative. Fires, electrical problems, downed equipment, and many other problems can bring a network down. The system manager should develop plans to keep the system up and running, and to ensure adequate backup and restoration procedures. Backup sets should go in fireproof safes or be carried off-site. A manager should do a trial backup and restore before the LAN is put into actual use. This provides confidence that the procedures work and may reveal hidden problems.

Large networks should use disk mirroring and duplexing techniques to ensure that the network will keep running if a primary drive should fail. Future versions of NetWare 386 will allow an entire server to be mirrored to another server. An alternative to this method is to establish a second file server with the same file system, user, and security structure as the primary system. Backups can then be made to this server, and it can be put into use if the primary server should fail.

Network Management Tools

The larger a network, the harder it is to manage, but network management tools can help. A whole range of software utilities and analysis products are available to track performance and isolate problem areas. While the purchase price of most of these tools is within the scope and budget of most LANs, others may be too expensive to have in house, so it may be necessary to rely on an outside consulting service.

Problems can be isolated with tools that "watch" the flow of network traffic. The Sniffer by Network General is a good example. It monitors the cable system and determines if a particular station is not responding, either due to a faulty interface card, cable, or workstation.

The performance of networks can also be monitored with various packages that can spot bottlenecks in the system or other problems that might be affecting performance. The NetWare MONITOR utility is one example.

Cable testers can be used to locate faulty wiring. For example, a bus topology network may not work properly due to a kink in a wire. Often the kink is not easy to spot. Cable testers can display the distance to a defect in the cable, which helps isolate a defective cable segment for replacement.

Network managers often find themselves running around the installation site to assist users with simple requests or questions. Several products are available that allow a manager to log into and operate a user's workstation from his or her own workstation.

Hardware and Software Support

As networks grow, support for users and the hardware they operate becomes an increasingly important issue. Each new user may need to be trained in basic PC operations, as well as network usage. Deciding who performs this support is important. If the supervisor is left with the task of training new users or helping existing users, he or she is drawn away from other tasks such as maintaining the efficiency of the network or the filing system.

Hardware support is also important. This support should be available as the network is being planned, during its installation, and after it is up and running. Vendors of network products should have experience with the type of network you are installing, a competent staff of trained people, and a good stock of loaner equipment.

Planning System Security

Novell NetWare servers provide many security features that make them a safe place to store information. Not only can it be made difficult for a would-be snoop to log into the server, it can also be made difficult for authorized users to explore outside the areas they have been designated to use.

Security and access rights are important to prevent users from accidentally erasing files or viewing the files of other users. For example, it is a good idea to keep unauthorized employees out of payroll information. Security may be even more important in companies that need to protect files from industrial spies.

Other reasons for maintaining security include the threat of computer viruses. A virus is a small program or piece of code written by an irresponsible programmer that can corrupt any or all aspects of the file system. It may make its way to the server by accident or intentionally and begin to cause havoc immediately or over a period of time. Viruses are sometimes located on files obtained from diskettes of unknown origin. The danger of the virus is real. For example, a well-known software vendor recently unknowingly shipped packages of its software that contained viruses. Fortunately, those viruses were not damaging. Some viruses merely display heart-stopping messages or greetings and then go away, while others may erase entire hard drives.

Viruses usually attach to executable program files. Supervisors can prevent virus infection by flagging these files with the Execute Only attribute and then preventing users from copying these files into system directories.

Securing the Hardware

To ensure the security of a server and its data, it may be necessary to lock the servers up in special rooms that no one but the supervisor has access to. In most cases NetWare servers are not directly accessed except for service. All management activities can be handled from workstations. If special rooms are not available, secure the system and its cover.

Security at the workstation is another matter. Users should log out as soon as they need to leave the system unattended. A snooper could walk up to a station that is logged in and access the system with the rights of the currently logged-in user. An industrial spy could download a company's database to disk. It is especially important that the supervisor log out when leaving a workstation to prevent a user from accessing the system with full supervisory rights. Supervisors should create an account for themselves other than the supervisor account that is used for normal, nonsupervisory activities.

Diskless workstations are inexpensive alternatives to full-feature personal computers. They also provide useful security features. Since disk drives are not installed, users cannot download sensitive data files to disk and remove them from the building. At the same time, users cannot introduce viruses at the workstation. Diskless workstations are ideal for the data entry and editing tasks performed by temporary personnel. It is also a good idea to place diskless workstations in unsupervised areas.

Supervisors who have sensitive data should be aware that copper cables emit signals that can be monitored by sophisticated equipment. Cables can also be physically tapped. As a solution to these problems, NetWare 386 encrypts passwords before they are sent over the cable to prevent unauthorized users from learning access codes. To prevent the monitoring of signal emanation, fiber optic cable or data encryption techniques can be employed. Special equipment that can sense abnormalities in the cable signal can discover cable taps.

Securing Remote Connections

A remote connection is an off-site workstation. Since it is off-site, the potential for intrusion is high. An intruder who breaks into a system from a remote connection is hard to detect. Intruders can sit in the comfort of their own homes or offices with little chance of being apprehended. But there are steps you can take to protect your system.

NetWare provides login name and password security with its remote system software. To extend security further may require third-party packages. To prevent intruder break-ins from a remote site, a call-back system can be used. In this system an authorized user calls the host system and then hangs up. The host then calls the user back at a predefined phone number.

You can use data encryption techniques to prevent signals emitted from cables from being monitored. Data is encrypted before transmission. Decrypting algorithms at the receiving end then reconvert the file back to its readable state. Only authorized personnel are given the decrypting algorithm.

Networking with NetWare 386, Advanced Concepts

Network Architecture
And NetWare Open Systems

S
E
V
E
N

The Importance of Network Architecture
Traditional NetWare Communications
The OSI Model
Industry Standard Network Architectures
NetWare Open Systems

Because the computer industry builds systems around many standards, it has always been difficult to connect unrelated systems into useful networks. This will all change in the 1990s as more and more vendors make their products *interoperable,* a movement that attempts to give users on diverse systems equal access to the resources of a network. The Open Systems Interconnect (OSI) model was designed by the International Standards Organization (ISO) as a set of guidelines vendors can use to design products that work in a multivendor environment with different operating systems and protocols. While the standard has not been completely defined, many companies, including Novell, have adopted it as a guideline to define future products.

NOVELL's open protocol technology (OPT) opens NetWare to many different standards and protocols and provides a transition to OSI, which will develop into an industry standard over the next few years. Part of OPT is the open data-link interface (ODI), which provides an interface between network interface cards and multiple protocols. When network interface card drivers are written to the ODI interface, they can use one or more protocols, such as AppleTalk, TCP/IP, and IBM's System Network Architecture (SNA).

ODI provides the following benefits to those who need to interconnect with non-NetWare systems. A more detailed discussion of these topics is covered later for those unfamiliar with the terminology.

- A single interface card can be used to interface with different types of networks, such as AppleTalk (a protocol for Apple networks) and TCP/IP (a protocol originally developed by the Department of Defense primarily to link dissimilar computer systems across wide area networks).

- ODI creates a *logical network board* in which different protocol packets can be sent on the same card and over a single network cabling system. The workstation can use a different protocol stack without being rebooted.

- ODI allows NetWare servers and workstations to communicate with a variety of other systems, including mainframes, that use different protocol stacks.

Since you should understand protocols when you purchase network equipment and integrate other systems and peripherals, this chapter explains how protocols work and compares those supported by NetWare. The emerging OSI protocol standard is used as a reference to show the relationship between layers of each protocol stack. Anyone who needs to plan, install, or operate NetWare 386 networks in a multivendor, multiple-protocol environment will find this chapter of interest. A brief discussion of traditional NetWare communications methods is followed by a discussion of OSI protocols and the new open data-link specification.

The Importance of Network Architecture

A network architecture is a set of protocols, rules, and design criterion that define how the network works and how hardware and software products should be designed to work with it. If the rules are followed properly, products from many vendors can work on the network without problems.

Network protocols like the OSI model define layers of communications between different systems on the network. The layers define how information is presented on a user's workstation screen, down to the layer where it is packaged and sent across the network cable system. Part of the architecture defines how data is split into packets for transmission and how those data packets are transferred to different types of network interface cards for transfer over the network.

Each protocol layer can be used by a programmer to create different types of applications that work over networks. The higher the layer in the stack, the more sophisticated the applications. To make programming tasks easier at a particular protocol layer, an applications programming interface (API) may be used. An API contains programming hooks and routines that eliminate the need for programmers to write low-level communication routines, such as those required to send data from station to station. Programmers can concentrate on the higher-level aspects of a program, such as the user interface. Examples of APIs are NetBIOS for the Microsoft PC LAN network operating system, Named Pipes for the OS/2 LAN Manager, and Advanced Program-to-Program Communications (APPC) for IBM connectivity.

The support of industry standard APIs in NetWare will promote the development of server-based distributed applications such as databases and communications packages. Novell provides development tools that can assist developers in creating such applications.

Traditional NetWare Communications

How does communication take place between two systems on a network? To find out we need to look at how communication is initiated, the protocols and standards used, and the hardware involved in the process. Some networks allow peer-to-peer relationships in which any workstation can establish a communication session with any other workstation, providing the users of each allow this to happen. On a traditional NetWare network, a workstation usually connects with a file server, but applications may establish a session between two workstations.

An overview of the communication process is presented in the following sections. Each workstation connected to a NetWare network has two resident programs to handle network requests and send those requests over the network. At the server, workstation requests are processed and returned to the workstation using the reverse method.

The NetWare Shell

The IPX.COM command is used to initialize the LAN card in the workstation. It is usually executed when the workstation is first started. IPX.COM is customized for each different type of network card.

Network communication starts when a user needs to request a service from the server. All user commands are intercepted by the network shell program to determine if the request is for NetWare or the local workstation DOS. The shell is loaded on DOS systems by executing one of the following commands:

NETx.COM	Loads the shell into conventional memory
EMSNETx.EXE	Loads the shell into expanded memory
XMSNETx.EXE	Loads the shell into extended memory

The x in these commands is replaced with either 3 or 4, depending on whether DOS 3 or DOS 4 is running at the workstation. For example, to load a shell into conventional memory on a workstation running DOS 3.3, you would type **NET3.COM**.

If a command issued by a user is for NetWare, the Internetwork Packet Exchange (IPX) program is put into action, as shown in Figure 7-1. IPX specializes in establishing, maintaining, and terminating a network communication session. It packages information that must be sent over the network. IPX is an implementation of the Internetwork Datagram Packet (IDP) protocol designed by Xerox.

All commands sent to the server must match the format required by the NetWare core protocol (NCP). Workstations can use the NCP language to make service requests to the server. The server will then respond appropriately.

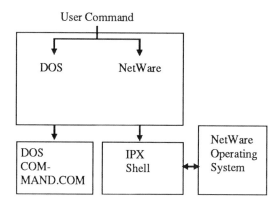

Figure 7-1.   The NetWare shell redirects network operating system requests over the wire to the server

Packets

Information is sent in packets in the same way that the mail service delivers letters in envelopes. If there is a large amount of information to be sent, more than one packet is used. Routing and reassembly instructions are added to each packet. Packets are usually around 618 bytes in size, but a new trend is to increase the packet size to improve network performance. Under NetWare 386, packet sizes can be between 618 to 4202 bytes. Vendors of network interface cards must supply drivers that allow different packet sizes, and you must specify a larger packet size when you set up the NetWare operating system.

It may appear that packets are casually sent over the network, but in reality, hundreds or thousands of packets may be sent per second, and these packets may have mixed destination addresses. Each receiving station must sort out the packets it is to receive and reject or forward the rest. A network is like a high-speed postal system in which packets are addressed, processed, sent, and received in microseconds with extreme accuracy.

Accessing the Network

When the packets to be sent reach the network interface card, they must be converted to electrical signals that can be transmitted over the cable. Every network card has an *access control method* it uses to transfer packets from memory to the physical cable system. The access method may be based on a carrier sensing scheme or a token passing scheme. With the carrier sensing scheme, like that used with Ethernet, the packet is broadcast like a radio transmission to all stations. The station with the proper address then accepts the packet. Token passing networks, like ARCNET and Token Ring, send packets from station to station, but only when they have possession of a "token."

Access control methods work at the data-link layer of the protocol stack and may be standardized by the Institute of Electrical and Electronics Engineers (IEEE). CSMA/CD (primarily Ethernet), Token Bus (primarily ARCNET but not standardized by IEEE), and Token Ring (primarily IBM Token Ring) are three of the methods discussed fully in Chapter 8.

The IPX.COM file that runs in each workstation must be customized to match the access methods and other features of the installed network interface card. This is done by linking the computer- coded driver supplied with the network card to the IPX.COM file using the NetWare SHGEN program. If every workstation uses the same card, only one IPX.COM file must be generated, but if workstations use different cards, an IPX file must be created for each. This makes a good case for using the same cards in all stations. However, Novell's strategy of media independence is based on the fact that any card and its driver can be linked to the IPX file.

As mentioned previously, packets contain source and destination addresses. Addresses are divided into three parts: the *network,* the *node,* and a *socket.* The network part of the address determines the physical LAN cable to which the workstation is attached. An internetwork may consist of two or more separate physical networks connected together, so the network address is important in routing the packet to the proper place. The node address identifies the exact workstation. Finally, a socket is used to identify a particular software process in the destination.

The Communications Session

In traditional NetWare network communications, a protocol stack defines how a session is established, how information is packaged, and how it is sent over the network. Part of the rules define how the information is delivered to the network interface card and how the interface card puts it on the network cable. At the receiving end of the transmission, the process is reversed. If a message is sent to another user, that message appears on his or her screen after being unpackaged and processed by the protocols.

With NetWare 386 this process can be expanded by using different protocol stacks, such as TCP/IP, OSI, and others. The next few sections discuss how this is done.

The OSI Model

The most prominent standards body today is the International Standards Organization, which has a membership of over 400. This broad membership prevents a single vendor from overly exerting its influence in defining standards in the computer industry.

ISO has developed the Open Systems International (OSI) seven-layer model for data communications, as shown in Figure 7-2. The model is usually viewed as a ladder of processes that take place when messages or data pass from an application running in a workstation to the physical network. In turn the model describes the reverse process when a packet is received from the network and is processed for use by an application. Each layer defines specific rules that programmers and vendors of network products use to design interoperable products.

The OSI standards are important to vendors throughout the computer industry. Not only are they being adopted in Europe and elsewhere, but as of August 1990, the federal government cannot buy a network system that is not compliant with the Government OSI Profile (GOSIP). In the early 1980s, the Department of Defense created and endorsed a similar standard called TCP/IP that they used for interfacing diverse

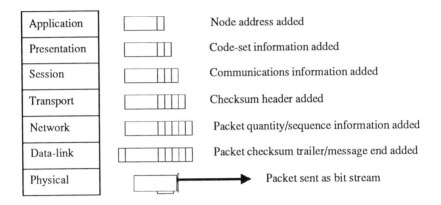

Application		Node address added
Presentation		Code-set information added
Session		Communications information added
Transport		Checksum header added
Network		Packet quantity/sequence information added
Data-link		Packet checksum trailer/message end added
Physical		Packet sent as bit stream

Figure 7-2.   The OSI protocol stack and its affect on packets

systems over wide area networks. While still in widespread use, it has some deficiencies and tends to be inefficient when used on local and metropolitan area networks. OSI will solve some of its problems.

The following describes each layer of the OSI protocol stack as illustrated in Figure 7-2. A message sent from one user to another is used to describe each layer in the discussion.

Application layer   The network operating system and its applications make themselves available to the user at this layer. A message is typed by the sender and addressed to the receiver.

Presentation layer   Interconnected stations may represent characters, numbers, directories, and other information in different ways. The presentation layer may serve as a translator between stations and determines the format for information displayed on the screen. For example, if the message is going from a DOS-based PC to a Macintosh, the way characters are displayed on the screen is slightly different. The presentation layer adds formatting information and passes the message to the session layer.

Session layer   The session layer coordinates the exchange of information between workstations. The layer gets its name from the communication session that it establishes and terminates. Coordination is required if one system is slower than another or packet transfer is not orderly. This layer adds beginning and ending brackets plus information about the communications protocol being used and sends the message to the transport layer.

Transport layer   This layer breaks information down into smaller segments and assigns a *checksum* to each segment for error checking. A copy is kept until the receiving station acknowledges receipt. The segments of the message are sent to the network layer.

Network layer   The network layer packetizes information. The size of each packet is determined by the cable access method or the operating system. Headers are added to record the total number of packets and their sequence. The packets are sent to the data-link layer.

Data-link layer   Each packet is assigned a checksum for error checking, and the checksum is added to a packet trailer. An address header is added to the front of each packet. A copy of each packet is held until receipt is acknowledged. The packet is then sent to the physical layer.

Physical layer   The packet is converted to digital bits for transmission over the cable system. The information is received by the physical layer of the receiving station.

OSI strives to provide a standard that could make other protocol stacks obsolete. It has limitations, but these are mainly due to the fact that the protocol set is not complete. For example, few applications have been written to take advantage of OSI. Additionally, directory services and internetwork routing specifications are not complete. The following standards are being developed for OSI.

OSI High-Level Standards

OSI File Transfer, Access, and Management (FTAM) provides file transfer and file access and management services across diverse, OSI-compatible systems. A file can be transferred from one network station to another, or created, written to, read, and deleted. File access and management functions provide protection features and the use of file attributes. File attributes include name, structure, size, and other information.

OSI application interfaces, such as X.500 directory services, X.400 electronic messaging, and CMIP network management, provide a link between the application and presentation layers. The X.400 standard defines communication with a variety of systems. X.500 directory services are based on the OSI Directory Services standard. These will be discussed in Chapter 11.

Industry Standard Network Architectures

As previously discussed, IPX/SPX is the standard used in Novell networks. When there is a need for interoperability among different operating systems and networks, network managers have reason to explore other standards. Novell and other network vendors have developed interim strategies that transmit several different packet types on a cable system at the same time. These strategies will be common until the OSI standard is in full use.

This section discusses the network operating systems, applications programming interfaces, and network communications methods NetWare supports as part of its open protocol technology, as was discussed in Chapter 5 and illustrated in Figure 5-2. Because the Open System Interconnection (OSI) model is a widely accepted standard, it can be used to explain and map the location in the protocol stack of the standards discussed in the following sections.

Distributed Filing Systems

The file systems discussed in the following sections allow stations on a network to access drives, directories, files, and other resources on other workstations as if they were local. In some systems, peer-to-peer connections can be made between workstations, which means that any workstation can make its resources available to another. With NetWare 386, only a dedicated file server or other server-type device can be used by another workstation for security reasons; however, by supporting other filing systems, peer-to-peer relationships can be established.

AppleTalk Filing Protocol (AFP) For Macintosh

NetWare 386 provides support for AppleTalk networks through a NetWare loadable module and a name-space facility that allows Apple Macintosh files to be stored on a NetWare server and used by non-Apple systems.

The AppleTalk system itself is implemented in every Macintosh, so it becomes a simple matter to configure an AppleTalk network. The appropriate cables are connected between systems to establish a simple print-sharing network. The AppleWork station software that comes with Apple's system software must be implemented. If more sophisticated features are required, such as file sharing and connection to NetWare networks, AppleShare must be implemented as well.

Sun Network Filing System (NFS)

NFS is a distributed file system protocol that allows a server to share its resources with another computer on a network. The operating system was developed by Sun Microsystems and is widely used to access files on Sun and other systems, including Unix-based minicomputers. Any system running Unix with NFS can be a server, while any PC or Macintosh can be a client. NFS is in the public domain and thus available for use by anyone.

Directories on the server can be made available, or *published,* for other users. Workstations then mount these directories, which appear as if they are local drives. Files can be transferred to and from the Unix server, but resources on workstations cannot be shared with other workstations, as is possible in a true peer-to-peer network.

Here is a summary of NFS features:

- A file-locking service similar to the Unix user authentication procedure can be used to limit or prevent file usage.

- Print jobs can be sent to the locally attached printer or a printer attached to the server.

- File conversion is available for converting DOS text files to Unix format or vice versa.

- Many commands are similar to those used in the Unix environment.

- PC-NFS LifeLine Mail is an electronic mail facility that allows mail to be sent to any workstation.

IBM Systems Network Architecture (SNA)

The IBM System Network Architecture (SNA) protocol is a seven-layer protocol that compares closely to the OSI protocol stack. SNA was developed in the 1970s by IBM to define communications between individual terminals and mainframes. IBM networks use the same SNA architecture. Although SNA was designed before the OSI model, IBM is working towards OSI compatibility. In the meantime, SNA is of importance to NetWare because Novell has announced support for it through the NetWare 386 Communications Manager, as covered in Chapter 10.

Microsoft Server Message Block (SMB) OS/2 Requester

SMB is a distributed file system protocol that allows a computer to share its resources with another computer on OS/2 networks. SMB was developed by Microsoft and is used by IBM and other vendors. IBM implements SMB in its LAN Manager program. SMB consists of a set of function calls used to send and receive messages, share printers, and share disks and directories. SMBs use NetBIOS or APPC to send messages across the network.

AT&T Remote File Service (RFS)

RFS is a distributed file system network protocol that allows a computer to share its resources with other computers on a network. RFS was developed by AT&T and is used in Unix system V. RFS is implemented using the STREAMS feature of Unix. Applications open streams to devices on the network such as a disk drive and communicate with it using a transport layer protocol called Transport-Level Interface (TLI). The TCP/IP protocol discussed later under "Transport Protocols" may also be used.

Interprocess Communications (IPC) Interfaces

Interprocess communications interfaces provide programmers with hooks and programming routines they can use to design products for networks. Because the interfaces are usually at a high layer on the protocol stack, programmers are insulated from lower-level programming tasks. NetBIOS is the exception that many programmers have found difficult to use because an awareness of lower-layer protocols is necessary.

IPC interfaces are supported by NetWare, so programs written for other environments can be run on NetWare. A NetBIOS emulator has been available for some time under NetWare 286. It is used to support programs written to NetBIOS for use on the IBM PC LAN program.

Advanced Program-to-Program Communications (APPC)

Advanced Program-to-Program Communications is an applications programming interface originally designed by IBM for communications between IBM mainframes and minicomputer systems. It is now used for communications between workstations on LANs. APPC has facilities for communicating with programs on hosts, such as IBM mainframes running CICS/VS, System/36, and System/38.

APPC is supported by the IBM System Application Architecture and is designed to establish a peer-to-peer communication level between programs on separate computers. The connection allows data to be transferred in one direction. APPC/PC is an alternative to NetBIOS, which was written for the IBM personal computer. It can be used to communicate with other APPC based programs.

Named Pipes

Named Pipes is an applications programming interface for interprocess communications that was originally designed by Microsoft for OS/2. It is used as a foundation for the OS/2 LAN Manager network operating system. When compared to the other programming interfaces described in this section, Named Pipes provides more hooks for programmers and requires less coding. Since many programs probably will be written to this interface, its support by NetWare is important.

NetBIOS

Network Basic Input/Output System (NetBIOS) was developed by Microsoft and IBM to provide a standardized high-level programming interface for peer-to-peer networks. This interface works mainly in the session layer. NetBIOS establishes a session between two workstations to provide data transmission. The session layer communications of NetBIOS is commonly emulated by vendors such as Novell in their own network products.

NetBIOS is harder to program than the other programming interfaces described in this section because more knowledge of the communication process is required. NetBIOS is *full duplex,* which means that both session partners can send simultaneously. A datagram service that does not require a session is also available. NetBIOS provides a naming facility that allows names to be given to workstations. Messages can then be directed to named stations rather than a network address.

NetBIOS does not normally provide support for the interconnection of separate LANs unless gateway products that run above NetBIOS are used. However, if Token Ring networks are connected, NetBIOS uses a *source-routing* method in which the sending station must provide routing information for messages that need to cross network boundaries. Methods are being developed to interface NetBIOS with TCP/IP for internetwork connections.

Transport Protocols

Transport protocols work at the transport and network layers of the OSI protocol stack. They provide low-level routines for transferring information during a network communications session.

SPX/IPX

Internetwork Packet Exchange (IPX) is a version of the Xerox network services protocol. It was created specifically for Novell NetWare. The protocol is optimized for use on LANs to provide low overhead and high performance, unlike TCP/IP, which was developed for wide area networks and contains many error-checking functions that add to its overhead. However, IPX is not a good protocol for wide area communications, and it is often necessary to use TCP/IP or X.25 when a reliable wide area transport protocol is required.

Sequenced Packet Exchange (SPX) is a connection-oriented interface that provides error checking, windowing, and flow control. SPX resides in the transport layer and partially in the session layer of the protocol stack. It is used instead of NetBIOS in Novell NetWare networks. SPX is used by applications when reliable data transfer is required. A virtual circuit is established between two connections, and special procedures are used to check for missing packets. Receipt of packets is acknowledged, and retransmission occurs if a packet is not received.

TCP/IP

TCP/IP is an acronym for Transmission Control Protocol and Internet Protocol. It was developed by the Department of Defense primarily to link dissimilar computer systems across large networks. TCP/IP was designed for long-haul, wide area networks that run over leased phone lines. TCP packages information for transmission and reassembles received packets, and IP handles the routing and transmission of data.

TCP defines a reliable method for transporting information between a computer site and a communications utility. Error recovery, flow control, and management features are available. TCP can also manage several connections (multiplex) at the same time without data loss. IP is an example of a datagram service; it handles data packets and fragments them if necessary. IP handles the functions at the network layer of the OSI model.

IEEE 802 Access Control Standards

The Institute of Electrical and Electronics Engineers (IEEE) has developed a set of standards for defining the way network interface cards transfer data from a system to the network. These protocols are accepted by ISO and work at the physical and data-link layers of the OSI reference model. The IEEE 802 body consists of a group of committees with the goal of producing technical standards open to all vendors so that a wide range of network interface products will work together. These products include network interface cards, bridges, routers, and other components used to create local twisted pair and coaxial cable-based networks or wide area networks using common carriers such as the phone system. The next few chapters discuss how the 802 specifications are used to design and implement these products.

The 802 committees are listed here. The physical and data-link layers are directly related to network interface cards and their drivers and are covered in the next chapter.

802.1	Internetworking
802.2	Logical link control (LLC)
802.3	CSMA/CD LAN
802.4	Token-Bus LAN
802.5	Token-Ring LAN
802.6	Metropolitan area network
802.7	Slotted-ring LAN
X.25	Wide area network protocol

The 802 standards allow computers and devices from many different vendors to be connected locally using twisted pair and coaxial cables, or over wide areas using high-speed cable systems—for example, fiber optic or common carrier services such as the phone system.

An important part of the 802 standard is referred to as *global addressing*. In this scheme every network card from every manufacturer is assigned a unique address, so no two cards on the same network have conflicting addresses. The addressing scheme provides a forwarding function important on internetworks to ensure packets reach their final destination on the local or remote LAN. The 802 addressing standards help vendors design compatible products to work over internetworks. More information is provided in the next chapter.

NetWare Open Systems

The traditional NetWare IPX communication method is ideal for networks that support only NetWare workstations. IPX is a fast and efficient packet delivery system. However, IPX is used only by Novell, which makes interoperability with other types of networks difficult. TCP/IP is an established standard used by many companies and government agencies as a way to provide multivendor networking and wide area networking. Because TCP/IP is seen as an important stepping-stone to the OSI standard, many vendors have invested money and development time in it. Thus, many TCP/IP products are available, and NetWare users have many good reasons to interconnect with those products.

In 1989, Novell acquired Excelan, a developer of TCP/IP products, and now supports the standard with a line of connectivity products. For example, LAN Workplace for DOS provides PC and PS/2 users with direct access to Unix systems, VAXs, IBM mainframes, and other resources that use the TCP/IP protocols. TCP/IP is an important standard because it was written with large multivendor internetworks in mind.

While TCP/IP is getting the most attention in the move to interoperability, other standards also exist, such as AppleTalk and IBM's System Network Architecture (SNA). Because of this, Novell developed its open protocol technology (OPT) to provide multiple-protocol capabilities.

With OPT, a single card can be used to communicate with multiple protocol stacks, as described earlier.

Although the OSI protocol set will be a major solution for those who need interoperability in the near future, the need to use multiple protocols exists today for those who want to connect to other computing platforms within an organization. Several network vendors, not just Novell, are using multiple protocol stacks. They allow NetWare users to choose among IPX/SPX, TCP/IP, and OSI. Through OPT, Novell will achieve protocol independence in the same way IPX allows independence in the selection of network interface cards.

Keep in mind that many products exist on the market today that allow Novell networks to interconnect to a wide variety of networks and networking products. The Novell Excelan products are a good example. Another is the Interlan NetWare TCP/IP Gateway which can be used for occasional access to a variety of multivendor TCP/IP products. Additional products are discussed in Chapter 9.

The Open Data-Link Interface

The Open Data-Link Interface (ODI) is a Novell NetWare 386 interface that allows multiple protocols to use the same network cabling system. Additional protocols are added to the server using the NetWare PROTO-COL command, and then one or more protocols, such as IPX/SPX and TCP/IP, are bound to a network interface card with the NetWare BIND command. A card that uses these protocols can then accept IPX/SPX or TCP/IP packets.

ODI first grew out of a need for protocol independence. The first step to interconnecting into other types of networks is to recognize their protocol stacks. ODI also standardizes the development of network interface card drivers; vendors no longer need to worry about writing their drivers to fit a specific protocol stack. Instead, drivers are written to attach to an ODI link called the link support layer (LSL). LSL is like a switchboard that is responsible for ensuring packets are directed to the proper protocol stack.

Through ODI, many of the protocols discussed earlier, such as Apple-Talk, Network Filing System (NFS), and IBM SNA, can be loaded, allowing messages and data from these systems to share the same cable. Multiple

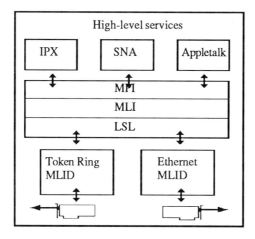

Figure 7-3.   Open Data-Link Interface (ODI)

protocol stacks allow the network medium to become a highway shared by different types of network traffic.

The ODI consists of the basic components shown in Figure 7-3. This figure illustrates a server with two interface cards, one supporting a Token Ring network and another supporting an Ethernet network. Workstations and bridges may also have a link support layer in which they can receive packets from any other workstation without the need to reload an operating system or change drivers.

The following sections briefly describe the ODI components.

Multiple Link Interface (MLI)   The MLI layer is an interface where device drivers for the network interface card are attached. The device drivers are written by vendors of network interface cards to match the Novell specification of the link support layer. Drivers are referred to as multiple link interface drivers (MLIDs).

Link Support Layer (LSL)   The LSL provides a link for drivers at the bottom and protocols at the top. It acts as a switching board, directing network traffic from MLIDs to the proper protocol, or vice versa.

Multiple Protocol Interface (MPI)   The MPI provides an interface for the connection of protocol stacks, such as IPX. Novell will also make available TCP/IP, AppleTalk, OSI, and SNA protocol stacks.

When a packet arrives at a network interface card, it is processed by the card's MLID and passed to the link support layer. The LSL determines which protocol stack the packet should go to and hands it to the protocol. The packet passes up through the protocol stack in the normal way, where it is handled by higher-level NetWare services.

Note: In some cases a packet may simply be routed through the LSL from one network to another, rather than being processed by the server (or bridge). The LSL takes the packet arriving from one MLID and passes it to another.

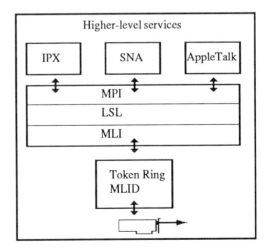

Figure 7-4   A link support layer (LSL) supports multiple protocols in a work-station

The link support layer can support up to 16 protocols and eight MLIDs. Figure 7-3 shows one of many ways to configure a server. Another example is shown in Figure 7-4. Here a single network interface card sends and receives multiple protocol packets across the network. This configuration is common in workstations that need to process different types of packets.

NetWare Streams

Streams is a set of tools used to establish an interface between NetWare and any Streams-supported protocols. This means NetWare services can be delivered across the network, no matter what transport protocol is used. It also provides support for server-based applications that use a variety of interprocess communications (IPC) mechanisms such as NetBIOS, Named Pipes, and AT&T's Transport Library Interface (TLI). In this way, the remote processes of distributed applications can communicate in a full-duplex mode (that is, communication takes place simultaneously in both directions).

Streams is implemented as a set of NetWare loadable modules that are loaded when the server is first installed or booted. When Streams is installed, interfaces are added at the top and bottom of the protocol stack (see Figure 7-3). The interface at the top of the stack is known as a *stream head* and interfaces with service protocol stacks such as NetWare core protocol, server message blocks, and AppleTalk Filing Protocol. The interface at the bottom of the stack connects to the link support layer.

Streams is a two-way data transfer path that can be manipulated through such operations as open, read, write, and close, and can be multiplexed so a single upper stream provides access to multiple lower streams. Each lower stream can lead to a different protocol stack with a different API. Btrieve and SQL requests can travel over a variety of transports (IPX, SPX, TCP/IP, OSI), using a variety of interprocess communications (IPC) mechanisms such as Advanced Program-to-Program Communications, NetBIOS, and Named Pipes.

Network Interface Methods
And Topologies

Network Connection Overview
Ethernet and IEEE 802.3
ARCNET
Token Ring

A network is a modular and adaptable communication system that can be customized to many different site requirements. Its modularity makes it easy to add new components or move existing ones, and its adaptability makes changes and upgrades easy.

The network methods discussed in this chapter are Ethernet, Token Ring, and ARCNET. The traditional methods of wiring these networks are described in the following list:

- Ethernet provides a linear bus topology with a CSMA/CD (carrier sensing multiple access/collision detection) access method using thin or thick coaxial cable and twisted pair.

- ARCNET provides a star or bus topology with a token passing access method using coaxial cable.

- Token Ring combines star and ring topologies and a token passing access method using shielded or unshielded twisted pair cable.

Many variations of these methods are appearing from vendors and distributors. For example, twisted pair is replacing coaxial copper cable in many installations, and attachments for fiber optic backbones are common.

129

Network Connection Overview

Networks consist of network interface cards and cables. The access method and topology used by a particular network method also are important considerations. These four factors are covered in the following sections.

Network Interface Cards

A network interface card is chosen after a decision is made on the access method, type of cable, and topology the card should use. Interface cards are available to fit AT-class machines with 16-bit industry standard architecture (ISA) bus slots or standard machines with 8-bit ISA bus slots. Whenever possible, 16-bit cards should be used. Cards are also available for microchannel architecture (MCA) systems like the IBM PS/2 systems, and for extended industry standard architecture (EISA) bus systems like the Compaq DESKPRO 486 and Compaq SYSTEMPRO. If possible, use MCA or EISA systems as servers in a NetWare 386 network to maximize performance due to their advanced bus structures. Chapters 13 and 14 cover server selection in more detail.

High-performance network cards are especially important in a NetWare 386 server because it handles large amounts of input from and output to workstations. Only MCA and EISA systems can deliver this performance. Older ISA systems, even those using 16-bit bus slots, do not perform well under the type of network traffic loads associated with the server.

Tasks of Network Interface Cards

Network interface cards must manage a number of tasks when a session is established between two workstations on a network. Some of these tasks are defined by the protocol stack and media access rules used by the particular card. In addition, the manufacturers of the card may build in performance improvements of their own, such as bus mastering, large buffers, or faster processors.

When packets need to be sent, a *handshaking* process takes place between workstations. This handshaking establishes communication parameters, such as the transmission speed, packet size, time-out parameters, and buffer size. Handshaking is especially important when two cards are not the same; one may attempt to send faster than the other can receive.

Once the communications parameters are established, the sending network interface card can begin transmitting, and the receiving card can begin capturing the data. Two types of conversions must take place on the packets of data formed by the protocol stack rules. The first is a *parallel-to-serial conversion,* which transforms the parallel data in the PC to a serial form that can be transmitted as electrical signals over a cable. The second has to do with encoding the data into a form that is compressed to enhance transmission speed. The receiving system must decode the data it receives.

The system that receives data may not be as fast as the system sending it; therefore, a memory buffer is needed to temporarily hold the information. If the buffer is large, the entire block of information being transmitted may fill the buffer. This frees the cable for other transmissions. Consequently, large buffers can increase network performance. Some interface cards have built-in buffers, while others use part of the PC's memory.

Once data has been received by a network interface card, it must be accessible by the PC's central processing unit (CPU). One of the following methods may be used to transfer the data on the card to a useful memory location.

Shared memory   When the shared memory method is used, the memory in the PC is used as a buffer. Data is placed directly in memory, so no intermediate shuffling is required. The shared memory method is the fastest for non-bus-mastering cards, but it is expensive.

DMA method   When the DMA method is used, a DMA controller on the PC takes control of the bus and transfers data from the network interface card's buffer directly into a designated memory location on the PC. This eliminates some of the work the CPU would normally perform and increases performance. While data is being transferred, the CPU may do some other task, but it cannot access memory. The DMA is sometimes referred to as bus mastering but it is not a true form of bus mastering, as discussed next.

Bus mastering   Bus mastering is similar to the DMA method, but more efficient. The card itself handles the task of the DMA controller without interrupting the CPU. True bus mastering is only possible on MCA and EISA machines due to their advanced bus design. Both the CPU and the card can operate simultaneously without the restrictions of the DMA method. Bus mastering cards have the potential to increase performance by 20% to 70%.

Network Interface Card Drivers

Almost all network interface cards are supplied with a disk that contains driver files used to install a card in a system and make it recognizable to NetWare. Driver files contain information about the card's configuration, its cable access method, and its communication features. For workstations, a driver is linked to the NetWare Internetwork Packet Exchange (IPX) file. For servers, the files are linked to the operating system itself.

Keep in mind that drivers for workstations are different than drivers linked to the operating system. Operating system drivers have an extension of LAN.

Global Addressing

Global addressing ensures that every network interface card has a unique identifying node address, or has a switch block used to ensure no duplicate addresses exist on a LAN. Token Ring and Ethernet card addresses are hard-wired on the card. ARCNET addresses can be selected by the user.

The IEEE committee is in charge of assigning addresses to Token Ring and Ethernet cards. Each manufacturer is given a code and a block of addresses. When installing cards, it is a good idea to determine the network address and write it down for future reference. The address may be on the card itself, or it may be determined by running the card's diagnostics program.

Network topology	Maximum segment distance
Thick Ethernet (10BASE5)	500 meters (1640 feet)
Thin Ethernet (10BASE2)	185 meters (607 feet)
Twisted pair Ethernet (10BASE-T)	100 meters (330 feet)
Fiber optic Ethernet	2 kilometers (6562 feet)
Twisted pair Token Ring	100 meters (330 feet) from MAU
Coaxial ARCNET (star)	609 meters (2000 feet)
Coaxial ARCNET (bus)	305 meters (1000 feet)
Twisted pair ARCNET (star)	122 meters (400 feet)
Twisted pair ARCNET (bus)	122 meters (400 feet)

Table 8-1.   Network Topologies and Their Maximum Segment Distance

Topology

Part of the decision for choosing a particular type of network involves the topology. Recall that the major forms of network topology are linear bus, star, and ring, but there are combinations of these. For example, ARCNET can take on both linear bus and star topologies, while Token Ring takes on a logical ring and physical star topology.

If all the workstations are in a row, such as in a classroom, for example, a linear topology works fine. If workstations tend to be in clusters, Token Ring should be considered. ARCNET is useful when clusters of machines are separated by long distances. For example, ARCNET allows a cluster of machines in a department to be connected in a star configuration, and then each cluster can be connected with a long stretch of linear cable. Table 8-1 lists the various forms of network topology and the potential distance of each.

Cabling

The choice of a cable is sometimes the determining factor when deciding on a network. In many cases coaxial copper cable or telephone twisted pair cable may already be in place. If not, the decision on the type of cable may be based on the cost of the cable and how much will be needed to wire the building. Cable shielding and security are also factors. Coaxial copper cable is protected from interference by its shielding, but it is expensive. Fiber optic cable is secure and does not require any shielding, but it is the most expensive of all. Twisted pair is cheap and provides some protection from interference, but data transmission rates and potential distance are low except with a new Ethernet standard. The use of twisted pair is expanding due to advances in network technology and communications methods. The IEEE 802 committee has developed a twisted pair Ethernet standard that has a 10Mbps rating.

Copper coaxial cable has the following characteristics:

- May be affected by outside interference.

- May act like an antenna as distance increases, picking up noise and interference from motors, radio transmitters and other sources of electric power.

- Has problems with grounding.

- Emits signals that can be monitored by intruders.

Fiber optic cable has the following characteristics:

- Is commonly used in combination with other cable types as a backbone connection.

- Although expensive, it has a greater potential distance and faster transmission.

- Does not emit signals and can be used in high-security areas.

- Cable taps can be detected by adjusting the amount of light through the cable. If a tap is made, the cable will fail because the system is not "tuned" for the addition of the tap.

Twisted pair wiring has the following characteristics:

- The most economical wiring system.

- May already be installed in the form of existing telephone twisted pair lines.

- Twisted pair has distance limitations, but these can be corrected by using coaxial or fiber optic backbones.

- Susceptible to some outside interference.

The telephone wiring closet can provide a place where different types of cabling schemes come together. For example, a coaxial backbone may be used to connect two distant groups of PCs. Twisted pair wiring can be used at either end of the backbone to connect workstations that radiate from the wiring closet. Table 8-2 describes and compares the three most popular types of cable.

Baluns

A balun (balanced-unbalanced) is a small device that allows coaxial cable to be intermixed with twisted pair cable. A simple transformer converts the signal and impedance between "balanced" and "unbalanced" circuits. A balanced circuit is one on which signals on one conductor are balanced by equal but opposite signals on the other conductor (twisted pair). An unbalanced circuit is one on which one conductor carries the signal, while the other (shielding in the case of coaxial cable) is grounded.

	Twisted Pair	**Coaxial**	**Fiber optic**
Cost	Low	Moderate	High
Band width	Moderate	High	Extra high
Length	100s of feet	1000s of feet	Miles
Interference	Some	Low	None
Reliability	High	High	Extra high

Table 8-2.   Comparison of the Three Most Popular Types of Network Cable

Baluns are in the price range of $25 to $50. In most cases they are used to provide flexibility with network wiring by allowing twisted pair and coaxial cable to be used on the same network.

Cable Access Method

Network interface cards use a specific access method when transferring data for transmission on a cable. The way packets are transferred to the cable affects transmission speed. Recall from Chapter 2 that carrier sensing methods, like that used in Ethernet, use a broadcast method in which every station hears the signal and receives or rejects it. In token passing methods, like Token Ring and ARCNET, a workstation must have possession of a token before it begins transmitting. Carrier sensing is fast (Ethernet is rated at 10Mbps), but collisions can occur during heavy traffic that can slow the network, since crashed signals must be rebroadcast. Token passing methods are not susceptible to collisions, but they are more reliable. Newer token passing methods are available that improve performance. IBM offers a 16 Mbps Token Ring interface card (the original boards are 4 Mbps).

The Institute of Electrical and Electronics Engineers (IEEE) has developed a set of standards that have also been adopted by the International Standards Organization (ISO) as part of the OSI standard. Any discussion of network interface cards and networking methods must begin with the standards defined by this organization. The 802 committees for local area networks (LANs) are listed here:

802.2	Logical link control (LLC)
802.3	CSMA/CD LAN
802.4	Token Bus LAN
802.5	Token Ring LAN

Keep in mind that other committees exist to define internetworking in general, as well as metropolitan area networking (MAN) and wide area networking (WAN), which are discussed in the following chapters.

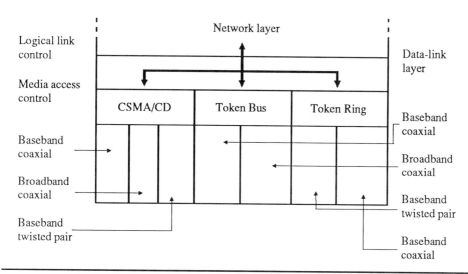

Figure 8-1.   The data-link layer has two sublayers used to interface network drivers and the physical layer to the protocol stack

These standards are used to define the physical and data-link layers of the OSI reference model, as shown in Figure 8-1. Note that the data-link layer is divided into two sublayers. The terminology used to describe these layers and their functions is widely used in computer industry journals and product literature for interface cards and other network devices; therefore, you should become familiar with the terminology.

Logical Link Control (LLC)

The logical link control layer provides a single standard interface between upper protocol layers and the lower-level media access control (MAC) layer. It is defined by the IEEE 802.2 committee. The LLC layer is like a switchboard that organizes how data flows between lower and upper layers. Notice that the MAC layer consists of the other 802.x specifications, which can be seen as modular in design. The LLC layer provides bridging between these modules. If, for example, a token bus and a Token Ring card are installed in a server, the bridging of data packets between them takes place at the LLC level.

Media Access Control (MAC)

The MAC layer defines the rules for accessing the network cable. These are the carrier sensing or token passing rules already discussed. The 802.3, 802.4, and 802.5 committees define these methods. The MAC layer allows multiple devices to access the cable, which means that several interface cards can be installed to form a *bridge*. If data needs to cross the bridge, it passes from the cable through the MAC layer up to the LLC layer and back down into another MAC layer to reach its destination.

The MAC layer is also concerned with the *framing* of data packets. Header and trailer information is added to a frame of data to identify the beginning and end of a message, routing information, and error detection controls.

The Physical Layer

The 802 committee supports the use of twisted pair, coaxial, and fiber optic cable. Specific types of cable are used by each of the media access methods. In addition, transmission methods, encoding methods, and data rates are defined. The physical layer is concerned with transmitting bits of information over the media. The frames from the MAC layer are converted to electrical signals and transmitted.

Ethernet and IEEE 802.3

Ethernet was originally created by Xerox, but was jointly developed as a standard in 1980 by Digital Equipment, Intel, and Xerox. This standard became known as DIX Ethernet in reference to the developers' names. Ethernet has a 10Mbps throughput and uses a carrier sensing (CSMA/CD) access method. The IEEE 802.3 standard also defines a similar standard with one slight difference that can cause those configuring Ethernet some headaches. The DIX Ethernet and IEEE 802.3 standard have a slight difference in the frame format. Because the 802.3 standard is the default for NetWare and is more commonly used, it is discussed in this section. NetWare does provide a way to use the DIX Ethernet standard if necessary by running the ECONFIG command.

The adaptations of the IEEE 802.3 standard all have transmission speeds of 10Mbps with the exception of 1BASE5, which transmits at 1Mbps but has long twisted pair segments. Only 10BASE5, 10BASE2, and 10BASE-T are discussed in this section due to their popularity. Here is a list of all IEEE 802.3 standard adaptations:

10BASE5	Coaxial cable with maximum segment lengths of up to 500 meters using baseband transmission
10BASE2	Coaxial cable (RG58A/U) with maximum segment lengths of up to 185 meters using baseband transmission
10BASE-T	Twisted pair cable with maximum segment lengths of up to 100 meters
1BASE5	Twisted pair cable with maximum segment lengths of up to 500 meters and transmission speeds of up to 1Mbps
10BROAD36	Coaxial cable (RG59/U CATV type) with maximum segment lengths of up to 3600 meters using broadband transmission
10BASE-F	Fiber optic cable segments with transmission at 10Mbps

The topology of 802.3 Ethernet is a linear bus with a CSMA/CD access method. Workstations are connected with segments of cable. The segments then form a single large cable system known as the *trunk cable*. The twisted pair version can be configured as a star since a concentrator that works as a hub can be used.

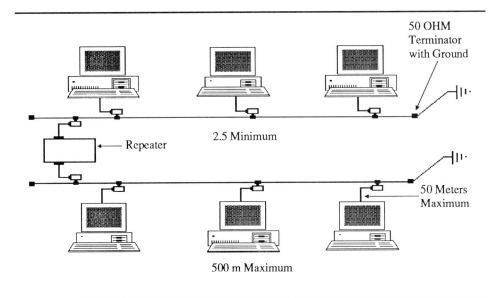

50 OHM Terminator with Ground

2.5 Minimum

Repeater

50 Meters Maximum

500 m Maximum

Figure 8-2.   Thick Ethernet topology and specifications

It is possible to combine different types of Ethernet cabling to achieve an optimum cabling system. For example, thick Ethernet may be used in a backbone configuration to connect two separate thin Ethernet trunks.

Thick Coaxial Ethernet 10BASE5

Thick Ethernet cable is often referred to as standard Ethernet since it was the original implementation. Figure 8-2 illustrates a thick Ethernet cabling scheme. Each station on a thick Ethernet trunk is attached with a transceiver and transceiver cable. The transceiver is not the same as a BNC T-connector like those used on thin Ethernet. It is a small box that provides electrical isolation of the workstation from the cable. A "heartbeat" test in the transceiver is used to determine if the station is connected properly.

The following components are part of a thick Ethernet network:

Network interface board   Most Ethernet boards support either thick or thin Ethernet cabling. The board should have a female DIX-type connector for the attachment of the thick Ethernet transceiver cable. If the interface card will be installed in a server, be sure to use a board with the best performance. Network interface cards are available in standard 8-bit ISA bus, AT-type 16-bit ISA bus design, MCA, and EISA. If installed in a diskless workstation, a remote reset PROM must be used.

Repeater   The repeater is an optional device used to join two Ethernet trunks and to strengthen the signals between them. A repeater attaches to a transceiver on each cable trunk with a transceiver cable.

Transceiver   The transceiver is a junction box on the thick Ethernet cable where workstations can be attached. It has three connectors: Two are the thick Ethernet in/out connectors and the third is used to attach the workstation to the transceiver using a transceiver cable. Transceivers attach to the network cable trunk in one of two ways. A clamping method pierces the cable, eliminating the need to cut the cable and mount connectors. Alternatively, a BNC version of the transceiver has a T-connector to which cable ends attach. This method requires that the cable be cut and connectors be attached to it.

Transceiver cable   Transceiver cables usually come with the transceiver units. A male and a female DIX-type connector are mounted on either end, along with slide locks to lock the cable to the network interface board and transceiver connectors.

Thick Ethernet cabling   The cabling used for thick Ethernet is a 50-ohm 0.4-inch-diameter coaxial cable and is not the same as that used for the transceiver cable. Thick Ethernet cable is available from many vendors in bulk or in precut lengths. A coaxial cable stripping and crimping tool is required to mount connectors. Note that cable is available as fireproof plenum cable, nonplenum interior cable, underground rated cable, and aerial rated cable.

N-series male connectors   These thick Ethernet cable connectors are installed on both ends of the cable when T-connector-type transceivers are used. Preassembled cables already have the connectors mounted.

N-series barrel connectors   These connectors are used to join two cable segments.

N-series terminators   Each cable segment must be terminated at both ends with a 50-ohm N-series terminator. For each cable segment you need one terminator with a ground wire attached and one without a ground wire.

Specifications and limitations of the network standard are described as follows:

- The maximum trunk segment length is 500 meters (1640 feet).

- Transceivers are connected to the trunk segment.

- The maximum workstation-to-transceiver distance is 50 meters (164 feet).

- The minimum distance to the next transceiver is 2.5 meters (8 feet).

- Up to five trunk segments may be joined using four repeaters. Workstations are allowed on only three of the segments. The others are used for distance.

- The maximum network trunk length is 2460 meters (8200 feet).

- You can have a maximum of 100 workstations on one trunk. Repeaters count as workstations.

- A 50-ohm terminator must be placed at the end of each trunk segment, and one end must be grounded.

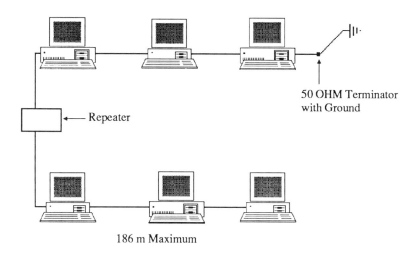

50 OHM Terminator
with Ground

Repeater

186 m Maximum

Figure 8-3.   Thin Ethernet topology and specifications

Thin Coaxial Ethernet 10BASE2

Thin Ethernet cable is physically easier to handle than thick Ethernet and does not require the use of transceivers at the stations. The cable is cheaper, but the maximum trunk length is not as high as thick Ethernet. Figure 8-3 illustrates a thin Ethernet network.

The following components are part of a 10BASE2 network:

Network interface board   Most Ethernet boards support either thick or thin Ethernet cabling. The board should have a BNC-type connector attached to the back and may have a thick Ethernet connector. A BNC T-connector is attached to BNC connectors on the back of the board to attach to the trunk cable. Network interface cards are available in standard 8-bit ISA bus, AT-type 16-bit ISA bus design, MCA, and EISA. If installed in a diskless workstation, a remote reset PROM must be used.

Repeater   The repeater is an optional device used to join two Ethernet trunks and to strengthen the signals between them.

Thin Ethernet cabling   The cabling used for thin Ethernet is a 50-ohm 0.2-inch-diameter RG-58A/U coaxial cable. Thin Ethernet cable is available from many vendors who have precut standard lengths ready to ship. Bulk cable can also be purchased, but BNC connectors must be mounted on the ends of the cable cuts. Note that cable is available as fireproof plenum cable, non-plenum interior cable, underground rated cable, and aerial rated cable.

BNC cable connectors   BNC connectors must be attached to the ends of all cable segments. The kits include a center pin, housing, and clamp down sleeve. A coaxial cable stripping and crimping tool will be required to mount connectors.

BNC T-connectors   T-connectors are attached to the BNC connector on the back of the Ethernet interface cards. The T-connector provides two cable connections for signal-in and signal-out. You will need a T- connector for each workstation.

BNC barrel connectors   These are used to join two cable segments together.

BNC terminators   Each cable segment must be terminated at both ends with a 50-ohm BNC terminator. For each cable segment you need one terminator with a ground and one without.
   The following rules and limitations apply:

- The maximum trunk segment length is 186 meters (607 feet).

- T-connectors are used to connect the cable to the network interface card.

- Up to five trunk segments may be joined using four repeaters. Workstations are allowed on only three of the segments. The others are used for distance.

- The maximum network trunk length is 910 meters (3035 feet).

- You can have a maximum of 30 workstations on one trunk. Repeaters count as workstations.

- A terminator must be placed at each end of a trunk segment, and one end must be grounded.

Combined Thick and Thin Cables

It is possible to combine a thick and thin Ethernet cabling system. This is usually done to save money on cable, because thin Ethernet is normally cheaper than thick. Thick cable may be used to extend the distance between two thin Ethernet cable trunks by using a repeater. A repeater can also be used to join two existing trunks. The maximum number of trunk segments is five.

Combination thick and thin cable segments can be created using a BNC to N-series adapter which is available with an N-series female or N-series male adapter at one end. Combination thick and thin segments are usually between 607 and 1640 feet long. The following equation is used to find the maximum amount of thin cable that can be used in one combination trunk segment:

$$\frac{1.640 \text{ feet} - L}{3.28} = t$$

where L is the length of the trunk segment you want to build, and t is the maximum length of thin cable you can use.

Twisted Pair Ethernet 10BASE-T

As of this writing the IEEE proposal for 10Mbps baseband twisted pair, called 10BASE-T, was ready for standardization. 10BASE-T offers most of the advantages of Ethernet without the need to use expensive coaxial cable. In addition, a star or distributed topology allows for clusters of workstations in departments or other areas. Many vendors have already released products that follow the proposed IEEE standard or will be compatible with it.

Part of the 10BASE-T specification is to make it compatible with other IEEE 802.3 standards. This makes transition from one media to another easy; existing Ethernet cards can be retained if converting from coaxial to twisted pair. In most cases twisted pair trunks can be added to existing trunks by using repeaters that support coaxial, fiber optic, and twisted pair Ethernet trunks. Many vendors make such products available as part of their Ethernet product line. The 10BASE-T specification includes a cable testing feature called link integrity testing. With this feature, the system constantly tests the twisted pair wiring for open wires and shorts. Monitoring is done from a central point.

A basic 10BASE-T connection is shown in Figure 8-4. Workstations are attached to a *central hub* or concentrator, which acts as a repeater.

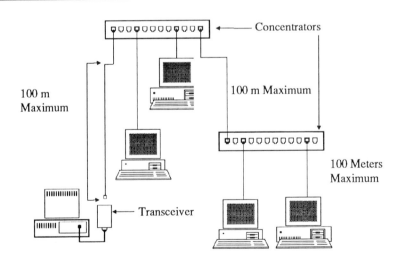

Figure 8-4.   Twisted pair Ethernet (10BASE-T) topology and specifications

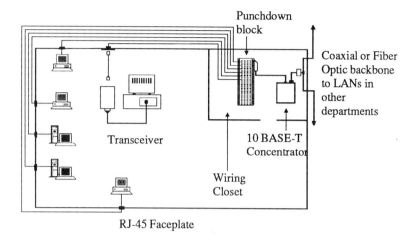

Figure 8-5.   Twisted pair Ethernet configuration with existing telephone wire

When a signal from a workstation arrives, the hub broadcasts it back out on all output lines. Note that hubs can be attached to other hubs in a hierarchical configuration. Workstations are attached with an unshielded twisted pair segment that cannot exceed 100 meters (328 feet). These cables connect to a transceiver near the workstation. The transceiver is then connected to the workstation with a 15-wire cable that can be up to 50 meters (164 feet) long.

One of the main reasons for using twisted pair is to take advantage of existing telephone wiring, as illustrated in Figure 8-5. In this example, a coaxial or fiber optic backbone connects the wiring centers or closets of different departments within a building. A 10BASE-T concentrator is connected to this backbone in the wiring closet. A 50-pin telephone jumper cable then connects the concentrator to a telephone punchdown block. Two pairs of existing unused twisted pair wires are put into use to establish a connection between the punchdown block and the telephone faceplate near the workstation. At the workstation, a cable is strung from the faceplate to a transceiver, which then connects to the workstation.

The following components may be used in a 10BASE-T network. Keep in mind that a basic system may not need the components to connect to a backbone cable or telephone wiring block.

Network interface card   An Ethernet card with a DIX-type 15-pin connector is required. Network interface cards are available in standard 8-bit ISA bus, AT-type 16 bit-ISA bus design, MCA, and EISA. If installed in a diskless workstation, a remote reset PROM must be used.

Hub   The hub (also called a concentrator) may have up to 12 ports; some have 10 or 11. A port for attachment to coaxial or fiber optic backbones should also be included. Some hubs do not have separate plugs for each workstation. Instead an "octopus" cable with lines for each of the stations is used.

Twisted pair cables   Twisted pair cable with RJ-45 connectors up to 100 meters long can be used. Bulk cable and connectors can be purchased to make custom cables. Be sure to purchase an RJ crimp tool.

Transceiver device   The transceiver device has an RJ-45 connector on one side and a DB-15 connector on the other.

Transceiver cable   The transceiver cable attaches between the transceiver device and the back of the network interface card.

Punchdown block connector cable   If existing telephone cable is to be used, a cable that connects the concentrator to a telephone punchdown block is useful.

Wall plate   A wall plate with an RJ connector can be used to mount the twisted pair cable to the wall. If a phone connection is also required, dual plates can be purchased.

The 10BASE-T specifications are listed next:

- Unshielded twisted pair (20 to 24 AWG UTP) wire is used.

- RJ-45 connectors are generally used. Pins 1 and 2 are used to transmit and pins 3 and 6 are used to receive.

- A transceiver and a 15-pin transceiver cable may be attached to each workstation. Some cards have built-in transceivers.

- Distances from transceiver to hub cannot exceed 100 meters (328 feet).

- A single hub can connect up to 12 workstations.

- Up to 12 hubs can be attached to a central hub to expand the number of network stations.

- Hubs can be attached to coaxial or fiber optic backbones to become part of larger Ethernet networks.

- Up to 1023 stations are possible on a network without using bridges.

ARCNET

ARCNET is a baseband token passing network system that offers flexible star and bus topologies at a low price. Transmission speeds are 2.5Mbps. ARCNET uses a token bus access method but is not an IEEE standard. ARCNET was developed by Datapoint (San Antonio, Texas) around 1970 and has been licensed to other companies. In 1981, Standard Microsystems Corporation (SMC) developed the first single-chip LAN controller based on the ARCNET token passing protocol. In 1986, a new chip set supporting bus topology was introduced. Most industry standards, including those used by Novell, are based on the new chip set technology.

A typical ARCNET configuration is shown in Figure 8-6. While ARCNET is generally considered to have a slow throughput, it does

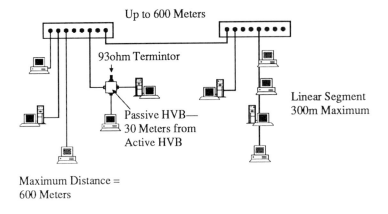

Up to 600 Meters

93ohm Termintor

Passive HVB—
30 Meters from
Active HVB

Linear Segment
300m Maximum

Maximum Distance =
600 Meters

Figure 8-6.   ARCNET cabling configuration

support long cable lengths of up to 2000 feet when *active hubs* are used. Fiber optic and twisted pair versions are available. Its flexible wiring scheme that allows long trunks and star configurations on the same LAN makes ARCNET an important consideration when speed is not a factor. However, recent tests have shown that ARCNET can be as fast as Ethernet and Token Ring in some environments.

Datapoint, SMC, and NCR recently announced ARCNETplus, a 20Mbps version of ARCNET that is compatible with 2.5Mbps ARCNET. Both versions can be on the same LAN. ARCNETplus supports larger packet sizes and eight times as many stations.

These components may make up a standard ARCNET network:

Network interface board   ARCNET boards are available from many vendors, including Standard Microsystems Corporation, Thomas Conrad, and Puredata. Standard coaxial boards should have a BNC connector attached to the back. When ARCNET is configured as a linear bus,

T-connectors are used on the cards. Network interface cards are available in standard 8-bit ISA bus, AT-type 16-bit ISA bus design, MCA, and EISA. If installed in a diskless workstation, a remote reset PROM must be used.

Active hub   The active hub is a network relay that conditions and amplifies the signal strength. Distances from active hubs can be 2000 feet. Most active hubs have eight ports to which workstations, passive hubs, or additional active hubs can be attached. It is not necessary to terminate unused ports on an active hub.

Passive hub   The passive hub is a four-port connector with BNC jacks used as a wiring center. Workstations cannot be further than 100 feet from a passive hub. Each unused port must be terminated.

ARCNET cabling   The cabling used for ARCNET is a 93-ohm RG-62/U coaxial cable. BNC connectors are used to attach cable segments to active hubs, passive hubs, and network interface cards. ARCNET cable is available from many vendors who will have precut standard lengths ready to ship. Bulk cable can also be purchased, along with BNC connectors that must be mounted on the cable ends. A coaxial cable stripping and crimping tool is required to mount connectors. Note that cable is available as fireproof plenum cable, nonplenum interior cable, underground rated cable, and aerial rated cable.

BNC coaxial connectors   Connectors can be purchased to mount on the ends of specially cut bulk cable. The kits include a center pin, housing, and clampdown sleeve.

BNC T-connectors   T-connectors are attached to the BNC connector on the back of the ARCNET interface cards when used in a bus topology. The T-connector provides two cable connections for signal-in and signal-out. You will need a T- connector for each workstation, plus two for each repeater being used.

BNC terminators   A 93-ohm BNC terminating cap must be placed on all passive hub ports that are not in use.
     The following rules and limitations apply:

- Most active hubs have eight nodes. Workstations on active hubs can extend as far as 600 meters (2000 feet) from the hub.

- Active hubs can be connected to form a hierarchical configuration. The maximum distance between two active hubs is 600 meters (2000 feet).

- Up to four workstations can be grouped around a passive hub. Each workstation cannot be further than 30.5 meters (100 feet) from the hub.

- Passive hubs cannot be connected to other passive hubs. They can be attached to active hubs at a maximum distance of 30.5 meters (100 feet).

- Unused nodes on passive hubs must be terminated using a 93-ohm terminator cap.

- The maximum distance between stations at opposite ends of the network is 20,000 feet.

- When stations are wired in a bus configuration, the maximum trunk length of the bus segment is 305 meters (1000 feet).

- The maximum number of stations is 255.

Token Ring

Token Ring is an IBM network implementation based on the IEEE 802.5 standard. It is a token passing ring network that can be configured in a star topology. Up to eight workstations radiate from a central hub, called a multistation access unit (MAU), which contains a logical ring wiring configuration as shown in Figure 8-7. If a station fails, the MAU immediately bypasses the station to maintain the ring of the network. Note that unconnected stations are bypassed.

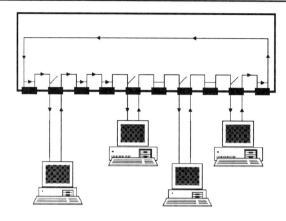

Figure 8-7.   The Token Ring multiple access unit (MAU) showing bypass switches

Additional MAUs can be added to the network as shown in Figure 8-8. A ring-in and ring-out receptacle is provided on each MAU for connection to other MAUs. The ring formation is maintained when MAUs are connected in this way. In addition, a fault tolerance feature maintains the ring if one of the cables becomes disconnected, as shown in Figure 8-9. Signals

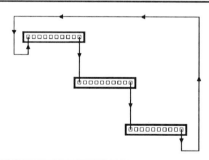

Figure 8-8.   Multiple Token Ring MAUs are connected together to form an expanded ring

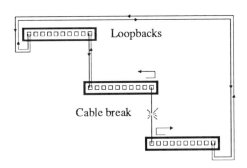

Figure 8-9.   When a cable segment is broken in a Token Ring network, a loop-back ring is formed

simply reroute in the opposite direction to create a loop-back formation. Repeaters are also available to extend the distance of a Token Ring network. Figure 8-10 shows how a large office or multistory building might be configured. The main ring connects all the MAUs in a circular fashion.

IBM Token Ring cards are available in 4Mbps versions and 16Mbps versions. The faster version has an increased frame length that requires fewer transmissions for the same amount of data. Token Ring networks that follow the IEEE 802.5 standard are now available from several manufacturers with connection methods that expand on the IBM design. Unshielded twisted pair and MAUs with 16 ports are common. In addition, two- and four-port hubs are available from some vendors. These hubs branch from an eight-port MAU and provide for the connections of two or more workstations in a cluster.

IBM Token Ring specifications allow for the following cable types:

Type 1   A shielded cable containing two twisted pair 22 AWG wires.

Type 2   A shielded cable containing two twisted pair 22 AWG wires with four twisted pairs of 26 AWG wires added outside the shield.

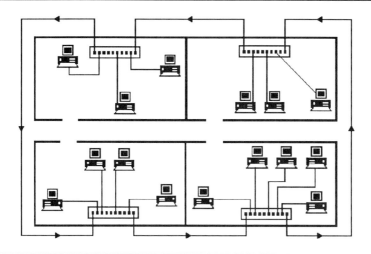

Figure 8-10.   A large main ring may interconnect MAUs in multiple departments of a building

Type 3	Unshielded telephone twisted pair 22 or 24 AWG cable. A media filter is required for use with Token Ring. Cannot be used with 16Mbps Token Ring cards.
Type 5	Fiber optic (100/140 micron) cable.
Type 6	Shielded twisted pair patch cables of 26 AWG wire. Distance is limited to two-thirds that of type 1.
Type 8	Shielded twisted pair 26 AWG cable for use under carpets. Distance limits are half of type 1.
Type 9	Shielded twisted pair 26 AWG plenum cable. Distance is limited to two-thirds that of type 1.

While Type 1 is the most common, Type 3 is becoming more popular. Type
3 cannot be used with 16Mbps Token Ring cards. Note that most types are

available as fireproof plenum cable, nonplenum interior cable, underground rated cable, and aerial rated cable.

A standard Token Ring network using Type 1 cable may consist of the following components:

Token Ring adapters   Token Ring cards are available in 4Mbps and 16Mbps models. If a 16Mbps card is used on a 4Mbps network, it must be operated at 4Mbps. A bridge should be established if both cards are to be used so that one network will consist of 16Mbps cards and the other 4Mbps cards. If used in diskless workstations, order a remote reset PROM.

Multistation access units   The multistation access unit (MAU) connects up to eight workstations using network adapter cables. Up to 12 MAU devices may be connected following the rules discussed below. Each IBM MAU is shipped with a setup aid, which is a small device that tests the ports of the MAU. Many non-IBM MAUs have built-in testing devices and up to 16 ports.

Token Ring adapter cable   The IBM Token Ring adapter cables have a nine-pin connector on one end to attach to the network interface card and a special IBM cabling system connector called a Type A data connector on the other end to connect into the MAU. Adapter cables are usually only eight feet in length, but patch cables can be used to extend them.

Patch cables   A patch cable for use on IBM Token Ring should be Type 6 cable of any length up to 150 feet. Patch cables can be used to extend the distance of the workstation from the MAU device, or to cable two or more MAU devices together. When used they halve the potential workstation-to-MAU distance.

Connectors   Type 1 cable uses the IBM cabling system Type A data connectors, which are hermaphroditic. By flipping a connector over, it can be connected to another, as done when patching two cables together.

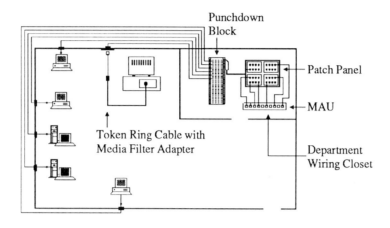

Figure 8-11.   Token Ring network using existing telephone twisted pair

Media filter   When Type 3 telephone twisted pair cable is used, a media filter is required at the workstation, as shown in Figure 8-11. It converts cable connectors and reduces line noise.

Patch panel   A patch panel is useful for organizing cable between the MAU ring and a telephone punchdown block. A standard telephone connector is used to connect the patch panel to the punchdown block, as shown in Figure 8-11. Another method is to wire the MAU directly to the punchdown block.

The maximum number of stations on one ring is 260 for shielded cable and 72 for unshielded telephone twisted-pair cable. The maximum distance from workstation to MAU with Type 1 cable is 101 meters (330 feet). This assumes that the cable is one continuous segment. If cable segments are joined using patch cable, the maximum workstation to MAU distance is 45 meters (150 feet).

If multiple MAUs are to be used, they should be stacked together and cabled locally. Calculating the maximum distance of a Token Ring network can be complicated because of its ring nature. The total length of the LAN may vary as each station logs in. For example, if a station connected to an MAU with an 8-foot patch cable logs in, 16 feet is added to the total ring distance due to the loop-back of the cable.

Anyone who intends to cable IBM Token Ring over large areas should refer to IBM publication GA273677-2, "Introduction and Planning Guide for the Token Ring Network." If other vendors are used, refer to their specification sheets or catalogs. Black Box, Andrews, Star-Tek, and Nevada-Western are vendors of non-IBM Token Ring products who have excellent catalogs and planning guides. Refer to Appendix D for addresses.

Telephone Twisted Pair

Token Ring equipment is available from many vendors using Type 3 telephone twisted pair cable. Stations can be directly wired to the MAU units with RJ-45 connectors and cable, or the existing telephone cable can be used. As shown in Figure 8-11, patch panels provide an in-between connection from the MAUs to the telephone punchdown block. Existing telephone wire provides the connection to workstations, where a media filter adapter is needed to convert from a Type 3 cable connector to a DB-9 connector that attaches to the Token Ring network adapter card. It also reduces noise that may be picked up by the Type 3 cable.

Internetworking

Internetworking Methods
Repeaters
Bridges
Routers
Backbones
Gateways

This chapter describes how to expand a network using repeaters, routers, and various internetworking methods. While managers of small unchanging networks need not be concerned with these issues, managers of large and growing networks must. You may want to familiarize yourself with the discussion in Chapter 7. LANs are expanded to allow more users to gain access, and they are interconnected to allow data to be exchanged with other LANs and allow users to communicate with electronic mail (E-Mail) software. If users on different types of systems need to share E-mail, systems on the network must be aware of different protocols. NetWare's open protocol technology (OPT) provides solutions for multiple protocols, while some of the equipment described in this chapter provides ways to share multiprotocol packets over diverse LANs.

The following topics are covered in this chapter:

- Expanding the number of stations

- Expanding the distance of a network

- Maintaining network throughput (performance) as networks expand

- Building internetworks with bridges and routers

- Building gateways to minicomputers, mainframes, and systems that use other operating systems

Most topics in this chapter are concerned with local area networks within a single building or several nearby buildings. A discussion of wide area networks, in particular remote connections using phone lines or other means of communications, are covered in Chapter 10.

Internetworking Methods

This chapter discusses repeaters, bridges, routers, brouters, backbones, and gateways. Figure 9-1 illustrates how each product relates to the ISO reference model and the tasks they perform on the network. The higher in the protocol stack a product works, the more expensive and complex it is.

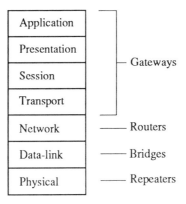

Figure 9-1. A comparison of various networking devices to the OSI protocol stack

Repeaters   Repeaters work at the physical layer. They repeat packets from a primary network trunk to an extended network trunk. They do not interact with higher-level protocols.

Bridges   Bridges interconnect two or more networks and pass packets among them.

Routers   Routers are similar to bridges, but in addition, they look deeper into a packet's address and become involved in routing it to its destination.

Brouters   Brouters are combinations of bridges and routers. They may allow multiple connections, some bridged and some routed. Brouters tend to have proprietary routing schemes that enhance performance but make them incompatible with routers.

Gateways   Gateways work at the highest levels of the protocol stack to allow systems and networks using incompatible protocols such as IBM SNA, IPX and TCP/IP to interconnect.

Bridges, routers, and gateways can be established within the same building or in a campus-size area that may include several buildings. They may also be established over long distances using remote connections, as discussed in the next chapter.

Repeaters

A repeater is a simple add-on device that boosts a cable's signal so that the length of the cable can be extended. The repeater does not normally change a signal in any way except to boost it for retransmission in the extended cable. Some repeaters filter noise. Repeaters have the following characteristics:

- They are primarily used in linear cable systems like Ethernet. Networks with token passing topologies rely on each station to retransmit signals they receive. An ARCNET active hub is a form of repeater. Repeaters are available to expand the distance of Token Ring networks.

- Repeaters operate at the lowest level of a protocol stack—the physical level. Protocols and access methods are not considerations with repeaters since they simply boost a signal for transmission over an additional trunk. Both segments must use the same media access method.

- Repeaters usually are used within a single building.

- Node addresses on the extended segments cannot be the same as addresses on the existing segment.

Repeaters normally operate at the same transmission speed as the networks they connect. When rated in packets per second, this speed is in the range of 15,000 for a typical Ethernet network. Repeaters range in price from $1500 to $3000.

Bridges

A bridge is established when two or more network interface cards are installed in a NetWare server or a machine dedicated as a bridge. The bridge allows workstations on physically distinct networks to communicate, thus establishing an internetwork. Examples of bridges are illustrated in Chapter 3, Figures 3-1 and 3-2.

One of the most important features of bridges is that they work at the media access control (MAC) layer. Any device that conforms to the MAC layer specifications can connect with other similar devices to form a bridge. Even devices that use different protocols can be connected. Any type of protocol packet can cross the bridge.

A bridge may be established for the following reasons:

- To extend an existing network when the maximum distance has been reached.

- To remove traffic bottlenecks caused by too many workstations attached to a single network. This puts a smaller number of users on each LAN to increase performance.

- To connect different types of networks together, such as Token Ring and Ethernet.

NetWare bridges are more like routers, however, because IPX is capable of performing routing functions. When a bridge is established in a NetWare server, it is referred to as an internal bridge. When a bridge is established in a separate system, it is referred to as an external bridge. Bridges from non-Novell vendors are generally external bridges.

NetWare internal or external bridges can consist of interface cards for similar or dissimilar networks. For example, a bridge might consist of a Token Ring card and an Ethernet card. When distance limitations are reached with an existing network cabling system, a bridge can be used to split the network in half and thus allow additional expansion on each side.

When a bridge is established, each network has a distinct *network address*. The network address can be thought of as a street. Each workstation on the network then has a distinct *node address,* similar to a house number. Network addresses are assigned during network installation and are used when routing packets between networks. A network may have more than one server and, if so, each server is given a special IPX internal number to distinguish it from other servers.

Bridges work at the data-link layer so that packets can be transferred between different types of network cards, as shown in Figure 9-2. Recall that the data-link layer is subdivided into two layers, logical-link control (LLC) and media access control (MAC). The MAC layer is modular; a network interface card driver supplies access control routines that plug into it, as shown in Figure 9-2. The upper LLC layer then serves as a switchboard and bridge between the modules in the MAC layer. Packets flow between networks by passing through the LLC layer.

Types of Bridges

Bridges do not need to be confined to the NetWare server. Many vendors supply bridges that offer additional features over those provided by NetWare's bridges. In most cases these bridges offer advanced management

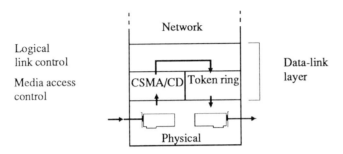

Figure 9-2. A bridge links MAC layer devices through the logical link control

features that are necessary when a network becomes large and hard to manage, or when performance of a network begins to deteriorate due to overloading. Routers, as discussed in the next section, provide even more network traffic management by giving managers control over exactly where network traffic goes.

The following features may be available in non-NetWare bridges:

Learning or adaptive bridges   Learning bridges "learn" the addresses of other stations on the LAN, making it unnecessary for the bridge installer or manager to create a table of these addresses in the bridge. Most bridges on the market are now learning bridges. Workstations constantly broadcast their identification signals, and the bridge builds tables from these addresses.

Spanning tree bridges   When a bridge connection is critical, it may be necessary to create fault tolerant redundant bridges. If one bridge goes down, the other can then assume its traffic. However, when two links exist, there is a possibility that traffic will travel across one and loop back over the other, creating a circular traffic pattern that could continue endlessly. Spanning tree bridges detect and break circular traffic by disabling certain links. The IEEE 801.2-D spanning tree protocol (STP) inhibits loops in redundant bridges by maintaining the secondary bridge as a backup. If the first bridge should go down, the secondary is immediately put into place.

Load balancing bridges   The load balancing bridge is the most efficient form of bridge. It uses a spanning-tree-type algorithm, but also uses a dual link to transfer packets, thus improving internetwork performance.

Bridge Forwarding
And Filtering Functions

A Novell bridge/router reads the destination address of a packet and determines whether the packet belongs to one of its workstations or should be sent on. The bridge filters all packets and forwards those not meant for its workstations. Novell often calls its bridges routers because they are capable of routing packets addressed to other networks.

Filtering helps avoid bottlenecks on bridges by keeping local traffic off the internetwork. Since network and node addresses are the only information available to bridges, this is the only method they have of filtering. Routers should be used if more advanced filtering is required. Since they work at the network layer, they have access to more information about the packet and its destination and can use this information to filter packets. For example, a router to an IBM host system may filter out non-IBM packets.

IBM Token Ring networks use a special source routing routine that tells the bridge not only where packets should go but how to get there. This feature puts routing tasks in the network protocol, rather than in a dedicated routing device.

Bridge Products and Vendors

One bridge currently on the market is the ISOLAN Managed Bridge, which is designed to the IEEE 802.1 bridge standard, filters at a rate of 21,800 packets per second, and forwards at a rate of 13,800 packets per second. It uses the spanning tree protocol and is priced at $7500. A network management package called the ISOVIEW Network Manager is $5995.

Bridges are available from the following vendors. Complete address information can be found in Appendix D.

Black Box; Pittsburgh, PA

Eicon Technology; Montreal, Quebec, Canada

Gateway Communications; Irvine, CA

Retix Corp; Santa Monica, CA

RND/RAD Network Devices; Rochelle Park, NJ

Vitalink; Fremont, CA

Routers

With routers you begin to move into the domain of wide area networks and remote communications links. Routers are primarily used on large networks of 20 or more interconnected LANs to keep traffic flowing efficiently over defined paths. They are especially important when leased lines are used to interconnect the LANs. Because these connections can be slow and expensive, filtering should be used to keep unwanted traffic off the connections. Many routing products are designed to support communication strategies such as T1 and X.25.

Routers may be used instead of bridges for the following reasons:

- Advanced packet filtering is required.

- The internetwork has multiple protocols and there is a need to filter traffic with specific protocols to special areas.

- Intelligent routing is required to improve performance. An intelligent router knows the network layout and can easily find the best path for a packet.

- Routers with advanced filtering are important when slow but expensive remote communications lines are used.

A router examines routing information fields in packets and determines the best route for each packet. It can forward packets to networks not directly attached to the router, because routers have addresses at the network layer that can be seen by other devices on the internetwork, including other routers. Routers can also be managed from other locations.

Routers are either protocol specific or they can handle multiple protocols. A protocol-specific router can only handle one type of packet; other packets are rejected. A *multiprotocol router* can handle multiple protocols, but tends to be slower and more expensive. Multiprotocol routers may be essential on networks that have a variety of systems and protocols and where internetwork traffic needs to be shared, such as an E-Mail system.

Routers allow networks to be segmented into logical networks. These logical networks are then easier to manage. Segmenting can be used to prevent a network occurrence called a *broadcast storm*. Broadcast storms occur when nodes are connected improperly and the network becomes saturated with broadcast messages attempting to locate the nodes. This situation occurs primarily on TCP/IP networks.

Routers send data over the best path, which may be the least costly, the fastest, or the most direct. This may be the one with the least number of hops, or it may be one based on line speed. For example, a router may send packets with higher priority over a 56Kbps link instead of over a 19.2Kbps link.

When you purchase routers, make sure the routing methods and protocols match between routers. Some routers use data compression techniques to increase the throughput of packets. Receiving routers must know how to translate information from these routers. It may be best to use the same routers in all locations to avoid problems. While routing methods are generally standardized, a mismatch may prevent connections between LANs.

Routers are available from the following vendors. See Appendix D for complete vendor information.

Advanced Computer Communications; Santa Barbara, CA

Black Box; Pittsburgh, PA

Cisco Systems; Menlo Park, CA

Eicon Technology; Montreal, Quebec, Canada

Gateway Communications; Irvine, CA

Halley Systems; San Jose, CA

Proteon; Westborough, MA

Retix Corp; Santa Monica, CA

RND/RAD Network Devices; Rochelle Park, NJ

Ungerman-Bass, Santa Clara, CA

Vitalink Communications; Fremont, CA

Brouters

Brouters combine features of both bridges and routers. They maintain the protocol transparency of a standard learning bridge while making intelligent path selections like a router. This allows for one or more protocols to be routed while bridging all other network traffic. Some brouters can perform load-balancing tasks between redundant connections and determine alternate routes in case of link failures.

The key difference between a brouter and a router is that a router uses an industry-standard routing protocol, while a brouter uses a proprietary method of routing. The proprietary method is developed by vendors to gain more features and efficiency out of their routers, but in doing so compatibility with other brouters and routers is lost. To maintain interoperability on large LANs, it may be best to stick with routers that use industry-standard protocols.

Backbones

A *backbone* is nothing more than a cable that connects two or more network servers together. Whereas a bridge can be formed by placing two or more network cards in a server (as shown in Chapter 3, Figures 3-1 and 3-2), backbones are formed by "connecting" multiple servers using a high-speed link (as shown in Chapter 3 in Figures 3-4 and 3-5). Backbones can segment large NetWare internetworks and make them easier to manage. They are useful alternatives to third-party bridges and routers for internetworks with 10 to 20 LANs. Networks may be connected to backbones with server bridges or external bridges. Figure 3-3 shows three servers connected with a backbone cable; two of the servers have a branching network segment.

Backbones for Centralized Management

Backbones can be used to group servers in one location for management purposes. For example, the servers for every department in an organization can be grouped together in an information systems (IS) department, where the staff can perform monitoring and service tasks. Network cabling is then run from the servers to each department. The ARCNET topology lends itself to this design since long linear cable runs that end in fan-out workstation connections can be used. Such a configuration is shown in Figure 9-3.

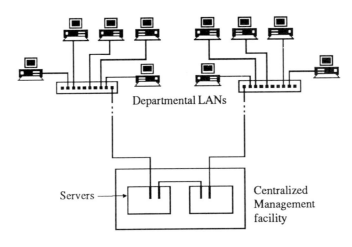

Departmental LANs

Servers

Centralized
Management
facility

Figure 9-3.   Servers can be grouped in a common management area using
backbone cabling

These are the advantages to using the short backbone:

- Servers are centrally located to improve monitoring and maintenance.

- Security is enhanced since the server area can be locked and fireproofed if necessary.

- Servers are not locked into individual departments where maintenance personnel may have trouble accessing them during off-hours.

- Performance is easier to monitor and improve when servers are centrally located.

- Backups and other services can be performed in one area by trained personnel.

- Backup power requirements and electrical filtering can be optimized for the server area.

Backbones for Campus-Wide
Or Metropolitan Area Networks

A backbone cable may be used to connect servers in a campus-wide area. Fiber optic cabling that operates as high as 100Mbps is commonly used to form a ring topology backbone to connect networks in several buildings. The backbone may contain a redundant secondary ring that is put into use should the main ring go down. For more information see Chapter 10.

Network Distribution Systems

Network distribution systems are wiring control centers used to manage and monitor the network wiring for a complete building or campus-wide area. The systems consist of repeater devices that allow many different types of networks to be connected to a modular system. A PC running a proprietary management program is usually connected to the devices. From the PC, managers can monitor network traffic, reroute traffic past faulty lines or bottlenecks, and track the resources of the entire network.

A typical example is the ISOLAN Ether Connect system by BICC Data Networks. The central component of the system is a modular repeater into which various interface cards can be installed. These cards can include twisted pair, Ethernet, and fiber optic network interface cards. All wiring is then distributed from this central point to different departments, building levels, or other buildings. Fiber optic ports can be added to build backbones to other ISOLAN Ether Connect systems.

Similar systems are available from Fibronics (Hyannis, MA) and LANNET Communications (Rochelle Park, NJ).

Gateways

Gateways provide links into minicomputers and mainframe (herein called host systems) environments. Through a gateway, any user on a LAN can access a host system by using the communications link already established by the network. Gateways under NetWare 386 are handled by the Novell NetWare 386 Communication Services products, which must be purchased separately. The products are designed to work in a NetWare 386 server as a NetWare loadable module.

NetWare 386 Communication Services is designed to support any combination of LAN-to-Host, LAN-to-LAN, or remote LAN access services. Users of DOS, Windows, OS/2, and Unix workstations can access corporate mainframe resources and wide area networks through Communication Services. The product is modular in design and consists of a platform in which other products are added. The basic platform is known as the *NetWare Communications Executive.* It supports the following add-on modules:

- *NetWare 386 Services for SAA* Provides a gateway into IBM host systems.

- *NetWare 386 Communication Services Manager* Provides management tools for network administrators.

- *NetWare 3270 LAN Workstation for DOS* Provides multiple host access from PCs.

- *NetWare 3270 LAN Workstation for Macintosh* Provides multiple host access from Apple Macintosh systems.

- *NetWare 3270 LAN Workstation for Windows* Provides multiple host access from DOS workstations running Microsoft Windows 3.0.

- *NetWare Communications Services Developer's Kit* A complete set of Application Programming Interfaces (APIs) for the NetWare 386 Communication Services.

- Future products will include plug-in modules to support OS/2, Unix workstations, other host systems, LAN-to-LAN connections, and wide area networking technologies such as T1 and X.25.

NetWare 386 Communication Services is an expandable platform. A communications engine runs in the server with any combination of NetWare Loadable Modules (NLM). The open programming interface, which is based on the AT&T Unix System V Streams environment, will promote the development of third party applications and services. The NetWare Communications Services Developer's Kit provides the tools developers need to quickly create customized applications for the NetWare 386 environment.

NetWare 386 Communication Services supports any combination of Ethernet, ARCNET, or Token Ring adapters in a single server. It also supports any combination of IPX/SPX, TCP/IP, or AppleTalk network transport protocols. Each protocol is implemented as an NLM and can be permanently loaded and bound to a network adapter, or dynamically loaded and bound as required.

Management software allows network administrators to control the entire network from a central location. The wide area computing resources that NetWare 386 Communication Services can make available demand this type of control since qualified personnel may be in short supply or not available at remote sites. Any Microsoft Windows based workstation can function as a management console and provide real-time monitoring and real-time control of multiple communication services.

Other features of NetWare 386 Communication Services are as follows:

- Built as a set of NLMs that can be loaded and unloaded from the server.

- Supports native workstation protocols and takes advantage of NetWare 386's ability to concurrently support multiple transport protocols.

- Works with NetWare 386's System Fault Tolerance (SFT) and Transaction Tracking System (TTS).

- Uses NetWare 386 security, network management, data encryption, and security audit trails.

- Uses NetWare name services to address communication resources such as hosts and links by name.

- Allows users to access communication resources without explicitly knowing which route to take.

NetWare 386 Services for SAA

NetWare 386 Services for SAA is an add-on module for NetWare 386 Communication Services. It provides the following features:

- Provides LAN-to-IBM host connectivity and provides access to applications such as OfficeVision, NetView, DB2, CICS, TSO, and CMS.

- Supports IBM's APPC and LU6.2 distributed application environment.

- Provides AS/400 connectivity.

- Supports DOS, Microsoft Windows 3.0, Apple Macintosh, OS/2, and Unix workstations.

- Supports 1000 host sessions on a single server.

- Supports connectivity to multiple hosts with a single server.

- Supports SDLC and Token Ring host connections.

- Works with other NetWare 386 Communication Services features and modules to provide management, security, and name services.

NetWare 386 Communication Services Manager

NetWare 386 Communication Services Manager is an add-on module for NetWare 386 Communication Services. It provides the following features:

- Provides network management capabilities for configuring, monitoring, and maintaining communication services on the NetWare network.

- Provides tools for fault, performance, and configuration management.

- Allows centralized management of NetWare 386 Communication Services throughout the corporate network from a single console.

- Provides a user-friendly, Microsoft Windows 3.0 environment that is open to third party development.

- Includes trace and diagnostic facilities for fault isolation and resolution.

- Allows collection of performance statistics for trend analysis.

- Allows remote configuration of communications resources from anywhere on the internetwork.

- Requires an 80286 or 80386 system with Color VGA monitor and mouse, as well as Windows 3.0.

- Works with other NetWare 386 Communication Services features and modules to provide management, security, and name services.

NetWare 3270 LAN Workstation Software Products

NetWare 3270 LAN Workstation Software is designed to run in LAN workstations and provide connection to the NetWare 386 Communication Services platform when the NetWare 386 Services for SAA module is installed. Three versions exist, as described in the following sections.

NetWare 3270 LAN Workstation for DOS

- Provides IBM host access for DOS-based personal computers via NetWare 386 Services for SAA.

- Supports up to five concurrent sessions (LU1, 2, 3) with multiple hosts.

- Emulates IBM 3278 and 3279 terminals (Models 2, 3, 4, and 5) and IBM 3287 Model 2 printers.

- Supports IBM APPC Protocol Boundary, allowing LU6.2-based SAA applications to run using minimal personal computer resources.

- Supports Extended Attributes (EAB), including extended highlighting, seven colors, and APL/APL2.

- Supports file transfer with IBM IND$FILE and NVL$FILE host file transfer programs.

NetWare 3270 LAN Workstation
For Windows

- Provides IBM host access for personal computers running Microsoft Windows 3.0 via NetWare 386 Services for SAA.

- Supports up to 26 concurrent sessions (LU1, 2, 3) with multiple hosts, each in its own windows.

- Emulates IBM 3278 and 3279 terminals (Models 2, 3, 4, and 5).

- Supports IBM APPC Protocol Boundary, allowing LU6.2-based SAA applications to run using minimal personal computer resources.

- Supports Extended Attributes (EAB), including extended highlighting, seven colors, and APL/APL2.

- Supports function keypad for convenient mouse activation of host function keys.

- Provides mouse support for cursor repositioning, copying and pasting of text to and from host session windows, and light pen emulation.

- Provides option for automatic font selection to fit host session window.

- Supports file transfer with IBM IND$FILE and NVL$FILE host file transfer programs.

- Requires an 80286 or 80386 system with graphics adapter and mouse to run Microsoft Windows.

NetWare 3270 LAN Workstation
For Macintosh

- Provides IBM host access for Apple Macintosh personal computers via NetWare 386 Services for SAA.

- Supports up to 26 concurrent sessions (LU1, 2, 3) with multiple hosts, each in its own window.

- Supports all major Macintosh networking platforms.

- Supports IBM APPC Protocol Boundary, allowing LU6.2-based SAA applications to run using minimal Macintosh resources.

- Supports Extended Attributes (EAB), including extended highlighting, seven colors, and APL/APL2.

- Emulates IBM 3278 and 3279 terminals (Models 2, 3, 4, and 5).

- Provides mouse support for cursor repositioning, copying and pasting of text to and from host session windows, and light pen emulation.

- Supports file transfer with IBM IND$FILE and NVL$FILE host file transfer programs.

- Provides option for automatic font selection to fit host session window.

Metropolitan and Global LAN Expansion

**T
E
N**

Types of Remote Links
Remote Workstation Connections
Campus-Wide Backbones
   and Metropolitan Area Networks
Wide Area Network (WAN) Connections

Local area networks can be expanded into metropolitan area networks (MANs) and wide area networks (WANs) with remote connections or high-speed fiber optic backbones. A remote connection may link two LANs on opposite sides of the street as well as on opposite sides of the globe. The methods used to make remote connections may depend on the following:

- Transmission speed requirements

- Required link distance

- Amount of internetwork traffic

- Network traffic patterns

- Cost

As the demand for MAN and WAN links increases, phone companies and other carriers are developing newer and faster methods for linking computer systems. Also the price of these links is going down, which makes networking over wide areas more feasible for organizations who could not justify it in the past.

Type	Speed	Use
ARCNET	2.5Mbps	Local area networks
Token Ring	416Mbps	Local area networks
Thin Ethernet	10Mbps	Local area networks
Thick Ethernet	10Mbps	Extended LANs
Dial-up line	2400-19,200bps	Single-user remote connections
Packet-switching	less than 64Kbps	Low to medium use WAN links
Fractional T-1	64Kbps	WAN use or redundant links
T-1	1.544Mbps	High use WAN links
T-3	44.184Mbps	High use WAN links
Fiber optic	10-100Mbps	High use MAN connections

Note: Worldwide fiber optic networks with transmission speeds in the 50 to 150Mbps range are under development.

Table 10-1.   Comparison of Network Transmission Speeds

A wide area network can be effective only if users can operate at a reasonable speed. While fiber optic connections can provide speeds of 10Mbps to 100Mbps and higher, they are currently limited to campus or metropolitan areas. Remote connections over phone lines or high-speed data links provide long-distance connections, but may be limited in transmission speed. A communications band-width in the 56Kbps to 1.544Mbps is essential for LAN-to-LAN connections. Anything below this range is suitable for only a single user or occasional connections. Table 10-1 provides a comparison of network transmission speeds as a point of reference.

Another important consideration when establishing MAN and WAN connections is the need to manage network security and performance. Building remote links may require the involvement of a telephone company and communication consultants. Routing products must ensure that local traffic stays local and does not cross the remote connections for cost and performance reasons. They can also keep sensitive data secure within a network boundary. Routers provide ways to segment networks to create more manageable logical networks; they also provide monitoring features so managers can accumulate valuable performance statistics.

Types of Remote Links

The current telephone network in the United States uses a combination of all-digital lines and analog lines. The links to many homes and businesses use copper voice-grade lines similar to those used at the turn of the century. Eventually the entire phone system will be completely digital and rely on a combination of copper and fiber optic cables. Until then many computer connections are made over voice-grade lines using modems. Since these lines do not allow transmission rates to increase above a certain rate, it may be necessary to acquire special digital lines from a phone company or other carrier to establish MANs and WANs. In some metropolitan areas, high-speed fiber optic cable is being installed by companies who then lease the lines to others.

Data communications over the phone system is handled in two ways. *Asynchronous communications* is a character-based method that transmits at speeds of up to 19.2Kbps. *Synchronous communications* is a block-oriented method that transmits at up to 64Kbps. The main difference is that synchronous communication is faster because it eliminates the need to transmit stop and start bits. You can use asynchronous communications over standard phone lines without contacting your local phone company. However, when higher transmission rates are required, the need for special lines is almost certain.

Remote Workstations

A remote workstation is used to dial into a LAN over dial-up or dedicated voice-grade telephone lines. The link connects a single user at a remote workstation to a LAN, or it connects LANs to other LANs for occasional use, such as the delivery of store-and-forward electronic mail. Simple file transfers are acceptable over such connections, but they are not suitable for establishing real-time connections for more than a few users.

Modems are required at each end of the transmission to convert computer digital signals to analog signals and then back again. Communication rates are typically 9600 to 19.2Kbps.

Campus-wide Links

A campus-wide area is defined as an area in which LANs can be interconnected using coaxial cable or fiber optic cable and in which a phone company or other carrier does not need to be involved. A university campus or industrial park is an example. Because the areas are usually privately owned, installation is easier because you do not need to run cable across properties or other public access areas. On a university campus, for example, fiber optic cabling could be installed between buildings by inhouse staff without the approval of outside organizations.

The emerging standard for campus-wide connections is the Fiber Distributed Data Interface (FDDI) standard, which is being developed by the American National Standards Institute (ANSI) X3T9.5 committee. FDDI defines a 100Mbps transmission rate over fiber optic cable using a token passing ring topology. A dual ring can be established for fault tolerance: one ring is primary and the second is a backup.

Metropolitan Area Links

A metropolitan area network may interconnect LANs as close as the building across the street or on the other side of town, but because it is difficult or impossible for a company to install private cable in public areas, a phone company or other carrier with established lines is involved. These carriers may use fiber optic, microwave, or satellite techniques for transmission.

Metropolitan area networks are being defined by the IEEE 802.6 committee, which probably will adopt a MAN standard by the end of 1990. The International Standards Organization (ISO) will then adopt the standard. The 802.6 standard specifies a dual bus topology, rather than the ring topology of FDDI, and it specifies a different protocol scheme at the MAC layer. The dual buses transmit in opposite directions and provide full duplex communications between two nodes. A range of speeds and media are also supported, including a digital signal level 3 (DS-3) rate of 45Mbps and an optical fiber rate of 155Mbps.

The 802.6 standard will begin to appear in 1991 and 1992. Because IEEE 802.6 is an emerging standard, few products exist at this writing, so it is not covered further in this chapter. Further information can be obtained from your local phone company.

Wide Area Networking (WAN)

One definition of a wide area network is that it involves the use of local, regional, and international phone companies or public data networks (PDNs) to establish connections between two or more diverse LANs. Because many different types of media may be used, including fiber optics, microwave, and satellite, the wide area network could span the globe. The most popular services are described here and later in the chapter; however, other services are available. Keep in mind that LANs are more intercity or international in scope.

X.25 packet switch   X.25 is an international standard for sending packets over PDNs like Tymnet and Telenet. Medium to high data rate links can be made for occasional or continuous use. A typical application would be store-and-forward electronic mail systems that dial out once or twice a day. The service is affordable because many users share the cost of the X.25 transmission lines. X.25 is popular for international networking because it spans the globe.

T-1 high-speed digital lines   T-1 provides high-speed digital phone links used to make continuous LAN-to-LAN connections for wide area networks. T-1 establishes and maintains specific lines between two points, unlike X.25, which can form a mesh of LANs over public data networks. T-1 is a digital line that offers 1.544Mbps of full duplex bandwidth in the United States and 2.048Mbps in Europe. Full duplex means that data can be flowing in either direction. A T-1 line in the United States has an actual capacity of 3Mbps. The cost of T-1 is high, but the amount of traffic on an internetwork may justify its use. T-1 may be used when regional sales offices access a remote company's database. T-1 may also be justified when considering the cost and productivity of employees who need to access information on remote systems. A T-1 line can also be *multiplexed,* which means it can be divided into multiple channels that can carry data and voice information.

T-3 high-speed digital lines   T-3 is similar to T-1, but provides more services. T-3 has a bandwidth of 44.184Mbps, which can be divided into 28 T-1 channels.

Emerging Technologies

Network planners and managers should be aware of emerging high- speed digital communications techniques when designing MANs and WANs for the future. The amount of data traffic on networks will increase as the power and speed of computing systems improve. Here are several trends to watch:

- An access method known as *frame relay* is succeeding X.25 packet switching networks. It provides a much faster and more efficient traffic flow by minimizing error checking and other overhead. Users of public data networks will realize immediate benefits.

- T-1 multiplexing will be replaced with high-speed optical fiber networks using Synchronous Optical Networks (SONET) standards and operating at speeds of 51 to 1,200Mbps. The following standards are being defined:

Optical Carrier 1 (OC-1)	51Mbps
Optical Carrier 3 (OC-3)	155Mbps
Optical Carrier 12 (OC-12)	620Mbps
Optical Carrier 24 (OC-24)	1,200Mbps

- A physical level *cell relay* method that defines a fixed-length packet of 48 bytes with a 5-byte header is being defined with the goal of providing a worldwide standard for voice, data, and image communications at 51Mbps.

- The Integrated Services Digital Network (ISDN) standard has a goal of linking every home and business with high-speed digital data services over phone lines. When and if the standard takes hold, the entire telephone system will become completely digital, which means that modems will not be required to interconnect computers over phone lines.

Anyone interested in more information on these emerging technologies should contact AT&T, Telenet, Tymnet, MCI, and other carriers. The addresses of product vendors such as Cisco Systems, Vitalink Communications, or Stratacom can be found in Appendix D.

Remote Workstation Connections

A remote workstation is a single PC at a remote site that dials into a LAN using an asynchronous communications method. The workstation may be used by an employee working at home, a manager at a remote site, or a field representative who needs to check the company database.

Connections made with voice-grade phone lines imply that a modem (modulator/demodulator) be used on both sides of the connection to convert digital signal for analog transmission and then back again to digital. Because the speed of such transmissions is limited, voice-grade lines are only recommended for occasional use to establish remote workstation-to-LAN connections or low- traffic LAN-to-LAN connections.

The following are two methods that can be used to establish remote workstation sessions.

Remote execution   With the remote execution method, all processing takes place at the remote workstation. All programs and data files the user needs must be transferred over the communication lines for processing in the user workstation, unless the files are copied to the workstation in advance. This method is not recommended if large amounts of information must be transferred over the lines. This method is useful for occasional connections by a user who uploads or downloads one or two files to or from the LAN.

Local execution   The local execution method connects a dedicated workstation on the LAN with the remote workstation. All processing takes place at the dedicated workstation; screen displays are echoed at the remote workstation and the user can enter keyboard commands. This method is very efficient because only keyboard and screen information is transferred over the remote connection. It does require the use of a dedicated LAN workstation during the communications session.

The following sections describe Novell products for establishing remote workstations that use the local execution method. NetWare AnyWare is designed for single-user use and is similar to third- party products like Norton-Lambert Close-Up/LAN or LAN Assist Plus from Fresh Technologies. The Novell NetWare Access Server package allows multiple NetWare AnyWare communication sessions.

Novell NetWare AnyWare

NetWare AnyWare is a remote-connection software package that provides satisfactory performance for users who need to gain remote access to a LAN. The following benefits are realized when NetWare AnyWare is used:

- Users at remote workstations operate as if they were sitting at the actual workstation attached to the LAN.

- Access to "in-use" database files is possible since users do not need to transfer whole files to their workstations. Instead, they can make changes to the database in the same way other users on the LAN do.

- File and database access are performed at LAN speeds, because all processing is handled by the local network workstation. Only keystrokes and screen displays are sent from the local PC to the remote workstation. The two machines function as one.

- Because this method does not perform any processing at the remote workstation, a dumb terminal can be used.

A NetWare AnyWare connection is illustrated in Figure 10-1. It requires the following components:

- A dedicated communications server running NetWare asynchronous communications server (NACS) software. This software allows up to 16 network workstations to simultaneously call in to or out of a NetWare LAN. NACS should not be run in the file server. It must be purchased separately from NetWare AnyWare.

- A workstation dedicated to running NetWare AnyWare. More than one workstation can be set up if multiple remote sessions are required. This station cannot be used for other tasks while a user is connected.

- A remote workstation running ATerm, a communications program that comes with NetWare AnyWare.

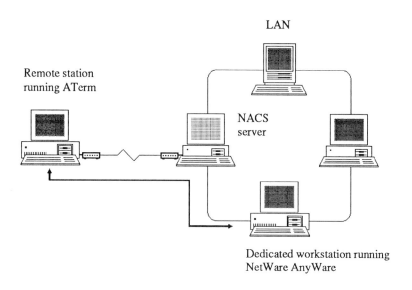

Figure 10-1. A NetWare AnyWare connection transfers only screen and keyboard information to optimize the performance of remote connections

The remote workstation starts a terminal program called ATerm; then it connects with the communications server through the modems. The communications server transfers the call to a local workstation running the NetWare AnyWare program. Each remote workstation calling in and using this method must have its own local workstation to do the processing, which can become expensive. However, since the remote workstation can be a dumb terminal, costs can come down. Many organizations may already have unused dumb terminals from a previously installed mainframe system. Separate modems are required for each incoming line.

NetWare Access Server Software

The NetWare access server provides a dedicated communications server that runs up to 15 NetWare AnyWare sessions. The software runs on

80386-based microcomputers. The software takes special advantage of the 80386 architecture by dividing its processing time into 15 virtual 640K PCs for multiuser remote access. The Wide Area Network Interface Module Plus (WNIM+) described below can be installed in the NetWare access server to provide four modem ports. Up to four of these cards may be installed. Figure 10-2 illustrates a NetWare access server configuration with two WNIM+ boards.

The WNIM+ board is a four-port asynchronous communications board for PC- and AT-type systems. Each board has four individual asynchronous ports that can communicate at speeds of up to 19.2Kbps. A modem may be attached to each port. The WNIM+ has its own on-board processor that frees the server's processor of communication I/O tasks.

Remote workstations dial directly into the NetWare access server through asynchronous modems. The ATerm software that runs in the remote workstations is included. Each remote workstation dials into a

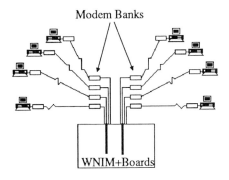

Communications server

Figure 10-2. The NetWare Access Server software allows up to 15 NetWare AnyWare sessions to take place within a dedicated 80386 communications server

dedicated session on the communications server. These sessions can each be configured for 640K of memory, depending on the memory available and the number of sessions in use. Each session requires a separate modem and phone line connection.

The NetWare access server provides some of the same features as NetWare AnyWare, with some saving on equipment when many connections are made. The single 80386 system can perform the same functions as 15 personal computers under the NetWare AnyWare system. In addition, local network stations are not tied up performing tasks for the remote users.

The software provides a dial-back security feature: The program calls back a user who has just signed on to verify phone numbers and locations.

Campus-Wide Backbones And Metropolitan Area Networks

Coaxial cable is an excellent choice for local area networks, but when LANs become large or need to span campus or metropolitan areas, fiber optic cabling becomes a viable solution. Fiber is often used to connect servers in a backbone configuration. For example, servers in two buildings that are reasonably close together might be linked with a single fiber optic backbone cable. Many vendors provide fiber optic Ethernet systems that run at 10Mbps and are especially designed for backbone use, but fiber can also be used to build large (100- to 200-kilometer) high-speed internetworks. Fiber optic cable standards specify data transmission rates of 100Mbps but it is possible to transmit at up to 1Gbps on some specialized systems.

Because fiber cable has the ability to support multiple transmissions at faster rates, it is stirring up a new communications revolution. Where microcomputers advanced personal computing, fiber optics will advance work group communications and productivity between many users on many different LANs. Design standards require that products be able to attach to multivendor networks. The current standard for privately installed fiber-optic backbones is the Fiber Distributed Data Interface (FDDI) standard, which is being developed by the American National Standards Institute (ANSI) X3T9.5 committee.

Note: The FDDI standard has been submitted to the American National Standards Institute (ANSI) for acceptance. It will be accepted simultaneously by the International Standards Organization (ISO).

FDDI defines a 100Mbps transmission rate over fiber optic cable using a token passing ring topology. A dual ring can be established to provide a backup connection should the primary fail. In addition, the FDDI standard defines protocols for management services to ensure that attachments to the LAN will work properly with LAN management packages from a variety of vendors. FDDI addresses the IEEE 802 physical and media access control (MAC) layers and links to the logical link control (LLC) layer.

FDDI can be used to connect not only high-speed networks, but mainframe computers and peripheral devices as well. While fiber is not normally used to connect directly to workstations, some high-performance systems such as those made by Sun and Apollo may need the added bandwidth when transferring large graphics files to a server. For this discussion, the use of FDDI for campus-wide and metropolitan area networks is discussed. FDDI can span areas of approximately 200 kilometers (120 miles) with a maximum distance between stations of 2 kilometers (1.2 miles) and support up to 500 workstations. The same ANSI committee is working on an advanced version called FDDI-II that will support voice and video.

The FDDI Standard

There are many similarities between the FDDI protocol and the IEEE 802.5 Token Ring protocol. Both use a token passing technique in a ring configuration, which is extremely reliable and suitable for use in high-speed network systems. The FDDI token passing scheme and topology are optimized for large interconnected networks.

- A token frame is passed around the network from one station to the next in a ring configuration. If a station needs to transmit, it acquires the token and holds it until done or a preset amount of time is reached in which it must relinquish the token.

- Each station retransmits frames it receives to the next station; thus, each station acts as a repeater.

- Multiple frames may exist on the network if a station relinquishes the token while its frames are still circulating. Another station could start transmitting in such a case.

- Two stations can enter into a dialog in which they can transmit data between themselves while other stations transmit the token in the normal way, thus improving network performance.

- FDDI networks can be created using a dual ring configuration. Two rings (primary and secondary) can be used with data flowing in a counterclockwise direction. Under normal conditions, only the primary ring is used. Should a link failure occur, the secondary ring is put into use and a loop-back ring is established similar to the 802.5 Token Ring method shown in Chapter 8, Figure 8-9.

- The FDDI standard also contains management mechanisms such as station management (SMT) that enable system administrators to manage and monitor FDDI networks, isolate faulty nodes, and route traffic.

A typical campus-wide FDDI backbone cabling system is shown in Figure 10-3. In this configuration, routers connect to the FDDI backbone. The routers then distribute traffic to one or more LANs within each building. Because several types of systems using different protocols are part of the internetwork in this example, routers that handle multiple protocols must be used to distribute network traffic to the proper LANs within each building according to packet protocol type.

FDDI Fiber Optic Specifications

Fiber optic cable has several advantages over copper cable, as listed here. In the past fiber cable was often more expensive, but in many cases it is comparable or cheaper in price when other factors such as installation and maintenance are considered.

- Fiber allows long distances between stations and repeaters because it is better at retaining its signal strength than copper cable.

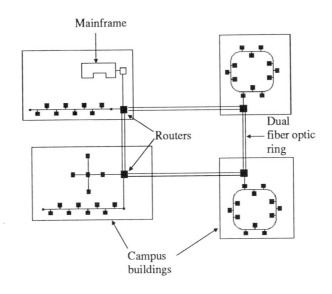

Figure 10-3. An FDDI network can span a campus-wide or metropolitan area

- Fiber is immune to electromagnetic interference, making it ideal in areas where such interference is common.

- Fiber has security advantages. Fiber does not emit a signal outside the cable, and intruder taps can be detected with the proper equipment.

- The length of fiber optic networks can reach miles with few repeaters, and fiber can replace microwave transmission techniques, buried cables, or telephone communications links.

The FDDI standard defines these cable and feature specifications:

- Core and cladding diameters of 62.5/125, 85/125, 50/125, and 100/140 micrometers are specified

- Maximum number of physical stations is 500

- Maximum distance between repeaters is 2 kilometers

- Maximum total length of the network can be 100 kilometers or more (depending on vendor configuration)

The three types of fiber optic cable and their properties are as follows:

- *Single fiber monomode cable*   Has a wide bandwidth but is difficult to splice.

- *Multiple fiber multimode cable*   Easy to splice, attach connectors to, and terminate because of its larger core diameter. It comes in 2 to 24 fiber variations.

- *Graded index multimode cable*   Provides the fastest transmission rates over the longest distances, but is the most expensive.

Cable should be selected after reviewing the interface cards, bridges, and router products available from different vendors. If cable is already installed, you will need to find a vendor that has products that can make use of the cable. A partial list of vendors is covered in the next section.

Planning for FDDI

It is not possible to discuss all the parameters you need to consider when planning or configuring a fiber optic network. You should contact several vendors for exact specifications and other information. Because of the existing installed base, FDDI embraces many types of multimode fiber. The 62.5/125-micron cable is used for testing and reference purposes.

While fiber optic networks and backbones may not be feasible for every installation, a future upgrade to such a system should be taken into consideration. Network administrators can design their existing cabling systems to allow for future fiber optic links by designing wiring systems around wiring centers or closets. Concentrations of workstation leads in such areas are much easier to connect to a network backbone.

Connections to FDDI backbones and networks can be made in several ways, depending on the vendor. Simple backbones can be made by installing cards in the NetWare server to form a bridge with an existing Ethernet, Token Ring, or ARCNET network. A more common method is to use a router device that allows several different types of local networks to be attached to an FDDI backbone. The FDDI backbone illustrated in Figure 10-3 uses routers to terminate several different types of networks in each building of a campus-size area.

The following vendors have FDDI products. Refer to Appendix D for the complete address.

CMC, Santa Barbara, CA

Cisco Systems, Menlo Park, CA

Codenoll Technology Corp, Yonkers, NY

Fibermux, Chatsworth, CA

FiberCom Inc, Roanoke, VA

Fibronics, Hyannis, MA

In-Net, San Diego, CA

International Data Corp, Framingham, MA

Network Systems, Minneapolis, MN

Wellfleet Communications, Bedford, MA

Wide Area Network (WAN) Connections

The wide area network (WAN) encompasses the connection of workstations and LANs over wide areas with telephone, satellite, microwave, direct digital synchronous (DDS) lines, and other connections. WANs may be hundreds or thousands of miles apart. While an asynchronous link can be established between LANs for occasional use and simple file transfers, the speed of such connections is not sufficient when multiple users must access resources on other LANs. X.25 networks can provide a mesh-like connection between remote LANs with a reasonable speed. T-1 and T-3 connections can provide a high-speed, point-to-point connection between two LANs.

The following sections describe common internetwork connections that are supported by products from Novell and other vendors.

X.25 Packet Switching Networks

The Consultative Committee for International Telegraph and Telephone (CCITT) recommendation for worldwide connection between communications terminals and public packet switching networks is X.25. It is a layered protocol consisting of the lowest three layers of the OSI protocol stack. The X.25 protocol is used to access public data networks (PDNs) that use packet switching such as Tymnet and Telenet. Each packet of data is sent individually over the best possible route to save costs.

While X.25 can transmit a maximum of 64Kbps, overhead reduces this rate to 56Kbps. X.25 is a pay-as-you-use service, which means that lines can be easily connected and disconnected as required. A flat rate is charged, in addition to a rate based on the amount of traffic sent.

To establish an X.25 line, you must contact one of the following public data services:

Accunet from AT&T

Tymnet from McDonnell-Douglas network

Telenet from Sprint

An X.25 gateway is established on the LAN. This gateway consists of both hardware and software for connecting into an X.25 network, which can often be reached through a local number. The gateway is often a plug-in board installed in a dedicated workstation that serves as a gateway and nothing else. Some vendors provide external gateways that deliver better performance because they are optimized for X.25 use.

The following sections discuss X.25 products available from Novell. Other vendors make similar products.

NetWare Link/X.25

NetWare Link/X.25 connects a NetWare LAN with up to 11 remote LANs simultaneously. The X.25 network is accessed through an X.25 gateway. Up to 11 connections can be made through the gateway to other LANs that are connected into the X.25 network. In this way, up to 11 LANs maintain connections over a "mesh" topoloogy formed by the X.25 network. NetWare Link/X.25 works as an external router. Once activated it becomes transparent to network users. All of the traffic for remote LANs is routed over the PDN.

Installation requires that one of the Novell X.25 adapters described in the next section be installed in an 80286 or 80386 system that is dedicated as a router. The X.25 adapter is then connected to a synchronous modem.

Novell X.25 Adapters
For PCs and IBM PS/2 Systems

The Novell X.25 communications interfaces are designed for PC- and AT-class machines, as well as the IBM PS/2 Micro Channel systems. The boards are used with several Novell communications packages discussed later. X.25 is a synchronous communications protocol. The boards have an on-board processor and 256K of memory to help minimize the use of resources in the attached system. The PC/AT board can provide through-put at up to 64Kbps and the PS/2 board can provide throughput at up to 19.2Kbps. Up to 32 X.25 virtual circuits are supported. An X.25 extended adapter also available for PC- and AT-class machines provides 512K of on-board memory and will support 254 X.25 virtual circuits.

LAN-to-LAN Connections Using T-1 Lines

T-1 is a common telecommunications method used to build private voice networks. The T-1 bandwidth of 1.544Mbps can be divided into twenty-four 64Kbps channels, each carrying one voice or data transmission. When T-1 is divided in this way, it is referred to as *fractional T-1*. T-1 connections can be acquired from the phone company or through private companies that offer microwave and satellite links. Both voice and data can be multiplexed over a T-1 line.

With T-1, the local telephone company serves as a hub for each network within a certain geographic area that is serviced by a central office of the local phone company. Networks at different company sites within the area serviced by the phone company (usually a metropolitan area) are then connected into the hub provided by the phone company. The area serviced by a phone company is known as its local access and transport area, or LATA. It is possible to connect to other LATAs by using links established by various long-haul carriers. You will then need to involve the local phone company, the remote phone company, and the long-haul carrier in your connection scheme.

In some cases T-1 services are cheaper than leased lines, especially when fractional T-1 is considered. Fractional T-1 allows customers to buy T-1 service in 64Kbps channels at an affordable price. If expansion is required, additional channels can be added easily because the phone company has already installed a full T-1 line without charging for the additional channels until needed. However, the cost of buying individual channels should be weighed against the cost of buying a full T-1 line. Prices are based on transmission speeds, distance, and other factors that the carrier determines when configuring and pricing the line.

A T-1 multiplexer is used to divide a 1.544Mbps T-1 line into multiple 64Kbps lines. Most T-1 multiplexers have ports for combining voice and data lines.

Novell T-1 Products

NetWare Link/T1 and NetWare Link/64 allow NetWare LANs to connect with remote LANs through synchronous communications lines. NetWare Link/64 is a down-sized, less expensive version of NetWare Link/T1 that supports a 64Kbps line. Only NetWare Link/T1 is discussed here.

NetWare Link/T1 supports transmission speeds from 9600bps to 2.048Mbps. It is capable of routing IPX, NetBIOS, and SPX over wide area networks. NetWare routing software dynamically determines the shortest path for each packet based on the current network topology. Inoperative links are automatically bypassed.

A Novell Synchronous/+ adapter is required in a dedicated external router. This board supports V.35, RS-422, and RS-232 interfaces to data service units/channel service units (DSU/CSUs), synchronous modems, multiplexers, and data switches. These devices must be purchased from third-party suppliers.

High Level Network
Standards and Applications

OSI Application Interfaces
Server-Based Applications
Groupware

This chapter discusses emerging network standards for software. It also discusses existing software standards and some of the packages that can be purchased for use on a LAN. LAN software is different than personal computer software in many ways: It is based on the fact that multiple users will access files and databases. It is also concerned with sharing information and elec-tronic messages. Many packages have been referred to as *groupware* because they are designed for use by people who communicate over networks.

OSI Application Interfaces

The following applications standards have been adopted or are in the process of being adopted by the OSI. They generally define high-level protocols in the OSI stack and determine the interaction between the application layer and presentation layer.

X.400 Electronic Message Handling System

The OSI X.400 standard defines an electronic system for exchanging personal messages between many types of electronic mail on many types of computer, assuming the mail systems are X.400 compatible. X.400 is an OSI model that is also accepted by the Consultative Committee for International Telegraph and Telephone (CCITT). It is compatible among multivendor products and interfaces with public and private message services.

Using the analogy of an envelope, X.400 electronic messaging provides a way to fill an envelope with information and send it to another user. Since message formats are the same, users can send messages to other users on different systems within their company, or even to users in different companies. Messages can include simple notes or data taken from an applications program such as a spreadsheet or word processor. A variety of communications systems such as X.25 public data networks can be used to exchange messages between users.

The following modules make up the message handling system:

- *User Agent (UA)* The UA prepares messages for routing to a destination by addressing them with names found in a lookup table. The table contains the names and addresses of other X.400 users on the network. The directory may follow X.500 specifications, as discussed later.

- *Message Transfer Agent (MTA)* The MTA accepts messages from the UA and routes them to other MTAs on the network.

- *Message Store (MS)* The MS is a storage area for messages that need to be distributed to other users. This store- and-forward feature is an important part of the system. It allows messages to be sent at convenient times.

- *Directory System* The directory system contains a complete list of names and addresses of other users on the network. If the network is a wide area network, this list can be large. At this time, the OSI

X.500 standard (described in the next section) is defining how such directories will be created and used.

Electronic mail systems that follow the X.400 standard are in development by Retix (Santa Monica, CA), Touch Communications (Campbell, CA), and Novell. Retix has developed a family of products called OpenServer 400 that can be ported to many environments, including NetWare, Unix, and the Macintosh. An X.500 directory service is provided. Ethernet LAN and X.25 WAN connections are supported.

Novell's X.400 mail software includes software supplied by Retix. It will also be implemented as a NetWare loadable module. Novell's Open-Server 400 system supports the older message handling system that was used in previous versions of NetWare.

X.500 Global Naming

Because of the growth in wide area networks and electronic mail systems, especially those implementing X.400, directory systems that help users locate other users and resources within a network are essential. The OSI X.500 standard is evolving to meet the demand.

Small networks with one or two servers and printers do not need naming services because it is easy to locate a particular device. Large networks, on the other hand, need a way for users to locate other users and resources. Global naming (X.500) provides a way to pull up a list of those resources and choose the appropriate one by name. Global naming is not as easy to implement as it may sound because the global database has to be constantly updated as devices are added and removed. This gets more complicated as the network gets larger and more diverse.

Novell's NetWare Name Service (NNS) links servers into domains of as many as 400 file servers. Once a domain is created, users can be added to it. When users log in they automatically receive access to the servers in the domain to which they belong, based on their security access rights. NNS should be considered a management tool for administering multiple servers.

NNS runs on both Novell NetWare 286 and NetWare 386 networks and requires an IPX/SPX connection. The package is free to new NetWare 386 buyers but sells for $1995 for users of NetWare 286.

Network Management

Network managers need tools to help them manage network users, resources, and interconnections. If network resources are in remote locations, network managers must travel to those locations to configure or reconfigure devices. An important issue with large internetworks is whether to centralize management or distribute it to the location of each network. In the past it was necessary to keep managers on hand at individual sites, but new developments in network software provide the means to centralize management. Network managers who use such applications can manage remote devices from the comfort of their own offices.

An evolving OSI network management protocol is called Common Management Information Protocol (CMIP). It defines how multivendor network management programs interact and how network managers can work with devices in remote locations without actually being there. Part of the standard is Common Management Information Services (CMIS). Applications that use this standard gather statistical information from devices and then present it to managers for evaluation. This information may be compiled from multivendor devices into a centralized management unit located in the network manager's office.

The proposed OSI network management protocols are currently supported by AT&T, IBM, and other vendors. Therefore, the protocols are quickly gaining world-wide acceptance, and vendors are beginning to design hardware and write applications for them. For example, IBM's NetView supports CMIP and CMIS. Several vendors have designed centralized management packages that communicate with and draw information from management packages on other networks.

The following management areas are defined by CMIP:

- Accounting management tracks the use of network resources for cost estimates, service schedules, and reporting

- Configuration management allows a manager to reconfigure a network resource

- Fault management provides ways to detect and correct faults in network equipment

- Performance management provides ways to monitor network traffic and the throughput of devices

- Security management allows managers to control access to network resources

A management information base (MIB) is maintained by the network management application. It contains information collected from remotely managed devices that can be used to perform the tasks just described. System management services include *management agents* and *reporters* in servers that communicate with all network services. The information is collected in the management information database. Management agents monitor *event alerts* from network components and track system operations.

Novell's overall strategy is to allow OSI-based network management tools to manage NetWare, but Novell provides tools of its own. NetWare 386 supports the remote management of resources through its Remote Management Facility (RMF). RCONSOLE (see Chapter 33) is a virtual console utility for workstation-based administration of 386 servers. Virtual console service allows administrators to see the server console and to monitor server information without leaving their workstations. Any command that can be given at the server can be given at the management workstation, which saves time and travel costs.

A network management agent NLM (NetWare loadable module) allows a service such as a LAN driver or router to share information dynamically with management agents. This feature will be used in future applications that rely on integrated management services.

Server-Based Applications

Applications software for networks can be divided into three categories. The first category is composed of *LAN-ignorant Applications,* which are applications written for use on a single-user computer. Even though they may run on a network, they do not contain features required in a multiuser environment to protect files and data. These features are included in the second category of software, known as *LAN-aware applications*. LAN-aware packages contain file- and record-locking features that prevent more than one user from using the same file or database record at the same time. This prevents one user from overwriting the work of another when the file or record is saved.

The third category is composed of *LAN-intrinsic applications*, which distribute various processing tasks between the server and workstations. They are also called *client-server applications* or *front-end/back-end applications*. The best way to visualize how an application splits up its processing load is to look at how a LAN-aware application, like a word processor, and a LAN-intrinsic application, like an advanced database program, work. Keep in mind that not all database applications are LAN-intrinsic, however.

When a user starts a word processing program, the program code is read from the server's hard drive into the memory of the workstation. The program code runs completely at the workstation. When the user accesses an existing document, it is transferred from the server to local memory in the same way. The server simply acts as if it were a local hard drive for the workstation.

When a LAN-intrinsic application is run, the workstation is referred to as the *client* (or *front-end*), and the server becomes the *server* (or *back-end*) in a client-server relationship. A LAN-intrinsic database program has separate program modules for the workstation and the server. The client portion is used to display menus and data and to accept commands executed by the user. Some commands are executed by the workstation's processor, such as a command to display new menus or list the data that is currently being worked on. Other commands are executed at the server, such as sorting or indexing commands that manipulate the entire database. After the request is processed at the back end, the results are sent to the front end for display. Front-end processing activities include formatting of the data and displaying it on the screen.

The important point is that the entire database is never transferred into the workstation's memory, only the portion the user needs. This has the following benefits:

- Network performance improves because there is less traffic on the network.

- If the server is a high-performance machine, some processing activities are better executed in the server where the processing and file system I/O can work together in a tight-knit arrangement.

- Security is enhanced because the entire database is not transferred over the network where it can be monitored.

In client-server relationships involving database applications, the back-end server process is sometimes referred to as the *database engine*. Such engines operate in accordance with certain rules. For example, relational integrity rules ensure that information in the database cannot be changed unless a user has the rights to do so. Managers can also apply such rules globally to the entire database.

Distributed or Centralized?

Those who are evaluating client-server applications should be aware that there are several definitions of how it should be done. Most of the current client-server database applications are really no different than centralized databases that perform all the processing. The workstations then display the data. But this method wastes the processing power available at the workstations and increases the load at the server. This may remind some readers of a centralized minicomputer or mainframe system using dumb terminals. In fact, many current client-server databases were ported over from those environments and still retain their characteristics.

A truly distributed client-server application places some of the processing in workstations. Obviously this method is harder to implement and is not widely available—yet. Novell's idea of a true client-server "model" is to distribute processing not directly related to finding and manipulating actual data records to the workstation. This processing includes managing an application's front end and the presentation of information. Basically the server farms out part of its workload. By doing this, client-server systems considered as a whole can approach the processing speeds of minicomputer and mainframe systems.

The idea of distributed processing can be taken a step further. Eventually applications that take advantage of the aggregate processing power of many different machines on a network will be common. Machines that sit idle during off hours will be given the mutual task of calculating extremely complex problems. They may also be used for everyday tasks. For example, if a user requests a report from the database, the database engine may find an idle processor on the network to do the job, thus freeing itself for other tasks. Keep in mind that this type of processing is still a few years down the road for NetWare servers, but it is something to look forward to.

SQL

SQL is an acronym for Structured Query Language. SQL is an English-like database language that was developed in the 1970s by IBM. Queries can be made in the form of verbs to retrieve information from a database. The language has virtually become a world-wide standard and is available for almost every operating system, including UNIX, DOS, Macintosh OS, OS/2, and others. Any database application that supports SQL can exchange data with any other SQL-compatible database.

Almost every client-server database system is based on SQL. Many of these applications hide the SQL commands with easy-to-use interfaces. Almost any type of application, such as electronic spreadsheets and accounting programs, can use SQL commands to access a database.

Novell makes SQL available as a NetWare loadable module. NetWare SQL allows many applications to share a common database, and it supports a variety of front ends, including Lotus 1-2-3 v3.0, Concentric R+R, and WordTech Quicksilver/SQL. NetWare's integrity and security features enhance the reliability of the database. The product can be used by developers to write applications, or it can be used in conjunction with the interfaces previously described to access information.

Available Applications

For those who need to investigate client-server applications further, the following list may provide useful information on vendors who are selling or working on such applications:

Advanced Data Servers, Boise, ID

Gupta Technologies, Menlo Park, CA

Informix Software, Menlo Park, CA

Oracle, Redwood Shores, CA

Microsoft, Redmond, WA

Novell, Provo, UT

Odesta, North Brook, IL

Sybase, Berkeley, CA

VIA Information Systems, Princeton, NJ

XDB Systems, College Park, MD

Groupware

Groupware is a network software concept that defines applications used by a group of people to increase the productivity of the group as a whole. It is based on the assumption that because networks connect users, those users should be able to interact as well. Beyond that, groupware is a term used in many different places to define many different things. This section explores several groupware packages that can be run on NetWare networks.

A true groupware package allows users to interact. For example, editing a file and then sending it to another user for review may not be groupware. On the other hand a manager who can tie into other users' workstations with a remote control program and help them through a tough situation is an excellent example of interactive groupware. This type of arrangement is often used in training classes where workstations are connected to a network. Any changes the instructor makes on his or her workstation is echoed on the students' workstations.

Taking this a step further, a group of users in different parts of a building may schedule a "meeting" to take place over the network. All members remain seated at their workstations while the meeting coordinator establishes a connection between their workstations. Once the connection is made, any activities on the main workstation are echoed to the other workstations. A simultaneous conference call can allow group members to talk together, or an on-screen dialog box can be used to type messages. Changes can be made to on-screen documents in real-time by a designated user, or if the package is really sophisticated, any user can make a change that is echoed to any other user's screen. This type of application is useful in engineering, architectural, or planning environments.

Another interesting groupware concept is interactive conferencing, which can best be described as an ongoing conference in which members hold on-screen conversations. Messages typed by users immediately appear on the screen. Members can respond to other members or simply watch as messages scroll by. Members can also sign in and sign out without disrupting the conference. CompuServe and other bulletin boards already provide this type of service on a world-wide basis. Several different conferences can be joined at any time of the day or night, assuming other users are "in conference." One aspect of the service is that members can remain anonymous. An organization can establish its own conferencing facility over a network to allow employees to discuss projects, weekend parties, or company policies.

The following sections describe other types of groupware.

Higgins from Enable Software

Higgins is an integrated group productivity package for networks. It includes E-Mail, group scheduling, calendaring, to-do lists, and expense reports. The main feature of Higgins is its scheduling feature, which allows users to schedule activities with other users. E-Mail can be used to request or confirm meetings; then Higgins coordinates the schedules of all those involved. For example, you can select meeting attendees from a list and then let Higgins go to work finding available times that the meeting can be scheduled without conflicts.

Together from Coordination Technologies

Together is an organizational tool for users that works on the principle of a desktop. Tasks and activities are placed on the desktop and appear as icons. Users then pick the activities or tasks they want to work on, which starts the appropriate application. Other users on the network can place icons on the desktops of their coworkers, in the same way a stack of work might be placed in an in-box on your desk. Together is still in development as of this writing.

Notes from Lotus   Notes is based on the assumption that users need to communicate basic types of information to their counterparts who may be in different offices or different cities. Notes replicates information databases on a continuing basis, so all users constantly have the most up-to-date information. As users make changes, updates are made to the databases of other users who have been designated as part of the same group. Notes is unique in that it works over many diverse types of networks.

Hardware Evaluation and
Performance Considerations

Network Planning
and Selection

Identifying LAN Needs
Developing Logs and Worksheets

This chapter is designed to help system designers and managers plan and purchase a network. Keep in mind that there may never be a final set-in-concrete plan for any network. Technology and user needs are constantly changing, and the modification of any plan is inevitable. But a plan is still needed, and it should be developed in the most professional and responsible way, no matter what the size of the LAN.

To begin planning a network, an organization may want to hire an outside professional who is experienced not only with network hardware, but also with the methods and procedures required to establish a network system. This systems analyst or consultant should be able to work among users, system supervisors, and organization managers who administer budgets and policies. The systems analyst can help bridge the gap between these groups as an unbiased mediator.

Part of any network system includes technical specifications, such as the type of interface card to be used, server hardware requirements, and so on. At the user end, multiuser software programs require new procedures, new personnel, and user training. The systems analyst can work with those familiar with specific aspects of the system and develop an overall system plan based on the information gathered.

Documentation is important as planning continues. If a systems analyst is used, management will want to know what is being done and will be concerned with why particular solutions have been chosen. Requests for proposals (RFPs) can be developed and sent to vendors and

T
W
E
L
V
E

213

retailers, who may then provide pricing and configuration information. At some point a complete drawing of the proposed system as well as an identification of exact components and cost can be developed. A cost-benefits report may be given to management for approval. If the system is approved, a detailed list of components is given to purchasing.

From that point on, installation and maintenance of the system can proceed as components and parts arrive. The system should be fully tested before it is brought on-line. Software and security features should be installed, and users should be trained. The remainder of this book covers installation and post-installation activities for Novell NetWare and will provide useful information to systems analysts or others in the process of planning and designing a network system.

Identifying LAN Needs

There are a number of reasons why a network system may be considered as a solution to a particular computing problem. In many cases, a network is a better solution than a minicomputer or mainframe system. The following problems or problem-related solutions may have already been identified by users, managers, or data processing personnel:

- Insufficient storage capacity of existing systems

- A multiuser software program is required

- Need to centralize a database

- Need to centralize backup of data

- Need to share peripherals such as high quality printers

- Users need to communicate with electronic mail

- Departmental managers need to manage work groups

Anyone trying to identify the requirements of a LAN must become familiar with any current system and its limitations. The following sections provide a brief outline that can be used to assess the current environment and determine problems and solutions.

Identify Existing Equipment

Using the worksheets provided at the end of this chapter, write down any information known about the current in- house systems, such as the types of PCs, their storage devices, backup systems, printers and plotters, and communications equipment.

Map the Potential LAN Environment

Draw a map of the complete installation site, including the location of the systems and peripheral devices defined in the previous step. Locate wiring closets, existing cable runs, wire outlets, and existing cable tracks.

In some cases, drilling holes may be prohibited or not practical. For example, asbestos ceilings may present a potential health threat to employees if drilled or opened. Measure the distances between potential workstations so cable cost can be estimated. Determine the location of future workstations as well as the location of the nearest cable these stations can tap into.

Evaluate Current Usage

Software on a network is as important as the hardware required to run it. The hard disk requirements of the software and the data files it will generate should be considered. If a company has multiple departments, elaborate filing structures and multiple software packages are probably needed. Department managers must be involved to help determine the number of users needing to access the system and the amount and type of data they need to store. Directory structures and security requirements should also be evaluated.

Evaluate Application Requirements

Software purchased for LANs should be either LAN aware or designed specifically for LAN use. LAN-specific software may monitor usage and prevent access when the maximum number of licensed users have started the program, so it is important to purchase multiuser licenses that allow several users simultaneous access.

Keep in mind that some programs are LAN ignorant. Some can be stored on the LAN server and used by several people, but they may not perform file- or record-locking, meaning there is no protection from overwrites if two users edit and save the same file or record simultaneously. LAN-aware programs keep track of how data files are being used and by whom, thus preventing data from being updated improperly.

When selecting LAN-based programs, check the level of their LAN awareness, or make sure the software designers plan to implement LAN support in the future. Also be aware of software licensing. You may need to purchase several versions of the software or simply an add-on LAN version.

Evaluate Performance Needs

Network performance depends on the number of users on the system and the type of work they are doing. This should be evaluated closely, perhaps during an evaluation period before hardware is specified. The types of server and network interface cards and cabling systems play an important part in how a network operates under heavy traffic conditions.

A *bottleneck* is a place or condition in the network environment that slows the entire network. The speed of a network is referred to as its *throughput,* which is the product of several different factors, including the cabling system, the performance of the server, and the performance of the workstation. However, a bottleneck can affect the throughput of an entire network. It is helpful to identify potential bottlenecks ahead of time and acquire equipment that will resolve them.

Bottlenecks that slow the entire system occur when large numbers of users are on the LAN at the same time and the cabling system, network interface cards, or server are not able to handle the load. On the other hand, few users may be logged on the system, but a bottleneck occurs because one user is intensively using the server and, in the process, the cabling system (for example, uploading large data files by a CAD system). Large database applications can also slow a server; such installations should use the highest-performance hardware.

If heavy throughput loads are anticipated, several solutions are possible:

- Increase the server memory as well as the size of the cache

- Upgrade the server hard drive to achieve better performance

- Select servers that use high-performance bus designs, like EISA and MCA, and that implement bus mastering, as discussed in Chapter 13

- Use high-performance super-servers like those discussed in Chapter 13

- Install high-performance network interface cards in the server that use 16- or 32-bit interfaces, large buffers, bus mastering, and increased packet sizing

- Use 10Mbps Ethernet cards and cable or 16MB Token Ring boards and cable

- Consider high-speed fiber optic backbones when connecting multiple servers or forming internetworks

- If the LAN has over 30 or 40 workstations, consider dividing these stations between two or more network interface cards in the server to increase performance or place heavy users on their own networks

- Add a second file server to distribute the file server load

The NetWare operating system uses extensive memory resources to increase its operating speed. Memory is used for cache buffers, communications buffers, directory caching, and various other tasks. It is recommended that 4MB of memory or more be installed in any server system to provide maximum performance. NetWare 386 provides memory statistics that managers can use to determine when more memory is required. It is feasible to run a network for some time to accumulate these statistics before adding more memory.

Evaluate Disk Storage Needs

The hard disk storage system of a server is a major factor that contributes to the overall speed of a network. Coincidentally, the larger a hard drive is, the faster it transfers data, due to the configuration of the internal components (number of disk platters and read/write heads). This makes the decision to buy large drives even more practical. In addition, Novell NetWare uses hard disk storage much more efficiently than DOS, so an increase in the speed of a server hard drive is realized when switching from a DOS environment to NetWare. In fact some workstations can access a NetWare server hard drive faster than their own.

Data storage requirements can be determined by the number of applications currently used by an organization and the number planned for future use. The disk storage required by these applications should be determined, as well as the size of the data files created with them. The number of data files depends on the number of users, of course. Users may also place various programs, utilities, or data files in their personal directories, so this should also be accounted for. Once the total disk usage space is determined, simply double or triple it to get an idea of future requirements.

Disk mirroring and duplexing requirements should also be evaluated. If volumes will span multiple drives, it is recommended that those drives be mirrored. Keep in mind that spanning volumes and mirrored drives can increase drive performance, since multiple reads can be performed simultaneously.

Backup Systems

A backup system for the LAN server is extremely important and at the same time convenient because network data can be backed up at one location. There are a number of ways to back up the system, including tape backup systems, optical systems, removable hard disk systems, and even floppy disk systems. Keep in mind that backup systems must be designed specifically for NetWare 386 to recognize the 16-bit attributes of the file system.

A third-party tape backup system can be conveniently mounted in a workstation and used to back up the server during off-hours. Many tape backup systems come with software that can be set to perform a backup at a specified time. Removable hard disk and optical systems can be used for backup. They provide quick access to archive files.

Selecting Network Hardware

The type of network interface cards, the cabling, the protocols used on the network, and the topology all combine to make up the network hardware. Be aware of your cabling options so you can choose the best for your installation. Availability of qualified installers may be an important factor in deciding the type of cable you want to use. Chapter 14 covers these topics in more detail.

Diskless Workstation Considerations

Diskless workstations are inexpensive computers that do not have either floppy disk drives or hard drives. They may be selected for price or for security. Since a local disk drive is not available, users of such workstations are unable to download files from the servers. This adds to the security of the system.

Make sure the station has at least 640K of memory and that the network interface card has a remote reset PROM available. These PROMs are usually available for less than $50. The PROM allows the workstation to boot from a boot file located in the SYS:LOGIN directory of the server. The boot file is created with the NetWare DOSGEN utility.

Cabling

A full understanding of the cable installation is important. The managers and installers should be familiar with the way the cable is assembled and connected to the various components, such as repeaters, hubs, and access units. A detailed map of the cable runs, including the location of all accessories, should be drawn. Planning for growth is also important. Mark the locations where future stations might be added. If existing telephone twisted pair wire is being used, it may be necessary to contact the phone company or owner of the cable before using it.

Cable can be purchased in bulk from many different suppliers. One-thousand-foot rolls are common. Make sure the cable is the exact type required by the network interface cards and topology you have chosen. The cable supplier should be able to furnish installation and handling information. Cable can also be ordered in preassembled lengths from various suppliers if you have a good idea of the distances between workstations.

If you are assembling your own cables, make sure to purchase the proper tools for mounting the cable connectors to the ends of the cables. Special crimping tools can be purchased from most cable suppliers or electronic stores. Adhere to the instructions for using these tools to prevent damage to the connector or cable. If necessary, order wall plates and other mounting brackets.

There are certain state and local codes that govern the type of cable that can be used in buildings. Cable that produces toxic gas when burned may be prohibited, or fire-retardant cable may be required. The code may also specify that cable be run through protective metal conduit. Plenum cable is fire retardant to some extent and may be used in place of cable requiring conduit protection, but its cost is higher than normal cable. The cost of plenum cable is usually less expensive than installing conduit. Check with your local building inspector for more details.

System Protection Equipment

Remember to plan for the purchase of system protection equipment, such as uninterruptable power supplies, surge suppressors, and line filters. Consider that workstations may need uninterruptable power as much as the server, so users can continue working at least long enough to save their files and exit from the network in a proper manner. The amount of time these units operate under backup power is an important consideration. A UPS monitoring board may also be required to provide a connection between the UPS and the server operating system. This connection alerts the server that the UPS is operating under battery power. Remember to order the cable that connects the UPS to the monitoring board.

Choosing the Right Vendor

The vendor or retailer you choose to purchase products from should be reputable and should have experience with a number of similar installations. It helps if they also have loaner equipment, as well as expensive and sophisticated cable testing equipment. Price is also a factor, but be aware that resellers that give the best price probably cannot afford to back up their service. You may want to purchase software and hardware from one organization and installation, service, and support from another.

Developing Logs and Worksheets

This section describes various worksheets and logs that can be created while planning, installing, and maintaining a network. Keep in mind that the categories listed here can also be used to create computerized databases. Use these only as a guideline to design forms for your own needs.

Initial Planning Worksheets

Worksheets should be used during the initial planning stage of a network to collect information about existing equipment and the needs of users and management. The following sections describe recommended worksheets.

Existing Equipment, Master Log

This log sheet is used to produce a master list for all equipment at the installation site. It cross-references to the workstation log, described next. List the following items, using one line for each existing system:

System number (to be assigned as required)

System (brand name or other identifier)

Department

Location

User or users (optional)

Workstation Log

Fill out a workstation log for each existing system at the installation site, and for each new system that will be added to the network.

System number (to be assigned as required)

System (brand name or other identifier)

Department

    Department Manager

Location

User or users

Date installed

Primary vendor

System resources

    Floppy drives and hard drives

    Software on hard drive

    Current backup procedures

    Monitor type

    Printers

    Memory

    Communications adapters

Service information

Service organization

Previous repair log (if available)

Needs Assessment Worksheet

A needs assessment worksheet may be necessary for each user or potential user of the system. Alternatively, a single sheet may suffice as a master worksheet for each workstation.

Existing software used

Required software

Server storage requirements

Usage for programs

Usage for data

Printing requirements

Printer type or quality

Forms

Network load estimates

Communication options

Other

NetWare Workstation Configuration Log

The workstation configuration log should be filled out and attached to the back of each workstation log.

Network information

Name of file server

Name and address of LAN that workstation is connected to

Network interface card installed

Brand and model

Option number

Interrupt line used (IRQ)

I/O base address

DMA line

RAM/ROM addresses

Additional resource sets

Option number

Interrupt line used (IRQ)

I/O base address

DMA line

RAM/ROM addresses

Information for remote workstations only

Network address

Remote boot filename

LAN Workstation Log

Obtain the following information for each workstation on each of the networks in an internetwork system:

Network name and address

Workstation ID

Type of computer

DOS version

LAN interface board

Station (Node) address

    Decimal

    Hex

Remote reset boot information

NetWare File Server Configuration Worksheet

This worksheet should be filled out for the server. A workstation log can be used to gather additional hardware information about the server. The two can be attached.

File server name

System supervisor

Internal IPX number

File server type

Memory

Disk drives

Hard disk information (fill out for each drive)

    Drive name

    Storage capacity

Channel

Controller

Type

Drive

Hot Fix size

Mirroring information

Volume information (fill out for each volume)

Volume name

Size

The following information should be collected for each LAN interface board in the server, each hard disk channel (0 through 4), other drivers, and resource sets:

Network addresses for LAN cards

Option numbers

Interrupt lines (IRQ)

I/O base address

DMA line

RAM/ROM addresses

Installation Parameters Worksheet

The information on the following worksheet should be collected and used during the NetWare installation phase.

UPS information

I/O address

Down time (minutes)

Wait time (minutes)

Battery low input setting (open/closed)

Battery on-line input setting (open/closed)

Network printer information

List type of printer

Connection method (serial/parallel)

Serial settings (baud rate, word size, stop bits, parity, Xon/Xoff)

Directory Structure Worksheet

The directory structure worksheet should be a map that shows all the directories and subdirectories of the system. Be sure to include the directories NetWare creates, which are SYSTEM, LOGIN, PUBLIC, and MAIL on the SYS drive. Also, remember to add the directories for other volumes.

Trustee Security Worksheet

The trustee security worksheet is used to log users and user rights in each directory. The worksheet is best if drawn as a matrix. Down the left side, list each directory on the system. Along the top, list each user or user group. In the corresponding boxes, list the security rights each user or user group has in the directory.

Resource List

The resource list is simply a log of user expertise that can be referred to by another user or the system supervisor when special assistance is required in a particular software package or procedure. List each user and the nature of the expertise he or she is willing to share.

Network Problems Log

Everything that happens on the network should be logged. The workstation logs have a place for problems occurring at the workstation, but if problems occur on the LAN, they should be recorded in the network problems log.

Evaluating Network Servers

Throughput, Performance, and Bottlenecks
Processors
The Server Bus
Memory Considerations
Disk Considerations
Network Interface Cards (NICs)
Workstations
Specialized Systems

NetWare 386 is a high-performance network operating system written specifically for the Intel 80386 processor. This chapter presents information you can use to evaluate various systems on the market that are candidates for NetWare 386 servers.

Of the many factors you must consider when evaluating systems, the type of bus used by the system is usually the most important. A bus is the "highway" used to transfer data between components in a server.

Other factors you must consider when selecting and configuring a server include the amount of memory and the type of hard drives used. This chapter explores these topics for those who are making a purchasing decision or people who are evaluating and recommending the purchase of equipment.

Throughput, Performance, And Bottlenecks

Throughput, performance, and bottlenecks are terms used to describe how a server and a network react under usage. Picture the server as a sort of Grand Central Station, and network cards are like tracks on which data moves in and out. Data moves from the cards to system memory for processing by the CPU. *Throughput* is a term often used when describing the combined performance of all componenets that transfer data. If there are *bottlenecks* in the system, throughput and performance suffer. Bottlenecks occur at the locations shown in Figure 13-1.

When data moves across a network, its fastest speed is often attained on the cabling system, so in some cases cable systems often considered slow actually transfer data faster than it moves in the server or workstations. In fact the throughput of 386 systems that use the Industry Standard

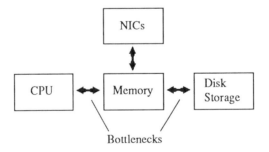

Figure 13-1.   Bottlenecks can occur at various points in the server to reduce performance

Architecture (ISA) bus designs has been estimated to be around 2Mbps, much slower than Ethernet's rating of 10Mbps.

To get the most performance out of NetWare 386, the weak links in the system must be eliminated. Weak links could be any of the following.

Processor   NetWare 386 runs only on systems that use an Intel 80386 processor, but newer 80486 systems can also be used to improve performance. Systems that run at 33MHz are preferred.

Bus design   The best way to provide enhanced performance in a server is through improvements in bus design and the use of intelligent network adapters.

Bus mastering   Bus mastering is a process of relieving the CPU of a task by shifting execution to another processor or controller. The CPU can then perform other tasks such as internal calculations.

Caching   Bottlenecks occur when data is not shuffled in and out of memory quickly enough. Cache memory can be used to reduce these bottlenecks. Exchanges between the CPU and memory or between disk storage and memory can be cached to improve performance.

Disk I/O   One of the most important considerations when evaluating performance is disk I/O. Bottlenecks can be reduced by increasing the disk channel size and decreasing the average access time of disks.

Network interface cards   Performance can be improved with the use of smart network interface cards that perform bus mastering or have improved buffering techniques.

Workstations   Workstations can cause bottlenecks when a system demands too much of the server's time, resulting in large amounts of network traffic. These bottlenecks can be reduced by improving the network interface card in the workstation or by improving the processor and bus size of the workstation.

Processors

The processor is the heart of any computer system. To run NetWare 386, a server based on the Intel 80386 or 80486 microprocessor is required. This section briefly describes the features of 80386 and 80486 systems as well as multiprocessing systems that use both chips. As a point of reference, Table 13-1 lists the performance of some common microprocessors using a rating method that compares millions of instructions per second.

Intel 80386

The 80386 is the successor to the Intel 8088, 8086, and 80286 family of processors. While previous processors were fine for single-user personal computers, the 80386 is the first in the family to provide effective multi-user, multitasking features. While the 80286 is capable of multitasking when running Unix and OS/2, the 80386 provides better performance and is more practical in such environments.

The 80286 has a 16-bit I/O port to the outside world while the 80386 has a full 32-bit I/O port. The 32-bit I/O port of the 80386 provides a connection point for high-speed 32-bit memory expansion on some ISA

System	Million Instructions per Second
Apple II (1979)	.04 MIPS
IBM PC (1981)	.25 MIPS
Apple Macintosh (1984)	.40 MIPS
16 MHz 80386 systems	4 MIPS
25 MHz 80386 systems	7 MIPS
DEC Microvax	2-3 MIPS
25 MHz 80486 systems	8-40 MIPS

Table 13-1.   Performance of Common Microprocessors

systems. On more advanced systems that use full 32-bit MCA and EISA buses, both memory and network interface cards can benefit from a full 32-bit path to the processor.

The speed of the 80386 is significantly faster than previous versions. Depending on the clock speed, the 80386 can run two to four times faster than the 80286. Other features include the following:

- The 80386 can address 4096MB of memory, whereas the 80286 was limited to 6MBs.

- The 80386 has built-in features that make task switching simple and efficient, thus allowing several programs to run at once.

- The 80386 can act like several 8086 processors running simultaneously. The exact number of 8086 processors depends on the amount of memory available, but each process gets its own protected block of memory.

- The 80386 is completely compatible with the 8088, 8086, and 80286, so software written for those processors also runs on the 80386.

- The 80386 contains a memory management unit (MMU) that is capable of speeding up access to memory.

One of the most significant benefits of the 80386 is that it has helped create a whole new level of sophisticated hardware and software, as well as multiuser, multitasking operating systems like NetWare 386.

Intel 80486

The Intel 80486 microprocessor is completely compatible with the 80386; therefore, software for the 80386 will work on 80486 systems without change. However, the 80486 is a completely redesigned processor that improves on the 80386's features and operational characteristics.

Many functions are now integrated onto the chip itself. For example, the functions of the Intel 80387 numeric coprocessor and the Intel 82385 memory cache controller are now integrated on the 80486 chip. The numerical processing functions can execute simultaneously with the 80486's normal functions.

The 80486 systems are so fast that special techniques must be used to keep data moving at the rate the processor can handle it. The 80486 has an 8K cache on the chip itself to improve performance. The 80486 has four write buffers that help keep the external bus from becoming a bottleneck. The buffers hold data until the external bus is free to transfer the data to external memory. Some 80486 systems come with external cache buffers to improve performance even further.

The 80486 also has a pipelined execution feature that breaks instructions into parts that can be executed simultaneously. While this feature is implemented on the 80386, it is more functional on the 80486. Operations normally done in four steps can be done in one step on the 80486.

The question is whether Novell NetWare 386 benefits from these added features. Numeric coprocessing and other features may be lost when an 80486 system is primarily used as a file server, but the 80486 systems are much faster and more efficient and have definite memory and file I/O benefits when used with the proper equipment. There are also advantages when processor-intensive server-based applications are running at the server.

Multiprocessing Systems

Multiprocessing systems have two or more microprocessors and, in some cases, specialized buses to improve performance. These specialized systems, sometimes referred to as super servers, have features designed to optimize throughput to each processor, disk storage, and the network. Multiprocessing systems that support a special version of NetWare 386 are available from NetFRAME and Compaq, as discussed at the end of this chapter. Super servers are designed for network use on the premise that most 80386 and 80486 systems are designed for personal computer use. The price tag is high, however—from $15,000 to $50,000. Disk I/O on these new super servers is rated at 19Mbps. This compares to about 6Mbps for normal 80386 systems that use high-performance components. LAN I/O is rated at about 8Mbps.

The Server Bus

The bus of any computer system is the communications channel used to transfer data between I/O devices, memory, disk storage, and the CPU. The type of bus selected is extremely important to the performance and throughput of a server.

The Industry Standard Architecture (ISA) bus used on the first IBM Personal Computer dominated microcomputer systems during the 1980s. But newer and faster microprocessors, storage devices, and I/O devices demanded better performance from the system bus. In the late 1980s, IBM introduced its Micro Channel Architecture (MCA) bus. In addition, a consortium of microcomputer vendors including Compaq, AST, Hewlett-Packard, Epson, Zenith, and others developed the Extended Industry Standard Architecture (EISA) bus. The MCA and EISA buses deliver increased performance over the older ISA bus, as shown in Table 13-2.

ISA Bus

The Industry Standard Architecture bus has been around since the introduction of the IBM PC. It was expanded from an 8-bit data path to a 16-bit data path in 1984 with the introduction of the IBM PC AT. This bus is used in many 80386 personal computers and some 80486 systems, but for reasons discussed here, it may not be adequate in servers running NetWare 386.

	Bus Size	DMA Transfer	Bus Master Speed	Clock Rate
AT Bus	16-bit	Up to 1.5Mbps	N/A	8 MHz
MCA Bus	32-bit	Up to 5Mbps	Up to 40Mbps	10 MHz
EISA	32-bit	Up to 33Mbps	Up to 32Mbps	8 MHz

Table 13-2.   Performance of Buses

Each card on an AT bus uses a different interrupt line to signal the CPU when it wants access to the bus. No two cards can share the same interrupt, and only 11 interrupts are available in the ISA bus. It is, therefore, important to plan ahead when building a server with an ISA bus since there is a possibility you may run out of interrupts when adding many different cards.

The biggest misconceptions about ISA systems are their processor speeds and actual throughput. Much of the advertising is misleading. Even though a 386 system may claim processor speeds of 16 to 33MHz, the 8MHz ISA bus can slow these systems down incredibly. That means data transfers to and from the processor hit a bottleneck at the bus. Couple the slow transfer rate of ISA with inefficient interface cards and you have a system that is unacceptable for use with NetWare 386 under heavy loads.

Bus mastering is supported on the ISA bus, but it is not a true form of bus mastering, as discussed later. Multiprocessing is not possible because of a lack of standard timing specifications. The exact timing information for the ISA bus was never published, so any attempts to push the performance of the bus would make it incompatible with the thousands of boards that are designed for it. Some ISA systems do have proprietary 32-bit expansion slots that are separate from the ISA bus itself, but these expansion slots are mainly designed for memory expansion.

EISA Bus

The EISA bus was designed by a consortium of industry manufacturers to provide a bus design that offered support for existing ISA expansion boards and to provide a platform for future growth.

To support ISA cards, an 8MHz clock rate is used, but the bus can provide direct memory access rates of up to 33Mbps. Because EISA has a separate I/O and processor bus, the I/O bus can maintain a low clock rate to support ISA boards while the processor bus runs at higher rates. EISA machines can provide high-speed disk I/O to multiple users.

The EISA is a full 32-bit bus, so it requires a new design to accommodate more pins than the ISA bus can handle. At the same time, the connector accepts both ISA or EISA cards. A two-tier slot design is used. The top tier makes contact with ISA boards, while the lower tier makes contact with newer EISA boards. While EISA maintains the 8MHz clock speed of ISA for compatibility, it supports a burst-mode method of quickly transferring data at up to three times the speed of an ISA bus.

As of this writing, most EISA machines are being designed for work group computing and client-server applications. A flood of EISA interface cards, many of which support bus mastering, as discussed later, are making their way to market.

MCA Bus

The Micro Channel Architecture bus was developed by IBM to help resolve the difficulties of combining fast processors with the relatively slow ISA bus. While MCA does not accept older ISA style boards, it provides a new 32-bit interface that is faster than ISA and is a better match to 80386 and 80486 processors.

The MCA bus is a single bus design that handles both memory and I/O transfers through multiplexing, which allows several processes to share the bus simultaneously. Multiplexing splits the bus into several channels that can each be used by different processes. This design does not compare favorably in speed when compared to multiple bus systems, but in many cases it is adequate for NetWare 386. If processor-intensive applications will be run at the server, super servers may be a better choice due to their superior throughput and multiprocessor capabilities.

The MCA bus is protected by patents and licensing agreements that inhibit its growth as a standard. Additionally, IBM has imposed some limitations in MCA to prevent it from competing with its minicomputer systems. In the meantime many vendors have jumped on the EISA bandwagon. For those who want to maintain IBM compatibility, however, MCA is important.

Bus Mastering

In most cases the central processing unit (CPU) has complete control of the entire system. However, it is beneficial to give other devices temporary control of the system so they can perform a specific task. For example, a network interface card can be given temporary control of the bus to transfer data in its buffer to system memory. Ideally, the CPU should be able to perform other tasks while data is transferred from the interface card into memory. This is the case to some extent when direct memory access (DMA) is used on ISA bus systems. In the DMA method, a separate DMA controller handles the transfer of data directly to the system's memory with little help from the CPU, thus increasing performance.

When a bus mastering card is used, a separate processor on the interface card can perform the entire task of transferring data into memory without any help from the main CPU. In this way the main CPU is not interrupted to perform such tasks and can better handle tasks assigned to it. This is true bus mastering.

A bus-mastering system requires an arbitration scheme that prevents two devices from using the same bus at the same time, and this becomes more important as additional bus mastering interface cards are installed in the system. With the EISA bus system, a bus master interface controller (BMIC) chip set is available to anyone who wishes to design such a card. A similar chip set is not available for the MCA bus.

Memory Considerations

NetWare 386 servers should have 4MB or more of memory for best performance, but the absolute minimum is 2MB. Memory is divided among the NetWare 386 operating system and units of cache buffers. The larger the cache, the better the performance of disk I/O. Cache buffers are used to improve performance by keeping often-accessed data in memory where it can be more easily accessed than data on disk.

Memory should also be located on 32-bit bus slots for faster access as it is on MCA and EISA systems. On ISA systems, a proprietary 32-bit slot separate from the bus is usually provided for memory expansion. This slot connects directly to the 32-bit input port on the 80386 for fast memory I/O. When using such systems, ensure that this slot is available.

Types of Memory

As processor speeds increase, RAM memory is being viewed as the bottleneck in many server systems. In the past, CPU, disk drive, and bus performance were not as efficient as memory, but as faster processors came into use, it became apparent that memory could not keep up with the performance of these systems. When memory cannot keep up with a processor's need for a continual flow of data, the processor must wait for one or more clock cycles. This waiting period is commonly referred to as a *wait state.* When memory is fast enough to operate in step with the CPU, a *zero wait state* condition can exists.

While zero wait state memory is the most ideal for use in any system, it is expensive. One type of memory, dynamic RAM or DRAM, commonly used in many personal computers, cannot keep up with the fastest 80386 and 80486 systems. Therefore, wait states are inevitable, unless faster types of RAM chips are used. RAM chips are rated according to their access time in nanoseconds (ns) with the slowest chips running at about 200ns and the fastest running at 35ns. The two types of memory chips are discussed next.

Dynamic RAM   DRAM chips are the most widely available chips. They are inexpensive and available in a range of speeds from 80 to 200 nanoseconds. DRAMs require a refresh cycle every 4 milliseconds to prevent stored memory from being lost. This refresh cycle further diminishes the speed of the chips. DRAM cannot match the speeds of any processor that runs above 16MHz, which prompts a need for wait states.

Static RAM   SRAM chips are much faster than DRAM chips and do not require constant refreshing. Their design contains flip-flop circuits that stay in one or the other state. Because SRAM chips have a more complex design, they are more expensive.

Many systems use a combination of DRAM and SRAM to hold cost down but provide reasonable performance. On many systems, an SRAM cache using 35ns chips is situated between the processor and normal memory. This cache holds the information that is most often accessed by the processor. Special circuitry moves data to and from DRAM memory to the SRAM cache as necessary. Thus the processor has fast access to the information it needs most. A cache controller chip like the Intel 82385 is commonly used to manage the cache systems.

Anyone evaluating systems for use as servers should ensure that memory performance is adequate for the number of users and applications running on the LAN. Most 80386 and 80486 systems that you would consider for server use have high-speed SRAM cache memories to improve performance. Be sure to check the specifications carefully on any system, and request product reviews from the manufacturer or dealer. These reviews are published often in computer and network trade journals and can be found in most libraries.

NetWare 386 Cache Buffers

NetWare sets up its own buffers to improve the performance of the operating system. These buffers are established in the common memory area of the server, not the high-speed cache used by the processor. Cache buffers are used in the following ways:

- NetWare loadable modules such as LAN drivers, disk drivers, and some utilities are "loaned" cache memory by the operating system. When the drivers are removed, the memory is returned for other uses.

- The file allocation table of each volume is cached.

- Part of each volume's directory table is allocated to cache buffers.

- Commonly accessed files are placed in cache memory for quick access.

- Directory names are placed in a hash table that requires some cache buffers.

- Buffers are allocated to turbo FAT indexing tables for all open files that have 64 FAT entries or more and are randomly accessed (database files).

Because NetWare provides caches for so many processes, it is advisable to install as much memory as possible. Memory utilization can be monitored by the network supervisor on an ongoing basis to ensure that each process is properly buffered; however, NetWare dynamically allocates memory, as discussed in the next section.

NetWare 386 Dynamic Configuration

NetWare 386 automatically and dynamically allocates memory to Net-Ware loadable modules, cache buffers, routing buffers, and other features based on the amount of memory available. The more memory available the better. Unlike previous versions of NetWare, managers do not need to make manual adjustments. All memory not needed by other buffers is allocated to disk file caching, but the size of the cache decreases as other features demand memory. When the situation becomes constrained, Net-Ware will warn of a low memory situation.

Disk Considerations

A common bottleneck on any server, even one that employs high-performance bus systems, is access to disk storage. Disk performance can be improved in the following ways:

- Disk caching is important, and NetWare 386 allocates all available memory to this task. In addition, NetWare uses techniques to improve the performance of the disk, such as elevator seeking and file allocation table caching.

- High-speed buses like MCA or EISA are important to quickly move data to and from other components in the server.

- The construction of the drive itself determines how quickly data can be read or written. As the capacity and number of disk surfaces in a drive increase, the access time improves.

- Various methods can be used to encode data being stored on the disk. Data that is efficiently encoded requires less disk space and is more quickly accessed.

Drives are normally rated by their access time, which is the average time it takes to store or retrieve data. NetWare 386 server drives should have access times of 22 milliseconds or lower.

Encoding methods and disk interfaces are available in several standards. The Enhanced Small-Device Interface (ESDI) or Small Computer Systems Interface (SCSI) drives and controllers are suitable for NetWare 386. Older technologies such as Modified Frequency Modulation (MFM) and Run Length Limited (RLL) may not be sufficient for NetWare 386. SCSI systems allow "daisy-chaining" of additional drives in an arrangement where one drive attaches to the back of another. Up to eight SCSI devices can be daisy-chained in this way. SCSI supports other types of devices such as tape backup units, CD ROMs, and other optical drives. ESDI supports a maximum of only two disk drive attachments.

DOS has traditionally imposed some limitations on the design of hard drives for PC systems. These limitations were in the number of cylinders and the sector size that DOS could address. SCSI has allowed manufacturers to overcome these limitations and in the long run provide superior drive systems, as summarized here:

- ESDI is limited to the range of 10 to 15Mbps data transfer rates, while SCSI has a virtually unlimited transfer rate. Current rates are in the 15Mbps range.

- SCSI systems put the drive controller circuitry on the drive itself instead of the controller, which optimizes the system when additional drives are attached. Only one SCSI attachment card is needed to daisy-chain up to 8 devices.

- ESDI uses a serial transfer method, while SCSI uses a faster parallel method.

- Because SCSI drives have their own controllers, they can independently complete disk read and write operations without intervention from the host CPU. During this time the CPU can perform other tasks.

Most manufacturers are now offering SCSI drives and interfaces for their high-end systems. The average access time of modern SCSI drives is in the range of 10 to 15 milliseconds. The more heads and disk surfaces a drive has, the faster it is. Western Digital, Seagate, and Quantum manufacturer SCSI drives suitable for NetWare 386.

Novell Disk Controller Board (DCB)

The Novell DCB is a 16-bit, high-performance disk interface that supports additional disk drives in NetWare servers. There are two models: the DCB and the DCB/2 for the MCA bus. An EISA version is in the works. The DCB offloads most disk I/O operations from the server CPU. When implementing large spanning volumes, disk mirroring and disk duplexing, DCBs are the logical choice for disk expansion.

The DCB and DCB/2 deploy SCSI features that allow the controllers to have multiple requests outstanding to multiple disk drives. Up to eight drives are supported on the DCB controller, and up to seven are supported on the DCB/2. These drives can be both internal and external. There are four different configurations of DCBs that can be ordered. Each DCB supports a different I/O address, as covered in Chapter 16. Hardware interrupts are jumper selectable.

Network Interface Card (NIC)

The performance of the network interface card is largely determined by the type of bus interface that is used. An MCA or EISA interface card gives better performance than a card designed for an ISA system. In addition, these cards can support bus mastering, which is increasingly important on high-traffic NetWare 386 networks. There are other features that determine performance, such as the method used to transfer data from the card to system memory. These topics are covered in Chapter 14, which evaluates network cards and cabling systems.

Workstations

Workstations normally do not affect the performance of the entire LAN, unless the workstation cannot accept the data sent to it due to inadequate buffering or slow throughput. Applications run in workstations at the speed and performance dictated by the hardware design of the station. It is only when users access the network that the network itself could be impeded. A workstation transferring large files could slow a network down.

The throughput of a workstation can be improved by upgrading to systems that use fast components. Managers should look at the workload and amount of network access performed at each machine. Systems that access the network often should move data quickly from the network to internal memory (or vice versa) to prevent bottlenecks. Some systems rarely access the network and are not candidates for upgrading.

To obtain good performance at a workstation, an 80286 system with a 16-bit ISA bus is recommended as a starting point. Systems that require more performance may need an 80386 or 80486 processor. To further improve performance, a system with an MCA or EISA bus is recommended. In addition, high-performance network interface cards should be used, as discussed in Chapter 14.

Specialized Systems

Several vendors are manufacturing systems designed for network use, including Compaq, NetFRAME Systems, and Datapoint Corporation. The architecture of these systems can be compared with minicomputer and mainframe systems. They support the use of multiple 80386 and 80486 processors and are characterized by multiple bus structures that separate the I/O of interface cards from the CPU and memory I/O. Multiple-bus systems communicate through common memory areas. In addition, the interface cards for these systems often have their own processors to handle data transfers without the help of the main CPUs.

NetFRAME Systems' NF/400 is an 80486 system that can be configured with up to eight separate I/O processors, each with a separate path with up to 16MB of system memory. The Compaq SystemPro can support two processors, either the 80386 or the 80486. Each processor has a separate path to memory. NetWare 386 must be optimized to take advantage of the multiprocessing, multifunction capabilities of these systems.

The NetFRAME and Compaq systems are briefly reviewed below.

NetFRAME Systems

NetFRAME Systems (Sunnyvale, CA) has several high-performance servers the company refers to as "network mainframes." The NetFRAME NF/100 is rated as capable of replacing three MCA- or AT-bus-based machines. The NF/300 can replace between four and five such systems, and the latest model, the NF/400, can replace eight such systems.

In personal computer systems using a single-bus structure, a single process takes control of the bus to perform a task, and then releases the bus for use by another process. The NetFRAME systems do not use the bus as a locking device to prevent processes from conflicting. Instead, multiple independent buses can run at the same time, and the system can be expanded by adding more buses, rather than redesigning the bus for each new generation of microprocessors or operating systems.

The NetFRAME systems use a high bandwidth bus that can coexist with older buses like the 16-bit ISA bus. Interprocess communications is performed in shared memory that all processors have access to, and each processor operates simultaneously to form a true parallel processing system. The NetFRAME systems are designed to take advantage of future client-server applications by allowing multiple processors to handle multiple server-based applications.

A NetFRAME server can start as a relatively inexpensive entry-level model. The system can then be expanded by adding plug-in cards that double the I/O capability or the computing capacity of the system. This type of expandability is possible through NetFRAME's *processor clustering architecture,* which allows processors and I/O processes to communicate through shared memory rather than conventional bus methods. Special boards dedicated to operating systems like Unix or OS/2 or dedicated applications like image processing and SQL databases can be added as they become available.

Compaq Systempro

The Compaq Systempro is designed to take advantage of both 33MHz 80386 processors and 33MHz 80486 processors in a system that has the architectural design of a minicomputer. Any combination of these processors can be installed. The 386 processor systems are optimized with a 64K cache memory design, and an optional 80387 or Weitek 3167 math coprocessor is supported. A second processor is added by installing a special processor board. The 80486 version can supply up to 40 million instructions per second of service. The Systempro uses Compaq's flex architecture with multiprocessing support (Flex/MP), which allows simultaneous processing I/O activity.

The EISA bus is used for I/O and the support of 32-bit expansion cards. Up to six 32-bit network interface controllers can be added to the system. A second bus that can transfer data as high as 100MB per second is used between the processor and memory. Fixed disk performance and reliability are enhanced with Compaq's unique *drive array technology*. The array distributes data across a series of synchronized fixed disk drives that are addressed as a higher-performing unit. A special intelligent drive array controller is used to transfer data up to four times faster than nonarrayed drive systems.

The drive arrays can also be used to implement hardware-level system fault tolerance. Mirroring can be done in hardware, thus separating it from software. A service person does not need to know about the operating system. Hardware mirroring also allows more control in the case of failure.

The initial system has 4MB of memory, expandable to 256MB without using an EISA slot. A total of 11 expansion slots are available. Up to 11 storage devices can be mounted internally in the system for up to 1.68 gigabytes of storage. External storage devices can increase capacity to 4.28 gigabytes.

Evaluating Network Topologies

Evaluating the Choices
Evaluating Network Interface Cards

This chapter discusses evaluation and selection methods for the various types of networks and network interface cards. Keep in mind that no system can ever be considered better than another, because each system has it own characteristics. One system may be selected because a particular type of cable is preferred, while another may be selected because the amount of traffic on the LAN dictates it.

Evaluating the Choices

This section provides you with information to evaluate which network system is best for your installation.

Methods for Evaluation

The following discussion ranks each network method according to cost, performance, and ease of installation. The following evaluations are based on coaxial-cable-based ARCNET and Ethernet, and shielded twisted-pair-based Token Ring systems. Metropolitan and wide area networking methods that use fiber optic backbones or remote connections are not considered.

Cost per Workstation

The cost of all three methods has been coming down in recent years. IBM is not the only vendor for Token Ring, so competitive pricing exists. Ethernet has seen the largest reductions in price.

Highest: Token Ring   Token Ring interface cards and shielded twisted pair cable are expensive. In addition, a multistation access unit is required for every eight users when the IBM system is used. Cost can be brought down by using non-IBM parts and unshielded twisted pair, especially if existing telephone cable is used.

Medium: Ethernet   Interface cards are usually more expensive for Ethernet, but the cabling is about the same as ARCNET. Ethernet cards have dropped in price due to competition.

Medium: ARCNET   The cost per workstation is lowest with ARCNET. Interface cards are generally inexpensive. A linear bus or star topology can be configured, which helps reduce the cost of cable since a topology can be designed that better fits the installation site.

Performance

Performance of a network is based on the access method used and the cable transmission speed. The higher the transmission speed, the shorter the supported distance. Keep in mind that network drivers with larger packet sizes are now available to increase overall performance. These larger packet drivers are blurring the performance distinction between Ethernet and Token Ring.

High: Ethernet   Transmits at up to 10Mbps. Under light loads, Ethernet performs well. Under heavy loads, Ethernet may slow down and match the throughput of Token Ring and ARCNET due to its collision detection access method.

Medium: Token Ring   Standard Token Ring transmits at 4Mbps while a newer, faster Token Ring transmits at 16Mbps. The faster version is actually the best performer of all the networks considered here, but it is more expensive.

Low: ARCNET   Transmits at 2.5Mbps. While the throughput of ARCNET may not be adequate for some NetWare 386 installations, recent tests have shown it can keep up with Token Ring and Ethernet under some conditions.

Ease of Installation

How easy a network is to install is really based more on the cable type than the network itself. The topology or layout of the cable is important, but installing connectors and hubs should also be considered. All networks rank high on the installation rating when the workstations are located in a single room, such as a classroom. Wiring a diverse network throughout a building is the real consideration here.

High: ARCNET   ARCNET is easiest to install because cables can be configured in a linear bus or star topology. Coaxial cable connectors are relatively easy to install.

Medium: Ethernet   A single cable run connects all systems.

Medium: Token Ring   Token Ring is relatively easy to install, but building custom cables with shielded twisted pair wire can be a chore because the Token Ring connector is hard to work with.

Evaluating Unshielded Twisted Pair

Because unshielded twisted pair wiring is now available as a wiring method for Ethernet, Token Ring, and ARCNET, it is worth evaluating on its own merits. Twisted pair has distance limitations, but it is inexpensive and already exists on most sites in the form of telephone wire. While not everyone will want to use existing telephone cable, it is a worthwhile consideration for those on a tight budget. Modern network hardware has noise filtering and signal conditioning features that make high-speed transmission over twisted pair possible. The new 10BASE-T Ethernet systems run at 10Mbps.

Networks are easy to move or rearrange when telephone twisted pair is used. Moving or installing a new station is a simple matter of tapping into unused telephone wires at the location of any existing telephone. Wiring is also simplified if the company moves—existing telephone wire at the new location can become the new network.

Wiring the telephone block in a phone closet is relatively simple. In most cases, a qualified installer can locate the lines coming from each phone. An "octopus" cable with a special block connector on one end and a multitude of cables on the other is attached to the wiring block. The cables then correspond to each workstation attached to the block and are plugged into the concentrator or multiaccess unit.

Telephone wire and modular jacks are also much simpler to work with than coaxial cables. Connections are a snap and cables can be built in seconds with a simple inexpensive tool.

Evaluating Ethernet

Ethernet is an excellent choice when data traffic tends to come in bursts, such as when workstations send and receive large files. Token Ring and ARCNET do better under constant traffic. However, if servers with ISA buses are used, bottlenecks can slow a fast Ethernet network down to speeds that match Token Ring and ARCNET. If you are considering Ethernet for its speed, make sure to install a fast server that uses an MCA or EISA bus.

Ethernet allows computers to be connected to a main trunk cable, which is usually made to fit the distances between each station. If the maximum distance is reached on one trunk, a new trunk can be connected by using a repeater. A disadvantage of Ethernet coaxial cabling is that a break or cut in the cable will cause the entire system to fail. A break or cut in a star wired network only affects the workstation connected to the broken cable run.

Because of its high throughput, Ethernet is often the best choice for high-volume applications, such as those in engineering or graphics environments where large file transfers to printing, plotting, and storage devices may demand high speed. Twisted pair 10BASE-T Ethernet products are an excellent choice for those who need to wire distant clusters of workstations.

If your budget for network equipment is not high, but you require speed, you have some alternative solutions. One is to use Ethernet cards and cable for only those stations that require high performance, such as graphics workstations. Then install a cheaper ARCNET network to wire stations with less traffic. In another situation a few workstations may generate so much network traffic that the entire network slows down. It may be necessary to install a separate network card in the server for these stations. In addition, high-speed FDDI fiber optic links may be considered to further improve performance. However, keep in mind that high-speed solutions should be considered only if a server has the proper throughput, which means it must be an MCA or EISA system with a fast processor.

In the future coaxial Ethernet probably will not be an important network method. Any attempts to increase its speed decrease its potential distance. The carrier sensing method used by Ethernet also proves inefficient as networks grow in size. Faster fiber optic networks are dropping in price and may replace coaxial networks completely after the year 2000.

Evaluating ARCNET

ARCNET's price and topology options make it a natural choice for those with simple installations who do not want to spend a lot of money. ARCNET also has a safe and reliable token passing access scheme, using a free-form topology that combines both a linear bus and star configuration. A linear bus configuration can be used when straight cable runs are required and star configuration can be used to distribute workstations from a central point.

ARCNET is easy to install, expand, modify, and service. The wiring scheme used by ARCNET will not disable the entire network if a station goes down, and fault isolation is easy. Workstations can be added or removed with little difficulty or configuration. The per station cost of ARCNET cards is low, sometimes under $100. For most workstations there is little need to spend more for cards to gain additional features or wider data buses.

Cost can be minimized if distances from a passive hub are kept under 100 feet. A more expensive active hub is required for distances over 100 feet. Active hubs allow workstations to extend to 2000 feet. A complete ARCNET system with multiple active hubs can extend as far as four miles. ARCNET systems are available that support thin coaxial cable, unshielded twisted pair cable, and fiber optic cable.

ARCNET provides a unique topology that gives planners more flexibility in configuring the wiring scheme for a building. As mentioned in the previous section, ARCNET can be used in combination with other network topologies. For example, high- performance systems like graphics workstations may be wired to the server using Ethernet, while slower workstations that generate less traffic can be connected to inexpensive ARCNET networks. This concentrates the heavy traffic into a high-speed system and separates it from workstations that use the network occasionally. This type of combining can help network planners stay within budget.

For those who like the topology of ARCNET or who have an ARCNET system with which they want to remain compatible, a newer 20Mbps ARCNET standard is in the works. It will provide high speeds, but it also will have distance limitations, as do Ethernet and other networks that have increased transfer rates.

Evaluating Token Ring

The most common Token Ring network is that made by IBM, although several other vendors now offer it. The IBM Token Ring transmits at 4Mbps or 16Mbps. Token Ring uses shielded or unshielded twisted pair wire to connect workstations to a central box known as the multistation access unit (MAU). In the IBM configuration, this box supports eight stations. It can be attached to other MAUs to form a ring. Other vendors offer more stations per MAU, and allow other types of cable, such as unshielded twisted pair (IBM now offers this also).

Maintaining the ring configuration is important in Token Ring but can sometimes be a nuisance when wiring a system. For example, to connect to distant MAUs, two cables are required to connect the ring-in and ring-out ports on each MAU. In many cases MAUs are stacked together in a wiring closet, so this is not a problem. In other cases MAUs are distributed in a logical loop around the building so that the last ring-out cable must connect to the ring-in port of the first MAU.

Token Ring uses a token passing scheme that provides reliability and a constant throughput, even under load. Each node waits for the token before transmitting. As the token is passed around the network, it is regenerated at each workstation, unlike ARCNET. Token Ring does suffer distance problems. The maximum distance between two stations using the IBM cabling system is about 700 feet.

The new 16Mbps Token Ring cards from IBM offer the fastest throughput of any system described here when larger packet sizes are used. They can be used when high speed is essential, such as in engineering or graphics environments. Both 4Mbps and 16Mbps networks can be established in the same server as long as each network remains separate.

Although Token Ring tends to be expensive, it is one of the most reliable and well thought out of the network designs. Fiber optic networks like FDDI are following in its footsteps with token passing ring designs that provide reliability at high speeds. Token Ring is easy to install, assuming premade cables are used. Telephone twisted pair can also be used to lower costs and simplify installation.

Evaluating Network Interface Cards

The first thing to consider when evaluating network interface cards is the card for the server—it should be the best possible card in the entire network, because all other workstations exchange information with it. It is a central hub. Depending on your budget, you may want to spend more money on the server card and less on those installed in workstations. The following rough guidelines can be used to evaluate and purchase cards:

Servers and workstations with high network usage   Use the best possible cards within your budget for these systems. This also implies that the server or workstation is a high-performance system, such as an 80386 or 80486 MCA or EISA bus system, that matches the performance of the card.

Medium-use workstations Workstations that generate occasional traffic, or burst-type traffic generated by large files (usually graphics files), should be 80286, 80386, or 80486 workstations with a 16-bit bus and network interface card.

Low-use workstations Stations that attach to the network to retrieve or store an occasional file are low-use workstations. They may access the server less than 10 times a day. Use inexpensive 8-bit interface cards in these systems if your budget is constrained.

Because of advances in processor technology, new network interface cards that transfer data more quickly and eliminate bottlenecks are becoming available. Most of the new cards will only work on EISA and MCA systems due to the need for higher throughput and faster processors.

As mentioned in the previous chapter, the 8MHz ISA bus in many 80286 and 80386 systems is a source of bottlenecks. Even though the processors in these systems run as high as 25MHz and 33MHz, the bus runs at 8MHz. Data that arrives from other stations on the network is placed in a temporary holding buffer on the network interface card. The buffer holds incoming data if the server or workstation is not able to process it immediately, thus freeing the network to service other workstations. If the buffer becomes full, network performance drops as it waits to service the workstation. Once the data is in the buffer, it must be transferred over the system bus to system memory, where it then may be sent to disk storage or the CPU for processing.

The methods used to move data from the interface card to its final destination in the server or workstation become an important consideration when purchasing not only cards but also the systems that will house them. Bottlenecks may be created by the way data is handled as it arrives and is sent to memory locations on the system. The network interface card interrupts the CPU when it has data to transfer. In NetWare the IPX protocol code is then run by the host CPU. The speed at which the protocol is executed depends on the processor speed, so a fast system delivers better performance.

Depending on the data-handling method used, data packets may be transferred from the buffer on the card to an area in memory where they are reassembled in the proper order. The packets then may be transferred again to an area in memory set aside by the network operating system and still another area used by an application. All of these memory transfers take time and are sources of bottlenecks. The following methods may be used to help eliminate bottlenecks:

On-board processors   Some interface cards have on-board processors that perform the tasks of packet assembly and then transfer the results directly to memory using a direct memory access (DMA) procedure. Multiple memory transfers are eliminated, but a bottleneck can still occur if an 8MHz ISA bus is used in the server. In addition, the on-board processor usually does not run as fast as the host processor, so there is a mismatch in performance.

Bus mastering   A network interface card installed in a system that supports bus mastering transfers incoming data directly into system RAM. The interface card interrupts the CPU and handles the data transfer, but the CPU runs the network protocol.

Pointer method   In this method data is transferred directly to a shared memory block used by both the network interface card and CPU using a bus mastering method. The interface card then supplies the CPU with a pointer indicating the location of packets to be processed. This method provides the best response and is normally only implemented in MCA and EISA. An Intel 82596 LAN controller chip is usually used to handle the transfer of data. Cards that support this method should be evaluated for server use.

The packet size of data transferred over the network is also important. A big improvement in throughput can be realized when packet sizes are increased. This reduces the amount of packet reassembly required and the amount of traffic on the LAN since there is less packet overhead. NetWare allows packet sizes to be set as high as 4K, but the driver for the network interface card in a particular machine must support it. Also, all cards on the network must be set to use the same packet size. However, some new cards are capable of working with multiple packet sizes.

Installing Netware

Preparing to Install NetWare

**F
I
F
T
E
E
N**

What You Need to Know
Overview of Major Installation Steps
Documenting Installation
Understanding Interrupts, Addresses, and Ports
Methods of Installing Netware
The NetWare 386 Disk Set
Server Boot Methods
Server Disk Drive Considerations
LAN Driver Considerations
Installing Other Server Options
Post-Installation Procedures

This chapter is designed to help you understand the steps involved in the installation of the NetWare operating system. NetWare 386 is easy to install, but don't plan on having it completed in an afternoon. Keep in mind that hardware must be configured, cable connected, and the software must be installed. In addition you must make sure you have the correct software drivers for the server and workstations. A large wide-area-network installation could take weeks if the equipment and workstations are spread out over a large area.

A new network can cause changes in the way people work and the procedures they follow. You may need to allow time to design and implement new procedures and to train users. Typically a LAN takes about three days to install, once the equipment is on hand. In a best-case scenario a small LAN can be installed in an afternoon, with proper planning and the cooperation of all those involved.

What You Need to Know

This chapter is designed to familiarize you with the terminology of the installation and help you fill out log sheets. The topics covered are

- How to boot the server

- How to configure disk drivers

- How to partition drives

- When and how to mirror drives

- How to establish volumes

- How to configure LAN drivers

- How to configure other drivers

Overview of Major Installation Steps

Once you have acquired the hardware and software for your network, you can begin the installation process. The following steps are recommended:

1. Install the hardware components in the server and workstations, making sure there are no hardware conflicts.

2. Install the network cabling. This is an optional step. You can do it before or after installing the server. It may be more convenient to install just one or two workstations near the server until the operating system, its users, and security are in place.

3. Install NetWare on the file server, following the procedures in Chapter 17. If you are upgrading an existing NetWare 286 installation, refer to Appendix B.

4. Generate the startup files and boot disks for the workstations attached to the LAN, as covered in Chapter 18.

5. Test the network to make sure all workstations can connect with the server.

6. Begin the task of managing a network, as described in Part V and Part VI of this book.

Documenting Installation

As you prepare your network, it is important to keep a log of everything you do, such as switch and jumper settings, network layout, and server configurations. Chapter 12 provides a list of log sheets you can use to collect information on your network, either before or during the installation. Have these log sheets at hand and make additions or changes to them as required.

The following log sheets are useful as you proceed with the installation:

- *Server log sheet* This chapter helps you determine how to configure various operating system parameters, such as hard disk partitions and volumes. Use the server log to record this information for later use. It also is important to track the settings of each board you install in the system. This helps you avoid conflicts when you install additional boards.

- *Workstation log sheets* The NetWare SHGEN program is used to generate the IPX.COM file for workstations. Use the workstation log sheets to record specific information about each workstation, such as node addresses, interrupts, I/O addresses, and ports. Much of this information is collected when you install network interface cards, as described in the next chapter.

- *Network map* Use the network map to help you locate specific workstations and record any pertinent information about those stations, such as their node address numbers and any changes you need to make to their startup procedure.

Remember that the information on these sheets is designed to help future installers and supervisors make sense of your network. Recording everything you do is a good idea; in a few months you probably will not remember how you set every feature. If you leave the company, would your successor be able to figure it out?

Understanding Interrupts, Addresses, and Ports

Some of the information you need to collect ahead of time has to do with the way switches and jumpers are set on the interface cards being installed in the server. No two devices can share the same settings, nor can any device use a setting already in use by the system. Chapter 16 explains how to install interface cards and avoid interrupt, address, and port conflicts between two or more boards. The following descriptions will assist you in gathering information about your hardware.

Note: Write special settings on a sticker attached to the back of interface cards for easy reference after the cards are installed.

- *Direct memory access (DMA) channel* A DMA channel is one of four channels controlled by a special chip called a DMA controller. It moves data directly from an interface card buffer to system memory. If an interface card uses DMA, a channel must be specified with switch settings or a SETUP program (it may also be hard-wired). The channel must then be supplied to the INSTALL program during installation.

- *Interrupt number* Interface cards need occasional but not full-time attention by the server's processor. To get the processor's attention, the card sends a signal through one of several interrupt lines. Think of a telephone line between the card and the processor. Each card must have its own number that does not conflict with those used by other cards. Interrupts are set with dip switches or jumpers and must be recorded on the log sheet for use during installation.

- *Base memory address* This is an address used by a card for its own memory usage. Two cards cannot share the same address, otherwise data is overwritten.

- *Input/output port address* An I/O port is a data line established to send information between the processor and an external device attached to an interface card. The port address must be unique for each device.

- *Slot* An IBM PS/2 system incorporating Micro Channel Architecture assigns numbers to the slots used by interface cards. You may need to know the slot number during installation.

Methods of Installing Netware

The method you use to install NetWare depends on whether you are upgrading an existing NetWare 286 server to NetWare 386 or you are installing a completely new NetWare 386 network. Those installing a new network need only perform the normal installation steps outlined in Chapter 17. Those upgrading an existing network must ensure that existing data is backed up and copied to the new NetWare 386 server. Refer to the appropriate sections in this chapter.

New Installation

If you are installing a new network, there is no existing data to back up, unless you use an existing machine. Back up any existing data to disk or tape before proceeding. Read through this chapter to become familiar with concepts you need while running the NetWare INSTALL program. Then refer to the next chapter to configure your hardware. Chapter 17 outlines the installation steps, and Chapter 18 explains how to prepare workstations.

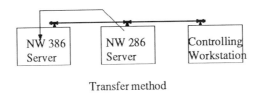

Transfer method

Backup method

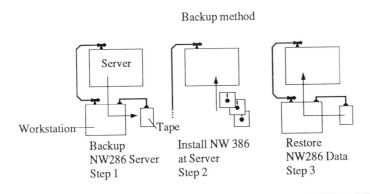

Figure 15-1. NetWare 286 can be upgraded to NetWare 386 using either the transfer or the backup method

Upgrade Installation

NetWare comes with a utility called UPGRADE, which is designed to help you make the transition from an existing NetWare 286 network to the NetWare 386 environment. UPGRADE preserves most of the existing user, security, login, and other information. The following two methods can be used for upgrading, as illustrated in Figure 15-1:

- *Transfer method* The transfer method is used if you have two servers, one old NetWare 286 server and one new NetWare 386 server. The information on the old server is transferred over a network cable to the new server. The transfer method is ideal because it does not affect the NetWare 286 server. If a problem occurs during installation, you can resume operating with the old system until the problem is resolved.

- *DOS device method* The DOS device method is for those who will use their existing NetWare 286 server as the server for NetWare 386. The data must be backed up and then restored after NetWare 386 has been installed on the server. This method must be used if you have only one file server, which must be an Intel 80386- or 80486-based system currently running NetWare 286.

Appendix B covers the upgrade methods in detail.

The NetWare 386 Disk Set

Before starting installation, make copies of the NetWare 386 disk set using high-density disks. Be sure to use the DOS DISKCOPY command to ensure that the copies are exact duplicates of the originals. The disks contain subdirectories, and have a volume label that must be transferred to its copy. Once the disks are created, you may need to copy certain files to them, as described next.

Copying Third-Party
Loadable Modules

Recall that NetWare loadable modules (NLMs) are software drivers NetWare uses to communicate with the hardware components you install in the server. While Novell includes a number of loadable modules, you'll need to copy loadable modules for the equipment you plan to install. These modules are normally stored on disks supplied with the equipment or can be obtained from your dealer or the manufacturer.

Copy the drivers to the NetWare Operating System-1 disk before beginning. Disk drivers have the extension DSK, and LAN drivers have the extension LAN.

Note: It is important that the drivers be located on this disk. During installation, they are copied from the disk to the SYSTEM directory on the NetWare SYS volume. Part of NetWare's security prevents drivers from being loaded during a normal startup if they are not in this directory.

Server Boot Methods

There are two ways to boot a NetWare 386 server. One method is to create a small DOS partition on the file server drive and load the file server startup files to it. The other method is to create a boot disk with the server startup files. The advantages and disadvantages of both methods are discussed in the following sections to help you decide on the method you want to use.

DOS Partition Boot Method

With this method a DOS partition of 1 to 3MB is created on the server hard drive. The remainder of the drive space is allocated to NetWare. The advantage of using this method is that the server boots quickly because files read from hard drives execute much faster. There is less risk of media failure if you use a DOS partition. In addition, creating a DOS partition gives you the ability to resort to the boot disk method, if you also create a boot disk.

Floppy-Disk Boot Method

This boot method stores the startup files on a floppy disk and allocates the entire drive to NetWare. The server takes much longer to boot using this method, but that may not be a moot point if you never turn the server off. One big advantage of this method is that you can store the boot disk in a secure location.

Server Disk Drive Considerations

The following information is important to know when you are configuring disk drives, establishing partitions, and creating volumes.

Disk Drivers

Disk drivers are loaded after the SERVER program is started. The Net-Ware LOAD command is used to place the driver information in memory. NetWare is shipped with the following disk drivers:

- ISADISK for drives using industry standard AT-compatible bus controllers

- PS2ESDI for IBM PS/2 or compatible microchannel machines

- DCB for external disk subsystems using disk coprocessor boards

- PS2MFM Microchannel MFM driver

- IBMSCSI Microchannel SCSC driver

Other drivers will be available with future versions. You can list the drivers that are shipped with your version of NetWare by placing the System disk in a floppy drive and executing the following command:

DIR *.DSK

Determine the DMA channel, interrupt number, memory address, I/O port and slot of any card you are installing in the server, and make sure these figures do not conflict with other cards. This is covered in the next chapter.

Partitions

Hard drives consist of either one whole partition or two or more smaller partitions. In the world of DOS, partitions have a limit of about 32MB, which means that large drives must be subdivided, with the first partition 32MB in size. You also can create partitions for different operating systems that reside on the same disk. If you decide to boot the hard drive instead of a floppy disk, you must create both a DOS partition and a NetWare partition.

To create partitions you must know about *cylinders,* which are divisions of a hard drive determined by the physical characteristics of the drive. To understand cylinders, first picture the platters of a hard drive as flat round disks with a double-sided magnetic recording surface. A hard drive may consist of two or more of these platters. Now stack the platters like poker chips, and on the top platter draw a large number of "bulls-eye" circles from the center to the perimeter of the disk. A cylinder is an extension of each circle down through the stack. If you could cut a cylinder out with a cookie cutter, it would appear as a stack of rings. Each ring has a top and bottom surface known as a track. The tracks in a cylinder can be seen here:

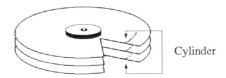

Cylinder

Now imagine enough space between each platter to fit a tiny arm fitted with two recording heads, one facing up and one facing down. Each makes contact with a respective surface of the platter above or below. Some degradation in access speed can occur because all heads move together on a single armature, even if only one is accessing information. However, cylinders are the key to eliminating this degradation. Since a cylinder extends down through the stack of platters rather than horizontally across a single platter surface, it is possible to write large files contiguously in one cylinder with no head movement.

The first part of the file is written on the top track of a cylinder. When the track is filled, the head on the opposite side of the platter continues writing. This process continues down through the cylinder stack. Only when the cylinder is full does the armature move the recording heads to the next cylinder. This eliminates head movement and improves access time. In fact, higher-capacity drives with four or more platters have faster file access times because they have more recording surfaces per cylinder.

Calculating Cylinders per Partition

You must determine how many cylinders are required to establish a DOS partition and the NetWare partition. This can be done with a simple calculation that indicates the number of cylinders in 1MB of disk space. You must know the cylinder count and size of the drive. The cylinder count of a drive can be displayed by the DOS FDISK command. Divide the total number of cylinders for the drive by the disk size. For example, if FDISK informs you that the drive has 1021 cylinders and you know the drive's capacity is 90MB, the following equation is used:

1021 cylinders/90MB = 11 cylinder per MB

You would specify 33 cylinders to create a 3MB DOS partition.

Hot Fix

Hot Fix is a feature of NetWare that sets aside 2% of a drive as a redirection area for bad blocks. In most cases the default Hot Fix size is sufficient, unless the drive is of unknown quality or has been in use for some time and is showing signs of degradation. You would then want to increase the Hot Fix size to anticipate a larger number of redirected blocks.

Disk Surface Test

After partitioning a drive, you may want to run a disk surface test. This step is unnecessary with most modern drives because they are thoroughly tested for bad sectors at the factory. If you have an older driver or one of unknown quality, run the disk test. Keep in mind that NetWare's Hot Fix feature is designed to detect and redirect data in bad blocks during normal operation of the server, so the need to do a surface test is further reduced.

Mirroring Partitions

Recall from Chapter 5 that disk mirroring and disk duplexing are used to ensure the protection of server data in the event of a hardware failure. Once the mirrored or duplexed pair is installed in the server, as discussed in the next chapter, you must partition the drives and establish them as mirrored pairs during installation.

Mirrors are established by creating partitions of the same size on two different drives and then pairing them during the installation process. All subsequent operations on the mirrored partitions, such as the establishment of volumes and Hot Fix, are duplicated on both drives.

Mirrors can be established between two drives on the same controller, or between two drives on separate controllers, which is known as disk *duplexing*. Duplexing provides additional security against failure of the first controller.

Volumes

Volumes are collections of directories, subdirectories, and files. NetWare allows more than one volume per server, but the first is always named SYS and contains the SYSTEM, PUBLIC, LOGIN, and MAIL directories. Volumes can be so small that up to eight fit on one hard disk, or volumes can be large enough to span several hard disks.

You can improve disk performance by spanning volumes over two or more hard drives, as shown here:

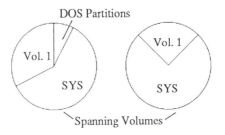

Both the SYS and VOL1 volumes span both drives. When a large file is written or saved to the SYS volume, for example, it may be split between the drive segments. In this way both drives handle the file operation simultaneously, halving the time of the operation. The only disadvantage to a file that exists on both drives is that it could be lost if one drive goes

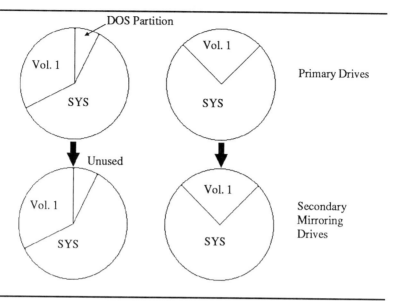

Figure 15-2   If volumes span drives, they should be mirrored, which will require a total of 4 hard drives

down. It is recommended that you mirror all drives that have spanning volumes, as shown in Figure 15-2.

In the same way that partitions are defined by specifying cylinders, volumes are defined by specifying the size of the segment they will use on a hard drive. The segment size is defined in blocks, which is the smallest number of bytes used to store a file.

Defining Block Sizes

NetWare volumes can be set to use block sizes of 4K, 8K, 16K, 32K, or 64K. The default block size is 4K, which means that the smallest area of disk space used to store a file is 4K, even if the file is only 1K in size. While this may seem to be an inefficient use of disk space, reducing the block size below 4K to accommodate such small files adds too much overhead to the filing system. However, increasing the block size can be beneficial in some cases. Consider the following:

- Small block sizes are useful if your volume will contain many small files. More disk space and overhead is required to keep track of the files, however.

- With large blocks, user access to information is much more efficient since a file access may be completed in one operation, rather than in multiple operations as would be required with smaller blocks.

- If large blocks are used, disk space is wasted when a small file is stored in a large block area.

- Large blocks are useful for databases.

In most cases the default 4K block size is sufficient, but you may want to consider creating a separate volume with a large block size for the sole purpose of storing a large database file.

Defining Volume Segments

When you set up a volume, you are requested to enter the volume segment size. If a volume will use only part of a hard drive, you must reduce the recommended segment size. If a volume will span several hard drives, you must define the segment size for each drive used by the volume.

The following rules apply when defining special segments:

- Up to 8 volume segments can be created on a single disk.

- A volume that spans hard drives can have up to 32 segments.

- A single volume can span up to 32 hard drives if each hard drive contains one volume segment.

- Volume size can be increased at a later date to expand the filing system by adding a new segment. It can never be decreased without reformatting the drive.

LAN Driver Considerations

An important task before installation is to obtain the latest LAN driver versions and to make sure they are compatible with Netware 386. Starting in late 1989, many LAN card manufacturers started providing NetWare 386 drivers on the disks that come with their cards. Many of these drivers can handle larger packet sizes. It may be worth your while to contact the manufacturer or your dealer to ensure you have the latest versions.

LAN drivers for the NetWare 386 server have an extension of LAN. Workstation drivers have an extension of OBJ. If you use a server driver that supports larger packet sizes, your workstation driver must match its capabilities. In some cases an entire network cannot use larger packet sizes if just one station does not support them. Some advanced network inter-face cards can operate in an environment with multiple packet sizes. Once again, check with the vendor to be sure.

During installation you use the NetWare LOAD command to install drivers for the LAN boards in the server. LOAD requests some information for each board, such as its interrupt and port address. You can also specify optional parameters to change the default settings for a driver. The settings you can specify include the DMA channel, interrupt number, node address, number of retries, frame type, memory address, port address, and slot number. Refer to the documentation for the board to determine if it requires special settings to run on a NetWare 386 network.

DOS ODI Workstations

Novell's Open Data-Link Interface (ODI) allows workstations to support multiple protocols and multiple drivers. While a normal DOS workstation can have only one network interface card and run only IPX, a DOS ODI workstation can have multiple protocols which allow it to communicate with not only IPX, but AppleTalk and TCP/IP protocols. Other protocols will be available in the future.

A number of configurations are possible. A workstation may have one or more network interface cards, each supporting a special protocol, or a workstation may have a single network card that is capable of supporting multiple protocols simultaneously. The second configuration requires special Multiple Link Interface Drivers (MLIDs) as discussed in the "NetWare Open Systems" section of Chapter 7.

DOS ODI workstations can communicate with a variety of workstations, file servers, and mainframe systems using different protocol stacks, without rebooting the workstation. In this strategy, the network cabling system becomes a platform for the interconnection of diverse systems.

The installation of DOS ODI workstation is covered in Appendixes H and I.

Configuring Ethernet Cards

Ethernet networks can use either the IEEE 802.3 or Ethernet II frame formats. The Ethernet II format contains a unique protocol number that is not contained in the IEEE 802.3 packet. The frame format of a workstation must match the frame format of the network it is connected to. By default, NetWare uses the IEEE 802.3 standard. If you want to maintain this standard, do nothing. If you want to change to the Ethernet II standard, specify the Frame option when loading the Ethernet driver module at the server. At the workstation use the ECONFIG command to alter the frame format of the IPX.COM file.

Sometimes none of the workstations come up on a new server, possibly because the workstations are using the default 802.3 format while the Ethernet card in the server is using the Ethernet II format. This may occur whenever a non-Novell card and driver are used. Before you check elsewhere for network problems, try loading the server driver with the following parameter:

```
FRAME=ETHERNET_802.3
```

To change the format at the workstations, refer to the discussion of ECONFIG in Chapter 18.

Internetwork Considerations

A new NetWare 386 server can be connected to an existing NetWare 286 network or even another NetWare 386 network. Among the considerations you must keep in mind is the need to change the login scripts of existing users to log them into the new NetWare 386 server. You will also need to copy the NetWare 386 commands and utilities to the NetWare 286 server. Other considerations are discussed in the sections that follow.

IPX Internal Network Number

When installation first begins you are asked for an IPX internal network number. Enter a unique number that is different from any other network address, including the DOS process number of a server running non-dedicated NetWare 286. What number you choose does not matter, as long as it is unique. The IPX number allows future versions of NetWare to support a system fault tolerant strategy in which an entire server is duplicated by a second server.

Network Addresses

Each network has a number that is the address of its cable system. This address is similar to the name of the street you live on. While each workstation or server attached to that "street" has a distinct node address, the "street" or network address must be the same for all workstations if they are on the same cable. If your new server is being attached to an existing cable system, use the network address for that system.

A bridge is established when more than one network interface board is installed in a server. Each card supports a separate and distinct network that must have its own network address.

Encrypted Passwords

NetWare 386 encrypts passwords as a security measure. Errors occur if a user on a NetWare 286 network attempts to log into a NetWare 386 server using the NetWare 286 LOGIN command. To resolve this problem, copy the NetWare 386 LOGIN command to the NetWare 286 server. You can also place a command in the NetWare 386 server startup files to set the encryption of passwords off.

Installing Other Server Options

The following server options are available in current versions of NetWare 386 or will be available with future versions.

Macintosh Support

NetWare 386 will support Macintosh systems with a future NetWare Loadable Module. Until then, you must establish a NetWare 286 server as a bridge using the NetWare for Macintosh VAP. This bridge must include two network interface cards: one that connects to the Macintoshes and one that connects to the NetWare 386 network. This bridge can be established at any time after NetWare 386 is installed.

Macintosh workstations need the AppleShare workstation software. This software comes with the Macintosh system software version 6.0 or above.

Name Space Support

To store non-DOS files on a NetWare server, you must install a name space support module. The Macintosh module is called MAC.NAM and is supplied with NetWare 386. Other name space support modules will be available in the future and will have the filename extension NAM.

Name space support requires additional memory from the file server to cache directory entries. For example, the Macintosh name space has two directory entries to match the filenaming conventions of the Apple filing system. Name space support cannot be removed from a volume once installed, and the volume cannot mount unless the loadable module that supports the name space has been loaded. In addition, a name space support command must be issued at the console for each volume used to store Macintosh files. This is performed during the operating system installation steps, which are covered in Chapter 17.

OS/2 Support

Workstations running OS/2 can connect to NetWare servers using the Novell NetWare Requester software. The Requester software is installed on the server and workstation hard drive. NetWare Requester can also be used to bridge to an OS/2 LAN manager server. The Requester provides the communications protocols and interprocess mechanisms such as Named Pipes, NetBIOS, and NetWare SPX to run applications. Once an application server is installed, any user on the NetWare network can access the application running on the OS/2 server. An example is the Ashton-Tate/Microsoft/Sybase SQL Server package.

You can install the NetWare OS/2 Requester after installing NetWare 386 and the DOS workstations. Instructions are given in Appendix G.

Other NetWare Loadable Modules

A number of other NetWare loadable modules are included with NetWare 386, and more will be available in the future. The UPS NLM is used to provide the software link between the operating system and an uninterruptible power supply. This link allows the UPS to warn NetWare that power has failed. Special options are required when the UPS NLM is loaded to establish the UPS link. For installation instructions refer to Chapter 35.

Future NLM will be based around NetWare services such as file and print, communications, database, store and forward, and management services. Refer to your NetWare documentation or vendor for additional information.

Loading PSERVER (Print Server)

PSERVER is a NetWare loadable module that allows you to establish printing services on the server. A print server can support up to 16 printers, but only five can be attached to the server itself. The rest can be attached to workstations and accessed by users at other workstations.

Attaching up to five printers at the server has its limitations. First, you must have five available ports. Most 386 systems come with only one parallel port and one or two serial ports, so you must add cards to expand the ports. This causes problems with interrupts on standard AT-type systems since only 11 are available. Some are used by disk drives, video cards, and other options. If you intend to install more than one network interface card and additional printers, you may run out of interrupts, and will need to attach printers to workstations or install another print server.

Post-Installation Procedures

The following sections describe some of the procedures and additional steps you may need to take after installation is completed.

Startup Options for the Server

The installation procedure creates two server boot files. These are STARTUP.NCF and AUTOEXEC.NCF. The commands and options you used to install the server are automatically inserted in the proper files for you. You can save these files for future boot sessions, or edit them to fit your network requirements.

When the server boots it first reads STARTUP.NCF, which contains commands to load the server's disk drivers and any name space support. The AUTOEXEC.NCF file is then read. It contains the following information, which is obtained from your installation procedure:

- Name of the server

- The IPX Internal Network Number

- LAN drivers loaded and bound

- Other NLMs loaded

The SERVER Command

You use the DOS SERVER command to start the server after booting DOS. You can place it in the DOS AUTOEXEC.BAT file so the server is automatically started. The command has several options you should be aware of. Three of the options are used to change or inhibit the AUTOEXEC.NCF and STARTUP.NCF startup files. This may be useful when you need to test or alter the startup configuration. These options are covered in more detail in Chapter 19.

-S	Include this option plus the name of an alternate startup file to use
-NS	Inhibits the use of STARTUP.NCF and prevents disk drivers from loading
-NA	Inhibits the use of AUTOEXEC.NCF and prevents LAN drivers from loading
-C	Used to specify a different block size for the cache buffer

Additional Startup Options

The NetWare console command SET changes the characteristics of the operating system. There are a number of options used to alter the settings of the file cache, directory cache, file system, communications, memory, file locks, transaction tracking system, encryption, and other features. Complete information is available in Chapters 35 and 36. A few SET options of importance during the initial installation are listed here. The first two should appear in the STARTUP.NCF file; the last goes in the AUTOEXEC.NCF file.

- *SET MAXIMUM SUBDIRECTORY TREE DEPTH=[10 to 100]* The default is 25. During an upgrade you must set this value higher if your existing subdirectory depth is greater than 25.

- *SET MAXIMUM PHYSICAL RECEIVE PACKET SIZE=[618 to 4202]* If you are using advanced network interface card drivers that support larger packet sizes, set this value to the size of the largest packet. Read the card or driver documentation for instructions on setting this option.

- *SET ALLOW UNENCRYPTED PASSWORDS=[ON or OFF]* The default is off. Set this option to on if you are adding a NetWare 386 server to an existing NetWare 286 network to allow the use of unencrypted passwords by 286.

- *SET CACHE BUFFER SIZE=[size]* If the server is dedicated to a special task, such as servicing a database, it may be beneficial to increase the block size to reduce the number of disk accesses. For example, you could increase the cache buffer block size from the default of 4K to 8K by including the number 8192.

Preparing and Starting Workstations

Workstations are attached to the network using the IPX.COM and the EMSNET*x*.EXE, or NET*x*.COM and XMSNET*x*.EXE files (*x* is a number that refers to the DOS version). The NetWare SHGEN program is used to link the IPX.COM file with drivers that match the network interface card installed in the workstation. After IPX is loaded, one of the shell files listed below is loaded. When the expanded or extended memory shells are used, the shell is loaded into high memory, leaving conventional memory free for applications.

NET3.COM	(DOS 3 shell for conventional memory)
NET4.COM	(DOS 4 shell for conventional memory)
EMSNET3.EXE	(DOS 3 shell for expanded memory)
EMSNET4.EXE	(DOS 4 shell for expanded memory)
XMSNET3.EXE	(DOS 3 shell for extended memory)
XMSNET4.EXE	(DOS 4 shell for extended memory)

Two additional files, NETBIOS.EXE and INT2F.COM may be required on workstations that will be running applications written for IBM-type networks.

Starting Diskless Workstations

Since diskless workstations have no way of booting on their own, a special boot PROM can be purchased and attached to the network interface card to allow them to boot directly from the server's hard drive. A program called DOSGEN creates a file used by the diskless workstations as they boot. This file is called NET$DOS.SYS and is stored in the LOGIN directory of the SYS volume.

The NET$DOS.SYS file mimics a floppy boot disk, complete with the DOS and network startup files. Creating the file is an interesting process since you must prepare an actual disk with all the files the diskless workstation needs to boot. This disk should include the version of DOS you want the workstation to start with, as well as the IPX.COM file that matches the interface board in the workstation. You should also create CONFIG.SYS and AUTOEXEC.BAT files on the disk. When DOSGEN is executed it scans this disk and creates an image of it in the NET$DOS.SYS file.

Workstation Startup Files

In addition to the files called IPX.COM, NETx.COM, EMSNETx.EXE, XMSNETx.EXE, CONFIG.SYS, and AUTOEX-EC.BAT, you can create a file called SHELL.CFG or NET.CFG to hold additional startup parameters for the workstation. These parameters can be different for each workstation and are used to customize them for use with NetWare. For example, one command specifies the type of DOS used by the workstation so a proper search path can be set to the same DOS version stored on the server.

Preparing the Network Hardware

Site Preparation
Preparing the Server
Preparing Workstations
Cable Installation
Checking Network Connections

This chapter gives you some insights into installing the hardware components of your system and helps you prepare for the installation. You must prepare the server location, the server itself, the workstations, and install the cable.

Site Preparation

The installation of a network is sure to disrupt the normal everyday activities of people at the installation site. Make sure these people are familiar with who you are and what you are doing, especially if you are crawling under their desks to install cable. A schedule of installation activities must be worked out with workers and managers. You will not win friends if you try to perform an installation when the company is trying to meet a sales quota or get its payroll out.

You can approach the installation in several ways. One method is to install all the hardware and cabling before installing the NetWare 386 operating system on the server. Another method is to install the operating system first. Still another method is to have groups of people installing hardware, software, and cabling at the same time.

The best method is to prepare the server in advance with at least one workstation attached. This helps you isolate server problems and assure that the server is working properly before you begin attaching workstations and users. Plan on taking some time to properly install directories, user accounts, login scripts, and applications before you put the network into use.

If several servers will be connected with a backbone cable, gather all the server equipment together and make the backbone connections. Of course, this may not be easy if the servers are in use. At some point all the servers must be downed so the new server can be attached to the network. If you are using the UPGRADE method, you also must make sure users are logged out so you can perform the transfer or backup operations.

It is best to streamline your task by having all the hardware components and the operating system installed and ready to go. Eliminate all hardware conflicts in the server and prepare the hard disk systems for use. Run the setup programs for your server to install additional hardware. These programs are not covered in this book, so refer to the owner's manual for details.

Once the server is installed, you can begin installing workstations. If they were already set up on an existing LAN, your job is easy. Simply make changes to the workstation's startup files and user login scripts as required for the new server. For example, you may want to change some login scripts so selected users are logged into the new server rather than the old server.

Power Requirements
And Conditioning

Backup power is essential to a network. You must have an available uninterruptible power supply before you put the server into actual use. Make sure this power supply can handle the server load. It also is a good idea to put a UPS on at least one workstation so you can close files, disconnect the workstation, and down the server in a proper manner if a power failure occurs.

Under NetWare 386, a UPS can attach to one of the following interface boards:

- Novell disk coprocessor board

- Novell standalone card

- Novell UPS keycard

- IBM PS/2 mouse port

A cable between the two devices must be obtained from the UPS manufacturer if it does not already come with the unit.

You must specify several parameters when you install the UPS NetWare loadable module. These parameters specify the port used (a number relating to one of the boards just listed), the number of minutes the network should operate on battery power, and the number of minutes it takes to recharge the battery after the network has been on battery power. Check the UPS documentation for details.

Power conditioning equipment is also essential. While most UPS units have built-in power conditioning, you may want to have surge protection devices available for workstations. These devices do not provide backup power, but they do protect against voltage spikes and electronic noise. If static electricity is a problem, grounded surfaces should be provided for the workstation. All equipment, including network cabling systems like Ethernet, should be connected to a good earth ground. Proper grounding can protect your equipment and guard against irregularities in the cabling system. Have the electrical system checked by a qualified electrician for proper grounding.

Note: Surges can reach a modem through either the power line or the telephone line and go directly to a PC. Look for power protection equipment that includes telephone jacks.

Problems with Surges to Ground

It has recently been discovered that many "phantom" network problems are caused by surges directed to the ground by power conditioning equipment. The network locks up for no apparent reason. The very devices that are protecting your workstation from fatal power surges may be redirecting those surges to the ground where they affect sensitive network cables. These cables are almost always attached to the ground, where they are susceptible to the surges. While the surge usually does not cause physical damage, the signals on the lines are disrupted enough to interrupt network communications.

Surge protection devices that divert surges to the ground line are known as *shunt-type devices*. Avoiding the use of these devices is hard because the ground shunting technique is used to protect the device itself from burning out. As more attention is given to this problem, manufacturers will develop products to resolve it. Be aware that strange network shutdowns may be caused by this problem.

Preparing the Server

Begin the installation of the file server by having the equipment and server log sheets at hand. Start by installing additional memory. You need at least 2MB of memory, but 4MB is recommended. Remember that NetWare loadable modules need to use a certain amount of memory that is taken away from the server cache. If you plan to load a number of these modules, increase the memory further.

If more than 16Mb of memory is installed in the server, use caution when installing AT bus-master disk adapter boards or boards that use on-line DMA. Such boards can only address up to 16Mb of Memory and can cause corruption of the file server's memory. If the board is an EISA board, refer to Auto Register Memory Above 16 Megabytes in Chapter 36. If the board is an ISA or MCA card, it must be replaced with a card that does not use on-line DMA or AT bus mastering.

Determine the hardware setting of components already in the server and those you plan to install. Refer to the previous chapter for a discussion of the settings you may need to make on interface boards. Keep in mind that some of these options are not used by some boards, may be self-configuring, such as those for Micro Channel machines, like the IBM PS/2.

A partial list of common base I/O addresses and interrupt lines is shown in Table 16-1. The recommended or default settings for some boards are listed for you to use or to help you avoid conflicts. Compare the addresses and lines on this list with those used by your board. Keep in mind that your system may not use all of these interrupts. If there are any

Device/Resource	I/O	Interrupt
Disk controllers		
AT hard disk	1F0-1F8	14
Floppy disk	3F0-3F7	6
Monochrome adapter	3B0-3BF	
Hercules mono adapter	3B4-3BF	
Color graphics adapter	3D0-3DF	
EGA adapter	3C0-3CF	2
VGA adapter	102, 46E8	
COMM1	3F8-3FF	4
COMM2	2F8-2FF	3
LPT1	378-37F	7
LPT2	278-27F	5
If LPT3 is used, then:		
LPT1	3BC-3BE	7
LPT2	378-37A	5
LPT3	278-27A	

Table 16-1.   Common Base I/O Addresses and Interrupt Lines

conflicts, change the switches and jumpers on your boards according to the boards' manuals. Use your server log sheets to write down the settings.

Keep the following in mind as you resolve interface board conflicts:

- See Table 16-2 for Novell disk coprocessor board settings.

- If you plan to install a print server that will use up to five printers, the ports and interrupts for LPT1, LPT2, LPT3, COMM1, and COMM2 will be used by the printers.

- VGA boards often use memory addresses that conflict with network interface cards. You know you have a memory conflict if the screen does not come up. Try changing the network card settings first since the VGA card may not be changeable.

- I/O ports and memory addresses may not conflict initially, but memory is used in varying amounts from the starting point on, and it could overlap memory used by other boards. You can install one card at a time and use the CONFIG command to determine the exact memory usage for the card.

Resolving Problems with CONFIG

CONFIG is a NetWare 386 server console command you can type to display useful information about the file server, protocols, network cards, and addresses. CONFIG can be extremely useful for resolving conflicts. Its use implies that your server is running NetWare 386. You may want to read through and perform the steps in Chapter 17 for starting the server and loading the LAN driver.

If a LAN driver has been installed, you can type the command to show the exact memory range used by a card. If you know the range, you can set other cards to ranges outside it. To use this method you must install one card at a time, start SERVER, load and bind the card's driver, and then run CONFIG to check its settings. You then down the server, remove the card, install a new card, and repeat the process until you are sure conflicts can be resolved.

Note: When you install new cards in the future, you can use CONFIG to determine the setting of existing cards.

Running Setup Programs

Use the SETUP program that comes with your system to set features such as the internal clock, memory size, and internal drive types. You should locate this program and run it before going further. On some systems you press one key while booting the system; on others you press ALT-ESC. Boot IBM PS/2 systems with the IBM Reference disk. Cards installed in PS/2 machines automatically avoid hardware conflicts, so you should install the cards and run the program before proceeding with NetWare installation.

Be sure to observe the following on IBM PS/2 systems:

- Do not choose "Set network server" mode. This feature disables the keyboard if set.

- Do not change the arbitration level of the MFM or ESDI fixed-disk driver from the factory default setting.

Note: Some early 80386 systems require a chip update due to a 32-bit multiply problem. You will receive an error during installation if your system has this problem.

Hard Disk Considerations

You can use two types of disk systems on a NetWare 386 server: internally installed drives and external disk subsystems. Most popular 80386 and 80486 systems come with a built-in controller and hard disks. You can usually add a second drive to these controllers, and in some cases you can add a second controller to support two more drives, making disk mirroring and duplexing possible. SCSI and the DCB controllers from Novell and other manufacturers support up to seven drives, each in a daisy-chain arrangement. These configurations are best when mirroring and duplexing. ESDI controllers normally support two devices.

A complete discussion of disk and controller technology is given in Chapter 13. The following sections of this chapter help you install disk hardware to take advantage of spanning volumes and disk mirroring.

Note: Be sure to keep track of all interrupt and address settings. You will be asked for this information during the installation of the operating system.

MFM Controllers

If your server system comes with an MFM controller, you can attach a second drive to the controller and use it for additional volumes or to mirror the first drive. As for disk duplexing, at this writing only Compaq systems support the use of two controllers when the ISADISK.DSK driver module is used. Since the boards are already installed in most cases, all you need to do is make sure no other interface card settings are already in use by the disk controllers.

SCSI and ESDI Controllers

Some advanced 80386 and 80486 systems are equipped with SCSI or ESDI controllers. You also can add these boards to an existing system. Refer to the manufacturer's specifications for board settings to avoid hardware conflicts. Special drivers may also be required to operate the boards under NetWare 386. These drivers should be located on a disk supplied with the controllers. If multiple boards are allowed, you must load a disk driver for each during the installation.

Disk Coprocessor Boards

Disk coprocessor boards (DCBs) from Novell and other manufacturers allow the most flexibility and greatest potential for expansion. Up to four Novell DCBs, EDCBs (enhanced DCB), or DCB/2s (for Micro Channel) can be installed in a server to support both disk mirroring and disk duplexing. Up to seven disk drives can be attached to each board. The Novell DISK-SET command places identification information on the PROM chips of the boards during installation.

Installation of the DCB/2 is simple. After the card is placed in the machine, use the system's reference disk to set the board's options. During NetWare 386 installation, load the DCB2.DSK loadable module for each DCB/2 controller installed in the server.

Use of the Novell DCBs requires some advanced planning. Which of the four possible boards you order depends on the I/O base address you want the card to fill, as shown in Table 16-2. If you already have one DCB, you should order the next card in the series. You also should order cards that do not interfere with I/O addresses used by other equipment. Interrupts are jumper selectable at either 10, 11, 12, or 15, so be sure to plan the use of those interrupts around those used by other boards. You can

	I/O Address	Interrupt
First DCB	340	B
Second DCB	348	C
Third DCB	320	A
Fourth DCB	328	F

Table 16-2.   Default Settings for DCB and EDCB

change only the preset I/O address of the DCBs by ordering special chips from Novell. During installation of NetWare 386, load the DCB.DSK loadable module for each DCB installed in the system.

Running Disk Surface Analysis

Once you have installed drives in the server and have run the setup programs, you can run DOS-level diagnostics and disk scanning utilities to test and format the drives. You also can run the test through an option of the INSTALL program, as covered in Chapter 17. Recall from Chapter 15 that this test may not be necessary on most modern drives.

Preparing Workstations

If you are adding the NetWare 386 server to an existing network, you should be able to log in from workstations with little or no changes. The setup of new workstations can proceed at any time during the installation. You may want to begin the task of installing cards and generating the boot files while the server hard drive is being surface tested or prepared by another installer. You must resolve interrupt and address conflicts when any card is installed in a computer, but this is less of a problem on workstations because usually you add only one card.

After installing the cards, you can make the network cable connection. If the server is already up and running, the IPX.COM and shell commands can be executed to establish the network connection. If the server is not up, you can check the connections between workstations by running the COMCHECK program, as covered under "Checking Network Connections" later in this chapter. Before you can attach the server or run COMCHECK, you must generate the IPX.COM files using the SHGEN program, as covered in Chapter 18.

Remember that diskless workstations boot from the server, so you cannot test their connection until the server is up and running and the NET$DOS.SYS file has been generated with DOSGEN.

Note: Network interface cards installed in diskless workstations must have a boot PROM attached. The PROM is usually purchased separately.

Isolating Network Connection Problems

When workstations do not make a network connection, you can use the following guide to determine where the problem is. It is a good idea to check station-to-station communications with COMCHECK, rather than station-to-server connections. A defective interface card or other component in the server may lead you to the incorrect assumption that the cable system is bad.

- *Errors appear when running IPX.COM* If IPX does not load properly, the board settings could be conflicting with other settings in the workstation or may not be matched with the settings of IPX.COM.

- *No workstations attach* The failure of all workstations during a network attach may be attributed to a faulty cable system or a defective server connection. Use the COMCHECK program to check connections between two or more workstations. If any two workstations connect, a faulty cable exists between those that do not connect. If all stations connect except the server, check the interface board or other features in the server.

- *The workstation hangs when executing NETx.COM, but other workstations attach correctly* This is an indication of an improper cable connection from the workstation to the cable distribution panel (active/passive hub or multiaccess unit) in star configured networks like ARCNET or Token Ring.

As the previous discussion indicates, most network problems are associated with cabling. It may be worthwhile to employ professional cable installers who have the proper equipment to isolate cable problems. Ethernet cable systems are most susceptible to system-wide communication failure. In many cases, the problem may be a kink, cut, or interference problem you cannot visually isolate because the cable is running through walls and ceilings. The exact location of such problems can be determined with proper testing equipment, however. This is covered later in this chapter and in Appendix A.

Important Advance Step
For Diskless Workstations

If all your diskless workstations will use the same interface board and the same DOS, your job is easy because you must create only one boot file. If any diskless workstation will use a different card, you must determine the address of that card and then create a separate boot file for it. Place the address in a log file on the server to indicate which workstations will use the special boot file. In some cases this address is set with a dip switch, so all you have to do is compare the switch setting with the card owner's manual to determine the current address or to change it. This is the case with ARCNET cards.

The node address is "burned" into a special chip on most Ethernet and Token Ring cards, so the only way to determine a card's node number is to temporarily place it in a PC with a disk drive and run the card's diagnostics. Refer to the instruction manual of the card for information on running the diagnostics program. The node address should appear on one of the screens; write it down to use when the DOSGEN program is run in Chapter 18. It is a good idea to place a sticker with the address on the back of each card.

Cable Installation

The cabling for small networks usually is easy to install and test. If the entire network is within one room, you often can run the cable and connect the entire system in less than an hour, assuming you don't need to drill holes or encase the cable in protective strips. With a professional cabling job, cable is hidden from sight and kept out of walkways or other areas where it may be damaged. Cable also should be kept away from devices, such as heavy electrical equipment, that might interfere with its signal transmission. The following sections provide a brief discussion of cable installation. Appendix A includes de-tailed information for installing and testing network cable.

Using Cable Installers

You might need to use an outside organization to install the cable, especially if the right tools are not available to you. Many employees do not want to climb through ceilings or under floors with cable in hand. A qualified installer will make sure the cable is fully tested and capable of transmitting signals by using proper test equipment.

Usually you can spot a cable installation done by in-house personnel. Cable is taped or tacked to walls and draped over equipment. Their primary concern was to get the system up and running, rather than be neat about the installation. An outside cable company can bid a cable job, including the installation of wall mounts and clean wire runs, at reasonable rates because they do it all the time and they have the equipment, parts, and expertise to do it well and do it right.

Do-It-Yourself Cabling

If cable will be installed by in-house personnel, everyone involved must understand the installation, wiring diagrams, and cable-handling procedures. You should also make sure you have the proper tools to cut, crimp, and fasten cable. Testing equipment is also useful if you can fit it in the budget. Refer to your cable supplier or catalogs you can obtain free from companies such as Glasgal Communications, South Hills Electronics, Specialized Products, Americable, Eazy, and Black Box. Refer to Appendix D for a list of these companies and their addresses.

Building plans are useful for locating where existing cable runs between floors, such as telephone wiring closets. When installing networks off-site, blueprints can help you map the topology with fewer trips to the installation site. This is especially useful when installing a wide area network at multiple locations.

Be prepared to follow building codes. The fire marshal may appear and order you to replace your normal coaxial cable with a nontoxic plenum cable—after all the cable is in place. Other problems can be avoided by simply doing a good job. If cable is draped over a wall and behind a desk, people may trip on it, pull it loose, or stretch it out. In some cases a stretched or kinked cable can cause signal transmission problems that you cannot locate if the cable appears to be normal.

Checking Network Connections

Novell supplies a program called COMCHECK on the SHGEN-1 disk that you can use to check the connections among workstations before the network server is up and running. This program is convenient for those installing cable and connections before preparing the server. The minimum you must do is install network cards in each station and generate an IPX file for them using the SHGEN program, as described in Chapter 18.

To run the program place the COMCHECK.EXE and COM-CHECK.HLP files on the disk you use to boot each workstation, and then type

IPX

COMCHECK.

COMCHECK requests a unique name for the workstation, and then displays a window that lists all other workstations currently running COMCHECK. Go to each workstation and repeat the above steps. You also can generate an IPX file for the network card in the server and then run COMCHECK to test its network connection.

As each station is brought up on the network, its name appears in the COMCHECK window. You may need to scroll through the list with the arrow or page keys. Information displayed by COMCHECK includes each workstation's unique name, the address of the network it is attached to, and the physical node address of the interface card in the workstation. Highlighted machines have not sent packets and may have gone dead. A sample screen is shown here:

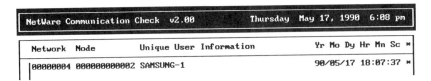

The following menu appears when you press ESC:

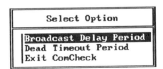

You can change the broadcast interval for the workstation and its timeout.

Cable installers can use COMCHECK to check the integrity of their installation before putting the server and the actual network into operation. It also helps isolate problems that might appear to be in the cable but are elsewhere on the network.

Installing NetWare 386

Installation Procedures
Create a DOS Partition
Ways to Start the NetWare 386 Server

This chapter is for those users who are installing NetWare for the first time or are upgrading from NetWare 286. If you need to upgrade your system from a previous version of NetWare, the material covered in this chapter is only part of the complete upgrade procedure. Refer to Appendix B before you start reading this chapter; you will be referred back here when appropriate.

In some cases it is beneficial to experiment with the installation process before making the "final" installation. A preinstall can help you avoid hardware conflicts and installation anomalies you did not anticipate. For example, additional software drivers may need to be acquired or existing ones may need to be updated. Because NetWare 386 is easy to install compared to previous versions of NetWare, a test-run of the installation is not an unreasonable proposition.

Note: Keep in mind that NetWare is very open to alterations, even while the network is up and running, so you may want to set advanced options later. Chapters 35 and 36 provide this information.

The steps and procedures involved in the installation of NetWare 386 are listed here:

1. Prepare the server and other hardware as discussed in the previous chapter

2. Create a DOS partition to boot from the hard drive or create a boot disk

3. Execute the SERVER command to start NetWare on the file server

4. Load any required disk drivers

5. Start the INSTALL program

6. Partition the server drives for NetWare

7. Mirror hard drives, if necessary

8. Create and mount volumes

9. Install the operating system files and utilities

10. Create the startup files

11. Load and bind the required LAN driver modules

12. Load any other required modules such as UPS support

13. Lock the server and begin setting up workstations, as covered in the next chapter

Installation Procedures

Follow the steps below to install the NetWare 386 operating system.

Prepare the Server

Install all equipment and peripherals in the server as described in the previous chapter, and then boot the server with a DOS disk.

To make the server startup process easier, create a small DOS partition for the storage of the server startup files. If your system does not allow DOS partitions on the hard drive, you must create a disk that will boot the system. You also can create a boot disk if you do not want the server startup files stored on the server. The boot disk can then be stored in a safe place away from the server. The following section describes how to create a server boot disk. To create a DOS partition on the server, skip ahead to "Create a DOS Partition."

Create a Server Boot Disk

The server boot disk must be a high-density disk. Use the DOS FORMAT command with the /S parameter to make the disk bootable, and then copy the NetWare 386 Operating System-1 diskette to the boot disk. You can create an AUTOEXEC.BAT file on this disk. Include the command **SERVER** in the file.

Note: Create a CONFIG.SYS file with the command "FILES=40" on the boot disk.

Create a DOS Partition

If the server has an old NetWare partition, refer to "Removing Old NetWare Partitions" in Chapter 16.

Use the DOS FDISK command to create a DOS partition of 2 to 3MB. This provides enough room for the NetWare boot files. Although the NetWare manual recommends a 1MB DOS partition, it is a good idea to create a slightly larger partition for any files you may need to add in the future.

DOS partitions are created by specifying the number of cylinders to use. See Chapter 15 for an explanation of cylinders.

To determine the number of cylinders required for 1MB, divide the number of cylinders for the drive by the disk size. FDISK displays the cylinder count for the server drive. For example, if FDISK informs you that the drive has 1021 cylinders and you know the drive capacity is 90MB, you would use the following equation:

$$1021 \text{ cylinders}/90\text{MB} = 11 \text{ cylinders per MB}$$

Use the Change Active Partition option of the FDISK command to make the C drive the bootable drive for the file server. Alternatively, you can leave it inactive and boot from a floppy disk for security reasons, as described earlier under "Create a Server Boot Disk." After creating the partition, the system reboots, so keep the DOS disk in the floppy drive.

Format the Partition

Once the DOS partition has been created, you can format it with the DOS FORMAT command. Use the /S option with the FORMAT command so the system files are copied to the partition. This makes it a bootable partition.

Copy the NetWare Files

When the formatting process is complete on the C drive, copy the contents of the NetWare 386 Operating System-1 disk to the formatted C drive. Copying these files to the hard drive speeds up the installation process and the normal server boot process.

Load NetWare 386

The next series of steps are performed while the NetWare 386 operating system is up and running. During this phase the operating system is not ready to support a network until you install the loadable modules, the NetWare partitions, and create the volumes. Type **SERVER** to start NetWare. You will be asked to enter the following as SERVER loads:

- *File server name*   Enter a unique name for the server from 3 to 47 characters long. The shorter the name, the easier it will be to type and refer to later. Do not use periods or spaces. If you are upgrading or have an existing network, be sure to use a different name than any existing server.

- *IPX Internal network number*   Enter a unique number that is different from other NetWare 386 servers attached to the network. The number can be 1 to 8 characters long in hexadecimal format. Be sure it does not conflict with any network or node address on the cable system, including the DOS process number of a server running nondedicated NetWare 286. The IPX number allows future versions of NetWare to support a system fault tolerant strategy in which an entire server is duplicated by a second server.

Register Memory Above 16MB

If the server has more than 16MB of memory, it must be registered with the REGISTER MEMORY command. Refer to "Registering Memory Above 16MB" and Table 36-1 in Chapter 36.

Load the Disk Drivers

After entering the IPX internal number, SERVER displays its colon prompt. You are now ready to load drivers that support the internal disk drives or external disk subsystems. Refer to one of the following sections that pertains to the type of disk controller you are installing. As the disk drivers are loaded, default I/O ports and interrupt settings are suggested. In some cases these settings are read from the board, so you should make the suggested selection. Refer to your worksheets for the correct settings made during hardware setup.

If you have more than one disk controller, load a driver for each. When two or more drivers exist, the settings for each must be different to avoid conflicts. When a driver is loaded more than once, only one copy of its code is placed in memory. A small block is used to differentiate between each board. You may need to use the parameters described in the next section when loading the drivers. Always load the driver for the internal disk controller first. Then load drivers for external disks if they are used.

Note: For additional information on loading disk drivers, refer to "Loading Disk Drivers" in Chapter 35.

Specify Disk Options

The following parameters can be specified with the LOAD command when installing disk drivers. Since some of the parameters are read directly from the controller boards, you need only accept the suggested settings. However, you can use the options to "force" a setting by specifying it with the LOAD command. When the commands are used in the STARTUP.NCF file, the options are used to initiate automatic loading.

DMA=#	Replace # with a DMA channel to reserve for the driver
INT=#	Replace # with the hardware interrupt set on the board
MEM=#	Replace # with the memory address to reserve for the driver
PORT=#	Replace # with the I/O port to reserve for the driver
SLOT=#	On Micro Channel machines and EISA systems with bus master slots, replace # with the number of the slot board is installed in. The interrupts, memory addresses, and I/O ports are set with the reference disk supplied with the board.

For example, the following specifies an interrupt of F and a port number of 170 when loading the ISADISK driver:

LOAD ISADISK INT=F PORT=170

Industry Standard AT-Compatible System

Server systems using the AT class of disk controllers must be installed using the ISADISK.DSK loadable driver module. Type **LOAD ISADISK** to load the disk driver. The default interrupt is E, but you can change it to B, C, or F using the INT= options. The default I/O port is 1F0, but you can change it to 170 using the PORT= option. Make sure the board settings are set appropriately if you make the optional settings.

Note: The ISADISK driver module can be loaded twice if two disk controllers are present. The first controller uses I/O port 1F0 and interrupt E. The second controller uses I/O port 170 and interrupt F.

IBM PS/2 Disk Drivers

Micro Channel Systems, like the IBM PS/2 line, uses either ESDI, MFM, or SCSI disk controllers. Use the reference disk that came with the system to determine exactly which controller is installed in the system, then use the appropriate load command listed below.

ESDI	LOAD PS2ESDI
MFM	LOAD PS2MFM
SCSI	LOAD PS2SCSI

The SCSII controller can be configured with the IBM REFERENCE diskette or the DISKSET command, as described under "Installing External Hard Disks" in Chapter 35.

External Disk Subsystem

External disk subsystems are drives attached to disk coprocessor boards, like Novell's DCB, EDCB, or DCB/2. Installation requires two steps. First, load the DCB driver module using the command **LOAD DCB**.

Next, run the DISKSET command as described in Chapter 35. DISKSET places information about the hard disks attached to the coprocessor board on the board's programmable chip.

Note: The Novell channel 2 DCB may produce hardware errors on Compaq machines due to a mouse port conflict at interrupt 12. You must disable the mouse port to correct it.

Load the INSTALL Program

The following steps are performed using the INSTALL program. INSTALL
is a menu-driven utility used to prepare disk partitions and volumes, and
to load the NetWare operating system files and utilities. To start INSTALL
type **LOAD INSTALL**. The Installation Options menu appears, as shown
here:

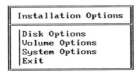

Note: Press the F1 key for INSTALL help or press F1 twice for an
installation overview.

Partition the Server

The server hard disks must be partitioned for NetWare in the same way
you installed the DOS partition earlier. Choose **Disk Options** from the
Installation Options menu. The following Available Disk Options menu
appears:

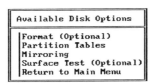

Choose **Format** if any of the hard drives have not been low-level
formatted by the manufacturer. Choose **Partition Tables** to create the
NetWare partitions. If more than one disk is installed, select the disk to
partition. A screen similar to the following appears:

```
  Partition Type                   Start    End     Size

DOS Partition (12 bit FATS)          0       24     2.1 Meg
Free Space                          25     1020     87.5 Meg
```

```
       Partition Options

  Change Hot Fix
  Create NetWare Partition
  Delete Partition
  Return to Previous Menu
```

Notice that the DOS partition is 2.1MB in size and that the remainder of the disk is available for NetWare.

Note: It may be necessary to remove old partitions using the Delete Partition option on the menu, since only one NetWare partition can exist per disk. See "Removing Old NetWare Partitions" in Chapter 16.

At the Partition Options menu, choose **Create NetWare Partition**. INSTALL selects the next available cylinder after the DOS partition as the default starting point and uses the remainder of the drive for the NetWare partition. A screen similar to the following appears to display the partition information:

```
              Partition Information

Partition Type: NetWare 386 Partition

Partition Size:    600    Cylinders,      52.7 Meg

Hot Fix Information:
  Data Area:            13229 Blocks,     51.6 Meg
  Redirection Area: 270    Blocks,         2.0 %
```

INSTALL automatically allocates 2% of the partition space as a Hot Fix redirection area. If you need to change the settings, refer to the next section. Press ESC and select Yes to create the partitions. Repeat the same steps with each additional drive you are installing. Finally, press ESC to return to the Available Disk Options menu and continue with the following steps that pertain to your installation.

Change the Partition Settings

In some cases, you may want to decrease the partition size or alter the Hot Fix area. This can be done by highlighting the appropriate fields on the Partition Information menu and altering the settings. INSTALL automatically calculates other settings based on your changes. Use the worksheets you developed in Chapter 15 to set the partition sizes.

Establish a Mirrored Pair

Disk mirroring is an optional feature you can use to ensure the integrity of the data in the NetWare filing system. A second drive mirrors the contents of the primary drive and automatically takes over if the primary drive fails. The secondary drive must have a capacity equal to or greater than the primary drive. Extra disk space on the secondary drive is not used.

To establish a mirrored pair, first partition both drives as previously discussed. Select **Mirroring** from the Available Disk Options menu. When the Drive Mirroring Status screen appears, select the primary drive. Next, press INS when the Mirrored NetWare Partitions menu appears, and select the secondary drive on the Available Partitions screen. The partitions then are paired for mirroring.

Create Server Volumes

Volumes hold collections of directories and files. NetWare volumes can span several disk drives, which means you can create extremely large volumes or increase the size of an existing volume by adding additional hard drives. For best performance a partition should include just one volume, but if a volume is to span multiple drives, Novell recommends mirroring the volume.

You can select the block size and volume configuration in this step. A discussion of blocks and volume creation can be found in Chapter 15.

Note: If you are performing the upgrade procedure described in Appendix B, try to create a NetWare 386 volume that is at least 6MB larger than the volume on your NetWare 286 server. You can use this extra space to accommodate duplicate directories or files that must be renamed.

To create volumes select **Volume Options** on the Installation Options menu. When the Volumes menu appears, press INS. If more than one drive is available, select the drive to hold the volume being created. The following New Volume Information screen appears:

```
┌─────────────────────────────────────────────┐
│        New Volume Information                 │
├─────────────────────────────────────────────┤
│                                               │
│  Volume Name: SYS                             │
│                                               │
│  Volume Block Size:  4 K Blocks               │
│                                               │
│  Initial Segment Size: 13209  Blocks          │
│                                               │
│  Volume Size: 51 Meg                          │
│                                               │
│  Status: Not Mounted                          │
│                                               │
└─────────────────────────────────────────────┘
```

The first volume is given the name SYS by default and should not be changed. The volume block size and segment size can be changed, as described next.

Define Block Sizes

NetWare volumes can be set to use 4K, 8K, 16K, 32K, or 64K block sizes. The default block size is 4K, which means that the smallest area of disk space used to store a file is 4K. Block size is discussed in Chapter 15. To change the block size, arrow to the Block Size field and press ENTER. The following menu of options appears. Make a selection and press ENTER to continue.

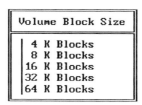

```
┌──────────────────────┐
│  Volume Block Size   │
├──────────────────────┤
│    4 K Blocks        │
│    8 K Blocks        │
│   16 K Blocks        │
│   32 K Blocks        │
│   64 K Blocks        │
└──────────────────────┘
```

Define Volume Segments

Volume segments are used to allocate disk space for multiple volumes on a single disk or for spanning a single volume over several disks. If you are creating a single volume, you can use the default segment displayed in the Initial Segment Size field and move on to the "Mount the Volumes" section.

Create Multiple-Volume Drives   To create multiple segments on a single drive, decrease the Initial Segment Size setting, and then create additional volumes in the available free space using the steps previously described.

Create Volumes that Span Multiple Drives   Creating volumes that span multiple drives is a matter of adding segments from other drives to the volumes you have defined. Press ESC until you return to the Volumes menu, and then select a volume you want to expand over other drives. When the New Volume Information menu appears, arrow down to the Volume Segments field and press ENTER. A list of current segments for the volume appears. Press INS to display a list of free areas on the current drive or other drives. If only one free area exists, it is added. Type the number of blocks to use for the segment, press ENTER, and answer Yes to create the new segments.

Mount the Volumes

Before you can continue with the NetWare installation, you must mount the volumes you just created. Although they are defined, the operating system has not opened them up for use. You use the MOUNT command to do this.

Return to the console prompt by pressing ALT-ESC, and then type the command **MOUNT ALL**. Press ALT-ESC again to return to the Installation Options menu.

Install the Operating System Files

You are now ready to copy the NetWare system and utilities files to the SYS volume. Press ESC until you return to the Installation Options menu, and then choose **System Options**. The following Available System Options menu appears:

```
╔══════════════════════════════════╗
║   Available System Options       ║
╠══════════════════════════════════╣
║ Copy System and Public Files     ║
║ Create AUTOEXEC.NCF File         ║
║ Create STARTUP.NCF File          ║
║ Edit AUTOEXEC.NCF File           ║
║ Edit STARTUP.NCF File            ║
║ Return To Main Menu              ║
╚══════════════════════════════════╝
```

Choose **Copy System and Public Files**. INSTALL asks for each of the disks in turn.

Create the NetWare Startup Files

The AUTOEXEC.NCF and STARTUP.NCF files are prepared by IN-STALL. You select each of the Create options on the Available System Options menu to view and save the files. An example is shown here:

```
╔══════════════════════════════════╗
║   File Server AUTOEXEC.NCF File  ║
╠══════════════════════════════════╣
║ FILE SERVER NAME COMPAQ-486      ║
║ IPX INTERNAL NET 486             ║
║ LOAD NE3200 PORT=4C80 SLOT=4     ║
║ BIND IPX TO NE3200 NET=4         ║
╚══════════════════════════════════╝
```

```
╔══════════════════════════════════╗
║   File Server STARTUP.NCF File   ║
╠══════════════════════════════════╣
║ LOAD ISADISK PORT=1F0 INT=E      ║
╚══════════════════════════════════╝
```

Notice that the options set in previous steps are automatically inserted into the files. You can make changes to the files before saving them if necessary.

   Note: When you create or edit the STARTUP.NCF file, you are asked for a drive letter. Type **C** if you created a DOS partition, or type **A** if you are booting from a DOS disk.

   You may need to add the following commands to the AUTO-EXEC.NCF file if a NetWare 286 network is attached. See Chapter 15 for details.

SET ALLOW UNENCRYPTED PASSWORDS = ON

Some advanced LAN drivers support larger packet sizes. You may want to add a command similar to the following to the STARTUP.NCF file:

SET MAXIMUM PHYSICAL RECEIVE PACKET SIZE=4202

The size is determined by the maximum packet size used on the LAN and is covered in the board's documentation.

If the server is dedicated to a special task, such as servicing a database, it may be beneficial to increase the block size to reduce the number of disk accesses. For example, to increase the cache buffer block size from the default of 4K to 8K, you would include the following in the AUTOEXEC.NCF file:

SET CACHE BUFFER SIZE = 8192

When you are done creating the files, press ALT+ESC to return to the console and load the LAN drivers.

Load the LAN Drivers

A number of LAN driver modules are supplied with NetWare to support many popular LAN cards. Be sure to copy the LAN driver for your cards to the C drive and the NetWare System disk. In addition, you should resolve interrupt, memory, and I/O port conflicts, as discussed in the previous chapter.

Note: The following commands are executed at the console (press ALT+ESC).

As the LAN drivers are loaded, default I/O ports and interrupt settings are suggested. In some cases, these settings are read directly from the board. Refer to your worksheets for the correct settings to use.

If you have more than one LAN card, load a driver for each, making sure the settings do not conflict. When drivers are loaded more than once, only one copy of the code is placed in memory. A small block is used to differentiate between boards. It may be necessary to use the parameters described in the next section when loading the drivers.

Refer to "Loading LAN Drivers in Chapter 35" for more on LAN driver parameters and special load options.

LAN Driver LOAD Commands

Before loading the LAN drivers, load the NMAGENT module by typing LOAD NMAGENT. The format for the command you use to load the LAN drivers for the network interface cards is

LOAD *driver-name*

Replace *driver-name* with the name of the driver. When you are asked for interrupt, memory, and I/O port information, supply it using your configuration sheets. Parameters can be used to specify information on the command line, as discussed in Chapter 35. For example, the following command specifies an interrupt of 3 and a memory address of C0000 when loading the Novell RXNET driver:

LOAD RXNET INT=3 MEM=C0000

The following drivers are shipped with NetWare 386 version 3.0. Others will ship with future versions. To list the drivers available on the NetWare 386 Operating System-1 disk, type **DIR A: *.LAN.**

TRXNET.LAN	Novell RX-Net, RX-Net II, and RX- Net/2 driver
3C503.LAN	3COM EtherLink II—ASS?Y 2227 driver
3C505.LAN	3COM EtherLink Plus—ASSY 2012 driver
3C523.LAN	3COM EtherLink/MC driver
NE2.LAN	Novell NE/2 Ethernet driver
NE232.LAN	Novell NE/2—32-bit Ethernet driver
NE1000.LAN	Novell NE1000 Ethernet driver
NE2000.LAN	Novell NE2000 Ethernet driver

NE3200.LAN   Novell NE3200 Ethernet driver

TOKEN.LAN   Driver for IBM Token Ring Adapters

Note: Token Ring adapters must be attached to the multiple access unit (MAU) before the Token driver will load.

Bind a Protocol to the LAN Driver

After the LAN driver module loads, you must bind it to a protocol. NetWare version 3.1 allows multiple protocols to be bound to a single board, but you may need to register the protocol before binding. This is done using the PROTOCOL command, as discussed in Chapter 35. Refer to that chapter now if you are installing additional protocols. The IPX protocol is always registered with NetWare.

In the following command replace *protocol* with IPX (Standard NetWare protocol) or another registered protocol. Replace *driver-name* with the name of the LAN driver loaded in the previous step.

BIND *protocol* TO *driver-name*

If you are installing more than one LAN board of the same type, you must tell the operating system which board to bind the communications protocol to. The operating system prompts you for the settings.

BIND asks you for a network number to use for the driver. The number must be a hexadecimal number one to eight digits long.

Note: If you are running the upgrade transfer method, set this number to the network address of the NetWare 286 server until the transfer is complete.

Load Other Modules

You can now install additional loadable modules to provide operating system support for other file systems, other communications protocols, or special LAN drivers. These options are briefly discussed below and covered in more detail in Chapter 35 and Chapter 36.

Loading Support for Non-DOS Files (Name Space)

Non-DOS files are those created by workstations like the Apple Macintosh that use different file-naming conventions. In order to store the files on a NetWare file system, support for multiple name spaces in the directory table must be loaded. Refer to "Supporting Non-DOS files" in Chapter 35 for a complete discussion. To load the Maciintosh name space support, type the following command:

LOAD MAC

Next, use the ADD NAME SPACE command at the console to specify the volume that will support non-DOS files. Use a volume besides SYS if possible. Type a command similar to the following:

ADD NAME SPACE *name* TO *volume*

where *name* is the name of the variable for the name space module loaded at the server (MAC, for example), and *volume* is the name of the server volume to support the name space.

Implementing STREAMS

The STREAMS environment provides mechanisms for integration of multiple communication protocols. To implement the environment, type the commands below. Not all commands are required; refer to "Implementing Streams" in Chapter 36 for more information.

LOAD STREAMS	(STREAMS support)
LOAD CLIB	(C Library support)
LOAD TLI	(Transport Level Interface support)
LOAD IPXS	(STREAMS-based IPX support)
LOAD CPS	(STREAMS-based SPX support)
LOAD MATHLIB	(Math library module)

Token Ring Remote Boot Support

Load the TOKEN Remote Program (TOKENRPL) module if you need to enable remote booting of diskless workstations that use Token Ring network interface cards. Type the command below to load the module.

LOAD TOKENRPL

After the module is loaded, you need to bind the TOKRPL support module to the Token Ring interface card in the file server. Type the following command to do so.

BIND TOKRPL

Loading Uninterruptible Power Supply Support

To install a UPS, the UPS.NLM module must be loaded. Several parameters are required, such as the interface board type used to connect the UPS to the server, the port number, the discharge time, and the recharge time. Refer to "Installing a UPS" in Chapter 35 for details.

Completion Tasks

Lock the server console from potential intruders by loading the MONITOR utility using this command:

LOAD MONITOR

Choose **Lock File Server Console** from the Available Options menu. Type in a password to lock the keyboard. Remember this password; you must know it to regain access to the console.

If you want to run the console from a remote workstation, load the Remote Console module as discussed in Chapter 33.

Working in a Multi-Server Environment

The following steps may need to be performed when a network consists of NetWare 286 and NetWare 386 servers.

- For NetWare 286 v2.0a servers, copy only LOGIN.EXE to the SYS:LOGIN and SYS:PUBLIC directories.

- For NetWare 286 v2.1x servers, replace the public utilities in the SYS:PUBLIC directory with the new NetWare 386 public utilities to allow for encrypted passwords.

The following steps outline how to copy files to the server.

1. Log into the NetWare 286 server.

2. Flag the files to be copied over with the Normal attribute by typing:

   FLAG *.* N

3. Protect the system login script in the SYS:PUBLIC directory from overwrites by typing:

   FLAG NET$LOG.DAT SRO

4. Log in to the NetWare 386 server if necessary.

5. Map a drive to the SYS:PUBLIC directory on the NetWare 386 file server by typing:

   MAP *drive:=servername*/SYS:PUBLIC

   where *drive* is an unmapped drive letter and *servername* is the name of the NetWare 386 file server.

6. From the NetWare 286 SYS:PUBLIC directory, type the following command to copy the files in the NetWare 386 SYS:PUBLIC directory, replacing *drive* with the drive letter assigned in step 5.

NCOPY *drive:*.*

7. Flag the files in the directory as Shareable and Read Only with the following command.

FLAG *.* SRO

Repeat steps similar to the above to copy files from the NetWare 386 SYS:LOGIN directory to the NetWare 286 SYS:LOGIN directory. Once the NetWare 286 servers are using the NetWare 386 files, you can type the following at the NetWare 386 console to begin encrypting passwords.

SET ALLOW UNENCRYPTED PASSWORDS = OFF

Remove the command SET ALLOW UNENCRYPTED PASSWORDS = ON from the AUTOEXEC.NCF file if necessary. You can now allow users to log into the new NetWare 386 server. Continue reading with Chapter 18, or Part V of this book.

Ways to Start the NetWare 386 Server

If you have not shut the server down, it should be ready to service the network at this time. In most cases you can leave the server on at all times. The longer the server stays on, the more information accumulates in the FCONSOLE and MONITOR utilities.

To start a downed server, you must boot the server with the DOS boot disk or from the DOS partition, then type **SERVER**. The server can be started automatically by including the SERVER command in an AUTO-EXEC.BAT file in the DOS partition or DOS boot disk.

You can use one of several options when booting the server. With these options you can change the startup procedure for testing purposes or temporarily disable an option.

To boot with an alternate STARTUP.NCF file, use the -S option. In the following example, TEMP.NCF is loaded instead of STARTUP.NCF:

SERVER -S TEMP.NCF

To boot without using the STARTUP.NCF file, use the NS option as shown here:

SERVER -NS

You may want to use this when testing a new disk subsystem.
To boot without using the AUTOEXEC.NCF file, use the NA option.

SERVER -NA

You may want to do this to test a different cabling system than the one that normally loads.
You can specify a different block size for the cache buffer when starting SERVER. This option may be used when a server is dedicated to a special task, such as servicing a database. It is beneficial to increase the block size for database access to reduce the number of disk accesses. For example, to increase the cache buffer block size from the default of 4K to 8K, you would type the following startup command:

SERVER -C8KB

Remember that you can use the NetWare SET command to make changes to the running mode of the operating system. These commands can be included in the AUTOEXEC.NCF or STARTUP.NCF server boot files. To make the changes load the INSTALL program and select **System Options** from the initial menu. Refer to Chapter 36 for information about the SET commands.

Installing Workstations

Installing Macintosh Workstations
Installing DOS Workstations
Starting a DOS Workstation
Configuring Diskless Workstations

When you have installed the network interface card in a workstation and attached the network cable, the IPX.COM and NET*x*.COM files execute to begin network communications. This chapter covers how to create startup files and get DOS workstations up and running.

Note: Refer to Appendix G to install OS/2 workstations. Appendix H covers the installation of DOS ODI workstations. Refer to this appendix if you need to run protocols besides IPX/SPX, run workstations with more than one network board, or use more than one frame type.

Installing workstations on the network can be a simple procedure when every workstation uses the same version of DOS and the same network interface card. You can create one IPX.COM file to work in every workstation using the SHGEN shell generation program. If they all use the same version of DOS, your management tasks are simple.

On the other hand, networks that use many different types of interface cards and many different types of DOS take a little more time and planning to prepare. For DOS systems, you must generate a different IPX.COM file for each different interface card on the network, and you must create a DOS directory on the server to support each version of DOS used at diskless workstations. A path to the appropriate DOS directory must then be set at workstations.

If you are installing OS/2 workstations, you must use the Novell OS/2 Requester to generate a network startup and attachment file for the workstations. The Novell OS/2 Requester also includes OS/2 versions of

319

many NetWare commands. Installing an OS/2 workstation is covered in Appendix G.

Installing Macintosh Workstations

Support for Apple Macintoshs and the Apple Talk File Protocol on Novell Networks is provided through the NetWare for Macintosh VAP that must run in a NetWare 286 server attached to the same network as the NetWare 386 server. Future versions of NetWare 386 will provide Macintosh support through a NetWare loadable module. (See the NetWare for Macintosh Installation Supplement.)

Macintosh computers connect to NetWare file servers via LocalTalk, Ethernet, or other media. Various manufacturers such as Thomas-Conrad provide network interface cards and drivers to support Macintosh workstations.

When the Macintoshs are connected to the network, Macintosh files can be stored on the network server. In addition, Apple printers can be shared by any user on the network, including those using DOS workstations.

For a complete description of the installation process, refer to the NetWare for Macintosh VAP manuals and your NetWare 286 installation manuals.

Installing DOS Workstations

The steps to installing a DOS workstation are covered in this section. You will see how to generate an IPX.COM file, a boot disk, and the diskless workstation boot files on the server.

The Master Boot Disk

The master boot disk holds the DOS system files and network startup files for a specific workstation configuration. If every workstation on your network uses the same version of DOS and the same network interface card, you need to create only one master boot disk. In addition, you need to run the SHGEN program only once to create a single IPX.COM file. If you have more than one type of workstation configuration, you must create a master disk for each configuration. You then duplicate the disk for each workstation that boots from a floppy drive, or copy its contents to a workstation with a hard disk. The disk can then be put in a secure place for future use.

For example, assume some workstations use an AST Ethernode card while others use a Novell NE2000 card. Further, some stations use DOS 3 while others use DOS 4. The following boot disks would be required to support every possible configuration:

- DOS 3 disk with IPX configured for AST Ethernode

- DOS 3 disk with IPX configured for Novell NE2000

- DOS 4 disk with IPX configured for AST Ethernode

- DOS 4 disk with IPX configured for Novell NE2000

The same disks can be used to create diskless workstation boot files, but you might want to make a separate copy since an alteration is made to the disk when DOSGEN is run. For example, if you install Novell NE2000 cards in the diskless workstations and you want to run DOS 4, you would use the fourth master boot disk (or a copy of it) to run DOSGEN. For more information on installing diskless workstations, be sure to read through "Configuring Diskless Workstations" later in this chapter.

Steps for Installing Workstations

The following steps briefly describe the creation of the master disks, workstation files, custom startup files, and the workstation boot process:

1. Create a master boot disk for each type of workstation on the LAN. Make the disk bootable with the version of DOS the workstations will use.

2. Run the SHGEN program to create an IPX.COM boot file for each type of network interface card on the network.

3. Copy the IPX.COM file and the NET*x*.COM file from the SHGEN disk or directory to the master boot disk.

4. Create a SHELL.CFG file and include any customization commands for workstations.

5. Create an AUTOEXEC.BAT file and a CONFIG.SYS file on the disk, if necessary.

6. Duplicate the master boot disk for each workstation that boots from disk, or copy its contents to hard drive systems.

7. Repeat steps 1 through 6 for each different workstation configuration.

8. Make alterations to the SHELL.CFG or NET.CFG file at each workstation that requires a special startup configuration beyond the one placed on the master disk. See Appendix I for more information on these files.

9. Run the DOSGEN program to create diskless workstation boot files on the server, if necessary.

10. Attach each workstation to the server by running the IPX.COM and NET*x*.COM programs.

11. Log into the server using the procedures covered in Chapter 19.

Creating Master Boot Disks

The first step to getting the workstations up and running is to create the master shell disks. Refer to your workstation log sheets to determine exactly how many master disks are required. Write down each combination of DOS and interface cards you will need for the workstation. Remember that DOS has incremental versions (DOS 3.2, DOS 3.3, DOS 4.0, DOS 4.1, and so on) that require separate boot disks. To maintain your sanity, it is recommended that you upgrade all workstations to a single DOS version before beginning this process.

The disk must be formatted using the FORMAT /S command, which copies the DOS system files and makes the disk bootable. Place a descriptive label on each disk that explains the exact configuration of the workstation.

Running the SHGEN Program

The SHGEN program is located on the NetWare SHGEN-1 disk. You can copy the contents of this disk to a hard drive for increased performance, or you can run it from the floppy disk. If you need to create only one IPX.COM file, run the program from floppy disk. If you need to create several files, or if you will be using the program often in the future, copy the program files to a hard drive. The procedure for copying is covered on the next page.

Using the SHGEN Menu System

Those unfamiliar with Novell's menu system may have trouble getting used to its peculiarities. The ESC key, rather than the ENTER key, is often used to accept an option because NetWare menus use pop-up windows to prompt for selections. You then press ESC to return to the previous "master" menu.

When a list of options is presented, you can use the arrow keys to highlight an option and then press ENTER to select it. If you need help, press the F1 key. Be sure to watch the abbreviated help screens that appear at the bottom of the screen.

Running SHGEN on a Hard Drive System

Boot the system and log into the hard drive to be used by SHGEN. If you have a workstation already attached to a server, you can use the network hard drive to run the SHGEN program.

Execute this command:

MD \NETWARE

Issue the following command to move to the NETWARE directory:

CD \NETWARE

Copy the file SHGEN.EXE from the NetWare SHGEN-1 disk to the new NETWARE directory using this command:

COPY A:SHGEN.EXE

Next, create a directory that branches from the NETWARE directory called SHGEN-1 using the following command:

MD SHGEN-1

Finally, you are ready to copy all the files on the SHGEN-1 disk to the SHGEN-1 directory. Enter this command:

COPY A:*.* SHGEN-1

Starting SHGEN

The command to start SHGEN is the same whether you are using the floppy disk or hard drive method. However, if you are using the hard drive method, make sure you are still in the NETWARE directory.

Execute the SHGEN command to start SHGEN. The SHGEN menu screen appears, similar to the one shown in Figure 18-1.

Selecting a LAN Driver from a List

If the LAN driver you need to use is included on the SHGEN-1 disk, you can choose the **Select LAN driver from list** option. If you are not sure,

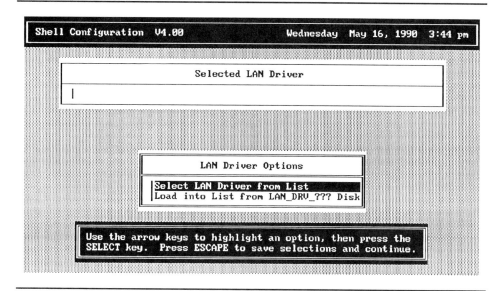

Figure 18-1.   The Shell Generation (SHGEN) programs main menus

select the option anyway to see if the driver is in the list. A LAN driver list similar to the following appears:

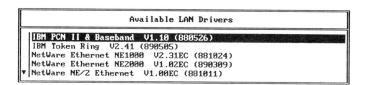

Scroll through the list with the arrow keys. When you find the required driver, highlight it and press ENTER to save the selection. Then proceed to the "Configuring the LAN Driver" section of this chapter. If the driver does not appear on the list, press ESC and refer to the next section.

Selecting a LAN Driver
From Another Disk

Since the Novell SHGEN-1 disk does not contain every available LAN driver, you may need to load a driver from a disk supplied with the card or obtained from your dealer. Place the disk in the floppy drive and select the **Load into List from LAN_DRV ??? DISK** option from the LAN Driver Options menu. If the disk is labeled properly and contains the correct files, a driver is transferred into the LAN driver list and you can skip to the "Configuring the LAN Driver" section of this chapter. If an error occurs, you must continue reading this section.

An error can occur when the disk does not have a label (the electronic name for the disk given by the LABEL command) in the form LAN_DRV_???, where the question marks may be a number or manufacturer identification code. For example, disks from Thomas-Conrad are labeled LAN_DRV_TCC. The disk must also contain valid NetWare 386 LAN driver files. There are normally two files, one with the extension OBJ and one with the extension LAN. Some disks ship with OBJ and LAN files for both NetWare 286 and NetWare 386; however, SHGEN knows which drivers are which.

Temporarily exit SHGEN by pressing ESC. The DOS prompt appears. Now you must determine the name you should give the disk. This name is usually included in the first line of the *.LAN file, so use the DOS TYPE command to display its contents. In the following example, *.LAN files are first listed with the DIR command to determine the name of the LAN files. The TCCSH.LAN file is then displayed with the DOS TYPE command. Notice that the name required for the disk, LAN_DRV_TCC, is displayed on the first line of the file.

```
F:\NETWARE>DIR A:*.LAN

 Volume in drive A is LAN_DRV_TCC
 Directory of  A:\

TCCSH    LAN     1412  11-29-89    2:10p
           1 File(s)         39936 bytes free

F:\NETWARE>TYPE A:TCCSH.LAN
δLAN_DRV_TCC2Thomas-Conrad Corp. ARC-CARD Accel. V2.20 (891129)
```

You can follow this series of steps to determine the required name for your disk.

Use the DOS LABEL command in a form similar to the following to rename the disk:

LABEL A:LAN_DRV_TCC

Replace LAN_DRV_TCC with the name you found previously. You can now reenter SHGEN and select the **Load into list from LAN_DRV ??? DISK** option from the LAN Driver Options menu. The driver is transferred to the SHGEN list of drivers. Scan through the list, press ENTER on the required driver, and then continue with the next section of this chapter.

Configuring the LAN Driver

After selecting a LAN driver, its name appears in the Selected LAN Driver window. You are then given a chance to change your selection. Press ESC to continue. The Available LAN Driver Configurations menu appears, similar to that shown here:

```
                    Available LAN Driver Configurations
  0:  IRQ = 3,  I/O Base = 300h,  no DMA or RAM
  1:  IRQ = 2,  I/O Base = 320h,  no DMA or RAM
  2:  IRQ = 4,  I/O Base = 340h,  no DMA or RAM
  3:  IRQ = 5,  I/O Base = 360h,  no DMA or RAM
  4:  IRQ = 2,  I/O Base = 300h,  no DMA or RAM
  5:  IRQ = 3,  I/O Base = 320h,  no DMA or RAM
  6:  IRQ = 5,  I/O Base = 340h,  no DMA or RAM
  7:  IRQ = 4,  I/O Base = 360h,  no DMA or RAM
```

If your LAN driver is self-configuring, you do not need to perform this step.

Select the top default setting or scroll through the list to select a configuration that matches the interrupts and addresses you set on the interface board.

Press ENTER to select the configuration. The next screen displays information about the LAN driver you selected and asks if you want to continue with the generation process. Select Yes to continue. The screen displays link and configuration messages, and then displays the following message box:

```
Valid shell files have been placed on SHGEN-1
           <Press ESCAPE to Continue>
```

Press ESC to exit from SHGEN.

Configuring IPX for Ethernet

Recall from Chapter 15 that DOS workstations on Ethernet networks can use either the IEEE 802.3 or Ethernet II packet formats. The IPX Ethernet frame you run at workstations needs to match the Ethernet frame running at the server, which is configured during server installation. By default, NetWare uses the IEEE 802.3 standard. If you want to maintain this standard, do not change IPX as described here. If you want to change to the Ethernet II standard, run the ECONFIG command as described next. This assumes that your network interface card is using Ethernet II by default or you changed it to Ethernet II during installation.

The ECONFIG.COM command is located on the SHGEN-1 disk or directory along with the IPX.COM file you want to change. To change the IPX.COM file to support Ethernet II protocols, execute the following ECONFIG command:

ECONFIG IPX.COM SHELL:E

Copying the Startup Files
To the Master Shell Disk

Copy the IPX.COM, NETx.COM, and other files on the SHGEN-1 disk or in the SHGEN-1 hard drive directory to the master shell disks. You may need to copy the following files on the disk:

IPX.COM	(required on all DOS workstations)
NET3.COM	(DOS 3 shell for conventional memory)
NET4.COM	(DOS 4 shell for conventional memory)
EMSNET3.EXE	(DOS 3 shell for expanded memory)
EMSNET4.EXE	(DOS 4 shell for expanded memory)
XMSNET3.EXE	(DOS 3 shell for extended memory)

XMSNET4.EXE   (DOS 4 shell for extended memory)

NETBIOS.EXE   (copy if NetBIOS support is required)

INT2F.COM   (copy if NetBIOS support is required)

Use the NET*x*.COM file associated with the version of DOS running on the workstation. Copy NETBIOS.EXE and INT2F.COM if the workstation will be running software products that require the IBM NETBIOS communications protocol. If a workstation has expanded memory, copy EMSNET*x*.EXE. If it has extended memory, copy XMSNET*x*.EXE.

Copy any additional files required by your network interface card or computer system, such as special drivers for network cards. Examples are the IBM LAN support drivers required for IBM Token Ring boards. You may need to create a CONFIG.SYS file with DEVICE commands to load the drivers.

If you have other master shell disks to prepare, run SHGEN again to create a new IPX.COM file configured for the systems associated with the disks.

The SHELL.CFG and NET.CFG Workstation Boot Files

Each workstation can have a configuration file that contains commands to customize it for the NetWare environment. The commands can be used to change the normal default setting for workstations. When the workstation logs into the server, the commands in the file execute. Not all workstations need configuration files. However, you should scan through the command list in Appendix I for commands that can be used to optimize the performance of a workstation. The most common commands (those used by the login script) are listed at the beginning of the Appendix.

There are two configuration files. The SHELL.CFG file was part of NetWare 286 and is included in NetWare 386. However, Novell is attempting to migrate users to a new file called NET.CFG, which has a more versatile format. The SHELL.CFG commands in Appendix I can be included in the NET.CFG file for those who are creating new configuration files. Workstations with existing SHELL.CFG files can continue to operate with the old files. However, commands for NET.CFG can only be placed in a NET.CFG file.

Both files can be created with a text editor or word processor. If you use a word processor, make sure the files are saved as ASCII text files (no formatting codes).

Starting a DOS Workstation

The following discussion assumes your server is still up and running after you performed the installation steps in the previous chapter. If the server is not running, refer to Chapter 17.

Initially, anyone can log into the server as a supervisor, but if login names and passwords have already been established, use your assigned name and password to log in. This discussion assumes that the network supervisor is signing on for the first time. The next chapter covers login procedures for users in more detail. In addition, this section describes how to automate the login process with batch files.

Basic Login Steps

The login procedure at a workstation can be performed from a boot floppy drive or from the hard drive. Diskless workstations cannot be used for the initial login procedure; you must have a bootable system. To configure diskless workstations, refer to "Configuring Diskless Workstations" later in this chapter.

The login steps are as follows:

1. Start the workstation with a copy of the master boot disk. If the workstation boots from a hard drive, copy the contents of the master boot disk to the root directory of the C drive.

2. Execute IPX.COM to initialize the network interface card.

3. Execute NET*x*.COM, EMSNET*x*.EXE, or XMSNET*x*.EXE to load the DOS shell.

4. If you need NETBIOS support, execute NETBIOS and INT2F.

5. Switch to the network F drive.

6. Type **LOGIN** to start the login procedure.

Note: If multiple file servers exist on the network, you can include the name of the file server you want to log into as part of the LOGIN command. For example, to log in as a supervisor on a file server called FS1, you would type **LOGIN FS1/SUPERVISOR**.

Logging in as the Supervisor

The first time anyone logs into the new server, password procedures will not be in force, unless the upgrade procedure was used. During an upgrade, the security and login features of the old NetWare server are transferred to the new server.

If you are logging in for the first time, type **SUPERVISOR** as your login name. A login screen similar to the following appears:

```
F:\LOGIN>login supervisor
Good evening, SUPERVISOR.

Drive  A:   maps to a local disk.
Drive  B:   maps to a local disk.
Drive  C:   maps to a local disk.
Drive  D:   maps to a local disk.
Drive  E:   maps to a local disk.
Drive  F: = FS1\SYS:  \SYSTEM
    -----
SEARCH1:  = Z:. [FS1\SYS:  \PUBLIC]
SEARCH2:  = Y:. [FS1\SYS:  \]

F:\SYSTEM>
```

The next chapter describes how to install security features such as a password for the supervisor. Always assign a supervisor password. Supervisors have special rights that no other user has. By assigning a supervisor password, the first level of system security is established.

Starting the Network Automatically

If the network is to be started every time the workstation boots, you can include the startup files in an AUTOEXEC.BAT file. Use COPY CON to create a new AUTOEXEC.BAT file or EDLIN to edit an existing file, and then include the following commands in the order shown:

```
PROMPT $P$G
IPX
NETx
F:
LOGIN
```

If NETBIOS support is required, include the commands NETBIOS and INT2F in the startup file after the NETx command.

Configuring Diskless Workstations

Diskless workstations cannot boot DOS on their own. To boot them from the network server hard drive, use remote reset PROMs. A file called NET$DOS.SYS is created in the LOGIN directory by the DOSGEN program. Diskless workstations then boot from the network hard drive using this file. The steps to running DOSGEN are described here.

Note: Diskless workstations must have a remote reset PROM installed on their network interface cards.

If all your diskless workstations use the same version of DOS and the same network interface card, you need to create only one boot file. If several different configurations exist, be sure to read through "Creating Multiple Remote Boot Files" to create additional boot files.

To create the NET$DOS.SYS boot file, obtain one of the master boot disks created earlier that matches the configuration of the diskless workstation and its DOS version. Make sure the disk has IPX.COM, NETx.COM, SHELL.CFG, AUTOEXEC.BAT, CONFIG.SYS, and any other startup files you will need for the workstation. This includes driver files like those required for Token Ring cards.

Once the disk is ready, place it in a network workstation with a floppy disk drive, and prepare to run DOSGEN. Log into the server as the supervisor, then follow these steps:

1. Enter the following commands to map the network SYSTEM and LOGIN directories:

    MAP F:=SYS:SYSTEM
    MAP G:=SYS:LOGIN

2. Change to the SYS:LOGIN directory by typing **G:**.

3. Place the boot disk in the A drive and type **F:DOSGEN**. NET$DOS.SYS is created and stored in the SYS:LOGIN directory.

4. Copy the AUTOEXEC.BAT file from the boot disks to the LOGIN directory:

    COPY A:AUTOEXEC.BAT

    Note: You also may need to copy this batch file to each user's default directory if login problems occur.

5. Type **FLAG *.* SRO** to make the files shareable and read-only.

DOSGEN reads the files on the disk and combines them into a new workstation boot file called NET$DOS.SYS in the LOGIN directory of the server. If you are not creating custom boot files, you can boot your remote workstations at this time.

Creating Multiple Remote Boot Files

When diskless workstations contain different interface boards, DOS versions, and startup commands, you must create a different remote boot file for each. A unique name is given to each customized file and each diskless workstation is linked to the file by its unique node address number. You should have this number marked on the outside of each network card, as instructed in Chapter 16.

The workstation-to-boot file links are made by matching a list of diskless workstation node address numbers with the boot file they are to use. This list is stored in a file you create called BOOTCONF.SYS.

You should have collected the card's addresses in Chapter 16, but if you did not, temporarily place the card in a disk-based system and run the diagnostics or utility software that came with the card. The diagnostics usually display the node address assigned to the card. Refer to the card's manual for more information.

Creating Multiple Boot Files

Perform the following steps to create additional custom remote boot files. These steps must be repeated for each custom file.

1. Place the master boot disk containing the boot files for the diskless workstation in a workstation with a floppy disk drive.

2. Enter the following command to rename the AUTOEXEC.BAT file on the master boot disk to a name that will uniquely identify the diskless workstation:

   REN A:AUTOEXEC.BAT A:*filename*.BAT

   Replace *filename* with a unique eight-character name. For example, a boot file for an AST diskless workstation could be called ASTBOOT.BAT.

3. Create a new AUTOEXEC.BAT file on the master boot disk to access the file renamed in step 2. Enter the following, replacing *filename* with the name you used in step 2:

   COPY CON A:AUTOEXEC.BAT *filename*.BAT

   Press F6 and ENTER.

4. Enter the following commands to map the network SYSTEM and LOGIN directories:

   MAP F:=SYS:SYSTEM
   MAP G:=SYS:LOGIN

5. Change to the SYS:LOGIN directory by typing **G:**.

6. Copy the unique startup file created in step 2 to the server's LOGIN directory by entering the following command, replacing *filename* with the name used in step 2:

COPY A:*filename*.BAT

7. Enter the following command, replacing *filename* with the unique name you used in step 2:

F:DOSGEN A: *filename*.SYS

Note: Be sure to leave a space between A: and the filename. Repeat steps 1 through 7 for each workstation or group of workstations that need unique boot files.

8. Enter the following command to make the new boot files shareable and read-only:

FLAG *.SYS SRO

Once you have created a remote boot file for each different type of diskless workstation, create the BOOTCONF.SYS file as explained next.

Locate the network and node address for each system and match it to the boot filename you just created. Make sure you are still logged to drive F and the LOGIN directory, and then enter the following COPY CON command to create the file:

COPY CON BOOTCONF.SYS

Create an entry for each diskless workstation using this format:

0x[*network address*],[*node address*]=[*remote boot filename*]

For example, the following would be typed for the AST workstation boot file if its network address is 1, its node address is 54321, and its remote boot filename is ASTBOOT:

0x1,54321=ASTBOOT.SYS

Post-Installation Activities And Management

Login and Startup Tasks
For New Servers

Network Login Methods
Drive Mappings and Search Drives
DOS Directories on the Server
Creating New Login Scripts Using SYSCON

This chapter covers the initial login and management tasks of supervisors. The methods used to log into a NetWare server are discussed as well as methods to attach to another server. The use of mapped drives and search drives is then explained. Also, the DOS directories required by workstations are then created, and a new system login script is presented.

This chapter is written for readers who are logging into a new NetWare 386 server. If you are working on a system that was upgraded from a previous version of NetWare, mapped drives, DOS directories, and login scripts may have been carried over from the previous system. It may be unnecessary to create the DOS directories and login script discussed here. In particular, the login script may be best left the way it is until you learn more about NetWare or consult with the administrator of the old system.

Network Login Methods

A network system may have several file servers attached to it. A workstation logs itself into the first available server, unless a particular one is specified in the LOGIN command. Once logged into a specific server, you can log into other servers using the ATTACH command. When two or more servers are in use simultaneously, it is important to map the directories to be used on each server to a drive letter. This helps avoid confusion and makes access to the directories easier.

Listing Available Servers
Before Logging In

You can use the SLIST command to list the servers currently available on the network prior to logging into a server or attaching to another server. After typing **IPX** and one of the shell commands (**NET*x*.COM, EMS-NET*x*.EXE,** or **XMSNET*x*.EXE**), type the drive specification **F:** to switch to the first available network drive. At this point, LOGIN is the current default directory.

SLIST is a convenient command for users who cannot remember the names of servers on the network. It displays a listing similar to the following:

```
Known NetWare Filer Servers    Network    Node Address
FS1                            454E44     640400454E44 DEFAULT
SALES                          454E44     640401454E44
ACCTG                          000010     000000000001
```

The information provided by SLIST can be used in LOGIN and ATTACH commands, as described in the next sections.

The LOGIN Command

After typing **IPX**, a shell command, and **F:**, users are placed in the LOGIN directory. To log into the first available server, simply enter the LOGIN command by itself:

```
LOGIN
```

LOGIN requests you to enter your user name. Alternatively, you can specify your account name with the following form of the LOGIN command:

LOGIN *username*

where *username* is your account name.

If you want to log into a specific server, the following form of LOGIN can be typed to designate that server as the login point:

LOGIN *server / username*

where *server* is the name of the server, which can be determined with the SLIST command. If you do not specify *username,* LOGIN asks for it, but you must include the slash (/), otherwise LOGIN interprets *server* as *username.* The proper form is

LOGIN *server /*

but in most cases it is best to type your *username* with the command.

Note: Passwords can be synchronized for all servers with the SETPASS command.

LOGIN Options

NetWare 386 provides three new options for the LOGIN command. These options are placed in the command as shown below and described in the following sections.

LOGIN *options server / username*

/S (Script)   Use this option to override both the system and user login scripts with a login script of your choice. Include the complete path and name of the overriding login script after the /S option. This feature is useful to a supervisor who is testing startup procedures or who needs to log into a user's station with different startup options. Users can also use the option to start a session with different drive and search mappings.

/N (NoAttach)   Use this option to execute a login script while logged into a server. You will not be logged out of the current server or attached to another. The option can be used with the /S option.

/C (Clearscreen)   Include this option to clear the workstation screen as soon as the login process is complete.

Login Script Parameters

Replaceable parameters like those used in DOS batch files can be included with the LOGIN command. These parameters are used by the IF...THEN statement in login scripts, as discussed in Chapter 28. The command would take the following form:

LOGIN *server / username parameters*

where *parameters* are keywords that replace variables in login scripts. The parameters are numbered: the file server name is always %0, the user name is always %1, and the remaining parameters are numbered sequentially, starting with %2. For example, in the following command, FCON is %2 and is used in the login script to execute the FCONSOLE utility. The supervisor can enter the option whenever he or she wants to start a session with FCONSOLE.

LOGIN FS1/SUPERVISOR FCON

Automatic Login

You can include the LOGIN command in the AUTOEXEC.BAT file of the boot disk or hard drive, along with the IPX.COM and shell commands. The following is an example of an AUTOEXEC.BAT file for the supervisor's workstation:

```
IPX
NET3
F:
LOGIN FS1/SUPERVISOR
```

Login Messages

Your initial login screen looks like the following unless the system login script has been changed:

```
F:\PUBLIC>login supervisor
Good evening, SUPERVISOR.

Drive  A:    maps to a local disk.
Drive  B:    maps to a local disk.
Drive  C:    maps to a local disk.
Drive  D:    maps to a local disk.
Drive  E:    maps to a local disk.
Drive  F: = FS1\SYS:  \SYSTEM
-----
SEARCH1:  = Z:. [FS1\SYS:  \PUBLIC]
SEARCH2:  = Y:. [FS1\SYS:  \]

F:\SYSTEM>
```

In this illustration, drives A through E are designated for the local workstation. Even though the drives might not be physically present, NetWare reserves their drive letters. The first network drive is drive F and is mapped to the SYSTEM directory. The last two lines show the search drives, which are basically the same as DOS path settings.

The ATTACH Command

You use the ATTACH command to attach to other file servers after first logging into the main server. You can enter the SLIST command to view a list of other servers on the network. The command takes the form

ATTACH *server* / *username*

where *server* is the name of the server to attach to and *username* is the user name for the server. If username is not included, ATTACH asks for it. You must include the slash if only *server* is included; otherwise AT-TACH interprets *server* as *username* and displays an error.

Once attached to another server, you must create drive mappings to use the directories on the server. This can be done with the MAP command, as discussed later in this chapter.

Working with more than one server can sometimes become confusing. To display your current status on any server, type **WHOAMI**.

Changing the Login Password

Until the supervisor is assigned a password, anyone can sign in as the supervisor with complete access to the entire system. This may not be a problem on a new system that does not yet include important data, but the supervisor should establish a password as soon as possible.

To establish a supervisor password, you can issue the SETPASS command at the NetWare command prompt. Make sure you are logged in as the supervisor before doing so. The form of the command is

SETPASS *fileserver*

If you have more than one file server, replace *fileserver* with the name of the server on which you want to set a password. The command first requests the old password. If you have not already assigned one, press ENTER, and then type your new password. You are asked to type it again for verification. If other servers exist on the network, you are then asked if you want to "synchronize" the password across all servers. Type **Y** to use the same password on all servers. Type **N** to use different passwords on other servers, and then repeat the SETPASS command for each server. Your display should look similar to the following:

Enter your old password:
Enter your new password:
Retype your new password:
Would you like to synchronize your passwords on all attached servers?

Note: To log into other servers, enter the LOGIN command in the form

LOGIN *server / username*

Replace *server* with the name of the server, and for *username* enter **SUPERVISOR**.

Drive Mappings and Search Drives

MAP is an important and useful command for anyone using a NetWare server. It is used to assign short drive letters to long directory names, making them easier to refer to. It is also used to create search paths to directories. A *drive mapping* refers to a directory that has been assigned a disk drive letter. *Search drives* refer to directories that are searched when commands are executed. Search drive mappings serve the same function as the DOS PATH command. They specify which directories the operating system should look in to find executable files.

Note: You can enter the MAP command without parameters to display the current mappings.

Drive Mappings

A drive mapping is a way of assigning a drive letter to a particular directory. The drive letter can then be typed on the command line to move into the directory, rather than typing the complete name of the directory. Mapping is especially useful when the directory is in another volume or on another server.

Mapping a drive is similar to using the SUBST command in DOS. For example, you could execute the following MAP command to map a directory called SYS:PUBLIC/APPS/DBASE to the K drive:

MAP K:=SYS:PUBLIC/APPS/DBASE

After mapping the drive, type **K:** to switch to the directory.

Drive mappings have the following characteristics:

- Each user can have a personal drive map. Drive K for one user may not be mapped to the same directory as it is for another user.

- You can use any drive letter, but using the letter of an existing drive map overwrites that map.

- You can create drive mappings at any time during a session, but they are lost when you log out.

- You can reestablish drive mappings for each session by including MAP commands in the system or user login scripts.

- MAP commands to establish drive maps for all users should be placed in the system login script.

- MAP commands specific to one user should be placed in that user's login script.

- Use special login script conditional commands to assign drive mappings to users according to the groups they belong to.

The DOS CD (Change Directory) command can cause some confusion to new NetWare users because its use changes a drive mapping. For example, assume Jim is working on the system and the current default drive K is mapped to SYS:ACCT\DATA. Now assume he uses the DOS CD command to change to the SYS:USERS\JIM directory, which is his personal directory. By doing so, he inadvertently remaps the K drive to his personal directory, which in most cases will already be mapped to drive F by commands in the login script. Jim becomes confused when he cannot return to the SYS:ACCT\DATA directory by typing **K:**. The MAP command would reveal the following:

```
Drive F: = FS1/SYS:USERS\JIM
Drive K: = FS1/SYS:USERS\JIM
```

This indicates that two driver letters are now mapped to the same directory. You must remember to use the mapped drive letter when switching between directories, rather than resorting to the DOS CD command.

You can use any available drive to map any available directory, but first use the MAP command to view the current mappings and see if a directory is already mapped. If an existing drive letter is used, the new mapping replaces the old mapping.

Each user can have a personal set of drive mappings. For example, Bob may map a data directory called PUB-DATA to his drive K, while Jane maps the same directory to her drive R. If Bob tells Jane that he has just placed a file in K, Jane should be aware that her drive R is where the file is located.

Search Drive Mappings

Search drive mappings establish pointers to directories that contain executable files. Through search drive maps, you can work in data directories and run programs located in program directories. Create a search drive map by specifying the number of the search drive and the directory to which it points. For example, the following command creates a search drive pointer to a directory called SYS:PROGRAMS:

```
MAP S2:=SYS:PROGRAMS
```

S2 designates the directory as the second search drive. It is searched by the operating system after S1, which is usually mapped to SYS:PUBLIC. Other search drives can be mapped as required.

Here are some points to remember about search drive mappings:

- Search drives can be established for all users by placing the MAP command in the system login script.

- All users can have their own personal search mappings.

- A search map is a pointer to a directory.

- A search drive mapping should always be set up for the SYS:PUBLIC directory so users can have access to the menu utilities and other commands stored there.

- Establish search drive mappings to applications directories so programs can be run from data directories.

- You must have proper security rights to run programs in directories on the search paths.

Avoiding MAP Confusion

The lettering system used by the NetWare MAP command is often a source of confusion. While you can choose a drive letter to map a directory, MAP automatically assigns its own drive letters when a search map is established. Search drive letters start with "Z" and work their way up through the alphabet. MAP uses this scheme to avoid conflicts with the letters you assign to mapped drives. Eventually, the mapped drive letters descending from letter "A" meet the search drive letters ascending from "Z." At this point, you must begin remapping existing letters. However, it is unlikely that you will assign this many mappings.

DOS Directories on the Server

You should create DOS directories on the server to support each different version of DOS used at the workstations. This is especially important for diskless workstations and workstations that boot from floppy disks. Hard drive systems, on the other hand, can efficiently return to their local hard drive for DOS files.

For DOS-based workstations you often need to reload a copy of COMMAND.COM when exiting an application or utility. It is more efficient to reload COMMAND.COM from the server hard drive than a local floppy disk. In the case of diskless workstations, you *must* reload COMMAND.COM from the server because it cannot be made available locally.

If every workstation is using the same version of DOS, create only one DOS directory. If workstations are using different versions of DOS (PC DOS or MS-DOS version 2, 3, or 4), each requires a separate directory. The directories should be created as subdirectories of SYS:PUBLIC.

Once you have created directories and copied the correct DOS to them, they can become part of the search path for a workstation. Search paths are created according to the *long machine type* of a workstation and the DOS version it uses. Recall from Chapter 18 that the long machine type is specified in the SHELL.CFG or NET.CFG file at each workstation. It is a name used to refer to the type of DOS running in the machine. The DOS version is its release number, such as version 3.20 or 3.31.

For example, assume IBM workstations need to access IBM PC DOS version 3.30. You create a directory called SYS:PUBLIC/IBMDOS/V3.30, and copy the DOS files to it. Place the line LONG MACHINE TYPE = IBMDOS in the SHELL.CFG file at the workstation, and then place the following command in the system login script:

MAP S2:=SYS:PUBLIC/%MACHINE/%OS_VERSION

NetWare replaces the parameter %MACHINE with the long machine name and %OS_VERSION with the operating system version to create a search path to the SYS:PUBLIC/IBMDOS/V3.30 directory. NetWare is capable of determining the OS version on its own. This command is actually a universal command you use to set DOS paths for any type of machine. The supervisor must ensure that a matching directory with DOS files exists on the server.

To help you assign long machine names and keep track of the DOS directories on the server, you may want to develop a DOS naming scheme, as shown here:

IBMDOS = IBM DOS
CPQDOS = Compaq DOS
ASTDOS = AST DOS

The diagram shown in Figure 19-1 illustrates a directory tree that matches these DOS versions.

To create each individual DOS directory, issue the following command:

MD SYS:PUBLIC/*machinename/osversion*

where *machinename* is a name similar to that shown in the previous example, and *osversion* is the version number in the form V#.##.

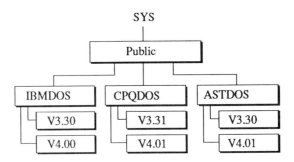

Figure 19-1. A sample directory tree for DOS directories

Copy the DOS files from disk to each new directory. You must also mark the files in the directory as shareable since more than one user may need to access them at the same time. Also, the files should be marked read-only as a protective measure. Enter the following command, replacing *machinename* with the name of the DOS directory and *osversion* with the version number:

FLAG SYS:PUBLIC/*machinename/osversion* SRO

Creating New Login Scripts Using SYSCON

You use login scripts to execute various NetWare commands when you first log into the system. These commands can be used to map directories to drives and to establish search drives. You can include a number of other commands in the login scripts, which are covered in detail in Chapter 28. For now, the system login script described here establishes maps and login messages that are preferable to those of the default login script.

There are two types of login scripts. The *system login script* is executed when all users log in, including the supervisor. *User login scripts* are executed after the system login script to run commands for a specific user. Every user can have a personal login script created by the supervisor, a work group manager, or themselves.

Creating a New System Login Script

The login script described here includes commands that display information about the workstation, such as the station address, the network node number, and the DOS version being run. This information is especially useful to supervisors or work group managers who may need to log into different stations to perform maintenance.

To begin creating the system login script, make sure you are logged in as the supervisor, and then enter the SYSCON command. At the SYSCON main menu, highlight Supervisor Options by typing **S** and pressing ENTER. At the subsequent menu, highlight System Login Script by typing **S** and pressing ENTER. A blank screen with the heading System Login Script appears.

Note: If a script already exists, you may want to leave it as is and read through the remainder of this section without making changes.

Type the login script shown in Figure 19-2. For the best results, press CAPS LOCK when creating or editing login scripts, because some command options must be in uppercase. Use the arrow keys to access parts of the display for editing.

The commands perform the following tasks in the order shown:

- *MAP ERRORS OFF* Prevents error messages from displaying. This command is used to hide unimportant messages.

- *WRITE "Good %GREETING_TIME, %LOGIN_NAME."* Displays a greeting message that includes the user's name.

- *SET PROMPT = "PG"* Sets the prompt to display the current directory.

- *MAP F:=SYS:USERS\%LOGIN_NAME* Maps drive F to the user's personal directory using his or her login name. This command assumes you have created the directories for each user. It also assumes that user names do not exceed eight characters, which is the maximum for a directory name.

- *IF "%LOGIN_NAME" = "SUPERVISOR" THEN MAP F:= SYS:SYSTEM* If the supervisor logs in, this command maps drive F to the SYS:SYSTEM directory. The command is ignored for all others who log in.

- *MAP INS S1:=SYS:PUBLIC* Maps the SYS:PUBLIC directory as a search drive.

Note: MAP INS (Insert) should always be used when specifying search drives. The Insert option saves any path settings made by DOS at the local workstation.

```
                          System Login Script
MAP ERRORS OFF
WRITE "Good %GREETING_TIME, %LOGIN_NAME."
SET PROMPT = "$P$G"
MAP F:=SYS:USERS\%LOGIN_NAME
IF "%LOGIN_NAME" = "SUPERVISOR" THEN MAP F:=SYS:SYSTEM
MAP INS S1:=SYS:PUBLIC
MAP INS S2:=SYS:PUBLIC\%MACHINE\%OS_VERSION
COMSPEC = S2:COMMAND.COM
WRITE "Workstation = %STATION"
WRITE "Workstation address = %P_STATION"
WRITE "Machine name = %MACHINE"
WRITE "OS type = %OS"
WRITE "OS version = %OS_VERSION"
```

Figure 19-2.   A suggested initial system login script

- *MAP INS S2:=SYS:PUBLIC\%MACHINE\%OS_VERSION*
Maps a DOS directory that matches the user's DOS version. Do not forget to create the directories.

- *COMSPEC = S2:COMMAND.COM COMSPEC* The location of COMMAND.COM. This command specifies it is in the directory mapped in the previous command (search drive S2).

- *WRITE "Workstation = %STATION"* Displays the workstation number.

- *WRITE "Workstation address = %P_STATION"* Displays the network node number of the workstation.

- *WRITE "Machine name = %MACHINE"* Displays the long machine name set in the SHELL.CFG file.

- *WRITE "OS type = %OS"* Displays the operating system being used.

- *WRITE "OS version = %OS_VERSION"* Displays the operating system version.

When you have finished entering the commands, press ESC. Answer Yes when asked if you want to save changes. You are returned to the Supervisor Options menu. Press ESC again to return to the Available Topics Menu.

Personal login scripts may overwrite some of the options set by the system login script. It may be necessary to disable it by placing an asterisk or other commands in the script. Follow this procedure to disable the supervisor's or other user's login script:

1. From the SYSCON Available Topics menu, select **User Information**.

2. Highlight Supervisor (or another user) and press ENTER.

3. Select **Login Scripts** and press ENTER.

4. Type * (asterisk).

5. Press ESC and answer Yes to the save option.

You can try the new system login script by logging in as the supervisor. You don't need to worry about logging out. Simply type **LOGIN SUPERVISOR** at the prompt. The greeting message should appear, along with the workstation information. Type **MAP** to make sure the drive mappings were set as described above. If you made any mistakes, re-enter SYSCON and the login script editing screen to make changes.

Startup Tasks for Supervisors

T W E N T Y

Exploring the NetWare Filing System
Initial Supervisor Tasks
Tasks Ahead for the Supervisor
Using the NetWare Menu Utilities

The fact that you are reading this section indicates that you have success-fully installed NetWare 386 and have logged in as a supervisor. Congrat-ulations! You can consider yourself a new member of the Fellowship of NetWare Supervisors. This is an unofficial group of elite people who have made it through the entire planning and installation phase. All the hard work and planning were your initiation rites into this special group. Now comes the task of managing the network system and its users.

Exploring the NetWare Filing System

Now that you are logged into the network, you can begin exploring its file system, create directories, add applications, and establish users on the system. To start, you must understand the terminology used on a NetWare network when referring to its servers, volumes, directories, and files.

Servers

Your network may have more than one server. Each server is given a specific name so you can switch between one or the other during your network sessions. In the screen display shown here, the server name is FS1, which can be seen in the drive F listing:

```
Good morning, SUPERVISOR
Drive A       maps to a local d:   .
Drive B       maps to a local d:   .
Drive C       maps to a local d:   .
Drive D       maps to a local d:   .
Drive E       maps to a local d:   .
Drive F    := FS1/SYS:SYSTEM
Drive G    := FS1/SYS:LOGIN
Drive H    := FS1/SYS:PUBLIC
```

The name of your server may be different and is set during installation or startup.

You can use the NetWare SLIST command to view a list of available servers, either before executing the LOGIN command or after. To log into a different server, use the LOGIN command or the ATTACH command, as explained in Chapter 19. You can also use the SESSION and SYSCON utilities to change servers, as discussed later in this chapter. When two or more servers are attached simultaneously, a drive letter should be mapped to the directories you want to use on each server for easy access.

You can see your current login connections and status by entering the NetWare WHOAMI command. This command displays your login name and time, along with the servers you are attached to.

Volumes

The network server file system may be divided into several volumes, the names of which may need to be included when referring to files or directories on other volumes.

You may use the NetWare MAP command to map directories on other volumes as well as other file servers for easy access.

Directories

Once you are logged into a NetWare server and a particular volume, you can begin to work with directories in the same way you would work with directories in the DOS environment. You can use the DOS CD (Change Directory), MD (Make Directory), and RD (Remove Directory) commands to work with directories, or you can use the NetWare menu utilities. The supervisor has rights to manipulate directories anywhere, but other users also need rights to do so.

The following NetWare commands are used when working with directories:

- The FILER menu utility is designed to manipulate both files and directories.

- MAP is used to convert a long directory name to a short, easy-to-use drive letter.

- NDIR is used to list directories. It lists directory creation dates, attributes, owners, and other information.

- RENDIR is used to rename directories.

- LISTDIR can be used to display a map of directories and subdirectories.

- FLAGDIR can be used to change subdirectory attributes to Hidden, System, Private, or back to Normal. You can also inhibit renaming and deletion with the command.

Note: Often you include the server name when referring to directories on a network server to distinguish between directories on other servers that might have the same name. For example, the SYS:SYSTEM and SYS:PUBLIC directories include the server name SYS throughout this text.

Files

Files are the basic units of storage for users on the network. Each file has a specific name and resides in a specific directory, on a specific volume, on a specific file server. Therefore, the complete name of the file is important and includes the server name, volume, directory, subdirectories, and the filename, as shown here:

File Server Name/Volume Name:Directory/Subdirectory/Filename

Note: The placement of the colon and slashes in the filename should follow the conventions shown.

Here are some points to remember when working with files:

- Only the filename needs to be specified for files in the current directory.

- To manipulate files in other directories, include the directory path.

- To manipulate files in other volumes, include the volume name and the directory path.

- To manipulate files on other file servers, include the file server name, the volume name, and the directory path.

- If you need to do a lot of work with files in other directories, map a drive letter to these directories for easy reference.

The System and Public Directories

The SYS:SYSTEM and SYS:PUBLIC directories hold most of the NetWare commands and utilities used by the supervisor and network users. The following sections help you explore the directories.

Note: If the prompt is not showing the name of your current directory, type **PROMPT pg** at the command line.

The SYS:SYSTEM Directory

As the supervisor, you have complete rights to the entire system. In addition, the SYS:SYSTEM directory is reserved for use by the supervisor or those with equivalent rights to the supervisor. If you are working with a new NetWare 386 server that has not had its drive mappings changed, you should be located in the SYS:SYSTEM directory. If you are not in this directory, you can list the current drive assignments by typing **MAP**.

Determine the drive letter of the SYS:SYSTEM directory and switch to the directory. Next, enter the NDIR command to display the files in the directory.

Press the spacebar to bypass the menu if it appears. In a second a list of files in the directory appears, along with their size, modification dates, access dates, flags, and owner information. Keep in mind that these commands are meant for supervisors only because they are used to handle the system security and accounting. Regular users should not have access to these files.

The SYS:PUBLIC Directory

SYS:PUBLIC contains the menu utilities and command files used by all users of the system. When you first log in, a search drive mapping is automatically created to this directory so the files in it can be executed from any other directory. Type **MAP** now to see the current search drive mappings for your system. If you upgraded from a previous server, your mappings may be different than those for a completely new server.

Type the following command to see the contents of the SYS:PUBLIC directory:

NDIR SYS:PUBLIC

You must ensure that all users have a search drive mapped to the SYS:PUBLIC directory if they are to use the commands and utilities in it. NetWare automatically gives all users rights to execute files in this directory, but not to alter or delete its files. You should never change these rights for any user.

The SYS:LOGIN and SYS:MAIL Directories

During the process of attaching to a NetWare server, you type **F:** to switch
to the NetWare server. At this point you are placed in the SYS:LOGIN
directory. This is the only directory you have access to before entering the
LOGIN command. After issuing LOGIN and logging in with the normal
procedure, you are given access to other directories on the system according
to your assigned rights and MAP commands in the login script.

The SYS:LOGIN directory holds the files LOGIN.EXE and
SLIST.EXE, along with NET$DOS.SYS and AUTOEXEC.BAT if diskless
workstations are present. Other commands may also exist, depending on
the configuration of the system. LOGIN.EXE is, of course, used to log into
the server. SLIST is used to display a list of file servers available on the
network. This is useful when you need to log into another server but cannot
remember its name.

The SYS:MAIL directory is primarily used by the NetWare MAIL
program, which is available as a separate option. When a user is created,
a subdirectory is created in the MAIL directory that corresponds to the
user's ID. Each user's personal login script is also stored in the SYS:MAIL
subdirectory.

Initial Supervisor Tasks

The system supervisor has a few matters to take care of before allowing
other users on the system. These are outlined in the following sections.

A Word About Security

Security features are an essential component of any multiuser operating
system, and NetWare's features make no exception to this rule. Unlike
personal computers that store files for one user, NetWare stores files for
many users. Methods are required to separate files and keep users from
viewing, copying, or erasing those of other users. Intruder detection and
lockout methods are also required to keep unwelcome users off the system.

There is the possibility that an intruder could copy a valuable company database or introduce a computer virus that could destroy data.

NetWare's security features are comprehensive and reliable when used properly. Because of this, NetWare is authorized for use by government and military agencies with sensitive data. But NetWare's security features are designed to provide more than security. They also assist in keeping the file system organized. Supervisors and managers can create directory structures that mimic the organizational chart of a company. Through the security features, users can be limited to working and storing files in their specific areas. While many small companies might consider the security system unessential and possibly a nuisance, this is a mistake. It should always be used, if only for its organizational effects. The security system offers the following benefits:

- Each user can be given a safe and secure directory on the server for their own use. Users who entrust their files to a shared filing system will feel secure in knowing other users cannot tamper with them.

- The security features keep intruders out of the system and provide an effective barrier to computer virus infections.

- The password feature ensures that only authorized users can log into the system. It also ensures that each user is properly identified so specific login scripts and drive mappings can be run.

- Users can be restricted to one specific workstation. This prevents users from logging into unsupervised areas.

- Users' access time can be restricted to a certain period, preventing them from accessing the server during unauthorized or unsupervised hours. Supervisors may want to restrict certain hours so backups and maintenance procedures can take place.

- File uploading can be prevented to keep users from overburdening the file system with unnecessary files.

Of course, there are many other reasons for using the security system. Its advanced features can be used according to your security needs. For example, the password security system may be sufficient for one company, while another company may require the use of directory and file security rights.

Supervisor Password Considerations

Once the supervisor's password has been established, only the actual supervisor can log in as the user SUPERVISOR. In this way the supervisor has complete control over the system. Management will probably want to develop a method to gain supervisor access in case something should happen to the supervisor. One fail-safe method is to compose the supervisor's password of two unrelated words and give two people one-half of the password. In this way, those two people must be in agreement before the system can be accessed without the supervisor.

Management should always be aware that the supervisor can change the password at any time. This can be a problem if the supervisor leaves the company suddenly. Keep in mind that a normal task for a supervisor is to change passwords on a regular basis for security reasons. In one case a supervisor got wind of news that he would be fired during the next week. On Friday he changed all the passwords on the system as part of his normal procedure, and then did not show up for work on Monday. Frantic users made every attempt to contact him, but he had already left for an extended vacation.

Using the Console

The *console* is the session running on the NetWare 386 file server. You cannot log in and use the file services of NetWare on this station, but supervisors can monitor and make changes to the operating system itself from the console.

Console commands can send messages to users, manage printers and print queues, and down the server. The console can also monitor the activities of various workstations. Commands are also available for handling mirrored drives, mounting or unmounting volumes, and loading or unloading interface card drivers.

You used the console during installation to install the NetWare operating system and drivers. During normal operations, you can use the console to monitor the network by loading the MONITOR program. This is done by typing **LOAD MONITOR** at the console prompt.

Note: If you previously locked the console, type your password at the password prompt and press ENTER.

The MONITOR display appears showing file server information at the top and a list of available options at the bottom. Take a few minutes to browse through the options on the Available Topics menu. The information that MONITOR makes available about connections, module information, and memory usage is extremely useful when monitoring the performance of your system, isolating problems, or evaluating the need to purchase additional equipment. The options on the monitor menu will be covered in Part VI of this book.

Note: Be sure to select the **Lock File Server Console** option before leaving the server.

Network Printing

Printing on a NetWare 386 network is accomplished through print queues instead of directly to a printer. You send your print job to a specific queue, rather than a printer. Queues have the following characteristics:

- A queue can direct its printing to more than one printer for greatest efficiency.

- A single printer can be serviced by several queues, each with different printing parameters.

- If a printer is serviced by several queues, one queue might have a higher priority than another. VIPs are then given access to the high-priority printers.

- Supervisors can assign users and groups to specific print queues, each with a different priority.

- Queues can define different printing forms. For example, queue PAYROLL might be connected to a printer that has paychecks loaded. Users in the accounting department would then be assigned the use of this queue.

Printers on a NetWare 386 network can be attached in the following ways:

- A total of 16 printers are supported by each print server, but additional print servers can be installed.

- The file server can be set up as a print server. It can then manage up to five directly connected printers and printers attached to other workstations.

- A workstation can be set up as a dedicated print server to handle all of the printing jobs. It can then manage up to five directly connected printers and printers attached to other workstations.

- A printer attached to a workstation can be used for network-wide printing. A queue on the print server can be directed to send its print jobs to the workstation's printer.

Printing is covered completely in Chapter 27.

Tasks Ahead for the Supervisor

As the system supervisor, you must perform various tasks to manage the operating system, file system, users, and groups. The system security also must be managed. These topics are outlined in the sections that follow, and then will be covered in more detail in the next few chapters.

Defining and Establishing Users, Groups, and Operators

As a supervisor you must establish each user on the system, including yourself. It is usually a good idea to log in as a regular user if you are using the system as everyone else does. You can then establish various login scripts and directories for your own use. This lets you work in a normal way on the system without accidentally issuing a command (with full supervisor privileges) that you might regret. Supervisors should be cautious of logging in under the supervisor name and then leaving the workstation unattanded.

You can then create groups of users. A user group has a specific name and is used to assign rights to directories and files. In almost all cases you assign security rights to groups, rather than to individual users. A user is assigned rights to his or her personal directory, but beyond that most directories are also used by other people, who are usually part of a group. For example, the use of an accounting directory can be assigned to users who belong to the ACCTG group.

Supervisors can create *work group managers* to make their job much easier. A work group manager can be given specific rights to create, remove, and grant rights to a group of users for a directory. In this way supervisors can unload part of their task to the work group managers. Likewise, work group managers can create *user account managers* who control users within a specific group but are not allowed to create or remove users.

The next few chapters explain the hierarchy of network users and explain how to assign security, directory, and file rights to them.

Defining System Security

System security starts with the login procedure. If you created a password for the supervisor, you have already established the first line of security. The next step is to create new users and require that they use passwords when logging in. No users can log in unless an account has been created for them.

Once users are created, they can be assigned to groups and given security rights to directories and files. Supervisors or group managers can also develop user restrictions such as the allowed login time or workstation number.

NetWare security is not just a matter of taking away a user's rights. Supervisors and group managers also must grant users rights so they can run applications and create files—basic tasks that NetWare does not let them do without the proper rights. New managers often forget to grant users rights and, as a result, the users and sometimes even the manager attribute the inability to run an application to other problems.

Creating Directories
And Loading Applications

You must design a directory structure that fits in with the applications you plan to use, the users and groups that will access them, and the security of the system. Try to avoid storing data in the same directory as applications because the access rights for each type of file are different. You also must make sure that users have at least Read and File Scan rights in directories used to access programs. They will need at least Create, File Scan, Write, and Read rights in directories in which data are stored.

You will learn in the next few chapters that directory structures, file access rights, group membership, and work group managers closely parallel the organization of most businesses. Therefore, you usually can include the employees of departments in a group that is managed by the department manager. Directories can then be created to hold the program and data files normally used by the department.

Accounting

If you plan to establish the accounting feature on your network, you must read Chapter 31. The accounting feature must be activated before it can be used. You can then perform the following:

- Track users' login activities
- Charge for system resources used, such as disk storage and printer time
- Charge users for the amount of time they use the system

Using the NetWare
Menu Utilities

This section gives you an overview of the NetWare menu utilities used by both supervisors and users. You should become familiar with their use since they make many tasks easier to perform. In the next few chapters, the menus are used to create users, groups, work group managers, and user account managers. They also are used to create directories and the security rights of users or groups for those directories.

The illustrations throughout this chapter show the main menu of each NetWare menu utility. Once a utility is loaded, you can access help information by pressing the F1 (Help) key. Information about the currently selected option is displayed. Pressing F1 twice displays a list of function key assignments, as shown in Figure 20-1. The function key assignments are listed in Table 20-1 for your convenience and explained in the following paragraphs.

Selecting Options

When a menu appears with a list of options, scroll down to the option you want and press ENTER. Alternatively, you can begin typing the first letter of the option to select it. If two options appear with the same first letter, type the second letter of the option you want to select and then press ENTER.

Some menus that display lists of files may extend beyond the bottom of the menu, in which case an arrow appears at the bottom of the screen. Use the arrow keys or PGUP or PGDN to move through the list. If a list is long, type the first or second letter of the option you want. The highlight jumps to the item or its immediate area, where you can then scroll using the arrow keys.

```
┌─────────────────────────────────────────────────────────────────────┐
│ NetWare System Configuration  V3.00           Sunday  May 20, 1990  9:33 pm │
│                    User SUPERVISOR On File Server FS1                  │
└─────────────────────────────────────────────────────────────────────┘

┌─────────────────────────────────────────────────────────────────────┐
│The function key assignments on your machine are:                      │
│                                                                       │
│ESCAPE            Esc                 Back up to the previous level.    │
│EXIT              Alt F10             Exit the program.                 │
│CANCEL            F7                  Cancel markings or edit changes.  │
│BACKSPACE         Backspace           Delete the character to the left of│
│                                      the cursor.                      │
│INSERT            Ins                 Insert a new item.                │
│DELETE            Del                 Delete an item.                   │
│MODIFY            F3                  Rename/modify/edit the item.      │
│SELECT            Enter               Accept information entered or select│
│                                      the item.                        │
│HELP              F1                  Provide on-line help.             │
│MARK              F5                  Toggle marking for current item.  │
│CYCLE             Tab                 Cycle through menus or screens.   │
│MODE              F9                  Change Modes.                     │
│UP                Up arrow            Move up one line.                 │
│DOWN              Down arrow          Move down one line.               │
│LEFT              Left arrow          Move left one position.           │
└─────────────────────────────────────────────────────────────────────┘
```

Figure 20-1.   The function key menu is available by pressing F1 twice

ESC	Backs out of the current menu.
ALT-F10	Quickly exits the menu utility.
F5	Marks multiple items for selection. In a list, scroll to each item to be selected and press F5. When editing, press F5 to begin marking a block, and then move the arrow keys to extend the block.
F7	Cancels markings made by the F5 key.
F3	Renames, modifies, or edits a selected item. For example, a current drive mapping or search mapping can be selected and then altered using the F3 key.
INS	In most menus that request additional information about directories and files, this key can be pressed to display a list. The F5 key can then be used to mark multiple items in a list for selection.
DEL	Removes items from a list. You can mark multiple items with the F5 key, then strike the DEL key.
TAB	Cycles through menus or items on some menu utilities.

Table 20-1.   List of Function Key Assignments

NetWare Main Menu

NetWare has a main menu that can be accessed by typing the following command on the NetWare command line:

MENU MAIN

The following menu appears and can be used to access all other menu utilities:

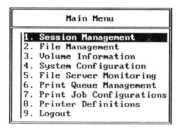

```
                    Main Menu
        ┌─────────────────────────────────────┐
        │ 1. Session Management                │
        │ 2. File Management                   │
        │ 3. Volume Information                │
        │ 4. System Configuration             │
        │ 5. File Server Monitoring            │
        │ 6. Print Queue Management            │
        │ 7. Print Job Configurations          │
        │ 8. Printer Definitions               │
        │ 9. Logout                            │
        └─────────────────────────────────────┘
```

The top five options on the menu are discussed in the following sections. Keep in mind that the menu simply starts utilities like SYSCON, FILER, and SESSION. You can just as easily start these menu utilities from the prompt and never use the main menu.

You can include the following command on the last line of the system login script to display this menu whenever the system starts. You can also include the command in personal login scripts.

EXIT "MENU MAIN"

System Console:
The SYSCON Menu Utility

The SYSCON menu utility is used to create users, groups, work group managers, and user account managers. It can also be used to define directory rights. You already have seen how SYSCON is used to create the system login scripts. Most of the tasks performed in SYSCON require supervisor rights, although users will find the utility useful for displaying information about their status on the system. They can also use it to create or change their personal login script.

The SYSCON main menu is shown here:

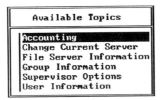

The menu options and their functions are listed here:

Accounting
: Used to install or access the NetWare accounting features.

Change Current Server
: Used to switch to another file server.

File Server Information
: Displays information about the current file server, such as the NetWare version, number of current users, network address, and version serial number.

Group Information
: Used to create groups or access information about groups.

Supervisor Options
: Provides options for setting default restrictions on the network and for creating special console operators as well as creating or editing the system login script. The Supervisor Options menu is shown here:

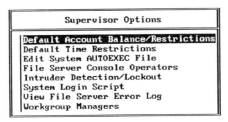

User Information   Used to create new users and to access information about them.

Note: Keep in mind that you can get help when setting or altering any options by pressing the F1 (Help) key.

Session Manager:
The SESSION Menu Utility

The SESSION menu utility is used to handle activities and settings in the current session. Any changes made with the utility are lost when the user logs out. The SESSION main menu is shown here:

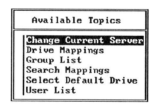

```
  Available Topics
┌──────────────────────┐
│Change Current Server │
│Drive Mappings        │
│Group List            │
│Search Mappings       │
│Select Default Drive  │
│User List             │
└──────────────────────┘
```

The SESSION menu options and their functions are described here:

Change Current Server   Allows users to change to a different server.

Drive Mappings   Provides menu-assisted help in creating drive maps.

Group List   Lists the current groups and allows the user to send messages to them.

Search Mappings   Provides menu-assisted help in creating search drive mappings.

Select Default Drive   Allows a user to switch to another drive.

User List   Lists the current users on the system and allows the user to send messages to those users.

File Manager: the FILER Menu Utility

You can use the FILER menu utility to work with volumes, directories, and files. Supervisors can use the utility to create directories and assign security. Files can be listed, deleted, renamed, and copied. File attributes can also be changed. Users do not have as much control in FILER as the supervisor, but they can view useful information about various directories and files. The FILER main menu is shown here:

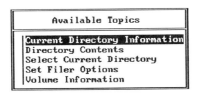

The FILER menu options and their functions are given in the following list. Note that information is displayed for the current directory unless another directory is selected with the Select Current Directory option.

Current Directory Information	Displays information about the current directory, such as its creation date, current effective rights, and the inherited rights mask. The rights displayed are for the current user. Other users may see a different display.
Directory Contents	Displays a list of files in a directory. When one or more files from the list are selected, they can be copied, moved, and viewed. The user can view or set file information, such as copy inhibit, delete inhibit, and others.
Select Current Directory	Allows users to switch the directory.
Set Filer Options	Sets the options that FILER uses when listing, copying, and deleting files. For example, you can have FILER warn you before overwriting a file with a COPY command.

Volume Information	Displays information about the current volume.

File Server Console Utility: FCONSOLE

The FCONSOLE menu utility is used by supervisors to view information about the network and to analyze and fine-tune its performance. Supervisors have full access to the features and functions of FCONSOLE, while users can only view limited information about the system. The supervisor can give other users rights to the FCONSOLE utility by making them *console operators*. They have rights similar to those of the supervisor.

The FCONSOLE main menu is shown here and is described in the list that follows.

Broadcast Console Message	Allows the operator to broadcast messages from the utility menu. This is important if the supervisor intends to bring the server down and needs to warn users to log off.
Change Current File Server	Allows the operator to switch to a different server to perform FCONSOLE tasks.
Connection Information	Displays a list of current users. The operator can view users' login information and network addresses, as well as send them messages.
Down File Server	This option can only be used by the supervisor.

File/Lock Activity	Displays the status of files and whether they are locked by a user or application.
LAN Driver Information	Displays information about LAN drivers. This information is helpful when trying to determine the network and node address of each card, or the board settings.
Purge All Salvageable Files	Removes all files that could possibly be recovered. This option is used to prevent any file from possibly being recovered by an unauthorized person.
Statistics	Displays the statistics of the file server, including its cache and network packet transmission information. The console MONITOR command can also be used.
Status	Displays the current status of the server, including the date and time. Can be used to change the date and time, and to disable login by new users. Login is usually disabled if you need to work on the server or down it. The Transaction Tracking system can also be disabled.
Version Information	Displays volume information.

Other Menu Utilities

There are several other menu utilities, such as those used to control printers and print queues, that are covered in separate chapters. You use the PRINTDEF menu utility to define printers, and you use PRINTCON to specify which printers to use for different types of print jobs. You can use the PCONSOLE command to control the print queue.

Network Hierarchy
And Security

Hierarchy of a NetWare System
NetWare Login and Account Security
NetWare File System Security
Directory and File Attributes

NetWare provides system managers with a full set of tools and features to control access to information on the server. Users are given rights to programs and information based on needs determined by the user, supervisor, and manager. A user may request access to files in a particular directory; the supervisor then enables them to access the directory, as if unlocking a door to it. Under NetWare, the task of managing and maintaining a network is distributed to a hierarchy of users. This chapter discusses the hierarchy as well as the security features used to control user access to the system.

Keep in mind that NetWare servers are used by many different people. Files created by users are stored in a central location, rather than at their personal workstations. These users put their trust in the supervisor or network managers to ensure that the file system is secure, reliable, and adequately backed up. After all, they are keeping their valuable data on the server and expect the network to be operational on a continuing basis.

TWENTY ONE

375

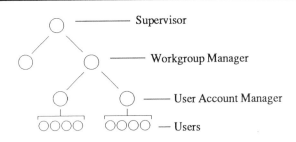

Figure 21-1.   Hierarchy of a NetWare 386 file system

Hierarchy of a NetWare System

Network hierarchy is established by the supervisor. It is unreasonable to expect the supervisor of a large network to manage the entire system, so NetWare allows management tasks to be assigned to other users. This hierarchy is shown in Figure 21-1. At the top is the supervisor and at the bottom are users with limited rights. Between them are two levels of

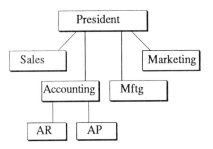

Figure 21-2.   A typical company organizational chart

managers who have control over users and the filing system. This control is almost always within a specific branch of the directory tree. A NetWare system may also have *operators* who are responsible for various hardware components, such as printers, and the operating system features that control them.

The hierarchy and directory structure of a NetWare file server can be compared to the organizational structures of a company, as you can see in Figures 21-2, 21-3, and 21-4. Figure 21-2 shows a company organizational chart with four departments. The manager (vice-president or controller) of each department is in charge of activities and personnel. The accounting department has two sub-departments—accounts receivable and accounts payable. Each department is headed by a separate department manager.

The user hierarchy of NetWare 386 translates this hierarchy into a structure similar to that shown in Figure 21-3. The supervisor is at the top with complete control. Deborah is assigned work group manager status over the users in the accounting department. As a work group manager, she can create new users on the network, a task that relates to her ability to hire new employees. To help her manage the departments, Deborah

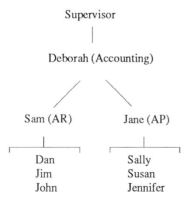

Figure 21-3.   The organizational chart transformed into a NetWare filing system

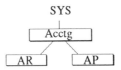

Figure 21-4.   A directory structure to match the organizational chart

designates Sam and Jane as user account managers for the accounts receivable and accounts payable departments, respectively.

Work group managers and user account managers are the two levels of management below the supervisor that can control users and their access to directories. The rights and responsibilities of each are similar, but work group managers have the additional abilities to add new users and create print queues.

Figure 21-4 shows how the organizational chart and user hierarchy translate to a directory structure on the NetWare 386 filing system. This is where NetWare's security features come into play. Deborah is given supervisor status in the accounting directory, which means she controls users and their access to the directory and its subdirectories. Deborah can then give Sam control of users in the AP (accounts payable) directory and Jane control of users in the AR (accounts receivable) directory. The three accounting clerks in each department are given rights in their respective accounting directories, but nowhere else on the system.

Keep in mind that users assigned as managers on the network may not always be real-life departmental managers. It may be better to designate people who are more familiar with the network as go-betweens for the departmental managers. These people may be better at interpreting the actual needs of the department manager into the requirements of the network.

Each level of user in the NetWare 386 hierarchy is discussed in the following sections.

Users

Everyone on the system starts out as a user with an account. A user is a person who has limited rights to the system, unless that user is the supervisor. Each user is created individually with the SYSCON menu utility. When a large number of users need to be created at the same time, the MAKEUSER or USERDEF utilities can be used. These are discussed in Chapter 25.

All new users automatically get a mailbox in the SYS:MAIL directory. This mailbox is a subdirectory named with the user identification. Each user also can have a personal login script that is stored in the mailbox directory.

User accounts can be restricted and controlled in the following ways:

- *Login restrictions* Users can be blocked from using the system, either completely or during a specific time frame. They can also be restricted to using a specific workstation. Login restrictions are used to control who gets on the system and when. Supervisors can set default login restrictions that affect all users, or they can set individual user restrictions.

- *Directory access rights* Users are blocked from using most directories until they are assigned certain rights. These rights may include the ability to list, read, write, create, and delete files, among others. A user's directory rights are inherited in the subdirectory, unless they are blocked by the supervisor or manager.

- *File access rights* Supervisors and managers can assign special properties to files that prevent users from copying, editing, or deleting them. Even though users may have access to a directory, their access to certain files can be blocked with *file attributes*. A number of attributes are available to protect or flag files in various ways.

The User GUEST

The user GUEST is created automatically by the operating system and can be used by anyone needing temporary access to the network. The account can be used to allow new employees to log into the system and run a training program, for example.

In most cases, supervisors may want to delete the GUEST account, or greatly restrict its rights. Since GUEST is a member of the EVERYONE group, users logging in as GUEST have any rights you assign to EVERYONE. As a security precaution, you can remove GUEST from the EVERYONE group, and then assign access rights to GUEST as needed.

Always require a password for the GUEST account, and require that the password be changed on a regular basis. If a new employee is temporarily assigned to the account, be sure to change the password before they log in.

System Supervisor

The supervisor has full access to the system files and control over the security system. He or she manages the user accounting system if it is installed and sets default login and account restrictions. The supervisor also designates users as work group managers, user account managers, and operators.

Part of the supervisor's responsibility is to determine who will have access to the system and at what level. In this role the supervisor may need to interact with company managers and the users themselves. Users may request access to certain files or directories, but it may be necessary for the supervisor to get approval before granting the user those rights.

Supervisors who manage large networks undoubtedly keep busy training managers and users, answering questions, and resolving problems. They also are involved in maintenance and performance monitoring. Because of these tasks, supervisors may find it necessary to assign some tasks to work group managers and user account managers. These tasks may include the following:

- Managing users

- Backing up the server

- File archiving and purging

- Management of print servers, print queues, and the attached printers

- Disk management and optimization tasks

- Emergency activities such as system shutdown

In addition, supervisors may need to delegate user training to company-trained staff or an outside firm. Proper training is crucial to the operation of a network.

Groups

Groups are collections of users put together to make the task of managing a network easier. A group typically correlates to a departmental work group or a group of managers. Groups are usually given access to specific directories and the files in those directories. In Figures 21-3 and 21-4, the clerks in each of the accounting departments represent separate groups. By including the clerks in a group, it becomes easy to grant them rights in their respective directories.

While groups are normally used to grant and revoke directory and file access rights, they are also convenient for messaging and mail systems. For example, you can send a message to a group of users called MANAGERS, or a group of users called TEMPS. To send a message to every user on the network, you can use the system- created group EVERYONE.

In most cases directory and file access rights are assigned to groups of users, rather than one user at a time. Rarely is any other directory set up for use by a single user, except for personal directories. In fact directory structures should be designed for group use. For example, programs can be stored in directories that are available to all users, while data files can be stored in directories that are only accessible to special groups.

Typically a group is created after users are created. Users are then added to groups. Any number of groups can be created, and any user can be added to any group. In this way you can easily match group structures to directory structures or company organizational charts. For example, you can create a group called MANAGERS to include departmental managers. On the other hand, you could create a group called GOLFCLUB for users who belong to the company golf club.

As an example, Figure 21-5 shows the users in the accounting department from the previous example. Users can belong to more than one group, as shown in the figure. The AR group includes the four users in the

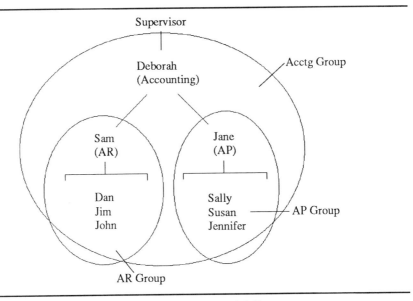

Figure 21-5. Users can be placed into several different groups

accounts receivable department, and the AP group contains the four users in the accounts payable department. The ACCTG group includes all users in the accounting department, including the pivotal work group manager, Deborah, who can manage or send messages to either AP, AR, or the entire ACCTG group.

The EVERYONE Group

All users belong to the group EVERYONE. They are assigned to this group when initially created as a user by the supervisor or supervisor equivalent. Supervisors can then grant directory rights to the EVERYONE group or broadcast system-wide messages. Since the group EVERYONE is automatically assigned Read and File Scan rights in the SYS:PUBLIC directory, all members have access to the NetWare programs and utilities in the directory, unless they are removed from the EVERYONE group.

Work Group Managers
And User Account Managers

Workgroup managers can be assigned the task of creating new users and managing the accounts of users in their group. A user account manager cannot create new users but can perform the other tasks of the work group manager. Work group managers are analogous to department managers who can hire employees; user account managers are analogous to assistant managers who take some of the load off the manager.

Work group managers are created by the supervisor to assist with the creation of users and to manage those users. In some cases the supervisor may prefer to create all users so work group managers would not be required. User account managers would then be created to manage the users of the system.

Keep the following in mind with regard to work group or user account managers:

- Managers should be created to parallel the management structure of the company and be put in charge of users who belong to specific departments or divisions.

- The Supervisor or Access Control right must be given to managers who need to assign user access rights in directories.

- Managers can only control the users and groups they create or those assigned to them by the supervisor.

Work group managers can perform the following tasks that user account managers cannot perform:

- Create new users

- Create, manage, and delete print queue

Work group managers and user account managers both can perform the following:

- Manage the accounts of users they create or those that have been assigned to them

- Change user account balances in the accounting system

- Change account restrictions, such as login time and designated workstations

- Change a user's password

- Change group status

- Change security equivalences

- Assign a user to a group

- Assign a user as a user account manager, but only for users they manage

Work group managers and user account managers must be assigned file rights before they can do any of the following:

- Modify trustee directory assignments

- Modify trustee file assignments

- Modify volume restrictions

- Modify disk space restrictions

Some restrictions do apply to the managers:

- Work group managers cannot create a user and make that user security-equivalent to the supervisor, nor can they create another work group manager

- Work group managers and user account managers can manage only the users they create or that have been assigned to them

- Both the work group manager and the user account manager are restricted from modifying the login restrictions of their own accounts, unless they have been allowed to manage them by the supervisor

Keep in mind that both work group managers and user account managers must be assigned Supervisor or Access Control directory rights. You should create a directory structure to match the users and applications they manage, and then assign them the appropriate rights to that structure. Rights are covered under "NetWare File System and Security" later in this chapter.

Operators

A network operator is a regular user who has been assigned additional privileges to a particular service of a Novell NetWare server, such as the console or a printer. An operator is more of an attendant than a manager. For example, the queue operator makes sure the printer has the right forms or is working properly.

FCONSOLE Operator

The FCONSOLE operator can run the FCONSOLE utility, which monitors the activity and efficiency of the network and makes adjustments to it. Typically FCONSOLE is used by maintenance personnel who are enhancing or repairing the system or by programmers who are developing special applications. The FCONSOLE operator status is given to a user by the supervisor using a special option in the FCONSOLE menu utility. Note, however, that only the supervisor can down the server with FCONSOLE.

MONITOR Operator

MONITOR is a NetWare loadable module that runs on the server console. Any user can select options on the screen if it is not locked. MONITOR provides many of the same features as FCONSOLE.

Print Server Operator

The print server operator has rights to manage a print server, including the ability to disable and reenable it in order to change or add to the printer configuration.

Queue Operator

A queue operator is given the right to control the activities of a print queue. A print queue is like a waiting line for print jobs at the printer. Each job sent to the printer is stacked in the queue. The queue operator can rearrange the jobs in the queue or remove them. The supervisor assigns queue operators for each queue that exists using a special menu option in the PCONSOLE menu utility. Typically each printer has one queue. However, a printer might have more than one queue to receive print jobs from different sources at a different priority. A queue can also service more than one printer.

Operators should be chosen wisely. Like any manager, they should be well trained, trustworthy, and accountable for managing the resources to which they are assigned.

NetWare Login and Account Security

Security on a network is administered in four ways. The first restricts how and when users can log into the system itself, and the rest control user access to directories and files. The methods are listed here and described in the following sections:

- *Login restrictions* Used to control access to the server.

- *Trustee rights* Used to grant or revoke a user's rights in a directory.

- *Inherited rights mask* Assigned to a *directory* by a supervisor or manager to control access to the directory by users.

- *File access rights* Used to control access to specific files in a directory.

Login Security

The first level of security protects the entire server from unauthorized users, or users who may attempt to log in at unauthorized machines. To log in, a user must specify a login name and an optional password, as described here:

- *User name* The name of a user's personal account in the NetWare filing system. In most cases a user's actual name is used. For reasons discussed later, try to limit the user name to eight characters.

- *Password* An optional access keyword that is known only to the user. The supervisor has the ability to change a user's password at any time. Although passwords are optional, their use is recommended.

If a user enters the wrong user name or password, he or she is denied access to the system but can try again. The supervisor can regulate how often a user can attempt to log into the system by using the Intruder Lockout feature. This feature prevents an unauthorized user from trying several different names and passwords in an attempt to gain access. After a while the system locks out further attempts.

When a user gains access to the system, the system login script is executed, as well as the user login script if it exists. At this point the user comes under the security umbrella of the filing system.

Password and Account Restrictions

The supervisor or account manager can control the login procedure in a number of ways. The most important tool is the password. The SYSCON menu utility is used to create users and establish password and account restrictions. The options to require passwords and define their use are

```
┌─────────────────────────────────────────────────────────┐
│          Account Restrictions For User BONNIE             │
├─────────────────────────────────────────────────────────┤
│ Account Disabled:                   No                    │
│ Account Has Expiration Date:        No                    │
│    Date Account Expires:                                  │
│ Limit Concurrent Connections:       No                    │
│    Maximum Connections:                                   │
│ Allow User To Change Password:      Yes                   │
│ Require Password:                   Yes                   │
│    Minimum Password Length:         5                     │
│ Force Periodic Password Changes:    Yes                   │
│    Days Between Forced Changes:     40                    │
│    Date Password Expires:           June 30, 1990         │
│    Limit Grace Logins:              Yes                   │
│       Grace Logins Allowed:         6                     │
│       Remaining Grace Logins:       6                     │
│ Require Unique Passwords:           No                    │
└─────────────────────────────────────────────────────────┘
```

Figure 21-6.   The Account Restrictions menu

available on the Account Restrictions menu shown in Figure 21-6. This menu is accessed after selecting a specific user, or the supervisor can access a similar screen to set default login restrictions for all users. The following options appear on the menu:

- *Account Disabled* Set this option to Yes to disable a user's account. This may be necessary if the user is on vacation or leave.

- *Account Has Expiration Date* Can be used to set an expiration date for temporary accounts.

- *Limit Concurrent Connections* Prevents users from logging into more than one machine.

- *Allow User to Change Password* This option is used to specify whether users can change their own passwords or not. Most user accounts, except GUEST, should have this right.

- *Require Password* A password can be required for a specified user. If Yes is selected, values can be specified for the remaining options described here.

- *Minimum Password Length*   The supervisor can specify the minimum length of a password to increase security.

- *Force Periodic Password Changes*   To improve security, the supervisor can force periodic password changes for periods specified in days. The default is to force changes every 40 days if the option is selected. You can also select a password expiration date.

- *Limit Grace Logins*   Grace logins are the number of times a user can log in with an expired password. This gives them a chance to change the password. The default is six times if the option is chosen.

- *Require Unique Passwords*   If this option is set, the system will not let users specify a password used as one of the last 10 passwords.

Intruder Detection and Lockout

An intruder may attempt to log into the system if they know another user's account name. They may try several likely passwords, such as a user's middle name, the name of a friend, or the name of a spouse. Intruder detection lets you limit the number of unsuccessful attempts that can take place during a login.

The Intruder Detection/Lockout screen shown here can be accessed by the supervisor by choosing Supervisor Options on the SYSCON main menu. When Yes is selected in the Detect Intruders field, the feature is activated. The threshold number of attempts is specified, which is the number of times an intruder can attempt to access the system before they are locked out. The system prevents further attempts beyond this number and for the amount of time specified in the menu.

```
┌─────────────────────────────────────────────────────────────┐
│              Intruder Detection/Lockout                       │
├─────────────────────────────────────────────────────────────┤
│Detect Intruders:              Yes                             │
│                                                               │
│Intruder Detection Threshold                                   │
│Incorrect Login Attempts:      7                               │
│Bad Login Count Retention Time: 0  Days   0  Hours   30 Minutes│
│                                                               │
│Lock Account After Detection:  Yes                             │
│   Length Of Account Lockout:  0  Days   0  Hours   15 Minutes │
└─────────────────────────────────────────────────────────────┘
```

Station Restriction

The SYSCON utility presents a User Information menu for each user account. The options on this menu are discussed in future chapters. One option, called Station Restrictions, restricts the physical station a user logs into. This can be done to prevent users from logging into an unsupervised station or to ensure that users log into a diskless workstation. For example, you can prevent sensitive data from being copied to disk and carried from the building by requiring users to log into diskless workstations.

Time Restrictions

Time restrictions can be set to prevent users from logging in during specific times, such as scheduled maintenance or backup periods. The system manager can set default time restrictions for all users on the system or for individual users.

Time restrictions are set in the SYSCON menu utility using a screen similar to that shown here:

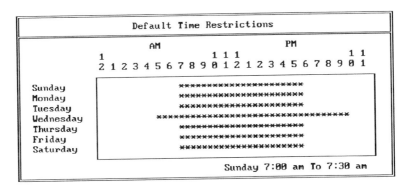

In the example, the login times are set for 7:00 AM to 6:00 PM, except for extended maintenance periods on Wednesday.

Volume Restrictions

The amount of space a user can access in a specific volume can be controlled by selecting the Volume Restrictions option on an individual's User Information menu. The menu shown here appears:

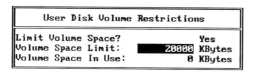

To limit space, answer Yes to Limit Volume Space, and then specify the amount of space to limit in KBytes.

NetWare File System Security

The NetWare filing system is protected with three levels of combined and effective security, as outlined here:

- *Trustee rights* Users must be granted trustee rights to a directory before they can access it. Once granted, the rights trickle down to subdirectories unless blocked by the inherited rights mask. The GRANT and REVOKE commands as well as the SYSCON and FILER menu utilities can be used by supervisors or managers to give or take away these rights.

- *Inherited rights mask* When users are granted trustee rights in directories, those rights trickle down to subdirectories, unless the supervisor or manager applies an inherited rights mask to the subdirectory. Rights that a user might inherit from the parent directory are then blocked. The inherited rights mask is like a barrier applied to all users in the subdirectory. However, the barrier can be overridden for users if the supervisor or manager grants them specific trustee rights in the directory that was masked. The ALLOW command and the FILER utility can be used to set the inherited rights mask of a directory.

- *File rights*   The right to access specific files within a directory can be granted or revoked for all users or specific users.

The actual rights a user has to a directory and its files are determined by examining all the rights just outlined at each individual directory and subdirectory level. These rights are referred to as *effective rights*. The effective rights a user has in a subdirectory are the trustee rights of the parent directory, less the rights revoked by the inherited rights mask, if any. However, a new set of trustee rights can be granted to a user in the subdirectory to override an inherited rights mask.

Keep in mind that supervisors or managers use the inherited rights as a general purpose security mask to limit the access of *all* users to a subdirectory. Trustee rights grant or revoke rights to *individual* users and can override the inherited rights masks of a subdirectory. Each set of rights is discussed in the following sections.

By default, all rights are allowed by the inherited rights mask, unless the mask is changed for a directory. Therefore, the trustee rights a user has in a directory carry down to a subdirectory if the mask is not changed.

Note: The maximum rights mask for NetWare 286 is functionally different than the inherited rights mask in NetWare 386. If working on a mixed system, refer to your NetWare 286 system manual for an explanation of the maximum rights mask.

Trustee and Inherited Rights

The following list shows the rights that can be assigned or revoked with trustee rights or the inherited rights mask.

A (Access Control)	The Access Control right is similar to the Supervisor right in its scope, but it can be blocked in subdirectories by the inherited

rights mask. Thus, the Access Control right can be used to give a user complete control within a single directory. The supervisor can modify the trustee list and inherited rights mask of the directory.

C (Create)   Users with this right can create new files and subdirectories.

E (Erase)   Users with this right can remove files and subdirectories.

F (File Scan)   Users with this right can list the files in the directory.

M (Modify)   Users with this right can change the name and attributes of a directory and its subdirectories.

R (Read)   Users with this right can open and read a file in the assigned directory and subdirectory.

S (Supervisor)   The Supervisor right gives a user complete control in a directory and its subdirectories. The right cannot be removed by an inherited rights mask. A user with Supervisor status in a directory controls its subdirectories without limitations. Note that the Access Control right is similar, but it can be blocked in subdirectories by the inherited rights mask. Users with Supervisor rights can grant other users rights to the directory, its subdirectories and its files, including the Supervisor right. The Supervisor right is usually granted to work group managers and user account managers.

W (Write)   Users with this right can open and write to files in the directory and subdirectory.

Effective Rights

The effective rights of users in a directory are the rights they inherit from a parent directory, or the trustee rights they have been granted specifically in the directory. Trustee rights override all other rights, but inherited rights can be blocked by the inherited rights mask. Unless a user has been granted specific trustee rights, his or her rights in a directory are the inherited rights from the parent directory, less those rights blocked by the inherited rights mask.

Because users may have the Erase trustee right does not mean they can remove directories or files. The supervisor may limit this right in the directory for all users by applying an inherited rights mask.

The following examples help explain how effective rights are established:

- Initially a new directory called ACCTG and a new user called John are created. The directory is shown in Figure 21-7 under A. The blank square brackets indicate that John has not yet been granted rights in the new directory.

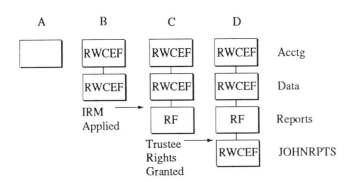

Figure 21-7. How trustee rights and the inherited rights mask affect effective rights

- John is granted the Read, Write, Create, Erase, and File Scan rights in the ACCTG directory. A subdirectory called DATA is then created. The supervisor does not alter the inherited rights mask in the new directory, so John's rights in the ACCTG directory carry down to the new directory. The default inherited rights mask allows all rights. This is shown in Figure 21-7 under B.

- In example C, a subdirectory of DATA called REPORTS is created by the supervisor and an inherited rights mask is applied to block the Write, Create, and Erase rights. John's effective rights in the REPORTS directory are Read and File Scan, due to the mask.

- In example D, John has requested that he would like to change some of the reports for his personal use. A subdirectory of REPORTS called JOHNRPTS is created. Initially, John's Read and File Scan rights in reports copy down. These rights are insufficient for editing files in the directory, so the supervisor grants John the trustee rights Read, Write, Create, Erase, and File Scan, which effectively override the limitations imposed by the inherited rights mask in the REPORTS directory.

As you can see, the system is practical and flexible. John could be given the Supervisor right in the JOHNRPTS directory, granting him complete control of the directory and any subdirectories he creates. This would be appropriate since the directory is used only by John.

Assigning Rights to Users

It is important that you evaluate the rights users need in each program and data directory on the system. The following sections point out some of the factors you need to consider when assigning rights.

Program directory   Users must be able to execute applications in program directories. Program directories may include the DOS directories or the directory that holds the program files for a word processing program. The minimum required rights for running programs are Read and File Scan. Since all users are members of the EVERYONE group, they already have Read and File Scan rights in the SYS:PUBLIC directory. If you create

DOS subdirectories in the SYS:PUBLIC directory, the same rights are in effect.

Data directory   Since files need to be created and altered in the data directory, users must have the Read, Write, Create, and File Scan rights. The Erase right is also useful in some cases, but could be damaging in the hands of the wrong users.

Work group managers   A work group manager is generally given complete control of a directory and its subdirectories and should be granted the Supervisor or Access Control right.

User account managers   User account managers can be granted the Access Control right, which gives them the ability to modify the trustee rights of other users, and the inherited rights mask of a directory. The supervisor or the work group manager can limit a user account manager's access to subdirectories with the inherited rights mask.

Groups   Groups usually are given Read and File Scan rights in program directories and Read, Write, Create, Erase, and File Scan rights in data directories. Chaos may result if you give an entire group Access Control, Modify, and Supervisor rights. Group members should be granted these advanced rights individually.

Directories and subdirectories   If a user is to be given complete control of a directory, including its subdirectories, give that user the Supervisor right. To give a user rights that can be limited in subdirectories, give the user the Access Control right. If that user needs to create subdirectories, give him or her the Create right.

Drop box directories   A drop box directory is created by granting only the Create right to a user. In this directory a user can create a file and write to it, but when the file is closed, it can no longer be seen or listed. The file can be viewed only by users with Read and File Scan rights.

User personal directories   In most cases, users should have complete access to their personal directory so they can create subdirectories and files as they please. They may even want to give other users access rights to their subdirectories, assuming they have rights to do so.

Controlling file access   The Read, Write, Create, Erase, and File Scan rights can be granted to or revoked from users at the file level. A user with the Access Control right can modify another user's access to a file. Users with the Modify right can rename the file and change its attributes, which are discussed later. A user with Supervisor rights has all rights to all files in a directory and its subdirectories.

Security Equivalence

A quick method that supervisors can use to grant rights to a directory is to make one user *security equivalent* to another, which means the other user inherits all of the first user's trustee rights and security restrictions, except for the password. The SYSCON menu utility has an option for assigning security equivalence. This option is available on the User Information menu for each user.

Another more informal method of making a user equivalent to another is to add them to a group. The user then automatically inherits all the trustee rights in the directories assigned to the group.

Directory and File Attributes

The rights or restrictions a user has in a directory are determined by their effective rights. In addition, directories can be given certain properties that prevent users from renaming and deleting them. Directories also can be designated as hidden or system directories. These attributes are assigned with the FLAGDIR command or the FILER utility.

At the file level, attributes can be assigned to prevent files from being copied, deleted, or even attacked by viruses. File attributes are applied with the FLAG command or the FILER utility.

Directory Attributes

Directories can be given the attributes listed here by those who have Modify and Parental rights in the parent directory. The FLAGDIR command is used to assign these attributes.

D (Delete Inhibit)	Prevents users from erasing directories, even if they have the Delete right.
R (Rename Inhibit)	Restricts users from renaming a directory, even if they have the Modify right.
P (Purge)	Causes files in the directory to be purged immediately if they are deleted. Purged files cannot be recovered with SALVAGE.
H (Hidden)	Hides the directory so it cannot be seen in a directory listing by any users. The directory cannot be removed as long as it has the H attribute. The directory appears when NDIR is used if the user has File Scan rights.
S or Sy (System)	Indicates the directory is used by the system and will not appear in a directory listing. The directory appears when NDIR is used if the user has File Scan rights.
V (Visible)	This attribute applies only to Macintosh directories and relates to the inaccessible gray folders.

File Attributes

You can protect the files in a directory in various ways by changing file attributes. File attributes can prevent accidental erasures or changes in specific files. Files used by several network users at once should be marked Shareable. The complete list of file attributes is shown here. These attributes are assigned with the FLAG command or with the FILER utility. A complete discussion can be found in Chapter 24.

A (Archive Needed)	Automatically assigned to files by Net-Ware if they have been modified since the last backup. The attribute is used during a modified-only backup to determine which files should be backed up.
C (Copy Inhibit)	Restricts the copy rights of users logged in at a Macintosh workstation, even if the user has Read and File Scan trustee rights in the directory. If users have the Modify trustee right, they can remove the Copy Inhibit attribute and copy the file.
D (Delete Inhibit)	Prevents users from deleting a file, even if the user has Erase trustee rights in the directory. If users have the Modify trustee right, they can remove the Delete Inhibit attribute and erase the file.
E (Execute Only)	Prevents EXE and COM files from being altered or copied and can be used to prevent virus infections. The attribute can be assigned only by the supervisor, but should be used with caution and only if a complete backup of the EXE or COM files exists. Files not written to Novell NetWare specifications may lock up.
H (Hidden)	Files with this attribute do not appear in DOS DIR listings and cannot be deleted or copied. The files appear when the NetWare NDIR command is used, however.
I (Indexed)	Indexes the FAT (file allocation table) entry of large files to improve access from the hard drive. NetWare automatically in-

	dexes files when they exceed 64 regular FAT entries.
P (Purge)	When the Purge attribute is assigned to a file, it is automatically purged from the system when deleted. The SALVAGE command cannot be used to recover the file.
Ra (Read Audit)	The Read Audit attribute is associated with the NetWare Audit Trail System used to track who reads from a database file. It is the "Big Brother" attribute. Read Auditing is used in conjunction with the Write Audit attribute.
Ro/Rw (Read Only/ Read Write)	When files are marked with the Read Only attribute, they cannot be written to, erased or renamed, even if the user has Write and Erase trustee rights in the directory. The attribute automatically assigns the Delete Inhibit and Rename Inhibit attributes. Users with the Modify trustee right can remove the Read Only attribute and then write to, rename, or erase the file. The Read Write attribute can be set to remove the Read Only attribute.
R (Rename Inhibit)	The Rename Inhibit attribute restricts users from renaming a file. If users have the Modify trustee right, they can remove the Rename Inhibit attribute and rename the file.
S (Shareable)	The Shareable attribute allows files to be used by more than one user. The attribute is usually assigned to database files, which are normally accessed by two or more network users.
Sy (System File)	Files marked with the System attribute do not appear in DOS DIR listings, but ap-

pear when the NDIR command is used. The attribute also prevents files from being deleted or copied.

T (Transactional)

Indicates that the file is protected by the transaction tracking system.

W (Write Audit)

The Write Audit attribute is associated with the NetWare audit trail system used to track who writes to a database file. Write auditing makes continuous backup possible, and when combined with the Read Attribute, provides greater security.

Introduction to User, Directory, And File Management

Steps to Creating a New User with SYSCON
Creating Directories for Groups
Creating Groups
Limiting Directory Access with the Inherited Rights Mask
Creating Work Group and User Account Managers
Managing Files
Installing Applications

This chapter shows how to create users and their personal directories. Through exercises you learn how to use the SYSCON and FILER menu utilities. Both supervisors and work group managers should read through this chapter to gain an understanding of the process. More detailed information on users, directories, and files is presented in the next few chapters.

Steps to Creating
A New User with SYSCON

Before proceeding with the steps to create a user, you should know that there are reasons for limiting user account names to eight characters. If you created the system login script in Chapter 19, recall that it maps drive F to a user's personal directory with the following command:

MAP F:=SYS:USERS\%LOGIN_NAME

The parameter %LOGIN_NAME is replaced with the user's login name, causing the command to create a drive mapping to the user's personal directory. However, since directory names are limited to eight characters, an error occurs if the login name exceeds eight characters. For example, if a user named ALEXANDRA logged in, the command would attempt to map a directory named SYS:USERS\ALEXANDRA, which cannot exist because the name exceeds eight characters.

As a point of interest, a similar error occurs when a supervisor logs in because the user name exceeds eight characters. However, the following command detects the supervisor login and maps drive F to the SYSTEM directory:

IF "%LOGIN_NAME" = "SUPERVISOR" THEN MAP F:=SYS:SYSTEM

Creating a User with SYSCON

To create a new user with SYSCON, follow the steps outlined here:

1. Start the SYSCON (System Console) utility by typing the command **SYSCON**.

2. In a moment, the SYSCON Available Topics menu appears, as shown here:

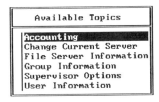

3. Select **User Information** to display the User Names menu. A screen similar to this one appears:

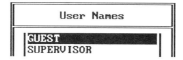

Other names may appear in the menu if you upgraded from another server.

4. The User Names menu gives you a chance to select an existing user and edit the account parameters, or to create a new user. Press INS to create a new user. When the User Name box appears, type a name for a new user, such as your own name, and press ENTER. For the examples in this chapter, CLYDE is created.

The name appears in the User Names menu when you press ENTER. A new user account with the following features now exists, but the rights and restrictions of this account are limited.

- New users automatically are included in the group EVERYONE and have all the rights of this group, including the Read and File Scan rights in the SYS:PUBLIC directory.

- New users are assigned an ID number.

- The user ID number also identifies a subdirectory of the SYS:MAIL directory used to hold their personal login script and files from electronic mail.

- Login restrictions such as password requirements and time restrictions may exist if system-wide default settings have been set by the supervisor. Default settings are discussed in Chapter 25.

Modifying the User's Account

Once a user is created, the account can be restricted in various ways through the User Information menu. First select the user's name from the User Names menu. Press ENTER to display the User Information screen shown here:

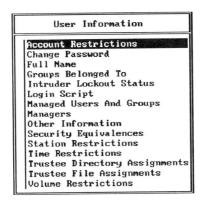

The options on the User Information menu are briefly described in the following list. Most of the options are set by a supervisor or manager and can be viewed by the user. Each option is discussed in more detail in Chapter 25.

- *Account Restrictions* Used to set security options such as the requirement for unique passwords, forced periodic password changes, and minimum password length. Note that default settings can be imposed on all users by the supervisor from the Supervisor Options menu, which will be discussed in Chapter 25.

- *Change Password* Changes the selected user's password.

- *Full Name* Used to specify the full name of the selected user.

- *Groups Belonged To* Lists the groups the selected user belongs to or allows the user to be added to an existing group.

- *Intruder Lockout Status* The supervisor or manager can lock the user's account with this option. Additionally, the number of unsuccessful login attempts can be changed as a security feature to prevent intruders from gaining access to the system if they know the user's login name but not the password.

- *Login Script* Used to create or edit the selected user's login script.

- *Managed Users and Groups* Used to view or change the users and groups managed by the selected user.

- *Managers* Used to view or change the managers who have control over the selected user's account.

- *Other Information* Displays information about the selected user's last login date, console operator status, disk space allocation, and identification number.

- *Security Equivalences* Used to view or change the security equivalence of the selected user.

- *Station Restrictions* Used to view or change the selected user's station restrictions.

- *Time Restrictions* Used to view or change the time the user is allowed to login to the server.

- *Trustee Directory Assignments* Used to view or change the selected user's trustee directory assignments.

- *Trustee File Assignments* Used to view or change the selected user's trustee file assignments.

- *Volume Restrictions* Used to view or change the selected user's disk space restrictions.

Personal Login Script

Personal login scripts can be created for each user, or users can create or edit the script themselves. In most cases users create and edit personal login scripts to match their own needs. The system login script should be maintained by the supervisor as a means of setting generic login options according to the groups or workstations logging in. These options are covered fully in Chapter 28.

Supervisors should be aware that each login script requires a minimum of approximately 4K of disk space. This may prohibit the use of personal login scripts on large networks that have limited disk space. For example, it would be a waste of disk space to create personal login scripts in an educational environment where hundreds of users have temporary accounts.

For those systems that do require the use of personal login scripts, an example is shown here. From the User Information menu, type **L** to highlight the Login Script option and press ENTER. Type the command shown here and press ESC to save it.

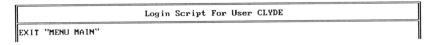

Login Script For User CLYDE

EXIT "MENU MAIN"

This command displays the main menu. When the user's personal login script executes, the main menu is displayed to assist in using the system. Press ESC after typing the command and answer Yes to the save request.

Creating the User's Personal Directory

Users can have personal directories where they have full access to create new files and subdirectories. All users' personal directories should branch from a directory called SYS:USERS or SYS:HOME, as Novell recommends. To create a personal directory for a user, follow these steps:

1. From the User Information menu, select **Trustee Directory Assignments**. A screen similar to the following appears:

Trustee Directory Assignments

SYS:MAIL/4000002   [RWCEMF]

2. The user's access rights to the SYS:MAIL directory rights are listed on the right. Press INS to create a new directory. The following window appears:

Directory In Which Trustee Should Be Added

3. You can type the full name of the directory, including the server and volume name, or you can press the INS key to select from the list. When you press INS the first time, a list of possible servers appears. Select the server to create the directory on and press ENTER. The file server name is inserted in the directory path. A list of available volumes then appears.

4. Highlight the volume you want to use (SYS for this example) and press ENTER. The Network Directories screen appears, as shown here:

```
NetWork Directories
▲ NETWARE
  PIX
  PUB-DATA
  PUBLIC
  SYSTEM
  TEST
  TOM
  USERS
  WORD
```

If a SYS:USERS directory already exists, type **U** to select it. If not, press ESC and type **USERS** after the colon in the directory path window.

5. Type / (slash) and the new user's account name—**CLYDE** for this example, as shown here:

```
Directory In Which Trustee Should Be Added

FS1/SYS:USERS/CLYDE
```

6. Press ENTER when the full directory path is specified. NetWare asks if you want to create the new directory. Select Yes and press ENTER.

The new directory appears in the Trustee Directory Assignments window, as shown here.

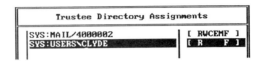

SYSCON always assigns the Read and File Scan trustee rights to new directories created for a user. The next section explains how to grant additional rights to the user.

Granting Trustee Rights to Directories

After creating a personal directory for users, you can grant them trustee rights to the directory. Remember that these rights are inherited in subdirectories unless blocked with an inherited rights mask. In most cases you can grant users supervisory rights in their own directories. For this example, assume CLYDE must have the Read, Write, Create, Erase, and File Scan rights in his new directory.

1. With the Trustee Assignments menu still open, highlight the directory created in the last section and press ENTER.

2. The Trustee Rights Granted menu appears, as shown on the left in the following illustration. Press INS to see the Trustee Rights Not Granted menu, as shown on the right.

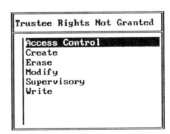

3. The File Scan and Read rights are automatically granted. To grant additional rights, arrow key to each and press F5 (Mark). For this example, the Create, Write, and Erase rights are marked. Press ENTER to add the new rights to the Trustee Rights Granted menu.

Once you have assigned all the rights, you can return to the Trustee Assignments menu by pressing ESC. The directory now displays the rights you granted as single characters to the right of the directory name, as shown here:

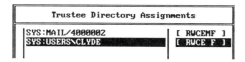

Repeat these steps to assign trustee rights to additional users. However, keep in mind that many directories are shared by other users, so it may be easier to add the new user to a group that already has trustee rights in directories.

Assigning a Password to a User

Each user should have a password to improve system security. There are two ways to do this. With the first method, you assign the initial password. With the second method, you require the user to enter a password the first time they log in.

To assign a password to a user, choose the **User Information** option of the SYSCON menu and select a user from the list. At the User Information menu, select **Change Password**. Type a new password, and then type it again for verification.

To have users create their own passwords the first time they log in, follow these steps:

1. Choose the **User Information** option of the SYSCON menu and select a user from the list.

2. At the User Information menu, select **Account Restrictions** to display the menu shown in Figure 22-1. Arrow down to Require Password and type **Y** in the field.

This initiates password security for the user and causes other password options to appear in the menu. The first time the user logs in, the user is asked for a password. You can assign a password now by selecting **Change Password** from the User Information menu. You can also change

```
┌─────────────────────────────────────────────────────┐
│         Account Restrictions For User CLYDE           │
├─────────────────────────────────────────────────────┤
│Account Disabled:                    No                │
│Account Has Expiration Date:         No                │
│   Date Account Expires:                               │
│Limit Concurrent Connections:        No                │
│    Maximum Connections:                               │
│Allow User To Change Password:       Yes               │
│Require Password:                    Yes               │
│   Minimum Password Length:          5                 │
│Force Periodic Password Changes:     Yes               │
│   Days Between Forced Changes:      40                │
│   Date Password Expires:            July 2, 1990      │
│   Limit Grace Logins:               Yes               │
│      Grace Logins Allowed:          6                 │
│      Remaining Grace Logins:        6                 │
│Require Unique Passwords:            No                │
└─────────────────────────────────────────────────────┘
```

Figure 22-1.   The Account Restrictions menu

some of the password options that appear on the menu. These options are discussed further in Chapter 25.

Creating Directories for Groups

Directories can be created in NetWare using the SYSCON or FILER utilities or the DOS MD (Make Directory) command. While any of these methods may be used, SYSCON makes the job easier because you can create directories and grant rights at the same time. The methods for doing this are covered in this section.

Creating a Data Directory
For the Group EVERYONE

It is a good idea to create a directory in which users can store files to share with other users. With the following steps you create such a directory called SYS:PUB-DATA. You grant all users Read, Write, Create, Erase, and File

Scan rights in the directory by assigning those rights to the EVERYONE group.

1. Type **SYSCON** to start the SYSCON menu utility if it is not already running.

2. At the main menu, select **Group Information**.

3. Since the object is to create a new directory for the group EVERY-ONE, select **EVERYONE** from the Group Names menu and press ENTER.

4. The Group Information menu appears, as shown here:

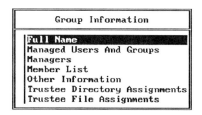

Select **Trustee Directory Assignments** from the menu to display a menu similar to the following:

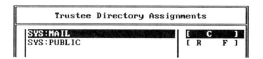

Note that EVERYONE already has Create rights in the SYS:MAIL directory as well as Read and File Scan rights in SYS:PUBLIC.

5. Groups can be made trustees of directories in the same way users are granted trustee rights to a directory. Press INS at the Trustee Assignments menu.

6. A screen appears where the path of the trustee directory can be typed. You can simply type the path, or press INS to get help from SYSCON. If you press INS, SYSCON displays a list of servers, then a list of volumes, and then one or more lists of directories

for you to choose from. For this example, simply type the text as shown in the following illustration and press ENTER.

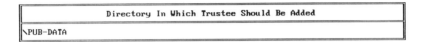

Note: that you must type the file server and volume names only if they are not the current defaults. You can type **\PUB-DATA** if the directory is on the current server and volume.

7. Answer Yes when asked to verify the creation of the directory.

The new Trustee Directory Assignments menu appears similar to the following:

Note that NetWare automatically grants Read and File Scan rights in the directory. To add rights, follow these steps:

1. Highlight the new directory and press ENTER.

2. When the Trustee Rights Granted menu appears, press INS to display the Trustee Rights Not Granted menu.

3. Use the arrow keys to highlight the Create right and press F5 to mark it.

4. Repeat this step for the Erase and Write right. Press ENTER when done and press ESC to return to the Trustee Directory Assignments menu. The final screen looks similar to the following:

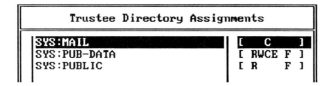

Note: You need not grant the EVERYONE group additional rights, but a work group manager or user account manager may need the rights to manage users and the directory.

Now users in the EVERYONE group can create and edit files in the SYS:PUB-DATA directory. Consider the directory a place where users can store files others need to view, copy, or edit. Note that the Erase right is optional because some users should not be able to erase files.

Mapping the New Public Directory

You can include a MAP command in the system login script to map the new SYS:PUB-DATA directory to drive G (use another letter if G is taken). Placing the mapping in the system login script and using a specific drive letter allows users collectively to make reference to the directory. Select **Supervisor Options** from the SYSCON Available Topics menu, and then select System Login Script. Arrow down below the first MAP command and insert the following command:

MAP G:=SYS:PUB-DATA

Creating Groups

Groups are created to make the job of assigning directory rights easier and to make group messaging and electronic mail possible. All users belong to the EVERYONE group by default. By granting trustee rights to EVERY-ONE, you grant rights to all users, and by sending messages to EVERY-ONE, you send messages to all users. Other useful groups might consist of departmental employees, managers, temporary personnel, or users working on special projects.

This section demonstrates how to create a group of departmental managers. The group is granted full trustee rights to the PUB-DATA directory so they can be designated as work group managers or user account managers by the supervisor. The managers then can control the activities and rights of other users in the directories. For example, a department manager can be granted control of the employees they manage and can erase files or modify their attributes.

Creating a Manager Group

You can substitute any group name or user name in the example shown here to fit your own needs. To create a group, follow these steps:

1. Start the SYSCON program if it is not already loaded.

2. Select **Group Information** from the Available Topics menu.

3. When the Group Names menu appears, press INS to add a new group.

4. Type **DEPT-MGR** in the New Group Name box, as shown here, and then press ENTER.

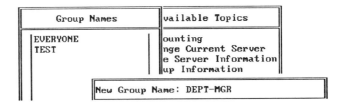

5. After creating the new group, select it and press ENTER to display the Group Information menu. You can enter a full name for the new group by selecting **Full Name** from the menu. Full names

are useful for identifying groups in various NetWare reports and system management functions.

6. Select **Member List** from the Group Information menu.

7. Press INS to add users to the group. In the following example you make CLYDE a member of the group when you select his name from the Not Group Members list and press ENTER.

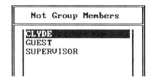

Granting the Group Trustee Rights

Once members are added to the DEPT-MGR group, a special directory can be created for their use. Follow these steps to create a directory called SYS:MGR-DATA:

1. Select **Trustee Directory Assignments** from the Group Information menu.

2. Press INS to add a new directory to the menu. The window shown here appears where the path to the directory can be entered.

3. Type the name shown in the illustration and press ENTER.

4. Select **Yes** when asked to verify creation of the directory.

The new directory appears in the Trustee Directory Assignments menu with the Read and File Scan rights. To give the group complete rights in the new SYS:MGR-DATA directory, grant the Supervisor right, as described here:

1. Select the SYS:MGR-DATA directory and press ENTER.

2. Press INS when the Trustee Rights Granted menu appears.

3. Select the **Supervisor** option and press ENTER. The new right appears in the Trustee Directory Assignments window.

The DEPT-MGR group should also be given supervisory rights to the SYS:PUB-DATA directory. Follow these steps:

1. Press INS at the Trustee Directory Assignments menu.

2. Type the directory name shown in the following illustration, and press ENTER to add the directory.

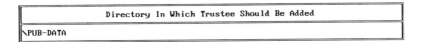

3. Select the directory name and press ENTER to grant trustee rights.

4. Press INS at the Trustee Rights Granted menu, and select the **Supervisor** right on the Trustee Rights Not Granted menu. Press ESC to return to the Trustee Directory Assignments menu.

When you are done, the Trustee Directory Assignments menu looks like this:

The DEPT-MGR group now has full supervisory access to the SYS.MGR-DATA and SYS:PUB-DATA directories.

You may want to map the MGR-DATA directory to a drive letter so the managers can easily switch to it when necessary. Add the following command to the system login script following the last MAP command. It uses the IF...THEN command to map the SYS:MGR-DATA directory to drive H only if a user is a member of the DEPT-MGR group. In this example it is assumed drive H is the next available drive.

IF MEMBER OF "DEPT-MGR" THEN MAP H:=SYS:MGR-DATA

Limiting Directory Access
With the Inherited Rights Mask

The inherited rights mask limits user access to specific subdirectories. The mask blocks a user's trustee rights in a parent directory that would normally be inherited from the subdirectory. Initially all new directories have a default inherited rights mask that allows all trustee rights to pass.

The exercises in this section demonstrate how you can use the inherited rights mask to block a user's rights in a directory. You create a subdirectory of the SYS:PUB-DATA directory called ARCHIVE, and then you apply an inherited rights mask to the directory to block the Write, Create, and Erase rights. Members of the EVERYONE group (all users) inherit these rights from the SYS:PUB-DATA directory because EVERYONE was previously made a trustee of the directory.

You can use the FILER utility to create the new subdirectory and apply the inherited rights mask to it. Be sure you are logged in as a supervisor, and then follow these steps:

1. Start FILER by typing its name on the command line.

2. When the FILER Available Topics menu appears, choose **Select Current Directory** to change to the SYS:PUB-DATA directory. Type a response similar to the following:

```
                      Current Directory Path
 FS1\SYS:PUB-DATA
```

3. Choose **Directory Contents** on the Available Topics menu and press ENTER.

4. At the Directory Contents window, press INS.

5. Type **ARCHIVE** in the New Subdirectory Name box, as shown here:

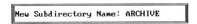

```
New Subdirectory Name: ARCHIVE
```

The ARCHIVE subdirectory appears in the Directory Contents window for the SYS:PUB-DATA directory, as shown here:

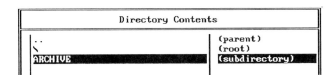

```
                    Directory Contents
  . .                              (parent)
  \                                (root)
  ARCHIVE                          (subdirectory)
```

6. Highlight the new ARCHIVE subdirectory and press ENTER. The following Subdirectory Options menu appears:

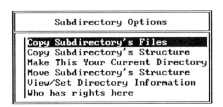

```
              Subdirectory Options
  Copy Subdirectory's Files
  Copy Subdirectory's Structure
  Make This Your Current Directory
  Move Subdirectory's Structure
  View/Set Directory Information
  Who has rights here
```

7. Select the **View/Set Directory Information** option from the menu to display the Directory Information window shown in Figure 22-2.

8. Scroll down to the Inherited Rights Mask option and press ENTER. To remove inherited rights, highlight the following options and press F5.

Access Control
Create Directory/File
Erase Directory/File
Modify Directory/File
Write To File

```
┌─────────────────────────────────────────────────────┐
│          Directory Information for ARCHIVE            │
├─────────────────────────────────────────────────────┤
│ Owner: SUPERVISOR                                     │
│                                                       │
│ Creation Date:  May 24, 1990                          │
│                                                       │
│ Creation Time:  9:25 am                               │
│                                                       │
│ Directory Attributes: (see list)                      │
│                                                       │
│ Current Effective Rights: [SRWCEMFA]                  │
│                                                       │
│ Inherited Rights Mask: [SRWCEMFA]                     │
│                                                       │
│                                                       │
│ Trustees:  (see list)                                 │
│                                                       │
└─────────────────────────────────────────────────────┘
```

Figure 22-2.   The Directory Information menu

Note: The Supervisor right cannot be removed because a user or group who has this right is not affected by the inherited rights mask in the first place. This is the case for the DEPT-MGR group created earlier. Since the group has the Supervisor right in PUB-DATA, its members still have full rights in ARCHIVE, even though you have applied an inherited rights mask. Only regular users are affected by the mask.

9. After marking the rights to remove, press DEL. FILER asks for confirmation that you want to remove the rights. Select **Yes** to revoke the rights.

You can view the rights a user has in these directories by logging in with the user's name and entering the RIGHTS command in either the SYS:PUB-DATA directory or the SYS:PUB-DATA/ARCHIVE directory. You can also load FILER to view the user's rights in the directory. Keep in mind that the information displayed by FILER is dependent on the current user. If the supervisor is logged in, an additional category for viewing directory trustees is available on the Directory Information window. Chapter 23 provides more information on the use of FILER.

Creating Work Group
And User Account Managers

Recall from Chapter 21 that work group managers and user account managers can be given control of users and groups. This section explains how this is done. To avoid confusion in the following discussion, work group managers and user account managers are referred to simply as managers, and the users or groups they control are referred to as accounts.

Managers can grant or revoke rights to accounts in the directories and subdirectories they control, assuming they have control of the account. The supervisor usually grants managers supervisory rights in the directories they control. They are then given control over selected accounts. Once a manager has control over these accounts, they can create their own user account managers (but not work group managers) to manage subsets of those accounts.

The main difference between a work group manager and a user account manager is the work group manager can create new accounts. If a supervisor wants to have complete control over the creation of new accounts, user account managers should be created instead of work group managers.

Both work group managers and user account managers are created with the SYSCON utility. The option for creating work group managers is in the Supervisor Options menu. Options for creating user account managers are in the Group Information and User Information menus.

Designating a Work Group Manager

You must be signed on as the supervisor to designate a work group manager. Follow these steps:

1. Start SYSCON if necessary.

2. Select **Supervisor Options**.

3. Select **Workgroup Managers** from the Supervisor Options menu.

4. When the Workgroup Managers menu appears, press INS to select an existing user from the Other Users And Groups menu.

5. Highlight the target user or group and press ENTER. The new name appears on the Workgroup Managers menu.

You can now assign accounts for the manager to control.

Designating a User Account Manager

Designating a user (or group) as a user account manager is really a process of placing accounts under his or her control. To designate an individual user account manager you use options under User Information on the SYSCON menu; for a group of user account managers you use options under Group Information.

Only the supervisor can give managers control over existing accounts. However, a work group manager can create new user accounts of their own. Once a manager is given control of a set of accounts (either users or groups), he or she can then control the restrictions, trustee rights, and other features of the accounts.

To assign accounts to a manager, perform these steps:

1. Select **User Information** from the SYSCON Available Topics menu.

2. Select the user to manage accounts from the User Names list.

3. When the User Information menu appears, select **Managed Users And Groups** to add accounts.

4. Press INS to see a list of possible user or group accounts.

5. Highlight each user to be added and press F5 (Select). Then press ENTER. The new accounts are added to the manager's list of controlled accounts.

Note: You can view the managers who control a user or group account by selecting **Managers** from the User Information or Group Information menu.

Managing Files

Most of the same trustee rights and inherited rights you set for directories can also be assigned to individual files within directories. These rights override any rights a user may have in a directory. In this way you can give users control of a directory while limiting their use of specific files. Alternatively, you can limit user access to a directory, but grant trustee rights to a single file.

Note: Do not confuse file access rights with file attributes. Access rights are designed to limit user access to files, while attributes are used to mark files as Shareable, Read Only, Read Write, and other features.

Follow these steps to grant or revoke trustee rights to a file:

1. From SYSCON, either select **Group Information** to grant or revoke file rights to an entire group, or choose **User Information** for individual users.

2. When the Group Information or User Information menu appears, select the **Trustee File Assignments** option to display a corresponding menu.

3. Press INS to add new entries to the list. You are asked for the directory that holds the files and to select a file in that directory. Keep pressing INS to see a list of possible options.

4. When the file appears in the Trustee File Assignments menu, you can select it and grant or revoke rights for the user or group using the methods described earlier for directories.

Installing Applications

When installing new software applications on the server, you must consider who should use the applications and where you want to store the data. In most cases the program files should be stored in one directory and the data files in another. Users should have Read and File Scan rights in program directories so they cannot change or accidentally delete files.

Users should have rights to work with data files in their personal directories or in special data directories.

After installing the software in the program directories, you should mark the files with the Shareable and Read Only attributes with the FILER utility or the FLAG command, as discussed in Chapter 24. The Shareable attribute allows multiple users to access the files, and the Read Only attribute protects the files from being accidentally erased or altered by those who have rights in the data directory, such as the users.

In some cases you may want to mark program files with the Execute Only attribute to protect them from virus infections. This should be done only to programs that are written to NetWare's specifications. Check with the manufacturer before proceeding, and make sure you have adequate backup.

Note: Some programs require that users have Create, Write, and Erase rights in a program directory if the program creates temporary files while the program is running. If a program cannot be executed, users probably don't have proper rights in its program directory. Some programs create these files in data directories so there will be no problems with access rights.

The next step would be to create a data directory for the managers. The steps for doing this were outlined earlier when you created the MGR-DATA directory. The minimum rights for the directory should be Create, Open, Read, Search, and Write.

Once programs and data directories are created, make sure users have the proper rights in those directories, and then add MAP commands to the system login scripts to point to the directories. Create a search drive to the program directory and a drive mapping to the data directory. In this way users can switch to the data directory by typing a single letter, and the program can be run because a search drive points to the program directory.

Note: Some application programs write only to the root directory. You can include the ROOT option in the MAP command to make the program think a directory is the root directory. Here is an example:

MAP ROOT J:=SYS:PUB-DATA

Working with Directories

Mapping Directories
Directory Activities with FILER
NetWare Commands for Working with Directories
Controlling Directory Trustees and Inherited Rights

This chapter provides useful and detailed information on working with directories and subdirectories. The discussion of the FILER menu utility in Chapter 22 is elaborated on, and the SESSION utility is discussed. You also see how the following NetWare commands are used to view, set, or change various options:

NDIR	Used to view directory and file lists
CHKDIR	Used to view directory information
TLIST	Displays the trustees for a directory
RIGHTS	Displays the rights of the current user
MAP	Maps drive letters to directories
GRANT	Grants trustee rights to a user in a directory
REVOKE	Revokes trustee rights in a directory
REMOVE	Removes a trustee from a directory
RENDIR	Renames a directory
FLAGDIR	Changes directory attributes

427

As you work with FILER, SESSION, SYSCON, and other menu utilities, keep in mind that many of their functions are duplicated in other menus, so you do not have to jump from one menu utility to another. This is often confusing to new users who assume the functions in each menu utility perform different tasks. In some cases one menu utility may present a different way to do a task, based on how you approach it. For example, you can assign trustees to a directory after creating the directory, or you can create directories and assign rights after creating users.

Note: With NetWare, either the slash (/) or backslash (\) symbols can be used when referring to directories because the operating system interprets them in the same way (unlike DOS, which uses only the backslash).

Mapping Directories

Drive mappings make access to NetWare directories easier and are vital when working between servers and volumes. A drive mapping lets you refer to directories on other servers or volumes without switching to or specifying the server or volume. You can use drive mappings to gain easier access to directories by referring to a directory name with a drive letter.

You use search drives to create drive pointers to directories that contain executable program files you want to run from other directories. You create search drives by assigning a search drive number to the directory that holds the programs. The number of the search drive is important because it specifies the order in which the operating system searches through the drives. The order is sometimes critical to program execution speed, but only if many search drives need to be searched. The search order can also give executable files in one directory precedence over those with the same name in another directory.

All maps are temporary and are lost when a user logs out. To make drive mappings permanent, you can add them to the system login script, or the personal login script of the user who requires them. In most cases permanent maps should be created to public directories like SYS:PUBLIC, the DOS directories, and data directories like PUB-DATA discussed in the previous chapter.

You will need to create program directories for users and groups who need access to them. In addition, the directories used to store files created by the application should also be mapped as a drive.

The discussion that follows describes how the MAP and SESSION commands for mapping drives are used at the command line. In fact, the SESSION utility makes settings in the current session only. No permanent changes are made to the operating system. However, users often need to map a drive to gain temporary access to a directory. This is especially true for the supervisor, who may need temporary access to directories for maintenance purposes, such as removing or archiving old files.

Using SESSION to Map Drives

The SESSION utility can be useful for viewing and mapping drives. The MAP command produces quicker results, but SESSION is menu driven and may be easier to use for first time users. To start the utility, type **SESSION** on the command line. The following screen appears:

Select **Drive Mappings** from the menu to see a list of current drive mappings like those shown in Figure 23-1. You can highlight any drive and press ENTER to see its effective rights as shown on the right. This is useful for users other than the supervisor whose effective rights depend on trustee rights and the inherited rights mask.

From the Current Drive Mappings window, press INS to create new drive mappings. Simply enter the drive letter and then the server, volume, and path for the new drive map or use the INS key method to bring up a list of names.

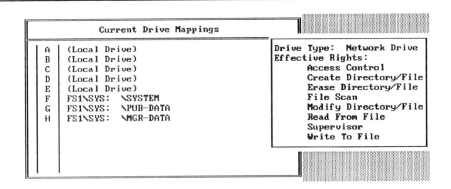

Figure 23-1.   The Current Drive Mappings menu

Press ESC to return to the SESSION main menu and select **Search Mappings**. A screen similar to the following appears:

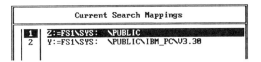

You can also press INS to create additional search drive maps. If you create a search drive using a number already in use, SESSION inserts the new drive and increments the numbers of the next drive.

Return to the SESSION main menu and choose **Select Default Drive**. A screen showing all available mapped drives appears. To switch to another mapped drive, highlight the drive and press ENTER.

Using the MAP Command

Use the MAP command to create drive mappings and search drive mappings from the command line. In the following examples, replace *drive* with the letter you want to use and *path* with the complete path to the directory.

Displaying the Current Maps

To display the current drive mappings and search drive mappings, type the MAP command by itself, as shown here:

MAP

If you want to display how a particular drive is mapped, type the following command, where *drive* is the letter of the drive map to view:

MAP *drive*:

Remapping the Current Drive

Your current directory always is mapped to a drive letter. You can change the mapping for the drive letter and switch to another directory by using the DOS CD (Change Directory) command. The destination directory becomes the new mapped directory for the drive letter. You can also use the MAP command as shown here, replacing *path* with the new directory path to map. *Path* can include a server and volume name as well.

MAP *path*

Mapping a New Drive

The form of the MAP command used to map new drives is shown here. Replace *drive* with the drive letter to use, and replace *path* with the directory to map. Remember that *path* can include server and volume names.

MAP *drive:=path*

For example, the following command maps drive J to the SYS:PUB-LIC\APPS\LOTUS directory:

MAP J:=SYS:PUBLIC\APPS\LOTUS

If the directory were on the ACCTG server in the VOL1 volume, you would type

MAP J:=ACCTG/VOL1:PUBLIC\APPS\LOTUS

If you were already in drive J assigned to LOTUS and you wanted to map drive L to the same directory, you would simply type

MAP L:=

Mapping a Root Drive

Some applications work only in the root directory. You can create a false root by using the ROOT option in MAP commands. The applications then think they are working in the root directory of a drive. The following ROOT command maps the SYS:PROGRAMS directory to drive K:

MAP ROOT K:=SYS:PROGRAMS

Mapping Search Drives

To map a search drive, you may need to enter the MAP command to determine the next available search drive. For example, search drive 1 (S1) and search drive 2 (S2) may already be mapped to a directory. The following command illustrates how the SYS:LOTUS directory is mapped to search drive 3.

MAP S3:=SYS:LOTUS

If you want to create a new search drive 1 or 2 but retain the existing search drives, use the INS (Insert) option. It increments the numbers of existing search drives and inserts the new search drive. For example, the following command makes the SYS:LOTUS directory the second search drive and changes the existing search drive 2 to search drive 3:

MAP INS S2:=SYS:LOTUS

Removing Drive Mappings

The following command removes a network drive mapping:

MAP DEL H:

This command removes a search drive mapping:

MAP DEL S3:

You cannot remove the mapping of the default drive.

Directory Activities with FILER

The FILER utility is used to create and alter the owners, trustees, and inherited rights masks of directories. You also can use it to move, copy, delete, and change the attributes and inherited rights mask of files. This section explores FILER's directory options. File options are covered in the next chapter.

Type **FILER** on the command line and press ENTER to display the FILER Available Topics menu shown here:

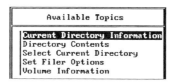

Selecting a Work Directory

The first thing to realize when working in FILER is that you can move to any directory and perform any task. The directory you are in when you execute FILER is the default current directory; however, you can change to any directory during the FILER session. When you exit FILER, your original directory is still the default directory.

You can change to a new directory by choosing **Select Current Directory** from the main menu. A window similar to the following appears:

```
                        Current Directory Path
FS1/SYS:USERS\CLYDE
```

You can use BACKSPACE to delete the current path and then type a new path to the directory you want to work in.

Another way to move around in the directory structure of your system is less conventional but may be more practical. Select Directory Contents to display a window similar to the following:

```
                     Directory Contents
 ..                                   (parent)
 \                                    (root)
```

Assume SYS:USERS\CLYDE is the current directory. If you highlight the double-dot (..) entry and press ENTER, FILER makes the parent directory USERS the current directory. If you highlight the backslash entry (\) and press ENTER, FILER makes the root directory the default. Select the root directory symbol and press ENTER. FILER displays the following:

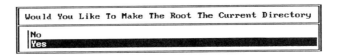

```
 Would You Like To Make The Root The Current Directory
 No
 Yes
```

Select **Yes** to make the root the current directory. The contents of the root directory are now displayed, as shown in Figure 23-2. You can highlight any directory and press ENTER to transfer to that directory. For the next

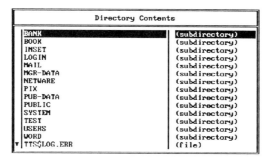

Figure 23-2.   FILER's Directory Contents display

few examples, select the SYS:PUBLIC directory. The Subdirectory Options menu appears, as shown here:

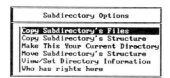

Highlight the **Make This Your Current Directory** option to move to the SYS:PUBLIC directory. Its contents are then displayed.

This method of moving through the directory structure is extremely efficient. For example, you can move to any subdirectory of the current directory using this method, or you can move back to the parent or root directory by selecting the .. or \ entry.

Viewing or Changing Directory Information

Return to FILER's Available Options menu by pressing ESC, and then select **Current Directory Information** and press ENTER. A menu similar to that shown in Figure 23-3 appears. It lists the owner, creation date and time, attributes, rights, and trustees of a directory. You also can change some of these options, as described later.

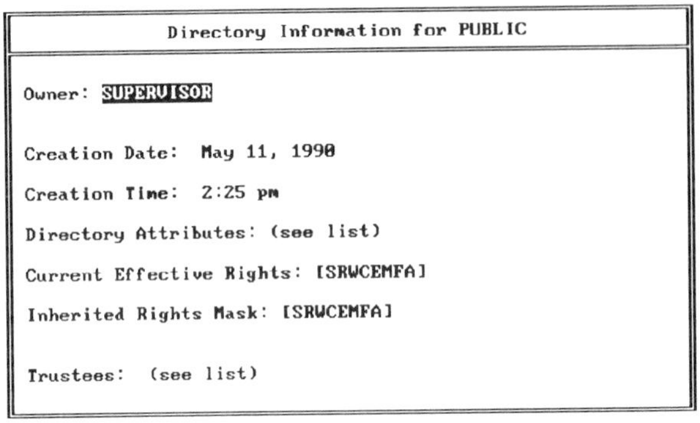

```
┌─────────────────────────────────────────────────────┐
│          Directory Information for PUBLIC             │
├─────────────────────────────────────────────────────┤
│  Owner:  SUPERVISOR                                   │
│                                                       │
│  Creation Date:  May 11, 1990                         │
│  Creation Time:  2:25 pm                              │
│  Directory Attributes: (see list)                     │
│  Current Effective Rights: [SRWCEMFA]                 │
│  Inherited Rights Mask: [SRWCEMFA]                    │
│                                                       │
│  Trustees:  (see list)                                │
│                                                       │
└─────────────────────────────────────────────────────┘
```

Figure 23-3.   The Directory Information window for the SYS:PUBLIC
directory

When displaying this information, be sure to keep track of the current
directory name, which is displayed at the top of the menu. The last four
options are described briefly here and discussed in detail in the next few
sections.

- **Directory Attributes** Used to view or change the directory
  attributes Delete Inhibit, Hidden, Purge, Rename Inhibit, and
  System.

- **Current Effective Rights** Displays the effective rights for the
  current user, in this case the supervisor. Other users who view this
  screen may see different settings.

- **Inherited Rights Mask** The supervisor can use this field to
  change the inherited rights mask. Regular users can only view the
  mask settings.

- **Trustees** This field is available only when a supervisor or manager is logged in. Current trustees can be viewed, added, or deleted.
  The rights of the trustees can also be changed.

Viewing and Changing
Directory Attributes

You can view or change directory attributes by selecting **Current Directory Information** from the FILER main menu and selecting the **Directory Attributes** option from the Directory Information menu. The Current Flags window appears and may be initially blank. Press INS to see a list of attributes that can be applied, as shown here:

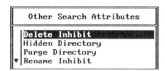

The attributes are defined here for your convenience. You can apply any attribute by highlighting it and pressing ENTER; select multiple attributes with the F5 key. The attributes then appear in the Current Flags window.

D (Delete Inhibit)	Prevents users from erasing directories even if they have the Delete right.
R (Rename Inhibit)	Restricts users from renaming a directory, even if they have the Modify right.
P (Purge)	Causes files in the directory to be purged immediately if they are deleted. Purged files cannot be recovered with SALVAGE.
H (Hidden)	Hides the directory so it cannot be seen in a directory listing by any users. The directory cannot be removed as long as it has the H attribute. The directory appears when NDIR is used if the user has File Scan rights.
S or Sy (System)	Indicates the directory is used by the system and does not appear in a directory

listing. The directory appears when NDIR is used if the user has File Scan rights.

V (Visible)

This attribute applies only to Macintosh directories and relates to the gray folders. The directory can be seen, even if the user does not have scan rights.

Viewing and Changing the Directory's Inherited Rights Mask

A directory's inherited rights mask can be changed by selecting **Current Directory Information** from the FILER main menu and selecting the **Inherited Rights Mask** option from the Directory Information menu. An Inherited Rights window similar to the following appears. The current rights depend on the directory and previous changes, if any.

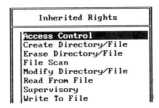

To add rights, press INS and select one or more rights to add. To delete rights, select one or more rights and press DEL. A supervisor may want to remove one or more of the inherited rights in a given directory, thus removing those rights for all users.

Keep in mind that a user's trustee rights may limit access to the current directory. You need to look at the Trustee option on the Directory Information window to see who currently has rights in the directory, as discussed next. Then you must compare those rights with the inherited rights mask to see if they have proper access in the directory. You can also log in as the user and start FILER to view the effective rights of the user on the Directory Information window.

Managing the Trustee of a Directory

When you select **Trustees** from the Directory Information screen, you can add or remove trustees from the directory or change the rights of the trustees. This option is similar to the user's options in the SYSCON utility. However, with SYSCON you start by selecting a user and then selecting a directory. With FILER a directory is already selected; you then add, remove, or alter the rights of a user or group in the directory.

When you select **Trustee**, a list of existing users and groups appears on the screen. The following actions are possible:

- You can add new users and groups as trustees of the directory by pressing INS and then selecting names of users or groups from the list.

- You can delete existing users or groups as trustees by selecting a name and pressing DEL.

- You can grant or revoke Trustee rights for any user or group account by selecting the account and pressing ENTER. Add or remove rights from the list using the normal method.

Viewing User Directory Rights

It is sometimes important to view the users and groups who have rights in a directory. For example, you might want to know the names of users who could delete files. Viewing the trustees of a directory with FILER or the TLIST command (discussed later) may not always provide you with this information.

Recall that a trustee listing like that provided by the Trustee option on FILER's Directory Information screen only provides a list of users who have been granted rights in a specific directory. However, other users who have rights in a parent directory may have inherited those same rights in the current directory. These users do not show up on a trustee list.

FILER has an important and convenient option that lets you view every user who has effective rights in a directory. The option, called **Who has rights here**, is on the Subdirectory Options menu. You must first move to the parent directory of the subdirectory you want to view, and then select the subdirectory and press ENTER. The Subdirectory Options menu appears with the **Who has rights here** option at the bottom. All users or groups are listed along with their effective rights.

Managing Subdirectories

While in a directory you can view and change the attributes, inherited rights mask, and trustees of any branching subdirectory. First, return to the FILER Available Topics menu, and then select **Directory Contents**. Choose any subdirectory and press ENTER. When the Subdirectory Options menu appears, select **View/Set Directory Information**. You are presented with a Directory Information window for the subdirectory that has the same options as those previously described for a directory. You can make the same kinds of changes to the subdirectory as you did to the directory.

New subdirectories can be created by pressing INS, and old subdirectories can be removed by highlighting them and pressing DEL. When you press INS you can type the name of the new subdirectory.

Copying, Moving, And Deleting Directories

FILER has several unique features that allow you to copy or move an entire branching directory, including subdirectories, to another location. You can also delete an entire directory branch, including all its subdirectories. To do this you must move to the starting directory, as described here:

- If you need to copy, move, or delete an entire branching directory tree, starting at its first level, move to the root directory.

- If you need to copy, move, or delete only part of a directory structure, move to the parent of the subdirectory that you want to change.

To begin, return to the FILER Available Topics menu and choose **Directory Contents**. Highlight the backslash (\\) and press ENTER. Answer Yes when asked if you want to make the root the current directory. From the root you can choose any directory and press ENTER. If you need to move further up into the directory, you can do so by starting at this first level.

Copying or Moving a Directory Structure

Select a directory from the list and press ENTER. The Subdirectory Options menu appears, as shown here:

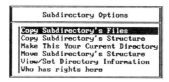

From this menu you can choose one of the following options:

- **Copy Subdirectory's Structure** Makes a duplicate of the entire directory structure in another location. This option is useful if you need to copy the directory structure of an existing user to a new user. When this option is selected, you must specify the path to which the directory is to be copied. If you specify a directory other than the root, it must already exist.

- **Move Subdirectory's Structure** Moves a branching subdirectory from one parent directory to another. This option is useful when reorganizing the file system.

Deleting a Directory Structure

You can delete an entire directory structure by selecting the directory and pressing DEL. The Delete Subdirectory Options box shown here appears:

```
    Delete Subdirectory Options
 Delete Entire Subdirectory Structure
 Delete Subdirectory's Files Only.
```

If you choose Delete Entire Subdirectory Structure, the entire subdirectory—its files and its subdirectories—are removed. If you choose Delete Subdirectory's Files Only, only the files within the subdirectory are removed; the subdirectory itself is left intact.

Setting FILER Options

Press ESC to return to the FILER main menu, and then select **Set Filer Options** from the menu. The Filer Settings menu appears, as shown in Figure 23-4. You can use this menu to change the way FILER handles copy and delete operations. For example, if you set Confirm Deletions to Yes, you are prompted before files are deleted. The include and exclude patterns for directories and files are similar in use to wildcard characters in file listings. For example, you can specify in Exclude Directory Patterns that directories starting with ARC not be included in the Subdirectory Information listing. The same technique holds for files. The opposite is to specify the pattern you want to list by using the Include options. When selecting one of these options, press INS to insert a new include or exclude pattern.

NetWare Commands
For Working with Directories

The commands described in the remainder of this chapter can be used to work with directories on the NetWare command line. Some of the commands covered here can be used when handling both directories and files. The file features are covered in the next chapter. DOS redirection com-

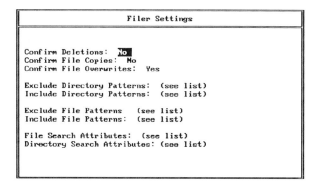

Figure 23-4.   The Filer Settings menu is used to change the way FILER handles file copies and deletes

mands can be used to output the listings from NetWare commands to a printer or a file.

DOS Directory Commands

The DOS directory commands can be used in NetWare to create directories and subdirectories from the command line. These commands offer an easy way to quickly create a directory. Keep in mind that trustee rights and other security features must be applied through the menu utilities or some of the commands listed later in this chapter. The DOS directory commands are shown here:

MD (Make Directory)	Creates a directory that branches from the current directory. Simply type **MD** followed by up to an eight-character directory name.
CD (Change Directory)	Moves to a different directory. Specify the path to the directory after the command.
RD (Remove Directory)	Removes a directory. The directory must be empty before it can be removed.

Checking Volumes and Disk Space

The CHKVOL and CHKDIR commands provide useful information about the current volume or directory, such as the amount of space in use and space available.

CHKVOL

The CHKVOL command displays information about a specified volume, such as the name of the file server where the volume is located, the total volume space, space used by files, deleted file space, and remaining space. The command is entered in the following form, where *volume* is the file server name and volume name of the volume you want to check:

CHKVOL *volume*

CHKDIR

The CHKDIR command displays information about a specified directory or the volume where the directory is located. This information includes the space limitations of the file server, volume, and directory. It also displays directory restrictions if any, the space in use by files in the volume, and the space available. The command takes the form shown here, where *path* is the directory to check:

CHKDIR *path*

Listing Directories with LISTDIR

The LISTDIR command is used to list the subdirectories of a directory, their inherited rights mask, the user's effective rights, and the creation date. The command takes the following form:

LISTDIR *path options*

Replace *path* with the directory name and *options* with one of the following:

/R (Rights)	Include this option to view the inherited rights mask of the directories' subdirectories.
/E (Effective rights)	Users can specify this option to view their effective rights in subdirectories.
/D (Date or Time)	Include this option to view the creation date.
/S (Subdirectories)	Include this option to view all subdirectories.
/A (All)	Include this option to view all the options just described.

To view a list of subdirectories for the current directory, you type **LISTDIR**. To view the subdirectory list of another directory, specify its path. For example, subdirectories of the SYS:PUB-DATA directory are listed with the following command:

LISTDIR SYS:PUB-DATA

If the SYS:PUB-DATA directory is mapped to drive G, type the following:

LISTDIR G:

To view all the information available from LISTDIR for a particular directory, use the /A option, as shown here:

LISTDIR G: /A

Listing Directories with NDIR

The NDIR command is equivalent to the DIR command in DOS, except NDIR is much more extensive, as you can see by the options described in this section. You can use NDIR to display information about files as well as directories. This section explains NDIR's directory specific options.

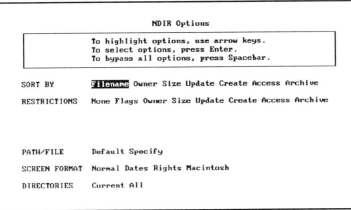

Figure 23-5.   The NDIR options menu

From any directory, type **NDIR** to display the NDIR options screen, as shown in Figure 23-5. From this screen you can select the many options available with NDIR. You also can type the options on the command line with the NDIR command, as explained in the remainder of this section. After you read through the section, you will be more prepared to use the options menu. To bypass the menu, press the spacebar; in a moment, a listing of files appears for the current directory.

Any directory can be listed by specifying its path. Use the following command to list the PUBLIC directory:

NDIR SYS:PUBLIC

The mapped drive letter of a directory can also be used to display the contents of a directory. The following example produces a list of files in the directory mapped to drive F:

NDIR F:

What NDIR Displays

The NDIR command displays a sorted list of files in a directory, and then finishes with a listing of subdirectories of the requested directory. NDIR pauses the listing one screen at a time, unless you type **C** to request continuous scrolling.

The examples in this section list subdirectories only, not files. A typical screen might look like the partial listing shown here:

```
                  Inherited   Effective
  Directories:    Rights      Rights      Owner       Created
  ------------    ---------   ---------   ----------  -----------
  BANK            [SRWCEMFA]  [SRWCEMFA]  SUPERVISOR  5-22-90  10:35a
  BOOK            [SRWCEMFA]  [SRWCEMFA]  SUPERVISOR  5-17-90   5:49p
  DELETED    SAV  [--------]  [SRWCEMFA]  SUPERVISOR  5-11-90   2:25p
  INSET           [SRWCEMFA]  [SRWCEMFA]  SUPERVISOR  5-11-90   2:39p
  LOGIN           [SRWCEMFA]  [SRWCEMFA]  SUPERVISOR  5-11-90   2:25p
  MAIL            [--------]  [SRWCEMFA]  SUPERVISOR  5-11-90   2:25p
  MGR-DATA        [SRWCEMFA]  [SRWCEMFA]  SUPERVISOR  5-23-90   7:24p
  NETWARE         [SRWCEMFA]  [SRWCEMFA]  SUPERVISOR  5-16-90   3:38p
  PIX             [SRWCEMFA]  [SRWCEMFA]  SUPERVISOR  5-17-90   6:12p
  PUB-DATA        [SRWCEMFA]  [SRWCEMFA]  SUPERVISOR  5-23-90   6:44p
```

At the top of the screen are column headers that describe the information in the listing. This screen is only listing directories; if files were also listed, the filename and its size would be listed first, along with file access date information. Note that the inherited rights and effective rights are listed. The effective rights differ according to which user is listing the directories.

NDIR Options for Directories

NDIR has a large set of optional parameters that can be typed on the command line after the path or filename. Only those options used with directories are discussed here. Additional options for files are covered in Chapter 24.

The NDIR command takes the following form:

NDIR *path/filespec options*

where *path* or *filespec* might include the path to a directory, a filename, or a path and filename. The *options* are typed last, and more than one option can be specified on the command line. Here is a list of possible options you can use with the NDIR command when working with directories:

DO (Directories Only)	Used to view only directories and subdirectories, not files.
SUB (Subdirectories)	Includes all subdirectories of the specified directory in the NDIR command.
OWNER (Owner)	Lists directories owned by a specific user. A NOT option is available to exclude an owner from a listing.
CREATE (Create)	Displays directories created before, on, or after a specified date. A NOT option also is available to exclude directories created before, on, or after the specified date.

Some examples help to illustrate the use of these options. In addition, the options BEFORE and AFTER are also available for filtering.

To view only the subdirectories of a directory, specify the DO option. The following command lists the subdirectories of drive H:

NDIR H: DO

If you want to see the subdirectories branching from the H drive, type the following command:

NDIR H: DO SUB

To list another volume, specify the volume name in the command. The following command lists the directories and subdirectories on the VOL1 volume:

NDIR VOL1: DO SUB

To list directories on other servers, specify the server name also. The next command lists directories and subdirectories in the SYS volume on the server SALES:

NDIR SALES/SYS: DO SUB

The complete path to a directory can also be specified. For example, to list the subdirectories of the user JOHN's directory, type the following command:

NDIR SYS:USERS\JOHN DO SUB

Since the listings display the inherited rights and user effective rights for each directory, users can type the NDIR command with the DO and SUB options to view the rights they have in directories. You can view the entire directory structure for the current volume by specifying the root directory in the NDIR command, as shown here:

NDIR \ DO SUB

or

NDIR SYS: DO SUB

Note: Use the backslash character (\) to indicate the root directory, as you do with DOS.

You can use the OWNER = *name* option to list the subdirectories owned by a particular user. The following command displays all subdirectories owned by user JOHN:

NDIR \ DO SUB OWNER = JOHN

To list all owners' subdirectories except JOHN's, type the following command:

NDIR \ DO SUB OWNER NOT = JOHN

List all directories not owned by the supervisor by typing:

NDIR \ DO SUB OWNER NOT = SUPERVISOR

The CREATE option lists directories created before, on, or after a certain date, and the NOT option gives you the opposite listing. The BEF (before) and AFT (after) options specify how the listing should treat the specified date. For example, the following command displays all directories created before 6-20-90 in drive H:

NDIR H: CREATE BEF 6-20-90 DO

To view files after the date, replace BEF with AFT. To view all branching subdirectories, include the SUB option.

The CREATE option filters the NDIR listing so it does not include directories created on a certain date. The following command lists all directories and subdirectories in the volume, except those created on 6-20-89:

NDIR \ CREATE NOT = 6-20-89 DO SUB

The next command may be more elaborate than most users care to type, but it illustrates the power of the NDIR command combined with the right options. The command lists all directories on the volume except those created on 6-20-89 and those created by the supervisor.

NDIR \ CREATE NOT = 6-20-89 DO SUB OWNER NOT = SUPERVISOR

Applying Directory Attributes
With FLAGDIR

You can use the FLAGDIR command to flag a specified directory with one of the following attributes, which have been discussed in previous chapters as part of NetWare's security features. Note that the single characters are used with the FLAGDIR command on the command line.

N (Normal)	Cancels other directory attributes that have been set.
D (Delete Inhibit)	Prevents users from erasing directories even if they have the Delete right.
R (Rename Inhibit)	Restricts users from renaming a directory, even if they have the Modify right.

P (Purge)

Causes files in the directory to be purged immediately if they are deleted. Purged files cannot be recovered with SALVAGE.

H (Hidden)

Hides the directory so it cannot be seen in a directory listing by any users. The directory cannot be removed as long as it has the H attribute. The directory appears when NDIR is used if the user has File Scan rights.

Sy (System)

Indicates the directory is used by the system and will not appear in a directory listing. The directory appears when NDIR is used if the user has File Scan rights.

Note: You must have the Modify right to change a directory or volume's attributes. You also must have the Erase effective right in a directory to set the Delete Inhibit and Purge attribute.

The FLAGDIR command is typed on the command line in the following form:

FLAGDIR *path options*

Replace *path* with the directory name or its mapped drive letter and replace *option* with one of the directory rights discussed in the "Applying Directory Attributes with FLAGDIR" section.

If you want help with the FLAGDIR command, use the HELP option, as shown here:

FLAGDIR HELP

Viewing Directory Attributes

Type the FLAGDIR command by itself to determine the status of the current directory. Type **FLAGDIR** * to view the status of any subdirectories that branch from the current directory.

The asterisk is a wildcard character that lists all filenames that do not have extensions, which is normally the case with directory names. To view the attributes of other directories, specify the name or mapped drive letter of the directory. The following command displays the directory attributes of drive K:

FLAGDIR K:

To view the subdirectory attributes of drive K, type the following command:

FLAGDIR K:*

If a directory is not mapped to a letter, you must specify the full path to the directory. For example, the following command lists the attributes of subdirectories that branch from the USER directory:

FLAGDIR SYS:USER*

Changing Directory Attributes

To change the attributes of the current directory, simply enter the FLAGDIR command followed by the attribute. Normally, the P and H attributes are assigned together to hide a directory in file listings and to prevent users from viewing its contents. The following command makes the SYS:PUBLIC\PROGRAMS directory both private and hidden:

FLAGDIR SYS:PUBLIC\PROGRAMS P H

If the directory were mapped to drive K, for example, you could type the following command to assign the P and H attributes:

FLAGDIR K: P H

It is possible to assign the P and H attributes to all subdirectories of the current directory by typing the following command in the parent directory:

FLAGDIR * P H

To assign the P and H attributes to the subdirectories of a directory other than the current directory, specify the path or mapped drive letter of that directory. For example, if the current directory is SYS:SYSTEM and drive K is mapped to SYS:PUBLIC\PROGRAMS, the following command assigns the P and H attributes to all subdirectories in drive K:

FLAGDIR K:* P H

To flag directories on other volumes, be sure to specify the volume name or the server name. For example, the following command assigns the P and H attributes to the TRAINING directory on VOL1:

FLAGDIR VOL1:TRAINING P H

If you ever become frustrated because you cannot find a directory in a listing, you probably have hidden it with one of the FLAGDIR commands. To return it to normal, use the N option, as shown here:

FLAGDIR K: N

Renaming Directories with RENDIR

The RENDIR command renames a directory and has a relatively simple format:

RENDIR *oldname* TO *newname*

where *oldname* is the complete pathname to the directory to be renamed, and *newname* is the new directory name. It is not necessary to specify the complete path for *newname*. Those attempting to use RENDIR must have the Modify right within a directory to rename its subdirectories. Directories can be renamed only on the current server. To change directory names on other servers, you must first log in or attach to that server.

To rename the current directory, use the period, which represents the current default directory. The following command renames the current directory to TESTING:

RENDIR . TO TESTING

The TO in the command is optional, so the following could be typed to rename the directory TEST2:

RENDIR . TEST2

To rename directories other than the current directory, specify the full name of the directory in the RENDIR command. If the directory is already mapped to a drive, the RENDIR command is much easier. For example, assume the SYS:USERS\TRAINING directory is mapped to drive L. Either of the following commands rename the directory to TUTO-RIAL:

RENDIR SYS:USERS\TRAINING TO TUTORIAL

or

RENDIR L: TO TUTORIAL

Remember that the TO in the commands is optional.

Controlling Directory Trustees And Inherited Rights

You use the commands discussed in this section to display a list of directory trustees and trustee rights, to grant trustee rights, and to revoke those rights. The trustee rights used by the commands described in this section are summarized here for your convenience:

A (Access Control)   Similar to the Supervisor right in its scope, but Access Control can be blocked in sub-directories by the inherited rights mask. Thus, the Access Control right can give a user complete control within a single directory. The user can modify the trustee list and inherited rights mask of the directory but cannot grant the Supervisor right to other users.

C (Create)   The user can create new files and subdirectories.

E (Erase)   This right can be assigned to a trustee of the directory, who can remove files and subdirectories.

F (File Scan)   Allows users to list filenames. Users who are file trustees can see the filename of only the files they are assigned trusteeship to.

M (Modify)   A user can change the name and attributes of a directory and all child subdirectories.

R (Read)   The user can open and read a file in the assigned directory and subdirectory.

S (Supervisor)   The Supervisor right gives a user complete control in a directory and its subdirectories. The right cannot be removed by an inherited rights mask. A user with Supervisor status in a directory controls all its subdirectories without limitations. Note that the Access Control right is similar, but can be blocked in subdirectories by the inherited rights mask. Users with Supervisor rights can grant other users rights to the directory, its subdirectories, and its files, including the Supervisor right. The Supervisor right is usually granted to work group managers and user account managers.

W (Write)   The user can open and write to files in the
                                   directory and subdirectory.

Setting Inherited Rights Masks
With ALLOW

The ALLOW command displays or sets the inherited rights mask of a
directory or file. Anyone can use the command to view the inherited rights
mask, but a user must have Access Control rights to set or change the
mask.

Type the ALLOW command on the command line in the following
form:

ALLOW *path option*

where *path* is the path or drive letter of the directory or files to be changed,
and *option* is one of the trustee rights discussed in the previous section.
Note that you can use wildcard characters when specifying files. You also
can specify the following:

ALL   Assigns an inherited rights mask that al-
                                  lows all eight trustee rights to be inherited

N   Assigns an inherited rights mask that al-
                                  lows no rights to be inherited

The rights you specify with ALLOW are not added to any existing
rights. Instead, ALLOW replaces the existing inherited rights mask with
the new mask you specify. Because of this, specifying just one new right
revokes all others not specified.

To view the inherited rights mask for subdirectories that branch from
the current directory, simply type **ALLOW**. The inherited rights mask of
each file is displayed, followed by the inherited rights mask of each
directory.

To create a new inherited rights mask for a directory, specify it by name or complete path name. In the following example the mask of the SYS:PUB-DATA\ARCHIVE directory is changed to Read and File Scan:

ALLOW SYS:PUB-DATA\ARCHIVE R F

The next command achieves the same results if the directory were mapped to the J drive:

ALLOW J: R F

In the next example, a mask that allows only Read and File Scan rights is applied to all files in the ARCHIVE directory with the extension TXT:

ALLOW J:*.TXT R F

Viewing Trustees with TLIST

The TLIST command displays the trustee list for any directory. Only users who have the Parental right for a specified directory may use the TLIST command to view the trustee list for that directory. Only trustee lists for directories on the current server may be viewed.

Note: Viewing the trustees of a directory does not give you sufficient information about user rights in a directory. The inherited rights mask may allow user rights in a parent directory to be inherited. You will not see these rights with TLIST since it only lists users who have been given specific trustee rights in the directory. Refer to the "Viewing User Directory Rights" section earlier in this chapter.

The command takes the following form:

TLIST *path* USERS GROUPS

where *path* is the path or mapped drive name for the directory to be viewed. If USERS is included, only the user trustees of a directory are listed. If GROUPS is included, only the group trustees of a directory are listed.

To view the trustees for the current directory, type **TLIST**. Information similar to the following is displayed:

```
User Trustees:
      JOHN          [SRWCEMFA]        (JOHN JONES)
      -----
Group Trustees:
      EVERYONE   [SRWC F ]
      MANAGERS   [SRWCEMFA]      (DEPARTMENT MANAGERS)
```

If no users or trustees exist, the display says so. The trustee rights in the directory are listed next to the user name.

You can view the trustee list in any directory by specifying the full path to the directory or by using a mapped drive letter if one has been established. In the following examples, drive K is mapped to the SYS:PUBLIC\PROGRAMS directory.

TLIST K:

or

TLIST SYS:PUBLIC\PROGRAMS

Both commands produce the same listing of the trustees for the directory.

To view only the user trustees of the current directory, type the following command:

TLIST . USERS

To view only the group trustees of the current directory, type the following command. A mapped drive letter or directory path can be typed instead of the period to specify another directory.

TLIST . GROUPS

RIGHTS

The RIGHTS command displays a user's current rights in any directory. The command takes the following form:

RIGHTS *path*

where *path* is the full directory path or mapped drive letter of the directory of which you want to display the rights. To display the rights for the current directory, type **RIGHTS**. To view rights in other directories, simply specify the path or search drive. For example, the following commands display the user rights in the SYS:PUBLIC\PROGRAMS directory, which is mapped to drive K:

RIGHTS SYS:PUBLIC\PROGRAMS

or

RIGHTS K:

Keep in mind that the rights displayed for users are the effective rights they have in the directory—a combination of the inherited rights mask assigned to the directory by the supervisor and the trustee rights assigned to the user for the directory.

Note: The NDIR commands for listing directories may be more beneficial to users who are interested in viewing their rights for the entire directory structure.

GRANT

The GRANT command can be used in place of the SYSCON and FILER utilities to assign trustee rights to users and groups, assuming those users and groups have already been created by the SYSCON utility. The rights that can be granted to users and groups are listed at the beginning of this section. In addition, the GRANT command has a NO RIGHTS option that revokes all rights to the user.

The GRANT command takes the following form:

GRANT *option* ... FOR *path* TO [USER or GROUP] *name*

where *option* is one of the trustee rights discussed earlier. FOR *path* designates the directory where trustee assignments are to be granted. TO *name* designates the user or group to be granted the rights. Two additional options are ONLY and ALL BUT, which you can use to grant only the specified right or all but the specified right. These options are placed in front of the rights designators.

Note: USER and GROUP are necessary when a user or group share the same name.

The GRANT command must be issued for each user or group to be granted rights. To grant rights in the current default directory, type the command followed by the letter of the rights to grant and the user name. For example, to grant the Read and File Scan rights to JOHN in the current directory, type the following:

GRANT R F TO JOHN

To grant rights in another directory, the full path to the directory must be specified, or the directory must have a mapped drive letter. In the following examples, the SYS:PUBLIC\PROGRAMS directory is mapped to drive K and JOHN is granted the Read and File Scan rights:

GRANT R F FOR SYS:PUBLIC\PROGRAMS TO JOHN

or

GRANT R F FOR K: TO JOHN

To grant all but certain rights, use the ALL BUT option. Assume you want to grant JOHN all rights except Supervisor and Modify in the current directory. Type the following command:

GRANT ALL BUT S M TO JOHN

To grant specific rights and revoke all others, use the ONLY option. To grant John the File Scan right only in the K drive, type the following:

GRANT ONLY F FOR K: TO JOHN

To grant all rights to JOHN in the K drive, type the following:

GRANT ALL FOR K: TO JOHN

Granting rights to groups is the same as granting rights to users. If a group and a user have the same name, you must specify whether the name used in the command is the user or the group. Precede the user name or group name with USER or GROUP in the command.

The GRANT command enrolls users or groups into the trustee list of a directory. You can use the commands discussed in the next two sections to revoke the rights of a user in a trustee list and to remove the user from the trustee list altogether.

REVOKE

Use the REVOKE command in place of the SYSCON and FILER utilities to revoke trustee rights from users and groups, assuming those users and groups have already been created by the SYSCON or MAKEUSER utility. The rights that can be revoked from users and groups are listed at the beginning of this section.

The REVOKE command takes the following form:

REVOKE *option* ... FOR *path* FROM [USER or GROUP] *name*

where *option* is the first letter of one of the trustee rights listed earlier. FOR *path* designates the directory where trustee assignments are to be revoked. FROM *name* designates the user or group whose rights are to be revoked. The additional option ALL can be used to revoke all the rights of a user or group.

Note: USER and GROUP are optional and are used when a user or group share the same name.

You must issue the REVOKE command for each user or group whose rights will be revoked. To revoke rights in the current directory, type the command followed by the letter of the rights to revoke, and then the user name. For example, to revoke the Read and File Scan rights from JOHN in the current directory, type the following:

REVOKE R F FROM JOHN

Do not forget to include FROM in the command. To revoke rights in another directory, the full path to the directory must be specified, or the directory must have a mapped drive letter. In the following examples, the SYS:PUBLIC\PROGRAMS directory is mapped to drive K and the Read and File Scan rights are revoked from JOHN:

REVOKE R F FOR SYS:PUBLIC\PROGRAMS FROM JOHN

or

REVOKE R F FOR K: FROM JOHN

To revoke all rights, use the ALL option. If you want to revoke all rights from JOHN, type the following command:

REVOKE ALL FROM JOHN

To revoke all rights for JOHN in the K drive, type

REVOKE ALL FOR K: FROM JOHN

Revoking rights from groups is the same as revoking rights from users. If a group and a user have the same name, you must specify whether the name used in the command is the user or the group. Precede the user name or group name with USER or GROUP in the command.

The GRANT command enrolls users or groups into the trustee list of a directory. The REVOKE command revokes the rights of a user in a trustee list. The command discussed next removes a user or group from the trustee list entirely.

REMOVE

The REMOVE command removes a user or group from the trustee list of a directory. The command is different than the REVOKE command, which revokes a user's rights in a directory, but does not remove them from the trustee list. The command takes the following form:

REMOVE *user/group* FROM *path*

The *user / group* options specify the name of the user or the group to remove. If a user and group have the same name, precede the name with USER or GROUP to indicate which to use. Only those users who have Parental effective rights in a directory can remove users in that directory.

To remove a user from the current directory, the name of the user is specified. For example, to remove JOHN from the current directory, type the following:

REMOVE JOHN

A similar command is used to remove a group.

To remove a user or group from another directory, you must specify the full path name of that directory or map the directory to a drive. The following command removes JOHN as a trustee of the SYS:PUBLIC\PROGRAMS directory:

REMOVE JOHN FROM SYS:PUBLIC\PROGRAMS

If the directory is mapped to the K drive, type the following command:

REMOVE JOHN FROM K:

Working with Files

Using FILER
Listing and Copying Files
Changing File Attributes with FLAG
Assigning Search Modes to Executable Files with SMODE
File Trustees and Inherited Rights
Salvaging Deleted Files

NetWare allows security and protection on several levels, as discussed in the last few chapters. Users can be given trustee rights so they can work in certain directories, and supervisors can protect subdirectories by applying inherited rights masks. This chapter discusses ways to apply attributes to individual files to provide protection, sharing, and other features.

You use the FILER utility to work with files. It can be used to apply attributes and to help supervisors and users list, copy, delete, and modify files. This chapter covers FILER first, and then discusses various forms of command-line utilities for those who prefer to work at the command level. Some tasks can be performed only by command-line utilities, as covered in the last few sections in this chapter.

Using FILER

With NetWare's FILER menu utility you can create new directories, assign trustees to those directories, and control the rights of those trustees, as discussed in Chapter 23. This section covers how you use FILER to work with files. You can view or change file attributes, creation date, owner, size, and contents. You also can copy files to another directory or duplicate them. The supervisor or a user with the Modify right can change the attributes of the file.

Select multiple files for modification or deletion with the F5 (Mark) key. You can also set FILER options so only specific files in a directory can be viewed or included in copy and delete operations. Note that most operations involving modifications can be performed only by the supervisor. Normal users can view file information and change files they have created or have been given access to.

Choosing a Directory to Work In

The current directory and its files are available when FILER is started. If you want to use another directory, you can switch to the directory before or after starting FILER. To change directories after starting FILER, use one of the following methods:

- *Direct Method* Select **Current Directory** from the FILER menu. Type the name of the directory in the window, or press INS to insert the names of the server, volume, and directory you want to work with. Press ENTER when the full directory name is specified.

- *Step Method* Choose **Directory Contents** from the FILER Available Topics menu. The window displays options similar to these:

Choose (..) to move to the parent directory or (\) to move to the root directory. When the Subdirectory Options menu appears, choose **Make This Your Current Directory**.

```
                    Directory Contents
 ┌──────────────────────────┬───────────────────────┐
 │..                        │(parent)               │
 │\                         │(root)                 │
 │IBM_PC                    │(subdirectory)         │
 │MS_DOS                    │(subdirectory)         │
 │!NETWARE.NFO              │(file)                 │
 │!NETWARE.WIN              │(file)                 │
 │$RUN.OVL                  │(file)                 │
 │ALLOW.EXE                 │(file)                 │
 │ATTACH.EXE                │(file)                 │
 │CAPTURE.EXE               │(file)                 │
 │CASTOFF.EXE               │(file)                 │
 │CASTON.EXE                │(file)                 │
 │CHKDIR.EXE                │(file)                 │
 │CHKVOL.EXE                │(file)                 │
 │▼CMPQ$RUN.OVL             │(file)                 │
 └──────────────────────────┴───────────────────────┘
```

Figure 24-1.   The FILER file list for the PUBLIC directory

Note: To follow along with the examples presented here, select the SYS:PUBLIC directory. Those using the step method should first select the root directory from the list and then select PUBLIC.

Accessing File Information

When you select the correct directory, you are presented with a list of files, or from the Filer Available Topics menu select **Directory Contents** to see the list. (The SYS:PUBLIC directory is used for these examples.) A screen similar to Figure 24-1 appears.

Note: Only supervisors or those given the Modify right in a directory can change the attributes.

You can view and set options for any file by selecting its filename from the list. The File Options menu appears, as shown here:

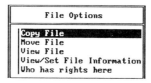

```
 ┌─────────────────────────────┐
 │        File Options         │
 ├─────────────────────────────┤
 │Copy File                    │
 │Move File                    │
 │View File                    │
 │View/Set File Information    │
 │Who has rights here          │
 └─────────────────────────────┘
```

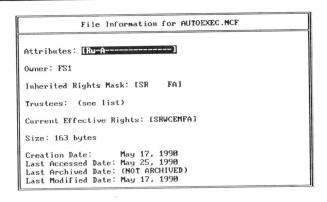

Figure 24-2. File information displayed by FILER

Select **View/Set File Information** from the File Options menu to display the File Information window shown in Figure 24-2. This window lets you view or change the options discussed in the following sections.

Changing File Attributes

The attributes of files can be viewed or changed from the File Information window. These attributes are used to make files shareable, read-only, read-write, and more. The complete set of attributes is listed in Table 24-1 for your convenience.

To change the attributes, highlight the Attributes field and press ENTER. The Current File Attributes window appears, as shown here:

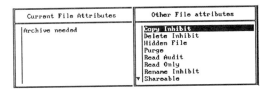

A (Archive Needed)	Automatically assigned to files by Net-Ware if they have been modified since the last backup. The attribute is used during a modified-only backup to determine which files should be backed up.
C (Copy Inhibit)	Restricts the copy rights of users logged in at a Macintosh workstation, even if the user has Read and File Scan trustee rights in the directory. If users have the Modify trustee right, they can remove the Copy Inhibit attribute and copy the file.
D (Delete Inhibit)	Prevents users from deleting a file, even if the user has Erase trustee rights in the directory. If users have the Modify trustee right, they can remove the Delete Inhibit attribute and erase the file.
E (Execute Only)	Prevents EXE and COM files from being altered or copied and can be used to prevent virus infections. The attribute can be assigned only by the supervisor, but should be used with caution and only if a complete backup of the EXE or COM files exists. Files not written to Novell NetWare specifications may lock up.
H (Hidden)	Files with this attribute do not appear in DOS DIR listings and cannot be deleted or copied. The files appear when the NetWare NDIR command is used, however.
I (Indexed)	Indexes the FAT (file allocation table) entry of large files to improve access from the hard drive. NetWare automatically indexes files when they exceed 64 regular FAT entries.
P (Purge)	When the Purge attribute is assigned to a file, it is automatically purged from the system when deleted. The SALVAGE command cannot be used to recover the file.

Table 24-1.   List of File Attributes

Ra (Read Audit)	The Read Audit attribute is associated with the NetWare audit trail system used to track who reads from a database file.
Ro/Rw (Read Only/ Read Write)	When files are marked with the Read Only attribute, they cannot be written to, erased, or renamed, even if the user has Write and Erase trustee rights in the directory. The attribute automatically assigns the Delete Inhibit and Rename Inhibit attributes. Users with the Modify trustee right can remove the Read Only attribute and then write to, rename, or erase the file. The Read Write attribute can be set to remove the Read Only attribute.
R (Rename Inhibit)	The Rename Inhibit attribute restricts users from renaming a file. If users have the Modify trustee right, they can remove the Rename Inhibit attribute and rename the file.
S (Shareable)	The Shareable attribute allows files to be used by more than one user. The attribute is usually assigned to database files, which are normally accessed by two or more network users.
Sy (System File)	Files marked with the System attribute do not appear in DOS DIR listings, but do appear when the NDIR command is used. The attribute also prevents files from being deleted or copied.
T (Transactional)	Indicates that the file is protected by the transactional tracking system.
W (Write Audit)	The Write Audit attribute is associated with the NetWare audit trail system used to track who writes to a database file.

Table 24-1. List of File Attributes (*continued*)

To add attributes, press INS to view the Other File attributes window. Highlight the attributes to add in the Other File Attributes window, and mark them by pressing F5. When you have selected all the attributes, press ENTER.

To remove attributes, select the attributes to be removed and mark them with the F5 key. Press DEL to remove them.

Remember that users with the Modify right in a directory are allowed to alter file attributes. Users can be given Modify rights to a specific file in any directory even though they do not have Modify rights in the directory.

Changing the Inherited Rights of a File

The inherited rights mask of a file can be changed to block rights from being inherited from parent directories. Like the directory-level inherited rights mask, a file inherited rights mask can be used to prevent users from accessing a file, but a supervisor or manager can give the rights back to specific users by granting file trustee rights.

To change the inherited rights mask of a file, select **Inherited Rights Mask** and press ENTER. The current list of rights appears.

To delete rights Highlight any right and press DEL. To remove several rights, highlight each and press F5 (Mark), and then press DEL.

To restore rights Press INS to display the Other Rights menu. Highlight any right and press ENTER. To add several rights, highlight each and press F5, and then press ENTER.

Changing the Trustees of a File

A user or group can be designated as a trustee of a file. Since trustee rights override any blockage of rights by the inherited rights mask, users can effectively be given complete control of a file, if necessary.

To change the trustees of a file, select **Trustee** from the File Information window and press ENTER. The current list of trustees appears; however, the screen may be blank. Press INS to add new trustees, and the Others list appears. You can highlight any user in the list and press ENTER to add them as trustees. To add several users, mark the names with F5, and press ENTER when done.

Once users are in the list of trustees, you can highlight any name and press ENTER to change their trustee rights to the selected file.

To add rights   Press INS to display the Other Rights menu. Highlight any right and press ENTER. To add several rights, highlight each and press F5, and then press ENTER.

To delete rights   Highlight any right on the Trustee Rights window and press DEL. To remove several rights, highlight each and press F5, and then press DEL.

Setting FILER's Options

From the FILER Available Topics main menu, you can select **Set Filer Options** to control how FILER handles confirmations during copies. You can also control the types of files that are listed. The Filer Settings menu is shown in Figure 24-3.

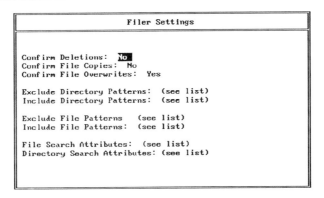

Figure 24-3.   The Filer Settings menu

Setting Exclude and Include File Patterns

Use the Exclude File Patterns and Include File Patterns options to specify the types of files you want to include and exclude from a file list. The options are useful for removing the "clutter" from a listing so you can easily see the files you need to work with.

Here is an example to demonstrate how you can use the Filer Settings menu. Suppose you want to see files only in the SYS:PUBLIC directory (presumably your current directory) that have the extension DAT. Scroll down to the Include File Patterns field and press ENTER. When the Included File Patterns window appears, press ENTER on the asterisk. In the Edit Pattern box, type **.DAT**, as shown here, and press ENTER.

```
Edit Pattern:*.DAT
```

Only files with the DAT extension appear in the file listing. Press ESC to return to the FILER Available Topics menu and select **Directory Contents**. When the Directory Contents list appears, only files with the DAT extension are visible.

You can select **Exclude File Patterns** from the Filer Settings menu to list files that do not have the pattern you select. For example, you could list all files except those with the extension COM or EXE by specifying COM or EXE as an exclude pattern.

Setting FILER Confirmations

The first three options on the Filer Settings menu, listed here, add protection to file operations that might delete or overwrite existing files:

- *Confirm Deletions* Type **Yes** at Confirm Deletions to protect against accidental file deletions. When this option is set, FILER asks if you really want to remove a file.

- *Confirm File Copies* This option is useful when copying multiple sets of files. FILER asks you to confirm before copying any file in a group, giving you a chance to reject the copy if need be.

- *Confirm File Overwrites* When this option is set, FILER warns you before copying over an existing file with the same name.

Setting File Search Attributes

Files that are marked as Hidden and System do not show up in file listings. You can add Hidden or System as a search file attribute to make these files show up. To do so, select **File Search Attributes** and press ENTER. The Search File Attributes window appears. To add attributes, press INS, highlight the attribute to add, and press ENTER.

Copying, Moving, and Viewing Files

FILER provides an easy way to copy or move files to other locations, or you can view the contents of text files. First, display the Directory Contents list for the desired directory, and then highlight a file to work with. Press ENTER to display the following menu:

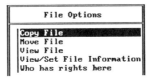

When a file is copied, the original stays where it is. When a file is moved, the original is erased. Select either **Copy File** or **Move File**, and enter the destination drive and directory in the Destination Directory box. When you press ENTER, the file is copied or moved.

To view the contents of a file, select the **View File** option. Text files are the only files that will be readable when this option is used.

Multiple File Operations

If you select more than one file using F5 (Mark) from the Directory Contents window, FILER displays the following menu, which includes some of the options already discussed in the previous sections. You can now use these options on the multiple set of files you have selected.

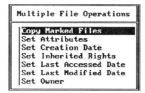

Arrow down to any option, and press ENTER to make changes. FILER asks you for appropriate responses with each option. You can change file attributes and inherited rights using the same method discussed earlier. The accessed and modified dates of files can be changed for reasons having to do with backup and include/exclude patterns when NDIR is used. For example, some accounting systems may require file dates to fall within a certain range before they can be processed.

Listing and Copying Files

You use the commands presented in this section to list, copy, and set file attributes at the command line, rather than from a menu system. The commands are powerful because they provide you with a number of options that can make the job of supervisor or manager much easier. Because of the number of options, the commands take a little getting used to. This section presents examples you can type at a workstation to experiment with each command.

Network managers can be overwhelmed by the thousands of files on a file server. The more control the supervisor has over these files the better. The listing and copying commands can become quite specific in their use. Files can be listed according to their owners, creation date, or archived status, for example. It benefits any supervisor to become familiar with the command options for future use.

Listing Files with NDIR

The NDIR command is equivalent to the DOS DIR command but is much more extensive. NDIR displays information about files as well as directories. This section explains NDIR's file-specific options. Chapter 23 explains NDIR's directory-specific options.

NDIR can play an important role in organizing or cleaning up a filing system. For example, you can print a listing of all files created by a user before or after a certain date. A manager or the user can then scan this list to determine which files should be kept on the system, which should be archived, and which should be purged. The listing is useful because it shows the exact directory location of the files.

One of the first things you can do with NDIR is list its help screen by typing the following command:

NDIR HELP

The help screen describes how to use the command. Another way to get help is to type the command by itself to display the NDIR Options menu. You use this menu to create an NDIR command. This method may be useful in the future if you cannot remember the NDIR options described here. The sections that follow will help you understand how the NDIR options are used on the command line.

The NDIR command takes the following form:

NDIR   *path/filename   options*

where *path /filename* is the directory path, filename, or directory path and filename to list, and *options* are special filters you can use to control the sort order, date, owner, and other information about files.

From any directory, you can simply type **NDIR** to see the NDIR Options menu. Press the spacebar to bypass the menu and see a listing of files and subdirectories for that directory.

Any directory can be listed by specifying its full path. The following command includes the path to the PUBLIC directory to list its contents:

NDIR   SYS:PUBLIC

The mapped drive letter of a directory can also be used to display the contents of a directory. The following example assumes that the PUBLIC directory is mapped to drive G. It produces the same listing as the previous command.

NDIR G:

Note: For clarity, mapped drive letters are used in the examples for the remainder of this section.

What NDIR Displays

The NDIR command displays a sorted list of files in a directory, and then finishes with a listing of subdirectories for the requested directory. The listing is paused on the screen, unless you type **C** to request a continuous listing.

NDIR displays the following information:

Files	Each file is listed in alphabetical order.
Size	The size of the file is listed in this column.
Last Modified	The last modification date of the file is listed. This information is useful to supervisors and managers who are removing unused files based on their modification dates. Users can also view the date to determine the most current version of a file.
Flags	The Flags column lists the current attributes of the files.
Owner	The owner or creator of the file is listed.

Subdirectories are listed after the file listing. The inherited and effective rights of each subdirectory are listed, along with the owner and creation date.

NDIR Options

The following options can be included with the NDIR command to control how and which files are listed. An option called NOT can be included to list files that do not fit the requested option. There are four categories of options, as described here. Examples are given in the following section.

- *Basic File Information Options*   The basic file information options control how files are listed in relation to their filenames, owner, last accessed date, last update date, creation date, and size.

- *File Attributes Options*   Files can be listed according to their attributes.

- *Sorting Options*   Files can be sorted by owner, last-accessed date, date of last update, creation date, size, and alphabetical or reverse-alphabetical order on the filename. The REVERSE option is used to reverse the order.

- *View Options*   You can choose to list only files, only directories, only subdirectories, or only Macintosh files. Some options can be combined, such as the directories only and subdirectories options.

Basic File Information Options

OWNER   The OWNER option lists files owned by a specified user. The NOT option can be used to exclude files owned by the user. The option takes the following form, where *name* is the owner's name:

NDIR *path/filename* OWNER = *name*
NDIR *path/filename* OWNER NOT = *name*

ACCESS   The ACCESS option lists files accessed on, before, or after a specified date. The BEF (Before) or AFT (After) option is used to specify listings before or after the specified date. The NOT option is used with the ACCESS command to specify dates not within the range. The option takes the following forms:

NDIR *path/filename* ACCESS *mm-dd-yy*
NDIR *path/filename* ACCESS NOT *mm-dd- yy*
NDIR *path/filename* ACCESS BEF *mm-dd- yy*
NDIR *path/filename* ACCESS NOT BEF mm- dd-yy
NDIR *path/filename* ACCESS AFT *mm-dd- yy*
NDIR *path/filename* ACCESS NOT AFT *mm- dd-yy*

UPDATE   The UPDATE option lists files updated on, before, or after a specified date. The BEF (Before) or AFT (After) option is used to specify listings before or after the specified date. The NOT option specifies dates not within the range. The option takes the following forms:

NDIR *path/filename* UPDATE *mm-dd-yy*
NDIR *path/filename* UPDATE NOT *mm-dd- yy*
NDIR *path/filename* UPDATE BEF *mm-dd- yy*
NDIR *path/filename* UPDATE NOT BEF *mm- dd-yy*
NDIR *path/filename* UPDATE AFT *mm-dd- yy*
NDIR *path/filename* UPDATE NOT AFT *mm- dd-yy*

CREATE   The CREATE option lists files created on, before, or after a specified date. The BEF (Before) or AFT (After) option is used to specify listings before or after the specified date. The NOT option specifies dates not within the range. The option takes the following forms:

NDIR *path/filename* CREATE *mm-dd-yy*
NDIR *path/filename* CREATE NOT *mm-dd- yy*
NDIR *path/filename* CREATE BEF *mm-dd- yy*
NDIR *path/filename* CREATE NOT BEF *mm- dd-yy*
NDIR *path/filename* CREATE AFT *mm-dd- yy*
NDIR *path/filename* CREATE NOT AFT *mm- dd-yy*

SIZE   The SIZE option lists files according to their size, or it can exclude files less than or greater than a certain size using the LE (Less than) or GR (Greater than) option. The NOT option can be used to exclude files of the specified size. The option takes the following forms, where *nnn* is the file size in bytes:

NDIR *path/filename* SIZE *nnn*
NDIR *path/filename* SIZE NOT *nnn*

NDIR *path/filename* SIZE GR *nnn*
NDIR *path/filename* SIZE NOT GR *nnn*
NDIR *path/filename* SIZE LE *nnn*
NDIR *path/filename* SIZE NOT LE *nnn*

ARCHIVE   The ARCHIVE option lists files archived on, before, or after a specified date. The BEF (Before) and AFT (After) options are used to specify listings before or after the specified date. The NOT option specifies dates not within the range. The option takes the following forms:

NDIR *path/filename* ARCHIVE *mm-dd-yy*
NDIR *path/filename* ARCHIVE NOT *mm-dd-yy*
NDIR *path/filename* ARCHIVE BEF *mm-dd-yy*
NDIR *path/filename* ARCHIVE NOT BEF *mm-dd-yy*
NDIR *path/filename* ARCHIVE AFT *mm-dd-yy*
NDIR *path/filename* ARCHIVE NOT AFT *mm-dd-yy*

File Attributes Options

A (Archived)   To list files with the Archive attribute, use the A option; use NOT A to exclude the files. The option is used as follows:

NDIR *path/filename* A
NDIR *path/filename* NOT A

EX (Execute Only)   To list files with the Execute Only attribute, use the EX option; use NOT EX to exclude the files. The option is used as follows:

NDIR *path/filename* EX
NDIR *path/filename* NOT EX

H (Hidden)   To list files with the Hidden attribute, use the H option; use NOT H to exclude the files. The option is used as follows:

NDIR *path/filename* H
NDIR *path/filename* NOT H

I (Indexed)   To list files with the Indexed attribute, use the I option; use NOT I to exclude the files. The option is used as follows:

NDIR *path/filename* I
NDIR *path/filename* NOT I

P (Purge)   To list files with the Purge attribute, use the P option; use NOT P to exclude the files. The option is used as follows:

NDIR *path/filename* P
NDIR *path/filename* NOT P

RA (Read Audit)   To list files with the Read Audit attribute, use the RA option; use NOT RA to exclude the files. The option is used as follows:

NDIR *path/filename* RA
NDIR *path/filename* NOT RA

RO (Read Only)   To list files with the Read Only attribute, use the RO option; use NOT RO to exclude the files. The option is used as follows:

NDIR *path/filename* RO
NDIR *path/filename* NOT RO

S (Shareable)   To list files with the Shareable attribute, use the S option; use NOT S to exclude the files. The option is used as follows:

NDIR *path/filename* S
NDIR *path/filename* NOT S

SY (System)   To list files with the System attribute, use the SY option; use NOT SY to exclude the files. The option is used as follows:

NDIR *path/filename* SY
NDIR *path/filename* NOT SY

T (Transactional)   To list files with the Transactional attribute, use the T option; use NOT T to exclude the files. The option is used as follows:

NDIR *path/filename* T
NDIR *path/filename* NOT T

WA (Write Audit)   To list files with the Write Audit attribute, use the WA option; use NOT WA to exclude the files. The option is used as follows:

NDIR *path/filename* WA
NDIR *path/filename* NOT WA

Sorting Options

SORT OWNER   File lists can be sorted by owner with the SORT OWNER option. Use REVERSE to change the sort order. The option is used as follows:

NDIR *path/filename* SORT OWNER
NDIR *path/filename* REVERSE SORT OWNER

SORT ACCESS   Files can be listed according to their last access date using this option. Use REVERSE to change the sort order. The option is used as follows:

NDIR *path/filename* SORT ACCESS
NDIR *path/filename* REVERSE SORT ACCESS

SORT UPDATE   Files can be listed according to the date of their last update using this option. Use REVERSE to change the sort order. The option is used as follows:

NDIR *path/filename* SORT UPDATE
NDIR *path/filename* REVERSE SORT UPDATE

SORT CREATE   Files can be listed according to the date of their creation using this option. Use REVERSE to change the sort order. The option is used as follows:

NDIR *path/filename* SORT CREATE
NDIR *path/filename* REVERSE SORT CREATE

SORT SIZE   Files can be listed according to size using this option. Use REVERSE to change the sort order. The option is used as follows:

NDIR *path/filename* SORT SIZE
NDIR *path/filename* REVERSE SORT SIZE

SORT ARCHIVE   Files can be listed according to the date of their last archive. Use REVERSE to change the sort order. The option is used as follows:

NDIR *path/filename* SORT ARCHIVE
NDIR *path/filename* REVERSE SORT ARCHIVE

View Options

FO (Files Only)   The FO option is typed on the NDIR command line to specify that only files should be listed.

DO (Directories Only)   The DO option is typed on the NDIR command line to specify that only directories should be listed. This is often used with the SUB option to display the entire directory structure, as discussed in the previous chapter.

SUB (Subdirectories)   The SUB option is typed on the NDIR command line to include subdirectories in the listing of the specified directory. This is often used with the DO option to display the entire directory structure, as discussed in the previous chapter.

MAC (Macintosh)   The MAC option lists files created in the Macintosh environment for the specified directory.

DATES   Use this option to view all time and date stamp information about a file. The last modified, last archived, last accessed, and creation date are listed.

RIGHTS   Used to view user access rights of files.

NDIR Examples

While most of the command options just listed can be used by themselves in NDIR commands, you can combine them, often in productive ways, to list files. This section concentrates on combinations of NDIR options. Keep in mind that these examples represent a small sampling of possible combinations.

Note: Chapter 29 shows you how to place long, extensive, hard-to-remember NDIR commands on menus similar to the NetWare menu utilities, making them much easier and more practical to use on a regular basis.

The following example lists files on drive K that include *.DOC in their filenames and are owned by JOHN:

NDIR   K:*.DOC   OWNER = JOHN

The next example lists files on drive K that include *.DOC in their filenames and have a size greater than 3000 bytes:

NDIR   K:*.DOC   SIZE   GR   3000

The following command lists files on drive K that include *.DOC in their filenames and are owned by JOHN. The list is then sorted by size.

NDIR   K:*.DOC   OWNER = JOHN   SORT   SIZE

The next example lists files on drive K that include *.DOC in their filenames, are owned by JOHN, and were created after 12-25-89:

NDIR K:*.DOC OWNER = JOHN CREATE AFT 12-25-89

The following command lists all files in the SYS volume owned by JOHN. All files in all subdirectories are listed.

NDIR SYS: OWNER = JOHN SUB

The following command lists all files in the SYS volume owned by JOHN in all subdirectories with a size greater than 3000 bytes:

NDIR SYS: OWNER = JOHN SUB SIZE GR 3000

The next command lists all files owned by JOHN in all subdirectories of SYS that have a size greater than 3000 bytes. The SORT FO option produces a list of files only.

NDIR SYS: OWNER = JOHN SUB SIZE GR 3000 SORT FO

The following NDIR command lists all files on drive K that are shareable (S):

NDIR K: S

The next NDIR command lists all files on drive K that have the Shareable and Read Only attributes and that were accessed after 12-25-89:

NDIR K: S RO ACCESS AFT 12-25-89

The next example lists all files in the SYS volume that have the Shareable and Read Only attributes. The list is displayed in reverse sorted order by creation date for all subdirectories. Only files are listed.

NDIR SYS: S RO REVERSE SORT CREATE SUB FO

Pattern Matching with NDIR

Wildcard characters can be used with NDIR to specify a range of files. For example, *.DOC is used in the previous examples to specify all files with the DOC extension. NetWare also allows you to use the asterisk when you are trying to locate files that have a certain pattern within the filename itself. For example, assume the files ACCT16-1.DAT, SAL16-1.DAT, and MKT16-3.DAT exist in a directory. Each file has the string 16 in common, but the string does not hold the same place in each filename. To list the files, use the following command:

```
NDIR   K: *16*
```

Other NDIR Operations

The output of the NDIR command can be sent to a file or printer. If sent to a file, the listing can be saved for later use or included with an archive disk. Supervisors or users who want to clear old files from the server can print a list of files filtered for a particular owner or last-accessed date. Date filtering may help users locate old or unnecessary files for deletion.

The redirection symbol (>) directs the NDIR listing to a file. It may be necessary to edit the file to remove the comments that normally appear on the screen during a listing. In the following example, a listing of all files is sent to the file FILELIST for further editing:

```
NDIR   SYS:  OWNER = JOHN   SUB   FO > FILELIST
```

In the next example, the same list is sent to the printer LPT1:

```
NDIR   SYS:  OWNER = JOHN   SUB   FO > LPT1
```

Note: This command assumes printing is directed to the local printer. To print on a network printer, refer to Chapter 27.

Copying Files with NCOPY

The NCOPY command, like the DOS COPY command, is used to copy files between drives and directories and to duplicate files. The NCOPY command works with Macintosh files as well and can copy both the data and resource forks associated with those files.

The NCOPY command is superior to the DOS COPY command because it transfers groups of files in a more efficient way. Note that files in use cannot be copied. The NCOPY command takes the following form:

NCOPY *source-filename* TO *destination-filename options*

where *source-filename* is the file or group of files to be copied, and *destination-filename* is the destination directory.

The following options can be included with the NCOPY command:

/S (Subdirectories)	Specify this option to copy the subdirectories in the specified directory.
/E (Empty subdirectories)	Specify this option to copy subdirectories, even if they are empty. You must use this option in conjunction with the /S option.
/F (Force sparse files)	Specify this option to force the operating system to write to sparse files.
/P (Preserve file attributes)	Use this option to preserve the existing file attributes when the file is copied.

Note the following:

- Both the source and destination can include a path or mapped drive letter.

- Files can be renamed during a copy by specifying a new filename in *destination-filename.*

- The TO option is not required in NCOPY commands, but it can be used for clarity.

- When a file is copied, it retains the last date and time of the original file; however, the date and time the new file was created and accessed changes.

- The wildcard characters * and ? can be used in commands to designate sets of files. These characters can act as placemarkers when targeting sets of files that have parts of their filenames in common.

- The Purge attribute is not preserved when files are copied with NCOPY. You must reassign the attribute in the new directory if you want to keep it.

- When copying to drives on the workstation, only the Shareable and Read Only attributes are preserved.

The next three examples are commands for copying files between directories. The full path of the directories is used in the first command:

NCOPY   SYS:PUBLIC\PROGRAMS*.DAT   TO   SYS:PUBLIC\DATA

If SYS:PUBLIC\PROGRAMS is the current default directory, only the names of the files need to be specified:

NCOPY   *.DAT   TO   SYS:PUBLIC\DATA

Assuming that drive K is mapped to SYS:PUBLIC\PROGRAMS and L is mapped to SYS:PUBLIC\DATA, the following command copies files from K to L:

NCOPY   K:*.DAT   TO   L:

Copying Between Servers

Files can be copied between file servers, as shown next. In the following command, files in the PROJ-1 directory are copied from server MKTG-1 to the PROJ-2 directory on the MKTG-2 server:

```
NCOPY   MKTG-1/SYS:PROJ-1   TO      MKTG-2/SYS:PROJ-2
```

Assuming that drive S is mapped to MKTG-1/SYS:PROJ-1 and T is mapped to MKTG-2/SYS:PROJ-2, the following command copies *.DAT files between the servers:

```
NCOPY   S:*.DAT   TO   T:
```

Renaming While Copying

In the following command, the file YOURFILE.DOC is duplicated in the same directory by using NCOPY to copy it to another filename. Two files reside on the disk after executing the command.

```
NCOPY   YOURFILE.DOC   TO   MYFILE.DOC
```

Files can be copied and renamed between directories and servers using a similar command, but you must insert the mapped drive letter or full path name of the source or destination directory.

Copying an Entire Directory Structure

An entire directory structure, including all files and all subdirectories, can be copied to another directory, another volume, or another server. In the following command, files and subdirectories in the PROJ-1 directory are copied from server MKTG-1 to the PROJ-2 directory on the MKTG-2 server. The /S option specifies that subdirectories should be copied, and the /E option ensures that even empty subdirectories are copied.

NCOPY   MKTG-1/SYS:PROJ-1   TO   MKTG-2/SYS:PROJ-2 /S/E

Changing File Attributes with FLAG

FLAG commands are used to change the attributes of files at the command line, rather than using the FILER utility. For example, files can also be hidden so they do not appear in directory listings. Each attribute is listed here. A complete description of file attributes can be found under "Changing File Attributes" earlier in this chapter.

RO	Read Only
S	Shareable
H	Hidden
SY	System
T	Transactional
P	Purge
RA	Read Audit
WA	Write Audit
CI	Copy Inhibit
DI	Delete Inhibit
RI	Rename Inhibit

The following options can be used with the FLAG command:

ALL

N (Normal)

SUB (Subdirectory)

The SUB option in the FLAG command specifies that the attributes assigned to files in a directory also be assigned to files in its subdirectories. The Normal option clears all attributes. The ALL option flags a file with all attributes.

To flag files users must have the Read Only, File Scan, and Modify trustee rights in the directory. Users must also be attached to the server where the files are located.

Note: You can use the plus (+) or minus (-) sign in front of each attribute option to add and remove file attributes in the same command.

Viewing File Attributes

To view the file attributes for all files in the current directory, you type **FLAG**. To view attributes for specific files, type the filename, as in the following example:

FLAG MYFILE.DOC

Use wildcard characters to specify a group of files. For example, the following command lists the attributes of the EXE files in the current directory:

FLAG *.EXE

If the files reside in other directories, you must specify the mapped drive letter to those directories or the complete directory path. For example, the first command below displays the attributes of the DOC files in JOHN's user directory:

FLAG SYS:USERS\JOHN*.DOC

If this directory is mapped to drive **F**, the following command performs the same operation:

FLAG F:*.DOC

Changing File Attributes

You can change the attributes of files by specifying the name of the file to change followed by the attributes to assign to the file. The following command changes the attributes of MYFILE.DOC in the current directory to Read Only:

FLAG   MYFILE.DOC   RO

Note: Files should be marked Read Only if you do not want them to be altered or erased by other users.

Wildcard characters can also be used to specify a group of files. For example, the following command changes the attributes of the EXE files in the current directory to Shareable and Read Only:

FLAG *.EXE S RO

Note: Since most program files used on a network should be marked with the Shareable and Read Only attributes, you should use a command similar to the previous one after installing applications in a directory.

If the files reside in other directories, you must specify the mapped drive letter or the complete directory path to those directories. For example, the following command changes the attributes of the DOC files in JOHN's user directory to Normal:

FLAG   SYS:USERS\JOHN*.DOC   N

If this directory is mapped to drive **F**, the following command performs the same operation:

FLAG   F:*.DOC   N

You can mark all files in a directory by specifying the asterisk (*) in the FLAG command. For example, the following command assigns the Shareable and Read Write attribute to the files in the PUB-DATA directory:

FLAG   SYS:PUB-DATA*   S RO

To add and remove attributes in the same command, use the plus (+) and minus (-) signs. In the following command, the Read Only attribute is removed and the file is marked Purge. This makes it possible to delete the file.

FLAG   SYS:USERS\JOHN\REPORTS.DOC   -RO   +P

Flagging Program and Data Files

When you install a program you should create one directory for the program files and another for the data files. Flag the files in these directories differently, as described in the following sections.

Program Files

Mark the program files for the application as Shareable and Read Only. In this way trustees of the directory can use the files but not alter or erase them. The following command changes the program files in the DBASE directory to Shareable and Read Only:

FLAG SYS:DBASE*.* S RO

Remember that anyone using program files in a directory must have at least the Read and File Scan trustee rights. Some programs that create temporary work files may require that users also have the Create, Write, and Delete rights.

Data Files

Mark the data files used by programs as Shareable and Read Write so users can share the files and make changes to them. Be careful when marking files Shareable, however. Some non-database applications do not support shareable files, nor would you want two people working on the same file at the same time. One user could write over the file that has just been changed by another user. In most cases, files used by database programs such as dBASE III and dBASE IV are marked Shareable because each user works on only one record at a time. This is referred to as *record-locking.* Some applications support *file-locking* which prevents two users from accessing a file simultaneously.

Assigning Search Modes
To Executable Files with SMODE

The SMODE command is used to assign a search mode to an executable file or to view the current search mode of a file. An executable file (program file) has the extension EXE or COM. Some program files need to access data files when they run, and if both types of files are in the same directory, the executable files have no trouble finding data files when necessary. However, if the data files are stored outside the program directory where executable files are stored, you must take steps to supply a search path for the data files. The SMODE command assigns one of the following search methods to executable files:

0   Mode 0 is the default setting that specifies no special search instructions. Instead, the executable file looks for instructions in the SHELL.CFG file, as discussed in Chapter 11. The command SEARCH MODE = n is placed in CONFIG.SYS, where n is equal to modes 1 through 7, described here.

1   The executable file uses a path of its own, or if that path is not specified, the executable file searches the default directory and the current search drive mappings.

2   The executable file searches only the default drive.

3   The executable file uses its own path, or if such a path is not defined and if the executable file opens Read Only data files, the default directory and the current search drive mappings are searched.

4   Reserved.

5   The executable file searches the default directories and search drives.

6   Reserved.

7   If Read Only data files are used by the executable file, it searches the default directory and all search drives.

The SMODE command takes the following form:

SMODE *path/filename option*

where *path* is a mapped drive letter or the full path to a directory, *filename* is the name of the file to assign the mode to, and *option* is one of the search modes. For example, the following command assigns mode 5 to the START.EXE file in a directory called SYS:PUBLIC\PROGRAMS:

SMODE SYS:PUBLIC\PROGRAMS\START.EXE 5

To view the search modes of files in a directory, type the command without specifying a search mode.

File Trustees and Inherited Rights

NetWare 386 provides four commands that grant users trustee rights to individual files as well as directories, and that supervisors and managers can use to apply an inherited rights mask to a file to prevent users from inheriting rights to access the file. A complete discussion of the commands and how they are used with directories is covered in Chapter 23. You can specify filenames in the commands in the same way you would specify directory paths.

ALLOW   The ALLOW command applies an inherited rights mask to a file. The form of the command used with files is

ALLOW *path/filename   rights*

where *path / filename* is the file to change and *rights* is one of the rights listed in the TLIST section of Chapter 23.

TLIST   The TLIST command lists the trustees of the specified file. The form of the command for files is

TLIST *path/filename*

GRANT   The GRANT command grants trustee rights to a user for a directory or file. In the following form the command grants rights to a file:

GRANT *rights* FOR *path/filename* TO *name*

Rights is the list of rights found in Chapter 23, *path / filename* is the file, and *name* is the user to receive the rights.

REVOKE   The REVOKE command removes a user's trustee rights to a directory or file. It is used in the same way as the GRANT command.

Salvaging Deleted Files

Most computers have limited disk space, so it is helpful to remove unnecessary files. That a delete function exists at all can be a danger on a filing system that holds extremely valuable information. Often an inexperienced or weary user accidentally erases the wrong files.

With NetWare, this is not always a serious problem if you recover the files as soon as possible using the RECOVER menu. Files cannot be recovered under certain conditions. The following rules apply to erased files that you may want to salvage:

- Do not log out of the file server. Logging out eliminates the possibility of restoring the erased files with RECOVER.

- Do not create or erase any more files on the volume where files were erased. SALVAGE cannot recover a file once another file has been created or deleted on the same volume.

- Do not issue a PURGE command, which would render all erased files irrecoverable.

- Only files deleted by the current workstation can be salvaged. Activities on other workstations do not affect the salvageable status of the deleted files on the current workstation.

- The SALVAGE command should be issued at the workstation where files were originally deleted.

The SALVAGE menu should be brought up immediately after accidentally deleting files. When you type **SALVAGE** the SALVAGE main menu appears, as shown here:

There are two possible types of salvageable files: those deleted in existing directories and those that existed in directories that have been deleted. When a directory is deleted, its salvageable files are saved in a hidden file called DELETED.SAV. The directory file is accessed by choosing the **Salvage From Deleted Directories** option. Recoverable files in the current directory can be salvaged by selecting **View/Recover Deleted**

Files. To salvage files in other directories, choose **Select Current Directory**. To set SALVAGE's options, choose **Set Salvage Options**.

Changing Directories

If you need to switch to a different directory, choose the **Select Current Directory** option. A box appears in which you can enter the path to the target directory. Recall that you can use INS to insert server, volume, and directory information.

Setting Salvage Options

You can change the way files are listed when SALVAGE shows you a list of salvageable files by selecting **Set Salvage Options** from the main menu. The following menu appears:

Select the sort order most appropriate to the types of files you need to recover. In most cases you will choose **Sort List by Filename**, but you may need to recover files based on the deletion date (which would list the most recently created file).

Salvaging Files

To salvage files in the current directory, select **View/Recover Deleted Files** from the SALVAGE main menu. To salvage files in a deleted directory, choose the **Salvage From Deleted Directories** option on the SALVAGE main menu. A box appears in which you can enter the filename pattern you want to match. For example, to list salvageable files with the extension DAT, you type *.**DAT**. To see all files, type the asterisk by itself. A screen listing salvageable files appears, similar to the one shown in Figure 24-4.

```
                        30 Salvageable Files
┌─────────────────────────────────────────────────────────────┐
│..              3-00-80 12:00:00am <DIR>                        │
│/               0-00-80 12:00:00am <DIR>                        │
│00000002        5-20-90  1:00:06pm <DIR>       UNKNOWN          │
│00000001.QDR    5-20-90 12:46:44pm <DIR>       UNKNOWN          │
│TCCTOK          5-23-90 11:10:00am <DIR>       UNKNOWN          │
│AUTOEXEC.NCF    5-17-90  5:48:08pm        130  FS1             │
│AUTOEXEC.NCF    5-17-90  5:47:34pm        100  FS1             │
│DCB.DSK         5-11-90  2:25:46pm      16034  FS1             │
│FIG18-6.PIX     5-16-90 10:02:42pm       2106  SUPERVISOR      │
│FILELIST        5-25-90  6:24:28pm          0  SUPERVISOR      │
│GO001.BAT       5-20-90 11:22:44pm          0  SUPERVISOR      │
└─────────────────────────────────────────────────────────────┘
```

Figure 24-4.   SALVAGE lists the files that can be salvaged

To salvage files, scroll through the list, marking those to recover with F5 (Mark). You can mark a set of files with similarities in their filenames by pressing F6. Enter a filename pattern using wildcards. All files that match the pattern are marked. When all the files are marked, press ENTER. SALVAGE asks for confirmation to recover the files.

Note: Selected files can be purged from the list by pressing DEL. When a file is purged, it can no longer be salvaged. This may be important for security reasons.

Purging Files with PURGE

In some cases you may want to completely remove files that have been deleted without any chance of recovering them. This is often the case where security is a concern and you do not want someone possibly salvaging the files you have just erased. The PURGE command removes the possibility of recovering any files that were deleted by your workstation. The command does not affect files deleted by other workstations.

The command takes the following form:

PURGE *path/filename* /ALL

where *path/filename* is the path to a directory or a file. You can specify that an entire directory be purged, or you can specify a single file. The ALL option purges all files in the current directory. For example, to purge all files in the SYS:PUB-DATA directory, you would type

PURGE   SYS:PUB-DATA   /ALL

Creating and Managing Users

Setting Default Restrictions
Steps to Creating New Users
Defining Operators
Command Utilities for Managing Users
The MAKEUSER and USERDEF Commands

Chapters 20, 21, and 22 provided an overview of the initial steps a supervisor goes through when setting up a NetWare system, including adding users, directories, and system security. This chapter provides more information on creating users. Also covered are the MAKEUSER and USERDEF utilities, which simplify the task of creating multiple users in educational or large system environments.

Setting Default Restrictions

As a supervisor you can set password, time, station, and other restrictions for each user individually, but to set default restrictions that apply to all users you use the SYSCON utility. Choose **Supervisor Options** from the SYSCON main menu to display the following Supervisor Options menu:

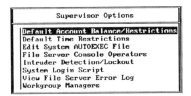

The Default Account Balance/Restrictions option, Default Time Restrictions option, and the Intruder Detection/Lockout option may be set by managers to create default settings before setting options for individual users.

Setting Default Account Restrictions

The Default Account Balance/Restrictions menu is shown in Figure 25-1. Keep in mind that a similar menu is available for each user or group account. You must decide whether to set the options on this menu as a system default or for individual accounts. Each option is discussed in the following sections.

```
          Default Account Balance/Restrictions
Account Has Expiration Date:        Yes
    Date Account Expires:           June 1, 1990
Limit Concurrent Connections:       Yes
    Maximum Connections:            1
Require Password:                   Yes
    Minimum Password Length:        5
Force Periodic Password Changes:    Yes
    Days Between Forced Changes:     40
    Limit Grace Logins:             Yes
        Grace Logins Allowed:       6
Require Unique Passwords:           Yes
Account Balance:                    0
Allow Unlimited Credit:             No
    Low Balance Limit:              0
```

Figure 25-1.   The Default Account Balance/Restrictions menu is used to set restrictions for all users

Account Has Expiration Date

The Account Has Expiration Date field specifies a date when all accounts expire. When the expiration date is reached, no one can log in except the supervisor. The accounts are not removed from the system. The supervisor can add new expiration dates to accounts or remove those accounts no longer needed.

It is not recommended that you set this option as a system default, unless you need it for security reasons or if the system is used in a temporary environment such as a classroom. The default setting is No. If you set this field to Yes, you can set the expiration date for all accounts.

To set account expiration dates for individual users, choose **User Information** from SYSCON's main menu, select a user, and then select **Account Restrictions** from the User Information menu. The Account Restrictions menu for the user appears. Note that you can also disable the account if necessary.

Limit Concurrent Connections

The Limit Concurrent Connections option on the Default Account Balance/Restrictions menu limits how many stations any user can log into at the same time. The default setting is No, which means that users are not limited. Set this field to Yes to limit users, and then specify the number of stations they can simultaneously log into. This option can be useful for security reasons or to prevent workstation and system resources from being overused.

Require Password

Set the Require Password field to Yes to require all users to enter a password when logging in. This field should normally be set to Yes if you want to ensure adequate security. The Minimum Password Length field specifies the number of characters in a password. The more characters you require, the better your security.

When the Require Password field is set to Yes, the remaining fields in the menu become active or are changed to default settings.

Force Periodic Password Changes

The supervisor can force users to change their passwords at the specified interval to enhance system security. Set the Force Periodic Password Changes field to Yes, and then specify the number of days between changes. The Limit Grace Logins field limits the number of times users can log in with an expired password. Normally, several login attempts should be allowed to give users a chance to change their password. Specify the number of grace logins in the Grace Logins Allowed field.

Require Unique Password

If you specify the Require Unique Password field, you can require all users to specify passwords that have not been used in the last 10 password changes.

Account Balance

You can use the last three fields of the menu to specify account balances for all users, whether they have credit, and their low balance limits. The accounting features of NetWare are discussed in Chapter 31.

Default Time Restrictions

From the Supervisor Options menu, select **Default Time Restrictions** to change the default times when all users except the supervisor can log in. You can use the F5 (Mark) key to mark the times you do not want users to log in, and then press DEL to remove the asterisk characters from the marked area. Times that do not have asterisk characters are times that no users can log in.

Intruder Detection Lockout

From the Supervisor Options menu, select **Intruder Detection/Lockout** to set the default conditions for recognizing intruders. Intruders may attempt to log in with unrecognized user names and passwords. You usually want to set the Detect Intruders field to Yes to initiate system-wide intruder detection. Each individual user's account can also be set using the Intruder Lockout Status option on the User Information menu.

The intruder detection feature sets a limit on attempted logins. For example, assume a user is trying to break into the system with Joe's login account name. The intruder assumes that Joe might be using the name of one of his children as a password and attempts to log in, using each child's name. If Joe does use a child's name as a password, there is a good chance the intruder will gain access. The default number of incorrect login attempts is 7. This number can be reduced, but it is not recommended; instead, users should be encouraged to use passwords that are not obvious.

The Intruder Detection/Lockout menu is shown here:

```
┌─────────────────────────────────────────────────────────┐
│              Intruder Detection/Lockout                   │
│                                                           │
│ Detect Intruders:              Yes                        │
│                                                           │
│ Intruder Detection Threshold                              │
│ Incorrect Login Attempts:      7                          │
│ Bad Login Count Retention Time: 0  Days   0  Hours   30 Minutes │
│                                                           │
│ Lock Account After Detection:  Yes                        │
│   Length Of Account Lockout:   0  Days   0  Hours   15 Minutes │
└─────────────────────────────────────────────────────────┘
```

Set the Detect Intruder field to Yes to enable the feature. You can then set the detection threshold and the length of lockout in the remaining fields. The initial threshold level is set to 7, but you can change this to any level you wish.

The Bad Login Count Retention Time field is set to the amount of time the operating system keeps track of incorrect logins. After the time has been exceeded, the incorrect login count is reset to 0.

The Lock Account After Detection field specifies the amount of time an account is locked after an intruder has been detected.

Users may find their accounts locked when they need access. This is possible if they forgot their passwords and attempted to log in using the guess method. To unlock a user account that has been locked, select **User**

Information from the SYSCON main menu, and then select the user that needs access to an account. Select **Intruder Lockout Status** and change the Account Locked field to No.

Steps to Creating New Users

The steps for creating a user discussed in this section explain how to give a user proper access to the system. MAKEUSER and USERDEF, described at the end of this chapter, can be used to perform most of the steps described here for a large number of users. If you are establishing a new network or a new group of users, you should refer to these utilities now. Supervisors running a school network that changes its network users every semester or quarter can use the utilities for defining new users.

Use the following steps as a guide to creating new users with commands other than MAKEUSER and USERDEF. Most of the options covered are available on the User Information menu shown here (although they are not discussed in the order shown):

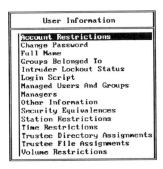

Add the user.   You must use the SYSCON utility to create new users, unless you use MAKEUSER or USERDEF. Select **User Information** from the SYSCON main menu, and press INS to begin adding new users. Type the new user's name and press ENTER. The name appears in the User Names window. Press ENTER on the new name to display the User Information window. Select **Full Name**, type the user's full name in the window, and press ENTER.

Assign the user to a manager.   To save yourself some steps, you may want to assign the user to a work group or user account manager before going further. You can then delegate the remaining tasks to the manager. Remember that work group and user account managers can change account restrictions, trustee rights, and other user account options discussed in the remaining steps.

Add the user to groups.   You can reduce the steps to creating new users by adding them to groups that already have trustee rights and work group or user account managers. Doing so may save you the need to perform some of the remaining tasks in this section.

New users automatically belong to the group EVERYONE. They can be added to other groups and receive the same trustee rights as those groups. Select **Groups Belonged To** from the User Information window, and press INS to select new groups. It may be convenient to increase the trustee rights and other features of the EVERYONE group if directory security on your system is not critical. You could assign EVERYONE trustee rights to any number of program and data directories. New users then automatically gain these rights when created.

Assign account restrictions for users.   From the User Information window select **Account Restrictions** to assign password and login restrictions to the user. Recall from the previous section that these restrictions may have been set using the supervisor's default options for the entire system.

Assign station and time restrictions to users.   Add station restrictions by selecting **Station Restrictions** from the User Information window. Add time restrictions by selecting **Time Restrictions** from the User Information window.

Change the intruder lockout status.   If you need to change the lockout status for the user, select **Intruder Lockout Status** from the User Information menu. You can lock or unlock the account and change the number of incorrect logins allowed. Use the Account Reset Time option to change the amount of time it takes to reset the account to an unlocked state after it has been locked due to intruder detection.

Apply disk volume restrictions.   If you are limiting space on the file server, you can apply a disk space limitation to the user by selecting **Volume Restrictions** on the User Information menu, as shown here:

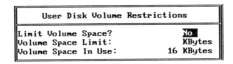

```
┌──────────────────────────────────────┐
║    User Disk Volume Restrictions       ║
╠──────────────────────────────────────╣
║Limit Volume Space?            No       ║
║Volume Space Limit:            KBytes   ║
║Volume Space In Use:        16 KBytes   ║
└──────────────────────────────────────┘
```

After selecting a volume, the Disk Volume Restrictions window appears. Type **Yes** to limit space, and then enter the amount of space to allocate to the user.

Make the user a manager if necessary.   To make the user a work group manager, return to SYSCON's Available Topics menu and select **Supervisor Options**. From the Supervisor Options menu, select **Workgroup Managers**. When the Workgroup Managers window appears, press INS to add the new user to the list.

     To make the user a user account manager, select **Managed Users and Groups** from the User Information menu. Press the INS key to display a list of possible users and groups. Select one or more users, and press ENTER to add them to the Managed Users and Groups list.

Create the user's personal directory.   Most new users need a personal directory in which they can store files and programs of their own. The steps for creating this directory can be performed while assigning trustee rights in the next step. Personal directories may branch from SYS:USERS if you have been following the examples in this book. Users can be granted full supervisory rights starting at the personal directory.

Assign trustee rights.   Users must have rights in the directories they need to access. In some cases users inherit all the rights they need in a directory. In other cases the supervisor or manager must grant specific trustee rights. For example, users inherit Read and File Scan rights in the DOS subdirectories that branch from SYS:PUBLIC because of their membership in the EVERYONE group. Recall that NetWare grants EVERYONE Read and File Scan rights to SYS:PUBLIC.

To add additional trustee rights, select **Trustee Assignments** from the User Information menu and press INS. Create a personal directory for the user by pressing INS at the Trustee Directory Assignments menu. You can type the full path of the directory, or press INS to select server, volume, and directory names from lists. Once the directory is created, highlight it and press ENTER to assign rights. Press INS and add the Supervisor right to grant users full access to their directory.

If necessary, add additional directories and assign trustee rights using the methods just described. Remember to specify at least the Read and File Scan rights in program directories and the Read, Write, Create, Erase, and File Scan rights in data directories.

Create a login script.   You can create a login script for each user by selecting **Login Scripts** from the User Information menu. Login scripts are discussed in Chapter 28.

Train users.   Once users have been added to the system, they can be trained on its use. Make sure users know their limitations on the system. They must know where programs and data are located and how to start programs. They should also be familiarized with printing techniques. Chapter 26 discusses commands used by all network users, which is helpful information for new users. Users can type **Help** at the command line to use the NetWare Help facility.

Defining Operators

Users can be defined as console, print server, or queue operators. This section explains how to define a console operator. Chapter 27 explains how to create print server and queue operators.

Console operators are users who have been given rights to access and use the FCONSOLE menu utility and the file server console. Only the supervisor is allowed to assign FCONSOLE rights to a user. Normal users and console operators have the following FCONSOLE rights:

- Users can use FCONSOLE to change file servers, view current user connection information, view a file server's LAN driver information, and view the version of NetWare currently running on the server.

- Console operators have the additional rights to broadcast messages, purge salvageable files, view more detailed current user connection information, view file and lock activity, see and alter the status of the file server, and view statistics about the file server's performance.

- Supervisors are the only operators who are given the right to down the server from the FCONSOLE utility.

To designate a console operator, supervisors should start the SYSCON menu utility and select **Supervisor Options** from the main menu. Select **File Server Console Operators** from the menu. Press INS to see a list of users and groups. Select a user or group, and press ENTER to add them to the list.

Command Utilities for Managing Users

Most command utilities listed in this section have already been discussed. They are briefly covered here to describe their usefulness in managing users.

Viewing the Trustee List with TLIST

Supervisors can use the TLIST command to view the current trustee list for any directory. Only trustee lists for directories on the current server may be viewed.

To view the trustees for the current directory, type **TLIST**. Information similar to the following is displayed:

```
User Trustees:
    JOHN            [ RWCE F ]              (JOHN JONES)
    -----
Group Trustees:
    EVERYONE    [ R  F ]
    DEPT-MGRS  [SR  F ]                    (DEPARTMENT MANAGERS)
```

If no users or trustees exist, the display says so. The trustee rights in the directory are listed next to the user name.

You can view the trustee list in any directory by specifying the full path to the directory or by using a mapped drive letter if one has been established. In the following examples, drive K is mapped to the SYS:PUBLIC\PROGRAMS directory:

```
TLIST   K:
```

or

```
TLIST   SYS:PUBLIC\PROGRAMS
```

Both commands accomplish the same operation, which is to list the trustees for the directory.

Supervisors can use the TLIST command to determine who is using a directory and what rights each user has in the directory. If a user is having trouble accessing programs or files, that user may not have the proper rights. The supervisor can use TLIST to determine exactly what a user's rights are, and then use the GRANT command to assign additional rights.

Viewing Current Users with USERLIST

The USERLIST command displays the current users and their connection information, such as connection numbers, login times, node addresses, and network addresses. The command also assists in sending messages since it lists the name of each user on the system. The command takes the following form:

USERLIST *server/user* */option*

where *server* is the optional name of the server to list and *user* is the optional name of the user to list. The *options* are described here:

/A (All)	Displays the connection number, login time, network address, and node address. This information is useful to a supervisor who needs to know where a particular user is working. This option also provides information a supervisor may need to disconnect a workstation from the server because it has locked up.
/O (Object)	Displays the type of object attached. In most cases this is USER.
/C (Continuous)	Use this option to make the list scroll continuously.

To begin using the command, simply type **USERLIST** on the command line. A screen similar to the following appears:

Connection	User Name	Login Time
1	*SUPERVISOR	12-25-89 7:00 am
2	JOHN	12-25-89 9:00 am
3	JANE	12-25-89 10:00 am

An asterisk appears next to the current user's name. To view information for only one user, type the user's name. For example, information about JOHN's connection is listed with the following command:

USERLIST JOHN

Use the option /A to list network and node address information about a user. In the following example, network and node information for JOHN is displayed:

USERLIST JOHN /A

To view the user list of another file server, specify the name of the file server in the command. In the following example, users on the ACCTG server are listed:

USERLIST   ACCTG/

To view information about the user TIM on the ACCTG server, type the following command:

USERLIST   ACCTG/TIM

To view node and network information for the user TIM on the ACCTG server, type the following command:

USERLIST   ACCTG/TIM   /A

GRANT

You can use the GRANT command in place of the SYSCON and FILER utilities to assign trustee rights to users and groups, assuming you have already created those users and groups with the SYSCON utility.

The GRANT command takes the following form:

GRANT *option* ... FOR *path* TO [USER or GROUP] *name*

where *option* is the first letter of NetWare's trustee rights. FOR *path* designates the directory where trustee assignments are to be granted. TO is used to designate the user or group to be granted the rights. Two additional options not shown above are ONLY and ALL BUT, which you can use to grant only the specified right or all but the specified right. Place these options in front of the rights designators. Replace *name* with the user's account name.

Note: USER and GROUP are optional and are used when a user and a group share the same name.

The GRANT command must be issued for each user or group to be granted rights. To grant rights in the current default directory, type the command followed by the letters of the rights to grant and the user. To grant rights in another directory, the full path to the directory must be specified or the directory must have a mapped drive letter.

For a complete discussion of the GRANT command, refer to Chapters 23 and 24.

REVOKE

You can use the REVOKE command in place of the SYSCON and FILER utilities to revoke trustee rights to users and groups, assuming those users and groups already have been created by the SYSCON utility.

The REVOKE command takes the following form:

REVOKE *option* ... FOR *path* FROM [USER or GROUP] *name*

where *option* is the first letter of one of the rights listed earlier. FOR *path* designates the directory in which trustee assignments are to be revoked. FROM is used to designate the user or group whose rights are to be revoked. An additional option not shown above is ALL, which can be used to revoke all the rights of a user or group. Replace *name* with the user's account name.

Note: USER and GROUP are optional and are used when a user and a group share the same name.

You must issue the REVOKE command for each user or group whose rights you want to revoke. To revoke rights in the current default directory, type the command followed by the letters of the rights to revoke and the user.

A supervisor can use REVOKE to quickly remove users' trustee rights in various directories. It may be necessary to prevent a user from accessing a file if the user has changed positions in the company. If temporary help is used, rights can be removed from temporary user accounts in various directories according to the type of work and the directories the users need.

For a complete discussion of REVOKE, see Chapters 23 and 24.

REMOVE

You use the REMOVE command to remove a user or group from the trustee list of a directory. The command is different from the REVOKE command, which revokes users' rights in directories but does not remove them from the trustee list.

The command takes the following form:

REMOVE *user or group* FROM *path*

The *user or group* option is used to specify the name of the user or the group to remove in the directory specified by *path*. If a user and group have the same name, precede the name with USER or GROUP to indicate which to use. Only those users who have Parental effective rights in a directory can remove users in that directory.

To remove a user from the current directory, specify the name of the user after the command. To remove a user or group from another directory, you must specify the full path name of that directory, or map the directory to a drive.

Checking the System Security

The supervisor can use the SECURITY command to determine how secure the network is. The command must be run from the SYS:SYSTEM directory or the supervisor must have a search drive mapped to the directory.

The SECURITY command is extremely useful for locating holes in security. SECURITY lists each user or group one by one and reports on the conditions described in the following sections.

Password assignments   If an account does not have a password, anyone can sign in under that account name and use the system with all the trustee rights assigned to the account. The SUPERVISOR account should always be given a password, as well as those users who have rights to valuable or sensitive data. The SECURITY listing helps you find holes in password security and fix them. You may want to use the Default Account Balance/Restrictions menu under the Supervisor Options selection in the SYSCON menu to specify that passwords are required by all users, as discussed in the first part of this chapter.

Insecure Passwords   Insecure passwords are passwords that might be easy to guess or that do not require periodic changes. The following password options are checked by SECURITY:

- Passwords similar to the login names

- Accounts that can use passwords of less than five characters

- Accounts that do not require password changes at least every 60 days

- Accounts that have unlimited grace logins

- Accounts that do not require new and unique passwords when passwords are changed

Supervisor Security Equivalence   SECURITY lists all accounts that are equivalent to SUPERVISOR. In most cases, only one supervisor should have these rights. If the rights are given to another user, they should only be temporary.

Root Directory Privileges   Users should never have privileges in the root directory. Users with parental rights in the root directory can grant themselves rights in all other directories.

No Login Scripts   Users who do not have personal login scripts are listed.

Excessive Rights   SECURITY lists users with excessive rights in the SYSTEM, PUBLIC, LOGIN, and MAIL directories. Only the supervisor should have rights in SYSTEM. Users normally should have only the Read and File Scan rights in PUBLIC and LOGIN, and only the Write and Create rights in MAIL.

Using the SECURITY Command

The SECURITY command is located in the SYSTEM directory; therefore, only the supervisor can use the command. To invoke the command, type **SECURITY**. The screen scrolls by quickly, so press PAUSE. It may be beneficial to redirect the output of SECURITY to a file for printing or viewing. The following command redirects the listing produced by SECURITY to a file called SECUR.DOC:

SECURITY > SECUR.DOC

To print the file, use the NetWare NPRINT command as shown here:

NPRINT SECUR.DOC

To view the file in paged mode, type

MORE < SECUR.DOC

Clearing a Connection

It may sometimes be necessary for a supervisor to clear a user's connection. This usually is necessary when a workstation crashes but the server has not yet released its files. In other situations, a user is no longer welcome on the system, or an intruder has managed to gain access, in which case the supervisor may find it necessary to shut the workstation down. Use the CLEAR STATION command from the console to perform these tasks. The command should be used with caution since it clears all file server resources allocated to the specific workstation.

Before using the CLEAR STATION command, you must determine the station number to shut down. Type **USERLIST** from another workstation to determine the number. Once you know the workstation number, you can clear the station. For example, the following command clears station 3:

CLEAR STATION 3

The MAKEUSER And USERDEF Commands

The MAKEUSER and USERDEF commands create or delete large groups of users. Both commands are designed to make a supervisor's or manager's task easier. The commands are especially useful in corporate or educational environments where large numbers of users are added and removed on a regular basis. A school might add new users at the beginning of a semester or quarter, and then remove the users at the end of the period.

The following descriptions outline the difference between the commands.

- *MAKEUSER* The MAKEUSER command processes a script file that contains a series of commands that define exactly how user accounts should be set up. The script can contain commands to create multiple users. MAKEUSER is preferable in an environment where users have different types of account requirements, but it requires more planning to create the script files.

- *USERDEF* The USERDEF command provides an easy way to create accounts for individual users as needed. Templates are created that contain standard values as to how accounts should be set up. The names of new users to be added to the system are typed in a list. When the command is executed, an account for each user in the list is created with the values in the template.

The MAKEUSER Command

The MAKEUSER command allows you to create or edit a script file that contains various commands for defining new users, setting up their accounts, assigning them to groups, assigning a login script, and other common tasks. The script file is then processed by MAKEUSER to create each user. The MAKEUSER main menu is shown here:

You use the first option to create a new script file and the second option to edit an existing script file. Use the last option to process the file. When a new script file is created, MAKEUSER asks you to name the file. It is then saved on disk with the extension USR. It is recommended that you create a directory for processing script files.

Creating a USR File

The USR file contains a list of users you want to create, along with the rights and restrictions to be assigned to each user. Special keywords are used to define each user's parameters. These keywords are covered under "MAKEUSER Keywords" later in this chapter.

To begin creating users, type the command **MAKEUSER**. When the MAKEUSER main menu appears, select **Create New USR File** from the menu and press ENTER. The MAKEUSER editing screen appears. All of the commands and keywords required to create a user can be typed on the editing screen. When the USR file is complete, press ESC, and a prompt asks you to name the new USR file.

Each keyword in a MAKEUSER script file is typed on a separate line. Keywords define specific user parameters and are followed by one or more CREATE keywords. The CREATE keyword defines the users who are to receive the parameters just listed. In the following example, the keywords above the CREATE statements define the accounts for HENRY and JANE:

```
#REM File to create clerks
#PASSWORD_REQUIRED
#PASSWORD_LENGTH 5
#UNIQUE_PASSWORD
#CONNECTIONS 1
#HOME_DIRECTORY SYS:USERS
#GROUPS CLERKS
#CREATE HENRY;Henry Jones;kokomo;;SYS:PUB-DATA RWCFE
#CREATE JANE;Jane Beach;plymouth;;SYS:PUB-DATA RWCFE
```

You can define another group of users that has different settings within the same script file. To start a new group, first type the CLEAR keyword, and then type a new set of parameters. Below the parameters, include CREATE statements with the names of the user accounts. You can repeat this process for each new set of users. When the script file is processed, MAKEUSER creates accounts for each of the users defined in the CREATE statements.

Note: If a USR script is being created to delete users or sets of users, replace the CREATE keyword with the DELETE keyword.

Processing USR Files

Once you have created the USR file, you can process it by selecting **Process USR File** from the MAKEUSER main menu. You are asked to specify the name of the file to process, which should be the name you used in the CREATE statement. The processing phase of MAKEUSER first scans the file to determine if any commands are incorrect or typed wrong. If so, an error occurs with an appropriate description. You can then select **Edit USR File** from the MAKEUSER main menu to make the required changes to the file.

Once the file is correct, processing continues normally. MAKEUSER creates a report file with the same name as the USR file and the extension of RPT. You should scan this file to determine if any other errors occurred during processing. You can use the TYPE command to view the file.

MAKEUSER Keywords

The CREATE and DELETE keywords are covered first in this section since they are required to define or remove any user. The keywords also have special options that you should know about before learning the other options.

CREATE   The CREATE keyword is used to create users and specify information about them. It takes the following form:

#CREATE *username;fullname;password;group..;directory* [*rights*]

You must specify the *username* variable; all others are optional. The variables are described here:

username	The account name to be given to the user.
fullname	Defines the full name of the user.
password	Assigns a password to new users.
group	Defines the groups the new user will belong to. Several groups can be specified.
directory	Specifies a path to a directory that the user will have trustee rights to. The trustee rights are typed within the square brackets. ALL can be used to specify all rights. The default rights are Read and File Scan.

Follow these rules when using the CREATE command:

- Separate all fields with a semicolon.

- If a field contains more than one variable, separate each variable with a comma.

- If the command reaches the end of the line, type **+** (plus sign) to extend the field to the next line.

- A user name can only be used once per USR file.

- Use a semicolon as a placeholder for fields that are not used. Use a caret (^) to terminate a line at any point. For example, to specify a user name and password but not a full name, type the following:

#CREATE JUNE;;OKIDOKI^

DELETE The DELETE keyword deletes users and related information. You can use DELETE to remove a set of users, and it can be used in the same file that contains a CREATE statement. The keyword takes the form

#DELETE *username;username...*

Replace *username* with the account name of the user to delete. User names must be separated by semicolons. This command is useful in an academic environment where a teacher may want to delete the names of a previous class. Since the command can be used in the same file as a CREATE keyword, old students can be removed while new ones are created.

Use the CLEAR or RESET command to separate statements that use the CREATE keyword from those that use the DELETE keyword. It may also be necessary to include the HOME_DIRECTORY and PURGE_USER_DIRECTORY keywords before the DELETE keyword in order to remove the users' special directories. Refer to the keywords below for more details.

ACCOUNT_EXPIRATION This keyword specifies when a user's account expires. If ACCOUNT_EXPIRATION is not used, the account never expires. The keyword takes the form

#ACCOUNT_EXPIRATION *date*

where *date* is specified in the full, formal date format, such as June 15, 1990. The keyword applies to all users until a CLEAR or RESET keyword is encountered.

ACCOUNTING   The ACCOUNTING keyword specifies the amount of accounting services a user can use. The account balance and low balance limits are specified. The server must support the accounting system. To install accounting, select the **Accounting** option from the SYSCON main menu. The keyword takes the form

#ACCOUNTING *balance;lowlimit*

where *balance* and *lowlimit* are numeric values used by the accounting system, as discussed in Chapter 31. Both must be specified, and *balance* cannot be less than *lowlimit*. The ACCOUNTING keyword affects all users until a RESET or CLEAR keyword is encountered.

CLEAR or RESET   The CLEAR or RESET keywords start a new set of keywords in the same USR file. Using these keywords is equivalent to starting a new file. Any keywords previously entered no longer have any effect on new CREATE or DELETE keywords.

CONNECTIONS   The CONNECTIONS keyword specifies the maximum concurrent connections each new user can have. If not specified, each user can have as many concurrent connections as possible on the network. The keyword takes the form

#CONNECTIONS *x*

where *x* is the number of concurrent connections.

GROUPS   Use the GROUPS keyword to assign users to groups. The groups must have already been created in SYSCON. The command takes the form

#GROUPS *group;group;...*

You must specify each group after entering the keyword. Several groups can be specified, but they must be separated by semicolons.

HOME_DIRECTORY   The HOME_DIRECTORY keyword creates home directories in a specified directory path. The user's name becomes the name of the new directory. It will branch from the specified home directory. The command takes the form

#HOME_DIRECTORY *path*

where *path* is the home directory. Be sure to specify the full path, including the volume name. If a path is not specified, a user directory is created that branches from the root directory. The keyword automatically assigns all rights to the user's home directory.

If you use the HOME_DIRECTORY command when creating the user, you must use it again to delete the user. To do so, type it before the DELETE keyword.

LOGIN_SCRIPT   The LOGIN_SCRIPT keyword specifies the login script for each user, and the login script must already exist. The keyword takes the form

#LOGIN_SCRIPT *filename*

where *filename* is the name of the login script. The script can be created with a text editor. The login script is stored in the MAIL directory under the new user's ID number.

MAX_DISK_SPACE   The MAX_DISK_SPACE keyword specifies the maximum amount of disk space available to a user. Disk space is allocated in blocks of 4K each. If not specified, users have unlimited disk space. The command takes the form

#MAX_DISK_SPACE *x*

where x is the number of disk blocks.

PASSWORD_LENGTH   The PASSWORD_LENGTH keyword specifies the minimum length of a new user's password. The length must be between 1 and 20 characters, and the default is 5. The command takes the form

D_LENGTH *x*

where *x* is the length of the password. PASSWORD_LENGTH can help in keeping the system secure by preventing passwords that might be easy to guess.

PASSWORD_PERIOD   The PASSWORD_PERIOD keyword specifies the number of days between password expirations. The command takes the form

#PASSWORD_PERIOD *days*

where *days* is the number of days between expiration periods. If this keyword is not used, the password never expires. The range is from 1 to 365 days.

PASSWORD_REQUIRED   The PASSWORD_REQUIRED keyword specifies that users must have passwords. You type the command without parameters in the USR file above the CREATE keyword.

PURGE_USER_DIRECTORY   Use the PURGE_USER_DIRECTORY keyword with the DELETE keyword to specify that the user's special home directory be deleted along with the account. Place the keyword before the DELETE keyword.

REM   You use the REM keyword to place comments in the USR file. All text after the REM keyword is ignored during processing.

RESTRICTED_TIME   The RESTRICTED_TIME keyword specifies when the user cannot log into the file server. The command takes the form

#RESTRICTED_TIME *day,start,end;...*

where *day, start,* and *end* are normal day and time formats, as shown in the following example:

#RESTRICTED_TIME mon,8:00 am,2:00 pm

STATIONS   Use the STATIONS keyword to specify the stations the user can log into. The command takes the form

#STATIONS *network,station...*

More than one *station* can be typed for each *network,* and more than one *network* can be typed. Each *station* in a network set is separated by a command and network sets are separated by semicolons. The addresses must be the hexadecimal addresses of stations created during installation.

UNIQUE_PASSWORD   The UNIQUE_PASSWORD keyword forces a user to create a unique password. A unique password is one that is not the same as the last ten passwords.

Defining Users with USERDEF

The USERDEF command creates user accounts with parameters defined on a template. The same template can be used to create additional users at any time. Several templates, each with different values, can be created and used to define different types of users. You can use this utility to create multiple users, provide simple login scripts, and set up home directories, minimal login/password security, account restrictions, and print job configurations.

The supervisor may need to complete the following steps before running USERDEF, depending on the features of the accounts.

1. Install the accounting option in SYSCON if the feature is to be used.

2. Create additional user groups in SYSCON if groups other than EVERYONE will be required.

3. Create the applications directories for the programs you will install.

4. Create the USERS directory (or suitable equivalent) where the user's personal directories can be created.

5. Create print job configurations in PRINTCON so the configurations will be available for new users.

To use the USERDEF utility, first define a set of user names. Then edit the template, or use it as is with its default settings. For each user define a default personal login script as well as special disk restrictions. Once the settings are correct, you can create the accounts. During the processing a default password is created for each user. You must write down the password and give it to each new user. They will be asked to change it the first time they log in.

Running USERDEF

To start the USERDEF program, type **USERDEF** on the command line. In a moment the Available Options menu appears, as shown here:

The first step is to decide whether you want to use the default settings, as shown in Figure 25-2, or create your own templates. If you need to change the settings, refer to "Altering the Template" before proceeding with these steps.

1. Select **Add Users** from the Available Options menu. The Templates window appears.

2. The window lists the standard template DEFAULT along with any others you may have created by referring to the "Altering the Template" section. Select the template you want to use and press ENTER.

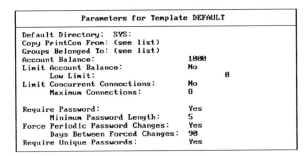

Figure 25-2.   The USERDEF template parameters menu

3. At the Users window, press INS to include new names. The names of existing users appear in the list; however, only those marked as (new) on the right are processed.

4. USERDEF asks for the user's full name, and then the user's login name. The name then appears in the Users window.

5. Press ESC after inserting the new users. The Create New Users Using Template DEFAULT window appears. Select **Yes** to create the new users.

6. USERDEF suggests a password, which you should accept. Give the password to the new user.

7. When the USERDEF process is complete, a log appears to show its activities.

8. If you want to limit a user's available disk space, return to the Available Topics menu and select **Restrict Users**. Select the user and press ENTER. At the disk space limitation window, type **Yes** in the Limit Space field, and then type the disk limitation size.

Altering the Template

The default template and its parameters are shown in Figure 25-2. You can create other templates with different values. Each of the parameters is described under "USERDEF Template Parameters."

To create a new template and a default personal login script for each new user, follow these steps:

1. Select **Edit Template** on the Available Options menu.

2. At the Templates window, press INS to create a new template. Type in the new template name and press ENTER.

3. You then are asked to edit the login script or the template parameters. Choose **Edit Login Script** to define a default personal login script for each user. You could enter the command **EXIT "MENU MAIN"** to start the utilities menu, for example.

4. To change the parameters of the template, choose **Edit Parameters**.

5. Change the settings in the Parameters window according to the descriptions supplied in the next section.

6. When done, press ESC and type **Yes** to save the changes.

7. The template is now ready to use. Now refer back to "Running USERDEF."

USERDEF Template Parameters

The following parameters can be changed on the template window:

Default Directory   Users' personal directories branch from this directory. This may be SYS:USERS or SYS:HOME.

Copy PrintCon From   This field allows you to specify where to copy print job configurations from. Type **SUPERVISOR** in the field.

Groups Belonged To   Press ENTER on the field, and then press INS to enter the groups the users will belong to. When done, press ESC to return to the menu.

Account Balance   If accounting is installed, the Account Balance option appears. Enter the number of services a user can use. The default setting is 1000 charges.

Limit Account Balance   The default setting is No, which means that depleted accounts can still be used. To limit a user's credit, change the setting to Yes. The Low Limit setting is used to specify how low the account balance can go.

Limit Concurrent Connections   The default setting is that users will have no limitations on concurrent connections. Type **Y** in the limit field and enter the number of connections in the Maximum Connections field.

Require Password   The default setting is Yes, meaning that users will require a password. You can change this to No, and then skip ahead to Limit Disk Space below. If a password is required, you can change the minimum number of characters in the Minimum Password Length field.

Force Periodic Password Changes   The default setting is Yes, meaning that passwords must be changed at fixed intervals. You can change this field to No. If the default setting is used, you can change the interval by changing the Days Between Forced Changes field.

Require Unique Password   Unique passwords are passwords that have not been specified by a user for the last ten changes. The default setting is Yes but can be changed to No.

Commands for Everyday Use

NetWare Menu Utilities for Users
Command Line Utilities for Users
Communicating with Other Users

This chapter covers commands and menu utilities used on a daily basis. The commands are covered with reference to normal users rather than the supervisor; however, the supervisor can also use these commands. Network users can gain a better understanding of working with NetWare by reading through this chapter.

NetWare Menu Utilities for Users

All the menu utilities can be accessed by users, but the functions available to nonsupervisors are limited. In most cases users can view only existing settings, but this information can be important during a NetWare session. For example, users can see who else is on the system, or they can view their trustee rights in a directory. The following sections cover each menu utility, except the printing utilities, which are covered in Chapter 27.

SESSION for Users

The SESSION utility helps you manage your current session. You can change servers, drive mappings, and search drive mappings. You also can view the current user list and send a message to another user or group of users. SESSION's features are described here.

Change Servers   Select **Change Current Server** to switch to another server. All servers appear in a list. To switch to another server, select a server from the list.

Add Drive Mappings   To add a new drive map, select **Drive Mappings** from the SESSION menu. A list of currently mapped drives appears. Press INS to add a new drive map. After selecting the drive letter, you can press INS again to insert the names of servers, volumes, and directories.

Send Group Messages   Select the **Group List** option to display available groups. You can send a message to any group by selecting the group name from this menu.

Add Search Mappings   To add a new search drive map, select **Search Mappings** from the SESSION menu. A list of currently mapped search drives appears. Press INS to add a new search map. After selecting the drive letter, press INS again to insert the names of servers, volumes, and directories.

Select Default Drive   You can choose **Select Default Drive** to switch to another mapped drive that appears on a list.

Send Messages to Users and Display User Information   Select **User List** from the menu to display information about currently logged users. You can send a short message to any user on the list by selecting the user's name, or press F5 to select multiple users. This option is covered in more detail later in this chapter.

FILER for Users

The FILER utility is a convenient tool for working with directories and files. The effective rights a user has in a directory determine what FILER features are available. Users can view and copy files, create new subdirectories, change file attributes, and perform other useful tasks depending on their rights.

The first thing to do after FILER loads is to switch to the desired directory by choosing **Select Current Directory** from the menu. Enter the path to the target directory. The following options are available.

Display Current Directory Information   Choose **Current Directory Information** to display rights, trustees, and other information about the directory.

Work with Files   Select the **Directory Contents** option on the FILER main menu to work with files in the directory. When a file is selected, the following menu appears:

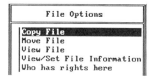

The File Options menu offers these options:

- Copy files with the Copy File option. A duplicate is made in another directory or drive.

- The Move File option moves files from one location to another. The original files are removed.

- The View File option displays the contents of files.

- The View/Set File Information option displays the File Information menu, which displays attributes, trustee rights, and the inherited rights mask of the file. Users must have Modify or Access privileges to change the options on this menu.

- Select **Who has rights here** to display a list of users who have trustee rights to the file.

If you use the F5 (mark) key to select several files and then press ENTER, the following menu appears:

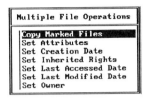

The Multiple File Operations menu offers these options:

- Use the Copy Marked Files option to copy the selected files to a specified directory.

- Use the Set Attributes option to set the marked files attributes. You must have the Modify right to do so.

- Use the Set Inherited Rights mask option to change the inherited rights if you have authority to do so.

- Use the remaining options to change the file's date and owner information.

Select Directories   You can select any directory using the Select Current Directory option, but you are limited to what you can do in the directory based on your access rights.

Set Filer Options   You can set options to control the way FILER operates, such as confirmation of copies and deletes, and inclusions and exclusions in directory and file listings.

Volume Information   You can view volume information using the Volume Information option.

SYSCON for Users

The SYSCON command displays information about a user's rights on the system, as well as disk usage, last login time, and station restrictions. Users can change some settings for their personal accounts, but the amount of information they can view about the system is limited. For example, users can change their passwords and customize their personal login scripts.

You can use SYSCON to view the full name of other users and the groups they belong to. This information can be important when working in shared directories or sending messages to groups.

Note: Normal users cannot access the Accounting and Supervisor options on the SYSCON menu.

Change Current Server   Switch to another server by selecting this option. A list of currently available servers appears.

Viewing File Server Information   Select this option from the menu to view information about a particular server. You first are given a list of servers to choose from. The information displayed includes the NetWare version, network address, and node address.

Viewing Group Information   Select **Group Information** to view information about any group. A group member list is presented for the selected group, which can be useful when sending messages or creating and copying files.

Viewing and Changing User Information   When you select **User Information**, you can perform the following tasks:

- View but not change your account restrictions

- Change your password

- View the groups you currently belong to

- View and change your login script

- Use the Other Information option to view

    Last login date

    If you have console operator status

    Disk space you are using

Your user ID, which is also the name of your personal directory in the MAIL directory

- View your station and time restrictions

- View your trustee assignments

Command Line Utilities for Users

Users may be interested in current connection information, such as who else is logged on the system, the system's time, or its volume and version information. The commands discussed in this section are typed on the command line.

Viewing User Information
With WHOAMI

The WHOAMI command displays information about a user, such as login name, login date and time, current file server, and connection information. The command displays additional information when special options are used, as described next.

The command takes the following form:

WHOAMI *server options*

where *server* is the server to view. The *options* for the WHOAMI command are listed here:

/G (Groups)	Used to view membership in groups on the current server.
/S (Security)	Used to view security equivalences on any file server.

/R (Rights)   Used to view rights in the directories of the file
                       server.

/S (System)   Used to view system information.

/A (All)   Used to view the combined information in the
                       four other options.

If you type the command by itself, you receive information regarding the current user's name and server connection. For example, when user GEORGE types **WHOAMI**, information similar to the following appears:

You are user GEORGE attached to server STARSHIP connection 3
Login Time: Friday September 1, 1990 11:25 am

To view information on another file server, include the name of the file server. In the following command, GEORGE views his status on the ACCTG server:

WHOAMI ACCTG

Information similar to the following appears:

You are user GEORGE attached to server ACCTG connection 5
Login Time: Friday September 1, 1990 11:30 am

Viewing Group Membership

To view membership in a group, use the /G option. In the following example, GEORGE views his group membership on the STARSHIP server:

WHOAMI STARSHIP /G

Information similar to the following appears:

You are user GEORGE attached to server STARSHIP connection 3
Login Time: Friday September 1, 1990 11:25 am
You are a member of the following Groups:
    EVERYONE (group)
    ENGINEERING (group)
    BRIDGE (group)
    COMMUNICATIONS (group)

If you do not specify a server, information about all servers is displayed.

Viewing Security Equivalences

Use the /S option to view security equivalences. Specify the file server name if you require a list for a particular server. If you leave out the server name, security equivalences are displayed for all file servers. In the following command, GEORGE views his security equivalences on STARSHIP:

WHOAMI STARSHIP /S

Information similar to the following appears:

You are user GEORGE attached to server STARSHIP connection 3
Login Time: Friday September 1, 1990 11:25 am
You are security equivalent to the following:
    EVERYONE (group)
    OFFICERS (group)

Viewing Effective Rights

The /R option displays the effective rights a user has in the server's directories. All directories accessible by the user are listed. The rights on all servers are displayed, unless you specify a particular server. In the following example, GEORGE views his effective rights on the STARSHIP server:

WHOAMI STARSHIP /R

Information similar to the following appears:

You are user GEORGE attached to server STARSHIP connection 3
Login Time: Friday September 1, 1990 11:25 am
You have the following effective rights:
[C]   STARSHIP/SYS:MAIL
[RWCEMF]   STARSHIP/SYS:MAIL/A005D
[R   F]   STARSHIP/SYS:PUBLIC
[RWCE F]   STARSHIP/SYS:PUB-DATA

You can use CTRL-S or PAUSE to pause the screen listing if a long list of rights appears.

Viewing All Rights

Use the /A option to view all rights for the default server, or the rights for a specified server. In the following command, GEORGE requests to see all rights for the STARSHIP server:

WHOAMI STARSHIP /A

Viewing Current Users with USERLIST

The USERLIST command displays a list of current users, including their connection numbers and login times. The command is useful when you need to address messages to other users. The command is also useful to supervisors and managers to determine who is logged into various workstations.

When you type **USERLIST** a screen similar to the following appears:

Connection	User Name	Login Time
1	SUPERVISOR	5-25-90 7:00 am
2	JOHN	5-25-90 9:00 am
3	JANE	5-25-90 10:00 am

To view information about one user, type the user's name. For example, information about JOHN's connection is listed with the following command:

USERLIST JOHN

To view the user list of another file server, you must specify the name of the file server in the command. The following command lists users on the ACCTG server:

USERLIST ACCTG/

To view information about the user TIM on the ACCTG server, you would type the following command:

USERLIST ACCTG/TIM

To view node and network information for TIM on the ACCTG server, you would type the following command:

USERLIST ACCTG/TIM   /A

Note: The /A option is used to view additional user information.

Viewing the Current Rights
With RIGHTS

You use the RIGHTS command to view your current rights in a particular directory. Simply type **RIGHTS**. To view rights in another directory, specify the mapped drive letter or full directory path of the directory to view, as in the following example:

RIGHTS F:

or

RIGHTS SYS:USERS\JOHN

Communicating with Other Users

NetWare offers you a number of menu utility options and commands for communicating with other users, including a simple message broadcasting system discussed in this section.

Sending Messages
To Users and Groups

You can send messages to users or groups with the SESSION utility. Start the utility, and then choose **Group List** to send messages to an entire group, or choose **User List** to send messages to a single user.

When the list of groups or users appears, select one or more and press ENTER. You can choose to view information about the users, such as their login times and node addresses, or you can choose **Send Message** to send the user a message. When you select **Send Message**, a message box similar to the following is displayed. In this example, BONNIE is sending a message to her work group.

```
Message: From BONNIE[2]:
```

The message appears on the bottom line of a user's screen, along with the name of the person who sent the message. The message can be cleared by pressing CTRL-ENTER.

Sending Messages
With the SEND Command

In place of the SESSION menu utility, you can use the SEND command to send messages to other users or groups. The message sent by SEND cannot exceed 45 characters, minus the number of letters in your user name. The command takes the following form:

SEND *message* TO USER *server/user* ...

or

SEND *message* TO GROUP *server/user* ...

or

SEND *message* TO USER *server/user* ... GROUP *server/user*

You use the first form to send messages to users, the second form to send messages to groups, and the third to send messages to both users and groups. The ellipsis indicates that you can specify more than one user or group with the command.

To send a message to the file server, use the following form:

SEND *message* TO *server/* CONSOLE

To send a message to all workstations, use this form:

SEND *message* TO USER *server/* EVERYBODY

To send a message to specific workstations, use the following form, replacing *n* with the workstation numbers. A comma or blank space must separate the numbers.

SEND *message* TO STATION *server/n* ...

Use the USERLIST command to determine the names of users currently logged on the system, as discussed previously. You can exclude the USER and GROUP options in the SEND command if no users and groups share the same name.

The following example illustrates how a message would be sent to JOHN:

SEND John, can we meet today at 2:00? TO USER JOHN

Since a group named JOHN is unlikely, the USER option can be left out, as in the following command:

SEND John, can we meet today at 2:00? TO JOHN

A message similar to the following appears on the sender's display:

Message sent to SERVER/JOHN (station 7)

To send a message to a user or group on a different file server, you must specify the name of the file server before the user name. In the folllowing example, a message is sent to the group CLERKS on the ACCTG server:

SEND We're closing at 3:00 today! TO ACCTG/CLERKS

To send a message to several users or groups, specify each user or group on the command line. In the following example, the message is sent to the user JOHN and the group MANAGERS on the current server and the user BERT on the ACCTG server:

SEND This is a stickup... TO JOHN MANAGERS ACCTG/BERT

Note that users and groups on the current server do not require the server name in the SEND command. To send a message to all users on the ACCTG server, you would type the following:

SEND Lunch is on the boss today! TO ACCTG/EVERYBODY

To send messages to users at workstations 2, 3, and 4 on the same server, you would type the following command:

SEND Let's play SNIPES! TO 2,3,4

Blocking Messages

The CASTOFF command can block any messages that might be sent to a workstation, and for good reason. Some computing jobs are best left unattended until finished. This is common when running program compilers, recalculating a spreadsheet, or sorting and indexing a database. You may go to lunch, expecting the job to be complete when you return. However, a message sent from another station would interrupt that processing and put it on hold until you read and clear the message. When you return to your station, you may find your machine has been sitting idle for some time.

To block messages sent from other workstations, enter the command **CASTOFF**. The following message appears on the screen:

Broadcast messages from other stations will now be rejected.

To block messages sent from all network stations, including those from the console, use the ALL option in the command, as shown here:

CASTOFF ALL

The CASTON command returns a workstation to its normal message-receiving mode. Type **CASTON** on the command line.

Printing

How NetWare Printing Works
Features of NetWare Printing Services
Configuring NetWare Printing Services
Queue and Print Server Operator Tasks
Customizing the Printing Environment
Command-Line Utilities for Printing

NetWare allows you to print at your locally attached printer or on printers attached to file and print servers that are shared by other network users. Shared printers can be located on servers and workstations anywhere on the network. It makes sense to share printers to maximize printer investment and eliminate printer idle time. Printer sharing also allows users to choose from a variety of different printers. For example, some printers may be high-quality laser printers, while others may be lower-quality but faster dot matrix printers.

The following features describe NetWare printing:

- All network printing is directed to queues that are serviced by print servers. Print servers can be located in the file server or special dedicated workstations.

- A printer server can service 5 directly attached printers and up to 11 printers attached to workstations on the network.

- A dedicated workstation print server can service up to 8 file servers.

- Unlike previous versions of NetWare, the printing environment can be altered easily at any time and does not need to be set up until after the file server is running.

- A workstation printer can become a shared network printer while still remaining available to the local user.

How NetWare Printing Works

NetWare printing is handled by a NetWare loadable module and several commands and menu utilities, all of which combine to form the NetWare printing services. Each module is described here:

PCONSOLE	Used to set up the print server and to control and view information about network printing.
PSERVER.NLM	Loads a print server on the file server after services have been defined by PCONSOLE. A print server running in a NetWare 386 file server is referred to as an *NLM print server*.
PSERVER.EXE	Dedicates a workstation as a print server after services have been defined by PCONSOLE. A print server running in a dedicated workstation is referred to as a *dedicated workstation print server*.
RPRINTER	Used to share a workstation printer with other users on the network. These printers are known as *shared printers*.
PSC	PSC is a quick alternative to PCONSOLE for controlling print servers and network printers.

PRINTDEF	Used to define a printer and its special control codes.
PRINTCON	Defines print job configurations using the printers defined with PRINTDEF.
CAPTURE	Intercepts local printing and sends it to the server printers. CAPTURE is used for NetWare-ignorant applications.
ENDCAP	Ends the CAPTURE command.
NPRINT	Prints files to file server printers.
SPOOL	Used to create, change, or display the current spooler mappings. Spooler mappings are used to set up default print queues for NPRINT and CAPTURE. SPOOL is a file server console command.

When a user prints a file (using network printing, not local printing), the information is sent to a *queue* in the file server. A queue stores a print job until it can be printed and is usually created for each printer on the network. If you want to print on a laser printer instead of a dot matrix printer, you send the print job to the appropriate queue. The printers may be locally attached or attached to workstations on the network. Figure 27-1 illustrates how files are printed on the network.

Keep in mind that a print server running in a file server (PSERVER.NLM) can service 5 local printers and 11 workstation printers. A print server running in a dedicated workstation (PSERVER.EXE) can also service the same amount of printers and accept print jobs from up to eight separate file servers. Note that the dedicated workstation print server in Figure 27-1 services two separate file servers. Using dedicated workstation print servers in addition to print server NLMs allows the total number of shared printers to be quite large on a network.

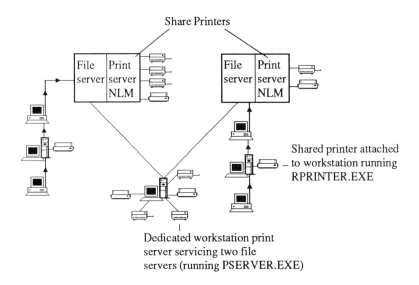

Share Printers

File server | Print server NLM

File server | Print server NLM

Shared printer attached to workstation running RPRINTER.EXE

Dedicated workstation print server servicing two file servers (running PSERVER.EXE)

Figure 27-1.   An example of printing services under NetWare

Features of NetWare Printing Services

The PCONSOLE command establishes print queues, print servers, and printers to be shared on the network. Each of these are described in the following sections.

Print Queues

A print queue is a storage area for a print job. Because network printers are used by more than one user, queues prevent conflicts between users who attempt to access the same printer simultaneously. Print jobs are sent to queues and stored until printed. Each queue is assigned a directory for storing its print jobs. Jobs are printed in the order received, unless the order is rearranged by a queue operator or preempted by another queue as described here:

- A single queue may service more than one printer. In this way if one printer is busy, the queue simply sends the print job to the next available printer. The printers must be exactly the same since users have no control over which printer is used.

- Multiple queues may be serviced by one printer. This arrangement allows some users' print jobs to have priority over others. For example, managers may be given access to a queue that has higher priority than a queue used by clerks. Print jobs in the manager's queue are always printed before print jobs in the clerk's queue.

PCONSOLE must be used to create queues before a print server can be installed. A queue should be given a name that identifies the printer or its location so users can differentiate between queues. The right to use a queue can be granted or revoked to, for example, ensure that printers with corporate stationery are not used by clerks who produce accounting reports. The EVERYONE group is automatically granted rights to new print queues, but these rights can be revoked in the PCONSOLE utility.

Queue Operators

Normally the supervisor is the only person who can change the parameters of a queue, but these tasks can be assigned to users who become *print queue operators*. Queue operators can rearrange the order of jobs to be printed in a print queue or remove print jobs altogether, even if they are currently printing.

Print Server Operators

One of the main tasks of the *print server operator* is to ensure that the printers are working properly and that each is loaded with paper or forms. The print server operator may need to change the forms in a printer in order to print a job. This is common when an organization has only one or two printers that handle many different types of printing tasks, such as printing paychecks or accounting reports.

Print server operators may also perform the following tasks:

- Attach the print server to other file servers

- Choose a user to be notified if the printer needs service

- Change the queues serviced by a printer

- Change queue priority

- Down the print server

Queue Users

Users must have access rights to queues in order to print. In most cases this is automatic since the EVERYONE group is given access to new queues. Access rights can be revoked by the supervisor or queue operator at any time, however.

Print Servers

Once queues and other print features have been established, the supervisor installs PSERVER.NLM in the file server or PSERVER.EXE in the dedicated workstation's print server. Recall that workstation print servers can service queues from up to eight file servers, while the NLM print server can service only queues from the file server in which it is running.

Because a dedicated workstation print server can service jobs from other file servers, the print server manager must have supervisor privileges on the other file servers, or enlist the help of the file server supervisor to establish printing services. A print server account must be created on each file server before you can attach to it.

When print servers are configured, the following must be specified in a print server configuration file, which is read every time the print server is started:

- File servers that the print server services (dedicated workstation print servers only)

- Printers attached to the print server

- Queues serviced by each printer

- Users who must be notified when the print server needs service

Print Forms

Most companies use many different forms for printing, such as payroll checks, accounting sheets, and company letterhead. Users who are not located next to a printer need to know that their print jobs are being printed on the proper form. Some companies use a separate printer for each type of form so that form changes are never required. Other companies may have only one or two printers that require periodic form changes.

NetWare allows supervisors to define what a form looks like and how it is printed, and then give the form a name and number. When a user sends a print job to a printer, they specify by number which form to use. Print server operators are then responsible for changing the forms in the printer to service a print job. Every time print server operators change a form in a printer, they must use PCONSOLE to tell the print server that a new form is currently in the printer. The print server knows which jobs it can print and which jobs to hold for proper forms, based on the form numbers.

Some installations may prefer to put all other print jobs on hold while a job that uses a different form is being printed. After the original forms are reinstalled in the printer, the print jobs on hold can be released for printing.

Configuring NetWare Printing Services

You must follow several steps to initially set up printing on NetWare print servers. NetWare printing services are not even required if users print from their workstation printers only. However, if printers are to be shared, you must establish print servers as discussed here. Each step of the configuration process is listed here and described in the sections that follow.

1. Set up the hardware

2. Create print queues

3. Create print servers

4. Set up the print server configuration file

5. Assign printers to print queues

6. Create spooler mappings

7. Load PSERVER.NLM at the file server or execute the file called PSERVER.EXE at the dedicated workstation print server

8. Execute RPRINTER on a workstation that shares printers with other network users

Setting Up the Hardware

You can set up the hardware for a print server in a number of ways. Most systems used in the personal computer and networking environment are limited to three parallel printers (LPT1, LPT2, and LPT3) and two serial printers (COM1 and COM2). NetWare does not support more than five printers because of attachment port limitations (however, some systems do allow four serial ports). To add more printers you must share printers attached to workstations on the network using the RPRINTER command. Up to 16 printers can be set up in this way, although the additional printers must be attached to workstations. To install more than 16 printers on the network, you must add another print server. This print server can be in another file server or in a dedicated workstation print server that runs the PSERVER.EXE program.

On systems that have more than one file server, it may be necessary to install two or more print servers to handle printing from multiple file

servers. Remember that an NLM print server can handle only the printing
of the file server to which it is attached, whereas a dedicated workstation
print server can handle the printing from eight separate file servers.

Attaching five printers to one system may not be convenient, especially since three must be parallel and two must be serial. If you use only
parallel printers, you can install additional printers on other workstations
or print servers and avoid serial printers altogether. The same is true if
you prefer to use serial printers. Serial printer cables can be longer than
parallel printer cables (up to 100 feet), so it may be advantageous for you
to use serial printers.

Adding more printer ports in a server has implications in the number
of interrupt request (IRQ) ports available for network cards and other
devices. It may be more important to use the available interrupt lines
(there are a total of 11 on ISA systems) for network interface cards, which
means you must connect printers to workstations or dedicated workstation
print servers.

Creating Print Queues

Print queues are created in the PCONSOLE utility. Start the utility now
and select **Print Queue Information** from the menu, as shown here:

Press INS to create a new print queue. Type a name for the print queue
that describes the printer it supports or other descriptive information. A
queue should be created for each printer, and some printers can be
assigned more than one queue.

Changing Queue Information

You can view or change information about any queue by highlighting the
queue from the Print Queue list and pressing ENTER. The following Print
Queue Information menu appears:

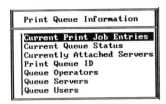

Most of the options on this menu are discussed later. At this time you may want to change the queue operators and users. The supervisor is automatically assigned as print queue operator, and each member of the EVERYONE group is assigned as a queue user.

- To add new operators select **Queue Operators** from the menu, and press INS to choose from a list of candidates.

- To add or remove users select **Queue Users** from the Print Queue Information menu and press INS to add a user. To remove the EVERYONE group, highlight it and press DEL.

Creating Print Servers

You use the PCONSOLE command to create a print server and define its configuration file. To create a new print server, select **Print Server Information** from the PCONSOLE main menu. When the Print Server's menu appears, press INS to add a new print server. Type a descriptive name for the print server and press ENTER. Select the new print server from the list and press ENTER. The Print Server Information menu appears, as shown here:

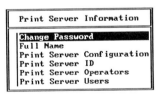

To change the password for the print server, select **Change Password** and type the new password. The supervisor is automatically designated the operator of new printer servers, and each member of the EVERYONE group is designated a user. To change these configurations, select either **Print Server Operators** or **Print Server Users** from the Print Server Information menu.

You can also assign a full name to the print server by selecting the **Full Name** option. To view the print server ID, select **Print Server ID**.

Setting Up Print Server Configuration Files

Print server configuration files must be set up before the NLM print server or dedicated workstation print server can be started. The information in the file specifies print server operators, users, and password information, as just discussed, but also contains configuration information. Remember that the print server configuration file must specify the following:

- The file servers that the print server will service (dedicated workstation print servers only)

- The printers attached to the print server

- The queues serviced by each printer

- The users who must be notified when the print server needs service

Select **Print Server Configuration** from the Print Server Information menu. The following screen appears, and each of its options are discussed in the order you use them to install a print server.

```
┌──────────────────────────────────────┐
│ Print Server Configuration Menu      │
├──────────────────────────────────────┤
│ File Servers Serviced                │
│ Notify List for Printer              │
│ Printer Configuration                │
│ Queues Serviced by Printer           │
└──────────────────────────────────────┘
```

File Servers Serviced

Select this option to configure a dedicated workstation print server, not an NLM print server. You can use it to specify up to eight file servers that the print server should attach to for servicing print jobs. To add file servers to the list, select the option and press ENTER, and then press INS on the menu to add the servers. Select any server that appears in the list. Note the following:

- The file servers must contain queues that the print server can service.

- You need not include the name of the server to which the dedicated workstation print server is attached.

- To service queues on other file servers, you must create a print server account and configuration file on the file server to be serviced. Refer to the section "Configuring File Servers for Dedicated Workstation Print Servers" later in this chapter.

Notify List for Printer

The **Notify List for Printer** option displays a list of network users who should be notified if the printer needs service. To select a user, choose **Notify List for Printer**, select a printer from the list that appears, and then press INS to select a user from a list of candidates.

Printer Configuration

Select the **Printer Configuration** option on the Print Server Configuration Menu screen to define each of the printers attached to the print server or workstations on the network. When the option is selected, a list of 16 potential printers appears. Highlight the first printer and press ENTER to display a printer configuration screen like that shown in Figure 27-2.

To configure the printer, fill in the following information as described here:

- *Name*   Enter a descriptive name for the printer.

- *Type*   Press ENTER on the Type field to display a list of possible printer types. You can select a parallel or serial port on the print server or a port on a remote workstation. Select **Remote**

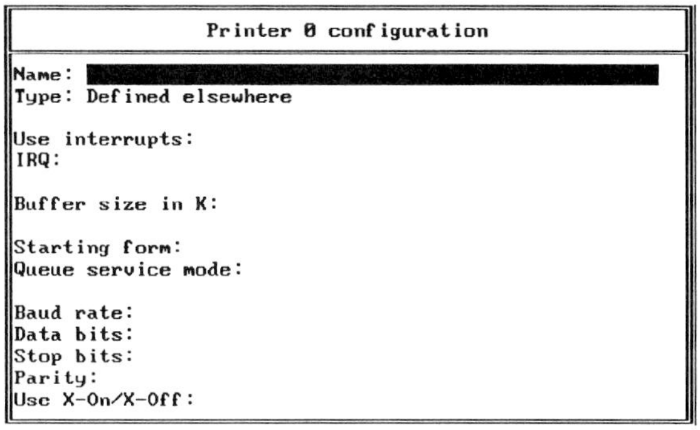

```
┌──────────────────────────────────────────────┐
│              Printer 0 configuration           │
│ ┌─────────────────────────────────────────────┐│
│ │Name: ███████████████████████████████████████ ││
│ │Type: Defined elsewhere                       ││
│ │                                              ││
│ │Use interrupts:                               ││
│ │IRQ:                                          ││
│ │                                              ││
│ │Buffer size in K:                             ││
│ │                                              ││
│ │Starting form:                                ││
│ │Queue service mode:                           ││
│ │                                              ││
│ │Baud rate:                                    ││
│ │Data bits:                                    ││
│ │Stop bits:                                    ││
│ │Parity:                                       ││
│ │Use X-On/X-Off:                               ││
│ └─────────────────────────────────────────────┘│
└──────────────────────────────────────────────┘
```

Figure 27-2.   A printer configuration menu

Other/Unknown if you want to configure a remote printer later when running the RPRINTER command. Select **Defined elsewhere** if the printer has already been defined on another file server and you are defining printers on additional file servers. In this situation you would enter the type on the first file server, and then select **Defined elsewhere** on subsequent file servers.

Note: If you select a serial printer, you can change the Baud rate, Data bits, Stop bits, Parity, and X-On/X-Off fields at the bottom of the screen to match the printer settings.

- *Use interrupts* Enter the interrupt used by the printer port if additional printer ports have been added to the system or if you are defining remote workstations. If you select **Yes** in the Use interrupts field, enter the interrupt number in the IRQ field.

- *Buffer size in K* Enter the memory size of the printer buffer, if you know it. Refer to the printer manual for information.

Working with forms   The next two options on the printer configuration screen are used when forms have been designed with the PRINTDEF utility. Forms allow users to tell the print server operator when their print jobs require the paper form in the printer to be changed. Each form has a number and a specific layout that defines its margins, paper size, tab size, and other features. One form might be payroll checks while another might be company letterhead. Forms are not required if several printers are available and each is dedicated to printing on a specific form. Users simply select the queue that sends jobs to the printer that has the form they need already installed.

- *Starting form*   Enter the form number that will be used initially. This field can stay as is until forms are defined in PRINTDEF, which is optional.

- *Queue service mode*   When users print, they can specify the number of the form to use. The print server operator then is alerted that the form in the printer needs to be changed to match the users' print requests. Printers can handle forms in several ways, as described in the following list. One of these methods can be selected from the Service Modes menu, which is displayed when you press ENTER on the Queue service mode field.

  - *Change forms as needed*   The printer prints all print jobs in the order they are received, regardless of the form.

  - *Minimize form changes across queues*   This option is used if several queues are sending print jobs to the printer. Any print job that uses the form currently installed in the printer is printed.

  - *Minimize form changes within queues*   If one queue is servicing the printer, the printer prints jobs that use the form currently installed before printing others.

  - *Service only currently mounted form*   The printer prints only those print jobs that require the currently installed form. All others are put on hold until the correct form is installed.

Queues Serviced by Printer

Once the queues have been created and the printers have been defined, you can map queues to printers. Select **Queues Serviced by Printer** from the Print Server Configuration Menu screen. A list of defined printers appears. Select a printer and press ENTER. You can then press INS to select a queue from a list of those available.

Remember that one printer can be assigned more than one queue. When you select a queue for a printer, you are given a chance to specify the queue's priority at the printer. If only one queue is selected, accept 1 as the priority by pressing ENTER. Priority levels can be between 1 and 10. Queues with a priority of 1 are serviced before queues assigned larger numbers. Base a queue's priority on the total number of queues assigned to the printer. For example, if three queues are assigned to a single printer, set priorities between 1 and 3.

Assigning Queues to Printers

Now that queues and printers have been defined, and queues have been linked with printers, it is necessary to "authorize" a print server to service a print queue.

Select **Print Queue Information** from the PCONSOLE main menu. A list of previously defined print queues appears. Select a print queue and press ENTER. On the Print Queue Information menu, select **Queue Servers**, and then press INS to view a list of queue server candidates. Select the print server to service the queue and press ENTER.

Configuring File Servers for Dedicated Workstation Print Servers

This section is optional and is not necessary to those running NLM print servers.

When a dedicated workstation print server is used, it is necessary to configure the queues established on other file servers to the printers on the print server.

The first thing to do is attach to the file server that has queues to service. You must be a supervisor on these other file servers or enlist the help of the current supervisor. If queues and printers are not defined on the server, follow the steps as outlined in the previous sections, starting with "Creating Print Queues," for each queue you want to be serviced by a print server.

Creating Spooler Mappings

The CAPTURE command redirects printing from a workstation to a network printer and is normally used when an application is NetWare ignorant. Use NPRINT to send text files from the NetWare command line. Both of these commands send their print jobs to whichever queue Spooler 0 has been mapped to.

To create a spooler mapping, type the SPOOL command at the NetWare 386 console in the following form:

SPOOL *nn* TO QUEUE *queuename*

where *nn* is the spooler number and *queuename* is a previously defined queue that is serviced by a network printer. For example, to designate the queue HP-LASER as the default queue, you would type the following at the file server console:

SPOOL 0 TO HP-LASER

If the print server is servicing queues from multiple file servers, issue the SPOOL command on each file server. Spooler mappings are lost if the server is brought down. They can be placed in the AUTOEXEC.NCF file and executed every time the file server is booted. To list spooler mappings, type **SPOOL**. You can do this by accessing Supervisor Options in SYS-CON.

Starting the Print Server

Now that printing services have been configured, you are ready to install PSERVER.NLM in the file server or PSERVER.EXE at a dedicated workstation print server. Follow the steps described in one of the following sections.

Starting an NLM Print Server

The PSERVER.NLM file is located in the SYS:SYSTEM directory, so only the supervisor may load the print server at the file server. Type the following form of the LOAD command at the file server console:

LOAD PSERVER *printserver*

where *printserver* is the print server name that exactly matches the name you specified during the PCONSOLE configuration session. The print server is installed every time the file server is booted if you include this command in the AUTOEXEC.NCF file. You can do this by accessing Supervisor Options in SYSCON.

Starting a Dedicated Workstation Print Server

For a workstation to operate properly as a dedicated workstation print server, you must include the following command in the SHELL.CFG or NET.CFG file of the workstation. This allows the workstation to have enough open connections for packet transmission. If problems occur, increase the number you specify.

SPX CONNECTIONS = 70

Reboot the station if necessary to initialize the new SPX settings, and then log into the file server as normal. The PSERVER.EXE command is in the SYS:PUBLIC directory, so you must be mapped to the directory or have a search drive mapped to the directory to execute it. Type the following form of the command to start the print server:

PSERVER *printserver*

where *printserver* is the name of the print server to start. Be sure this name exactly matches the name defined in the PCONSOLE session.

Sharing Workstation Printers

If printers on workstations are to be shared by other network users, the RPRINTER.EXE command file must be executed at the workstation. RPRINTER.EXE is a *terminate-and-stay-resident program,* which means it loads and stays active in the background until removed. Print jobs from the print server are automatically serviced by the printer without intervention from the user at the workstation.

Before beginning, make sure the workstation is logged into the network and has a search drive mapped to the SYS:PUBLIC directory. At the workstation type **RPRINTER**, and a menu-driven program appears. Select the print server to use, and then select a printer number from the list of printers you defined in the PCONSOLE session. If you did not configure the printer in the PCONSOLE session, select Other/unknown type, and then configure the printer as serial or parallel.

To disconnect a remote printer, type the command **RPRINTER -R** at the workstation.

Queue and Print Server Operator Tasks

Once printing services have been established, periodic maintenance or changes to the printing environment may need to be performed by the queue or print server operators. These tasks are covered here.

Changing Queue Operator Flags

The queue operator flags can be changed to prevent users from submitting jobs to a queue, to prevent the print server from servicing jobs in the queue, and to prevent the print server from attaching to the queue. Start PCONSOLE and select **Print Queue Information** from the main menu. Select a queue to change, and then select **Current Queue Status** from the Print Queue Information menu. The following menu appears:

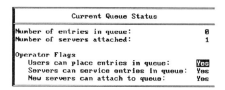

Enter **No** in any of the fields to prevent queue usage by users, printers, and print servers.

Listing, Changing, and Holding
Print Job Entries

Print queue operators can list and change the jobs in a queue. To list a queue, start PCONSOLE and select **Print Queue Information** from the main menu. Select a print queue to view, and then select **Current Print Job Entries** from the Print Queue Information menu. A list of jobs waiting to print is displayed. To remove a print job, highlight it and press DEL.

Once the print queue list is visible, you can select any job and press ENTER to display the Print Queue Entry Information menu, shown in Figure 27-3. The following information can be changed on the menu:

- To change the order of a print job, type a number in the Service Sequence field that corresponds to its new position in the list. For example, type **1** to make it the next print job.

- To hold a print job for later printing, type **Yes** in the Operator Hold field. Note that users can place holds on their own print jobs by typing **Yes** in the User Hold field.

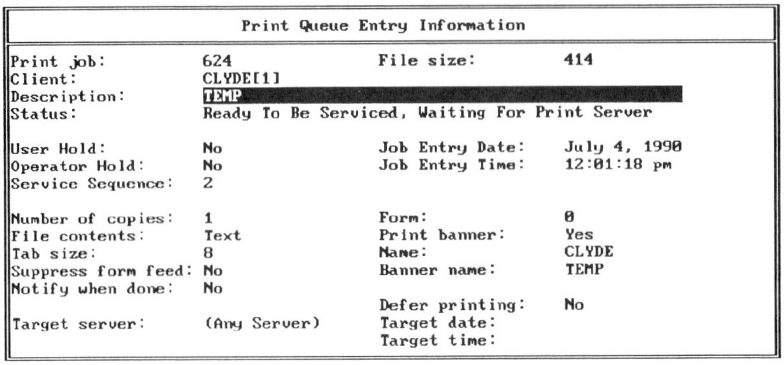

```
┌─────────────────────────────────────────────────────────────────────┐
│                      Print Queue Entry Information                    │
├─────────────────────────────────────────────────────────────────────┤
│Print job:        624              File size:      414                 │
│Client:           CLYDE[1]                                             │
│Description:      ▓TEMP▓▓▓▓▓▓▓▓▓▓▓▓▓▓▓▓▓▓▓▓▓▓▓▓▓▓▓▓▓▓▓▓▓▓▓▓▓▓▓▓▓       │
│Status:           Ready To Be Serviced, Waiting For Print Server       │
│                                                                       │
│User Hold:        No               Job Entry Date:   July 4, 1990      │
│Operator Hold:    No               Job Entry Time:   12:01:18 pm       │
│Service Sequence: 2                                                    │
│                                                                       │
│Number of copies: 1                Form:             0                 │
│File contents:    Text             Print banner:     Yes               │
│Tab size:         8                Name:             CLYDE             │
│Suppress form feed: No             Banner name:      TEMP              │
│Notify when done: No                                                   │
│                                   Defer printing:   No                │
│Target server:    (Any Server)     Target date:                       │
│                                   Target time:                        │
└─────────────────────────────────────────────────────────────────────┘
```

Figure 27-3. The Print Queue Entry Information menu

The other options on the Print Queue Entry Information menu are covered in the next section.

Printing a File from Within PCONSOLE

Files in the queue are usually sent from user applications. In some cases a user may print a text file from the NetWare command line using the NPRINT command. The CAPTURE command may also direct printing to a queue. Another way to print files is from within PCONSOLE. When you use PCONSOLE to set up the print job, a number of parameters must be set in the Print Queue Entry Information menu.

To print a file, start PCONSOLE and select **Print Queue Information** from the main menu. Select **Current Print Job Entries**, and then press INS to create a new print job. When the Select Directory to Print From dialog box appears, enter the full path and name of the file to print, or use the INS key method to select from a list of options.

You are then asked to select a print job configuration. These configurations are designed in the PRINTDEF utility. For now, select **PCon-**

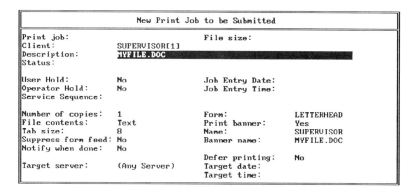

Figure 27-4. The New Print Job to Be Submitted menu

sole Defaults to define a custom print job. A screen similar to that shown in Figure 27-4 appears. Each parameter is described in the following list:

- *Print job* The print job field displays the number of the print job after it has been submitted.

- *File size* The size of the submitted print job.

- *Client* The user who submitted the print job.

- *Description* The description of the print job, which can be its filename or other descriptive information.

- *Status* The status of a print job is displayed, such as whether it is on hold or currently being serviced.

- *User Hold* Type **Yes** in this field to put your print job on hold, either when you create it or after you submit it.

- *Operator Hold* The queue operator can type **Yes** in this field to hold any user's file from printing.

- *Service Sequence* The service sequence is the position of the print job in the queue.

- *Number of copies* The number of copies to print.

- *File contents* Files can be specified as either Text or Byte Stream. Select **Text** when special formatting characters, such as tabs, are to be interpreted and formatted by NetWare. Select **Byte Stream** if the document contains control codes that can be interpreted by the printer to format the document. Print files created by applications like WordPerfect and Microsoft Word are examples of files that should be printed in this way.

- *Tab size* If you select **Text** in the File contents field, specify the character width of the tabs.

- *Suppress form feed* If you want the printer to advance to the top of the next page after your print job, type **No** in this field; otherwise type **Yes** to prevent form feeds.

- *Notify when done* The configuration can send a message to the user when the print job is done if **Yes** is entered in this field.

- *Defer printing* Type **Yes** in this field to print the job at a later time. If **Yes** is chosen, you must enter the target date and time.

- *Target date* The date of deferred printing is specified in this field.

- *Target time* The time of deferred printing is specified in this field.

- *Target server* The target server can be specified in this field. Select **Any Server** if a specific server is not required.

- *Form* Choose the form number as created in the PRINTDEF utility.

- *Print banner* Type **Yes** to print a banner, which is a separate sheet that has information about the document and serves to separate one print job from another.

- *Banner name* Specify the name or other text to appear on the banner; otherwise the name of the currently logged user prints on the banner.

Viewing and Changing Print Server Status and Controls

Using the options described in the following sections, you can view information about a print server and change its status. The options are only available after a print server has been installed. From the PCONSOLE main menu, select **Print Server Information**, and then select a print server to display the Print Server Information menu. From this menu select **Print Server Status/Control** to display the Print Server Status and Control menu, as shown here:

File Servers Serviced

The File Servers Serviced option is used to attach a file server to a print server temporarily. Using this method to attach a file server does not make a permanent entry in the default configuration file (which tells the print server which file server to attach when it is started). To create permanent file server attachments, refer to the "Setting Up Print Server Configuration Files" section earlier in this chapter.

When you select this option, you are presented with a list of currently attached file servers. Press INS to attach other file servers.

Notify List for Printer

When you select this option, you are presented with a list of printers. Select a printer from the list and then press INS. A Notify Candidates list appears.

Printer Status

You can use the Printer Status option to view the current status of a printer. It may be out of paper or out of service for another reason. You also can change the printer's service mode or change the number of its currently mounted form. Note that it is important to notify the print server when a new form has been installed in the printer so print jobs waiting for the form can begin printing.

Queues Serviced by Printer

This option lets you view the current print queues assigned to a printer and change their priority as needed. When you select the option, you are presented with a list of active printers. After selecting a printer, a list of queues appears. To change the priority of a queue, highlight it and press ENTER.

Server Info

With the Server Info option you can view information about the print server, such as its version number, number of printers, and queue service modes. You can also view and change the current status by pressing ENTER on the **Current server status** option. The following menu appears, which allows you to down the print server immediately, down it after the current job finishes, or keep it running.

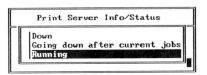

Customizing the Printing Environment

The PRINTDEF and PRINTCON menu utilities are used to customize the printing environment. If you are printing from applications that already recognize the printers attached to the print server, you may not need to customize with PRINTDEF and PRINTCON and can move on to the next section. Use PRINTDEF and PRINTCON for the following reasons:

- If the printer settings of a previous print job are not cleared.

- If different forms or print configurations need to be specified when using CAPTURE and NPRINT, which are used when print jobs need to be redirected from local printers to network printers. This is usually the case when applications are not aware of NetWare's printing methods.

- When different forms are used and changed often at a network printer.

PRINTDEF and PRINTCON are relics from older versions of Net-Ware that provided a convenient way for mangers to ensure users printed with the proper page layouts and could make font changes. Most modern applications allow the user to specify many different types of layout and font changes from within the application, so it is not necessary to define forms for users outside of their applications. In fact it may be detrimental to use defined forms with applications that do their own formatting.

In some cases information or files may not be formatted. For example, files from remote online services may not have margin settings and other features used to define how it should be printed on a page. You can use PRINTDEF to create a definition of a printing device like a printer or plotter and to create forms (page layouts) to use on the printer. PRINTCON uses the information set up in PRINTDEF to create customized print job configurations.

PRINTDEF

The PRINTDEF utility defines network print devices and print forms. A print form consists of a predefined layout and paper size. Each form is assigned a name and number. For example, payroll checks can be called CHECKS and accounting forms can be called REPORTS. A form also specifies the number of lines and character width so a printer knows when to insert page breaks. When a new form needs to be installed in a printer, the print server must be made aware of the new form number using the technique described earlier under "Printer Status." Jobs waiting in the queue for a particular form are made aware that the form has been installed in the printer.

When an application cannot set print modes, PRINTDEF allows you to create your own print drivers, assuming you know the control codes that must be sent to the printer to activate its modes. These usually are found in the printer owner's manual. NetWare comes with 30 predefined definitions for the most popular printers to make this task easier. You can use PRINTDEF to load one of these existing drivers if they match your output device, or you can create your own.

The design of forms can be simple in that only the paper size and margins are specified. More complex forms define the type of printer used and its control codes, so you can include formatting changes like underline and boldface in your documents. As mentioned earlier, this type of definition is rarely needed outside of an application, since most modern applications have extensive printer definition files of their own. The following section illustrates how to define a printing device. If you are using applications that provide adequate print device definitions, skip ahead to "Defining Print Forms."

Using PRINTDEF to Create Print Devices

The PrintDef Options menu is shown in the following illustration. To define print devices select **Print Devices**. The Print Device Options menu then appears.

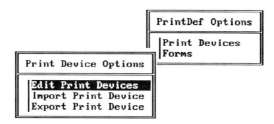

Select **Import Print Device** to import a predefined print device. In the Source Directory dialog box, type **SYS:PUBLIC** and press ENTER. If there are no printer definition files (PDFs) in the SYS:PUBLIC directory, insert the Print Services and Utilities disk in the workstation disk drive and type **A: /PDF** in the Source Directory dialog box.

The Available .PDFs menu appears, as shown in the following illustration:

Scroll through this list to find the driver that matches your printer. The drivers are given names that approximate printer brand names and model numbers. The following list will help you determine the brand code for your printer:

APP = Apple

CIT = Citizen

CITO = CItoh

DIAB = Diablo

EP = Epson

HP = Hewlett-Packard

IBM = IBM

NEC = NEC

OKI = Okidata

PAN = Panasonic

STAR = Star Micronics

TOSH = Toshiba

Select a device that matches or closely matches your printer. You can make changes to the device file if it does not match exactly. To edit a device file, select **Edit Print Devices** from the Print Device Options menu. A screen similar to the following appears, listing the printer driver you selected. In this example the Hewlett-Packard LaserJet and IBM Pro-Printer II/XL device drivers have been imported.

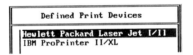

To view or edit the current modes and functions of a printer, select a printer from the Defined Print Devices list and press ENTER. At the Edit Device Options menu, select **Device Modes** to display a list of predefined modes for the printer. The following example lists five predefined modes for the IBM ProPrinter.

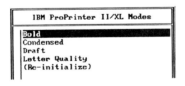

Device modes are sets of functions that invoke a change in the printing mode, such as a type style change. To invoke mode changes, special *escape codes* are sent to the printer. Each printer has its own particular set of escape codes to invoke mode changes, thus almost every printer requires a special printer driver. Some printers use the drivers of other more popular printers and are said to be compatible with those printers.

When using the PRINTCON utility, parameters for special print jobs can be defined using the modes established in PRINTDEF for a particular printer. For example, to create a print form for the accounting department, a printer and then a form is selected. This form defines the type style and print method used by the printer using the print modes defined here. For example, you can use the condensed mode when printing wide accounting reports.

Note: The selected modes apply to the whole document. It is not possible to apply them to individual parts of a document.

Some modes may consist of sets of separately defined functions. For example, the following screen shows the list of functions that make up the Hewlett-Packard LaserJet printer's condensed mode:

```
┌─────────────────────────────────────────┐
│          Condensed Functions             │
├─────────────────────────────────────────┤
│ Reset                                    │
│ End-of-Line Wrap - Enable                │
│ Orientation - Landscape                  │
│ Pitch - 16.66                            │
│ Vertical Motion Index - 5.4              │
└─────────────────────────────────────────┘
```

If you want to edit this mode by adding functions, press INS. The following functions appear for the Hewlett-Packard LaserJet:

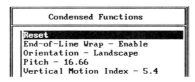

```
┌──────────────────────────────────────────────────────────────┐
│    Additional Hewlett Packard Laser Jet I/II Functions         │
├──────────────────────────────────────────────────────────────┤
│ Big Font                            <ESC>z$3g                  │
│ Character Set - Line Draw           <ESC>(0B                   │
│ Character Set - Roman Extension     <ESC>(0E                   │
│ Character Set - Roman-8             <ESC>(8U                   │
│ Character Set - USASCII             <ESC>(0U                   │
│ End-of-Line Wrap - Disable          <ESC>&s1C                  │
│ Font - Courier                      <ESC>(s3T                  │
│ Font - Helv2                        <ESC>(s4T                  │
│ Font - Letter Gothic                <ESC>(s6T                  │
│ Font - Linedraw                     <ESC>(s0T                  │
│▼Font - Lineprinter                  <ESC>(s0T                  │
└──────────────────────────────────────────────────────────────┘
```

Keep in mind that functions are the lowest level of control that can be sent to a printer. Modes are sets of these functions, and a printer definition file is a collection of modes. For example, you could build a mode used to create lecture notes by combining the Big Font function with others such as the Reset and End-of-Line Wrap functions.

Note: Press the F1 key to display instructions for creating functions.

Defining Print Forms

When you select **Forms** from the PRINTDEF main menu, a blank Forms screen appears, unless forms have already been defined by another user. To define new forms, press INS to display the Forms Definition Form screen.

For example, to define a form for letterhead stock, type a form name in the Name field and a form number in the Number field. If the form is for standard 8 1/2-by-11 sheets, type **66** for the number of lines in the Length field and **85** for the character width in the Width field. Press ESC and answer Yes to save the new form. The Forms Definition Form window now looks like this:

Remember that forms are defined so NetWare knows how to handle page breaks and page width. They also inform NetWare when a new form has been installed in a printer, as described earlier under "Printer Status." Jobs waiting in the queue for a particular form are made aware that the form has been installed in the printer. NetWare can delay print jobs that are requesting a particular form when it knows that a different form is installed. The print server operator is responsible for informing the print server when a form has been changed. Keep in mind that forms only need to be used in this way if the forms in the printer are being changed often. In many cases, several printers each use a permanent form, and users can simply direct their print jobs to the printer with the form they want to use. In other cases, jobs that require special forms may be printed while other print jobs are put on hold. When the jobs are finished, the original form is reinstalled in the printer and the waiting queues are released for printing.

The supervisor or print queue operators should define a form for each different type of paper or form that might be placed in printers, including normal 8 1/2-by-11 or 14-by-11 green bar paper, paychecks, accounting forms, and others. The number of lines and character widths of these forms must be specified. Paper that is 11 inches long prints up to 66 lines. Paper that is 8 1/2 inches wide normally prints 85 characters across, and 14-inch-wide green bar paper normally prints 140 characters across.

Once forms have been created, they are further defined by PRINTCON, as described in the "PRINTCON" section.

Exiting PRINTDEF

When all print devices, functions and forms have been defined, you can press ESC to leave the PRINTDEF menu. You must select **Save Data Base, then EXIT** to save any additions or changes you have made in PRINTDEF.

PRINTCON

The PRINTCON utility creates customized print job configurations, using the devices, functions, and forms created in PRINTDEF. Once printer configurations are defined, they can be used on a regular basis by PCONSOLE, NPRINT, CAPTURE, and other printing utilities. Print job configurations are created to establish various printing parameters for jobs that are printed on a regular basis and eliminate having to set these jobs up every time. Print job configurations can be created for common printing tasks such as month-end accounting reports, paychecks, and mailing labels.

To start the PRINTCON program and create or edit a print job configuration, type **PRINTCON** on the command line. The following Available Options menu appears. Use the first option to create or edit new configurations, the second to select which configuration will be used by default, and the third to copy print job configurations to other users.

Select **Edit Print Job Configuration** from the Available Topics menu. The Print Job Configurations window appears. Initially this window is blank; press INS to add a new configuration, giving it a name of your choice. After naming the new configuration and pressing ENTER, a screen similar to the following appears:

```
┌─────────────────────────────────────────────────────────────────┐
│            Edit Print Job Configuration "SCRIPTS"                 │
│  ┌─────────────────────────────────────────────────────────────┐ │
│  │ Number of copies:      1        Form name:      LETTERHEAD   │ │
│  │ File contents:         Text     Print banner:   Yes          │ │
│  │ Tab size:              8        Name:           SUPERVISOR   │ │
│  │ Suppress form feed:    No       Banner name:                 │ │
│  │ Notify when done:      No                                    │ │
│  │                                                              │ │
│  │ Local printer:         1        Enable timeout: No           │ │
│  │ Auto endcap:           Yes      Timeout count:               │ │
│  │                                                              │ │
│  │ File server:           FS1                                   │ │
│  │ Print queue:           HPLASER-1                             │ │
│  │ Print server:          (Any)                                 │ │
│  │ Device:                Hewlett Packard Laser Jet I/II        │ │
│  │ Mode:                  Letter Quality                        │ │
│  └─────────────────────────────────────────────────────────────┘ │
└─────────────────────────────────────────────────────────────────┘
```

Note that this screen has already been partially modified. The Hewlett-Packard LaserJet has been added as a printer in the Device field, and Letter Quality has been selected for that printer in the Mode field. The fields contain the printer and mode settings created in the PRINTDEF menu utility, as discussed in the previous section.

The following list describes each field in the configuration window and how each can be used to create custom print job configurations. Once a configuration is complete, press ESC to exit and save it.

- *Number of Copies* From 1 to 65,000 copies can be printed, with a default setting of 1.

- *Form Name* Press ENTER to display a list of forms created with the PRINTDEF utility. These forms define the paper size in lines per page and characters of width.

- *File Contents* Files can be specified as either Text or Byte Stream. Select **Text** when special formatting characters, such as tabs, are to be interpreted and formatted by NetWare. Select **Byte Stream** if the application of origin can handle the formatting commands at the printer. Use Byte Stream with applications such as WordPerfect and Microsoft Word.

- *Print Banner* Type **Yes** in this field to print a banner, which helps separate print jobs in the output bin of the printer.

- *Tab Size* Use this field to specify the character width of tabs, which may be a number from 1 to 18. The default is 8.

- *Name* The name to appear on the banner.

- *Suppress Form Feed* Form feeds ensure that the final page of a print job ejects fully. You may need to enter **Yes** to suppress form feeds if an application already performs this action.

- *Banner Name* If you decide to print a banner, you can specify a banner name. If no name is specified, the name of the user is printed on the banner.

- *Notify when done* The configuration can send a message to the user when the print job is done if **Yes** is entered in this field.

- *Local Printer* Used with the CAPTURE command. This field can specify the local printer port to capture printer output from.

- *Auto Endcap* Use this field with the CAPTURE command. Enter **Yes** to cause printing of captured data when a program is exited or when the program closes the print device. If you enter **No**, the file is printed only after running the ENDCAP command.

- *Enable Timeout* Use this field with the CAPTURE command. Enter **Yes** to capture data to be sent to a print queue after the number of seconds specified in the Timeout Count field. If you enter **No**, printing performs according to the settings of the Auto Endcap field.

- *Timeout Count* The number of seconds of wait time between 1 to 1000 before queuing the saved file. The default is 5. You need only specify a timeout count if ENDCAP has not been used.

- *File Server* Press ENTER on the field to select a file server to use. Remember that queues are located on file servers and these queues are serviced by print servers.

- *Print Queue* Press ENTER to select a print queue on the selected server.

- *Print server*   Press ENTER to see a list of print servers authorized to service jobs in the selected print queue.

- *Device*   Press ENTER to select a print device as defined in the PRINTDEF menu utility.

- *Mode*   Press ENTER to select a print mode, as defined in the PRINTDEF menu utility.

Copying and Selecting Default Print Job Configurations

Choose Select Default Print Job Configuration from the PRINTCON main menu to select the print job configuration that will be used as a default. Each existing print job is displayed. Simply highlight the print job to be used by default and press ENTER.

Print jobs can be copied to users' mail directories so that the jobs in the configuration can be used every time they print. To copy the configurations, select the third option from the PRINTCON main menu and press ENTER. You must specify the source user and target user to copy the file.

Command-Line Utilities for Printing

NetWare has four command-line utilities used for printing: The CAPTURE and ENDCAP commands control whether printing occurs on local or network printers, NPRINT can send print jobs to network printers, and PSC lists the status of network print jobs.

PSC (Printer Server Command)

The Print Server Command (PSC) is used by print server operators to quickly control print servers and network printers. It performs most of the same tasks as PCONSOLE, but from the command line. Network users can also use PSC to see the status of print servers and network printers.

The PSC command takes the following form:

PSC PS=*printserver* P=*printernumber* *flaglist*

where *printserver* is the name of the print server, *printernumber* is the number of the printer, and *flaglist* is one of the following flags. Type only the capital letters when entering one of the flags.

- *STAT (Status)* Displays the status of one or all printers installed on the specified print server. If a printer number is not specified, all are listed. A number of possible status messages can appear, most of which are self explanatory, such as "Waiting for job", "Printing job", and "Paused". "Not connected" means a configuration file for a printer at a workstation has not been connected (use RPRINTER to connect it). "Not installed" means a configuration file has not been set up for a printer. "In private mode" means a workstation printer is not available because it is being used locally.

- *PAU (Pause)* Use this flag to temporarily stop a printer. Keep in mind that a printer may not actually stop until its built-in buffer is depleted.

- *AB (Abort)* Use this flag to stop printing the current job. The next job in the queue then begins printing.

- *STO k (Stop keep)* Use this flag to stop a printer. Enter **STO k** to resubmit the current print job at the top of the queue; otherwise it is deleted from the queue.

- *STAR (Start)* Use this flag to restart a printer after it has been paused or stopped.

- *M character (Mark)* Use this flag to align a printer. Replace *character* with an asterisk or other character. This character is printed on the form so you can see where printing will begin.

- *FF (Form Feed)* Use this flag to advance the paper to the top of the next page.

- *MOF=n (Mount Form)*   Use this flag to inform the print server that a new form has been mounted, where *n* is the new form number.

- *PRI (Private)*   This flag is used when a user wants to use a locally attached printer for private use and not share it with the network.

- *SH (Shared)*   Reverses the Private flag.

- *CD (Cancel Down)*   Include this flag if you have selected the "Going down after current jobs" option in PCONSOLE and want to cancel that command before the print server goes down.

Setting a Default Print Server and Number

Use the DOS SET command to set a default printer number and print server name to use with the PSC command. You then use the default name and number throughout your login session. By including the SET command in your personal login script, it executes every time you log in.

To use SET at any time from the command line, use the following form:

SET PSC=PS*printserver* P*printernumber*

To include a SET command in a login script, use the following form:

SET PSC="PS*printserver* P*printernumber*"

Once these settings are made, you can use PSC in the following form, including only the flags just discussed.

PSC *flaglist*

CAPTURE

Many applications are not designed specifically for network use. With such applications, print jobs are automatically sent to local printers, usually the parallel ports LPT1, LPT2, and LPT3. The CAPTURE command is used to "capture" the data being sent to a local printer on the workstation and redirect it to network printers.

In its simplest form CAPTURE can be entered at the workstation by typing **CAPTURE** just prior to entering an applications program that requires its printer output be sent to a network printer. This CAPTURE command automatically redirects printer output sent to LPT1 to the default network printer. The special options described in the following section can be used with the CAPTURE command to enhance its capabilities. Examples of using CAPTURE follow this section. The ENDCAP command is used to end capturing and return printing to the local printer.

Options Used with CAPTURE

The following options can be included immediately following the CAPTURE command on the command line. In most cases, more than one option can be included with the command.

- *SH (Show)* The Show option is used to view the file server, the queue, and the printer that the local printing port (LPT) has been redirected to. This option cannot be used with any other CAPTURE option.

- *NOTI (Notify)* Include this option if you want to be notified when a print job is complete.

- *NNOTI (No Notify)* Include this option if you do not want to be notified when a print job is complete. This option is used if a print job configuration already specifies that you should be notified.

- *A (Autoendcap)* Include this option to send data to a network printer when, but not until, you exit an application. The option is useful if you want to save several different screens or files from the same application to the same network file.

- *NA (No Autoendcap)* Cancels the Autoendcap option. Prevents data from being sent to a network printer or file when entering or exiting an application.

- *TI=n (Timeout)* Enables the timeout feature. Replace *n* with a number from 1 through 1000 to represent the number of seconds between the moment you initiate printing and the moment the job is queued for printing. The default timeout is 0, which means that the timeout feature is disabled.

- *L=n (Local)* Include this option to indicate which LPT port to capture. Replace *n* with 1, 2, or 3 to indicate LPT1, LPT2, or LPT3, respectively.

- *S=server (Server)* Include this option along with the server name to indicate which file server will be used to handle the print job.

- *J=job (Job)* The name of a predefined print job configuration can be specified with the Job option. Print job configurations are defined with the PRINTCON utility.

- *Q=queuename (Queue)* Include this option to indicate which queue the print job should be sent to. Replace *queuename* with the name of the queue.

- *F=form or n (Form)* The Form option specifies the predefined form or form number, as defined by the PRINTDEF menu utility.

- *C=n (Copies)* Copies specifies the number of copies of a print job to print. Replace *n* with a number from 1 to 256.

- *T=n (Tabs)* The Tabs option is used to specify the number of spaces to be used in tabs. The option is used for applications that do not have print formatters, which is rare.

- *NT (NoTabs)* Include this option only if an application does not have a print formatter (most applications do). This option ensures that all the tabs in your print job arrive at the printer unchanged.

- *NAM=name (Name)* The Name option specifies the user name that will appear on the upper half of a banner page. Replace *name* with a user name if it should be different than the login name of the current user.

- *B=bannername (Banner)* Replace *bannername* with the name to appear on a banner, which is used to separate print jobs at the output bin of the printer.

- *NB (No Banner)* Use the No Banner option to prevent banners from printing.

- *FF (Form Feed)* The Form Feed option enables a form feed upon completion of the print job.

- *NFF (No Form Feed)* The No Form Feed option is used to disable form feed upon completion of a print job.

- *CR=filename (Create)* Include this option to send data to a file instead of to a network printer. The file server, volume, and directory name should be included if the destination is other than the current directory.

- *K (Keep)* The Keep option is a safety feature. It is used when data is captured over several hours or more. The option ensures that the file server keeps all data it receives from a workstation, even if the workstation crashes. The server sends the data to a printer 15 minutes after a system crash. If the option is not used, the server discards any data received from the crashed workstation.

Using CAPTURE

The following examples represent basic uses of the CAPTURE command to capture printing on a network. Remember that the CAPTURE command should be typed before starting an application with print jobs that are printed on a network printer. Also, use ENDCAP when network printing has finished to resume printing on a local printer.

Note: Subsequent CAPTURE commands override the settings of previous CAPTURE commands.

In the following example local printing is redirected to the ACCTG queue using print job 2:

CAPTURE Q=ACCTG J=2

In the next command any print jobs sent to LPT2 by the application are sent to the ACCTG queue. Print jobs sent to LPT1 by the application are sent to the local printer as normal.

CAPTURE L=2 Q=ACCTG

In the next example three copies are made of each print job sent to the default network print queue.

CAPTURE C=3

In the next command any print job sent to LPT2 in the applications program is sent to the default queue on the SALES server.

CAPTURE L=2 S=SALES

Data can be saved in a network file using the Create option. In the following example, data is saved to a file called DATAHOLD on drive G of the server. The NA (No Autoendcap) option is used to disable the Autoendcap option. This then allows the user to enter and exit applications without prematurely closing the file that is capturing data on the server. The option is often used to collect screen captures in a file.

CAPTURE CR=G:DATAHOLD NA

The current status of the LPT ports on a workstation can be listed by typing the following command:

CAPTURE SH

The screen displays information similar to the following, depending on the options that are set:

LPT1: Capturing data to server SALES queue LASER

Capture Defaults:Enabled		Automatic Endcap:	Enabled
Banner	None	Form Feed	:Yes
Copies	1	Tabs	:8 spaces
Form	0	Timeout Count	:2 seconds

LPT2: Capturing Is Not Currently Active.

LPT3: Capturing Is Not Currently Active.

ENDCAP

The ENDCAP command ends the capture of a workstation's LPT ports established by the CAPTURE command. The command is typed as shown here,

ENDCAP *option*

where *option* is one of the following options:

- *L=n (Local)* The Local option is used to specify the LPT port (either LPT1, LPT2, or LPT3) to end capturing. The *n* option is either 1, 2, or 3.

- *ALL (All)* The All option is used to end the capture of all LPT ports on the workstation.

- *C (Cancel)* The Cancel command is used to end capturing of the LPT1 port and to discard any data without printing it.

- *CL=n (Cancel Local)* This option is used to end the capture of the specified LPT port and to discard any data without printing it. The *n* option is replaced with 1, 2, or 3 to designate one of the LPT ports.

- *CALL (Cancel All)* This option is used to end capturing on all LPT ports and to discard any data without printing it.

Before entering an ENDCAP command, it is useful to list the current capture information with the following command:

CAPTURE SH

From the information listed, you can use an ENDCAP command to cancel capture at a printer port.

As an example, the following command ends capturing of the LPT2 printer port on the workstation:

ENDCAP L=2

To cancel the capture and delete any captured data that might be ready to print to LPT2, enter the following command:

ENDCAP CL=2

NPRINT

The NPRINT command sends files to a network printer. The CAPTURE command does not need to be active since NPRINT automatically sends to network printers, bypassing any local printers. Files sent to a server with NPRINT are placed in print queues and printed in the order received unless rearranged by the supervisor or queue operator.

Files sent by NPRINT must be ASCII files, or print files, to be printed properly. NPRINT does not have any special formatting tools, as most word processing programs do; therefore, the text of a file is printed exactly as it is stored. This is usually fine for straight ASCII text files but not appropriate for files created by applications that may contain control codes and other formatting information that cannot be interpreted by NPRINT. Files created by applications can be printed as files, however, which means the application sends all printing information to a disk file instead of the printer. The disk file then contains information that can be interpreted by the printer, and the NPRINT command can send the file to the printer at any time. In some cases, a print file can be created by one user for printing on another person's printer. The user who creates the file must load a print driver that matches the printer of the user who will receive the file, and then NPRINT is used to print the file when it is received. The file is printed correctly because it contains the correct formatting codes for the users' printer.

The NPRINT command takes the following form:

NPRINT *filename options*

where *filename* is the name of the file to be printed and *options* is one or more of the options listed in the following section. Note that *filename* must include the mapped drive letter or complete path specification of the file's location. A few examples of the NPRINT command follow the options listings.

Options Used with NPRINT

The following options can be included immediately following the NPRINT command on the command line. In most cases more than one option can be included with the command.

- *PS=printserver (Print Server)* Use this option to specify which print server should be used for printing. Replace *printserver* with the name of the server.

- *NOTI (Notify)* Use this option if you want to be notified when a print job is complete.

- *NNOTI (No Notify)* Use this option if you do not want to be notified when a print job is complete. This option is used if a print job configuration already specifies that you should be notified.

- *S=server (Server)* Include this option along with the server name to indicate which server will be used to handle the print job.

- *J=job (Job)* The name of a predefined print job configuration can be specified with the Job option. Print job configurations are defined with the PRINTCON utility.

- *Q=queuename (Queue)* Include this option to indicate which queue the print job should be sent to. Replace *queuename* with the name of the queue.

- *F=form* or *n (Form)*   The Form option specifies the predefined form or form number, as defined by the PRINTDEF menu utility. Replace *form* with the name of the form, or *n* with the number of the form.

- *C=n (Copies)*   The Copies option specifies the number of copies of a print job to print. Replace *n* with a number from 1 to 256.

- *T=n (Tabs)*   The Tabs option is used to specify the number of spaces to be used in tabs. The option is used for applications that do not have print formatters, which is rare.

- *NT (No Tabs)*   Include this option only if an application does not have a print formatter (most applications do). This option ensures that all the tabs in your print job arrive at the printer unchanged.

- *NAM=name (Name)*   The Name option specifies the user name that appears on the upper half of a banner page. Replace *name* with a user name if it should be different than the login name of the current user.

- *B=bannername (Banner)*   Replace *bannername* with a word or phrase up to 12 characters long to appear on the banner page of printed documents. Banner pages separate print jobs in a printer's output bin.

- *NB (No Banner)*   Use the No Banner option to prevent banners from printing.

- *FF (Form Feed)*   The Form Feed option enables a form feed upon completion of the print job.

- *NFF (No Form Feed)*   The No Form Feed option is used to disable form feed upon completion of a print job.

- *D (Delete)*   The Delete option is used to automatically erase the file after printing.

Examples of NPRINT

Files in the current default drive do not require a drive or path specification in order to be printed with NPRINT. In the following example, the file MYFILE.DOC is printed on the default network printer:

NPRINT MYFILE.DOC

If the file is in another mapped drive, such as drive G, the following command is used:

NPRINT G:MYFILE.DOC

Initially files are printed with the network printing defaults, which are as follows:

- The default printer is used

- A banner page is printed and includes the name of the user

- A last sheet is ejected (form feed)

The NPRINT options are used to change the default settings of network printing. For example, the following command causes the file MYFILE.DOC to be printed on the queue ACCTG, using the LETTERS print job configuration:

NPRINT MYFILE.DOC Q=ACCTG J=LETTERS

The next example inhibits the banner and form feed options:

NPRINT MYFILE.DOC Q=ACCTG J=LETTERS NB NFF

In the next example, the file is deleted after it is printed:

NPRINT MYFILE.DOC Q=ACCTG J=LETTERS NB NFF D

Login Scripts

The Default Login Script
Creating or Changing Login Scripts
Login Script Identifier Variables
Login Script Commands
Login Script Examples

Login scripts are designed to establish the network environment when users first log in. A login script contains a set of commands that execute one after another and are similar to DOS batch files. Most login scripts contain mapping commands for drives and search drives, but you can also include commands that display greeting messages, attach users to other servers, or display a menu of selections. Keep in mind that every server can have its own login script, but if you are using NetWare's global naming service, one login script may suffice for a number of servers.

Recall that there are three types of login scripts. The first login script is the *default script* used by NetWare if a system login script has not yet been created. This script sets up the basic drive mappings to the SYSTEM and PUBLIC directories. If you have been following the examples in this book, the default script has already been replaced by your custom script. The default login script is covered here only as an example.

The other two types of login scripts are the system login script and the user login scripts. The *system login script* is designed to set various network parameters for all users. It executes when any user logs on the system, so it should contain generic commands for any user logging into the server. A *user login script* can be written for each individual user. It executes after the system login script. The system login script can be modified only by the supervisor, but users can modify their user login

591

scripts to include commands important to their use of the network; for example, commands that map drives in their personal directory. The NetWare SYSCON menu utility is used to edit login scripts.

The Default Login Script

The commands in the default login script are examined here to help you understand their usage. Since many login scripts have similar commands, it is worthwhile to review the script. Note that each line is numbered for reference only.

1. WRITE "Good %GREETING_TIME, %LOGIN_NAME."
2. MAP DISPLAY OFF
3. MAP ERRORS OFF
4. Remark: Set 1st drive to most appropriate directory.
5. MAP *1:=SYS:; *1:=SYS:%LOGIN_NAME
6. IF "%1"="SUPERVISOR" THEN MAP *1:=SYS:SYSTEM
7. Remark: Set search drives (S2 machine-OS dependent).
8. MAP S1:=SYS:PUBLIC; S2:=S1:%MACHINE/%OS/%OS_VERSION
9. Remark: Now display all the current drive settings.
10. MAP DISPLAY ON
11. MAP

1. The first line includes the WRITE login script command, which displays a greeting message. Two variables, %GREETING_TIME and %LOGIN_NAME, display the current time ("morning," "afternoon," or "evening") and the name of the user who logged in.

2. The MAP DISPLAY OFF command prevents extraneous messages from displaying on the screen while the script commands execute.

3. The MAP ERRORS OFF command prevents error messages from displaying during the login process.

4. This remark statement is used only to document the contents of the login script. It has no effect when the script is executed.

5. The MAP command maps the first network drive (represented by *1) to the user's personal directory. This option is used for workstations that run DOS 2. For DOS 3 and 4, the first network drive always is F.

6. When the supervisor logs in, this command maps the first drive to the SYS:SYSTEM directory.

7. Another remark.

8. The SYS:PUBLIC drive is mapped to search drive 1, and the DOS directory for the workstation is mapped to search drive 2, all in the same command.

9. Another remark.

10. Messages displayed by commands as they execute are made visible again with the MAP DISPLAY ON command.

11. The current drive mappings are displayed using the MAP command.

The remainder of this chapter explains additional commands and features you can use in login scripts to improve their functionality.

Creating or Changing Login Scripts

Both the system and user login scripts are changed with the SYSCON menu utility. To change the system login script, select **Supervisor Options** from the main menu, and then select **System login script** from the next menu. Note that user login scripts are changed by selecting **User Information** from the SYSCON main menu. The **Login Script** option is then selected from the User Information window.

In the login script edit window, editing keys such as HOME, END, DEL, and the arrow keys can be used to make changes to the file. You can use the F5 (Mark) key to highlight a block of text to be copied or deleted. After pressing F5, use the arrow keys to move through the text and highlight the portions you want to move, remove, or change. Text removed with the DEL key can be inserted elsewhere with the INS key.

There are only a few rules for working in the login script edit window:

- Only supervisors can edit the system login script, but users can create or edit their own scripts.

- Only specific login commands can be placed in the script. DOS commands can be included but they must be preceded by a pound sign (#).

- Text in a command line cannot exceed 150 characters. For clarity, try to use only 78 characters, which is the width of the edit window.

- Only one command can be entered per line.

- The login script command must be the first word on the command line.

By pressing the F1 (Help) key, you can view several screens of login script help, including a listing of editing keys, commands, and the special identifiers (%LOGIN_NAME, %MACHINE, %OS_VERSION, etc.) that can be used with many of the login script commands. Use the PGDN and PGUP keys to scroll through the help screens. You will find login scripts easy to create and edit if you use the help screens for reference.

Once a login script is complete, press ESC to return to the menu. You will be asked if you want to save changes.

Login Script Identifier Variables

Variables are used in login scripts to display or operate on values that exist at the time a user logs into the server. Each variable is described briefly in Table 28-1. As an example, any workstation can be assigned a long machine name in the SHELL.CFG file, as discussed in Chapter 19. This name can then be used to establish a path to the directory on the server that holds the correct version of DOS for the workstation. In this way each workstation can be assigned a different name and thus assigned a different DOS path. The SHELL.CFG file is read when the station logs into the network, and the variables in the file are used to establish parameters for its login session.

Not all variables are set in the SHELL.CFG file. Some are automatically set by NetWare, such as the date and time. For example, the following WRITE command displays the message "Good Morning", "Good

Time and Date

SECOND	Holds the current second (00-59)
MINUTE	Holds the current minute (00-59)
HOUR	Holds the current hour (1-12)
HOUR24	Holds the current hour in 24 hour time (00 - 23)
AM_PM	Holds the day or night specifier (AM or PM)
GREETING_TIME	This variable is either morning, afternoon, or night, depending on the time of day
DAY	Holds the current day as a number (01 - 31)
NDAY_OF_WEEK	Holds the current weekday number (1 - 7, Sunday is 1)
DAY_OF_WEEK	Holds the day of the week in full format (Sunday, Monday, and so on)
MONTH	Holds the current month as a number (01 - 12)
MONTH_NAME	Holds the current month's name in full (January, February, and so on)
YEAR	Holds the year in full format (for example, 1990)
SHORT_YEAR	Holds the short format of the year (for example, 90)

Table 28-1.   Login Script Identifier Variables

User Information

LOGIN_NAME	Holds the current user's login name
FULL_NAME	Holds the current user's full name
USER_ID	Number assigned to the current user

Workstation Information

STATION	Holds the number of the login workstation
P_STATION	Holds the 12 digit hex number of the physical workstation
MACHINE	The long machine name given to a workstation in the SHELL.CFG file with the command LONG MACHINE TYPE =
SMACHINE	The short machine name given to a machine by the SHELL.CFG file with the command SHORT MACHINE TYPE =

Network Information

NETWORK_ADDRESS	Network number of the cabling system
FILE_SERVER	Name of the file server

Operating System Information

OS	Holds the workstation's operating system (PCDOS, MSDOS)
OS_VERSION	Holds the version of the workstation's operating system (for example, v3.3, v4.01)
< >	Use a DOS environment variable between the brackets.

Conditional Commands

ACCESS_SERVER	Returns True if access server is functional; otherwise it returns False
ERROR_LEVEL	A value indicating errors that have occurred; the error 0 indicates no errors
MEMBER OF "group"	Returns True if user is member of group; otherwise returns False

Table 28-1.   Login Script Identifier Variables (*continued*)

Afternoon", or "Good Evening". The variable %GREETING_TIME inserts "Morning", "Afternoon", or "Evening" based on the current time of day.

WRITE "Good %GREETING_TIME"

The majority of the variables are used with the WRITE command. WRITE displays any message between quotation marks, and variables can be included in the message, as demonstrated in the previous example.

Note: When variables are used with MAP commands or placed within the quotations of a WRITE command, they must be preceded by a percent sign. Variables within quotes must be all uppercase.

Identifier variables are used to make the system login script generic. Commands that contain variables may execute in a different way for each user. For example, a command may map a directory for users if they belong to a specific user group, such as clerks or managers. The supervisor can more easily manage the login process for all users with one script, rather than tailoring individual login scripts for each user.

Note: For best results and to avoid problems, type all variables in uppercase at all times.

Login Script Commands

The following commands can be used in login scripts. Each is explained in detail, and examples are given for each. See the section "Login Script Examples" for examples of login scripts that use a combination of these commands.

ATTACH

Use the ATTACH command to attach to another file server. The command takes the following form:

ATTACH *servername/username*; *password*

where *servername* is the name of the server to attach to, *username* is the login name of the current user on the server, and *password* is the password required to gain access to the system.

If the variables are not specified, the following messages appear:

```
Server:
Username:
Password:
```

ATTACH can be used in the system login script to attach all users to another server, but do not include the *username* and *password* variables in the command. In this way each user is prompted for a personal user name and password. When users need to attach to another server, they can do so individually at any time by executing ATTACH at the NetWare command line. Users who need to attach to other servers on a regular basis should place the command in their personal login scripts.

If *username* and *password* are the same on the server a user is attaching to, they are said to be synchronized, and ATTACH does not ask for a user name and password.

Example

The following command is placed in a user's personal login script to attach him to the server ACCTG with the login name TED and the password TOPGUN:

```
ATTACH ACCTG/TED;TOPGUN
```

BREAK

The BREAK ON command allows a login script to be terminated by pressing CTRL-BREAK or CTRL-C. The BREAK OFF command is used to prevent a break in the login script. It is not recommended that this command be placed in the system login script.

In some cases it is necessary to stop a user login script from executing further. For example, a user could place a command in a login script that may need to be executed only occasionally. By placing a PAUSE or WAIT command before the command, the user has a chance to break out of the script before it executes. The BREAK ON command can also be used to test a login script. The execution of further commands can be stopped if a problem or error occurs.

The commands take the following forms:

BREAK ON

BREAK OFF

When BREAK ON is active, type-ahead keyboard input is not saved in the buffer.

Note that BREAK can be turned on for small segments of a login script, and then turned off again to prevent a user from breaking out if the login script is allowed to continue beyond the BREAK OFF point.

COMSPEC

Use the COMSPEC command to specify the directory where the DOS COMMAND.COM file exists. When you enter an application, some of the DOS code in memory is discarded to create room for the application. When you exit the application, this DOS code must be replaced by executing COMMAND.COM again. COMSPEC indicates to the operating system where COMMAND.COM can be found. The file may be stored on the server or may be located on a drive at the workstation. The DOS files are often placed on the server to enhance performance.

If workstations are using different versions of DOS, you can create a directory for each version on the server and then specify a path to the directory that is appropriate for each workstation. In most cases these directories branch from the PUBLIC directory. For example, the following directories are created for IBM DOS 3.3, Compaq DOS 4.01, and Tandon DOS 3.2:

SYS:PUBLIC\IBM33

SYS:PUBLIC\CPAQ401

SYS:PUBLIC\TAND32

The COMSPEC command takes the following forms:

COMSPEC = *drive*:COMMAND.COM

where *drive* is a local drive or mapped server drive. You also can enter the command in the following form:

COMSPEC = S*n*:COMMAND.COM

where S*n* is the number of a previously mapped search drive. Another form is shown below:

COMSPEC = **n*:COMMAND.COM

where *n* is the directory where the *n*th network drive maps. This is further explained under the MAP command.

Examples

The following examples show how you can use the MAP command to map a search drive before you execute the COMSPEC command. In this way the COMSPEC command can include the letter of the search drive. Note that the %MACHINE variable holds the name of the directory specified in the workstation's SHELL.CFG file with the LONG MACHINE TYPE command.

```
MAP S3:=SYS:PUBLIC\%MACHINE
COMSPEC = S3:COMMAND.COM
```

In the next example, the third network drive is mapped to a subdirectory of PUBLIC that matches the name specified in the identifier variable %MACHINE.

```
MAP *3:=SYS:PUBLIC\%MACHINE
COMSPEC = *3:COMMAND.COM
```

In this example, COMSPEC is specified on the local A drive:

COMSPEC = A:COMMAND.COM

DISPLAY and FDISPLAY

The DISPLAY and FDISPLAY commands display the contents of text files. These text files, which are read by the person logging in, can contain messages or instructions such as meeting announcements or server maintenance schedules. The text files must be created using an editor or word processor. Use the DISPLAY and FDISPLAY commands when you need to display large blocks of text. The WRITE command, covered later, displays a line or two of text.

The difference between DISPLAY and FDISPLAY is that FDISPLAY filters out any formatting codes that were inserted by a word processor. It does a good job of this most of the time. The DISPLAY command displays every character in the file, including "junk" characters. For best results, create the text files using an editor that allows files to be saved as text only, such as an ASCII text editor like EDLIN.

A supervisor can use the DISPLAY and FDISPLAY commands in several ways. For example, daily messages for everyone to see could be written in a text file called DAILY.DOC and displayed by placing the following command in the system login script:

DISPLAY DAILY.DOC

Message files can also be displayed using the IF...THEN...ELSE statement, which is covered later. This statement allows messages to be displayed only under certain conditions; for example, if the user is the member of a group or if the day is Friday.

The commands take the following forms:

DISPLAY *path/filename*

FDISPLAY *path/filename*

where *path* is the full path to the file (or a mapped drive letter), and *filename* is the name of the text file created by an editor or word processing program.

Examples

The FDISPLAY command is used in the following examples because filtering of control codes in the text files is preferable in most cases. In the following command the file NEWS.DOC in the SYS:PUBLIC directory is displayed during the login script:

FDISPLAY SYS:PUBLIC\NEWS.DOC

The next example assumes a text file exists in a directory called SYS:NEWS for each day of the week. The %DAY_OF_WEEK identifier variable is replaced with the name of the current day, which then matches a text file of the same name, such as MONDAY.DOC or TUESDAY.DOC. These files can be updated on a regular basis as required. Note that the percent sign is used in front of the identifier variable to differentiate it from a filename.

FDISPLAY SYS:NEWS\%DAY_OF_WEEK.DOC

The following example uses the IF...THEN...ELSE statement in another form to display a message if the day is Monday:

IF DAY_OF_WEEK = "MONDAY" THEN FDISPLAY SYS:NEWS\MEETINGS.DOC

The next example displays the message file COMPAQ.DOC in the SYS:NEWS directory if the workstations logging in have the machine name COMPAQ:

IF MACHINE = "COMPAQ" THEN FDISPLAY SYS:NEWS\COMPAQ.DOC

DOS BREAK

Use the DOS BREAK command to specify that you can interrupt DOS commands with CTRL-BREAK or CTRL-C. This command is different from BREAK ON command, which is used to interrupt a login script. The commands take the forms:

DOS BREAK ON

DOS BREAK OFF

The default DOS BREAK is OFF. See your DOS manual for more information.

DOS SET

The DOS SET command creates variables that can be used in batch files after the login script has completed. You can use these variables in many of the same ways that you use identifier variables. The command takes the form:

DOS SET *name* = "*value*"

where *name* is the name you want to give to a variable, and *value* is the value that is held in the variable name. Note that *value* must be enclosed in double quotation marks. If you use backslashes, enter two to avoid conflicts, since the backslash is used as a special programming character in NetWare commands.

Because NetWare has an extensive set of its own identifier variables, you may not use the DOS SET command much. On the other hand, you can use it to create variables from the NetWare identifier variable that can be used in DOS batch files or with the MENU utility discussed in the next chapter. In the following example, the NetWare identifier variable LOGIN_NAME is made equal to the DOS variable USER. USER can then be used to customize batch files for each user logging into the system.

DOS SET USER = LOGIN_NAME

The DOS SET command can also change the system prompt, as shown here. This causes the prompt to display the current directory.

SET PROMPT = "PG"

$P displays the directory and $G displays the > sign, similar to the standard DOS prompt.

The SET command places variables in a memory area called the *environment space*. If too many variables are set, the environment space may become full. To increase the size of the environment space, place a command similar to the following in the CONFIG.SYS file on the boot disk or hard drive of the workstation:

SHELL=COMMAND.COM/E *xxx*/P

This command increases the size of the environment space from 127 bytes to *xxx* bytes. Replace *xxx* with a suitable environment size, depending on the amount of space required by your new variables. The SHELL command is described in your DOS manual.

DRIVE

Use the DRIVE command in a login script to switch users to a mapped drive. In most login scripts the user's personal directory becomes mapped to the first network drive (drive F). If other drives are mapped and you wish to change a user to one of those drives, you use the DRIVE command. It is sometimes necessary to do this when running commands that execute only if the user is in the directory where the commands are located. After the commands are executed, the DRIVE command can place the user back in the personal directory.

The DRIVE command takes the form:

DRIVE *n*:

where *n* is a drive letter, or

DRIVE *n*:

where *n* is a drive number. In the first form the command switches to a drive that was mapped earlier in the login script. In the second form, the user is switched to the *n*th drive, as specified by a previous MAP command.

Example

The following command switches a user to drive R, which was mapped by a previous command in the login script.

DRIVE R:

EXIT

The EXIT command stops the execution of the remaining commands in a login script. Usually you use the command with an IF...THEN...ELSE statement after a condition is evaluated as True or False. For example, an EXIT command may stop the login script for a user if that user is a member of a group, such as a group called TEMPORARY that includes the temporary personnel for a company. Any commands that follow the EXIT command are executed only for regular company employees.

Note: If you use EXIT, include the PCCOMPATIBLE login script command anywhere in the script before the EXIT command. This tells NetWare that you have changed the long machine name to a name other than the default, which is IBM PC.

The EXIT command takes the following forms:

EXIT

EXIT "*filename*"

In the second form *filename* is replaced by an executable file with the extension COM, EXE, or BAT. In this way a program can be run immediately upon exiting the login script. It is common to run a menu system, as described in the next chapter.

Examples

While the standalone form of the command has limited usage, you can use it while writing and testing login scripts to exit the script before certain commands are actually executed.

The following command can be used in any login script to start a command line utility, batch file, or DOS command. In this example a batch file called MENU.BAT is executed.

```
EXIT "MENU"
```

The most common way to use the EXIT command is after evaluating a certain condition with the IF...THEN...ELSE command. The following command uses the temporary personnel example described earlier:

```
IF MEMBER OF "TEMPORARY" THEN EXIT "TEMPS"
```

In this command, TEMPS is the name of a batch file that switches temporary personnel to a special data directory and starts the applications program that they are assigned to work with, such as a database entry program.

The EXIT command has several strict rules:

- The PCCOMPATIBLE command must be placed before the EXIT command for non-IBM DOS systems.

- The command specified with EXIT must be located in the current directory or a mapped search drive.

- The path to a command can be specified with EXIT, but the complete path and command cannot exceed 14 characters. The next rule also applies in this case.

- If backslashes are used with commands, they must be typed twice to differentiate them from backslashes used in other NetWare commands. A double backslash counts as a single character.

- External Program Execution

You can execute external commands from a login script if you place the pound sign (#) in front of the command. The command takes the following form:

path/command parameters...

where *path* must be specified if the *command* is not in the current directory or default drive. *Parameters* can be specified as required by the command.

Since the login script is held in memory while the external program is running, the remainder of the script resumes execution when the external program ends or is exited. In this way the external program execution command is different than the EXIT command, because the remainder of the login script is executed, whereas EXIT aborts the login script.

Example

In the following series of commands, a program called INSET (a screen capture program) is executed during a user's login script. The script first maps the J drive to the INSET directory, then switches to that drive using the DRIVE command. The INSET program is started with the third command, and the fourth command switches the user back to drive F.

```
MAP J:=SYS:INSET
DRIVE J:
# INSET
DRIVE F:
```

One of the reasons for mapping and switching to the INSET directory is that the program must be started in the same directory where its supporting programs and startup files are stored.

In the next example the PCONSOLE program is started when a print queue operator with the login name SUE logs in. Note that the set of commands shown here can be inserted anywhere in the login script. Also note the form of the IF...THEN...ELSE BEGIN command, which allows multiple commands to be included between the BEGIN and END options. This is covered under the IF...THEN...ELSE statement.

```
(beginning login commands)
IF LOGIN_NAME = "SUE" THEN BEGIN
            # PCONSOLE
            END
(remaining login commands)
```

FIRE PHASERS

You can use the FIRE PHASERS command to generate the sound that is useful for alerting users to various conditions, such as the presence of mail when a mail system is used. Use FIRE PHASERS sparingly since users may become irritated by the sound or not pay attention to it. In most cases you should use the command only as an occasional attention-getting method. For example, if users normally do not watch the screen during login, they may not realize an important message has been displayed. You can draw attention to the screen with the sound created by FIRE PHASERS.

The command takes the following form:

FIRE PHASERS n TIMES

where n is the number of times you want to fire the PHASERS.

Example

The phasers are fired five times in the following example:

```
FIRE PHASERS 5 TIMES
```

You may want to fire PHASERS only under certain conditions. For example, you can use FIRE PHASERS to alert users. This is done in the following example, which also includes a WRITE statement to display a message and a PAUSE command to pause the login script so users can read the message.

```
IF DAY_OF_WEEK = "Monday" THEN BEGIN
      WRITE "Don't forget, meeting at 3:00 today!"
      FIRE PHASERS 5 TIMES
      PAUSE
      END
```

The FIRE PHASERS command executes after a message is displayed, and the whole series of commands is placed between an IF...THEN...ELSE and END statement, as covered next.

IF...THEN...ELSE

The IF...THEN...ELSE command is one of the most useful commands for login scripts. You can use it when you want to execute commands only when a specific condition is met. An IF...THEN...ELSE command evaluates the truth or equality of various conditions. Commands may then execute, depending on how the condition evaluates.

You have already seen the IF...THEN...ELSE command used in previous examples. For example, in the FIRE PHASERS command example, a WRITE command and FIRE PHASERS are executed if the day of the week is Monday.

The IF...THEN...ELSE command takes the two forms shown below:

IF *conditional*(s) [AND;OR;NOR] THEN *command* ELSE *command*

IF *conditional*(s) THEN BEGIN

   (*commands*)

   (*commands*)

   END

In the first example, the *conditional* argument is evaluated, and if True the *command* following the THEN statement is executed. If False, the command following the optional ELSE is executed. In the second example, if *conditional* is True, a series of *commands* are executed on one or more lines following a BEGIN statement until the END statement is encountered. If *conditional* is False, the commands are skipped, and processing of the login script continues with commands following the END statement.

The IF...THEN...ELSE command can evaluate the condition of an identifier variable, which was listed earlier in this chapter. The following examples may help to explain how IF...THEN...ELSE works. One or more commands are placed behind the THEN option in all cases.

```
IF DAY_OF_WEEK = "Monday" THEN ...
IF MEMBER OF TEMPS THEN ...
IF NOT MEMBER OF TEMPS THEN ...
```

The first example is similar to the statements previously described under the FIRE PHASERS command. The commands following THEN are executed if the day of the week is Monday. In the next example, commands are executed if the user is a member of the group TEMPS. The last example is just the opposite of the previous example: commands are executed only if the user is not a member of the group TEMPS. Note that the first example uses an identifier variable DAY_OF_WEEK, whereas the second and third examples use the MEMBER_OF variable.

How to Use the IF...THEN...ELSE Command

You can place the IF...THEN...ELSE command anywhere in a login script, and you can use it more than once. As mentioned earlier, there are two versions of the command. The first is typed on one line and includes the command to be executed on the same line. The following example represents a single-line IF...THEN...ELSE statement:

```
IF DAY_OF_WEEK = "Monday" THEN WRITE "Wake up, you!"
```

The second version includes a block of commands placed on separate lines between BEGIN and END options. All commands between the BEGIN and END statements are executed if the IF...THEN...ELSE statement evaluates as True. Each command must be typed on a separate line. In the following example MAP commands are executed if a user is a member of the group MANAGERS. Note that indenting is used in the following example only to distinguish commands between BEGIN and END options.

```
IF MEMBER OF "MANAGERS" THEN BEGIN
    MAP H:=SYS:MGR-DATA
    MAP I:=SYS:ACCTDATA
    MAP INS S3:=SYS:MGR-PROG
    END
```

Since the mapped drives and search drives are only meant for managers, users who belong to the group MANAGERS will get the drive mappings. Other users can be given drive mappings of their own, depending on the groups they belong to.

Conditional Relationships

Six relationships can be evaluated with the IF...THEN...ELSE command. These are listed in Table 28-2. In addition, you can use AND, OR, and NOR to form compound conditionals, which are true only if the conditions joined by the expressions are True. In the following example, the manager's news file is displayed if the user belongs to the manager group and if the day is Monday.

```
IF MEMBER OF "MANAGERS" AND DAY_OF_WEEK = "Monday" THEN
FDISPLAY SYS:NEWS\MGRNEWS
```

> *Note:* The above command should be typed on one line.

Evaluating Command-Line Parameters

The parameters you type with the login command such as the server name, your user name, and the password can be used in the login script. Each parameter is given a number: the server name is %0, the user name is %1, and the password is %2. For example, in the following command, STARSHIP is parameter %0 and JOHN is parameter %1.

```
LOGIN STARSHIP/JOHN
```

Symbol	Relationship
=	Equal to
< >	Not equal to
>	Greater than
<	Less than
>=	Greater than or equal to
<=	Less than or equal to

Table 28-2. Six Relationships Evaluated by IF...THEN...ELSE

You can now use these parameters in your login script. For example, JOHN could automatically attach to another file server when logging in. First the following login command is typed.

LOGIN STARSHIP/JOHN ACCTG

JOHN has included the name of the ACCTG server on the command line in the parameter's %2 position. If the following command is placed in the login script, JOHN is attached to the server.

IF %2 = "ACCTG" ATTACH ACCTG

This command would be interpreted as "IF ACCTG is equal to ACCTG ATTACH ACCTG." Since the statement is True, John is attached to the ACCTG server.

Evaluating Group Membership Conditions

You can evaluate whether a user is or is not a member of a group using the MEMBER OF or NOT MEMBER OF options with your IF...THEN...ELSE commands. The commands take the following forms:

IF MEMBER OF *"groupname"* THEN *command*

IF NOT MEMBER OF *"groupname"* THEN *command*

where *groupname* is the name of the group the user belongs to and *command* is the command to execute if the user is a member (or is not a member). The following examples demonstrate how to use these commands on a single command line. They can also be used with block commands that use BEGIN and END.

```
IF MEMBER OF "SALES" THEN MAP T:=SYS:SALEDATA
IF NOT MEMBER OF "TEMPS" THEN MAP J:=SYS:USERNEWS
```

Evaluating Error-Level Conditions

Various command execution errors produce error codes that can be evaluated with an IF...THEN...ELSE command. The %ERROR_LEVEL identifier variable holds the latest error code from a command that did not successfully execute. An error level of 0 always represents a successful command completion. Other error codes can be evaluated and commands or messages can be displayed if they are greater than 0.

The command takes a form similar to the following command, which exits to a batch file called ERRORS.BAT if a problem occurs:

```
IF "%ERROR_LEVEL"<>"0" THEN EXIT "ERRORS"
```

Another way to use the command is to determine whether a file server is on-line before attempting to map drives to it. In the following example the ATTACH command is placed ahead of the IF...THEN...ELSE statement. If the ATTACH command fails to attach to the ACCTG server, an error code other than 0 is produced and the commands following BEGIN are not executed.

```
ATTACH ACCTG
IF "%ERROR_LEVEL"="0" THEN BEGIN
    MAP I:=ACCTG/VOL1:DATA
    MAP INS S5:=ACCTG/VOL1:PROGRAM
    END
```

Note: The %ERROR_LEVEL identifier variable uses the last error code generated in the program by an ATTACH or # (External Program

Execution) command. Make sure the last error code generated is appropriate for your login script.

INCLUDE

The INCLUDE command makes the login script execute an external set of login script commands, or subscripts. Programmers usually use subscripts to make large programs easier to use and create. Code routines that are frequently used can be written to an external file and then included in a login script program when you call the file containing the code. The technique is often used when a set of code is used on a regular basis by many programs. While the INCLUDE command is not too useful for the system login script, it is useful for user login scripts, which can be numerous.

The command takes the form:

INCLUDE *path\filename*

where *path* is the full path or drive specifier to the directory holding the external code file, and *filename* is the name of that file. You can nest INCLUDE statements up to 10 levels deep.

Note: Users of INCLUDE files must have Open and Read rights in the directory where the files reside.

Example

In the following example the file LOGIN2.DAT in the SYS:PUBLIC directory is included in the login script:

INCLUDE SYS:PUBLIC\LOGIN2.DAT

It is the opinion of this author that the INCLUDE command is of little use and adds confusion to login scripts. The system login script should be as integrated and generic as possible for maintenance purposes and should therefore not use the INCLUDE command.

MACHINE

Use the MACHINE command to set the machine name of the station logging into the name specified in the command. The name may contain up to 15 characters.

The command takes the form:

MACHINE = "*name*"

where *name* is the name, in quotation marks, you want to assign to the machine. The MACHINE command is often necessary for some programs written to run under PC DOS. The name can include identifier variables, as described earlier.

Example

The following command assigns a machine name of IBMPC to a machine:

MACHINE = "IBMPC"

MAP

The MAP command, as discussed in Chapter 16, is used extensively in login scripts to establish the mappings for all users and selected users. (Remember, the IF...THEN...ELSE command can be used to map drives based on the groups a user belongs to and other identifier variables.) For more information on MAP, see Chapter 23, or refer to the examples at the end of this chapter.

Keep in mind that the MAP command can be used by itself to display the complete set of drive and search drive maps to a user. This is sometimes done at the end of a login script.

There are four additional MAP commands you can use in login scripts that have not been covered elsewhere. These are described here:

MAP DISPLAY OFF   As drives are mapped in a login script, they are displayed on the screen. Use this option to turn this display off to avoid screen

	clutter. Remember that a MAP command can be included at the end of the login script to display the final mappings to a user.
MAP ERRORS OFF	When errors are encountered during a login script, the error messages are not displayed if this command is used. In some cases you might use the IF...THEN...ELSE commands that may produce errors, even though the errors are not serious, since processing would continue with the next statement. You can use the MAP ERRORS OFF command to suppress the error messages. It is recommended that you not use this command until the login script has been completely tested and debugged.
MAP DISPLAY ON	Reverses the effect of the MAP DISPLAY OFF command.
MAP ERRORS ON	Reverses the effect of the MAP ERRORS OFF command.

These commands can be used anywhere within a login script; however, the OFF command must be used before the ON commands.

PAUSE

You can use the PAUSE command to introduce a temporary stop in the login script. You usually place PAUSE after a message is displayed. Simply type the command as it is. Processing continues when you press a key.

Example

In the following example the PAUSE command is placed after the WRITE command, which displays an extended message on the screen.

WRITE "All users on this system are required to follow software
licensing rules and regulations."
PAUSE

PCCOMPATIBLE

Use the PCCOMPATIBLE command if the EXIT command does not work
properly. The command designates non-IBM systems as compatible machines. If your machine is an IBM PC compatible but you have changed
the long machine type in the SHELL.CFG file to another name in order to
access a different version of DOS, you must use PCCOMPATIBLE in the
login script.

Type the command in the login script before any EXIT commands, as
follows:

PCCOMPATIBLE

REMARK

You can use the REMARK command in a login script to include comments
for your own use or for other users who may need descriptions of the
routines in the script. Programs and scripts should always be documented,
out of common courtesy to others who may need to manage and edit them
in the future. The command takes the following forms:

REMARK *text*

REM *text*

* *text*

; *text*

where *text* is the text to include in the remark. The REMARK command
and text cannot reside with other commands on the command line. The
following example documents part of the MAP section of a login script:

REM The following MAP commands are for managers only

WRITE

The WRITE command displays messages and other text. It can also be used with the identifier variables in a number of ways. The command takes the following forms:

WRITE "*text*"; *variable*

WRITE "*text* %VARIABLE"

In the first form the text to display is in quotation marks. An identifier variable can then be added to display one of the system variables. A semicolon separates text and variable. In the second form the same results are achieved, but all options are included within the quotation marks. When an identifier variable is used within quotation marks, it must be capitalized and preceded by a percent sign.

The following character strings can also be included to perform specific tasks:

\r   Carriage return

\n   New line

\"   An embedded quotation mark

\7   A beep

The identifier variables that can be used with the WRITE command are listed in Table 28-1. Enter each variable as shown, including the underscore characters that separate those with multiple words. WRITE replaces the identifier variable with the text or value identified by the variable.

There are two important rules when using identifier variables within text strings:

- The identifier variable must begin with a percent sign.

- The identifier variable must be in all uppercase letters.

Examples

The following example creates four blank lines, displays a greeting message for a user, and then creates four more blank lines:

WRITE "\n\n\n\nGood %GREETING_TIME, %LOGIN_NAME\n\n\n\n"

In the next command identifier variables are used to display month, day, and year. Note that percent signs and uppercase letters are used because the identifier variable is within quotes. Also notice the use of the comma, which appears when the text is displayed.

WRITE "Today is %MONTH_NAME %DAY, %YEAR"

Login Script Examples

This section provides examples of login scripts which you can use when creating your own login scripts. The first script is the most basic. It can be used on networks where supervisors and users create personal login scripts to execute commands for their own use. The second example is a system login script that sets the parameters used by all users. Keep in mind that these scripts are only examples that you can adapt for your own use. The lines are numbered only for convenient reference.

```
1. SET PROMPT = "$P$G"
2. MAP F:=SYS:USERS\%LOGIN_NAME
3. MAP G:=SYS:PUB-DATA
4. MAP INS S1:=SYS:PUBLIC
5. MAP INS S2:=SYS:PUBLIC\%MACHINE
6. COMSPEC = S2:COMMAND.COM
```

The first command in this example sets the system prompt to display the current directory. The second command maps drive F to the user's personal directory using the LOGIN_NAME identifier variable. Line 3 maps the PUB-DATA directory to drive G. Line 4 maps the first search drive to the

SYS:PUBLIC directory. Note that the search drive is inserted with the INS command. This means that the user's current DOS path settings are saved. The fifth line maps a DOS directory according to the long machine name specified in the SHELL.CFG file. The last line sets the COMSPEC to the S2 search drive. This batch file is useful to each user because it maps the user's personal directory and COMSPEC drive according to the login name and machine type.

The next example is a system login script that adds various greeting messages and maps drives and search drives according to the groups users belong to. This login script places more emphasis on the use of the system login script rather than individual user login scripts. Keep in mind that it is best to let users manage their own personal login scripts, since this task can be too time consuming for managers.

```
1. WRITE "\n\n\n\nGood %GREETING_TIME, %LOGIN_NAME\n\n\n\n"
2. SET PROMPT = "$P$G"
3. PCCOMPATIBLE
4. MAP F:=SYS:USERS\%LOGIN_NAME
5. MAP G:=SYS:PUB-DATA
6. MAP INS S1:=SYS:PUBLIC
7. MAP INS S2:=SYS:PUBLIC\%MACHINE
8. COMSPEC = S2:COMMAND.COM
9. IF MEMBER OF "TEMPS" THEN BEGIN
10.     MAP F:=VOL1:ACCTDATA
11.     MAP INS S1:=VOL1:ACCTPROG
12.     EXIT START
13. IF MEMBER OF "MANAGERS" THEN BEGIN
14.     MAP H:=SYS:MGR-DATA
15.     MAP INS S3:=SYS:MGR-PROG
16.     END
17. IF LOGIN_NAME = "PCON" THEN BEGIN
18.     # PCONSOLE
19.     END
20. FDISPLAY SYS:NEWS\%DAY_OF_WEEK.DOC
21. PAUSE
22. IF DAY_OF_WEEK = "MONDAY" THEN FDISPLAY
    SYS:NEWS\MEETINGS.DOC
```

```
23. PAUSE
24. IF MACHINE = "CPAQ" THEN FDISPLAY SYS:NEWS\CPAQ.DOC
25. PAUSE
26. DOS SET USER = LOGIN_NAME
27. IF P_STATION = "000025478525" THEN EXIT "FIX.BAT"
28. EXIT "MENU MAIN"
```

This login script makes effective use of group names to assign drive and search mappings to users according to the groups they belong to. Lines 9, 13, and 17 start commands that perform tasks only if the user is a member of a group. For example, the PCONSOLE command is executed in line 16 if the user signs in with the user name PCON (Print CONsole operators). News and messages are then displayed with the commands in lines 20 through 24. The PAUSE command is used to pause the screen for reading. Messages are displayed based on the day or the machine number. Line 26 sets the external variable USER to the user's login name so it can be used in batch files later in the user's NetWare session, if necessary. Line 27 runs a special fix program for the station that matches the number shown in the IF...THEN...ELSE command. The last command then displays a main menu.

Lines 9 through 12 place personnel belonging to the TEMPS groups directly into an accounting program, and the rest of the login script is aborted. This assumes that the users who belong to this group are not regular employees of the company and should not view any of the messages or have any of the drive mappings that might be set in subsequent login script commands. The command in line 9 maps the data directory to their default drive, and line 10 maps a search drive to the accounting program. Line 11 starts the accounting program by first exiting the login script. In this way, the remaining login script commands do not execute for temporary personnel.

The messages displayed by the commands in lines 20 through 23 are kept in the SYS:NEWS directory and should be managed by the system supervisor. The meeting message files are updated according to the requests of different department managers. It is important for the supervisor to continually update messages displayed by the system login script, otherwise users will begin to ignore them.

Displaying Login
And Station Information

You can place the following commands in the system login script to display information about a system and the user who logs in. This information may be useful to the supervisor or technician who is attempting to resolve problems or assist a user. Insert the commands at the end of the login script so the information they display is not overwritten by other commands. It may be useful to insert a PAUSE at the end of the commands so the information can be viewed or written down.

```
WRITE "Login name = %LOGIN_NAME"
WRITE "User ID = %USER_ID"
WRITE "Workstation = %STATION"
WRITE "Workstation address = %P_STATION"
WRITE "Machine name = %MACHINE"
WRITE "Network address = %NETWORK_ADDRESS"
WRITE "File server = %FILE_SERVER"
WRITE "OS type = %OS"
WRITE "OS version = %OS_VERSION"
```

The NetWare Menu System

Using MENU
A Menu Example
Running MENU on Standalone Computers

The NetWare MENU command is an extensive menuing system that can be used to create your own custom menus similar to those of the NetWare menu utilities like SYSCON, SESSION, and FILER. To see how MENU works, type **MENU MAIN** on the command line. The menu shown here is displayed:

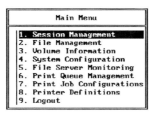

MAIN is a separate file that contains commands executed by MENU. It has the filename extension MNU. MAIN.MNU contains definitions of the menu's size, color, location, and items to select. It is supplied with NetWare not only as an example menu, but also as a useful utility for accessing the other NetWare menu utilities. By making a selection on the menu, another NetWare utility is started, unless Logout is selected. Once you start MAIN.MNU it stays active, even while working in other menu utilities. When users exit a utility started from the main menu, they are returned to the main menu. You may want to start the main menu every time a user logs on the system by including its startup command in the system login script as follows:

1. Log in as the supervisor

2. Start the SYSCON menu utility

3. Select **Supervisor Options** from the SYSCON main menu

4. Select **System Login Script** from the Supervisor Options menu

5. Include the PCCOMPATIBLE command if this is a non-IBM system or if you used the command LONG MACHINE TYPE in your SHELL.CFG file

6. Go to the last line of the script and type **EXIT "MENU MAIN"**

Note: Starting a menu from the system login script disables the user login script.

For more information on the EXIT login script command, refer to Chapter 28. Note that other menu files you create can be substituted for MAIN in the previous example. The following section explains how the MAIN menu works and how to build menus of your own.

Note: The MENU command cannot be used from within a DOS batch file.

Using MENU

The MENU command is a tool that supervisors can use to make the computer environment easier for users to access. In addition, commands that are frequently used but not easy to remember can be placed on menus. Users can create their own menus to automate the startup of programs they use or to perform tasks they do often.

A menu selection can display a submenu, which is an additional list of items. In this way an entire system of menus may exist. Submenus help to organize menus that have many selections. For example, the main menu might include a selection called Applications. Selecting this item would display a submenu with a list of applications available on the system.

Since the commands to create and display a menu are contained within separate files, you can create as many menus as you like. Menu files must be text-only files that have a filename extension of MNU, unless you specify another extension when running the MENU command. Recall that text-only files contain only text, not control codes or formatting characters. You can use an editor like EDLIN to create the files, or you can use a word processor, but be sure to save the files in text-only format. MENU looks for its MNU files in the current directory, and then in the PUBLIC directory. To use a file in another directory, specify its mapped drive letter or path.

Novell's MENU command is both easy to use and of infinite benefit to both users and supervisors. The rest of this chapter introduces the menu creation process by presenting example menus you will find useful.

The Main Menu Revisited

This section examines the MAIN.MNU file, the contents of which are listed here. This file is a standard ASCII text file located in the SYS:PUBLIC directory. It can be displayed with the DOS TYPE command and edited with EDLIN or other text editors.

```
%Main Menu,0,0,3
1. Session Management
       SESSION
2. File Management
       FILER
3. Volume Information
       VOLINFO
4. System Configuration
       SYSCON
5. File Server Monitoring
       FCONSOLE
6. Print Queue Management
       PCONSOLE
```

```
7. Print Job Configurations
        PRINTCON
8. Printer Definitions
        PRINTDEF
9. Logout
        !LOGOUT
```

The first line is the menu title. It begins with a percent sign and ends with numbers that describe the menu's location on the screen and its color arrangement. The numbered items 1 through 9 are displayed as selections on the menu. Under each selection is the command that is executed when the selection is made. Menu titles are distinguished by percent signs, menu items are left justified, and commands for menu items are indented or preceded by at least one space. This menu does not contain a submenu, which is discussed later.

The four parts of the main menu and the rules for using each are discussed in the following sections.

Menu titles   The percent sign indicates a main menu title. The position and color palette of a menu can be specified at the end of the title using horizontal and vertical coordinates and color palette numbers.

Menu selections   Statements that define menu selections are placed under the menu titles and are left justified. MENU sorts these items in alphanumeric order. If you want to determine the order of items on a menu, you must precede each item with a number; otherwise MENU sorts them in alphabetical order.

Commands   Any item that is indented with a tab or a space is treated as a command for the menu selection item directly above, unless it includes a percent sign, which indicates it is a submenu, as discussed next. In the main menu the first selection (Session Management) is followed by the command SESSION, which starts the SESSION utility.

Submenus   Any item that is indented with a tab or space and preceded by a percent sign is the title for a submenu. The commands for submenus are typed in a separate location of the file. Submenus are described in more detail later.

Notice that in the main menu listing, the first line starts with a percent (%) sign, which indicates it is a menu title. The title of the menu is Main Menu. Notice also that each menu selection starts with a number and is left justified. The commands executed by each menu selection are directly beneath the selections and indented.

Note: Since the selections in MAIN.MNU are numbered, the items on the menu remain in numeric order, which is the order the menu's creator wanted.

Planning and Creating Menus

You can begin creating your own menus immediately. Menus usually are created in the SYS:PUBLIC directory so they can be used by all users, but you can create personal menus by storing menu files in your own directory. The MENU command always searches the current directory and then the PUBLIC directory when searching for a menu file, unless a path to a specific directory is included. The following sections can help you plan the contents of menus. They present examples and help you prepare menus of your own. Selections in the example menus can be substituted with selections that fit your own needs.

Menu Planning

Menus should be planned to determine what they will display and what actions are performed when an item is selected. Recall that a main menu can have selections that display submenus. As the supervisor, you could create one menu system for all users. This menu could present a selection of programs, commands, and tasks commonly performed on the system. If there are a number of these selections, you must divide them up into categories and place them on submenus. For example, the main menu categories might be Applications, NetWare Menu Utilities, NetWare Commands, and Miscellaneous Utilities, among others. These categories then open to submenus that display complete listings.

The following types of users should be considered when planning menus. A particular menu can be displayed for a user, depending on that user's name or group.

- *Supervisors* Menus for supervisors can include commands and options for managing network accounting, security, diagnostics, and maintenance.

- *New users or temporary help* Menus for new users may contain help information or selections for starting tutorials, as well as programs they will be using.

- *Groups* Menus can be created for specific groups of users. For example, clerks might see a menu to start a database program or word processing program. A menu for a management group can list applications or management utilities used by managers.

- *Individual users* Users can create menus in their own directories for their own use.

To plan a menu, write down the following:

1. Who the menu is for: Supervisor, Users, Groups, or other type of user.

2. What the menu will do. Will it have submenu categories?

3. When a menu has many selections, categorize them to see if submenus can reduce screen clutter.

4. Determine the menu selections on the main menu and its submenus. If an item directly executes commands rather than displaying a submenu, write down the commands it executes.

5. Include PAUSE commands so users can read messages or other information displayed on the screen.

7. Make sure users have security rights that allow them to run the commands executed by a menu selection. In addition, if a selection switches them to another directory, make sure users have the proper rights in the directories to perform the intended task.

8. Variable requests can be used to request information from users before they execute a command. For example, it may be necessary to request a document filename before starting an application.

9. Plan the screen spacing and colors, if necessary, although MENU's default settings are adequate in most cases.

Creating Menus

As an example, a menu called User is created below using the DOS EDLIN line editor. You can create this menu for your own use by substituting the applications on your system for those shown on the menu. The User menu and its Applications submenu are shown here:

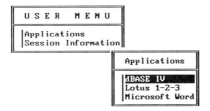

A listing of the USER.MNU file is shown here:

```
%USER MENU,8,22,0
Session Information
        WHOAMI /A
        PAUSE
        USERLIST
        PAUSE
        MAP
        PAUSE
Applications
        %Applications
%Applications
Microsoft Word
        WORD
```

Lotus 1-2-3
    123
dBASE IV
     DBASE

To create the file, start EDLIN by typing **EDLIN USER.MNU**. You can refer to the DOS manual for details on using EDLIN. The asterisk is the EDLIN prompt, and most of its editing commands are single-letter commands, such as I (Insert) or L (List). At the asterisk, type **I** and press ENTER. Each line is numbered and only one line can be edited at a time. On the first line, type the following text:

%U   S   E   R   M   E   N U,8,22,0

Notice that the percent sign is used to indicate a menu header and that spaces occur between each letter to spread the header out. Type three spaces between the words. The numbers at the end of the menu determine its vertical and horizontal placement on the screen and its color. Press ENTER to edit the second line, and type the following without indents:

Session Information

On the third line, press TAB or the spacebar to create a command. Type the following commands, one on each line, with a tab or space before each. When the menu is run and you select Session Information from the menu, these commands execute.

WHOAMI /A
PAUSE
USERLIST
PAUSE
MAP
PAUSE

On lines 9 and 10, type the following:

Applications
   %Applications

Do not type a space or press TAB before the header in line 9, because this is the heading for the Applications submenu. In line 10 press TAB and type the percent sign in front of the line that will execute the Applications submenu. When the menu is run, this command will search further in the file for a menu header that matches Applications. In this example, the submenu routine immediately follows. On line 11 type %**Applications** without an initial tab or space. It is important that the case, spacing, and spelling of the command that calls a submenu and the submenu routine match exactly.

Next, you can begin adding the selections for the submenu. You can change these to match the programs you want to run on your network. In the following example, dBASE IV, Lotus 1-2-3, and Microsoft Word are used. The commands to execute each application are included after the selection name and indented with a tab.

```
Microsoft Word
        WORD
Lotus 1-2-3
        123
dBASE IV
        DBASE
```

At the end of the last line, press CTRL-BREAK to end the Insert mode. At the EDLIN asterisk prompt, type **E** to end editing and save the menu. At the operating system prompt, type the command **MENU USER** to display the menu.

The first thing you may notice is that MENU has rearranged the items on the menu into alphabetical order. Try each of the menu items to see how they work. The Session Information selection is a useful way to display information about the current session. It uses the WHOAMI, USERLIST, and MAP commands to display information about trustee rights, other users, and current drive and search drive mappings. Notice the PAUSE commands give you a chance to read the information displayed by a command before executing the next command.

Try running one of the software applications from the menu. After the application loads, exit the program and the menu should be restored. If you have problems running applications, refer to the section "Running Software Applications from Menus" later in this chapter.

Menu Selection Order

MENU rearranges the items you place in MNU text files into alphabetical or numeric order when the menu file is run. If you arrange the menu items in the order you prefer and then place numbers in front of each line, MENU keeps the order.

As you have probably noticed from using other NetWare menu utilities, you can make selections on menus by typing the first few letters of a selection. In most cases you land on a selection by typing its first letter, but if two selections have the same first letter, you can type the second or third letter to get to the correct selection. If you do not want to use numbers but want to maintain a particular order, you may need to be creative in the names you use for menu selections so a specific order can be maintained.

Running Software Applications From Menus

If a software application is run from a menu, a search drive should be mapped to the application. The user runs the application from the current directory or mapped drive, unless you place commands in a menu selection that switches to another directory. In the example at the end of this chapter, each software application has two selections. One switches users to their personal data directories, and the other switches them to a public data directory before starting the program.

If a selection switches a user to another directory, the user must have the proper rights in the directory. The MENU program writes a temporary file to the directory that is deleted, so Create, Read, Write, and Erase rights are essential. Also note that some applications write temporary files as they execute in the directory where the program file exists.

Note: Do not include terminate-and-stay-resident (TSR) commands in your menus. Load these programs from the DOS command line; otherwise serious errors may occur.

Creating Submenus

A main menu can have submenus, and each submenu can have its own submenus, thus allowing multilevel menu systems. When a submenu is to be displayed from a "parent" menu, an indented command preceded by a percent sign is used to call the submenu. MENU then searches the rest of the file for a line that exactly matches the command that called the submenu. The menu selections and commands for the submenu should immediately follow this line.

Notice in the previous example that the Applications submenu is called with the command %Applications. When MENU sees this command, it "jumps" to the line in the file that matches this command exactly. The rules that apply to defining the main menu also apply to defining submenus. Submenu selections should not include preceding spaces or percent signs. Commands then follow the selections and should be indented with a tab or space.

If a submenu itself has additional submenus, create them in the same way you created submenus for the main menu. You may need to be concerned with the placement of the menus when a number of submenus are displayed. Submenus may overlap other menus, but this can be avoided by specifying vertical and horizontal coordinates.

Screen Placement of Menus

As just mentioned, you may want to stagger the placement of menus on the screen so users can view menus or other information underneath. The location is specified by vertical and horizontal coordinates at the end of each menu header line. In the previous example, the menu placement for the User menu is 8,22, which specifies the vertical and then the horizontal placement of the menus. The placement numbers are calculated using the following methods.

Vertical placement   Vertical lines are counted from the top of the screen to the center of the menu. You must first determine how many lines your menu requires from top to bottom, and then divide that number by two. Add that number to the number of lines you want between the top of the menu and the top of the screen.

Horizontal placement   Horizontal placement is specified in characters or columns from the left edge of the screen to the center of the menu. You must first determine the character width of your menu, and then divide that number by two. Add that number to the number of columns you want between the left of the menu and the left screen border.

As an example, assume you have a menu that is 10 lines long and 20 characters wide, and you want to place the top of the menu 5 lines down from the top of the screen and the left menu border 20 columns from the left screen border. The following formulas can be used to determine the vertical and horizontal placement numbers:

menu lines/2 + top-of-screen distance = vertical placement number

or 10/2 + 5 = 10, and

menu columns/2 + left-screen-distance = horizontal placement number

or 20/2 + 20 = 30.

The menu header using these values would appear as follows:

%A MENU HEADER,10,30,0

Note that the last digit is the menu's color specification. If values are left out, MENU uses its default parameters, which centers the horizontal or vertical placement. If a single value is left out, you must still insert the comma as a placeholder. In the following example, the default horizontal placement is used:

%A MENU HEADER,10,,0

Menu Variables

Variables can be used in your menu commands to request information from users, such as filenames and drive letters. For example, you could place the NCOPY command in a menu and then ask for the source filename and destination filename. These names are inserted into numbered variables for use in the current command or subsequent commands within the same menu selection.

Use the at symbol (@) to request a numbered variable from the user. A remark or statement is typed in quotation marks following the variable. When the menu is run, the remarks appear in a box on the screen. When the user types the appropriate information in the box, it is saved in the variable for later use. For example, the following command could be used to sort a specified directory in creation date order.

NDIR @1"Enter the drive letter or path" SORT CREATE

If the user enters **H:**, the following command executes and lists the files in drive H in creation-date order. Note that the variable is inserted in the command exactly where the variable is placed in the command.

NDIR H: SORT CREATE

Note the following:

- There is a 100-character limit on the length of any command, so keep your variable messages short.

- Variables are only saved for the current group of commands under one menu selection heading. As soon as a new menu selection is made, previous variables are lost.

- Do not use the symbols @ or \ in your variable messages.

Menu Colors

If you want to select different colors for your menus, you must use the COLORPAL program covered in Appendix E to generate new menu color configurations.

Running and Testing Menus

You may need to run a menu several times before it works the way you want. Most of the problems can be easily fixed and have to do with leaving out characters or using incorrect command syntax. The following problems may occur:

- An error message may occur initially because MENU cannot run your menu script. Make sure the script was saved as an ASCII text file and that the first line is a menu header that starts with a percent sign.

- A selection may not be accessible because the command is left out or has incorrect syntax.

- A submenu may not be accessible because its parent selection name does not match the menu header exactly.

- A submenu may not contain selection options. Go back and add the options.

MENU displays several descriptive error messages you can use to debug your menu files.

A Menu Example

The following menu system contains several submenus and menu techniques you may find of use when designing your own menu. Since the options on this menu are quite useful, you may want to create the entire menu for your system. Later you can make copies of the file and edit it to create new menus. You can change the options in the applications submenu to fit the applications you have installed on your system.

The User menu is designed to provide useful information to all users on a system; therefore, it can be placed in the system login script. Figure 29-1 shows the submenus for the options on the User menu where appro-

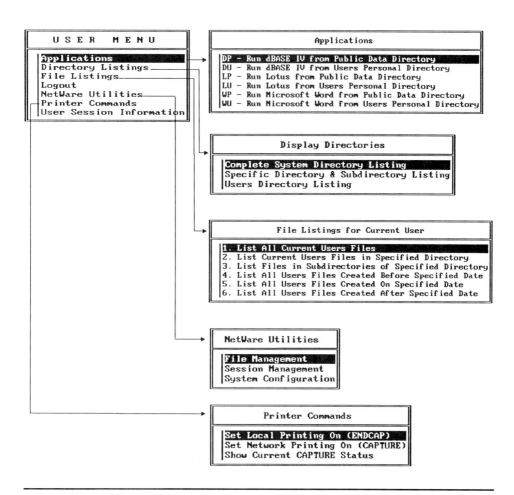

Figure 29-1.   The User menu with its submenus

priate. Two options, Logout and User Session Information, execute commands directly.

The complete script file for the menu system is as follows:

%U S E R   M E N U,5,20,0
User Session Information
 WHOAMI /A
 PAUSE
 USERLIST
 PAUSE
 MAP
 PAUSE
Applications
 %Applications
Directory Listings
 %Display Directories
File Listings
 %File Listings for Current User
Printer Commands
 %Printer Commands
NetWare Utilities
 %NetWare Utilities
Logout
 !logout
%Applications
WP - Run Microsoft Word from Public Data Directory
 G:
 WORD
WU - Run Microsoft Word from User's Personal Directory
 F:
 WORD
DP - Run dBASE IV from Public Data Directory
 H:
 DBASE
DU - Run dBASE IV from User's Personal Directory
 F:
 DBASE
LP - Run Lotus from Public Data Directory
 I:
 123
LU - Run Lotus from User's Personal Directory
 F:
 123
%Display Directories
Complete System Directory Listing
 NDIR \ DO SUB
 PAUSE

Users Directory Listing
      NDIR \ OWNER=%USER% DO SUB
      PAUSE
Specific Directory & Subdirectory Listing
      NDIR @1"Drive/Path" DO SUB
      PAUSE
%File Listings for Current User
1. List All Current User's Files
      NDIR \ OWNER=%USER% SUB FO
      PAUSE
2. List Current User's Files in Specified Directory
      NDIR @1"Drive/path" OWNER=%USER% FO
      PAUSE
3. List Files in Subdirectories of Specified Directory
      NDIR @1"Drive/path" OWNER=%USER% SUB FO
      PAUSE
4. List All User's Files Created Before Specified Date
      NDIR @1"Drive/Path" CREATE BEF @2"Date" OWNER=%USER% SUB FO
      PAUSE
5. List All User's Files Created On Specified Date
      NDIR @1"Drive/Path" CREATE=@2"Date" OWNER=%USER% SUB FO
      PAUSE
6. List All User's Files Created After Specified Date
      NDIR @1"Drive/Path" CREATE AFT @2"Date" OWNER=%USER% SUB FO
      PAUSE
%Printer Commands
Show Current CAPTURE Status
      CAPTURE SH
      PAUSE
Set Network Printing On (CAPTURE)
      CAPTURE L=1 TI=2 NAM = %USER% NFF
Set Local Printing On (ENDCAP)
      ENDCAP L=1
%NetWare Utilities
Session Management
      Session
File Management
      Filer
System Configuration
      Syscon

You can easily locate the code for each submenu by finding the accompanying lines with percent signs in the first character position. The code for the main menu starts at the top and goes through to the !LOGOUT command. Note that this special command is used with the exclamation point to execute a system logout.

In the main menu block, the User Session Information option directly executes the six commands that follow it—the WHOAMI, USERLIST, and MAP commands, with a PAUSE command placed between each to buffer the screen display. The remaining lines in this block display the menu selections and execute the jumps to other parts of the menu script, as discussed in the following sections under their header names.

Note: Keep in mind that the selections in the menu script file are rearranged in alphabetical order by the MENU command.

Applications Submenu

The Applications submenu is displayed when a user makes the corresponding selection on the main menu. Locate the block of code that starts with %Application and ends with the 123 command just above the %Display Directories line. This code produces the Applications submenu shown in Figure 29-1. There are several interesting points here. First, the menu is sorted in the order of the codes placed before each menu item. These codes make it easy for users to type the letter corresponding to the desired menu selection. Also note that the menu selections allow users to work with either of the applications from their personal directories or the PUBLIC directory. Looking at the code for each menu option, you can see that the command logs users to the appropriately mapped drive. If this menu is to be generic, you must make sure that drive F always maps to user's personal directories and that drive G, H, and I always map to each application's directory.

Display Directories Menu

The Display Directories submenu is used to display directory information especially for the currently logged users. Take a look at the code section beginning with %Display Directories. Notice that three different versions of the NDIR command are used to display directories, as discussed in Chapter 23. Under the User Directory Listing option, a variable called %USER% is used to place the current user's name behind the OWNER option. This lists directories assigned to the current user. Include the following command in the system login script to create the %USER% variable:

DOS SET USER = LOGIN_NAME

File Listing Submenu

The lines in the script for the File Listing submenu start with the section in the text file that reads %File Listings for Current User. The NDIR command is used for each selection to display a list of files for the current user according to specific directories, matching strings, or dates. The selections are numbered so they will appear in the specified order in the menu. In this way the selections that list files by date are grouped together.

Printer Commands Submenu

The Printer Commands menu displays a submenu with various printer commands used to display the current status of a printer or queue, or to set Capture mode On or Off. The code for the Printer Commands menu starts with the line %Printer Commands.

NetWare Utilities Submenu

The NetWare Utilities menu displays three of the available NetWare utilities. The commands, which start at the line NetWare Utilities in the menu file, are the same type of commands used in the main menu supplied with NetWare. You can add the other menu utilities to this menu if necessary.

Running MENU
On Standalone Computers

You can use MENU on a hard-disk-based standalone computer without running the NetWare operating system. You can use the utility to create convenient menus for your DOS environment. Copy the following files to a directory on your hard drive. The file IBM$RUN.OVL must be renamed $RUN.OVL during the copy process or after the files have been copied.

```
SYS$MSG.DAT
SYS$ERR.DAT
SYS$HLP.DAT
IBM$RUN.OVL
MENUPARZ.HLP
MENU.EXE
MENUPARZ.EXE
```

Make sure the CONFIG.SYS file has at least the following parameter settings:

```
BUFFERS = 20
FILES = 30
```

Backup Topics

Backup Methods
Backing Up with the NBACKUP Menu Utility
Restoring Backed Up Data
Installing Non-DOS Devices

"Blessed are the pessimists for they have made backups,"
—(Anonymous)

This chapter aptly describes not only the importance of backups, but the reason for doing them. If you think your system is immune to failure, you are playing Russian roulette. Just take a moment to consider the amount of information that is or will be on your file server and the replacement cost of that information, if it even can be replaced. But this chapter is not written to convince you that backups are important. Instead it covers how and when you should do backups and introduces the NetWare NBACKUP command.

Because network servers are shared devices that constantly receive new files or file updates, they are candidates for daily backup. In fact most servers need constant real-time backup, which can be done with NetWare's system fault tolerance (SFT) strategies. SFT's mirroring and duplexing features duplicate entire hard drives and controller boards. SFT III, available in early 1991, allows an entire server and all its drives to be duplicated by another server. Even though these strategies provide convenient and real-time backup of data, managers still need to create alternate backup sets that can be taken off site in case of fire or other catastrophe. These backup sets may be stored on tape, removeable disk, or optical disk.

643

Backup Methods

There are several ways you can back up the server. One method might be to copy the entire hard drive to an optical disk or removeable hard disk cartridge, and then store the disk in a safe or a fireproof box. The methods discussed in this chapter use the NetWare NBACKUP command. NBACKUP can back files up to disk or to third-party tape drives installed in workstations. While the tape backup method is easier and requires less monitoring (disk swaps), the disk method is useful when a strategy is employed that only backs up changed files.

With any backup method, you must establish a backup strategy. Part of this strategy should include a test run of your backups, including a full restore to make sure you actually can use your server once it has been repaired or brought back up. Also keep in mind that backups like those done with the NetWare NBACKUP command may be done for reasons other than providing secure backups of data. NBACKUP is a useful command for copying sets of files to disk that can then be copied to other systems. You can also use NBACKUP to copy old unused files to archives, and its restore feature allows users to easily get at single files in the archive if necessary.

Consider the following regarding data backup:

- At least two backup sets are essential. These backup sets rotate from day to day and may be rotated to off-site locations for further protection. In this way if one set is defective you can always revert to the previous set. The smaller the interval between backups, the less data you must reenter to restore the system to its "precrash" state.

- A backup strategy should include a procedure to move backup sets off site or to fireproof safes. Keep in mind that fireproof safes have different ratings and some may not provide enough heat protection to keep disk or tapes from warping or melting.

- Backups taken off site are open to theft.

- A master backup of the entire system should be created at regular intervals, such as every week. Intermediate sets can then be created during the week. An intermediate backup consists of only those files that have been altered since the last backup. Intermediate backups are covered in the next section of this chapter.

- When you use a tape backup method, you may find it practical to back up the entire server to a tape every time a backup takes place. A tape should be available for each day of the week so that backups do not write over the previous day's backups. Tape backup systems from third-party vendors must be designed specifically for Net-Ware 386.

- When you use mirrored drives and one of the primary drives fails, the secondary takes over until a new primary is installed. You should allow NetWare to copy the information from the secondary drive to the new primary, rather than restore the drive from backups.

Incremental Backups
And the Rotation Method

There are many suggested methods for backing up, but all include some type of rotation method so that several backups are always available. In one scheme, 10 tapes are rotated over a two-week period, and each tape is marked for a different day of the week. One week's worth of tapes is always off site for protection. At the start of the first week, a complete backup is made. During the week intermediate backups are made of only those files that have changed. At the end of the week, the complete set is delivered to the off-site location, and the second set is brought on site to repeat the process. This rotation continues on a regular basis.

The Archive Needed Attribute

An important feature of the intermediate backup method is that changed files are backed up during the interval after the master backup. When a file is altered, its Archive Needed attribute is activated by the operating system. This attribute is like a flag which indicates the file needs to be backed up.

You can use this attribute in two ways. In the first method the flag is turned off after the file has been backed up. Therefore, the file is not backed up during the next day's incremental backup. The amount of disk or tape space required during an incremental backup is thus reduced, which is an important consideration if you are using disks. In the event of a restore, each day's disk sets must be restored in the order they were created—the master backup first and then the incremental backups. This ensures that all files are restored properly, even those files that were altered several times during the backup interval.

The second method does not turn off the Archive Needed attribute when a file is backed up. Each incremental backup then contains the complete set of changed files and is the only disk besides the master set that must be restored in the event of a disk failure. This method is prohibitive if floppy disks are used since it requires more disk space.

Backing Up to Hard Drives

The NetWare NBACKUP command gives you the ability to back up to a hard drive on a workstation or to a system that can become a server if the primary server fails. Here are some reasons why backup to hard drives is useful:

- Hard drive backup methods can be used in conjunction with tape and disk backup methods.

- If a single file is accidentally erased or lost, it can more easily be restored.

- You can have a stand-by server prepared in case the primary fails. Backups are then made to this server on a daily basis. Recovery after a failure is easy because the secondary server is ready to go. NetWare 386 SFT III uses this method but performs backups in real time. In addition, users may never know the primary server failed because the secondary takes over immediately.

Tape Backup Systems

Tape systems that use cartridge- and cassette-type media are becoming increasingly popular, due to their ease of use and integrity. They are more practical than floppy disk backup methods because most network servers have high-capacity drives that require too much disk swapping and time to back up.

Many tape backup systems use a quarter-inch tape that comes in lengths of 600 to 1000 feet. Common tape formats include the DC600 streaming tape made popular by 3M. The DC600 cartridge can store 60MB to 150MB of data on a cartridge. The maximum capacity of an extended length tape is 320MB. Another common format also standardized by 3M is the DC2000 streaming tape. This tape cartridge is about the size of an audio cassette tape and stores 40MB, 60MB, or 80MB of data. The DC2000 is a little lower in cost than the DC600.

Still another method of tape backup is the digital audio tape (DAT), which has storage capacities in the gigabyte range. The storage method used by DATs is different than that used by standard tapes such as the DC600 and DC2000 streaming tape methods. Streaming tape systems record all the way to the end of the tape on one track, and then reverse and record on the next track. This method is used for up to 32 tracks on quarter-inch tape. DATs use a combination of tape and head movements to record with a method called *helical scan*. Data is recorded in diagonal strips on the tape as it passes over a cylindrical drum containing several read-write heads. This method compresses data storage, which increases capacity and tape throughput simultaneously. Since data is compressed, it takes less time to scan a tape when trying to locate a file.

Optical Disks

Optical disks have a long shelf life and are not susceptible to problems inherent with magnetic media. Two types of technology are currently available: Write-Once-Read-Many (WORM) disks and the Write-Many-Read-Many (WMRM) disks. Optical disks have capacities in the gigabyte range, making optical drives a viable option for archive strategies. Hard drives in the 300MB range can be completely backed up several times to a single optical disk. The WMRM disks may be useful as on-line data storage devices as well as backup media. Because they allow both reads and writes to the disk, on-line data can be continually updated.

Some optical drives "play" stacks of disks and can be used to keep vast amounts of archive data on line to users. Files that are archived in this way are usually deemed old or not important enough for the main server drives. Because some users may still need to access this data occasionally, optical disks are useful for keeping it available.

One thing to consider about optical disk technology is its performance. Writes are often slower than floppy disk writes, but disk reads are usually as fast as normal hard drive reads. The process of "burning" data to the disk with the laser takes more time than traditional magnetic write methods. This technology should improve rapidly, however.

Backing Up with the NBACKUP Menu Utility

The NetWare NBACKUP menu utility is used to back up file servers and restore them if necessary. Supervisors and managers can back up entire servers with NBACKUP, while regular network users can back up files in their personal directories.

The NBACKUP command has the following features and functions:

- NBACKUP must be run from a workstation on the network.

- Both backup and restore functions are in the BACKUP utility.

- NBACKUP backs up and restores DOS files and Macintosh files.

- NBACKUP can be used to back up and restore other versions of NetWare. A backup must be restored to the same operating system type it was backed up from.

- If a Macintosh VAP on a NetWare 286 server was running during a backup, it must also be running during the restore.

- The following DOS devices can be used to back up files from a NetWare server:

  - Floppy drives on workstations

  - Hard drives on workstations

  - Another file server drive

  - Tape drives that operate as DOS devices

  - Optical drives that operate as DOS devices

Always make sure a target drive has enough room to hold the entire backup set of data with at least a 10% overhead; otherwise the backup procedure does not complete properly.

The NBACKUP command provides two methods of backup. The first method backs up an entire server to another device, but this method can be used only if the backup device can hold all the information on the server. The second method backs up individual directory trees or the NetWare bindery files. It is used when a backup needs to be done in several sessions because the backup device does not have the capacity to back up the entire server. It can also be used when there is a need to copy specific files for reasons other than backup.

The following section discusses how to use NBACKUP with DOS devices. You can also use NBACKUP to back up information to tape or DAT devices, which are generally non-DOS devices that require special drivers. The tape drivers listed in Table 30-1 are available with the initial release of NetWare 386 version 3.1. Additional drivers will be available in the future or can be ordered from the drive manufacturer. Because NetWare 386 stores files with 16-bit attributes, existing devices require new drivers to maintain compatibility.

When you use tape devices, be aware that tapes are rewound to the beginning and any existing data is overwritten. You should never use your most recent backup tape when starting a new session; instead, employ a tape rotation method in which you use a different tape each day of the

Company and device	Driver file	Cartridge size
ADIC Data 128	ADICSCSI.EXE	128M
ADIC LANBacker 4000	ADICLANB.EXE	600M
ADIC LANBacker 8000	ADICLANB.EXE	1.2G
GigaTrend Giga 1236T DAT	PC36.EXE	1.2G
Transitional Technology CTS-4 DAT	TTI.EXE	1.2G
Transitional Technology CTS-8000	TTI.EXE	2.2G
Wangtek 5099EN24	WANGTEK.EXE	60M
Wangtek 5150EN	WANGTEK.EXE	150M

Table 30-1. Backup Devices for NBACKUP

week, for example. Tape backup sessions also require two separate tapes if you decide to back up the bindery, because the directory information and bindery information are placed on two separate tapes.

Starting NBACKUP
And Preparing to Back Up

You can start NBACKUP from any directory by typing **NBACKUP** on the command line. You must be mapped to SYS:PUBLIC. The first menu to appear is shown here:

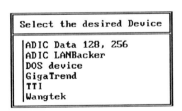

```
Select the desired Device

ADIC Data 128, 256
ADIC LANBacker
DOS device
GigaTrend
TTI
Wangtek
```

Use this menu to select the device to use for backup. If DOS Device is selected, backups can be made to floppy drives, local hard drives, or other devices that appear as DOS devices to the workstation. To back up to a tape drive, choose one of the tape drives listed on the menu.

When a tape drive is selected, its driver information is automatically linked with the NBACKUP utility. If you need to use a device not listed on the menu, refer to "Installing Non-DOS Devices" at the end of this chapter. The driver for the new device must be copied to the SYS:PUBLIC directory, and the NBACKUP menu must be updated.

Once you have selected the device to use for backup, the NBACKUP main menu appears, as shown here:

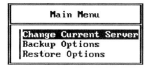

The first option is used to select a different server to backup. The next two options are selected for backup and restore, respectively.

To change to a different server, select **Change Current Server** from the main menu. Select a server from the list, or if the desired server does not appear on the list, press INS to select it from the Other File Servers menu. The next three sections present three different backup methods:

- Back up the entire server if the target device has adequate capacity

- Back up the NetWare bindery files

- Back up individual directories

To start one of these backup procedures, select **Backup Options** from the NBACKUP main menu. The Backup menu appears, as shown here:

Selecting a Working Directory

The Select Working Directory option on the Backup menu is used to select a working directory, which is where backup logs and error logs are stored.

These logs are files created during each backup session. The backup log contains information about a particular backup session, and the error log contains error messages generated by a session, if any. Because these files are required to restore the session, you should choose to store them on a device other than the server being backed up, such as floppy disks. Supervisors and managers can also review these logs at any time.

To select a working directory, choose the **Select Working Directory** option from the Backup menu. The dialog box that appears contains the names of the current file server, volume, and directory. Backspace over this and type the name of another device, or use the INS key method to select a new device. You may need to press ENTER on the double-dot symbol (..) several times before you see a list of other devices.

Backing Up the Entire Server

An entire file server can be backed up to another device if that device has the capacity to hold the files and other information. To use this method, select **Backup File Server** from the Backup menu. The Backup Options menu shown here appears:

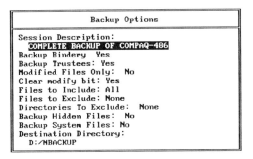

```
                         Backup Options

Session Description:
     COMPLETE BACKUP OF COMPAQ-486
Backup Bindery   Yes
Backup Trustees: Yes
Modified Files Only:  No
Clear modify bit: Yes
Files to Include: All
Files to Exclude: None
Directories To Exclude:   None
Backup Hidden Files:  No
Backup System Files: No
Destination Directory:
     D:/NBACKUP
```

The Backup Options menu is used to specify the parameters for the backup, as described in the following sections. You must fill in the Session Description and Destination Directory fields, but the other fields have default values that may be suitable. If you are backing up the entire server, the Modified Files Only field should be set to No.

Session Description   Type a unique description of the backup session in this field. It will be used later to identify the backup files and information required to do a restore. Keep in mind that the working directory may hold description files from several backup sessions.

Backup Bindery   Set this field to Yes if you are doing a complete backup.

Backup Trustees   This field has a default of Yes, which means trustee information for directories and files is backed up. This option is not usually set to No for a complete server backup.

Modified Files Only   Recall that there are two types of backups, complete and modified files only. Initially you should make a complete backup of the entire system by setting this option to No. Additionally, you may need to make a complete backup on a weekly basis. Modified file backups are made between complete backups. Since only files that have been modified are backed up, time and disk space is saved during the backup. You must make sure this option is set correctly for the type of backup you are doing.

Clear Modify Bit   Set this field to Yes to clear the modified bit. When the modified bit is clear, it is an indication that the file has been backed up. Future backup sessions will not back up the file unless the file is edited and the bit is set back on.

Files to Include   Press ENTER on this option to select specific files to back up. The default is All. When doing a complete backup, this option is normally not used. Press INS to type the name of files to include. Wildcard characters can be used to specify groups of files.

Files to Exclude   Press ENTER to prevent some files from being backed up. This option should be left at the default of None when doing a complete system backup. The option can be used to exclude program files, assuming they never change and you have the original disks in a safe place. Press ENTER on the option, and then press INS to type the names of files to be excluded. Note that if a file is in both the Files to Include list and the Files to Exclude list, it will be excluded.

Directories to Exclude   Press ENTER to exclude entire directories
from the backup. For a complete backup, leave this option at None. You
may want to exclude program directories or directories such as SYS:PUB-
LIC and SYS:SYSTEM.

Backup Hidden Files   The default is No. Enter **Yes** to back up any
hidden files during a complete system backup.

Backup System Files   The default is No. Enter **Yes** to back up any
system files during a complete system backup.

Destination Directory   Enter the name of the device and directory
where the backup set will be stored. This can be a floppy drive, hard drive,
or tape device on the local workstation. It can also be a drive on another
server. If you choose a non-DOS tape device, the destination is automatically selected.

After the Backup Options window is filled out, press ESC to save the
changes. The Start Backup menu then appears, as shown here:

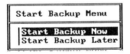

```
┌─────────────────────────┐
│ Start Backup Menu       │
├─────────────────────────┤
│ Start Backup Now        │
│ Start Backup Later      │
└─────────────────────────┘
```

You can start the backup immediately by selecting **Start Backup Now**,
or you can schedule it for a later time—for example, in the middle of the
night when no one is using the system.

When you select **Start Backup Now**, a session status window
appears to display what is currently being backed up, what has already
been backed up, and how much time has elapsed in the backup session. An
activity bar moves across the screen during the session. The bindery is
backed up first. Error messages appear at the bottom of the screen. If you
need to stop the session, press ESC. The backup stops as soon as the current
item is backed up.

If you use tapes or other removable media for backups, a Media ID
field displays the current cartridge number. Each new cartridge is indicated by an incremental number on the screen; write this number on each
cartridge so the order can be followed in the event of a restore. The bindery

is backed up to one tape and directories are backed up to another, so you may need two or more tapes.

Note: If you receive an error message during a backup session, refer to "Viewing Backup and Error Logs" later in this chapter.

Scheduling Backups for Later

If you want to schedule a backup for a later time, select **Start Backup Later** from the Start Backup Menu. The Start Backup Timer menu appears, as shown in the following illustration. Fill in the start date and start time as necessary.

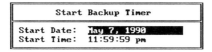

Backing Up in Multiple Sessions

A backup is done in multiple sessions if the device used for backup does not have the capacity to hold an entire server disk. The multiple session method allows you to choose sets of directories that fit on separate devices. Another reason for using this method is to back up a single directory of files for reasons other than backup protection. For example, you may want to send the files to another user. You can also use this method to back up your personal directory.

To begin select a working directory as described under "Select a Working Directory" earlier in this chapter. Then select **Backup By Directory** from the Backup menu. The screen shown here appears:

The Backup Options menu is used to specify the parameters for the backup, as described in the following sections. You must make specific entries in the Session Description, Source Directory, and Destination Directory fields; other fields have default values that may be suitable. Take special note of the Modified Files Only field description.

Session Description   Type a unique description of the backup session in this field. It will be used later to identify the backup files and information required to do a restore. Keep in mind that the working directory may hold description files from several backup sessions.

Backup Bindery   Select this option if you want to back up the bindery. The bindery must be backed up to a separate tape.

Backup Subdirectories   Leave this option at the default of Yes to back up all subdirectories of the selected directory. To back up just the specified directory, set this option to No.

Backup Trustees   This field has a default of Yes, which means trustee information for directories and files is backed up. Set this field to No if you are backing up files to copy to a system that does not require security information (also set Modified Files Only to No).

Modified Files Only   When this option is set to Yes (the default), only files that have been altered are backed up. To perform an incremental backup, as discussed in the section "Incremental Backups and the Rotation Method," leave this field and the Clear Modify Bit field set to Yes. If you want to back up all files in a directory, set this field to No.

Clear Modify Bit   When this option is set to Yes, the Archive Needed attribute of modified files is turned off, indicating to future backup sessions that the modified file has now been backed up. Leave this option set at Yes in most cases; however you might set it to No if you want to perform a duplicate backup.

Files to Include   Press ENTER on this option to select specific files to back up. The default is all files in the selected directories. Press INS to type the names of files to include. Wildcard characters can be used to specify groups of files.

Files to Exclude   Press ENTER to prevent some files from being backed up. For example, this option can be used to exclude program files, assuming they never change and you have the original disks in a safe place. Press ENTER on the option, and then press INS to type the names of files to be excluded. Note that if a file is in both the Files to Include list and the Files to Exclude list, it is excluded.

Directories to Include   Use this field to enter the directories to be backed up other than those already included in the Source Directory field. Press ENTER on the field, and then press INS to type the names of directories. All is the default.

Directories to Exclude   Press ENTER to exclude entire directories from the backup. You may want to exclude program directories or directories such as SYS:PUBLIC and SYS:SYSTEM.

Backup Hidden Files   The default is No. Enter **Yes** to back up any hidden files during a complete system backup.

Backup System Files   The default is No. Enter **Yes** to back up any system files during a complete system backup.

Source Directory   Press ENTER on this field to include the volume, directory, or subdirectory to back up. Only directories on the current server can be specified. Press INS to select a directory name from a list.

Destination Directory   Enter the name of the device and directory where the backup set will be stored. This can be a floppy drive, hard drive, or tape device on the local workstation. It can also be a drive on another server. If you choose a non-DOS tape device, the destination is automatically selected.

After the Backup Options window is filled out, press ESC to save the changes. The Start Backup menu then appears, as shown here:

You can start the backup immediately by selecting **Start Backup Now**, or you can schedule it for a later time—for example, in the middle of the night when no one is using the system.

When you select **Start Backup Now**, a session status window appears to display what is currently being backed up, what has already been backed up, and how much time has elapsed in the backup session. An activity bar moves across the screen during the session. The bindery is backed up first. Error messages appear at the bottom of the screen. If you need to stop the session, press ESC. The backup stops as soon as the current item is backed up.

If you use tapes or other removeable media to store the backup, a Media ID field displays the current cartridge number. Each new cartridge is given an incremental number on the screen; write this number on each cartridge so the order can be followed in the event of a restore. The bindery is backed up to its own tape; directories are backed up to another.

Note: If you received an error message during the backup session, refer to "Viewing Backup and Error Logs" later in this chapter.

Scheduling Backups for Later

If you want to schedule a backup for a later time, select **Start Backup Later** from the Start Backup menu. The Start Backup Timer menu appears, as shown in the following illustration. Fill in the start date and start time as necessary.

```
┌──────────────────────────────────┐
│         Start Backup Timer        │
├──────────────────────────────────┤
│ Start Date:  May 7, 1990          │
│ Start Time:  11:59:59 pm          │
└──────────────────────────────────┘
```

Message	Meaning
The file *filename* was not marked after backup!	The archive bit was not removed after the file was backed up.
The file *filename* was not backed up because it is in use.	If a file is in use by a user, it will not be backed up. You may need to have some or all users log off before backing up.
The file *filename* was not backed up because it is execute-only!	Files flagged with the execute-only attribute cannot be backed up.
The directory *directory* was not backed up because it has an illegal name!	Rename the directory with a legal directory name.
The file *filename* was not backed up because it has an illegal name!	Rename the file with a legal DOS name.

Table 30-2.   Common Error Log Messages

Viewing Backup and Error Logs

The backup and error logs provide information to users about the status of a backup session. To view a record of the files, directories, and volumes backed up during a backup session, view its backup log. If an error message is encountered during a backup session, read the error log. You can view either log by choosing the appropriate selection from the Backup menu. Table 30-2 displays some of the messages that may appear in the error log.

Restoring Backed Up Data

The Restore Options selection on the NBACKUP main menu is used to restore files from backup sets. All restores must be done to systems that are running the same operating system version. If a NetWare 286 system was running a Macintosh VAP when it was backed up, that VAP must also be running during the restore.

When the server hard drive that holds the NetWare operating system and the NBACKUP command files fails, a new drive is usually installed. Restoring is impossible until the operating system has been reinstalled on the server. Refer to Chapter 17 for details. The NBACKUP command and all its peripheral programs are copied to the SYS:PUBLIC directory during the installation.

Note: If you are replacing a failed mirrored drive, the restore should take place from the second drive, not the backup set.

While the primary purpose of backups and restores is to recover from failed servers or drives, files may be backed up and restored for many other reasons. For example, a set of files in a directory can be backed up on one system and then restored to another. Backups also may be made for archive reasons. Old unused files may be backed up and then removed from a server. If a user needs one or two of these files, a selective restore must take place so that only the desired files are recovered from the backup set.

To start a restore session, start NBACKUP by typing **NBACKUP** on the command line. In a moment the NBACKUP Main Menu appears. Select **Restore Options** from the menu to display the Restore menu, as shown here:

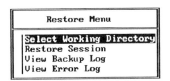

Choose **Select Working Directory** from the Restore menu, and enter the name of the directory that holds the log file for the backup session to be restored.

Next, select **Restore Session** from the Restore menu to display the Restore Session menu similar to that shown in Figure 30-1. This menu lists the available session files stored in the working directory. Highlight

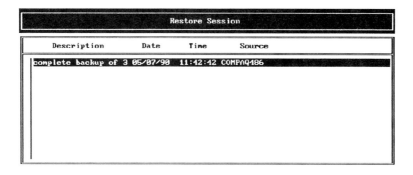

Figure 30-1.   The Restore Session menu displays a list of available backup
sessions

the appropriate session and press ENTER. The Restore Option menu shown
here then appears:

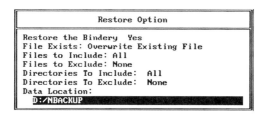

The following fields can be altered on the Restore Option menu:

- *Restore the Bindery*   The default is Yes. To restore a downed server
  or drive, always leave this at the default setting. You might set this
  option to No if you want to restore specific files to another drive in
  a nonrecovery situation.

- *File Exists*   Remember that not all restore sessions are performed
  to recover a failed server or hard drive. Occasionally you may need

to restore just one or two files from an archive. The File Exists option gives you control over which files are restored. Press ENTER on the field and select one of the following options:

- *Do Not Overwrite* Select this option if you do not want to restore files that already exist on the drive.

- *Interactive* Select this option if you want to be prompted with the name of each file to be restored.

- *Overwrite Existing File* Choose this option to overwrite existing files with files of the same name in the backup set.

- *Rename Existing Files* Choose this option to have existing files renamed with the B*nn* extension, where *nn* is an incremental number.

- *Rename Restored Files* Choose this option to rename files being restored with an extension of B*nn*, if files with the same name exist. B*nn* is incrementally numbered.

- *Files to Include* Press ENTER on this field and then press INS to choose a list of files to restore.

- *Files to Exclude* Press ENTER on this field and then press INS to choose a list of files to exclude from the restore. Excluded files override included files.

- *Directories to Include* Press ENTER on this field and then press INS to include the name of directories to include in a restore.

- *Directories to Exclude* Press ENTER on this field and then press INS to create a list of directories to exclude during the restore.

- *Data Location* The location of the backup set is inserted by NBACKUP in this field, based on the backup session file. If you have changed the location of the backup files, highlight the field, press F3 (Modify), and then type the path for the new location.

When the options have been filled out, press ESC to save changes, and select **Yes** to start the restore. You can stop the restore session by pressing ESC at any time. The session stops after the current file has been restored. Status information appears at the bottom of the restore screen to indicate the progress of the restore. If any errors occurred, be sure to select View Error Log from the Restore menu.

Installing Non-DOS Devices

When the NBACKUP command is executed, the first menu to appear displays the current device list. You can add the driver for your backup device to this list by copying the driver itself to the SYS:PUBLIC directory and then adding the name of the device to the list by updating a file called DIBI$DRV.DAT.

To copy the new driver file to the SYS:PUBLIC directory, use the NCOPY command in the following form:

NCOPY A:*driver*.EXE SYS:PUBLIC

where *driver* is the name of the new driver.

Next use a text editor to add the following line to the file called DIBI$DRV.DAT:

"*name*" DRIVER

where *name* is the name you want to appear in the NBACKUP opening menu, and *DRIVER* is the name of the driver.EXE file copied in the last step. For example, if you are installing an Emerald Systems VAST device, you would add the following line to the DIBI$DRV.DAT file:

"Emerald System VAST" EMSAVE.EXE

NetWare's Accounting System

Accounting System Overview
Installing the Accounting System
Setting the Accounting Charge Rates

NetWare's accounting system allows you to track the login and logout activities of every user, which in turn allows you to track how system resources are being used. You can then use this information to evaluate the quantity and quality of resources available to users. You can also use the accounting feature to monitor the way users access resources and possibly charge them for their use. In particular, educational institutions and time-sharing services often track the use of system resources and then charge for the time.

Accounting System Overview

The accounting system must be installed by the supervisor before it can be used. Most supervisors do install this system because the information that it tracks can be useful. Although accounting is typically associated with billing users for the time and resources they use on the system, NetWare's accounting system can provide other useful information. For example, the accounting system can track user logins and logouts, or supervisors can monitor usage logs to determine exactly how resources are being used and by what users. This information may be useful if supervisors are considering the addition of new equipment and must justify purchases with management.

The accounting system charges users for their time or the resources they use with a point system. Points can have monetary value, or they can be thought of as "tokens" or "credits" that users can spend. A supervisor may allocate a certain number of points to a temporary user. When the user depletes those points, the supervisor may grant more, but at the same time the supervisor is made aware of the amount of time and system resources the temporary person is using. Points can be limited or unlimited, depending on how the supervisor needs to manage the system.

Be careful when allocating points or placing limits on user accounts. Users that begin reaching their point limits may actually become less productive so as not to deplete the points. It does not make sense to limit resources when there are plenty available. However, it may be beneficial to put limits on some users' accounts, as well as their access rights, to prevent users from wasting time on the system, especially if workstations are in limited supply.

An educational site is a good example of where the accounting system can be put to use. Students can be given a certain amount of resources and charged for the resources they use. A report can be produced at regular intervals to establish charge rates. Conversely, students may buy a block of time and space at the beginning of the school term. When the block runs out, they must buy more. Students who are aware of their limits will be more productive on the system and waste less of its resources.

It is often hard to determine exactly what to charge for account usage or even to determine how much each resource is used. The best strategy is to establish a test period by installing the accounting feature and then tracking the system usage with users who have unlimited credit. At the end of the test period, you should have enough information to determine rates.

Types of Accounting

The accounting feature allows you to use several different options. Read through this section to determine the correct option for your network. Keep in mind that "charges" may represent monetary or tracking units.

User login and logout tracking is automatically performed when the accounting feature is installed. Each user has an account of charges for the system resources he or she uses. Each file server designated as a chargeable system makes entries into user accounts. Print servers may also make these entries.

Charges incurred by users fall into two main groups: those that use the server's disk file space and those based on work performed by the server. If charges are to be made for the disk space, a rate must be established, and you as the supervisor must specify how often and at what times the file server should measure the disk space accessed by the user. Charges for the amount of work performed by a server can be categorized five different ways, as listed here. You can charge using one or all of these methods.

- The amount of resources consumed from not only file servers but also gateways, print servers, and database servers

- The amount of time a user is logged on the file server

- The amount of information read from the file server disk

- The amount of information written to the file server disk

- The number of requests made to the file server for services

Installing the Accounting System

The accounting feature must be installed before it can begin tracking logins and logouts, and before you can use it to charge users for resources.

To start the SYSCON menu utility, type **SYSCON**. At the SYSCON main menu, select **Accounting** and press ENTER. In a moment the Install Accounting screen appears. Select **Yes** to install the accounting feature on the current server, and then press ENTER. Once the accounting feature is installed, the new Accounting menu appears, as shown here:

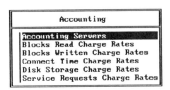

All accounting records are placed in a new file called NET$-ACCT.DAT, which is stored in the SYS:SYSTEM directory for security reasons. No one else should have access to this information.

Removing the Accounting System

If you need to remove the accounting feature for any reason, you can select the **Accounting Servers** option from the menu to see a list of servers currently set up to perform accounting. Each of these servers must be removed before you are given the option to remove the accounting system. Highlight each server, or use the F5 (Mark) key to select all servers, and then press DEL. Once the servers are removed, a confirmation box appears asking if you want to remove the accounting feature. Highlight Yes and press ENTER to remove accounting.

Activating Accounting On Other Servers

The supervisor of a server establishes accounting features on that server. If other servers exist, such as disk subsystems, you can establish accounting to track the usage of those systems as well. For example, you can grant users access to a server in the accounting department, and then track their usage on the system for security reasons or for interdepartmental expense tracking.

Start the SYSCON menu utility and select **Accounting** from the main menu. At the Accounting menu, select **Accounting Servers**. A list of available servers appears. Press the INS key to display the Select Server Type menu, which shows the types of servers available. Highlight the type of server you want to authorize to charge and press INS. In the Other Servers list, highlight the server to authorize for charging and press ENTER.

Perform this step for each server, or use the F5 (Mark) key to select multiple servers at once. When you are done, press ESC to exit.

To revoke an existing accounting server's right to charge, press DEL to remove the server you no longer want to charge from the Accounting Servers menu.

Setting the Accounting Charge Rates

You must determine the types of charges you want to make for services incurred by a user and the rate at which you want to charge the user for the services. In addition, you must set up an initial account balance and view the existing accounting information, either to help establish the initial rates or to bill users for usage.

Types of Charge Rates

The remaining selections on the Accounting menu are used to set the charge rates for the accounting feature. Each option is described in the following sections.

Blocks Read Charge Rates

The Blocks Read option sets the charge rates for the amount of information read from the server drive. This is not the same as the charge for storing blocks on the disk, which is covered later under "Disk Storage Charge Rates." Charges are specified in half-hour increments and are assigned per block read, with one block being equal to 4096 bytes or 4K.

Each read from the drive is charged to the user's account. The Blocks Read option is important for servers that supply information to other users, such as an on-line service or database system. Keep in mind that this option may inhibit users from using the system more productively if they know charges are being made.

Blocks Written Charge Rates

The Blocks Written option is similar to the Blocks Read option, except that users are charged for the amount of information written to the disk rather than read from the disk. Charges for blocks written to disk are not the same as charges for blocks of disk storage, which is covered later in this chapter. Charges are specified in half-hour increments and are assigned per block written, with one block being equal to 4096 bytes or 4K.

Each write to the drive is charged to the user's account. Be careful when using this option since some programs write to the disk continuously, and you would be unfairly charging users of the program. In addition, users may be less productive if they know they are being charged every time they write to the disk.

Connect Time Charge Rates

The Connect Time option charges users for each half hour of time they are logged into the server. It is important to consider the type of user and the resources available on the system before establishing this rate, however. If network usage is high, you may want to charge a higher rate to ensure that users do not tie up the system for too long or that users are more efficient with the tasks they perform on the system. This may not be appropriate for some systems, however, especially if the system is new and there are many first time users.

Disk Storage Charge Rates

The Disk Storage Time option allows you to set up charge rates for each block of disk storage. A block is 4096 bytes or 4K. A charge rate is established for every half-hour increment of disk storage use and is assigned on a block-day basis, which measures the number of blocks stored in a day. If the network has limited disk storage, charges can be established to encourage users to be more efficient in the way they store files and to keep their storage area clear of unnecessary files.

Service Requests Charge Rates

The Service Request option establishes charge rates for use of the server in general. Every time a request is made to the server for any operation, the user is charged. Charge rates are specified in half-hour increments, and the user is charged per request received. Users are charged for services from the moment they log in to the moment they log out.

Setting a Rate

The supervisor on each server can establish the charge rates for his or her server only. If your network uses a server controlled by another supervisor, charge rates on that server are controlled by its supervisor.

You can use the ATOTAL command to view the total usage for each service and to help determine the charge rates for accounting. The supervisor should run this command after an initial test period to get an idea of how the system is being used before establishing the actual charge rates. Use the PAUDIT command to view the system accounting records in detail. Since the NET$ACCT.DAT file becomes quite large, you should view its contents periodically or compile it with the appropriate accounting application (available from third-party developers), and then remove it from the system. A new file is then created by the accounting system.

After viewing the accounting totals provided by the ATOTAL command, you should have a good idea how services are being used. You can then begin establishing charges. A *charge ratio* is calculated with the following formula:

$$\frac{(Total\ you\ want\ to\ charge\ for\ a\ service)}{(Estimated\ total\ usage\ of\ a\ service)} = \frac{(Charge\ rate\ multiplier)}{(Charge\ rate\ divisor)}$$

This ratio is then assigned to specific times of the day, and up to 20 different ratios can be applied. In this way charges can be higher during the day than in the evening, for example.

Assume you are trying to determine the charge rate for block reads and you have determined that 100,000 blocks were read during a week.

Now assume you have determined that this usage is typical, and that $500 per week is sufficient income for this usage. Now assume that the points are equivalent to 1 cent. You must convert the $500 weekly charge to cents in order to establish the proper multiplier/divisor formula, which would be calculated in the following way:

$$\frac{50,000}{100,000} = \frac{1}{2}$$

This ratio is applied to the charge rate screen that appears when one of the charge rate options is selected from the Accounting menu. An example is shown in Figure 31-1. Note that a charge rate is applied to a selected block of time. In Figure 31-1, the number 2 charge rate is applied to the highlighted block of text. Note that the number 1 charge rate is No Charge. Other charge rates can be created, as discussed next. They appear in the Rate and Charge columns on the left side of the screen.

```
                                             Sun  Mon  Tue  Wed  Thu  Fri  Sat
       Service Requests Charge Rates  8:00am   2    2    2    2    2    2    2
                                      8:30am   2    2    2    2    2    2    2
                                      9:00am   2    2    2    2    2    2    2
   Sunday To Saturday                 9:30am   2    2    2    2    2    2    2
   8:00 am To 11:29 am               10:00am   2    2    2    2    2    2    2
                                     10:30am   2    2    2    2    2    2    2
   Rate  Charge      Rate   Charge   11:00am   2    2    2    2    2    2    2
    1   No Charge     11              11:30am   1    1    1    1    1    1    1
    2   1/2           12              12:00pm   1    1    1    1    1    1    1
    3                 13              12:30pm   1    1    1    1    1    1    1
    4                 14               1:00pm   1    1    1    1    1    1    1
    5                 15               1:30pm   1    1    1    1    1    1    1
    6                 16               2:00pm   1    1    1    1    1    1    1
    7                 17               2:30pm   1    1    1    1    1    1    1
    8                 18               3:00pm   1    1    1    1    1    1    1
    9                 19               3:30pm   1    1    1    1    1    1    1
   10                 20               4:00pm   1    1    1    1    1    1    1
   (Charge is per request received)    4:30pm   1    1    1    1    1    1    1
```

Figure 31-1.   A typical charge rates screen

Creating Rate Charges

The methods used to create Blocks Read, Blocks Written, Connect Time, and Service Request charges are similar and discussed in the following paragraphs. Select either one of the rate options from the Accounting menu to display a screen similar to that shown in Figure 31-1. The screen shows how much the file server charges for each request made by a workstation. Charges are shown for each half hour during a weekly period and are applied in the following ways:

Blocks Read Charge Rates	Charge is per block
Blocks Written Charge Rates	Charge is per block
Connect Time Charge Rates	Charge is per minute
Disk Storage Charge Rates	Charge is per block-day
Service Request Charge Rates	Charge is per request received

Block charges are assigned in blocks of 4096 bytes.

To assign charge rates to a specific time of the day or week, press F5 (Mark) and use the arrow keys to highlight the exact area that will be given a specific time charge. When the total area is highlighted, press ENTER. A Select Charge Rate screen similar to the one shown here appears:

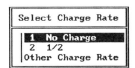

You can select an existing charge rate by highlighting one of the options, or you can define a new charge rate by selecting Other Charge Rate from the screen. The following New Charge Rate screen appears:

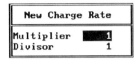

Use the arrow keys to highlight either Multiplier or Divisor and enter the ratio established for a particular service. It is applied to the highlighted block of time.

Assigning Disk Storage Charge Rates

Disk storage rates are assigned according to how often the system should charge for the disk space being used. For example, assume you have determined with ATOTAL that 500,000 blocks of space are normally in use, and you want to receive a $1000 fee for that use. Also assume that each charge point is equal to 1 cent. The $1000 weekly charge is converted to 100,000, which means the ratio is 1/5, as shown below.

$$\frac{100,000}{500,000} = \frac{1}{5}$$

You can now select **Disk Storage Charge Rates**, highlight the block of time to charge this rate, and press ENTER to create the ratio for the charge rate. The ratio specifies how much the file server charges for each block (blocks are measured in 4096 bytes or 4K) of storage on the disk for one day. The file server checks the disk storage space every half hour and charges a user for all the disk storage used in the last half hour according to the rate specified.

Establishing User Account Balances

The supervisor may want to assign account balances to users to provide some limits on the amount of system resources they can use. If the supervisor only wishes to monitor the use of the system for each user, he or she can set unlimited account balances. Caution should be taken when assigning balances to users since the system may log them out if their account balances are expended or come close to zero.

Default account balances for all users are assigned by selecting **Supervisor Options** from the SYSCON main menu. Individual account balances can be assigned by selecting a user from the User Information option on the SYSCON main menu. To assign default account balances, highlight **Default Account Balance/Restrictions** from the SYSCON main menu and press ENTER. When the menu appears, arrow down to Account Balance at the bottom of the screen and enter the default account balance you want to assign to users. Specify the account balance in points, similar to those used on the accounting screen. In this way users will be charged for each point according to the rates you specify, as discussed in the previous section.

Additional credit can also be specified by highlighting the options just below the Account Balance field. You can allow unlimited credit by highlighting Allow Unlimited Credit and entering **Yes**. You can assign a specified amount of credit by entering **No** in the Allow Unlimited Credit field and then entering a balance in the Low Balance Limit field. If a negative number is entered in the Low Balance Field, users receive services until the charges have been used up. Entering a positive number in the field always leaves some value in the field. The user can then go to the supervisor and request additional services.

To assign account balances to *individual* users, select **User Information** on the SYSCON main menu, select a user from the User Names list, and highlight **Account Balance** from the User Information screen. The procedure to assign individual user balances is the same as that described in the previous paragraphs.

Viewing the Accounting File

The ATOTAL and PAUDIT commands are used to view the accounting files. Supervisors must transfer to the SYS:SYSTEM directory or map a search drive to it before the commands can be executed. Both commands read and display information from the NET$ACCT.DAT file stored in the SYS:SYSTEM directory. ATOTAL lists totals only and can be used to view the way resources are used when establishing rates or determining new rate values.

The PAUDIT command is used to view the login and logout activities of the server or to view the resources used by users. This file can be quite large, so the following commands may be necessary to view it one page at a time. The first command redirects the screen display to a file:

PAUDIT > PAUDIT.DAT

The next command directs the file to the printer for a hardcopy printout:

NPRINT PAUDIT.DAT

Use the next command to view the file one page at a time on the screen:

MORE < PAUDIT.DAT

After you have viewed the accounting information, you may want to delete the NET$ACCT.DAT file to open up space on the hard drive. The accounting system immediately begins to build a new file.

Note: Third-party applications are required to compile the accounting information into user billings. Check with your dealer for suitable applications.

Managing and Maintaining
A NetWare Network

677

NetWare Management Issues

Tasks of the System Administrator
Network Security and Virus Protection
Fault Tolerance
Preparing for Emergencies
Training Users

A network administrator's job is to keep the network up and running and to ensure that users can access the resources of the LAN. Since LANs remove some aspects of standalone computing such as personal file storage, users rely on the system managers to ensure that the files they store on the LAN are safe and secure.

Tasks of the System Administrator

Many of the tasks expected of system managers are listed here. While some of these tasks have already been covered in previous chapters, others are covered here and in the remaining chapters of this book.

- Planning and installation

- Planning for future growth

- Administering users

- Securing software and data

THIRTY

- Securing the hardware

- Managing backup strategies

- Upgrading hardware and software

- Monitoring and maintaining performance

The last category is the topic of the remainder of this book. The next four chapters cover the many NetWare 386 commands that can be used to manage the server and its networks. Chapter 33 gives an overview of important commands used to monitor and manage the network. Chapter 34 then explains commands to view the network configuration and monitor performance. Chapter 35 covers techniques and commands for managing network hardware, including disk drives, LANs, cable systems, and uninterruptible power supplies. Finally, Chapter 36 presents commands for managing the operating system configuration.

Network Security and Virus Protection

One of the responsibilities of a network manager is to provide adequate security for the system and its data. While NetWare itself provides a number of security features, you should take additional steps to ensure that the installation is protected from accidents, natural catastrophes, and intentional harm. Computer viruses are most dreaded of all. They are constantly being written or improved by programmers whose only intention is to test their skill at cracking a security system and watching the results. And the results may be global, as was a recent virus in the telephone system.

While managers must be constantly aware of the presence of viruses, NetWare provides many features that can prevent virus infections.

- The SYS:SYSTEM directory should be locked to all users except the supervisor. In this way system files and other executable program files that affect the operating system cannot be accessed or affected by outside users who might introduce viruses. All executable files should be flagged as Read Only or Execute Only. Use Execute Only with caution because it may lock some files not written to normal network specifications. If so, you may need to recopy the files from their original disks.

- Minimize the number of users who have supervisor privileges. In reality there should be only one supervisor who has complete access to a file server. All other users should be classified as managers with restricted rights, especially to the SYS:SYSTEM directory.

- Flag all executable application files with the Read Only attribute, and do not give other users the rights to change the attributes.

- Secure all backups.

- Lock the file server console at all times.

- Use diskless workstations in remote or unsupervised areas to ensure data is not downloaded from the server to a disk and carried out of the building.

- Train users to log out of their workstations properly so unauthorized users cannot walk up and begin using their stations.

- Use physical locking devices to prevent theft of equipment. Even though a server system may be locked down, you still need to ensure that its internal hard drives are not removed. The data on those drives is the most important part of the network.

- Centralize servers and other network equipment into a single management area, and then lock the area. Use access devices such as fingerprint readers or magnetic cards to gain access to the area.

- Secure the cable system from unauthorized taps. This can be done with management software that monitors all nodes on the network. Fiber optic cable can also be used.

Fault Tolerance

The reliability of a network may be one of the most important considerations of a manager. When a component fails, how easy will it be to get the system back on line? The next section discusses hardware service, loaners, and backup equipment, but you may need to have instant, on-line recovery from faults. This is the case with banks, military operations, emergency, and other services. System fault tolerance (SFT) is a methodology of ensuring that data is always on-line and available to users.

With NetWare 386 and SFT Level III, an entire server and its data can be duplexed and mirrored by another server. If the first server goes down, the second immediately takes over. Users may be entirely unaware of the transition from primary server to secondary. Part of this strategy is to ensure adequate power to servers (and some workstations) through uninterruptible power supplies.

Preparing for Emergencies

A manager must evaluate the most critical components of the network and consider how those components will be replaced in the event of failure. It may be necessary to establish a relationship with a dealer or vendor who maintains a good supply of replacement parts. Same-day or next-day service contracts can be established that include loaner equipment. Some organizations may want to purchase their own backup components, or integrate these into workstations that can be "cannibalized" for parts if the need should arise.

A manager should also have emergency plans for resuming network operations should the entire network become unusable, for example, after a fire or earthquake. It is important to carry backups of the entire server, including the operating system files, to an off-site location. In this way you may be able to get a small network back up and running in a day or so with the help of software and hardware dealers.

With the growing use of LANs, many organizations are relying on outside consulting companies to handle their LAN management needs. These companies are equipped with loaner and test equipment that is too expensive to be practical for many companies. They also come with the expertise to manage the hardware, the software, and the users of a network.

Training Users

Making sure that users are trained on the network is important. Make them aware of the NetWare HELP command, which can be typed at the command line to provide on-line help. Users should also be aware of the way network security works. They need to know that some files cannot be accessed because they do not have the proper rights to the file or directory. If you prevent users from creating files in a directory and they cannot copy files to it, they will be calling you on the phone for assistance.

Network managers can provide assistance to users at remote locations with remote LAN software products. LAN Close-Up by Norton-Lambert (See Appendix D for the address) is a good example. It allows a manager to operate a user's workstation as if sitting at it without leaving his or her office.

Software for classroom network training is also useful. LANSchool from LANSystems (See Appendix D for the address) turns any Novell network into a computerized classroom environment. The instructor can broadcast his or her workstation session to students. Any activity on the instructor's station is echoed to the students' stations, including keyboard commands, menus, and screens.

Introduction to NetWare Management Commands

Users and Connections
Locking the File Server Console
Downing the Server
The SET Command
The LOAD Command
Remote Console
Editing the Startup Files

NetWare 386 has a large set of commands that can be used by system administrators to manage the server and its networks. This chapter introduces the basic commands used to load or work with most other commands, which are introduced in Chapters 34, 35, and 36. These chapters categorize the commands three ways to help you more easily locate the command you need to use for a particular task. Chapter 34 covers commands used to view network settings and monitor performance. Chapter 35 discusses techniques and commands you use to manage network hardware, including disk drives, LANs, cable systems, and uninterruptible power supplies. Chapter 36 introduces commands used for managing the operating system configuration.

This chapter covers topics related to the process of making changes to the server or network, including:

- Viewing and clearing user connections

- Disabling user logins so work can be performed

- Locking the server console

- Downing the server

- Editing the startup files to include commands and parameters discussed in the next three chapters

Most of the commands discussed in Chapters 34, 35, and 36 are entered at the file server console. However, you are not limited to using console commands strictly at the file server. The Remote Console feature can be loaded so console commands can be used from any workstation. A password security feature ensures that only authorized users can use a remote console. If you need to execute console commands from a remote workstation, refer to "Remote Console" at the end of this chapter.

Users and Connections

Refer to the following commands before you work on the console. In some cases you must disconnect current users and prevent new users from logging in. Before connecting any users, you can use the SEND or BROADCAST command to send a message to their consoles that they should log off properly. The first option helps you determine the number of the workstation being used by each user.

Determining a User's Workstation Number

It may be necessary to determine the connection number of a workstation. This can be done in the following way:

1. Type the following command to load the MONITOR module:

LOAD *path*\MONITOR

Replace *path* with a drive or directory where MONITOR.NLM can be found if it is not in the SYS:SYSTEM directory.

2. Select **Connection Information** from the MONITOR Available Options menu.

3. When the Active Users list appears, use the arrow keys to scan the list.

Note: You can disconnect a user by highlighting the user's name and pressing DEL. Answer Yes to the "Clear Connection?" prompt.

Using FCONSOLE
To View Network Connections

You can also view user connections and disconnect a user with the FCONSOLE command. Only supervisors or supervisor equivalents can disconnect another user in this way.

1. Type **FCONSOLE** at the workstation prompt.

2. Select **Connection Information** from the FCONSOLE Available Options menu.

3. When the Current Connections list appears, use the arrow keys to scan through it. Disconnect a user by highlighting the user's name and pressing DEL.

Disabling and Enabling User Logins

The DISABLE LOGIN console command is used to prevent users from logging in to the file server. Issue this command when you must perform maintenance on a server, when installing software, or when creating a backup. Type the command **DISABLE LOGIN**.

To allow users to log into the server after the DISABLE LOGIN command has been executed, issue the ENABLE LOGIN command by typing **ENABLE LOGIN**.

Enable and Disable Login with FCONSOLE

You also can use the FCONSOLE menu utility to disable login from a workstation. Start the command, and then choose **Status** from the Available Options menu. When the File Server Status window appears, select **No** in the Allow New Users To Login field.

Broadcasting and Sending Messages

The BROADCAST and SEND commands are used to send a message (55 characters maximum) to all or specific users, usually when work needs to be done on the server or a particular workstation. The message may alert users to log off the system so maintenance work can proceed. Both BROADCAST and SEND have the same form, so only SEND is discussed here. It takes the form

SEND "*message*" TO *user* (or *station number*)

Type the message between quotation marks, and then specify the user's name. If no user is specified, the message is sent to all currently logged users. The workstation number of a user can be specified instead of the user's name. Separate multiple user names and station numbers with commas. For example, to send a message to the user JOHN and workstations 4 and 6, you would type the following command:

SEND "Please log off the system soon" TO JOHN, 4, 6

To determine a user's workstation number, use the MONITOR command as described under "Determining a User's Workstation Number." Messages appear on the twenty-fifth line of the user's screen and are cleared by pressing CTRL-ENTER. You can use the CASTOFF command discussed in Chapter 26 to prevent messages from appearing on a workstation's screen.

Using FCONSOLE to Broadcast Messages

You can broadcast messages to all users or specific users with the FCONSOLE command. Begin by typing **FCONSOLE** at the workstation prompt. To broadcast to all users, select **Broadcast Console Message**.

To broadcast to a specific user, select **Connection Information**, and when the Current Connections list appears, use the arrow keys to scan the list and highlight a user. Press ENTER and select **Broadcast Console Message**.

Clearing Connections

The CLEAR STATION command is used to disconnect a workstation from the file server. You use this command for two reasons: to disconnect a workstation at a distant location that was left on by a user and to disconnect a crashed station that left files open on the server. Use the CLEAR STATION command with caution, however. It removes all file server resources allocated to a station, closes all open files, and erases internal tables used by the file server to track the station. If the workstation is in the middle of a transaction during a CLEAR STATION, data being written to a file may corrupt the file.

The command takes the form

CLEAR STATION n

where n is the number of the workstation that can be determined with the MONITOR command, as explained in "Determining a User's Workstation Number." For example, to clear workstation 10, you would type the following command at the console:

CLEAR STATION 10

Using FCONSOLE to Clear Connections

You can disconnect a user with the FCONSOLE command. Only supervisors or supervisor equivalents can disconnect another user in this way.

1. Type **FCONSOLE** at the workstation prompt.

2. Select **Connection Information** from the FCONSOLE Available Options menu.

3. When the Current Connections list appears, use the arrow keys to scan through it. Disconnect a user by highlighting the user's name and pressing DEL.

Locking the File Server Console

You can lock the file server console to prevent unauthorized users from using commands and equipment on the server. A keyboard password is required to regain access once the server has been locked. Lock the console by typing **SECURE CONSOLE** at the console prompt.

When you have secured a console, the following security measures are implemented:

- Loadable modules cannot be loaded from any directory except SYS:SYSTEM. This prevents intruders from introducing "Trojan horse" modules that might access or alter important information.

- Keyboard entry into the OS debugger is prevented.

- The date and time cannot be changed, which is important to some network accounting features.

- The option removes DOS from the file server, thus preventing a user from running DOS files. You should also implement the power-on password option (if available with the server) to prevent an intruder from restarting the system with a DOS disk and running a DOS program that could steal or alter data.

Locking the Console with MONITOR

Start the MONITOR loadable module with the following command, replacing *path* with the path to a directory if MONITOR.NLM is not in the SYS:SYSTEM directory.

LOAD *path*\MONITOR

When the Available Options menu appears, select **Lock File Server Console** from the menu. Type a password that can be used to regain access to the console. To regain access to a locked console, press a key to clear the screen saver, and then type the password used to lock the keyboard.

Downing the Server

NetWare provides a number of ways to shut the server down. You can use the FCONSOLE command at a workstation, the console at the file server, or a remote console at a workstation. It is important that you shut down the file server properly to ensure data integrity. Write all cache buffers to disk, close files, and update the directory and file allocation tables properly. Perform these tasks when you down the server using the methods discussed later.

If files are still open, you are asked if you still want to down the server. Always close files with the appropriate applications, unless you are sure the files will not be corrupted when the server is downed.

Note: Always use the SEND console command to warn users when a server will be brought down. You can also use the Broadcast Console Message option on the FCONSOLE Available Options menu or the workstation SEND command.

The Console DOWN Command

Type **DOWN** at the file server console or remote console to down the server. You then can invoke the EXIT command to return to DOS. If you use the REMOVE DOS command, the server is warm booted.

Downing the Server from FCONSOLE

The supervisor can use the FCONSOLE menu utility from a workstation to down the server. Select **Down File Server** from the Available Options menu, and then type **Yes** at the prompt.

The SET Command

Use the SET command to view and change the configuration of the operating system in the following categories:

Communications

Memory

File caching

Directory caching

File system

Locks

Transaction tracking

Disk

Miscellaneous

You can use SET to both display and change the current settings. When you type SET without parameters, a list of categories similar to the preceding list appears. Select one of the categories to display more detailed information about the category. If you type **SET** with one of its parameters, as listed in Chapter 36, the current setting of the parameter is displayed. If you type **SET** with a parameter and a new setting, the setting changes.

Most SET parameters have default values that do not need to be changed. Some you can change at the console, while some you can change only by including them in the startup files and rebooting the system. See Chapter 36 for a complete discussion of SET.

The LOAD Command

You use the LOAD command to install NetWare loadable modules (NLMs). These modules can include disk drivers, LAN drivers, name space support, and NLM utilities such as INSTALL and VREPAIR. A loadable module links itself to the operating system and uses part of the server's memory. Modules may be loaded and then unloaded. When a module is unloaded, its memory is returned to the operating system for other use. Utilities are commonly loaded and then unloaded, while disk drivers and LAN drivers are loaded and usually stay in memory the entire time the server is in operation.

If you must load a module every time the server boots, you should place its LOAD commands in the server startup files, AUTOEXEC.NLM and STARTUP.NCF. Modules loaded at boot time should also be placed on the boot drive or startup disk. It is important that Novell approve any module running in the server. An improperly written module can lock up the server or cause other problems. Novell has a NetWare loadable module testing program to which vendors can submit modules for testing and approval.

The following commands illustrate how the LOAD command is used in several situations. In the examples, the MONITOR module is loaded from the network or a boot disk.

If the loadable module is in the SYS:SYSTEM directory, type the LOAD command and the module name as shown here:

LOAD MONITOR

If the module is on another disk or has a path other than the SYS:SYSTEM directory, specify the drive letter and/or path before the module name, as in the following examples:

```
LOAD A:MONITOR
LOAD SYS:MODULES/MONITOR
```

If modules are located in a directory besides SYS:SYSTEM, you can specify the names of the directories using the SEARCH command as described under "Specifying Loadable Module Search Paths" later in this chapter. The NetWare disk set includes several modules, as described in the following sections.

Disk Drivers

Disk drivers are loadable modules that provide links between the operating system and disk controller boards. The following drivers are available on the NetWare 386 Operating System-1 disk. Disk driver loadable modules have the extension DSK.

DCB.DSK	Driver for Novell or other disk coprocessor board
ISADISK.DSK	Driver for industry standard architecture board
PS2ESDI.DSK	IBM PS/2 ESDI driver
PS2MFM.DSK	IBM PS/2 MFM driver
PS2SCSI.DSK	IBM PS/2 SCSI driver

LAN Drivers

LAN drivers are loadable modules that provide links between the operating system and network interface cards. The following drivers are available on the NetWare 386 Operating System-2 disk. LAN driver loadable modules have the extension LAN.

TRXNET.LAN	Novell RX-Net, RX-Net II, and RX-Net/2 ARCNET driver
3C503.LAN	3COM EtherLink II - ASSY 2227 driver
3C505.LAN	3COM EtherLink Plus - ASSY 2012 driver

3C523.LAN	3COM EtherLink/MC driver
NE2.LAN	Novell NE/2 Ethernet driver
NE232.LAN	Novell NE/2 32-bit Ethernet driver
NE1000.LAN	Novell NE1000 Ethernet driver
NE2000.LAN	Novell NE2000 Ethernet driver
NE3200.LAN	Novell NE3200 Ethernet driver
TOKEN.LAN	Driver for IBM Token Ring adapters

Note: Load the NMAGENT command before LAN drivers to allow them to register and pass network management parameters to the MONITOR utility for viewing. Refer to Chapter 34 for more information.

NLM Utilities

Many programs are available that run on the NetWare 386 server along with the operating system. The utilities may provide management, monitoring, maintenance, communications, and diagnostics functions. The following NLM utilities are available on the NetWare 386 Operating System-1, NetWare 386 Operating System-2, and print services and utilities disks. The utilities have the extension NLM.

DISKSET.NLM	Configures disk coprocessor boards
INSTALL.NLM	Installs disk partitions, volumes, and other features
MONITOR.NLM	Monitors server and network activity
NMAGENT.NLM	Allows tracking of network management parameters
PSERVER.NLM	The Print Server module
REMOTE.NLM	Remote file server console

RSPX.NLM	SPX communications module for REMOTE
TOKENRPL.NLM	Enables remote booting of Token Ring boards
UPS.NLM	Uninterruptible power supply support
VREPAIR.NLM	Volume repair module

The following loadable modules are part of the Streams environment:

STREAMS.NLM	Support for Streams-based protocol services
CLIB.NLM	C-library module
IPXS.NLM	Streams version of IPX
MATHLIB.NLM	Provides math coprocessor support
MATHLIBC.NLM	Used on 80386 systems without math coprocessors
TLI.NLM	Provides TLI communications services support

Name Space

Name space modules allow non-DOS operating systems to store files on NetWare servers. Because these files use different conventions and may require additional file table entries, drivers must be written and installed to support them. Currently, the only available name space module is MAC.NAM to support Apple Macintosh files.

Specifying Loadable Module Search Paths

Use the SEARCH console command to tell the file server where to look for loadable modules and NCF files. The default path is SYS:SYSTEM, but if you want to store these files in another directory, specify it in the SEARCH command. You can specify up to 20 search paths to local drives or directories on the file server. Each search path is given a number; the operating system searches paths in numerical order.

To display the current search path, type **SEARCH**. To add new search paths, use this format:

SEARCH ADD *number path*

where *path* is the path to add. *Number* is optional; use it to specify that the new path should be inserted in the list rather than added to the bottom. To delete a search path, use the following format, replacing *number* with the number of the search path to delete:

SEARCH DEL *number*

The INSTALL NetWare Loadable Module

The INSTALL module is used to initially install NetWare 386 and to make changes to the installation at a later time. You can use it to create and delete partitions, mirror and unmirror disks, create and modify volumes, format disks, and perform other tasks associated with server maintenance. The INSTALL module is used extensively in the disk maintenance section in Chapter 36. To start INSTALL, type **LOAD INSTALL** at the NetWare 386 console command line. When the Installation Options menu appears, you can choose between disk, volume, or system options. Select **Disk Options** to install hard disks and modify their partition and mirroring status. Select **Volume Options** to create and modify volumes. When you select **System Options**, you can choose to copy system and public files to the server, change the file server's name, change the file server's internal network number, and edit the startup files.

Remote Console

NetWare's Remote Console feature allows authorized users to execute console commands from a workstation rather than directly at the file server console. It is an extremely useful feature for large in-house networks or wide area networks that have their management centralized in an area away from the server.

The Remote Console feature consists of the following loadable modules and command:

REMOTE.NLM A module loaded at the server to initiate and handle remote console sessions.

RSPX.NLM A module loaded at the server after loading REMOTE.NLM to provide SPX communications support.

RCONSOLE.EXE A command executed at the workstation where the remote console session will take place.

Follow the steps below to load and run Remote Console:

1. Type the following command to load the REMOTE module:

   LOAD *path*\REMOTE *password*

   where *path* is the drive or directory where REMOTE.NLM can be found if it is not in the SYS:SYSTEM directory, and *password* is a password you use when starting a remote console (it can be the same as the supervisor's password). You will be asked for a password if you do not specify it.

   This command and the next can be placed in the AUTOEXEC.NCF file to load a remote console every time the server starts.

2. Type the following command to load the RSPX module, replacing *path* with a drive or directory where RSPX.NLM can be found if it is not in the SYS:SYSTEM directory.

LOAD *path*\RSPX

3. Go to the workstation that will be the remote console and type **RCONSOLE**. You must be logged in as the supervisor or a user with supervisor privileges in the SYS:SYSTEM directory where RCONSOLE.EXE is located. You may need to set a search path to this directory.

4. If multiple file servers are running REMOTE and RSPX, select a server to remotely manage.

5. Enter the password specified in step 1. The file server's console screen appears at the workstation.

Keep the following in mind when working at the file server's console screen:

- All activities performed at the remote console are mirrored on the screen of the file server. You may want to load MONITOR or another utility at the file server before leaving it unattended.

- You should always lock the file server console when leaving it unattended. Refer to "Locking the File Server Console" earlier in this chapter.

The following keys can be used to choose options at the remote console:

+ or -	Moves through any active screen currently available. If you loaded MONITOR at the file server before leaving it, you can jump between this display and the RCONSOLE menu.
* (on the keypad)	Displays the RCONSOLE available Options menu, which is discussed in the next section.
SHIFT-ESC	Lets you select a server from a list.

Note: To execute console commands, refer to "Selecting a Screen to View" in the next section.

The RCONSOLE Available Options Menu

The RCONSOLE Available Options menu shown here is displayed by pressing the asterisk (∗) on the numeric keypad.

```
                    Available Options
  Select A Screen To View
  Directory Scan
  Transfer Files To Server
  Copy System And Public Files
  End Remote Session With Server (SHIFT-ESC)
  Resume Remote Session With Server (ESC)
```

The following sections describe the tasks you can perform using the options from this menu.

Selecting a Screen to View

When you choose the **Select A Screen To View** option, a list of available screens appears. If you loaded MONITOR at the console, MONITOR SCREEN and SYSTEM CONSOLE appear in the Available Screens menu.

To enter console commands, select **SYSTEM CONSOLE**. The console colon (:) prompt appears so you can execute any console command as you normally would at the file server.

Scanning a Directory

Select the **Directory Scan** option to scan directories on the file server, a DOS partition, or a disk drive. Type the drive letter and/or path to scan. You can use the PGUP and PGDN keys to move through the list if it is long.

Transferring Files to the Server

Select the **Transfer Files To Server** option to transfer files from the workstation. When you are asked for the source path and then the destination path, type the path and the filename. You can use wildcards to specify groups of files.

Note: If the file is located in the currently logged directory of the workstation, simply type the filename.

Copying System and Public Files

Select **Copy System and Public Files** to copy the NetWare utilities to the file server, as you must do during an upgrade. Enter the NetWare 386 Operating System-2 disk in the floppy drive of the remote workstation to start the process, and follow the prompts on the screen.

Ending a Remote Session with the Server

Select **End Remote Session With Server** to end a remote console session. You are returned to the Available Servers menu, where you can select another file server if available. You can also press SHIFT- ESC to end the session.

Editing the Startup Files

The two startup files AUTOEXEC.NCF and STARTUP.NCF were created during the NetWare 386 installation procedure in Chapter 17. You can alter these files at any time using the procedures described here. As you read through the next few chapters or use them for reference, you may want to include some of the options in the startup files. This section presents tips and examples for doing so.

Most LOAD, BIND, and SET commands are candidates for inclusion in the AUTOEXEC.NCF and STARTUP.NCF files. Include them in the startup files to save yourself the trouble of typing them every time the server starts. In addition, startup parameters that you would normally be prompted for when executing commands at the console can be specified with commands in the startup files. In this way you or other users do not need to answer the prompts when starting the system.

Note: Keep in mind that any changes to the startup files do not take effect until the server is rebooted.

Both AUTOEXEC.NCF and STARTUP.NCF can be edited by loading INSTALL and selecting **System Options** from the main menu.

To place unexecutable comments in the startup files, precede them with the pound sign (#). Place the command ECHO ON at the beginning of the files if you wish to see commands as they execute during the boot sequence.

The following commands can be placed in the AUTOEXEC.NCF file:

LOAD INSTALL

LOAD MONITOR

LOAD PSERVER

LOAD *lan_driver*

BIND

SET

MOUNT

REMOVE DOS

SECURE CONSOLE

SPOOL

TRACK ON

UPS STATUS

The following commands can be placed in the STARTUP.NCF file:

LOAD *disk driver*

LOAD *name space*

SET

Monitoring Network Activity
And Performance

Console Commands for Viewing Network Information
The MONITOR Loadable Module

This chapter explains commands and loadable modules you can use at the console to view network settings and activity. In particular, the MONITOR module is used to view the performance of the LAN and to determine whether settings should be changed, as explained in Chapters 35 and 36.

Console Commands for Viewing Network Information

The following commands are typed at the file server console or the remote console to display information about the file server and its networks.

The VERSION Command

Type **VERSION** at the console to display the file server's version information and copyright notice.

The NAME Command

Type **NAME** at the console to display the name of the file server.

The VOLUMES Command

Type **VOLUMES** to display a list of currently mounted volumes.

The TIME Command

Type **TIME** at the console command line to display the current time and date settings of the server. To reset the time, refer to Chapter 36.

The CONFIG Command

Type **CONFIG** at the console to display the following information:

- File server name

- Internal network number of the file server

- Loaded LAN drivers

- Settings on network boards, which you need to know when installing additional boards

- Node addresses of network boards

- Protocol bound to each board (IPX or other)

- Network numbers of network boards

- Frame types assigned to network boards

- Names assigned to network boards

The MEMORY Command

The MEMORY command displays the total amount of installed memory that the operating system can address. Type **MEMORY** on the command line to display the memory information.

NetWare 386 addresses memory above 16MB on EISA computers. Use the REGISTER MEMORY command covered in Chapter 36 to enable the operating system to address memory above 16MB. On MCA and ISA computers, NetWare 386 can only automatically address memory up to 16MB.

The MODULES Command

The MODULES command displays information about the modules currently loaded in the file server. The short name used to load the module is displayed, along with a descriptive string or long name for each module. A version number may also be displayed. Type **MODULES** at the server console to display the list.

The DISPLAY NETWORKS Command

The DISPLAY NETWORKS command is a useful console command for displaying the currently available networks. Type **DISPLAY NET-WORKS** to display the following network information:

- The network number.

- The number of networks that must be crossed to reach the network is displayed in front of the slash. A 0 indicates the current network.

- The estimated time in ticks (1/18 of a second) for a packet to reach the network is displayed after the slash.

- The number of known networks is displayed at the bottom of the screen.

The DISPLAY SERVERS Command

The DISPLAY SERVERS command displays a list of currently available servers. Type **DISPLAY SERVERS** to list the servers and the number of networks that must be crossed to reach the server.

Clearing the Console Screen

The CLS (clear screen) command clears any text from the console screen. Simply type **CLS** to clear the screen. You can also type **OFF**.

The MONITOR Loadable Module

Use the MONITOR loadable module to view information about server and network activities such as the following:

- Overall activity and utilization

- Cache memory status

- Connections and their status

- Disk drives

- Mounted volumes

- LAN drivers

- Loaded modules

- File lock status

- Memory usage

The main MONITOR screen displays statistics about several important network functions. After one minute of nonactivity, a moving snake appears to prevent screen burn. As network usage increases, the snake moves faster and its tail gets longer. Press any key to retrieve the MONITOR display.

The Network Management Agent (NMAGENT)

The NMAGENT module allows LAN drivers to register and pass network management parameters to the MONITOR module. NMAGENT registers three resources for tracking:

- Network management triggers

- Network management managers

- Network management objects

You must load the module before loading any LAN drivers. Refer to Chapter 35 for more information.

Loading MONITOR

Load the MONITOR module at the file server console or at a workstation that is running in remote console mode, as discussed in Chapter 33. Enter the command in this form:

LOAD *path*\MONITOR *parameters*

where *path* is the path to the MONITOR.NLM file if it is located outside the SYS:SYSTEM directory. You can specify the following parameters:

ns (No Saver)   Turns off the screen saver option

nh (No Help)   Saves memory if you do not need the help functions

The Main MONITOR Screen

The main MONITOR screen, shown in Figure 34-1, displays the following information about the network functions. It also provides a menu for viewing other information, as described in the sections that follow.

- *File Server Up Time* The amount of time the server has been running.

- *Utilization* The percentage of time the processor is busy. A high percentage indicates an overworked server.

- *Original Cache Buffers* The number of cache buffers in blocks available when the server was first booted.

- *Total Cache Buffers* The number of blocks currently available for file caching. Check this number after loading NLMs to ensure adequate memory is available for caching.

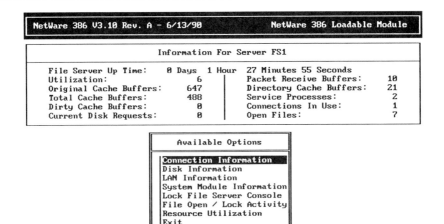

Figure 34-1. The main MONITOR screen

- *Dirty Cache Buffers* The number of file blocks waiting to be written to disk.

- *Current Disk Requests* The number of disk requests waiting for service.

- *Packet Receive Buffers* The number of buffers available for requests from the workstations. The default is 10.

- *Directory Cache Buffers* The number of buffers allocated to handle directory caching.

- *Service Processes* The number of "task handlers" allocated for station requests. The server may allocate additional processes when station requests run abnormally high, and these processes are not released unless the server is downed.

- *Connections In Use* The number of stations currently attached to the file server.

- *Open Files* The number of files that can be concurrently accessed.

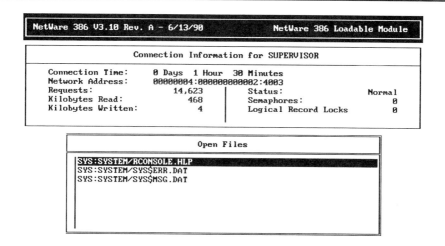

Figure 34-2.   The MONITOR Connection Information screen

Connection Information

Select **Connection Information** from the MONITOR Available Options menu. When the Active Connections menu appears, select a user from the list. You can clear a connection by pressing DEL on a user's name. After a user is selected, a Connection Information screen similar to that shown in Figure 34-2 appears. Any files that the user currently has open are displayed beneath the screen. You can highlight any file to view its record lock information, which is described later in this section.

The following options are available on the Connection Information screen:

- *Connection Time* Displays the amount of time the user has been connected.

- *Network Address* Displays the network address, station address, and socket address of the user's workstation. Sockets represent the address of processes running in multitasking operating systems like OS/2.

- *Requests* Displays the number of requests made by the connection since it was booted.

- *Kilobytes Read* Displays the number of kilobytes the connection has accessed for reading.

- *Kilobytes Written* Displays the number of kilobytes written by the station.

- *Status* Displays Normal (logged in and functioning), Waiting (waiting for a file to be unlocked), or Not-logged-in (attached but not logged in).

- *Semaphores* Displays the number of semaphores the connection has open. Semaphores are used to request the use of a resource and help limit how many tasks can use or change a resource at the same time.

- *Logical Record Locks* Displays the number of record locks a connection has. Records are locked to prevent other users from accessing them.

Listing a Connection's Physical Record Locks

Workstations can lock the records of a database so other workstations cannot access them simultaneously. It may be necessary to see which workstation has which records. This can be done by highlighting the database in use by the workstation in the Open Files window and pressing ENTER. The Record Lock screen appears with the following information:

- *Start* The offset in the file where the lock begins.

- *End* The offset in the file where the lock ends.

- *Record Lock* Displays one of the following:

  - *Locked Exclusive* Locked so no one else can access the record.

- *Locked Shareable*   Other stations can read but not write to the record.

- *Locked*   Logged for future locking; specified when the lock is completed.

- *TTS Holding Lock*   Unlocked by the application but locked by TTS because of incomplete transactions.

- *Status*   Displays one of the following:

  - *Logged*   A set of records is being prepared for locking to prevent deadlock.

  - *Not Logged*   A normal condition in which there are no pending requests for a set of locks.

Disk Information

Select **Disk Information** from the MONITOR Available Options menu to display information about hard disks. If more than one disk exists, you are asked to pick from a list. The Drive Status screen appears, as shown in Figure 34-3. The following information is displayed:

- *Driver*   The name of the driver for the disk.

- *Disk Size*   The size of the disk in megabytes.

- *Partitions*   The number of partitions on the disk.

- *Mirror Status*   The disk may be labeled Mirrored, Not Mirrored, or Remirroring.

- *Hot Fix Status*   The disk may be Normal (Hot Fix is functioning) or Not-hot-fixed (Hot Fix has failed).

- *Partition Blocks*   The total space on the partition shown in blocks.

- *Data Blocks*   The space in blocks available for data.

- *Redirection Blocks*   The block size of the Hot Fix redirection area.

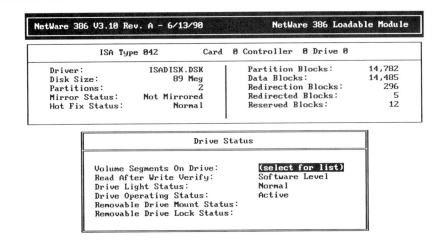

```
╔══════════════════════════════════════════════════════════════════════╗
║ NetWare 386 V3.10 Rev. A - 6/13/90        NetWare 386 Loadable Module  ║
╚══════════════════════════════════════════════════════════════════════╝
┌────────────────────────────────────────────────────────────────────────┐
│          ISA Type 042        Card  0 Controller  0 Drive 0               │
├────────────────────────────────────────────────────────────────────────┤
│  Driver:              ISADISK.DSK   │  Partition Blocks:      14,782      │
│  Disk Size:               89 Meg    │  Data Blocks:           14,485      │
│  Partitions:                 2      │  Redirection Blocks:       296      │
│  Mirror Status:      Not Mirrored   │  Redirected Blocks:          5      │
│  Hot Fix Status:          Normal    │  Reserved Blocks:           12      │
└────────────────────────────────────────────────────────────────────────┘
          ┌──────────────────────────────────────────────────┐
          │                  Drive Status                    │
          ├──────────────────────────────────────────────────┤
          │  Volume Segments On Drive:    (select for list)   │
          │  Read After Write Verify:     Software Level      │
          │  Drive Light Status:          Normal              │
          │  Drive Operating Status:      Active              │
          │  Removable Drive Mount Status:                    │
          │  Removable Drive Lock Status:                     │
          └──────────────────────────────────────────────────┘
```

Figure 34-3.   The MONITOR Disk Information screen

- *Redirected Blocks*   The number of blocks redirected to the Hot Fix area.

- *Reserved Blocks*   Blocks reserved for Hot Fix tables.

Additional Drive Status options are covered in Chapter 35. To view the volume segments on the drive, select **Volume Segments on Drive** from the Drive Status screen.

LAN Information

Select **LAN Information** from the Available Options menu to view information about LAN drivers. Multiple cards, if they exist, are listed on the LAN Driver Information screen. Select a card from the list and press ENTER to display information about the card, as shown in Figure 34-4. Use the arrow keys to view additional information. LAN information can help in determining if a LAN is overloaded or not working properly. The following

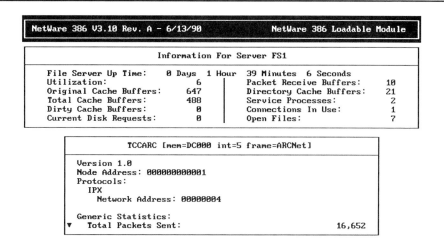

```
┌──────────────────────────────────────────────────────────────────────┐
│ NetWare 386 V3.10 Rev. A - 6/13/90            NetWare 386 Loadable Module │
└──────────────────────────────────────────────────────────────────────┘

┌──────────────────────────────────────────────────────────────────────┐
│                        Information For Server FS1                       │
│  File Server Up Time:    0 Days  1 Hour  39 Minutes  6 Seconds          │
│  Utilization:                6  │  Packet Receive Buffers:      10       │
│  Original Cache Buffers:   647  │  Directory Cache Buffers:     21       │
│  Total Cache Buffers:      488  │  Service Processes:            2       │
│  Dirty Cache Buffers:        0  │  Connections In Use:           1       │
│  Current Disk Requests:      0  │  Open Files:                   7       │
└──────────────────────────────────────────────────────────────────────┘

         ┌─────────────────────────────────────────────────────────┐
         │         TCCARC [mem=DC000 int=5 frame=ARCNet]            │
         │  Version 1.0                                             │
         │  Node Address: 000000000001                             │
         │  Protocols:                                             │
         │    IPX                                                   │
         │       Network Address: 00000004                         │
         │                                                         │
         │  Generic Statistics:                                    │
         │ ▼   Total Packets Sent:                        16,652    │
         └─────────────────────────────────────────────────────────┘
```

Figure 34-4.   The MONITOR LAN Information screen

items are listed in a section called Generic Statistics, but additional
information may be displayed depending on the specific driver used.

- *Driver Name* The name of the driver and its parameters.

- *Version* The current driver version.

- *Node Address* The address of the network board in the file server.

- *Protocols* The communications protocol bound to the driver with
  BIND.

- *Network Address* The network address assigned to the network
  card. This only appears if IPX is bound to the board.

- *Total Packets Sent* The number of packets sent from the file server
  through the LAN card. This number can be compared with other
  LAN drivers to determine which is handling more traffic.

- *Total Packets Received*   The number of packets received by the file server since last booted.

- *No ECB Available Count*   The number of packets that could not be received because a buffer was not available. The file server allocates more buffers after such incidents until a maximum limit is reached. The maximum limit can be set with the SET command.

- *Send Packet Too Big Count*   The number of packets that could not be sent because they were too big for the board to handle.

- *Send Packet Too Small Count*   The number of packets that could not be sent because they were too small for the hardware to handle.

- *Receive Packet Overflow Count*   The number of packets received that were too big to store in a cache buffer. This may indicate a need to update a software package that does not work well on the network.

- *Receive Packet Too Big Count*   The number of packets received that were too large.

- *Receive Packet Too Small Count*   The number of packets received that were too small.

- *Send Packet Miscellaneous Errors*   The number of errors that occurred when packets were sent.

- *Receive Packet Miscellaneous Errors*   The number of errors that occurred when packets were received.

- *Send Packet Retry Count*   The number of errors that occurred when the server tried to send packets but could not because of hardware errors. Errors of this sort may indicate a faulty cabling system or network hardware at the workstation.

- *Checksum Errors*   The number of data errors indicated by a mismatch in the checksum byte.

- *Hardware Receive Mismatch Count*   The number of errors when specified packet lengths do not match.

System Module Information

Select the **System Module** Information option on the Available Options menu to view information about each of the loadable modules currently running in the server. A screen appears similar to the one shown here:

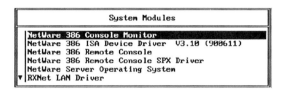

```
                    System Modules
┌────────────────────────────────────────────────────┐
│ NetWare 386 Console Monitor                          │
│ NetWare 386 ISA Device Driver  V3.10 (900611)        │
│ NetWare 386 Remote Console                           │
│ NetWare 386 Remote Console SPX Driver                │
│ NetWare Server Operating System                      │
│▼RXNet LAN Driver                                     │
└────────────────────────────────────────────────────┘
```

Note that the NetWare 386 operating system is not a module, even though it is listed on the screen.

When an option is selected, the following information can be viewed:

- *Tag* The name of the resource tag that the loadable module gave to a resource.

- *Module* The name of the module using the tag.

- *Resource* Displays the type of resource the tag is using. See Appendix B of the *NetWare 386 System Administration* manual for a complete description of resource types.

- *In Use* The amount of memory in bytes currently used or the number of resources being used.

File Open/Lock Activity

Select the **File Open/Lock Activity** option on the MONITOR Available Options menu to display information about the activities of a file, such as which connections are using the file, how it is being used, and whether it is locked.

When the option is selected, a list of directories appears. You may need to press the double dots (..) to return to a parent directory. When the correct directory is reached, you can select the file to view. A double menu appears with the following options:

- *Use Count* The number of connections that have the file open, logged, or locked.

- *Open Count* The number of connections that currently have the file open.

- *Open for Read* The number of connections reading the file.

- *Open for Write* The number of connections writing to the file.

- *Deny Read* The number of connections that have opened the file for exclusive use.

- *Deny Write* The number of connections that have the file and will not let other stations write to it.

- *Status* A file may have a status of Locked or Not Locked. Other users cannot access locked files.

- *Conn.* A list of connections using the file.

- *Task* A number assigned by the shell to an application program.

- *Lock Status* Displays the following information about the records of a file in use:

  - *Exclusive* No one else can read or write to the record

  - *Shareable* Others may read but not write to the record

  - *TTS Holding Lock* TTS has locked the file because transactions are not complete

  - *Logged* A set of records is being prepared for locking to prevent deadlocks

  - *Not Logged* The normal condition indicating that no requests have been made for the file

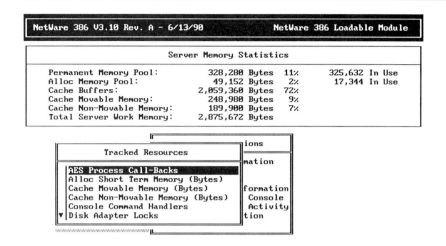

```
NetWare 386 V3.10 Rev. A - 6/13/90          NetWare 386 Loadable Module

                    Server Memory Statistics

Permanent Memory Pool:        328,280 Bytes   11%    325,632 In Use
Alloc Memory Pool:             49,152 Bytes    2%     17,344 In Use
Cache Buffers:              2,059,360 Bytes   72%
Cache Movable Memory:         248,980 Bytes    9%
Cache Non-Movable Memory:     189,900 Bytes    7%
Total Server Work Memory:   2,875,672 Bytes

              ┌─────────────────────────┬─────┐
              │    Tracked Resources    │ions │
              │                         │mation│
              │ AES Process Call-Backs  │      │
              │ Alloc Short Term Memory (Bytes)│formation│
              │ Cache Movable Memory (Bytes)   │Console│
              │ Cache Non-Movable Memory (Bytes)│Activity│
              │ Console Command Handlers │tion │
              │▼│Disk Adapter Locks      │     │
              └─────────────────────────┴─────┘
```

Figure 34-5.   The MONITOR Memory Statistics and Resource Utilization screen

Viewing Memory Statistics

Memory statistics appear when you select the **Resource Utilization** option from the MONITOR Available Options menu. A screen similar to Figure 34-5 appears.

The percentage column indicates the amount of available memory being used for a particular memory pool or buffer. The In-Use column indicates how many of the available bytes are being used by a particular memory pool. Memory is categorized in the following way:

- *Permanent Memory Pool* The statistics of both permanent and semipermanent memory are listed. The memory is used for long-term memory needs such as directory cache buffers and packet receive buffers and is not returned to regular memory unless the file server is rebooted.

- *Alloc Memory Pool* This pool is the Allocated Short Term Memory pool, which is available for use by loadable modules, mappings, user connection information, and server advertising. The memory is not returned to cache but is made available for use by other loadable modules. The Maximum Alloc Short Term Memory parameter of the SET command, which is discussed in Chapter 36, can be used to increase the pool if it ever reaches 2,000,000 bytes.

- *Cache Buffers* The total amount of memory available for cache buffers. If the figure reaches 20 percent, add more memory. More cache buffers can be made available by unloading loadable modules like INSTALL, MONITOR, and DISKSET. You can also down the server to recover memory locked by some processes, or use RE-MOVE DOS to free memory used by DOS.

- *Cache Movable Memory* This memory pool lists memory buffers that are "rotating free blocks" in a certain range of memory. NetWare can move these at any time to facilitate memory management. They are returned to the cache buffer pool when not in use.

- *Cache Non-Movable Memory* This memory pool lists memory buffers temporarily allocated to a program. They are returned to the cache buffer pool when not in use.

- *Total Server Work Memory* The total number of bytes available for the server to use.

Viewing Tracked Resources

The resources of the operating system are given names so they can be tracked. Loadable modules use these resources, which are returned to the operating system after use. To display information about the resources, select **Resource Utilization** from the Available Options menu. The Tracked Resources menu appears. Use the arrow keys to page through the list, and then select a resource to view. The Resource Tags list appears. When you select an option the following information can be viewed:

- *Tag* The name of the resource tag that the loadable module gave to a resource.

- *Module* The name of the module using the tag.

- *Resource* The type of resource the tag is using is displayed. See Appendix B of the *NetWare 386 System Administration* manual for a complete description of resource types.

- *In Use* The amount of memory in bytes currently used or the number of resources being used.

Managing Network Hardware

Managing the File System
Managing the LAN and Cable System
Installing a UPS

This chapter covers techniques and commands for managing network hardware, including disk drivers, LANs, cable systems, and uninterruptible power supplies.

Managing the File System

This section discusses how to manage and change the NetWare 386 filing system. Management tasks associated with the filing system include installing, removing, testing, partitioning, and formatting hard drives. Also discussed in this chapter are setting up hard disk mirroring and volumes.

You can view information about hard drives with the MONITOR loadable module and the CONFIG console commands (see Chapter 34 for more information).

Loading Disk Drivers

Disk drivers are loadable modules that provide links between the operating system and disk controller boards. The following drivers are available on the NetWare 386 Operating System-1 disk. Other drivers must be obtained from the specific manufacturer of the disk controller board.

DCB.DSK	This is the driver for Novell or for other disk coprocessor board
ISADISK.DSK	Driver for industry standard architecture (ISA) board
PS2ESDI.DSK	IBM PS/2 ESDI driver
PS2MFM.DSK	IBM PS/2 MFM driver
PS2SCSI.DSK	IBM PS/2 SCSI driver

Note: If more than 16MB of memory is installed in the server, use caution when installing AT bus master disk adapter boards or boards that use on-line DMA. Such boards can only address up to 16Mb of memory and can cause corruption of the file server's memory. If the board is an EISA board, refer to Chapter 36 for information. If the server is an ISA or MCA system, remove the REGISTER MEMORY command from the AUTO-EXEC.NCF file and reboot the file server.

The command to load a disk driver takes the following form:

LOAD *path / driver parameter*

where *path* is the path to the directory containing the loadable module if it is not in the SYS:SYSTEM directory. *Driver* is the name of the driver, and *parameter* is one of the following parameters, which are specified to configure each driver to match the settings of the disk adapter.

DMA=#	Replace # with a DMA channel to reserve for the driver.
INT=#	Replace # with the hardware interrupt set on the board. The operating system uses hexadecimal values for the interrupts (10=A, 11=B, 12=C, 13=D, 14=E, 15=F).
MEM=#	Replace # with the memory address to reserve for the driver.

PORT=#   Replace # with the I/O port to reserve for the driver.

SLOT=#   On Micro Channel machines and EISA systems with bus master slots, replace # with the number of the slot in which the board is installed. The interrupts, memory addresses, and I/O ports are set with the reference disk supplied with the board.

If you do not specify parameters, NetWare asks for those it needs (some are read directly from the board). If you include the LOAD commands in the startup files, use parameters so NetWare does not need to ask for them when it boots. Remember that no two cards can share the same interrupts and I/O ports. You can load a driver multiple times if more than one card exists, but the board setting and drive parameters for each must be different.

Note: The PS/2 drivers PS2ESDI and PS2MFM do not need parameters because they cannot be configured.

For example, the following command specifies an interrupt of F and a port number of 170 when loading the ISADISK driver:

```
LOAD ISADISK INT=F PORT=170
```

The following sections explain how to configure several drivers. Because MCA systems do not require configuration, they are not described here, except for the PS2SCSI driver.

Industry Standard
AT-Compatible Systems

Server systems using the AT class of disk controllers must be installed using the ISADISK.DSK loadable driver module. Type **LOAD ISADISK** to load the disk driver. The default interrupt is E, but you can change it to B, C, or F using the INT= options. The default I/O port is 1F0, but you can change it to 170 using the PORT= option. Make sure the board settings are set appropriately if you make the optional settings.

Note: The ISADISK driver module can be loaded twice if two disk controllers are present. The first controller uses I/O port 1F0 and interrupt E. The second controller uses I/O port 170 and interrupt F.

External Disk Subsystems

External disk subsystems are drives attached to disk coprocessor boards like Novell's DCB, EDCB, or DCB/2. Installation requires two steps. First, load the DCB driver module by typing **LOAD DCB**. Next, run the DISK SET command as described under "Installing External Hard Disks." DISK-SET is used to place information about the hard disks attached to the coprocessor board on the board's programmable chip.

Note: The Novell channel 2 DCB may produce hardware errors on Compaq machines due to a mouse port conflict at interrupt 12. You must disable the mouse port to correct it.

Microchannel SCSI Drivers

Microchannel systems like the IBM PS/2 line use three types of internal controllers: ESDI, MFM, and SCSI. Use the reference disk that came with the system to determine exactly which controller is in the system you are installing.

To install the driver, first down the file server, and then install the boards and connect the drive. Copy the configuration file (a file with the extension ADF) to the reference or setup disk for the MCA system. Configure the board with its reference disk, then use the DISKSET command as described under "Installing External Hard Disks." Load the driver with the following command:

LOAD *path*\PS2SCSI

where *path* is the drive or directory where the driver can be located if it is not in the SYS:SYSTEM directory.

Unloading Disk Drivers

If you need to upgrade a disk driver or remove it so a disk can be replaced or removed, use the following procedure. First, dismount all volumes that use the disk by typing the following command:

DISMOUNT *volume*

where *volume* is the name of the volume. Repeat this command for each volume.

Next, type the following command to unload the disk driver,

UNLOAD *driver*

where *driver* is the name of the disk driver to unload.

Installing Internal Hard Disks

You can install internal hard disks by following the steps described here. You are directed to further instructions later in the chapter for detailed information.

1. Down the server, and then install the drive.

2. Reboot the server and load the INSTALL module by typing **LOAD INSTALL**.

3. Run a disk surface test (optional), as described under "Testing Disks."

4. Format the disk (optional), as described under "Formatting Disks."

5. Partition the disk, as described under "Partitioning Disks."

6. Establish disk mirroring (optional), as discussed under "Mirroring and Unmirroring Disks."

7. Create and mount volumes, as described under "Managing Volumes."

If the volume to be mounted is the SYS volume for the NetWare 386 operating system, you should also install the operating system files, as discussed in Chapter 17.

Installing External Hard Disks

An external hard drive is a disk subsystem that attaches to a disk controller board (DCB). The drives have their own power supply, and additional drives may be attached in a daisy-chain fashion. Once you attach a drive to a NetWare file server, you then run the DISKSET command to configure the drive.

To install or replace a drive, refer to "Replacing or Removing Internal and External Hard Disks." Follow steps 1 through 12 to replace existing drives and steps 7 through 12 to mount new drives. Then return here to run the DISKSET procedures.

The DISKSET Command

The DISKSET command is used to place identification information about external hard disks on the EEPROM chip of Novell disk coprocessor boards as well as some third-party boards. You may perform the following tasks with DISKSET:

- Configure the EEPROM on disk coprocessor boards.

- Back up or restore the NetWare Ready configuration information (as described in the following pages) information for disks that are prepared for NetWare.

Load the DISKSET command at the console with the following LOAD command:

LOAD *path*\DISKSET

If DISKSET.NLM is not in the SYS:SYSTEM directory, you must specify *path* before DISKSET.

The Diskset Options menu appears with the following options for setting up DCBs and for backing up and restoring the NetWare Ready information.

DCB Set Up

1. Select **Disk Coprocessor Board SET UP** from the DISKSET menu to set up a DCB.

2. When the Select Desired Driver window appears, select the DCB driver and address settings that match the installed board.

3. The EEPROM Config screen then appears. Highlight the appropriate controller address in the window, and then press INS.

4. Highlight the name of the hard disk you are setting up from the Select Disk(s) and Controller Type menu, and press ENTER. The name of the drive appears next to the controller number in the EEPROM Config screen.

5. If a second hard drive will be attached to the same controller, press RIGHT ARROW to move to the Device 1 column, and then press INS and repeat step 4 to add the second drive.

6. Repeat steps 2 through 5 for each board to install.

NetWare Ready Backup

NetWare Ready hard disks contain the configuration information needed to install a drive in NetWare. Use the following procedure to back the information up to a floppy disk so you have another copy should the information become corrupted.

1. Format a disk with the volume label DISKDATA, and then place the disk in the server's floppy drive.

2. If the NetWare Ready disk driver is not loaded, load it with the following command, where *driver* is the name of the disk driver.

    LOAD *driver*

3. Load DISKSET by typing **LOAD DISKSET**, and then select **NetWare Ready Disk Backup/Restore** from the Diskset Options menu.

4. Select **Backup** from the Select Procedure menu.

5. Select the disk driver configuration to back up from the Select Desired Driver menu, and then select the hard disk's controller address from the Controller Address menu.

6. Select **Yes** to save the configuration, and then enter a filename. Press ENTER to save the file, and press ESC when you are done.

NetWare Ready Restore

The following steps are performed if you need to restore the NetWare Ready information to the DCB if it becomes corrupted.

1. Load DISKSET by typing **LOAD DISKSET**, and then select **NetWare Ready Disk Backup/Restore** from the Diskset Options menu.

2. Insert the DISKDATA disk in the server floppy drive.

3. Select **Restore** from the Select Procedure menu.

4. Select the disk driver configuration to restore from the Select Desired Driver menu, and then select the hard disk's controller address from the Controller Address menu.

5. Next select the configuration file from the Select Disk Data File to Edit list.

6. Press ESC if the configuration information is correct, and then select **Yes** at the Save Configuration prompt to restore the information.

Replacing or Removing
Internal and External Hard Disks

Hard disks need to be replaced when they become unusable or unreliable. This section explains how to replace or remove internal disks in file servers or external disks attached to disk coprocessor boards (DCBs). When drives are mirrored and the primary drive becomes unusable, the secondary drive takes over until the primary drive is replaced. After the drive is replaced, the data from the secondary drive synchronizes with (copies to) the primary drive. If mirroring is not used, files from the backup disk set or tape must be copied to the replacement drive.

1. Dismount any volumes that use the drive by invoking the DIS-MOUNT command. Execute the command in the following form for each volume, replacing *volume* with the name of the volume:

   DISMOUNT *volume*

2. Unmirror the drive, referring to "Mirroring and Unmirroring Disks" later in this chapter.

3. Delete the NetWare partition, referring to "Partitioning Disks" later in this chapter.

4. If the drive is internal, you must down the server and turn the power off before replacing the drive. If the drive is external, you can disconnect an old drive, and then connect a new drive without downing the server.

5. Replace or install new drives as necessary and reboot the server if it was downed.

6. For external subsystems, run DISKSET if the replacement drive is not the same as the replaced drive.

7. Unload the disk driver with the following command, replacing *driver* with the name of the driver for the disk coprocessor board:

UNLOAD *driver*

8. For internal drives, configure the drive with the system's Setup program.

9. Load the drivers unloaded in step 7.

10. Mount the volumes unmounted in step 4.

11. For disk subsystems, load the DISKSET utility and follow the procedure discussed in "The DISKSET Command."

12. Load INSTALL, and then refer to the following sections in this chapter as needed:

Testing Disks

Formatting Disks

Partitioning Disks

Altering the Hot Fix Area

Mirroring and Unmirroring Disks

Managing Volumes

Testing Disks

You can run a surface test on a hard disk to test for bad blocks. Run the test in the background so you can work on other disks. Normally the test should be run after hours or when there is no activity on the server. Tests can be either *destructive* or *nondestructive*. A nondestructive test can be performed on a drive that has data; it performs reads and writes to thoroughly test the surface, but restores data intact. The destructive test takes less time than the nondestructive test but destroys data on the disk. It should be run only on new disks or disks in which the data can be restored.

Follow these steps to test a hard drive:

1. Dismount any volumes on the hard drive with the following command, replacing *volume* with the name of volumes to dismount:

   DISMOUNT *volume*

2. Load the INSTALL module by typing **LOAD INSTALL**.

3. Select **Disk Options** from the main menu, and then select **Surface test** from the Available Disk Options menu.

4. Select the disk to test if more than one exists. The Disk Surface Test Status window appears, which displays information about the test. The Test Type field may show None, Failed, Completed, Terminated, Destructive, or Nondestructive.

5. Select **Begin Surface Test** from the menu. When asked for the type of test to run, you can choose either destructive or nondestructive.

The test may run for some time. If you stop the test, "Terminated" appears in the status window. If you need to perform other work such as testing other hard drives, press ESC to move to the other options in INSTALL, or press ALT-ESC to go to the console prompt.

Formatting Disks

Most modern drives are already formatted by the manufacturer; however, the manufacturer may recommend formatting for some drives, or a new format may be required if a disk controller has been changed. Drives that may be unreliable can be formatted to make them usable.

Before formatting a drive, you must make sure that all users are logged out. Use the SEND command to alert users, and then use the DISABLE LOGIN console command as discussed in Chapter 34 to prevent further login. Before proceeding, back up any data on the drive using NBACKUP or other utilities. Follow these steps to continue:

1. Dismount the drive using the command **DISMOUNT** *volume*, where *volume* is the name of the volume to dismount. Repeat this step for every volume that uses the drive.

2. Load the INSTALL module by typing **LOAD INSTALL**.

3. Unmirror the hard drive if necessary, and then delete the volumes on the hard disk. Refer to "Mirroring and Unmirroring Disks" and "Managing Volumes" later in this chapter.

4. Select **Disk Options** from the INSTALL Installation Options menu, and then select **Format** from the Available Disk Options menu. If more than one hard disk exists, select the hard disk to format from the Available Disk Drives list.

5. Select **Format Disk Drive** from the Format Options menu to proceed with the format.

6. Enter the interleave factor. The default is 2, but you should refer to the disk's documentation for information.

7. If the format is successful, recreate a NetWare partition on the drive, mirror the drive if necessary, and then create a volume on the drive or add it to an existing segment.

Partitioning Disks

Partitions are divisions of hard drives set aside for a particular operating system, as discussed in Chapter 15. Use the INSTALL loadable module at the console to create or remove a partition from a disk, as discussed in the following sections.

Creating Partitions

To create a disk partition, load the INSTALL utility in the normal way by typing **LOAD INSTALL** at the console prompt. When the Installation Options menu appears, select **Disk Options** and follow these steps:

1. Select **Partition Tables** from the Available Disk Options menu.

2. If multiple disks exist, select the disk to partition from the Available Disk Drives menu.

3. A screen similar to Figure 35-1 appears. Partitions are divided into cylinders, as discussed in Chapter 15. The size of a partition is shown by its starting and ending cylinder.

4. Select **Create NetWare Partition** from the Partition Options menu. The Partition Information screen similar to that shown in Figure 35-2 appears. NetWare automatically assigns all free space to its partition, with 2 percent of that space allocated to the Hot Fix redirection area.

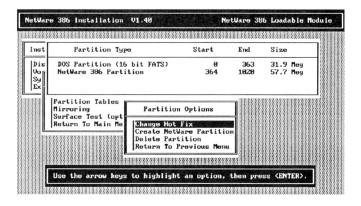

Figure 35-1.   The Partition Tables menu

5. To resize the partition, enter a new size in the Partition Size field.

6. Enter the number of blocks in either the Data Area or Redirection Area field. Any remaining space is automatically assigned to the other field.

7. When done, press ESC and select **Yes** to create the partition.

Deleting Partitions

Partitions are deleted when a disk used for another operating system is used for NetWare or you need to reconfigure the size of a partition because the Hot Fix redirection area has been used completely. Before deleting any partition, make sure you have good backups of the data.

Load the INSTALL module in the normal way at the console and follow these steps to remove a partition:

1. Unmirror the drive if necessary, as described in "Mirroring and Unmirroring Disks" later in this chapter. If the unmirrored disk is labeled "Not Mirrored," delete the volumes on the partition, as discussed under "Managing Volumes."

2. Select **Disk Options** from the Installation Options menu, and then select **Partition Tables** from the Available Disk Options menu.

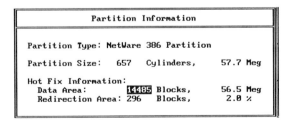

Figure 35-2.   The Partition Information screen

3. Select the hard disk with the partition to delete from the list if more than one drive exists.

4. Select **Delete Partition** from the Partition Options menu, and then select a partition to delete, if more than one exists.

5. Press ESC to delete the partition.

Altering the Hot Fix Area

If it is necessary to change the size of the Hot Fix redirection area, follow these steps:

1. Back up any data on the disk because the partition will be reconfigured and data will be lost.

2. Load the INSTALL module by typing **LOAD INSTALL** at the console.

3. Unmirror the disk if necessary, as described in "Mirroring and Unmirroring Disks" later in this chapter. If the unmirrored disk is labeled "Not Mirrored," delete the volumes on the partition, as discussed under "Managing Volumes."

4. Select **Disk Options** from the Installation Options menu, and then select **Partition Tables** from the Available Disk Options menu.

5. Select the hard disk with the partition to delete from the list, if more than one drive exists.

6. Select **Change Hot Fix** from the Partition Options menu. The Partition Information screen appears.

7. Enter the number of blocks in either the Data Area or Redirection Area field. Any remaining space is automatically assigned to the other field. Make sure at least 2 percent is assigned to the Redirection Area field.

8. Press ESC and select **Yes** to change the Hot Fix area and the partition.

9. If the disk is mirrored, repeat steps 3 through 8 for the other hard disk in the pair.

10. Remirror the hard drives, recreate the volumes, and restore the files and directories.

Mirroring and Unmirroring Disks

Mirroring duplicates the information in a partition on one disk to a partition on another disk for backup purposes. If the primary disk fails, the secondary disk can be used to establish a new primary disk. Mirrored hard disks should have partition sizes within a few megabytes of each other. When NetWare mirrors the drives, they are made exactly the same size, and any extra space on one drive is lost.

Mirroring Hard Drives

Follow these steps to establish a mirrored pair:

1. Load the INSTALL module by typing **LOAD INSTALL** at the console prompt.

2. Select **Disk Options** from the main menu.

3. Select **Mirroring** from the Available Disk Options menu.

4. The status window appears showing one of the following conditions for each partition:

   - *Not Mirrored*   The partition is not currently mirrored to another partition.

   - *Mirrored*   The partition is currently mirrored to another partition.

   - *Out of Sync*   The partition was mirrored to another partition, but is currently unmirrored from that partition.

5. Select one of the partitions to be the primary partition in the mirrored pair.

6. Press INS to select a hard disk to be the secondary hard disk in the mirrored set.

NetWare proceeds to synchronize the partitions. When the mirroring process is complete, the status of both disks should appear as In Sync.

Unmirroring Hard Disks

Disks may be unmirrored if it is necessary to delete a partition, conduct a surface test, or change the Hot Fix redirection area. Follow this procedure to unmirror disks:

1. Load the INSTALL module by typing **LOAD INSTALL** at the console prompt.

2. Select **Disk Options** from the main menu.

3. Select **Mirroring** from the Available Disk Options menu.

4. Select the mirrored partition you want to unmirror from the Partition Mirroring Status list.

5. Highlight the hard disk to unmirror in the Mirrored NetWare Partitions list, and press DEL.

6. You can now replace the drive or perform other actions as discussed in the previous sections.

Managing Volumes

The following sections explain the options and commands for managing volumes. You can view the currently mounted volumes with the VOLUMES command.

Creating Volumes

Volumes must exist on hard drives before they can be used for file storage. Volumes are created within the partitions of hard drives. Up to 64 volumes may exist on a NetWare 386 file server. The operating system uses the initial volume SYS as a storage area for its commands and utilities. Other volumes can be created to store files from specific applications or files from other operating systems such as the Macintosh. Chapter 15 discusses volumes in more detail.

To create a volume, follow these steps. (It is assumed the disk has been installed and partitioned as described in the previous sections.)

1. Load the INSTALL module at the console, and select **Volume Options** from the main menu.

2. When the Volumes list appears, press INS. If multiple hard disks are installed and have available space, you can select the disk on which you want to create the volume. The New Volume Information screen appears.

3. To name the new volume, highlight the Volume Name field and type a name.

4. Press ENTER to move to the next field, and enter a block size. Refer to the discussion of volumes in Chapter 15 for information on defining block sizes.

5. Press DOWN ARROW to get to the Initial Segment Size field. Volumes may span several drives, as discussed in Chapter 15. To use the entire drive, leave the field as is. To establish a special segment size, use the following formula:

   size-in-MB(1024/*block-size*)=block segment size

   where *size-in-MB* is the size you want the volume segment to be in megabytes, and *block-size* is the block size you specified in step 4. For example, the following calculates the number to insert in the Segment Size field when a 25MB segment with a block size of 4 is required.

   25(1024/4)=6400

6. Press ESC and select **Yes** at the prompt to create the volume specified.

7. Highlight the new volume name and press ENTER to return to the Volume Information screen. Highlight the Status field and press ENTER. Select **Mount Volume** to mount the volume, or refer to the next section.

Mounting and Dismounting Volumes

After you create a volume, you can use the MOUNT console command to make it available for use. If you are in the INSTALL utility, press ALT-ESC to switch to the console mode and type the MOUNT command in the following form:

MOUNT *volume*

where *volume* is the name of the volume, or enter **ALL** to mount all volumes.

Note: You can view which volumes are currently mounted by typing **VOLUME** at the console.

The console DISMOUNT command makes volumes unavailable to users so you can perform maintenance and upgrades. Be sure to use the SEND command to warn users before dismounting a volume. To dismount a volume, issue this command:

DISMOUNT *volume*

where *volume* is the name of the volume to dismount.

Expanding a Volume

You may need to increase the size of a volume as more information is stored on it. Since volumes can have multiple segments, expanding a volume is a simple matter of adding a new drive and creating a segment on the drive that becomes part of an existing volume. The segments must be duplicated on mirrored drives. The following limitations exist:

- Volumes are limited to 32 segments.

- A single hard disk can have 8 segments.

- The maximum number of volumes is 64.

- Segments can be added but not removed without destroying data.

Increase a volume by adding a new volume segment on the same hard disk as the volume, or by installing a new hard drive and creating a segment on the drive for the volume. Follow these steps to increase the size of a volume:

1. Load INSTALL and select **Volume Options** from the main menu.

2. From the Volumes list, select the volume to expand. The Volume Information screen appears.

3. Select the **Volume Segments** field to display a list of current segments.

4. Press INS to select a free area of disk for the segment. If more than one free area exists, you can pick from a list. If no free area exists, nothing happens (refer to the previous sections on installing drives).

5. Type the number of blocks for the new volume segment, and press ENTER. Use the formula in step 5 of "Creating Volumes" to calculate the segment sizes. The default is the whole area.

6. Select **Yes** at the prompt to add a new segment.

Deleting Volumes

To delete a volume, first make sure no one has files open on the volume, and back up any data to be saved. Then follow these steps:

1. Load the INSTALL module and select **Volume Options** from the Installation Options menu.

2. Select the volume to delete, and then highlight the Status Field and press ENTER.

3. Select **Dismount Volume** and press ESC to return to the Volumes list.

4. Highlight the volume, press DEL to remove it, and then select **Yes** at the prompt.

Disk Options Available in MONITOR

Disk options can be accessed by loading the MONITOR utility at the file server console or remote console. When the Available Options menu appears, select **Disk Information** to select a disk drive. The Drive Status screen appears, and you then can change one of the options described in the following sections.

Changing the Read After Write
Verify Status of a Disk

The Read After Write Verify option ensures that data written to disk matches the information in memory. Most disk drives support this feature. There may be a need to change the status to one of the following options. Select **Read After Write Verify** from the Drive Status screen to change the settings.

- *Software Level Verify* Selects the driver to perform the read-after-write verification.

- *Hardware Level Verify* Selects the controller to perform the read-after-write verification.

- *Disable Verify* Disables both driver and controller read-after-write verification and is used if the hard disk performs read-after-write internally. Check the hard disk's specification for details.

Flashing the Hard Disk Light

It may be necessary to physically identify which hard disk corresponds to the drive listed in the System Disk Drives window. The disk light can be set to flash at a time interval by selecting **Drive Light Status** from the Drive Status menu. Select **Flash Light** from the Drive Light Status screen. Some drives may display a "Not Supported" message, preventing the option from being used. To return the status to normal, select **Return to Normal**.

Activating or Deactivating a Hard Disk

You can set drives to active or inactive status by selecting **Drive Operating Status** from the Drive Status screen. When the Operating Status screen appears, select one of the following options:

- *Activate Drive*   Sets the drive to active, and displays information in the information window about the drive when it is selected.

- *Deactivate Drive*   Sets a drive to inactive, and removes information about the drive from the status window.

Mounting and Dismounting Removable Media

Removable media must be mounted and dismounted before it can be used. The driver for the disk must support removable media. Select **Removable Drive Mount Status** from the Drive Status window, and then select one of these options:

- *Mount Drive*   Mounts the media.

- *Dismount Drive*   Dismounts the media.

Locking or Unlocking
A Removable Media Device

The Removable Drive Lock Status option is used to lock or unlock a removable media to prevent the media from being physically removed. The driver must support this option. Select the **Removable Drive Lock Status** option from the Drive Status screen, and choose one of the following options:

- *Lock Drive* Locks the media so it cannot be removed from the device.

- *Unlock Drive*   Unlocks the media so it can be removed.

Repairing Volumes with VREPAIR

The VREPAIR utility corrects minor hard disk problems at the volume level, which means that the utility affects only the volumes you specify. If the primary file allocation table (FAT) or directory table becomes corrupted, VREPAIR compares the primary tables with their mirrored counterparts and makes corrections if necessary. VREPAIR may be required in the following situations.

Note: Do not use the NetWare 3.1 version of VREPAIR with a NetWare 3.0 version of the operating system.

- A hardware failure prevents a disk from mounting.

- Disk read and write errors are occurring.

- A power failure has corrupted a volume.

- A mirroring error occurs when the server boots.

- If a name space is loaded and there is not enough memory for the name space, VREPAIR returns volume tables to the size they were before the name space support was added (see the next section for more information on name space).

Note: Make sure a copy of VREPAIR.NLM is on the hard disk boot partition or floppy boot disk so the SYS volume can be repaired if it fails to boot.

In most cases you cannot mount a volume that requires VREPAIR, but if it is mounted, type **DISMOUNT** *volume,* replacing *volume* with the name of the volume. If the SYS volume is dismounted, you must run VREPAIR from the boot drive or floppy disk or place the NetWare 386 Operating System-1 disk into drive A. Type the VREPAIR command at the console in the following form:

LOAD *path*\VREPAIR

where *path* is the directory where VREPAIR.NLM exists if it is not in the SYS:SYSTEM directory.

Select the number 2 option to set VREPAIR options. The current settings are listed at the top of the screen, and other possible settings are listed and numbered at the bottom. Typing a numbered entry causes the current setting to change. You can switch between the following options by typing the appropriate numbered selection:

- *Remove All Name Space Entries / Retain Name Space Information* This option relates to name space support, as discussed in the next section. If name space failed to load because there was not enough memory, select **Remove All Name Space Entries** to return the volume tables to the size they were before the name space support was added. Removing the name space removes all information about the files supported by the name space.

- *Write Only Changed Directory and FAT Entries Out to Disk / Write All Directory and FAT Entries Out to Disk* The first time an attempt is made to repair a volume, choose to write only the changes. If the first attempt does not work, choose to write all to disk. Do not use this option if the file server crashed during the updating of important files. Contact your dealer or Novell advanced technical support for more information.

* *Keep Changes in Memory for Later Update / Write Changes Immediately to Disk*   If only a few errors exist, VREPAIR can run faster if changes are saved in memory, and then written to disk afterward. Do not use this method if you must make over 1000 changes. Instead, turn on the Write Changes Immediately to Disk option.

After selecting one of the options, return to the main menu and choose **Repair a Volume** from the Available Options menu. If more than one volume has been mounted, select the volume to be repaired. You can press F1 to change the current repair settings described here:

* Option 1 pauses VREPAIR after each error to let you view a screen that describes the error.

* Option 2 logs all errors in a text file. Any errors found are written to a file you specify. The repaired files may no longer be valid and may need to be restored from a backup.

When VREPAIR is done, a screen appears to display the number of FAT and directory repairs. Select **Yes** to write the repairs to disk, and press any key to return to the Options menu. Type **0** to exit VREPAIR. If the volume cannot be mounted, you must delete the volume, recreate it using INSTALL, and restore data to it from backup.

Supporting Non-DOS Files (Name Space)

Non-DOS files are those created by workstations such as the Macintosh. To support these files, a name space loadable module must be linked with the operating system. Name space modules have the extension NAM and are loaded at the server with the LOAD command. Once you load the module, use the ADD NAME SPACE command to configure the volume(s) so you can store the files. Name space support creates an additional entry in a directory table to hold the filenaming conventions of non-DOS files. Note that NetWare 386 supports OS/2 files without the need to load name space support.

If name space is already installed, you can type **ADD NAME SPACE** to view the current configuration.

Each volume configured for name space support requires extra memory. Although you can add name space support to a volume, the volume may not mount if enough memory is not available. To install the name space, add more memory to the server.

Loading Name Space Support

Use the LOAD command at the server to load the name space module. The command takes the following form:

LOAD *namespace*

where *namespace* is the name of the name space module, which is assumed to be stored in the SYS:SYSTEM directory. If the module is in another directory, specify the path before *namespace*. The name space module for Macintosh support is MAC.NAM, so you would type **LOAD MAC** to install Macintosh support.

Note: You may want to add the LOAD command to the NetWare startup files. If the SYS volume has a name space, add the command to the STARTUP.NCF file (type **LOAD INSTALL** at the server and select **System Options** from the menu). If a volume besides SYS has a name space, add the command to the AUTOEXEC.NCF file.

Adding Name Space to a Volume

After loading a name space with the LOAD command, use the ADD NAME SPACE command at the console to specify the volume that will support non-DOS files. The command takes the following form:

ADD NAME SPACE *name* TO *volume*

where *name* is the name of the variable for the name space module loaded at the server (MACINTOSH, for example), and *volume* is the name of the server volume.

Note: It is not recommended that you add name space to the SYS volume. Instead, create a volume especially for files from the non-DOS operating system.

Running MACINST
For Macintosh Workstations

You can use the MACINST utility to install AppleTalk driver support for the Macintosh. Run the MACINST utility to specify the server as a target file server. Refer to the *NetWare for Macintosh: Installation Supplement* for more detailed instructions.

Upgrading Name Space

It may be necessary to upgrade a name space module if the manufacturer produces a new version. You can update the module without downing the server. However, if the SYS volume is using the name space, or if SECURE CONSOLE or REMOVE DOS commands have been used, you must down the file server, copy the updated module to the file server boot directory, and then reboot the file server.

To update the name space module without downing the server, follow these steps:

1. Back up the data on all volumes that use the name space module.

2. Dismount all volumes that use the name space module.

3. Type **UNLOAD *namespace*** to unload the name space module, replacing *namespace* with the name of the module.

4. Copy the new module from its floppy disk to the directory that holds the existing module.

5. Load the new module by typing **LOAD *namespace***, replacing *namespace* with the name of the module.

6. Remount the volumes by typing **MOUNT ALL**.

Managing the LAN
And Cable System

This section provides managers with the information they need to view, monitor, install, remove, and make other changes to the network interface cards and drivers. When a new LAN card is installed, you must load its driver with the LOAD command. Then you must bind a communications protocol to the driver with the BIND command. To remove a card you reverse the process. The following sections provide details on using these commands with the drivers and protocols supplied with NetWare or those supplied with third-party network hardware.

Viewing LAN Information

You can view information about the LAN configuration with the CONFIG command, which displays the network number and LAN drivers currently installed. You also can view information about LAN drivers with the MONITOR loadable module, as described in Chapter 34. The DISPLAY NETWORKS command also displays useful information about networks attached to a server.

Adding and Removing LAN Cards

You can install a number of interface cards in a NetWare server, but it is important to avoid conflicts between interrupts and I/O ports. NetWare also allows you to install more than one of the same type of network interface card, but each card must have different settings. Keep in mind that interface cards are not the only components that use interrupts and I/O addresses. Use Table 35-1 to avoid conflicts when installing cards. The CONFIG command shows you the settings of existing boards so you can set new boards appropriately.

Note: If more than 16MB of memory is installed in the server, use caution when installing AT bus master disk adapter boards or boards that use on-line DMA. Such boards can only address up to 16MB of memory and can cause corruption of the file server's memory. The 3COM 3C505 ISA board is an example. If the board is an EISA board, refer to Chapter

Device/Resource	I/O	Int
Disk controllers		
AT hard disk	1F0-1F8	14
Floppy disk	3F0-3F7	6
Monochrome adapter	3B0-3BF	
Hercules mono adapter	3B4-3BF	
Color graphics adapter	3D0-3DF	
EGA adapter	3C0-3CF	2
VGA adapter	102, 46E8	
COMM1	3F8-3FF	4
COMM2	2F8-2FF	3
LPT1	378-37F	7
LPT2	278-27F	5
If LPT3 is used:		
LPT1	3BC-3BE	7
LPT2	378-37A	5
LPT3	278-27A	

Table 35-1.   Common Base I/O Addresses and Interrupts

36. If the server is an ISA or MCA system, remove the REGISTER MEMORY command from the AUTOEXEC.NCF file and reboot the file server.

Here are some tips on installing boards in EISA and MCA systems:

- *EISA systems* If the server is an EISA system, copy the *.CFG files from the disk that came with the board to the CONFIGURA-TION disk used to configure the server. Then configure the board with the EISA configuration utility.

- *MCA systems* If the server is a Micro Channel architecture system, copy the *.ADF files from the disk that came with the board to the setup or reference disk for the file server. Then run the setup or reference program. If RX-Net boards are used, the node address must not be 0.

The LOAD and BIND commands are used when installing a card and configuring it to the operating system. The UNBIND and UNLOAD com-

mands are used when removing a card from the server. These commands
are covered in the next few sections.

Loading LAN Drivers

NetWare supplies a number of LAN driver modules to provide support for
several common network cards. They are loaded with the LOAD command
at the console. The commands can be placed in the startup files so they will
execute every time the server starts. As the LAN drivers are loaded, default
I/O ports and interrupt settings may be suggested, or you may be prompted
to enter them. You can use the parameters listed later in this chapter to
specify the settings in advance. Parameters are usually specified when the
LAN drivers' LOAD commands are placed in the startup files.

The LAN driver LOAD command takes the following form:

LOAD *path\driver parameters*

where *path* is the driver and/or directory where the driver can be located
if it is not in the SYS:SYSTEM directory. Replace *driver* with one of the
drivers listed in this section, and replace *parameters* with one of the options
discussed in the next section, "Specifying LAN Driver Options."

The following drivers ship with NetWare 386 version 3.1. Others will
ship with future versions or can be obtained from Novell or third-party
sources. To list the drivers available on the NetWare 386 Operating
System-2 disk, specify the *.LAN options with the DIR command.

TRXNET.LAN	Novell RX-Net, RX-Net II, and RX-Net/2 ARC-NET driver
3C503.LAN	3COM EtherLink II - ASSY 2227 driver
3C505.LAN	3COM EtherLink Plus - ASSY 2012 driver
3C523.LAN	3COM EtherLink/MC driver
NE2.LAN	Novell NE/2 Ethernet driver
NE232.LAN	Novell NE/2 32-bit Ethernet driver

NE1000.LAN	Novell NE1000 Ethernet driver
NE2000.LAN	Novell NE2000 Ethernet driver
NE3200.LAN	Novell NE3200 Ethernet driver
TOKEN.LAN	Driver for IBM Token Ring adapters

Note: Token Ring adapters must be attached to the multistation access unit (MAU) before the Token driver can load.

Specifying LAN Driver Options

You can specify the following parameters with the LOAD command when installing LAN drivers at the console, or more importantly when including the commands in the startup files. Some of the parameters are read directly from the LAN boards, so you should accept the suggested settings. However, you can use the options to "force" some settings.

DMA=#	Replace # with a DMA channel to reserve for the driver.
INT=#	Replace # with the hardware interrupt set on the board. Some ISA drivers prompt for this parameter. For MCA and EISA boards, the parameters are set with the reference disk that comes with the computer.
MEM=#	Replace # with the memory address to reserve for the driver. Some ISA drivers prompt for this parameter. For MCA and EISA boards, the parameters are set with the reference disk that comes with the computer.
PORT=#	Replace # with the I/O port to reserve for the driver. Some ISA drivers prompt for this parameter. For MCA and EISA boards, the parameters are set with the reference disk that comes with the computer.

SLOT=#	On microchannel and EISA machines, replace # with the number of the slot in which the board is installed.
NAME=*boardname*	Assigns a unique name to a board's configuration so you can identify the board more easily when multiple boards of the same type are installed. *Boardname* can be as long as 17 characters.
FRAME=*string*	Replace *string* with the type of packet header to use with NetWare. The default for Ethernet is **Ethernet_802.3**, and the default for Token Ring is **Token-Ring**. Other standards are discussed under "Frame Formats."
NODE=#	Replace # with a node address that overrides the one set on the board, if the driver supports the change. Use this option only if you know the node address does not conflict with any other on the network.
RETRIES=#	Replace # with the number of retries to perform when a packet transmission fails. This optional parameter can be modified only at the command line when the driver is loaded.
LS=#	Sets the number of 802.2 link stations for the Token Ring driver. This optional parameter can be modified only at the command line when the driver is loaded.
SAPS=#	Sets the 802.2 service access point stations for Token Ring. This optional parameter can be modified only at the command line when the driver is loaded.
TBC=#	Sets the transmit buffer count for Token Ring. This optional parameter can be modified only at the command line when the driver is loaded.

TBZ=#   Sets the transmit buffer size for Token Ring. The default assigns the maximum packet size allowed by either the board or the operating system. This optional parameter can be modified only at the command line when the driver is loaded.

Frame Formats

Different types of packet headers can be specified with Ethernet and Token Ring drivers using the FRAME parameter just discussed. The type of frame you use depends on the communications protocol used on the network. All workstations must be set to the same standard or be able to support it along with others. The *string* parameter in FRAME can be replaced with one of the following:

Ethernet_802.3   The default frame type for Ethernet. It assigns the standard Novell frame and should be used on networks that use only NetWare.

Ethernet_II   Assigns a unique packet header that is used on networks connected to DEC or to computers using the TCP/IP protocol.

Ethernet_802.2   Assigns the IEEE and OSI standard frame type.

Ethernet_Snap   Use on networks that need to communicate with TCP/IP.

Token-Ring   The default frame type for Token Ring. It assigns the standard packet header 802.2 for use on an all-IBM network.

Token-Ring_Snap   Assigns the 802.2 with SNAP header for use on networks that need to communicate with protocols such as AppleTalk and TCP/IP.

If a name other than Ethernet_802.3 or Token-Ring is specified, workstations must be configured to match the frame type. If you use

Ethernet_Snap, Ethernet_802.2, or Token-Ring_Snap, you must use the DOS ODI drivers discussed in Appendix H.

Loading the Network Management Agent (NMAGENT)

Before loading LAN drivers, the NMAGENT module must be loaded to allow LAN drivers to register and pass network management parameters that can be viewed by the MONITOR module. NMAGENT registers three resources for tracking:

- Network management triggers

- Network management managers

- Network management objects

Type the following to load the module:

LOAD *path*\NMAGENT

If NMAGENT is not in the SYS:SYSTEM directory, replace *path* with the name of the directory where it is located.

LOAD LAN Driver Commands

Type the following to load the LAN driver for the network interface cards in your system. Replace *driver-name* with the name of the driver.

LOAD *driver-name*

You will be asked for interrupt, memory, and I/O port information as the driver is loaded, if it is required. To specify the information in advance, use the LOAD command parameters described earlier. Once the driver is loaded, you must bind a communications protocol to it as described under "Binding and Unbinding Protocols to Drivers." If you want the LOAD command to execute every time the server boots, include the LOAD command with appropriate options in the AUTOEXEC.NCF file, as discussed in Chapter 33.

As an example, the following specifies an interrupt of 3 and a memory address of C0000 for the Novell TRXNET driver:

```
LOAD TRXNET INT=3 MEM=C0000
```

Problems may occur on some LAN cards if they are not attached to the cabling system. Token Ring cards must be attached to the multistation access unit (MAU). If conflicts exist, the driver will not load. You must reconfigure the board to a different setting and try again. Once the board loads, bind it to a communications protocol as discussed under "Binding and Unbinding Protocols to Drivers."

If you need to change the parameters of a driver or upgrade the driver to a new version, refer to "Unbinding and Unloading Drivers" later in this chapter.

Installing and Registering Protocols (PROTOCOL)

This section applies to servers that are running communication protocols other than IPX. Use PROTOCOL to view the protocols registered on the file server, and use PROTOCOL REGISTER to register a new protocol for use by a LAN driver. The IPX protocol does not need to be registered because it is automatically registered with the operating system. Make sure any protocols you use are approved by Novell.

The command takes the following forms:

PROTOCOL

PROTOCOL REGISTER *protocol frame id#*

PROTOCOL by itself lists the currently installed protocols. To register a new protocol use the second example and replace *protocol* with the protocol name, and *frame* with the name representing the frame type that is to be bound to the communication protocol. This information is in the protocol module's documentation. Replace *id#* with the protocol identification (PID) number. This is a unique hexadecimal number that tells the server how to recognize data coming from a certain network board through a designated communication protocol such as IPX. The PID number is in the protocol documentation, or look for an SAP number in IBM documentation.

Binding and Unbinding Protocols to Drivers

The console BIND command links LAN drivers to a communication protocol such as IPX. Packets cannot be processed until the protocol link has been established. Before this step can take place, the LAN card must be installed in the server and the driver must be loaded with the LOAD command, as described under "Loading and Unloading LAN Drivers." The command takes the following form:

BIND *protocol* TO *name parameters*

where *protocol* is the name of the protocol to bind, and *name* is either the name of the previously loaded driver or the board name you assigned when loading the driver. The protocol IPX is always available. Other protocols need to be registered with NetWare before they can be bound to a driver, as discussed under "Installing and Registering Protocols (PROTOCOL)."

If you have more than one network board of the same type in the file server, you must supply the interrupt address, DMA channel, and other information when binding the card. If you do not supply the information on the command line, you are asked for it. Include the following parameters in the startup file so you are not prompted for the information every time the server starts. Not all parameters need to be specified.

DMA=#	Replace # with a DMA channel to reserve for the driver.
INT=#	Replace # with the hardware interrupt set on the board.
MEM=#	Replace # with the memory address to reserve for the driver.

PORT=#   Replace # with the I/O port to reserve for the driver.

SLOT=#   On microchannel machines, replace # with the number of the slot in which the board is installed.

FRAME=*string*   Either replace *string* with Ethernet_802.3 or Ethernet_II, depending on the type of packet header to use. Refer to "Loading and Unloading LAN Drivers" for a list of frame types.

NET-#   Replace # with a unique network number for the cabling system attached to the board when using the IPX protocol. If multiple boards are installed, each must have a different number.

Use the UNBIND command in the same way as the BIND command to remove a communications protocol from the LAN driver of a network board. The command takes the form shown here, and you can specify the parameters just described.

UNBIND *protocol* FROM *name parameters*

For example, the following command binds IPX to the NE2000 board:

BIND IPX TO NE2000

To unbind the IPX protocol from the NE2000 board, you would type the following command:

UNBIND IPX FROM NE2000

The LOAD command allows boards to be assigned names as a way to differentiate one from the other. The next example assumes that the name ACCTG was assigned to a LAN card with the LOAD command (using the NAME parameter). IPX is bound to the ACCTG interface card.

BIND IPX TO ACCTG

The BIND command should be included in the AUTOEXEC.NCF file so binding occurs every time the network starts. Specify parameters on the command lines so you or other operators do not have to specify them every time the server starts. In the following example, IPX is bound to the NE2000 board and the port, interrupt, frame, and network number parameters are specified.

BIND IPX TO NE2000 PORT=340 INT=4 FRAME=ETHERNET_802.3 NET=26

Unbinding and Unloading Drivers

It may be necessary to remove a communication protocol from a card or remove a driver from a card. This is the case if the protocol or driver has been updated, or if the card needs to be removed from the server. You can also change the cable number of a network by unbinding the protocol from the driver and then binding it again with a new network number. The UNBIND command is used to unbind a communication protocol from a driver, and the UNLOAD command removes a driver from a card. UN-LOAD automatically unbinds a protocol.

The UNBIND command takes the following form:

UNBIND *protocol driver parameter*

where *protocol* is the name of the protocol, and *driver* is the name of the LAN driver. Specify parameters if more than one network board of the same type is installed in the server. The parameters help identify exactly which board you want to unbind.

The UNLOAD command takes the following form:

UNLOAD *driver*

where *driver* is the name of the LAN driver to unload. If two cards of the same type are installed, use the UNBIND command instead of UNLOAD.

Installing Token Ring Remote Boot Support (TOKENRPL)

The Token Remote Program Load (TOKENRPL) loadable module is used to enable remote booting of diskless workstations that use Token Ring network interface cards. Follow these procedures to remotely boot a diskless workstation that uses a Token Ring network interface card:

1. Load TOKENRPL with the command

   LOAD *path*\TOKENRPL

   where *path* is the name of the directory that holds the file TOKENRPL.NLM if it is not in SYS:SYSTEM.

2. Bind the TOKRPL protocol to the network boards in the file server with the command

   BIND TOKRPL *driver*

   where *driver* is the name of the LAN driver. If a driver is loaded more than once, repeat this step for the second card.

3. Configure the workstation to boot from the boot file on the server, using the DOSGEN program discussed in Chapter 18.

You also should add these commands to the AUTOEXEC.NCF file so they execute every time the server starts. Be sure to include after the BIND command any parameters required by the board. Parameters can be found in the section "Binding and Unbinding Protocols to Drivers." Refer to Chapter 33 for more information.

Managing Token Ring Bridges With ROUTE

The ROUTE loadable module is used to allow NetWare to pass frames through bridges on an IBM Token Ring network. Frames that pass through an IBM bridge must have source routing information added to the frame header at the media access control (MAC) layer of the protocol stack. NetWare's bridging is normally done above this layer. The ROUTE.NLM module enables NetWare to track source routing information and to configure the information according to the parameters listed below. ROUTE needs to be loaded for each Token Ring board in the file server. Use the BOARD parameter to specify a second board.

The ROUTE module is loaded using the command

LOAD *path*\ROUTE *parameters*

where *path* is the drive and/or directory where ROUTE.NLM is located, if it is not in the SYS:SYSTEM directory.

The following parameters for the ROUTE module are all optional because default values can be used to configure simple bridges. If redundant bridges are installed, the parameters can be used to reduce traffic on some paths. For more information refer to the IBM publication *IBM Token Ring Network Architecture Reference*.

- *BOARD = number* Use this parameter to specify board number 2 if two boards are being loaded. If you need to change parameters on the second board, use this option to specify that you want to work on the second board.

- *CLEAR* This parameter manually clears the source routing table and forces the table to be rebuilt. Use this parameter to build a new route when a bridge has gone down and an alternate route is available.

- *DEF (Default)* Prevents frames with unknown destination addresses from crossing single route IBM bridges. If DEF is specified, frames without addresses in the source routing table are forwarded as all routes broadcast (ARB) frames. If DEF is not specified, frames without addresses in the source routing table are forwarded as single route broadcast (SRB) frames. If DEF has been used to specify ARB frames, using the parameter again specifies SRB frames.

- *GBR (General Broadcast)* Use this parameter to specify that all general broadcast frames are to be sent as ARB frames. If the parameter is not specified when ROUTE is loaded, all GBR frames are broadcast as SRB frames. If ROUTE has been previously used with GBR, using it again specifies ARB frames.

- *MBR (Multicast Broadcast)* Use this parameter to specify that all multicast broadcast frames are to be sent as ARB frames. If the parameter is not specified when ROUTE is loaded, all MBR frames are broadcast as SRB frames. If ROUTE has been previously used with MBR, using it again specifies ARB frames.

- *REMOVE = number* Use this parameter to remove a specified node address from the file server's source routing table, such as when a bridge has gone down. An alternate route is found. Replace *number* with a 12-digit hexadecimal number. If less than 9 digits are entered, ROUTE prefixes the address with 4000h.

- *RSP = value* Use this parameter to specify how the file server should respond to broadcast requests. Replace *value* with NR (indicating a response is not required), AR (to respond with an all routes broadcast frame), or SR (to respond with a single route broadcast frame). The default is NR.

- *TIME = number* Use this parameter to set the update interval for the routing table. The values for *number* are 3 to 255 seconds, with a default value of 3.

Tracking Router Information With TRACK ON

The TRACK ON console command displays the Router Tracking screen, which includes all network packet information coming into or going out of the server. Type **TRACK ON** to initiate tracking.

TRACK ON displays server, network, and connection requests. The information is listed on the screen as either IN, which indicates incoming information, or OUT, which indicates outgoing information. The sending or receiving network number and node address are also displayed.

To turn tracking off, type **TRACK OFF**.

Solving Router Problems
With RESET ROUTER

A routing table keeps track of interconnected networks and the nodes on them. If a server or bridge in the internetwork goes down, the routing table becomes inaccurate and must be rebuilt. Under normal conditions, the routing table is updated every two minutes to handle such situations. The RESET ROUTER command speeds up the process of rebuilding the table. To rebuild a routing table, type **RESET ROUTER** at the console.

Installing a UPS

The UPS loadable module is used to link an uninterruptible power supply (UPS) with the file server operating system for UPS monitoring. Monitoring allows the UPS to send a signal to the server when it is operating on backup power. The server can then warn users that the server may shut down and they should log off. In a local network environment, a loss of power at the server coincides with a loss of power at workstations, so warning messages are futile unless the workstations are also on battery backup. UPS monitoring is meant for users at remote locations who may not be affected by a power outage and who normally would not be aware that the server was running on battery backup power.

To load the UPS module, type the following command:

LOAD *path*\UPS *parameters*

where *path* is the directory where UPS.NLM can be found if it is in a directory other than SYS:SYSTEM. Replace *parameters* with one of the parameters listed on the next page. If these parameters are not specified, you will be prompted for them. In most cases you should place the LOAD UPS command in the AUTO-EXEC.NCF file so it loads every time the server starts. You therefore must specify the UPS parameters in the file.

- *TYPE=name* Replace *name* with the name of the interface board controlling the UPS. These boards come with special ports or cables for attachment to most UPS systems. Use one of the following names:

DCB	Novell disk coprocessor board (default setting)
EDCB	Novell enhanced disk coprocessor board
STANDALONE	A Novell UPS card
KEYCARD	Old-style serialization card
MOUSE	Mouse port on IBM PS/2 systems
OTHER	

- *PORT=number* Replace *number* with a hexadecimal number corresponding to the jumper setting on the board. This option is not required for the mouse port.

- *DISCHARGE=number* Replace *number* with the time in minutes that the server can run on battery power.

- *RECHARGE=number* Replace *number* with the time in minutes it will take for the battery to recharge after the network has been on battery power.

After the UPS is installed, run a test by logging all users out and unplugging the power line to the UPS. The UPS should begin supplying power to the server, and a message indicating that the server is running on backup power should appear within 20 seconds.

Checking the UPS Status

Use the UPS STATUS command to check the UPS and display information about its current status. Type **UPS STATUS** at the command line to display the UPS Status Information screen. The following information appears:

- *Power being used* This field indicates that UPS is using either commercial or battery power.

- *Discharge time requested / remaining* The first number is an estimate of the time the network can run safely on battery power. The second number is the time remaining if the network is currently on battery power.

- *Battery Status* This field will be either Recharged, Low, or Being Recharged. Repair or replace the battery when Low is indicated.

- *Recharge time requested / remaining* The first number is an estimate of the recharge time after a total discharge. The second number estimates the time needed to recharge; if battery power is being used, this number increases as the battery discharges.

- *Current network power status* One of the following messages is displayed:

Normal   Using commercial power
Server Down   Using battery power
Server going down in *xx* minutes.   The server is using battery power and will shut down in *xx* minutes.

Changing the UPS Time

Use UPS TIME to change the amount of time the server operates on battery power and the estimated time it takes the battery to recharge. Type the command

UPS TIME *discharge=n recharge=n*

where *discharge* and *recharge* are one of the following variables:

- *Discharge = n* Replace *n* with the estimated number of minutes battery power can be supplied to the server.

- *Recharge = n* Replace *n* with the estimated number of minutes required to recharge the battery.

Managing the Operating System Configuration

Altering SERVER Startup
Server Information
Implementing Streams
Memory Configuration
The SET Command

This chapter covers commands for managing the operating system and the network environment. The SET command is covered in particular. It is used both to monitor and to change parameters in the operating system, such as communications settings, memory allocation, and file system options.

Altering SERVER Startup

The commands discussed in this section are used to alter the server environment. Many of the commands are placed in the startup files so they are executed every time the server starts. You can use the options discussed here to prevent the server from reading the startup files. This may be done for testing purposes or due to a need to reconfigure the server.

You can use several options to change the way the server boots. To boot with an alternate STARTUP.NCF file, use the -S option. For example, use this command to load TEMP.NCF instead of STARTUP.NCF:

SERVER -S TEMP.NCF

To boot without using the STARTUP.NCF file, use the NS option, as shown here. You may want to use this when testing a new disk subsystem.

SERVER -NS

To boot without using the AUTOEXEC.NCF file, use the NA option, as in the following command. You may want to do this to test a different cabling system than the one that normally loads.

SERVER -NA

You can specify a different block size for the cache buffer when starting SERVER. This option may be used when a server is dedicated to a special task, such as servicing a database. It is beneficial to increase the block size for database access to reduce the number of disk accesses. For example, to increase the cache buffer block size from the default of 4K to 8K, you would type the following startup command:

SERVER -C8KB

Server Information

The following tasks can be performed to change the settings and parameters of the server.

Changing the Server Name

To change the server name, you must alter the setting of the FILE SERVER NAME command in the AUTOEXEC.NCF file, and then reboot the server through the INSTALL loadable module. At the console, type **LOAD INSTALL**. Select **System Options** from the Installation Options menu, and then select Edit **AUTOEXEC.NCF** file from the Available

System Options menu. Locate the FILE SERVER NAME command and change the name of the server. To initialize the new name, down the server and reboot.

Changing the Internal Network Number

To change the internal network number, you must alter the setting of the IPX INTERNAL NET command in the AUTOEXEC.NCF file, and then reboot the server. This can be done through the INSTALL loadable module. At the console, type **LOAD INSTALL**. Select **System Options** from the Installation Options menu, and then select **Edit AUTOEXEC.NCF file** from the Available System Options menu. Locate the IPX INTERNAL NET command and change the network number. To initialize the new name, down the server and reboot.

Setting the Date and Time

The SET TIME command is used to set the date and time kept by the file server. When you type **SET TIME**, the current setting is displayed. To change the date or time, type **SET TIME *date time***, replacing *date* and *time* with the appropriate values. Enter the date format as mm/dd/yy and the time format in standard or military format with the hours, minutes, and seconds separated by colons.

Setting the Time Zone

The SET TIMEZONE command is used to configure time zone information for the CLIB module. The default value is Eastern Standard Time, or Eastern Daylight Time, which is five hours from Greenwich Mean Time. The command does not automatically change the file server from standard time to daylight time.

Type the command in the following form:

SET TIMEZONE *zone*[*hours*[*daylight*]]

where *zone, hours,* and *daylight* are each one of the following, depending on the time zone. Note that *hours* is the number of hours from Greenwich Mean Time.

Time Zone	Zone	Hours	Daylight
Eastern	EST	5	EST
Central	CST	6	CDT
Mountain	MST	7	MDT
Pacific	PST	8	PDT

The parameters are placed together after the command with no spaces between. For example, to change the time zone for Pacific Daylight Time, you would type the following:

SET TIMEZONE PST8PDT

Displaying the Server's Speed

The SPEED command displays the speed of the processor. Type **SPEED** at the console. Speed ratings are determined by the CPU clock speed, type, and the number of memory wait states. Here are some examples for comparison:

Intel 80386SX at 16MHz	95
Intel 80386 at 16MHz	120
Intel 80386 at 20MHz	136

If a system gets a slower speed rating, check to make sure the CPU speed has not been reduced with an on-board switch or its configuration program.

Enabling and Disabling the Transaction Tracking System (TTS)

The TTS system is automatically enabled when a NetWare 386 server is booted. Some applications developers may want to disable it to test transactional applications. To disable TTS, type **DISABLE TTS** on the console command line. To enable TTS, type **ENABLE TTS** on the console command line.

Repairing the Bindery with BINDFIX

Use the BINDFIX command to repair the *bindery,* which contains information about the users, user groups, queues, accounting charge rates, and other information important to the operation of the network. The bindery information is included in the files NET$OBJ.SYS, NET$VAL.SYS, and NET$PROP.SYS, which are hidden files in the SYS:SYSTEM directory.

You can use the BINDFIX command to correct the bindery files that may be corrupted. Problems such as the inability to delete or modify user names, passwords, and user rights indicate problems with the bindery files that can be repaired with BINDFIX. If errors such as "unknown server" occur during spooling, or if general bindery errors occur, you may need to run BINDFIX.

Before running the utility, make sure all users are logged off the system. BINDFIX shuts down the bindery files so users cannot access them. It then rebuilds the bindery files and reopens them. Each task performed by BINDERY is listed, and you are asked if you want to delete the mail directories and trustee rights of users who have been deleted from the network.

Note: BINDFIX creates new NET$OBJ.SYS, NET$VAL.SYS, and NET$PROP.SYS files. The old files are renamed NET$OBJ.OLD, NET$VAL.OLD, and NET$PROP.OLD. The OLD files can be restored if problems occur while rebuilding the bindery. The BINDREST utility, covered in the next section, restores the original bindery files. Once the new bindery files are in place and working properly, you can remove the OLD files.

To run BINDFIX, type **BINDFIX** while logged into the SYS:SYSTEM directory. The BINDFIX program goes through a series of checks and displays messages on the screen as it does so. You are asked if you want to delete the directories of accounts that no longer exist. These directories branch from the SYS:MAIL directory. You then are asked if you want to delete the trustee rights for the user. If you type **Yes,** BINDFIX scans all mounted volumes and removes users that no longer exist from all trustee lists. Each volume is then checked.

If the BINDFIX command runs successfully, you will see a message that indicates the bindery check is successfully completed. If the command is unsuccessful, the following message appears:

Bindery check NOT successfully completed.

If the BINDFIX command is unsuccessful, you must run the BIND-REST command to return the bindery to its original state.

Restoring the Bindery with BINDREST

The BINDREST command is used to return the NET$OBJ.OLD, NET$VAL.OLD, and NET$PROP.OLD files to their original bindery file status. The command cancels the new bindery files that were unsuccessfully completed and renames the OLD files with the extension SYS. To run the command, type **BINDREST** on the command line in the SYS:SYSTEM directory.

Implementing Streams

The Streams environment provides the mechanism for integration of multiple communication protocols. To implement the environment, add the commands described in the following sections to the AUTOEXEC.NCF file so they are automatically loaded every time the file boots. Load the Streams modules in the following order:

STREAMS

CLIB

TLI

IPXS

Other Streams modules as required

The STREAMS Module

STREAMS is used if a loadable module requires the CLIB loadable module or uses Streams-based protocol services. STREAMS must be loaded before CLIB using this command:

LOAD *path*\STREAMS

where *path* is the path to the directory where CLIB.NLM is stored if it is in a directory other than the SYS:SYSTEM directory.

The C Library (CLIB) Module

The CLIB module is loaded if you have a NetWare loadable module such as PSERVER or BTRIEVE that requires it. CLIB is a library of routines and functions that loadable modules can use, but it must be loaded before the module that requires it. The STREAMS module must be loaded before CLIB.

To load the CLIB module, type the following command:

LOAD *path*\CLIB

where *path* is the path to the directory where CLIB.NLM is stored if it is in a directory other than the SYS:SYSTEM directory.

Transport Level Interface (TLI)

Load the TLI module if a loadable module requires TLI communication services. STREAMS and CLIB must already be loaded before TLI will load. You may also need to load one of the Streams-based NLMs listed in the following sections.

To load the TLI module, type

LOAD *path*\TLI

where *path* is the path to the directory where TLI.NLM is stored if it is in a directory other than the SYS:SYSTEM directory.

Streams-Based IPX (IPXS)

The IPXS loadable module is used if Streams-based IPX protocol services are required. Load the module after the STREAMS module, using the command

LOAD *path*\IPXS

where *path* is the path to the module if it is in a directory other than SYS:SYSTEM.

Streams-Based SPX

The CPS loadable module is used if Streams-based SPX protocol services are required. Load the module after the STREAMS module, using the command

LOAD *path*\CPS

where path is the path to the module if it is in a directory other than SYS:SYSTEM.

The Math Library Module (MATHLIB)

Use the MATHLIB module if the server has a math coprocessor. You must load CLIB before loading MATHLIB. To load MATHLIB, type the command

LOAD *path*\MATHLIB

where *path* is the path to the module if it is in a directory other than SYS:SYSTEM.

The Math Library Module (MATHLIBC)

Use the MATHLIBC module if the server is an 80386 system that does not have a math coprocessor. You must load CLIB before MATHLIBC. To load MATHLIBC, type the command

LOAD *path*\MATHLIBC

where *path* is the path to the module if it is in a directory other than SYS:SYSTEM.

Memory Configuration

The following sections describe commands you can use to alter the memory configuration of the file server.

Registering Memory Above 16MB

The REGISTER MEMORY command is used to register memory above 16MB if the operating system fails to recognize it. The starting address and length of the memory above 16MB is specified in the command. Typical addresses are listed in Table 36-1. The command takes the following form:

REGISTER MEMORY *start length*

where *start* is the starting address of the memory and *length* is the memory length, as shown in Table 36-1. When the memory is successfully added, the message "Memory successfully added" appears. If the memory is not added, make sure the parameters were specified correctly. Note the following two points:

Total Memory	Starting Address	Memory Length
20MB	1000000	250000
24MB	1000000	500000
28MB	1000000	750000
32MB	1000000	1000000
36MB	1000000	1250000
40MB	1000000	1500000

Table 36-1.   Memory-Starting Addresses and Lengths in Hex

- Use REGISTER MEMORY only with actual memory that is installed in the file server. Do not use "shadow" RAM, because it may be mapped to lower memory.

- If more than 16MB of memory is installed in the server, use caution when installing AT bus master disk adapter boards or boards that use on-line DMA. Such boards can only address up to 16MB of memory and can cause corruption of the file server's memory. If the board is an EISA board, refer to "Auto Register Memory Above 16MB" later in this chapter. If the board is an ISA or MCA card, it must be replaced with a card that does not use on-line DMA or AT bus mastering.

Freeing Memory with REMOVE DOS

Use the REMOVE DOS command to remove DOS from the server's memory. The memory is then made available for file caching. Use this command if memory is low or to increase security at the file server. When DOS is removed, loadable modules cannot be loaded from the file server's DOS drives. To remove DOS, type **REMOVE DOS**.

When REMOVE DOS is used, the file server will warm boot when the EXIT command is used to return to DOS. This feature allows a user running RCONSOLE from a remote workstation to reboot the server remotely.

The SET Command

You can use the SET command to view the current operating system parameters and configure the operating system environment. Keep in mind that you may never need to use many SET parameters. The NetWare 386 operating system can automatically adjust many of its settings to fit the needs of a changing network environment. With the SET command you can force changes to some parameters, as described in the following sections. Many SET commands can be typed at the console, while others can be used only by placing them in the STARTUP.NCF file, and then rebooting the server.

Many of the SET parameters are used to make adjustments on servers that have low memory or minimal disk space. To get around these problems and avoid having to make adjustments with SET, increase the server's memory or disk space. You can monitor memory utilization with MONITOR, as discussed in Chapter 34.

The SET command takes the form SET *parameter,* where *parameter* is a parameter in one of the following categories:

Communications

Memory

File caching

Directory caching

File system

Locks

Transaction tracking

Disk

Miscellaneous

Refer to one of the following sections that applies to the parameters you need to change. To change a SET parameter at the console, type the SET command followed by the parameter and the new setting. For example, the following command changes the Watchdog feature, as described under "Communications":

SET CONSOLE DISPLAY WATCHDOG LOGOUTS=ON

Some commands must be included in the startup files. Use the same form you would type at the console in the startup files.

Viewing Current SET Parameters

To view the current configuration, type **SET** at the console prompt. When the SET screen appears, you can type the number of the category you want to view. SET asks if you want to view both normal and advanced options. Type **Y** to view the advanced options or press ENTER to view normal options.

Communications

The following settings control the Watchdog feature and the packet receive buffer parameters.

Console Display Watchdog
Logouts=*value*

Set *value* to On to use the Watchdog feature, which helps locate stations not receiving or successfully sending Watchdog packets. These packets are sent if the Watchdog has not heard from a station in five minutes. If the station does not respond, the Watchdog feature sends packets every minute. At the end of fifteen minutes, the station connection is cleared if there is no response.

Maximum Physical Receive
Packet Size=*number*

This parameter can be used only in the STARTUP.NCF file. It sets the maximum size of packets that can be transmitted on any of the networks attached to the file server. The default is 1K. Set *number* to the largest packet size that can be transmitted by any board. The default value is 1130 buffers, and the range is 618 to 4202.

Maximum Packet Receive
Buffers=*number*

Set *number* to the maximum number of packet receive buffers the operating system can allocate. To determine the correct number, view the server packet use with the MONITOR LAN Information option. Increase *number* in increments of 10 if packet receive buffers is at its maximum. For EISA and MCA bus master boards, increase the parameter by 10 if "Not ECB available count" errors occur. The default is 100, and the range is 50 to 2000.

Minimum Packet Receive
Buffers=*number*

This parameter can be used only in the STARTUP.NCF file. Increase *number* if the server is slow immediately after booting. For EISA and MCA bus master boards, increase the number so that each board is allocated at least five packet receive buffers. The default is 10, and the range is 10 to 1000.

New Packet Receive Buffer
Wait Time=*time*

This parameter is used to prevent the operating system from granting too many packet receive buffers during a sudden peak in usage. Do not use this parameter if an EISA bus master board is installed in the file server. Set *time* to the amount of time the operating system should wait after receiving a request for packet receive buffer before granting another buffer. The default is 0.1 seconds, and the range is 0.1 seconds to 20 seconds.

Memory

The memory parameters control the size of the dynamic memory pool, the block size of the cache buffers, and the automatic registering of memory on EISA bus computers.

Maximum Alloc Short Term
Memory=*number*

Set number to the amount of memory to allocate to the short term memory pool, which stores information on drive mappings, service request buffers, open and locked files, user connections, and other operating system information. The 2MB default should be sufficient for 250 users that have 26 drive maps each. Increase the number in increments of 1MB if the operating system issues low short-term memory warnings. To view current settings, use MONITOR, as described in Chapter 34. The default is 2,097,152 bytes, and the range is 50,000 to 16,777,216 bytes.

Auto Register Memory Above
16 Megabytes=*value*

This parameter has a default setting of On, which registers memory above 16MB. Set *value* to Off for interface cards that use on-line DMA or AT bus mastering by including the command in the STARTUP.NCF file.

Cache Buffer Size=*number*

This advanced parameter controls the block size of the cache buffer. In some cases performance can be improved by matching the buffer with volume block sizes. Set *number* to the block size you are using on all volumes if the block size is larger than 4K (refer to Chapter 15 for an explanation of blocks). If volumes use different block sizes, set *number* no larger than the smallest block allocation size. This parameter can be included only in the STARTUP.NCF file. The default value is 4096 bytes, but values of 8192 and 16,384 bytes are supported. You also can set the cache buffer size when starting the server with the SERVER command, as described at the beginning of this chapter.

File Caching

The following parameters are used to make changes to the file cache buffer settings. The first parameter is most often changed, while the others are for advanced use.

Minimum File Cache Buffers=*number*

Most available memory is allocated to the file cache buffers, but loadable modules and other tasks may require some of this memory. Set *number* to the minimum number of file cache buffers that must always be available to prevent the operating system from allocating the buffers to other tasks. The default is 20, and the range is 20 to 1000. Keep in mind that if the minimum is too high, other tasks may not be able to load due to insufficient memory.

Maximum Concurrent Disk Cache Writes=*number*

This advanced parameter sets how many write requests for changed file data can be put in the elevator before the disk head begins a sweep across the disk. Set *number* high to service write requests more efficiently, or low to service read requests more efficiently. To determine a setting, use MONITOR, as described in Chapter 34, to monitor dirty cache buffers. If this number is above 70%, increase *number*. The default setting is 50, and the range is 10 to 100.

Dirty Disk Cache Delay Time=*time*

This advanced parameter sets the time a write request stays in memory before being written to disk. Reduce *time* to prevent data in buffers from being lost if the server should go down; however, this drastically reduces performance. *Time* can be increased to improve performance when many small write requests are handled, but the additional information in the cache is lost if the server crashes. The default value is 3.3 seconds, and the range is 0.1 to 10 seconds.

Minimum File Cache Buffer Report Threshold=*number*

Use this parameter if you want to be warned when memory normally available to the file cache buffers is getting close to the minimum specified with the Minimum File Cache Buffers parameter. Set *number* to the number above the minimum setting at which the operating system warns you of low buffers. The default setting is 20, and the range is 0 to 1000.

Directory Caching

Directory caching improves access to frequently used files by keeping a copy of the directory table entry in memory. The entry is overwritten by a new entry if the file has not been accessed after a certain period of time. The operating system automatically allocates 20 buffers for directory caching. Allocating additional directory cache buffers decreases the number of file cache buffers, so balance the two appropriately.

Directory Cache Buffer NonReferenced Delay=*time*

Set *time* to the amount of time a directory entry is allowed to be cached before being overwritten by another entry due to inactivity. The operating system allocates more directory cache buffers if the time is increased and file access improves. Performance decreases if *time* is reduced since directory entries are less likely to be in the cache, but the number of directory cache buffers is reduced. The default setting is 5.5 seconds, and the range is 1 second to 5 minutes.

Maximum Directory Cache
Buffers=*number*

Once directory cache buffers are allocated, they are not returned to memory for file caching unless the server is rebooted. Because of this, it may be important to set a maximum number of directory cache buffers. The default *number* setting is 500, and the range is 20 to 4000.

Minimum Directory Cache
Buffers=*number*

Set *number* to the minimum number of directory cache buffers that must be available at all times, but do not set it so low that the performance of file access is reduced. Keep in mind that the minimum number could be more than the server needs on small networks. These unused buffers may be better off allocated to the file cache. If the file server responds slowly to directory searches when first booted, the minimum directory cache buffers setting is too low. You can view this information in MONITOR, as discussed in Chapter 34. The default setting is 20, and the range is 10 to 2000.

Dirty Directory Cache Delay
Time=*time*

This advanced parameter sets how long the operating system keeps a directory table write request in memory before writing it to disk. Increasing the delay improves performance but increases the possibility of directory table corruption. Decreasing the delay has the opposite effect. The default is 0.5 seconds, and the range is 0 to 10 seconds.

Maximum Concurrent Directory
Cache Writes=*number*

This advanced parameter sets how many write requests for directory cache buffers can be put in the elevator before the disk head begins a sweep across the disk. Set *number* high to service write requests more efficiently, or low to service read requests more efficiently. The default setting is 10, and the range is 5 to 50.

Directory Cache Allocation
Wait Time=*time*

This parameter sets the amount of time the operating system waits before allocating a new directory cache buffer after it has just allocated one. During the wait time, all requests for a new directory cache buffer are ignored. If *time* is low, a peak in usage could cause more directory cache buffers to be allocated than are normally needed. If *time* is high, the operating system allocates directory cache buffers slower than is required to serve normal requests. Decrease the time if directory searches seem slow after the server has been running 15 minutes. The default value is 2.2 seconds, and the range is 0.5 seconds to 2 minutes.

File System

File system parameters control warnings about full volumes, file system purging, and the reuse of turbo FATs.

Immediate Purge of Deleted
Files=*value*

Set *value* On if you want to immediately purge deleted files without the possibility of salvaging them. The default setting is Off. This can be used to free disk space, but accidentally erased files are permanently lost.

Volume Low Warn All Users=*value*

The default setting is to warn users when a volume is full. To turn the feature off, set *value* to Off.

Volume Low Warning Threshold=*number*

Set *number* to the amount of free disk space (in blocks) that must remain before the operating system issues a low disk space warning to users. Block sizes are discussed in Chapter 15. The default value is 256 blocks, and the range is 0 to 100,000 blocks.

Volume Low Warning Reset Threshold=*number*

When a volume is almost full, its available disk space may move up or down in the warning messages range as users create and delete files. To prevent the warning message every time the volume dips below the threshold, set *number* to a minimum amount of space above the threshold before users are again warned of low space. This parameter can be set at the console when a volume becomes low on space. The default is 256 blocks, and the range is 1 to 100,000 blocks.

Minimum File Delete Wait Time=*time*

Set *time* to the amount of time a deleted file stays in a salvageable state on the volume. During this time range, deleted files will not be purged automatically even if the volume is full and users are unable to create new files. The default is 1 minute, 5.9 seconds, and the range is from 0 seconds to 7 days.

File Delete Wait Time=*time*

Set *time* to the amount of time the operating system waits before purging a file. When a file's delete wait time has been exceeded, it is marked as purgeable and is removed as soon as the volume needs additional space. The oldest purgeable file is removed first. Set this value high if there is a need to keep files in a salvageable state for long periods of time and if a volume is not limited on disk space. The default is 5 minutes, 29.6 seconds, and the range is 0 seconds to 7 days.

Maximum Subdirectory Tree Depth=*number*

This advanced parameter sets the number of subdirectory levels supported by the operating system. Replace *number* with the number of levels to support if it is over 25. When upgrading from a previous version of NetWare that has more than 25 levels, use this parameter to specify the number of subdirectories. The default is 25, and the range is 10 to 100.

Turbo FAT ReUse Wait Time=*time*

This advanced parameter determines how long a turbo FAT buffer remains in memory after an indexed file is closed. Once *time* has been exceeded, the buffer is allocated to another indexed file. The operating system automatically builds turbo FAT entries for files that have more than 64 FAT entries. Because these indexes take time to build, they should not be immediately removed if there is a chance you will need to open the file again, as is often the case with some accounting packages. Increase *time* to keep the index in memory longer, especially if plenty of memory is available. Decrease *time* to release the memory for other indexes. The default is 5 minutes, 29.6 seconds, and the range is 0.3 seconds to 1 hour, 5 minutes, 54.6 seconds.

Locks

Lock parameters are used to control the number of open files and the number of record locks the operating system and workstations can handle. With a file lock, a workstation has exclusive use of the file. With a physical record lock, other users are prevented from accessing a particular record in a file. With a logical record lock, an application assigns a name to each section of data that needs to be locked and then locks the name when the data is accessed.

Maximum Record Locks
Per Connection=*number*

Set *number* to the number of record locks a station can use at once. Increase this number if error messages occur because a workstation cannot lock enough records. The default is 500, and the range is 10 to 10,000.

Maximum File Locks
Per Connection=*number*

Set *number* to the number of opened and locked files a station can use at once. Increase this number when a station cannot open enough files. An OS/2 station may need a number higher than the default. It may also be necessary to increase the number of file handles in the SHELL.CFG file of the workstation. The default is 250, and the range is 10 to 1000.

Maximum Record Locks=*number*

Set *number* to the maximum number of record locks the operating system should handle. Increase *number* if users are having problems running applications because there are not enough record locks. Decrease *number* if users are using too many file server resources. MONITOR can be used to view record locks, as discussed in Chapter 34. The default is 20,000, and the range is 100 to 200,000.

Maximum File Locks=*number*

Set *number* to control the number of opened and locked files handled by the operating system. Use MONITOR, as discussed in Chapter 34, to view the number of open files during a peak usage period. If the number of current open files is near the default, increase the number. Decrease this number to restrict file server resources. The default is 10,000, and the range is 100 to 100,000.

Transaction Tracking

The following parameters can be used to control the transaction tracking system (TTS).

Auto TTS Backout Flag=*value*

This parameter determines if incomplete transactions are automatically backed out when a crashed server is rebooted. The default is Off, which means that you are asked if you want to back them out. Set *value* to On to automatically back out the transactions upon rebooting.

TTS Abort Dump Flag=*value*

Set *value* to On to create a TTS log file that contains the information that was backed out of a file. The file is called TTS$LOG.ERR and is stored in the SYS:SYSTEM directory. The default value is Off (which means the file is not created).

Maximum Transactions=*number*

Set *number* to the number of transactions that can occur at the same time. The default value is 10,000, and the range is 100 to 10,000.

TTS UnWritten Cache Wait Time=*time*

This advanced parameter specifies how long transactional data is held in memory. Some blocks of transactional data wait for other transactional blocks to be written first. If one of these blocks reaches its maximum time limit, it is written to disk as soon as possible. The default time of 1 minute, 5.9 seconds is usually sufficient, but a range of 11 seconds to 10 minutes, 59.1 seconds can be specified in *time*.

TTS Backout File Truncation
Wait Time=*time*

Set *time* to the amount of time allocated blocks remain available for the TTS backout file when the blocks are not currently being used. The default is 59 minutes, 19.2 seconds, and the range is 1 minute, 5.9 seconds to 1 day, 2 hours, 21 minutes, 51.3 seconds.

Disk

The following disk parameter controls a feature of Hot Fix redirection.

Enable Disk Read After Write
Verify=*value*

This parameter controls whether information written to disk is compared with that in memory and is normally not disabled. It helps determine when bad blocks exist. If they do, data is redirected to the Hot Fix redirection area. If disks are mirrored and thus more reliable, you can gain some speed advantage on disk writes by disabling this feature. Set *value* to Off to disable it.

Miscellaneous

The following parameters are used to control several aspects of the operating system, including the use of encrypted passwords, alerts, and other server processes. In most cases the first parameter is the only one ever changed, but the remaining parameters may be necessary under the conditions described.

Allow Unencrypted Passwords=*value*

Under NetWare 386, passwords are encrypted before they cross the wire. If the network has servers running NetWare 286, you may need to take one of the following actions, since NetWare 286 does not support encrypted passwords:

- Set this parameter to On so users can use both unencrypted and encrypted passwords.

- Copy the NetWare 386 utilities to the NetWare 286 server, and leave this parameter at its default Off setting. All users can then use encrypted passwords.

Display Spurious Interrupt Alerts=*value*

An interface card in the server may create spurious interrupts, indicating a malfunctioning card. To detect spurious interrupts, set this option to On, and then monitor the messages that appear on the screen. If a spurious interrupt message occurs, remove all cards from the server, and then remount them one-by-one until the message appears again. Report the problem to the card's vendor for additional assistance. A new driver or updated card may be available. The default setting is On.

Display Lost Interrupt Alerts=*value*

In some cases a card may request a service from the server by issuing an interrupt, and then lose track of the interrupt before the server can respond back. These lost interrupts indicate a hardware driver problem or defective board. This parameter will display messages when lost interrupts are detected if it is set to On. To test drivers and hardware, set the option On and monitor lost interrupt messages. To determine which driver or board is defective, unload all the drivers and then reload them one at a time until the problem resurfaces. The default setting is On.

Display Disk Device Alerts=*value*

Set this parameter to On if you want to display informational messages about hard disks when a disk driver is loaded or unloaded, when the file server is booted or downed, or when attempting to isolate disk driver or hardware problems. The default setting if Off.

Display Relinquish Control Alerts=*value*

This parameter is used by programmers writing NLMs. If set to On, a message appears if an NLM uses the processor for more than 0.4 second without relinquishing control to other processes. The default setting is Off.

Display Old API Names=*value*

This parameter controls messages that appear when a module is loaded that uses old applications programming interfaces (APIs). APIs were upgraded with NetWare 386 version 3.1. Programmers writing NLMs can set this parameter to On if they are upgrading 3.0 NLMs to the new 3.1 APIs. The default setting is Off.

Maximum Outstanding NCP Searches=*number*

This advanced option sets the maximum number of NetWare core protocol (NCP) directory searches that can be processed at once. Normally only one NCP directory search occurs at once, but you may need to increase the default to support applications that do multiple directory searches at the same time if you have problems with corrupted or invalid directory information. The default is 51, and the range is 10 to 1000.

New Service Process Wait Time=*time*

Set *time* to the amount of time the operating system should wait after receiving a request for another service process before making the allocation. The default setting is 2.2 seconds, and the range is 0.3 seconds to 20 seconds.

Maximum Service Processes=*number*

Set *number* to the maximum number of service processes that the operating system can create. The current number can be viewed with MONITOR, as described in Chapter 34. Decrease *number* if the server is temporarily low on memory. Increase *number* if the service process number in MON-ITOR is at its maximum. Increasing *number* helps only if more than 20 requests are waiting for disk I/O to complete. The default is 20, and the range is 5 to 40.

Appendixes

Cable Installation Tips

Cable Testing Equipment

This appendix provides some cabling suggestions for those who will be installing their own network cable. It also discusses cable testing equipment that can be useful to those with large networks.

It is recommended that you rely on professional cable installers any time you do not have a thorough understanding of the cable installation requirements or do not have the proper tools to install it or test it. Professional installation is especially recommended for fiber optic cable due to its complexities. The cable is hard to work with and tends to be more fragile than other cable. When using existing telephone twisted pair, tapping into punchdown blocks in wiring closets is not recommended unless you are familiar with procedures to isolate and test the cable runs going to each workstation from the wiring block. You may also need to contact the installers of the equipment for approval and information about the existing telephone system before proceeding.

If a cable system will be upgraded at any time in the future, consider designing special cable pathways and enclosures so that future cable can be more easily installed. Metal and plastic conduit or housing should be incorporated into the design of new buildings. Consider that a well-planned cabling system may have a higher up-front cost, but will require less maintenance. Retrofits will also be easier and cheaper to perform when the cable system is planned with this in mind.

If you plan to proceed with the cable installation and testing procedure yourself, be sure to take the following points into consideration:

- Document and map the entire installation. Documentation for existing telephone wiring may already be available from the telephone system installers and should include documentation for the punchdown blocks and the telephones it connects. After the cable system is installed, be sure to log all problems for future reference.

- Talk with administrators who have installed similar networks and inspect their cabling system.

- Get blueprints of the building. Know the location of telephone closets and other equipment rooms, as well as risers, conduits, and cable trays.

- Check the local building codes for cable types and installation requirements, otherwise the building inspector could make you reinstall the entire cable system.

- Know the ceilings and walls of a building. You could be in for a surprise if you find out a solid concrete wall exists between two offices. Check above ceiling tiles to ensure that cable can be strung from office to office without interference.

- Avoid running cable in walkways and other traffic areas.

- Make sure the cable attachment location is near a source of electricity to power the workstation itself.

- If possible, use a hierarchical wiring scheme in which departmental systems are attached to concentrators in wiring closets and interdepartmental connections are made with backbone connections. This can be accomplished with ARCNET, 10BASE-T Ethernet, and Token Ring, as well as some other configurations of Ethernet. The hierarchical method provides better troubleshooting and expansion.

- Set aside enough time to do the job right.

- Work during off-hours when employees are not bothered.

- When attaching connectors to twisted pair, make sure the correct wires go to the correct lead on the connector.

- When using telephone twisted pair, always test for continuity between wiring closet and workstation before proceeding. Also make sure that wires go to the planned workstation locations. You can rely on qualified electricians to check the cable, or purchase one of the testing tools discussed at the end of this chapter.

- Avoid bending, creasing, pulling, or stretching coaxial cable. Abnormalities may be introduced that change the electrical characteristics and signal-carrying capacity of the cable.

- Use the bouncing-ball and drop-rock approaches to cabling. By attaching a string to a ball, you have an object you can throw from one location to another when crawling around in a ceiling or other tight space. A string-attached rock or similar object can be dropped down to drill holes in walls. Lightweight rods or poles may also be useful when pushing wires through conduits or casings.

- Walkie-talkies are useful when communicating to a person on the other side of a wall or building.

- Stay away from fluorescent lights in drop ceilings. You may need to provide extra cable so you can work around the lights.

- Cable should not run alongside other electrical cable. Also avoid running two network cables next to each other since cross-talk could occur.

- Prop cable up with fasteners, staples, or clamps. Coaxial cable in particular should never hang on its own since it is not designed to support itself. Be careful not to damage the cable when attaching fasteners.

- Do not stretch cable when pulling it through openings or conduit. A stretched cable could lose its transmission properties.

- Make sure all cable lengths in a network are of the proper type of cable. Cables that look the same may have different numbers and thus different transmission characteristics. A single length of the wrong type of cable in a network can prevent its use.

- Be aware that moisture can corrode cable and possibly change its electrical characteristics. Protect it from wet conditions with conduit and other coverings, especially if it is exterior cable.

- You can check network connections before the NetWare server is up and running by using the COMCHECK program. This program requires installed interface cards and cable. In addition, the IPX.COM program must be running in each machine. IPX.COM is generated by running the SHGEN program, as described in Chapter 18.

- Interference problems may occur on long cable runs. Metal cables tend to act like big antennas that pick up stray fields and interference from devices along their paths. As a cable's length increases, its signal-carrying capacity decreases, which is one reason why cables with high transmission rates have shorter recommended distances. When problems occur, move the cable away from electrical devices.

- Intermittent network problems can occur if cables are run next to surge protection devices.

- Be sure a cable run is properly grounded at only one point so it can unload unwanted voltage peaks. Grounding in two locations can cause loops that may not suppress surges and can cause other problems. Some network problems have been solved by disconnecting the ground, which indicates the cable system is grounded elsewhere by accident.

- Cable problems are easy to isolate on star-configured networks like Token Ring, ARCNET, 10BASE-T, and others. If one workstation does not work, replace the cable or card to that workstation. If all workstations branching from a concentrator box or MAU do not work, check the concentrator or the cable that attaches it to the rest of a network.

- Cable problems on small Ethernet networks are harder to locate than those on star-configured networks, but can be done through a process of elimination if you do not have the testing equipment described later. First determine whether the problem is in the hardware or the cable by running the server and a single workstation through a separate cable. Be sure to entirely remove the existing cable system. If the workstation and server communicate, the problem is most likely in the cable system. Connect each workstation to the server, one-by-one, making sure to terminate the T-connector on each station as you go. You also must restart the server and workstation every time. When the network does not start, replace the cable segment between it and the previous workstation.

Cable Testing Equipment

You can use a number of devices to test cable. Some are quite affordable and should be part of any cable installer's tool kit. More expensive test equipment can be rented, or you can rely on the services of consultants who own the equipment.

Cable Tracers

A cable is *traced* to determine its path. It may also be traced to determine its source or destination. A typical application would be to determine which wire in a bundle belongs to a cable at a distant location. A device such as a tone generator is attached to the end of the cable and an amplifier is then used to "listen" for the tone at the other end, which is typically a punchdown block. The amplifier indicates when it is near the wire by producing a signal.

A popular product is the Microtest Tracer, which makes it easy to locate any coaxial, twisted pair, or other type of wire hidden inside a floor, wall, or ceiling. The Tracer's sending unit is connected to the wire or cable, and then its pocket-size receiving unit is run over the areas where the wire is suspected to run. When Tracer's receiving unit passes over the wire, an alarm sounds and grows stronger as you get closer to the wire.

Continuity Testers

A continuity tester is similar in operation to the cable tracer but is used to determine whether a short or break exists in a wire. It can also be used to check which lead going into a wall is connected to which lead coming out of a wall. The Microtest Checker is an example. It includes both a sending and receiving unit. If the green LED on Checker's receiver lights up, the cable is good. If only the red LED on Checker's sender lights up, there is a short. If neither LED lights, there is a break.

Time Domain Reflectometers

A time domain reflectometer (TDR) determines the location of breaks and shorts in cables. It sends a high-speed pulse down the length of a cable, and then measures the time it takes for the reflection of the signal to return. A reflection occurs at shorts and breaks, and the time of reflection gives a close approximation of where the shorts and breaks are. TDRs must be aware of the type of cable used since the pulse travels through different types of cable at different speeds. In the past, TDRs have been expensive, but Microtest has introduced products in the $1500 range.

The Microtest Cable Scanner is a standalone handheld tester used to determine if cabling is the cause of computer malfunctions. It helps you easily pinpoint the location of faults or breaks. A 32-character display reports the fault location in plain English, as in "Short at 306 ft." The Cable Scanner can print a hard copy to any serial printer. It can also save test results in memory for later review. You can test Ethernet, ARCNET, twisted pair, and Token Ring by making a selection from the keyboard. The Cable Scanner also provides real-time monitoring of a LAN's activity to help determine when a bridge or repeater may need to be added. LAN activity can be graphically displayed on any PC monitor to find faults while the network is running under normal conditions. The unit can also be attached to an oscilloscope. The Tracer product described earlier is included with Cable Scanner.

Diagnostics Software

Diagnostics software packages monitor and track the activity of a network. They consist of software that runs in a workstation on the network and are similar to the protocol analyzers discussed in the next section but provide fewer features and are lower in cost. An example is TXD from Thomas-Conrad, a menu-driven diagnostics utility that performs the following:

- Queries all nodes and performs point-to-point communication testing between any specified node and all other nodes on the internetwork.

- Determines the entire internetwork configuration.

- Analyzes critical data from one or all nodes and reports only unusual activity based on a user-defined set of thresholds.

- Performance data such as traffic volume and packets serviced by a bridge are displayed.

- Provides useful information about network efficiency, performance, possible hardware errors, noise problems, and problems with applications software.

The TXD package works with ARCNET, Ethernet, and Token Ring in the NetWare environment.

Protocol Analyzers

Network protocol analyzers connect as workstations to a LAN and are used to analyze the frames being transmitted over the network cable. Protocol analyzers are usually portable personal computers that contain network interface cards and run special software designed to analyze the types of frames crossing the LAN. A protocol analyzer can provide sophisticated interpretation and presentation of the information being analyzed. Other functions of the protocol analyzer are discussed here:

- Monitors large amounts of traffic and the filtering of unwanted traffic.

- Packets with specific source or destination addresses can be monitored and viewed.

- Provides alerts when critical traffic situations are occurring.

- Monitors and displays information about traffic on the network.

- Displays peak traffic loads and their times.

- Displays maps of the LAN and points out workstations that have been added or the addition of unauthorized workstations and possible taps.

A typical protocol analyzer is the Sniffer by NetWork General Corporation (Mountain View, CA). The Sniffer provides usage and statistical information about network traffic, network nodes, and the utilization of the network. Historical information can be captured at selected intervals and stored on disk. This information can be kept for the entire network as well as individual workstations. Sophisticated filtering functions allow packets with specific source or destination addresses to be monitored and viewed.

Protocol analyzers are also available from Cabletron Systems, Hewlett-Packard, Novell, Black Box, Digilog, and Excelan.

Upgrading to NetWare 386

Using UPGRADE
The Transfer Method
The Backup Device Method
Restoring Data
Follow-up Procedures for UPGRADE
Installing Non-DOS Devices

NetWare comes with a utility called UPGRADE that helps you make the transition from an existing NetWare 286 network to the NetWare 386 environment. UPGRADE preserves most of the existing user, security, login, and other information. There are two methods for upgrading: the transfer method and the backup device method. Both methods are illustrated in Figure 15-1.

You use the transfer method if you have two servers: one old NetWare 286 server and one new NetWare 386 server. The two servers are connected on a network, and the NetWare 286 server's data is transferred to the new server. The transfer method is ideal because it does not affect the NetWare 286 server. If a problem occurs during installation, you can resume operating with the old system until the problem is resolved.

When you install NetWare 386 on an existing NetWare 286 server, you use the backup device method. Because NetWare 386 has a new type of file system, the server drives must be initialized and all data is lost. Therefore, you must back up the NetWare 286 data before you install NetWare 386. The data is then restored. The UPGRADE utility makes these steps easy by providing backup and restore routines optimized for the upgrade process. You must use this method if you have only one file server, which must be an Intel 80386- or 80486-based system that currently runs NetWare 286.

Using UPGRADE

UPGRADE is designed to make either upgrade method simple. Keep the following in mind when performing an upgrade:

- Partition tables and file formats are different with NetWare 386. Existing servers must be reformatted to the NetWare 386 system. Since data is lost, you must have a good backup before proceeding.

- UPGRADE automatically reorganizes the bindery information into a new structure used by NetWare 386. The new bindery files are NET$OBJ.SYS, NET$PROP.SYS, and NET$VAL.SYS.

- All existing users are given new ID numbers.

- Passwords are encrypted over the cable with NetWare 386. If you are using the transfer method, you must set the Allow Unencrypted Passwords feature of NetWare 386 to On while transferring data from the NetWare 286 server, as discussed later.

- Security rights and file attributes have changed between NetWare 286 and NetWare 386. UPGRADE translates the old rights to the new rights. Refer to Tables 5-2 and 5-3 in Chapter 5 for a description of the differences between rights.

- The maximum rights mask of NetWare 286 is replaced by the inherited rights mask used in NetWare 386.

You must make the following changes when upgrading to the NetWare 386 environment:

- NetWare 386 allows only 8-character filenames with 3-character extensions, unlike NetWare 286, which allowed 14-character filenames. You must change names that are longer than 8 characters, otherwise UPGRADE truncates them for you.

- Private, system, and hidden directories on NetWare 286 servers cannot be upgraded with UPGRADE. Remove the directory flags before continuing, and then refer to the end of this appendix to restore the flags on the NetWare 386 server.

- The default subdirectory depth for NetWare 386 is 25 levels. If the NetWare 286 server exceeds this level, you must change the maximum directory depth allowance on the server. This is done during NetWare 386 installation, as covered in Chapter 17.

When merging two or more NetWare 286 servers to a new NetWare 386 server, be aware of the following:

- The values may not be accurate after merging, so record the accounting balances of users who have accounts on both servers.

- Users may have different account restrictions on different servers. Decide which server has the most important account restrictions, and then merge it last. You may need to edit account restrictions for users.

- Files with similar names, such as the system login script from each server, overwrite each other. The file from the last server is on the NetWare 386 server after the upgrade.

Handling Overwrites During Upgrades

During a transfer or restore, it is possible that duplicate directories, files, and objects (user information) may overwrite existing information. This is especially true if you are merging two existing NetWare 286 servers to the new NetWare 386 server. Directories, files, and objects from the first 286 server could be overwritten by those of the same name or type from the second 286 server. UPGRADE lets you control duplicates in the following ways.

Directories   You can choose to combine or rename duplicate directories interactively during the upgrade, or you can initially specify how duplicates should be handled when setting up the upgrade session. Renaming a directory prevents the original directory from being overwritten. If you choose to rename, make sure the new server has enough disk space to hold both sets of files.

Files   If you choose to combine directories, UPGRADE lets you control how duplicate files within the directory are handled. You can do this interactively during the session, or you can specify how the files should be handled before the session starts. Existing or transferred files can be renamed, or you can choose to overwrite existing files. Note that NetWare 286 VAPs are automatically excluded during a transfer. Also, renamed operating system files in the SYS:PUBLIC and SYS:SYSTEM directory are given the extension U*nn,* where *nn* is an incremental number starting with 00. This makes it easy to list or delete the duplicate files later, as covered at the end of this appendix.

Bindery Objects   If UPGRADE finds a NetWare 386 object with the same name as a NetWare 286 object, you are requested to resolve the conflict.

Resolving Bindery Conflicts

The bindery contains objects that represent user accounts, such as SUPERVISOR, EVERYONE, and GUEST, as well as other users on the NetWare 286 server. When the bindery is transferred, you must resolve how bindery objects with the same name are handled. In most cases the only duplicates are SUPERVISOR, EVERYONE, and GUEST, unless you merge two or more servers. You can choose to combine the objects or rename the NetWare 286 bindery objects. Login scripts, account balances, and account restrictions, if combined, are overwritten by the transferred object.

   Note: If you are transferring more than one NetWare 286 server with accounting features installed, obtain a list of current user account balances before proceeding, because they may be lost when combined.

   Here are some points to remember regarding object types.

SUPERVISOR   Each server in a transfer session has a SUPERVISOR object. You can choose to keep either the NetWare 286 or NetWare 386 SUPERVISOR object.

EVERYONE   You can choose to combine the rights of the NetWare 286 EVERYONE object with the NetWare 386 EVERYONE object, or to keep each group separate by renaming one. This is also true when merging two or more NetWare 286 servers. Keep in mind that the EVERYONE group on each server may hold group rights to directories specific to the server. Since these directories probably will be transferred to the new server, you must merge or rename each group to maintain the access rights to the directories.

GUEST   You can choose to combine the rights of the NetWare 286 GUEST object with the NetWare 386 GUEST object, or to rename the NetWare 286 GUEST object and keep the NetWare 386 GUEST object intact.

Other objects   When merging two or more servers to the NetWare 386 server, objects (user accounts) with the same name may exist. You can choose to rename one object, or if the objects are the same user, you can combine the objects.

The Transfer Method

The first step in the transfer method is to install NetWare 386 on the new server, as described in Chapter 17. After you install the operating system, you can continue the transfer procedure by referring back to this section. Keep the following in mind as you perform the installation.

- You will need to use a workstation on the network to manage the transfer session.

- Assign the NetWare 386 server the same address as the NetWare 286 server, because they must share the same cable system during the transfer. This number is specified when binding IPX (or other protocol) to the network interface card, as covered in Chapter 17.

- If the servers will share an Ethernet network, they must also use the same frame format (refer to Chapter 15).

- Make sure that the main SYS volume has at least 6MB more memory than the NetWare 286 SYS volume if you rename the operating system files that are transferred.

- If volumes on the NetWare 386 server will have the same names as existing volumes on the NetWare 286 server, make sure the new volumes have at least 10 percent more space.

- If you plan to merge volumes into a single NetWare 386 volume, make sure there is enough room for all the data that will be combined.

- Run the CHKVOL command to make sure the NetWare 286 disks are not more than 97 percent full. If they are, remove unnecessary files or back up some of the files, and then remove them from the drive. You can restore them to the NetWare 386 server after the upgrade if there is enough room after removing duplicate files.

- You might want to remove any unnecessary files at this time. Many programs create temporary files or files with the BAK extension that can be removed to conserve space.

Running the UPGRADE Transfer Method

Follow these steps to prepare for the UPGRADE transfer method. This section assumes you have installed NetWare 386 on the new server.

1. Before beginning the transfer, log all users out of the servers, and type **DISABLE LOGIN** at the server console to make sure no one else logs in.

2. At a workstation on the NetWare 286 network, type **BINDFIX** to delete any mail directories for users who were removed from the server.

3. Back up the NetWare 286 server to ensure adequate data protection.

4. Attach the servers to the same network. To transfer data, they must be attached to the same network cable system and must share the same network cable address.

5. Log into the NetWare 386 server as the supervisor from a workstation on the network. You should be able to do this from any DOS workstation attached to the original NetWare 286 network. If not, refer to workstation installation instructions in Chapter 18 for more details. Once the workstation is connected, make sure no terminate-and-stay-resident (TSR) programs are loaded, and then proceed with the instructions in the following section.

Starting and Running The Upgrade Transfer Method

You are now ready to start the UPGRADE utility located in the SYS:SYSTEM directory of the NetWare 386 server. Type **UPGRADE**, and in a moment the Select the Desired Device menu appears. Select either a DOS device or the Wangtek device. If you want to add your own device, refer to "Installing Non-DOS Devices" at the end of this appendix. After selecting a device, the main menu appears, as shown here:

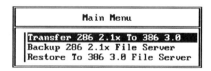

Select the first option from the menu to display the Transfer menu shown here:

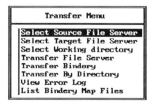

Now follow these steps:

1. Choose **Select Source File Server** from the Transfer menu to select the NetWare 286 file server to transfer. If it is not on the list, press INS to log in as supervisor.

2. Choose **Select Target File Server** from the menu and select the NetWare 386 server you just installed.

3. Choose **Select a Working Directory**. A working directory is the location where a session log file is stored. This file contains information about the upgrade session and may contain error messages you can view to resolve problems. Type the drive name and/or directory of a local hard drive, or a directory on the new NetWare 386 server. Do not select a directory on the source file server.

Selecting a Transfer Method

The Transfer menu lists three different methods for transferring the data. If you have sufficient disk space on the NetWare 386 server to hold the entire NetWare 286 server, you can choose the **Transfer File Server** option and refer to the next section, "Transferring the Entire File Server." If you do not have sufficient space on the NetWare 386 server, or if you want to transfer only specific directories, select **Transfer Bindery** to transfer the bindery, and then select **Transfer By Directory** to transfer specific directories. Refer to the appropriate sections of this chapter for instructions.

Transferring the Entire File Server

Select the **Transfer File Server** option from the Transfer menu to display a menu similar to the following:

Follow these steps to start and run the session:

1. Type a session description in the Transfer Description field.

2. If you want to exclude some files, press INS on the Files to Exclude field and type the name of a file to exclude. Press ENTER and repeat the process for each file to exclude.

3. To control how directories with the same name are handled, select **Directory Exists** and press ENTER, and then select one of the following options. Note that the SYSTEM, PUBLIC, LOGIN, MAIL, and DESKTOP directories are automatically combined regardless of the options and their settings. See step 4 to control how NetWare 286 commands and utilities are written to the NetWare 386 server.

   • *Combine Directory Contents* Combines the contents of two directories into one. To control duplicate filenames, see step 4.

   • *Rename Existing Directory* Rename the existing directory with an extension of U*nn*, where *nn* is an incremented number starting with 00.

   • *Interactive* When two directories have the same name, you are prompted to combine or rename the existing directory. If renaming, you can type a new name.

4. Select **File Exists** and choose one of the following options to specify how duplicate files should be handled. To prevent Net-Ware 286 files from copying over NetWare 386 files, it is recommended that you choose **Rename Restored File**.

   • *Interactive* When two files have the same name, you are prompted to overwrite or rename the existing file, or rename the restored file. If renaming, you can type a new name.

   • *Overwrite Existing File* The transferred file overwrites the existing file.

   • *Rename Existing File* Renames existing files with an extension of U*nn*, where *nn* is an incremented number starting with 00.

- *Rename Restored File* Renames restored files with an extension of U*nn,* where *nn* is an incremented number starting with 00.

5. When the screen is complete, press ESC, and then select **Yes** at the "Start Transfer" prompt.

Monitoring the Transfer Session

When the session starts, a status window appears to display information about file transfers and possible errors. You can press ESC to stop the session if necessary.

During the session a file with the BMF extension is created to store information about how each object in the NetWare 286 bindery is mapped to the new NetWare 386 ID number. The file must not be deleted until you have checked all the upgraded data. It contains information about the ownership of files, directories, and trustee assignments.

After the bindery is transferred, the volumes, directories, and files begin transferring. The information in the bindery map file is used to assign ownership to bindery objects. If you did not create a volume to match the NetWare 286 volumes during the NetWare 386 installation, you are prompted to enter a directory path where volume information can be placed. UPGRADE cannot create volumes, so you must create the volumes after UPGRADE is complete using INSTALL, and then copy the volume information with FILER.

Viewing Error Messages

When the transfer is complete, you can view error messages if any exist by selecting **View Error Log** from the Transfer menu. Some errors provide basic information, while others indicate that the transfer may not have been successful and you must repeat it.

Transferring the Bindery

Select the **Transfer Bindery** option from the Transfer menu if you are transferring the bindery only. This option may be selected if you are selecting specific directories to transfer from the NetWare 286 server, as covered in the next section.

You are asked to fill in the Transfer Options menu with a description of the session. When done, press ESC and select **Yes** to save the changes. Then select **Yes** to start the transfer.

As the session progresses, you may need to resolve conflicts between duplicate bindery objects. Refer to "Resolving Bindery Conflicts" earlier in this chapter.

Transferring Specific Directories

Select the **Transfer By Directory** option from the Transfer menu to transfer specific directories. The following menu appears:

Directories are transferred after the bindery is transferred, as described in the previous section. Each volume, directory, and file is mapped from the information in the BMF file created by the bindery transfer. If the NetWare 386 server has the same volume names as the NetWare 286 server, the contents of the directories are transferred into the new volumes. If the volumes do not exist, they are placed in a directory you specify. You can transfer them to a new volume at a later time using the FILER utility.

Follow these steps to start the session:

1. Type a session description in the Transfer Description field.

2. Type the name of the volume, directory, or subdirectory to transfer in the Source Directory field.

3. To accept the remaining default settings, press ESC, and the session immediately starts; otherwise, continue with step 4.

4. Type **No** in the Transfer Subdirectories field if subdirectories of the specified directories should not be transferred.

5. Type **No** in the Transfer Trustee Rights field if you do not want to transfer the trustee assignments in the specified directory.

6. To transfer only selected files, highlight Files to Include and press ENTER. Press INS, type the name of a file, using wildcards to specify file groups, and then press ENTER. Repeat this step for each file to include.

7. To exclude certain files, highlight Files to Exclude and press ENTER. Type the name of the file to exclude, using wildcards to specify groups of files, and then press Enter. Repeat this step for each file to exclude.

8. To control how directories with the same name are handled, select **Directory Exists** and press ENTER, and then select one of the following options:

   - *Combine Directory Contents* Combines the contents of two directories into one. To control duplicate filenames, see step 9.

   - *Rename Existing Directory* Renames the existing directory with an extension of U*nn,* where *nn* is an incremented number starting with 00.

   - *Interactive* When two directories have the same name, you are prompted to combine or rename the existing directory. If renaming, you can type a new name.

9. Select **File Exists** and choose one of the following options to specify how duplicate files should be handled. To prevent NetWare 286 files from copying over NetWare 386 files, it is recommended that you choose **Rename Restored File**.

   - *Interactive* When two files have the same name, you are prompted to overwrite or rename the existing file, or rename the restored file. If renaming, you can type a new name.

   - *Overwrite Existing File* The transferred file overwrites the existing file.

- *Rename Existing File*   Renames existing files with an extension of U*nn,* where *nn* is an incremented number starting with 00.

- *Rename Restored File*   Renames restored files with an extension of U*nn,* where the variable *nn* is an incremented number starting with 00.

10. When the screen is complete, press ESC, and then select **Yes** at the "Start Transfer" prompt.

When the session starts, a status window appears to display information about file transfer and errors if they occur. You can press ESC to stop the session if necessary.

Viewing Error Messages

When the transfer is complete, you can view error messages if any exist by selecting **View Error Log** from the Transfer menu. Some errors provide basic information, while others indicate that the transfer may not have been successful and you must repeat it.

The Backup Device Method

Use the backup device method when you want to install NetWare 386 on an existing NetWare 286 server. This assumes that NetWare 286 has been running on an 80386 or 80486 system. Because there are differences in file allocation and storage, the existing NetWare 286 server must be reformatted for the new operating system. This method helps you back up the data on the server, and then restore it after NetWare 386 has been installed.

The backup method involves three main steps. The backup step is performed first. Then refer to Chapter 17 to install NetWare 386. Finally, return to the section "Restoring the Data" later in this appendix to restore the backed up data to the new server filing system.

Keep the following in mind when you perform the NetWare 386 installation:

- During the installation make sure that the main SYS volume has at least 6MB more memory than the NetWare 286 SYS volume, if you plan to rename duplicate files.

- If you use a DOS device for backup, it must be attached to the workstation used to manage the UPGRADE session. You can back up to tape, floppy disks, hard drives, optical drives, or removable media.

- If the backup device is not large enough to hold the entire server's data, you can back up in multiple sessions to other devices. For example, you can back up the bindery and program directories to the hard drive on one workstation and back up data directories to the hard drive on another workstation.

- Because the server's hard drive is formatted, make sure you have adequate backups.

- If additional volumes on the NetWare 386 server will have the same names as existing volumes on the NetWare 286 server, make sure the new volumes have at least 10 percent more space.

- If you plan to merge volumes into a single NetWare 386 volume, make sure there is enough room for all the data that will be combined.

- Make sure the NetWare 286 disks are not more than 97 percent full by running the CHKVOL command. If they are, remove unnecessary files or back up some of the files to tape, and then remove them from the drive. You can restore them to the NetWare 386 server after the upgrade, if there is enough room.

- You might want to remove any unnecessary files at this time. Many programs create temporary files or files with the BAK extension that can be removed to conserve space.

Backing Up the NetWare 286 Server

The NetWare 286 server can be backed up to a local workstation floppy drive, a workstation hard drive, or a non-DOS device. Devices may be optical disks, removable drives, or tape drives. The backup devices should have at least 10 percent more space than the data to be backed up. If you are using a non-DOS device that is certified for use with NetWare 386, you can add its name and driver to the UPGRADE program by referring to "Installing Non-DOS Devices" at the end of this chapter.

To perform the backup, you must access a workstation on the network attached to the NetWare 286 server. This workstation should have one of the previously mentioned backup devices attached to it.

Note: It is recommended that you do a complete backup using your normal backup method before running the UPGRADE backup method. This ensures that you can recover the complete server should something go wrong.

Follow these steps to start the UPGRADE procedures:

1. Log into the network as the supervisor on a workstation that has a hard drive. Do not load any terminate-and-stay-resident programs or other utilities that might interfere with the backup process.

2. Log all users out of the NetWare 286 server. Prevent users from logging in by typing **DISABLE LOGIN** at the console.

3. Run BINDFIX to remove any mail directories for nonexistent users.

4. The UPGRADE disk is part of the NetWare disk set. You can run UPGRADE from the disk, or you can copy its contents to the workstation's hard drive.

5. Type **UPGRADE** to start the program.

6. Select the device to use for the upgrade from the initial menu. To include another device on the menu, refer to "Installing Non-DOS Devices" at the end of this appendix.

7. When the UPGRADE main menu appears, select **Backup 286 2.1x File Server**. The Backup menu shown here appears:

8. Choose **Select Source File Server** from the menu to select the NetWare 286 file server to back up.

9. Choose **Select Working Directory** from the menu, and type the name of the directory where a session log file will be stored. This file contains information about the upgrade session and may contain error messages you can view to resolve problems. Type the drive name and/or directory of a local hard drive, or a directory on the new NetWare 386 server. Do not select a directory on the source file server.

The three options available for doing the backup are as covered in the next few sections. You can back up the entire server using the Backup File Server option on the Backup menu, if you have sufficient room on the target device. If not, you can back up in multiple sessions using the Backup Bindery and Backup By Directory options. Refer to the appropriate section below.

Backing Up the Entire File Server

Choose **Backup File Server** to back up the entire file server to a single device. The Backup Options menu appears, as shown here:

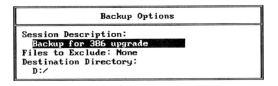

Follow these steps to back up the server:

1. Type a description of the session in the Session Description field.

2. If you want to exclude any files, highlight the Files to Exclude field and press INS to type the names of any files you want to exclude. Repeat this step for each file to exclude.

3. In the Destination Directory field, type the directory name if you are backing up to a DOS device.

4. Press ESC to start the session, selecting **Yes** at the "Start Backup" prompt.

If you need to stop the backup session, press ESC. During the session, the screen displays status information about the data being backed up and the elapsed time. If you are using tapes, be sure to mark each tape with the Media ID number that appears on the screen.

When the backup is complete, you can view the error log to see if there were any problems that would warrant another backup session. Select **View Error Log** from the Backup menu. Some errors provide descriptive information, while others may indicate that you need to repeat the session.

If the session was successful, you may want to run the backup again if you have room on a DOS device or if you have extra tapes. Then proceed to Chapter 17 and install NetWare 386. When the installation is complete, refer to "Restoring the Data" later in this appendix.

Backing Up the Bindery

You use the Backup Bindery selection on the Backup menu to back up only bindery information if you are doing the backup in multiple sessions. This is often the case when the backup device does not have enough room to hold the NetWare 286 files. You could, for example, back up the bindery to a hard drive on one workstation and back up directories on another. Follow these steps to back up the bindery:

1. From the Backup Options menu, fill in the Session Description field with information about the backup session.

2. Type the name of the target device in the Destination Directory field.

3. Press ESC when done and type **Yes** at the "Save Changes" prompt. Type **Yes** at the "Start Backup" prompt.

If you need to stop the backup session, press ESC. During the session, status information is displayed on the screen about the data being backed up and the elapsed time. If you are using tapes, be sure to mark each tape with the Media ID number that appears on the screen.

When the backup is complete, you can view the error log to see if there were any problems that would warrant another backup session. Select **View Error Log** from the Backup Menu. Some errors provide descriptive information, while others may indicate that you need to repeat the session.

If the session was successful, you can run the backup again if you have room on a DOS device or if you have extra tapes. Then proceed to the next section to back up specific directories.

Backing Up Specific Directories

The Backup By Directory option is used to back up specific directories on the NetWare 286 server to a backup device. Use this method when the backup device cannot hold the entire server's data. You can back up the data to multiple devices if necessary, and then restore it from each device to the server after you have installed the NetWare 386 operating system.

Select **Backup By Directory** to display the Backup Options menu. Fill in the Session Description field with information about the session, and then fill in the remaining fields as described here:

1. Fill in the Source Directory field with the name of the directory on the NetWare 286 server to back up.

2. Fill in the Destination Directory field with the local DOS device to use for the backup.

3. Press ESC now if the remaining fields should be set at their default settings, or continue with step 4.

4. Type **No** in the Backup Subdirectories field if subdirectories of the specified directories should not be backed up.

5. Type **No** in the Backup Trustee Rights field if you do not want the trustee assignments in the specified directory to be backed up.

6. To back up only selected files, highlight the Files to Include field and press ENTER. Press INS, type the name of a file, using wildcards to specify file groups, and then press ENTER. Repeat this step for each file to include.

7. To exclude certain files, highlight the Files to Exclude field and press ENTER. Type the name of the file to exclude, using wildcards to specify groups of files, and then press ENTER. Repeat this step for each file to exclude.

8. Press ESC when the fields are complete, and then select **Yes** at the "Start Backup" prompt.

When the session starts, a status window appears to display file status and errors, if they occur. You can press ESC to stop the session, if necessary.

You can make a second backup of the directory or back up other directories. When all the directories have been backed up, you can install NetWare 386 on the server, as described in Chapter 17. Then refer to "Restoring the Data" to copy the data to the new server.

When the Backup is complete, you can view error messages if any exist by selecting **View Error Log** from the Backup menu. Some errors provide basic information, while others indicate that the backup may not have been successful and you must repeat it.

Restoring the Data

Once the NetWare 386 operating system is installed on the server, you can restore the backed up data from the backup devices. Note the following before beginning:

- If the NetWare 286 system has a subdirectory depth greater than 25 levels, make sure the NetWare 386 system is set to handle greater levels, as discussed in Chapter 17.

- If you want to save the NetWare 386 login script, copy the file NET$LOG.DAT in the SYS:PUBLIC directory to disk. The NetWare 286 login script copies over it. You can decide which login script you want to use later.

To begin the restore, reboot the workstation used during the backup session and log into the NetWare 386 server as supervisor. Make sure you are in the SYS:SYSTEM directory and type **UPGRADE**. Select the device to use from the list and press ENTER. When the main menu appears, select **Restore to 386 3.x File Server**. The Restore menu appears, as shown here:

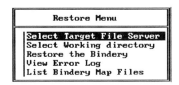

Read through the following sections to restore the data.

Restoring the Bindery

Follow these steps to restore the bindery:

1. Choose **Select Target File Server** from the Restore menu, and then select the NetWare 386 file server.

2. Choose **Select Working Directory** from the Restore menu, and type the name of a drive or directory that will hold the session log file.

3. You must restore the bindery before restoring any directories. The only option to appear is Restore the Bindery. Select this option, and then select the bindery session to restore and press ENTER.

Note: If you moved the backup files to another drive or directory between the backup and restore sessions, press F3 and type the new drive or directory path.

4. Type **Yes** at the "Start Restore" prompt. If you need to stop the session, press ESC; otherwise, monitor its progress. Refer to "Resolving Bindery Conflicts" at the beginning of this appendix for information about resolving duplicate bindery objects.

When the bindery has been restored, you can continue with the next section to restore the remaining data.

Restoring the Data

After the bindery has been restored, as discussed in the previous section, you can restore the remainder of the data from backup. Follow these steps to restore data:

1. Select the **Restore Session** option from the Restore menu. It appears only after restoring the bindery.

2. If you changed the location of the backup files between the backup and the restore session, press F3 to enter the new drive and directory location of the files.

3. To control how directories with the same name are handled when two or more NetWare 286 servers are restored, select **Directory Exists** and press ENTER, and then select one of the following options. Note that the SYSTEM, PUBLIC, LOGIN, MAIL, and DESKTOP directories are automatically combined, regardless of the settings of these options. See step 4 to ensure that NetWare 286 commands and utilities do not overwrite those commands and utilities for NetWare 386.

   • *Combine Directory Contents* Combines the contents of two directories into one. To control duplicate filenames, see step 4.

- *Rename Existing Directory* Rename the existing directory with an extension of U*nn*, where *nn* is an incremented number starting with 00.

- *Interactive* When two directories have the same name, you are prompted to combine or rename the existing directory. If renaming, you can type a new name.

4. Select **File Exists** and then choose one of the following options to specify how duplicate files should be handled. To prevent NetWare 286 files from copying over NetWare 386 files, it is recommended that you choose **Rename Restored File**.

- *Interactive* When two files have the same name, you are prompted to overwrite or rename the existing file, or rename the restored file. If renaming, you can type a new name.

- *Overwrite Existing File* The transferred file overwrites the existing file.

- *Rename Existing File* Renames existing files with an extension of U*nn*, where *nn* is an incremented number starting with 00.

- *Rename Restored File* Renames restored files with an extension of U*nn*, where the variable *nn* is an incremented number starting with 00.

5. When the screen is complete, press ESC and then select **Yes** at the "Start Restore" prompt.

Monitor the session, watching for error messages at the bottom of the screen. These errors can also be viewed by displaying the error log, which is an option on the Restore menu. If you need to stop the restore session, press ESC.

If necessary, restore other backup sessions. This is the case if you backed up individual directories using either the transfer or backup method. When done, continue with the next section.

Follow-up Procedures for UPGRADE

Before you allow users to log into the new NetWare 386 server, perform the following checks and tasks:

- If any of the NetWare 386 utility and command files in the SYS:LOGIN, SYS:SYSTEM, and SYS:PUBLIC directories were copied over by NetWare 286 files, load the install program, as discussed in Chapter 17, and recopy the NetWare 386 SYSTEM and PUBLIC files. When the Installation Options menu appears, select **System Options**, and then choose **Copy System and Public Files**. You are prompted for each disk.

- If you renamed any files during the upgrade, you may need to get rid of duplicate files. Recall that duplicates were renamed with the extension U*nn,* where *nn* is an incremental number. Switch to the SYS:PUBLIC directory and type **FLAG *.U* N** to flag the files with the Normal attribute so they can be erased. You may want to scan these files and keep some, such as the old login script (NET$LOG.U*nn*). Type **DEL *.U*** to delete any files you do not want.

Repeat the following steps for the SYS:SYSTEM and SYS:LOGIN directories.

- Check other directories for duplicate files by typing **DIR *.U*** in each suspected directory. Remember that files may have the same name but different contents. Use caution when removing files.

- User passwords from NetWare 286 v2.0a are transferred during an upgrade; however, passwords from NetWare 286 v2.1*x* are not. You must run SYSCON to change users' passwords.

- Copy program files that had the Execute Only flag from their original disk to the NetWare 386 server. These files are not copied during an upgrade. Make sure applications run properly.

- Recall that the NetWare 286 maximum rights mask has been replaced by the NetWare 386 inherited rights mask. The directory masks on the new server are set to allow all rights, because the two masks are completely different. You should refer to Chapter 6 and Part V of this book for more information on establishing the new masks.

- The Netware 286 v2.15 Private right is no longer available for directories. To create a similar directory under NetWare 386, use ALLOW or FILER to revoke all rights in the inherited rights mask, and then grant a user who needs a private directory the Create right in the directory with the GRANT command.

- Use FILER or FLAGDIR to flag system and hidden directories with the System and Hidden attributes, as necessary.

- Run the SECURITY command to check the account restrictions of users.

- Change the system login script to reflect any changes made to the server during upgrade. For example, error messages occur when a user is mapped to a directory in which they do not have rights. You should delete the drive mapping command in the login script or grant the users rights to the directories. You may also want to use other login script techniques to map users to directories, as discussed in Chapter 28.

- Create new workstation startup files as necessary. Refer to Chapter 18 for more information.

Working in a Multiserver Environment

You may need to perform the following tasks when a network consists of NetWare 286 and NetWare 386 servers:

- For NetWare 286 v2.0a servers, you only need to copy LOGIN.EXE to the SYS:LOGIN and SYS:PUBLIC directories.

- For NetWare 286 v2.1*x* servers, replace the public utilities in the SYS:PUBLIC directory with the new NetWare 386 public utilities to allow for encrypted passwords.

The following steps outline how to copy files to the server:

1. Log into the NetWare 286 server.

2. Flag the files to be copied over with the Normal attribute by typing **FLAG *.* N.**

3. Protect the system login script in the SYS:PUBLIC directory from overwrites by typing **FLAG NET$LOG.DAT SRO**.

4. Log into the NetWare 386 server if necessary.

5. Map a drive to the SYS:PUBLIC directory on the NetWare 386 file server by entering this form of the MAP command:

   MAP *drive:=servername*/SYS:PUBLIC

   where *drive* is an unmapped drive letter, and *servername* is the name of the NetWare 386 file server.

6. From the NetWare 286 SYS:PUBLIC directory, type **NCOPY *drive:*.*** to copy the files in the NetWare 386 SYS:PUBLIC directory, replacing *drive* with the drive letter assigned in step 5.

7. Flag the files in the directory as Shareable and Read Only by typing **FLAG *.* SRO.**

Repeat steps similar to these to copy files from the NetWare 386 SYS:LOGIN directory to the NetWare 286 SYS:LOGIN directory. Once the NetWare 286 servers are using the NetWare 386 files, you can type the following at the NetWare 386 console to begin encrypting passwords:

SET ALLOW UNENCRYPTED PASSWORDS = OFF

Remove the SET ALLOW UNENCRYPTED PASSWORDS = ON command from the AUTOEXEC.NCF file if necessary. You can now allow users to log into the new NetWare 386 server. Continue by reading Chapter 18 or Part V of this book.

Installing Non-DOS Devices

When the UPGRADE command is executed, the first menu to appear displays the current device list. You can follow the instructions presented here to add the driver for your backup device to this list. The procedure is to copy the driver itself to the SYS:PUBLIC directory, and then add the name of the device to the list by updating a file called DIBI$DRV.DAT.

To copy the new driver file to the SYS:PUBLIC directory, use the following command:

NCOPY A:*driver*.EXE SYS:PUBLIC

where *driver* is the name of the new driver.

Next, use a text editor (or word processing program) to add the following line to the DIBI$DRV.DAT file:

"name" DRIVER

where *name* is the name you want to appear in the NBACKUP opening menu, and *DRIVER* is the name of the *driver*.EXE file copied in the last step.

For example, if you are installing an Emerald Systems VAST device, you would add the following line to the DIBI$DRV.DAT file:

"Emerald System VAST" EMSAVE.EXE

External LAN Bridges

A bridge connection to another LAN may be made to extend the area of an existing LAN, to split a network for improved performance, or to connect with a LAN that uses different topologies and interface cards. Internal bridges are established in a NetWare file server; external bridges are established in a separate machine. This appendix covers the installation of external bridges.

An external bridge can be created in a dedicated or a nondedicated system. A *nondedicated bridge* is one that handles the bridging task in one portion of memory and acts like a normal workstation in another part of memory. A *dedicated bridge* is used for bridging purposes only. You can use a nondedicated bridge to run another application, but it is recommended that you use an 80286 or 80386 system running in protected mode. Both bridges are efficient at passing traffic between LANs, but a nondedicated bridge slows when a user executes an application on the workstation portion of the bridge.

Bridges can be run in real mode or protected mode. A dedicated bridge must be run in real mode, regardless of the computer type being used for the bridge. A nondedicated bridge can be run in either mode.

A protected-mode bridge accommodates up to 11MB of extended memory. The extra memory can be used to accommodate additional applications when the bridge is running in nondedicated mode. The protected mode establishes barriers around protected areas in memory that prevent applications running within the protected areas from crashing applications (such as the bridge software) that run in other protected areas. The additional memory can also be used to run a value added process (VAP), which is a NetWare 286 operating system enhancement comparable to a NetWare 386 NLM. These applications are linked into the NetWare operating system and executed while the bridge is running. Bridge systems that use 8088 or 8086 processors cannot run in protected mode. Protected-mode bridges must have at least 1.5MB of RAM and an 80286 or 80386 processor, and must boot as nondedicated bridges with 640K of memory set aside for workstation use if it is required. Such a bridge can be used to run an application in a pinch.

Real-mode bridges use the standard 640K base memory of most DOS machines, but are limited in the number of VAPs they can run. A dedicated bridge runs in real mode. If the bridge system uses an 8088 or 8086 processor, it must run in real mode.

Generating External LAN Bridges with BRGEN

The BRGEN program creates a file called BRIDGE.EXE that is copied to the boot disk used to start an external bridge. If the external bridge has a hard drive, you should copy this file to the root directory of the bootable hard drive.

Starting BRGEN

A bridge is established by running the NetWare BRGEN utility, which can be found on the BRGEN-1 disk that comes with the NetWare 386 package. The disk is enclosed in the manual *NetWare 286 External Bridges Supplement*. You *must* make a copy of the BRGEN-1 disk to a non-write-protected disk before beginning.

Insert the BRGEN-1 disk in drive A and switch to the drive. Type **BRGEN -N** (use -N only if you want a new session and do not want to save settings made in a previous BRGEN session). When the System Configuration Method window appears, choose the **Default Configuration** option. Custom Configuration is used by installers such as value added resellers who need to install bridges with special custom configurations.

Additional information on custom configurations can be found in the *NetWare 286 External Bridges Supplement*.

After starting the BRGEN program and selecting **Default Configuration**, the following menu appears:

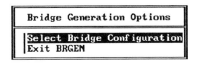

Choose the **Select Bridge Configuration** option from the menu to continue. The Available Options menu appears, as shown here:

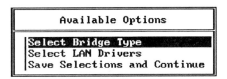

You can select the bridge type (real or protected mode) and LAN drivers for the bridge by making a selection from this menu.

Selecting a Bridge Type

Choose **Select Bridge Type** from the menu to display this screen:

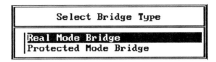

Select whether the bridge will be a real-mode bridge or a protected-mode bridge. The choice of dedicated or nondedicated mode is made when starting the bridge using the BRIDGE command, as you will see later.

Selecting LAN Drivers

Select LAN drivers by choosing the **Select LAN Drivers** option from the Available Options menu. You may select up to four different drivers, which means that the external bridge can support up to four networks. The following LAN Driver Options menu appears:

Choose the **Select Loaded Item** option from the menu if the LAN driver is for one of the following:

IBM PCN II and Baseband network interface card

IBM Token Ring

Novell NE1000 Ethernet card

Novell NE2000 Ethernet card

Novell NE/2 Ethernet card

Novell RX-Net card

Novell RX-Net/2 card

To install the driver for a different card, choose the **Load and Select Item** option. You will be asked to insert the disk that contains the driver for your interface card.

When the following Available LAN Drivers screen appears, select a driver from the list and press ENTER to continue.

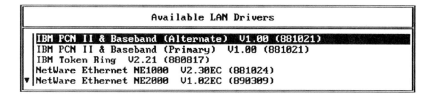

The driver name appears in the Select LAN Drivers window. Follow the same procedure to select the driver for the second card and any additional cards in the bridge. Note that the LAN Driver Options menu now has the

Deselect an Item option, which you can use to remove one of the selected drivers if necessary. When you are done press ESC to return to the Available Options menu.

Assigning Network Addresses

Once LAN drivers have been selected, they must be configured before proceeding. Choose **Save Selections and Continue** from the Available Options menu. A Network Information menu similar to the following then appears. This menu lists the drivers you have selected.

```
╔══════════════════════════════════════════════════════════════╗
║                      Network Information                       ║
╠══════════════════════════════════════════════════════════════╣
║ A: NetWare Ethernet NE1000  V2.30EC (881024)                   ║
║        Network Address: ██████████                             ║
║ B: NetWare Ethernet NE1000  V2.30EC (881024)                   ║
║        Network Address:                                        ║
║ Non-dedicated Bridge DOS Process                               ║
║        Network Address:                                        ║
║ Communication Buffers: 40                                      ║
╚══════════════════════════════════════════════════════════════╝
```

Type the network address for each card that coordinates with the rest of your network. You can also change the number of communications buffers used by the bridge. The range is from 10 to 150 and should be set according to the amount of memory your system has. Use the default if you are operating with standard 640K memory. Press ESC after assigning network addresses and buffers. The Selected Configuration screen appears and displays information about the card settings. If the settings on the screen do not match the card settings, you can either change the cards or change the BRGEN configuration. To change the configuration, choose **No** and refer to "Changing the Configuration" later in this appendix.

If the Selected Configuration screen settings match the card settings, press ESC. The Continue Bridge Generation Using Selected Configuration menu appears. Select **Yes** to configure the bridge or **No** to reconfigure the drivers. If you choose No to reconfigure the drivers, refer to the next section. If you select Yes, an executable file called BRIDGE.EXE is linked. When the linking process is complete, a message telling you that the BRIDGE.EXE file is complete and located on the disk is displayed. You can now exit the BRGEN program by selecting **Exit BRGEN**.

Note: If one of the bridge boards is an Ethernet board, you may need to run the NetWare ECONFIG command to reconfigure for a different packet type. Refer to Chapter 18 for more information.

Changing the Configuration

You may need to change the interrupts and other board settings for one or more of the interface cards in the bridge to match board settings and avoid conflicts. If you selected No in the last section to do this, the Abandon Bridge Generation and Exit menu appears. Select **No** to display the Available Options menu. A new option called Configure Drivers/Resources appears. Select this option to display the following menu:

```
┌─────────────────────────────────────┐
│ Configure Drivers / Resources        │
├─────────────────────────────────────┤
│ Review Selected Configurations       │
│ Set Network Addresses                │
│ Release LAN Configuration            │
└─────────────────────────────────────┘
```

Select **Release LAN Configuration** from this menu, and a list of configured LAN drivers appears. Select each item on the list, press ENTER to release them, and press ESC to return to the Configure Drivers/Resources menu. The top selection will now be Choose LAN Configuration. Select this option to display the list of unconfigured LAN drivers. Select each driver, and then choose a configuration from the Available LAN Configurations menu, similar to that shown here:

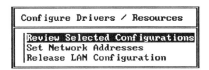

```
╔═══════════════════════════════════════════════════════╗
║              Available LAN Configurations               ║
╠═══════════════════════════════════════════════════════╣
║ 0: IRQ = 3, I/O Base = 300h, no DMA or ROM             ║
║ 1: IRQ = 2, I/O Base = 320h, no DMA or ROM             ║
║ 2: IRQ = 4, I/O Base = 340h, no DMA or ROM             ║
║ 3: IRQ = 5, I/O Base = 360h, no DMA or ROM             ║
║ 4: IRQ = 2, I/O Base = 300h, no DMA or ROM             ║
║ 5: IRQ = 3, I/O Base = 320h, no DMA or ROM             ║
╚═══════════════════════════════════════════════════════╝
```

Once you have configured each driver, you can press ESC until the Continue Bridge Generation Using Selected Configuration menu appears. Select **Yes** to configure the bridge.

Note: If one of the bridge boards is an Ethernet board, you may need to run the NetWare ECONFIG command to reconfigure for a different packet type. Refer to Chapter 18 for more information.

Starting the Bridge

To prepare to start the bridge from a floppy drive system, format a bootable disk with the version of DOS you will be using, and then copy the BRIDGE.EXE file from the BRGEN-1 disk. If the bridge has a bootable hard drive, copy the BRIDGE.EXE file to the root directory of the hard drive. If the bridge is a protected-mode bridge, you must also copy the CONSOLE.COM file from the BRGEN-1 disk to the boot disk or hard drive. If running a nondedicated bridge, copy the NETx.COM file created during the SHGEN configuration process in Chapter 18 so you can start NetWare and run the bridge as a workstation.

If value added processes (VAPs) are being installed in a dedicated bridge, copy the VAP files to the boot disk or hard drive. Then create a file called XBRIDGE.CFG that contains instructions for loading the VAP, as outlined in the instruction manual for the VAP. Two additional commands for VAPs can be included in the file, as outlined here:

- The VAP WAIT command instructs the server to wait before automatically loading the VAPs. The command has the format

    VAP WAIT *xxx*

    where *xxx* is the number of seconds, from 10 to 360, to wait.

- The VAP DISK command allows you to load VAPs from an internal hard disk or second floppy drive. The command takes the form

    VAP WAIT *path*

    where *path* is the drive letter and directory path to search.

Starting a Dedicated Bridge

After booting the system, type **BRIDGE** on the DOS command line. The Novell copyright message appears, and then the colon prompt is displayed, indicating the bridge is in dedicated mode.

Starting a Nondedicated Bridge

Nondedicated servers are started by specifying the amount of memory to allocate to the bridge task, with a minimum of 180K of memory. Type the command **BRIDGE** *xxx,* where *xxx* is the amount of memory to allocate. Novell recommends 288, so you would enter the following command:

BRIDGE 288

When the DOS prompt appears on the screen, type the NET*x* command to load the NetWare shell. You may then operate the workstation as normal.

Bridge Console Commands

The following commands can be executed at the colon prompt for bridges running in the console mode. Dedicated bridges always run in this mode. For nondedicated bridges, type **CONSOLE** at the DOS prompt to switch to the bridge console mode. Console commands can be used to view the bridge configuration, list loaded VAPs, and down the bridge, among other things. The following commands can be used at the console.

CONFIG	Displays information about the operating system's hardware configuration for each network supported by the bridge
CONSOLE	Used to select the console mode when running a nondedicated bridge
DOS	Used to return to the DOS command line from the console mode on nondedicated servers
DOWN	Brings the bridge down and is always used when shutting down a bridge
MONITOR	Displays the version number of the NetWare bridge software

OFF   Clears the bridge console screen

VAP   Displays a list of value added processes cur-
                       rently loaded into the NetWare operating sys-
                       tem

Resources

Backup Products
Communications Products
Data Protection Equipment
Distributors
Groupware
LAN Media
Management Products
Network Products
Publications and Organizations
Server Products
Company Addresses

The following companies are mentioned in this book or provide products useful to network administrators. Anyone planning or installing a network should contact the distributors listed here to obtain free and informative catalogs.

Backup Products

Digital Storage Systems, Inc.

Emerald Systems

Maynard Electronics

Mountain Computer, Inc.

Optical Data Systems

Palindrome Network Archivist

Communications Products

AT&T

CNet Technology, Inc.

Digital Equipment Corporation

Eicon Technology Corporation

Hughes LAN Systems

Infotron

J&L Information Systems

Microcom, Inc.

Network Products Corporation

Newport Systems Solutions, Inc.

ParaData Computer Networks, Inc.

Promptus Communications, Inc.

Retix

Verilink Corporation

Vitalink Communications Corporation

Data Protection Equipment

Elgar Corporation

Micronyx, Inc.

SAFE Power Systems

Tripp Lite Mfg.

Distributors

AMP

Belkin Components

Black Box

CPU Corporation

Glasgal Communications

North Hills Electronics

Specialized Products

Groupware

Action Technologies

Brightwork Development, Inc.

cc:Mail, Inc.

Da Vinci Systems

Dynamic Microprocessor Associates (DMA)

Enable Software, Inc.

Information Research Corporation

LAN Media

Andrew Corporation

Aquila Communication, Inc.

AT&T

BICC Data Networks, Inc.

Cabletron Systems, Inc.

Canary Communications, Inc.

D-Link Systems, Inc.

Fibronics International, Inc.

General Technology, Inc.

IBM

IMC Networks Corporation

IQ Technologies, Inc.

Madge Networks, Inc.

Mod-Tap Systems

Netronix

NetWorth, Inc.

Nevada Western

Proteon

Pure Data, Inc.

Star-Tek, Inc.

Synernetics, Inc.

Thomas-Conrad

Tiara Computer Systems, Inc.

Vertex Computer Cable & Products

Vitalink Communications Corporation

Xircom

Management Products

Cheyenne Software, Inc.

Fresh Technology Group

International Data Sciences

Saber Software Corporation

Network Products

Digital Equipment Corporation

Novell, Inc.

Publications and Organizations

Affiliation of NetWare Users

Data Communications

LAN Magazine

LAN Technology Magazine

LAN Times

NetWare Users International

Network World

Networking Management

Server Products

CMS Enhancements, Inc.

Cogent Data Technologies, Inc.

Compaq Computer Corporation

Core International, Inc.

Giga Trend Incorporated

IBM

Morton Management, Inc.

NetFRAME Systems, Inc.

Optical Data Systems

PROCOMP USA, Inc.

Storage Dimensions

Sysgen, Inc.

Company Addresses

Action Technologies
2200 Powell Street
Emeryville, CA 94608
(415) 654-4444

Affiliation of NetWare Users
75 Union Avenue
Sudbury, MA 01776
(508) 443-3330

AMP
Worldwide Headquarters
Harrisburg, PA 17105
(800) 638-2666

Andrew Corporation
2771 Plaza Delamo
Torrance, CA 90503
(213) 320-7126

Aquila Communication, Inc.
846 Del Rey Avenue
Sunnyvale, CA 94086
(408) 732-0700

AT&T
299 Jefferson Road
Parsipanny, NJ 07054
(800) 247-1212

Belkin Components
14550 South Main Street
Gardena, CA 90248
(213) 515-7585

BICC Data Networks, Inc.
1800 West Park Drive
Westborough, MA 01581
(508) 898-2422

Black Box
P.O. Box 12800
Pittsburgh, PA 15241
(412) 746-5565

Brightwork Development, Inc.
766 Shrewsbury Avenue
Jerral Centre West
Tinton Falls, NJ 07724
(201) 530-0440

Cabletron Systems, Inc.
35 Industrial Way
Rochester, NH 03867
(603) 332-9400

Canary Communications, Inc.
1435 Koll Circle
Suite 111
San Jose, CA 95112-4610
(408) 453-9201

cc:Mail, Inc.
385 Sherman Avenue
Palo Alto, CA 94306
(415) 321-0430

Cheyenne Software, Inc.
55 Bryant Avenue
Roslyn, NY 11576
(516) 484-5110

CMS Enhancements, Inc.
1372 Valencia Avenue
Tustin, CA 92680
(714) 259-9555

CNet Technology, Inc.
62 Bonaventura Drive
San Jose, CA 95134
(408) 954-8000

Cogent Data Technologies,
  Inc.
175 West Street
P.O. Box 926
Friday Harbor, WA 98250
(206) 378-2929

Compaq Computer
  Corporation
20555 SH 249
Houston, TX 77070
(713) 370-0670

Core International, Inc.
7171 North Federal
  Highway
Boca Raton, FL 33487
(407) 997-6055

CPU Corporation
1424 East North Belt, #100
Houston, TX 77032
(713) 987-0234

D-Link Systems, Inc.
5 Musick
Irvine, CA 92718
(714) 455-2521

Da Vinci Systems
4200 Six Forks Road
Suite 200
Raleigh, NC 27609
(919) 781-5924

Data Communications
1221 Sixth Avenue
New York, NY 10010
(212) 512-6050

Digital Equipment Corporation
30 Porter Road
Littleton, MA 01460
(508) 486-2690

Digital Storage Systems, Inc.
1234 Sherman Drive
Longmont, CO 80501
(303) 651-6312

Dynamic Microprocessor
  Associates (DMA)
1776 Jericho Turnpike
Dix Hills, NY 11746
(516) 462-6652

Eicon Technology Corporation
2196 32nd Avenue (Lachine)
Montreal, Quebec H8T 3H7
(514) 631-2592

Elgar Corporation
9250 Brown Deer Road
San Diego, CA 92121
(619) 450-0085

Emerald Systems
4757 Morena Boulevard
San Diego, CA 92117
(619) 270-1994

Enable Software, Inc.
Northway Ten Executive
  Park
Ballston Lake, NY 12019
(518) 877-8600

Fibronics International,
  Inc.
Communications Way
Hyannis, MA 02601
(800) 456-3279

Fresh Technology Group
1478 North Tech
  Boulevard, #101
Gilbert, AZ 85234
(602) 497-4200

General Technology, Inc.
415 Pineda Court
Melbourne, FL 32940
(407) 242-2733

Giga Trend Incorporated
2234 Rutherford Road
Carlsbad, CA 92008
(619) 931-9122

Glasgal Communications
151 Veterans Drive
Northvale, NJ 07647
(210) 768-8082

Hughes LAN Systems
1225 Charleston Road
Mountain View, CA 94043
(415) 966-7300

IBM
P.O. Box 1328
Internal Zip H420
Boca Raton, FL 33428
(contact your local IBM
  representative)

IMC Networks Corporation
1342 Bell Avenue
Unit 3E
Tustin, CA 92680
(714) 259-1020

Information Research
  Corporation
414 East Market Street
Charlottesville, VA 22901
(800) 368-3542

Infotron
Cherry Hill Industrial Center 9
Cherry Hill, NJ 08003-1688
(609) 424-9400

International Data Sciences
Seven Wellington Road
Lincoln, RI 02865
(401) 333-6200

IQ Technologies, Inc.
11811 NE First Street
Bellevue, WA 98005
(206) 451-0232

J&L Information Systems
9238 Deering Avenue
Chatsworth, CA 91311
(818) 709-1778

LAN Magazine
500 Howard Street
San Francisco, CA 94105
(415) 397-1881

LAN Technology Magazine
501 Galveston Drive
Redwood City, CA 94063
(415) 366-3600

LAN Times
151 East 1700 South
Suite 100
Provo, UT 84604
(801) 379-5800

Madge Networks, Inc.
1580 Oakland Road
Suite C206
San Jose, CA 95131
(408) 441-1300

Maynard Electronics,
  An Archive Company
460 East Semoran
  Boulevard
Cassel Berry, FL 32707
(407) 263-3500

Microcom, Inc.
500 River Ridge Drive
Norwood, MA 02062-5078
(800) 822-8224

Micronyx, Inc.
1901 North Central
  Expressway
Richardson, TX 75080
(214) 690-0595

Microtest, Inc.
3519 East Shea Boulevard
Suite 134
Phoenix, AZ 85028
(800) 526-9675

Mod-Tap Systems
P.O. Box 706
Harvard, MA 01451
(508) 772-5630

Morton Management, Inc.
12079 Tech Road
Silver Springs, MD 20904
(301) 622-5600

Mountain Computer, Inc.
240 Hacienda Avenue
Campbell, CA 95008-6617
(408) 3590-4300

NetFRAME Systems, Inc.
894 Ross Drive
Sunnyvale, CA 94086
(408) 745-0633

Netronix
1372 North McDonnell
  Boulevard
Petaluma, CA 94954
(714) 762-2703

NetWare Users International
122 East 1700 South
Provo, UT 84601
(801) 379-5900

Network Products
  Corporation
1111 South Arroyo Parkway
Suite 450
Pasadena, CA 91105
(818) 441-6504

Network World
161 Worcester Road
Framingham, MA 01701
(508) 875-6400

Networking Management
One Technology Park Drive
P.O. Box 988
Westford, MA 01886
(508) 692-0700

NetWorth, Inc.
8101 Ridge Point Drive
Suite 107
Irving, TX 75063
(214) 869-1331

Nevada Western
615 North Tasman Drive
Sunnyvale, CA 94089
(408) 734-2700

Newport Systems
  Solutions, Inc.
4020 Birch Street
Suite 107
Newport Beach, CA 92660
(714) 752-1511

North Hills Electronics
1 Alexander Place
Glen Cove, NY 11542
(516) 671-5700

Novell, Inc.
122 East 1700 South
Provo, UT 84606
(801) 379-5900

Optical Data Systems
1226 Exchange Drive
Richardson, TX 75081
(214) 234-6400

Palindrome Network
  Archivist
850 East Diehl Road
Naperville, IL 60563
(708) 505-3300

ParaData Computer
  Networks, Inc.
37525 Interchange Drive
Farmington Hills, MI 48331
(313) 478-8400

PROCOMP USA, Inc.
6801 Engle Road
Cleveland, OH 44130
(216) 234-6387

Promptus Communications,
  Inc.
207 High Point Avenue
Portsmouth Business Park
Portsmouth, RI 02871
(401) 683-6100

Proteon
Two Technology Drive
Westborough, MA 01581
(800) 545-RING

Pure Data, Inc.
1740 South I-35
Suite 140
Carrollton, TX 75006
(214) 242-2040

Retix
2644 30th Street
Santa Monica, CA 90405-
   3009
(213) 399-2200

Saber Software Corporation
5944 Luther Lane, #1007
Dallas, TX 75225
(214) 361-8086

SAFE Power Systems,
A Division of Acme
   Electric Corp.
528 W. 21st Street
Tempe, AZ 85282
(602) 894-6864

Specialized Products
3131 Premier Drive
Irvine, CA 75063
(800) 527-5018

Star-Tek, Inc.
100 Otis Street
Northboro, MA 01532
(508) 393-9393

Storage Dimensions
2145 Hamilton Avenue
San Jose, CA 95125
(408) 879-0300

Synernetics, Inc.
85 Rangeway Road
North Billerica, MA 01862
(508) 670-9009

Sysgen, Inc.
556 Gibraltar Drive
Milpitas, CA 95035
(408) 263-4411

Thomas-Conrad
1908-R Kramer Lane
Austin, TX 78758
(512) 835-1935

Tiara Computer Systems, Inc.
2700 Garcia Avenue
Mountain View, CA 94043
(415) 965-1700

Tripp Lite Mfg.
500 North Orleans
Chicago, IL 60610
(312) 329-1777

Verilink Corporation
145 Baytech Drive
San Jose, CA 95134
(408) 945-1199

Vertex Computer Cable &
   Products
420 Northboro Road
Marlborough, MA 01752
(508) 485-4202

Vitalink Communications
   Corporation
6607 Kaiser Drive
Fremont, CA 94555
(415) 794-1100

Xircom
22231 Mulholland
   Highway
Suite 114
Woodland Hills, CA 91364
(818) 884-8755

The COLORPAL Utility

COLORPAL Rules
Changing or Adding Color Palettes

The COLORPAL menu utility is used to create new color schemes for your menu utilities, including those provided with NetWare such as SYSCON, FILER, and SESSION.

You can use the COLORPAL menu utility to manage all palettes, which are numbered starting with palette 0. The first five palettes are the default palettes used by the NetWare menu utilities. Initially they are set to blue backgrounds with white letters. If you change the color schemes for these default palettes numbered 0 through 4, you permanently change the default colors for all the NetWare utilities. It is suggested, therefore, that you experiment with COLORPAL by creating your own palette files in directories other than SYS:PUBLIC. You can create your own color palettes starting with palette 5. To make a custom palette the color scheme for custom menus, you must include the palette number as a parameter on the menu header line in the menu text file, as discussed in Chapter 29.

The main color table used by COLORPAL is located in the file IBM$RUN.OVL in the SYS:PUBLIC directory. Any changes made with COLORPAL are stored in this file, assuming you make the changes while logged into the SYS:PUBLIC directory.

APPENDIX E

COLORPAL Rules

When menus are run they automatically use the color schemes specified by the IBM$RUN.OVL file in the SYS:PUBLIC directory, if that is the only color palette file stored on the server. However, menus first look for an equivalent IBM$RUN.OVL file in the current default directory before using the one in SYS:PUBLIC. Menu utilities then start searching through the mapped search drives for other palettes. The following rules apply:

- An altered version of IBM$RUN.OVL can be placed in any directory. Menus executed from that directory use the altered version of IBM$RUN.OVL.

- An altered version of IBM$RUN.OVL can be placed in any directory that is mapped as the first search drive. Menus then use this altered file before resorting to the IBM$RUN.OVL file in the SYS:PUBLIC directory. Note that this rule assumes the current default directory does not have an IBM$RUN.OVL file.

- You can specify a short machine type other than IBM in the SHELL.CFG file of a workstation to use a different color palette file during a session. For example, if you include the following command in the SHELL.CFG file

    SHORT MACHINE TYPE = AST

    NetWare uses a file called AST$RUN.OVL for its color palette specifications during the workstation's session. Only the station booting with this SHELL.CFG file is affected. The AST$RUN.OVL file can coexist with the IBM$RUN.OVL file in the SYS:PUBLIC directory.

- Whenever you run COLORPAL from the SYS:PUBLIC directory, alterations are made to the default IBM$RUN.OVL file. To create custom palettes, simply run COLORPAL from another directory.

COLORPAL automatically places an altered version of IBM$RUN.OVL in the new directory. Whenever menus are run from that directory, the colors of the altered palette file are used.

- You can add palettes to the default IBM$RUN.OVL file in SYS:PUBLIC by specifying palettes greater than 4. You then can call these palettes from your custom menu utilities by specifying the palette number as a parameter on a menu header line, as described in Chapter 29.

- Workstations running monochrome monitors are rarely affected by the COLORPAL settings. However, some monochrome monitors running on composite color video adapters may be unreadable. If this is the case, you should specify the CMPQ$RUN.OVL file in the SYS:PUBLIC directory for these stations by placing the following command in the SHELL.CFG file of the workstation:

SHORT MACHINE TYPE = CMPQ

The CMPQ$RUN.OVL file is designed for monochrome systems that may be affected by the contrast and intensity of the normal color palette file.

Default Color Palette

The default color palettes used by the NetWare menu utilities are the first five palettes specified in the IBM$RUN.OVL file. These palettes are listed here, along with the specific NetWare menus they affect:

Palette 0 affects lists, menus, and normal text

Palette 1 affects main headers and screen backgrounds

Palette 2 affects help screens

Palette 3 affects error messages

Palette 4 affects exit and alert menus

Changing or Adding
Color Palettes

Recall that a color palette is a color scheme used by the NetWare menu utilities or your own menu utilities. The first five color palettes in the IBM$RUN.OVL file are used by the NetWare menu utilities. If you change these palettes, you permanently change the color of the utilities. This section covers adding additional color palettes that can be used by your custom menu, as discussed in Chapter 29.

You can start COLORPAL from the SYS:PUBLIC directory to make changes to the default IBM$RUN.OVL file, or you can start COLORPAL from another directory to create a new version of IBM$RUN.OVL in the current directory. Menus run from the current directory then use the new color palette file instead of the one in the SYS:PUBLIC directory. This section assumes that you are logged into the SYS:PUBLIC directory and are adding new palettes to the default color file.

To start the COLORPAL utility, type **COLORPAL** while logged into the SYS:PUBLIC directory. The menu lists the current palettes in order. The NetWare default palettes 0 through 4 are listed first. Press INS to add a new color palette. Color palette 5 is added to the list of defined palettes.

To edit the new color palette, highlight it and press ENTER. When the "Edit Attribute" window appears, you will see a list of attributes you can change for color palette 5. These attributes are described here:

- *Background Normal*   The field on which menu titles and text are displayed.

- *Background Reverse*   The color of the highlight bar.

- *Foreground Intense*   The highlight for the text and borders of currently active menu options.

- *Foreground Normal*   The color of normal text and border displays.

- *Foreground Reverse*   The color of text covered by the highlight bar.

The Color Palette window shows how the various color attributes actually appear prior to making changes. This window reflects any color changes made as you proceed.

To make changes highlight the selection you want to change and press ENTER. A list of possible colors appears. This list is more extensive for foreground menu colors than background colors. The current color is highlighted. Simply highlight a new color and press ENTER. You can repeat this procedure for each menu attribute. When done, press ESC to exit from the menu, and be sure to enter **Yes** to save any changes you have made.

Games

NSNIPES is a network game that can be played by one or more users. The object of the game is to shoot and destroy snipes and the factories that make them before being shot by the snipes. If playing against others you shoot other players as well.

There are two versions of the game. NSNIPES is played on systems with monochrome screens, and NCSNIPES is played on systems with color screens. The commands to start the games take the following forms:

NSNIPES *option*

NCSNIPES *option*

where *option* is a number between 1 and 10 that specifies the skill level of the game. Increasing the skill level increases the number of snipes and how quickly they are produced.

The playing field is a maze. The object is to shoot and destroy snipes, and if two or more players are playing the game, players shoot other players. The following actions are available:

- To move through the maze, use the arrow keys on the keyboard.

- To move diagonally, press two arrow keys at once.

- To go faster, press the spacebar while pressing any of the arrow keys.

- Type **A** to fire left, **D** to fire right, **W** to fire up, and **S** or **X** to fire down. To fire diagonally, press two of the keys above that correspond with the direction you want to fire.

- The game is stopped by pressing CTRL-BREAK.

Note: The game is limited to five players who must have the Read, Write, Open, Create, and Delete rights in a given directory.

If two or more players want to play SNIPES in the same maze, they must map their default drives to the same directory on the same file server. One user executes the game by specifying the skill level after the NSNIPES or NCSNIPES command. Remaining users then enter the game from the same directory by typing the NSNIPES or NCSNIPES command without specifying a skill level. The game is started after all users have entered the command. If five people are playing, the game automatically begins when the fifth player enters the command.

Installing OS/2 Workstations

Installing the OS/2 Workstation Files
Installing OS/2 Requester on the Server
Named Pipes Support

The Novell OS/2 Requester allows OS/2 workstations to attach to the network. Files on the OS/2 Requester's disks are copied to the server and to the OS/2 workstations. This chapter outlines the hardware you need to run OS/2 and the installation steps to install the OS/2 Requester software, which ships with NetWare 386.

Note that Novell does not recommend using the NetWare utilities to manipulate files on a local OS/2 high performance file system (HPFS) drive.

Installing the OS/2 Workstation Files

Follow these four steps to install the OS/2 Requester files on an OS/2 workstation:

1. Make sure the OS/2 workstation is attached to the network, and boot it with OS/2.

2. Place the Requester disk in the floppy drive and type **INSTALL**.

3. Follow the installation prompts and the suggestions in the OS/2 Requester manual to copy files into directories on the OS/2 workstation.

4. Combine the CONFIG.PST file with the workstation's CONFIG.SYS file. The statements in this file are preceded by REM statements, so they will not execute until you remove the REM statements. Do so for the statement that loads the driver for your network interface card.

To edit the CONFIG.SYS file, first remove the REM statement from in front of the line that lists the interface card installed in the workstation. Then remove the REM statement from each command shown in the following list to activate the commands when the station is rebooted. Note that *directory* is the name of the directory the OS/2 files were copied to.

- To use the Token Ring driver with Communications Services Manager in IBM OS/2 Extended Edition v1.2, activate

  REM DEVICE=C:*directory*\TOKENEE.SYS

- To use SPX, activate

  REM DEVICE=C:*directory*\SPX.SYS
  REM RUN=C:*directory*\SPDAEMON.SYS

- To use OS/2 Named Pipes without specifying your workstation as an OS/2 Named Pipes server, install SPX and activate the following commands:

  REM DEVICE=C:*directory*\NMPIPE.SYS
  REM RUN=C:*directory*\NPDAEMON.EXE

- To use OS/2 Named Pipes and have your workstation act as an OS/2 Named Pipes server, activate the following commands:

  REM DEVICE=C:*directory*\NMPIPE.SYS
  REM RUN=C:*directory*\NPDAEMON.EXE *computername*

Replace *computername* with the name for the OS/2 Named Pipes server. Do not duplicate another name.

- To use NetBIOS, activate

  REM DEVICE=C:*directory* \NETBIOS.SYS
  REM RUN=C:*directory* \NPDAEMON.EXE

- Make sure the following lines are activated in the order shown here:

  DEVICE=C:*directory* \NWREQ..SYS
  IFS=C:\directory\NWIFS.IFS
  RUN=C:*directory* \NPDAEMON.EXE

Save the CONFIG.SYS file as a text file. When all the installation tasks are completed, you can reboot the workstation. If the workstation is attached to a working network, it should respond to the NetWare Requester. The NetWare Requester maps network drive L to SYS:LOGIN for that server. Refer to the next section to install the OS/2 NetWare utilities.

Installing OS/2 Requester On the Server

OS/2 cannot use DOS utilities, so the NetWare Requester comes with a set of utilities that you must install in a separate directory on the server. You need to create two new directories, and then copy the files to them. These steps must be performed only once to support any number of OS/2 workstations. The following steps outline the process:

1. Start the OS/2 workstation and choose OS/2 Full Screen mode. Place the OS2UTIL-1 disk in drive A and switch to the drive.

2. Log into the server as the supervisor.

3. Create two new directories using these commands:

   MD SYS:PUBLIC\OS2
   MD SYS:LOGIN\OS2

3. Map the new directories to drive P and drive L with the following commands:

    MAP P:=SYS:PUBLIC\OS2
    MAP L:=SYS:LOGIN\OS2

    Add these commands to the login script for OS/2 users.

4. Place the OS/2 Requester OS2UTIL-1 disk in the workstation's floppy drive and type **SERVINST**.

5. You must flag the files in the directories as Shareable and Read Only using the following commands:

    FLAG P:*.* SRO
    FLAG L:*.* SRO

6. As you add new OS/2 workstation users, you need to give them Read and File Scan rights in the two directories.

Named Pipes Support

If you need to use the NetWare DOS Named Pipes extender to run applications that require this type of communications media, copy the file DOSNP in the DOSNP directory of the Requester disk to the boot disk or directory of the workstation. Add the command DOSNP to the AUTO-EXEC.BAT file so it executes every time the workstation starts.

Installing ODI Workstations

Novell's Open Data-Link Interface (ODI) allows a workstation to use multiple communication protocols and drivers. A single card can use IPX/SPX, AppleTalk, or TCP/IP protocols at the same time. Communication can be established with other systems that use these protocols, without rebooting the system. Novell releases LAN drivers and protocols as required.

Note that ODI does not work unless the driver for a particular network interface card supports it.

The following files are required on the boot disk or boot directory of the ODI workstation:

- The LSL.COM (Link Support Layer) file that allows the workstation to use several protocols.

- The LAN drivers for the network interface cards.

- The protocol files that are linked to the LAN drivers, such as IPXODI.COM.

- The normal NetWare shells used to redirect network commands to the server instead of the local operating system. These files are NET*x*.COM, EMSNET*x*.EXE, and XMSNET*x*.EXE. Refer to Chapter 18 for more information on the shell files.

To install an ODI workstation, first set up the computer and install the network interface boards. Make sure the network board is not using any interrupts or settings used by other boards. Create a master boot disk for the workstation that contains the DOS files, startup files, and other configuration files the workstation needs to boot. These steps are similar to those in Chapter 18 for DOS workstations.

Follow these steps to make the workstation boot disk ODI compatible:

A
P
P
E
N
D
I
X

H

1. Copy either the NET*x*.COM (conventional memory), EMSNET-*x*.EXE (expanded memory), or XMSNET*x*.EXE (extended memory) files to the boot disk. Refer to Chapter 18 for information on these files. Do not forget to copy the files needed to initialize extended or expanded memory supplied with the board.

2. Copy the following files to the master boot disk from the DOS/DOS ODI Workstation Services disk:

   • LSL.COM

   • The LAN driver for the installed board

   • The protocol stack to be bound to the board (IPXODI.COM or other)

   You may also need the files NETBIOS.EXE, INT2F.COM, or ROUTE.COM (for Token Ring networks with routers).

3. Create an AUTOEXEC.BAT file that contains the commands you copied to the disk. Place the commands in the order shown here where *driver, protocol,* and *shell* are replaced with the appropriate names:

   ```
   LSL
   driver
   protocol
   shell
   ```

4. Create a CONFIG.SYS file on the master disk that contains the following commands:

   ```
   FILES = 20
   BUFFERS = 20
   ```

   The file and buffer settings can be higher to accommodate other applications. If you have existing CONFIG.SYS files, be sure to add these commands to the file.

5. Create a NET.CFG file if you need to change the default settings of the protocol, LAN driver, and network interface card. Refer to Appendix I for more information.

6. Create copies of the master disk for each workstation. You may want to customize the disk for each workstation with startup commands for the particular user or the workstation hardware.

The SHELL.CFG and NET.CFG Configuration Files

The SHELL.CFG Configuration File
The NET.CFG Configuration File

Each workstation can have a configuration file that contains commands to customize it for the NetWare environment. You can use the commands to change the normal default setting for workstations. When the workstation logs into the server, the commands in the file execute. Not all workstations need configuration files, but, you still should scan through the following lists for commands that can be used to optimize the performance of a workstation.

There are two configuration files. The SHELL.CFG file was part of NetWare 286 and is included in NetWare 386. However, Novell is attempting to migrate users to a new file called NET.CFG, which has a more versatile format. The SHELL.CFG commands can be included in the NET.CFG file for those creating new configuration files. Workstations with existing SHELL.CFG files can continue to operate with the old files, but commands for NET.CFG can only be placed in a NET.CFG file.

You can create both files with a text editor or word processor. If you use a word processor, make sure the files are saved as ASCII text files (which have no formatting codes).

The SHELL.CFG Configuration File

The SHELL.CFG file specifies changes to the startup configuration of a workstation. This file is similar to the DOS CONFIG.SYS file because the commands in it are executed when a workstation logs onto the network. Commands in the file can be used to alter IPX.COM, NET*x*.COM, and NETBIOS.

Note: Most of the options covered in this section are for advanced use, except those described under "Useful SHELL.CFG Commands." You can quickly scan the options for now, and then refer to them later if you need to add them to a station's SHELL.CFG file.

Useful SHELL.CFG Commands

While most of the commands for SHELL.CFG are used to set advanced options, there are a few commands you may want to set on every workstation. SHELL.CFG can be created on the root directory of the boot disk with the COPY CON command. It can include any of the following options:

LOCAL PRINTERS=0   Specifies the absence of a local printer at the workstation. All printing automatically is redirected to the default network printer.

READ ONLY COMPATIBILITY=ON   Specifies read-only compatibility for electronic mail programs. Use this option if it is required by the mail program.

LONG MACHINE TYPE=*name*   Replace *name* with a name that indicates the DOS type used on the workstation. For example, you could use IBMDOS3 for IBM DOS version 3, or COMPAQ4 for Compaq MS DOS version 4.1. A directory of the same name should then be created on the server for the DOS files. The command sets a variable used by the system login script to create a path for the workstation to the appropriate DOS directory on the server. This is covered in Chapter 19.

SHORT MACHINE TYPE=*name*   Replace *name* with a four-character (maximum) variable that specifies which overlay file the workstation should use for menus (color default, monochrome, or custom colors). To use the default color scheme, leave this option out. For monochrome systems, specify CMPQ.

PREFERRED SERVER=*name*   Set *name* to the name of the server to attach to when logging in.

Options for EMSNET*x*.EXE

The parameter ENTRY STACK SIZE=*number* should be set high for TSRs and other programs using expanded memory to ensure that the code residing in expanded memory is visible in the memory page frame. The default is 10, and the range is 5 to 40.

Options for Altering NET*x*.COM

The following commands are read by NET*x*.COM at boot time. Type those required by an individual workstation on separate lines in the SHELL.CFG file.

ALL SERVERS=ON/OFF   If set to On, an "End of task" message is sent to all connected servers, not just those interacting with a task. The default is Off.

CACHE BUFFERS=*number*   Sets the quantity of 512-byte buffers. The default is 5. Improves network performance by providing a buffer for disk data during sequential reads.

EOJ=ON/OFF   Sets to On or Off the end-of-job (closing of files, locks, semaphores, and so on). The default is On.

FILE HANDLES=*number*   Sets the number of possible open files. The default is 40.

HOLD=ON/OFF   Sets file hold On or Off. If On, all files opened by a program are not usable by others until the program ends. The default is Off.

LOCAL PRINTERS=*number*   Can be used to specify zero printers at the local workstation to prevent system lock if SHIFT-PRTSC is accidentally pressed.

LOCK DELAY=*number*   Sets the amount of tick times the shell should wait before retrying to get a lock. The default is 1.

LOCK RETRIES=*number*   Sets the number of times the shell should attempt to get a lock on the network. The default is 3.

LONG MACHINE TYPE=*name*   Assigns a six-character name to a machine that is later used by the %MACHINE variable in login scripts to establish the operating environment for a specific type or brand of machine and the DOS version it is running.

MAX CUR DIR LENGTH=*number*   Defines the "Get Current Directory" call to return 64 bytes of path. Set *number* to a configurable range of 64 to 255.

MAX PATH LENGTH=*number*   Specifies the maximum size of the path that can be specified. The default is 255, and the range is 64 to 255.

MAX TASKS=*number*   Specifies the maximum number of simultaneous active tasks. The default is 31, the minimum is 8, and the maximum is 50.

PATCH=*byte offset,value*   Allows an option in the shell to be patched with any value.

PREFERRED SERVER=*name*   Specifies the name of the server to attach to when you log in.

PRINT HEADER=*number*   Sets the size of the buffer holding the printer escape characters sent before a print job. The default is 65 bytes.

PRINT TAIL=*number*   Sets the size of the buffer holding the printer escape characters sent after a print job. The default is 16 characters.

READ ONLY COMPATIBILITY=ON/OFF   When set to On, the shell reverts to an older NetWare method of allowing read-only files to be opened with a write access call. Any attempt to write to the file fails, however.

SEARCH MODE=*number*   Sets the way EXE and COM files search for needed files in the directory structure. The default is 1. You can set the following search modes:

0   No search instructions.

1   Search on the path specified in the executable file itself. If a path is not specified, search the default directory and then all search drives.

2   Search on the default directory.

3   Search only the path leading to the data file specified in the EXE file itself. If a path is not specified and the executable file opens data files as read-only, search the default directory and then all search drives.

4   Reserved.

5   Search the default directory and all search drives whether or not the path is specified in the executable file.

6   Reserved.

7   Search the default directory and all search drives whether or not the path is specified in the executable file, if the executable file opens read-only data files.

SET STATION TIME=ON/OFF   The default setting of On synchronizes the workstation time with the file server's time. Set to Off if this should not occur.

SHARE=ON/OFF   Sets file-handle sharing. When set to On, the child process inherits the file handle of the parent process. The default is On.

SHORT MACHINE TYPE=*name*   Assigns a four-character short name to the variable %SMACHINE that specifies the color palette for menu utilities. The default color palette short machine name is IBM. Setting the short machine name to CMPQ sets black-and-white mode.

SHOW DOTS=ON/OFF   Set this option to on for Windows 3. It is used to emulate the . and .. directory entries of DOS.

SPECIAL UPPERCASE=ON/OFF   Set this parameter to On to have the shell call DOS to perform translations of ASCII characters above 128 (foreign language and special characters).

TASK MODE=*number*   This option determines the way in which the shell creates, switches, and destroys tasks. If you are using Windows 3.0 or any multitasking program, set TASK MODE to 1. If you are not, set to 0. The default is 1.

Options for Altering IPX and SPX

The following commands are read by IPX.COM at boot time. Type those required by an individual workstation on separate lines in the SHELL.CFG file.

INT64=ON/OFF   This option allows applications to use interrupt 64h to access IPX services and maintain compatibility with earlier versions of NetWare. If an application works on earlier versions of NetWare but not on NetWare 386, set this parameter to Off.

INT7A=ON/OFF   This option allows applications to use interrupt 7Ah to access IPX services and maintain compatibility with earlier versions of NetWare. If an application works on earlier versions of NetWare but not on NetWare 386, set this parameter to Off.

IPATCH=*byte,value*   Allows any location in the IPX.COM file to be patched with any value.

IPX PACKET SIZE LIMIT=*number*   Set *number* to reduce the maximum packet size set by each LAN driver. This saves memory if "out of memory" errors occur at the workstation. The optimum size for Token Ring is 4160 bytes and for Ethernet is 1500 bytes. Note that some drivers may not support this option since it is new with NetWare 386 v3.1. The range is 576 to 6500 bytes, and the default is 4160 bytes or the size set by the LAN driver.

IPX RETRY COUNT=*number*   Sets the number of times a packet should be resent if packets are lost. The default is 20.

IPX SOCKETS=*number*   Specifies the maximum number of sockets, or subaddresses, that IPX can have open at the workstation. The default is 20. Change if an application using IPX requests an increase in the default.

SPX ABORT TIMEOUT=*number*   Specifies the wait time before a session is aborted if responses are not being received from the other side. The default is 540 ticks (30 seconds).

SPX CONNECTIONS=*number*   Specifies the maximum number of SPX connections a workstation can use at the same time. The default number is 15.

SPX LISTEN TIMEOUT=*number*   Sets the amount of time SPX waits for a session packet before a request for a session packet is made. The session is still valid if the request for a packet gets a response. The default is 108 ticks (6 seconds).

SPX VERIFY TIMEOUT=*number*   Sets the interval at which SPX sends packets to determine if a session is still active. The default is 540 ticks (30 seconds).

Options for Altering NETBIOS

You can use the following options to alter the NETBIOS environment if it is being used. Type each on a separate line in the SHELL.CFG file.

NETBIOS ABORT TIMEOUT=*number*   Specifies the amount of time NETBIOS waits for a response before terminating a session. *Number* is in ticks (18.21 per second on IBM compatibles). The default is 540 ticks (30 seconds).

NETBIOS BROADCAST COUNT=*number*   Increase *number* if many LAN segment nodes need NetBIOS or a gateway cannot attach. The default is 2 to 4, depending on the setting of NETBIOS INTERNET, and the range is 2 to 65,535.

NETBIOS BROADCAST DELAY=number   Increase *number* if the packet loss rate is high or if traffic is high. The default is 18 to 36, depending on the setting of NETBIOS INTERNET, and the range is 18 to 65,535.

NETBIOS COMMANDS=*number*   The number of commands needed for applications may vary. Set this number higher than the default of 12 if NetBIOS command error 22 occurs.

NETBIOS INTERNET=ON/OFF   Set this parameter to Off to increase performance if only one network is used. If more than one network or LAN segment is running and a bridge is used, this parameter must be set to On, which is the default.

NETBIOS LISTEN TIMEOUT=number   Sets the amount of time NETBIOS waits for a session packet before a request for a session packet is made. The session is still valid if the request for a packet gets a response. The default is 108 ticks (6 seconds).

NETBIOS RECEIVE BUFFERS=*number* Sets the number of receive buffers NETBIOS uses. The default is 6, and the range is 4 to 20.

NETBIOS RETRY COUNT=*number* Determines the number of times NETBIOS sends a packet to establish a session with a remote partner. Increase the value if there are many LAN segments using NetBIOS or you cannot attach to a gateway.

NETBIOS RETRY DELAY=*number* Sets the delay (in ticks) between each packet sent when establishing sessions or registering names. The default is 10 ticks (0.5 second).

NETBIOS SEND BUFFERS=*number* Sets the number of send buffers NETBIOS uses. The default is 6, and the range is 4 to 20.

NETBIOS SESSIONS=*number* Sets the number of sessions NETBIOS supports at one time. The default is 10, and the range is 4 to 100.

NETBIOS VERIFY TIMEOUT=*number* Sets the interval at which NETBIOS sends packets to determine if a session is still active. The default is 54 ticks (3 seconds).

NPATCH=*byte offset,value* Used to patch any location in the NETBIOS.EXE data segment with any value.

The NET.CFG Configuration File

The NET.CFG file must be created with special header sections and indented commands, unlike the SHELL.CFG file that is all left-justified.

The section headers are as follows, and the options that are indented and placed under each header are described in the following sections.

LINK SUPPORT

PROTOCOL "protocol_name"

LINK DRIVER "drivername"

LINK DRIVER LANSUP (IBM LAN Support Program)

An example file is shown here:

```
LINK SUPPORT
    BUFFERS 5
LAN DRIVER NE2000
    DMA 3
    INT 5
```

Link Support Options

The header for the link support options is

```
LINK SUPPORT
```

Left justify the header, and then type one of the following options under it, making sure to indent each option.

BUFFERS *number size*   Replace *number* with the number of receive buffers and *size* with the size of the buffers. The default size is 1130, and the minimum is 586. The number of buffers must be large enough to hold all media headers and the desired maximum data size.

MEMPOOL *number*   Some protocols set *number* to the size of the memory pool buffers that the link support layer will maintain. The IPXODI protocol stack does not use this option. Refer to the protocol documentation for more information.

Protocol Options

The following information is used to configure protocols. Refer to the protocol documentation for more information. The header for the protocol options is

PROTOCOL *name*

Left justify the header, and replace *name* with the name of the protocol. Then type one of the following options under it, making sure to indent each option.

BIND *name*   The IPXODI protocol usually binds to the first network board it finds. The search order is the order of the slots in the workstation. To specify a specific board, replace *name* with one of the following:

TRXNET	Novell RX-Net
NE2	Novell Ethernet NE/2
NE2-32	Novell Ethernet NE/2-32
NE1000	Novell Ethernet NE1000
NE2000	Novell Ethernet NE2000
LANSUP	IBM LAN Support Program
3C503	3Com EtherLink Series 503
3C523	3Com EtherLink/MC

Check your board documentation for the names of other boards. The following parameters can be used for non-IPXODI protocol stacks.

DEFAULT *name*   Replace *name* with one of the LAN driver names just listed. It configures the protocol to a default stack.

PRESCAN *name*   Replace *name* with one of the LAN driver names previously listed. It configures the protocol to a default prescan stack.

SESSION *number*   Set *number* to the number of sessions that the protocol stack must maintain, as outlined in the protocol's documentation.

Link Driver Options

The following options are used to change the setting of network interface cards and how they link with protocols. Refer to the LAN driver or protocol documentation for more information. The header for the Link Driver option is as follows:

LINK DRIVER *drivername*

Type is left justified on a line, and *drivername* is replaced with the name of the driver you are using. The names are listed under the BIND parameter in the "Protocol Options" section. Enter one of the following parameters under the header and indent.

DMA *number*   Use this option to configure either one or two DMA channels, replacing *number* with the DMA channel number. If a second channel is configured, type **#2** before the channel number, as shown in the following example:

DMA 3
DMA #2 4

The first DMA option configures the first board and the second option configures the second board.

INT *number*   Use this option to configure the interrupts used by the board, replacing *number* with the interrupt number. If a second interrupt is configured, type **#2** before the number, as shown here:

INT 2
INT #2 3

The first INT option configures the first board and the second option configures the second board.

MEM *number length*   This option specifies the memory range to be used by the network board. Replace *number* with the hexadecimal physical (absolute) address of the memory used by the network board. Replace *length* with the hexadecimal paragraph length.

NODE ADDRESS *number*   Replace *number* with a node address that overrides any hard-coded node address on the network interface card if the card allows it.

PORT *address ports*   Use this option to specify the starting port and number of ports in the range. Replace *address* with a hexadecimal I/O starting port number and *ports* with a hexadecimal number that represents the ports in the range. You can specify two ranges, if the board supports it, by typing the command a second time with **#2** in front of the *address* parameter.

PS/2 SLOT ?   Use this option if only one of the same type of board is installed. It causes the LAN driver to scan for its board.

PS/2 SLOT *number*   Use this parameter to specify exactly which slots two boards of the same type occupy. Replace number with the slot number of the second board.

FRAME *type*   Use this option to specify the frame type for a network interface card. Replace *type* with one of the following frame types, which are discussed in Chapter 35:

ETHERNET_802.3

ETHERNET_II

ETHERNET_802.2

ETHERNET_SNAP

TOKEN-RING

TOKEN-RING_SNAP

LOOK AHEAD SIZE *number*   Replace *number* with the number of bytes in the packet that the LAN driver sends to the link support layer to determine how to route the packet. The range is 0 to 128 bytes, depending on the protocol.

PROTOCOL *name type*   Use this option to allow existing LAN drivers to handle new protocols. Replace *name* with the hexadecimal protocol ID number for the new protocol name. Replace *type* with the frame type. Frame types were previously listed under the FRAME option.

SEND RETRIES *number*   Replace *number* with the maximum number of times the driver resends a packet following an error. The default is determined by the driver.

Link Driver LANSUP Options

Use the following options if you use the LANSUP (IBM LAN Support) driver with a network interface card. Refer to the LAN Support Program documentation for additional information. The header for the LANSUP option is

LINK DRIVER LANSUP

Left justify the header, and then type one of the following options under it, making sure to indent each option.

SAPS *number*   Replace *number* with the number of service access points needed. The default is 1.

LINK STATIONS *number*   Replace *number* with the number of link stations needed. The default is 1.

MAX PACKET *number*   Replace *number* with a larger packet size if necessary.

Description: AmeriCorps Members will serve at Opportunity Centers, located at public housing and school sites, tutoring and mentoring to promote school success, and recruiting and training parents and community volunteers to assist children at-risk of academic failure.
Contact: Mr. Dale Rice; 313/487-0028; 313/487-7153 (fax)

State Priorities:

Its mission is to encourage volunteerism, especially among young people, as an effective means of meeting the serious social challenges that face our communities today. The Commission has been designated as Michigan's lead agency in applying for federal dollars from the Commission on National and Community Service.

MINNESOTA

State Lead Contact:

Mary Jo Richardson
Department of Education
683 Capitol Square Building
550 Cedar Street
St. Paul, MN 55101
Phone: 612/296-1435
Fax: 612/297-3348

State Commission:

Minnesota Commission on National and Community Service

1995-96 Programs

National Service Network

MN-1

Statewide:
Program: USDA Rural Development Team
AmeriCorps Members: 21
Description: AmeriCorps Members will help communities protect watersheds, improve housing, promote economic development, boost sustainable agriculture and respond to disasters.
Contact: Joel Berg; 202/720-6350

MN-2

Statewide:
Program: USDA Rural Development Team
AmeriCorps Members: 78 in the 9 Flood States
Description: Responding to the environmental and economic damage caused by last year's flood, AmeriCorps Members will assess flood-relief needs, explain wetlands delineation to land owners and work to reduce ground water pollution.
Contact: Joel Berg; 202/720-6350

MN-3

Statewide:
Program: USDA Public Lands and Environment Team
AmeriCorps Members: 73 in the 9 Flood States
Description: AmeriCorps Members will engage a variety of flood relief work by assessing damage, restoring wetlands, and restoring flood control facilities.
Contact: Joel Berg; 202/720-6350

MN-4

Duluth:
Program: YMCA Earth Service Corps Fellowship
AmeriCorps Members: 40 Nationally
Description: AmeriCorps Members will address local environmental concerns coordinating park cleanups, urban gardening projects and environmental symposia.
Contact: Celeste Wroblewski; 312/269-0506

MN-5

St. Paul:
Program: National Multiple Sclerosis Society/"Bridge to Independence"
AmeriCorps Members: 8 (144 Nationally)
Description: AmeriCorps Members, many of who have Multiple Sclerosis will work to build awareness about Multiple Sclerosis while coordinating volunteers in extensive living assistance programs—helping disadvantaged people to make it on their own.
Contact: Colleen Bjerke; 612/870-1500; 612/870-0265 (fax)

State and Local

MN-6

Minneapolis:
Program: Two or More, Inc./Twin Cities Youth and Housing Initiative
AmeriCorps Members: 25
Description: AmeriCorps Members will provide quality, affordable housing to 150 low-income families by rehabilitating and building housing, repairing nearly 60 apartments, and assisting residents in achieving self-sufficiency.
Contact: Earl Rogers; 612/521-8736; 612/521-4809 (fax)

MN-7

Minneapolis:
Program Pillsbury Neighborhood Services, Inc./Community Works
AmeriCorps Members: 26
Description: AmeriCorps Members will address inner city poverty, crime, and low educational achievement by linking 500 area families to community services, providing employment support, tutoring adults and youth, and creating safe havens in high-crime communities.
Contact: Andrea Breen or Edwin Espino; 612/338-5282; 612/338-8421 (fax)

MN-8

Owatonna:
Program: Southeastern Minnesota Initiative Fund/Southern Minnesota Youth Works Coalition
AmeriCorps Members: 55
Description: AmeriCorps Members to address the needs of large, low-income immigrant populations to adjust to area life by linking families to human services, mentoring and tutoring youth, tutoring adults and youth in English language skills, and assisting at homeless and domestic abuse shelters.
Contact: Mr. Keith Luebke; 507/455-3215; 507/455-2098 (fax)

MN-9

Red Lake:
Program: Red Lake Tribal Council/Partners in Service to America

AmeriCorps Members: 55
Description: Planning grant developed by the Red Lake Tribal Council in partnership with the Bois Forte Indian Reservation to address poverty, substance abuse, and environmental needs of Red Lake through tutoring, substance abuse education, life skills straining, and restoration and conservation of area land.
Contact: Red Lake Tribal Council; 218/679-3959

MN-10

St. Paul:
Program: Neighborhood Housing Association/Multicultural Communities in Action
AmeriCorps Members: 26
Description: AmeriCorps Members will address high crime and poverty in increasingly multicultural communities by mentoring and tutoring 500 area children, creating safe havens by restoring area green spaces, and providing alternatives to violence activities for youth.
Contact: Eric Adams; 612/227-9291; 612/227-9291 (fax)

MN-11

St. Paul:
Program: City of Saint Paul/Future Force-St. Paul
AmeriCorps Members: 76
Description: AmeriCorps Members will address high poverty, crime, and low educational achievement by tutoring and mentoring 250 youth, teaching conflict resolution skills to 500 youth, organizing neighborhood clean-ups, and linking the elderly to independent living services.
Contact: Don Long; 612/641-8704

MN-12

City of Lakes:
Program: City of Lakes Minneapolis Public Schools
AmeriCorps Members: 25
Description: AmeriCorps Members will be involved in many services with children including tutoring, enrichment programs, and conflict resolution.
Contact: Kathy Marker; 612/371-8700

MN-13

St. Paul:
Program: Minnesota Department of Natural Resources-Minnesota Conservation Corps
AmeriCorps Members: 77
Description: AmeriCorps Members will address the environmental quality of low-income communities.
Contact: Larry Fonnest; 612/296-8195

MN-14

Statewide:
Program: Minnesota Department of Economic Security/Service Delivery Areas/Community Action Agencies
AmeriCorps Members: 70
Description: AmeriCorps Members will provide child care, tutoring, and housing support services to low-income families.
Contact: Susan Lauer; 612/296-7134

State Priorities:

In addition to the federal priorities, Minnesota state priorities include the following:

EDUCATION

Family literacy: Providing literacy training for children and their families; and

School-to-work transition: Training and developing youth for a high performance work force.

ENVIRONMENT

Raising environmental consciousness through recycling and other conservation approaches.

HUMAN NEEDS AND PUBLIC SAFETY

Providing an approach that is most likely to reduce arrest rates, incarceration rates, teenage pregnancy, and other indicators of troubled youth.

MISSISSIPPI

State Lead Contact:

Marsha Meeks Kelly

Mississippi Committee for National and Community Service
3825 Ridgewood Rd.
Jackson, MS 39211
Phone: 601/982-6779
Fax: 601/982-6790

1995-96 Programs

National Service Network

MS-1

Statewide:
Program: Delta Service Corps
AmeriCorps Members: 50
Description: Through a partnership with local community agencies, AmeriCorps Members will assist low-income residents in finding low income housing, tutor children to enhance their literacy skills and work with state parks to conserve and restore the environment.
Contact: Jerry Robinson; 601/742-3410; 601/846-4016 (fax)

MS-2

Statewide:
Program: USDA Rural Development Team
AmeriCorps Members: 17
Description: AmeriCorps Members will help communities protect watersheds, improve housing, promote economic development, boost sustainable agriculture and respond to disasters.
Contact: Mr. Bennie Hutchings; 601/833-5539; 601/835-0054 (fax)

MS-3

Clarksdale:
Program: Children's Health Fund/AmeriCorps Community Outreach
AmeriCorps Members: 4 (15 Nationally)
Description: The Children's Health Fund was designed to meet the complex health care needs of medically under-served, homeless, and impoverished children. AmeriCorps Members will work to this end by encouraging families to take advantage of available primary health care resources.
Contact: Aurelia Jones-Taylor; 601/624-2504; 601/627-3629 (fax)

MS-4

Oxford:
Program: Teach for America
AmeriCorps Members: 58 (1000 Nationally)
Description: AmeriCorps Members will respond to an acute need for educators and role models in under-served urban and rural areas by introducing innovative teaching methods to the classroom.
Contact: Anne Ferris; 601/236-4000; 601/236-6206

MS-5

Jackson:
Program: USDA Anti-Hunger Team
AmeriCorps Members: 72
Description: Several local service agencies will join AmeriCorps Members in performing food assistance outreach aimed primarily at needy seniors.
Contact: Alfred Martin; 601/353-3111 (phone & fax)

State and Local

MS-6

Jackson:
Program: Operation Shoestring, Inc./Metro Jackson Service Corps.
AmeriCorps Members: 27
Description: AmeriCorps Members will help prepare disadvantaged children for school and help teen and low-income parents develop their parenting skills. AmeriCorps Members will also assist with community revitalization efforts, including housing rehabilitation.
Contact: Mr. Warren Yoder; 601/353-6336; 601/353-5369 (fax)

MS-7

Oxford:
Program: North Mississippi Regional Center/Interactive Community Transitions (InterACT)
AmeriCorps Members: 23
Description: AmeriCorps Members will help people of all ages with disabilities to help them achieve self-sufficiency. Members will tutor, mentor, and provide in- and after-school learning opportunities to children, as well as pre-employment and job training to

adults with developmental disabilities.
Contact: Dr. Carol B. Haney; 601/234-1476; 601/234-1699 (fax)

MS-8

Jackson:
Program: National Council on the Aging/Christian Children's Fund/AmeriCorps Neighbor-to-Neighbor Program
AmeriCorps Members: 20
Description: AmeriCorps Members will teach immunization education and provide preventive health care education to young mothers.
Contact: Wendell Paris; 601/355-7497; 601/355-1506 (fax)

MISSOURI

State Lead Contact:

Steve Schad
Director
Missouri Community Service Commission
Lt. Governor's Office
State Capitol, Rm. B-14
Jefferson City, MO 65101
Phone: 314/751-0382
Fax: 314/751-9422

1995-96 Programs

National Service Network

MO-1

Kansas City:
Program: Local Inititatives Support Corporation/Campaign for Communities
AmeriCorps Members: 4
Description: AmeriCorps Members will work in community development corporations and engage in comprehensive community revitalization activities, including housing outreach and education, job training, community policing, youth education programs, affordable housing finance and development, neighborhood planning, and human services planning.
Contact: Ms. Katrina Jackson; 816/753-0055

MO-2

Kansas City:
Program: Legal Aid of Western Missouri/
National Legal Service Corps
AmeriCorps Members: 3
Description: AmeriCorps Members will provide conflict mediation training for families
and individuals involved in child custody
and visitation disputes. The goal is to mediate problems rather than have disputes reach
the courts.
Contact: Ms. Anna Marie Merritt 816/474-
6750

MO-3

Program: USDA Mid-Missouri Water Qual-
ity Project
AmeriCorps Members: 5
Description: AmeriCorps Members will
research, develop, and conduct water quality
testing and education efforts in rural mid-
Missouri counties.
Contact: Mr. Ross Braun; 314/876-0912

MO-4

Kansas City:
Program: Kansas City Consensus/Bridges
Across the Heartland
AmeriCorps Members: 76 Members
Description: Supported by a coalition of
experienced non-profit agencies, Ameri-
Corps Members will serve Kansas City urban
communities by providing a comprehensive
response to interrelated community needs.
Contact: Mr. Shawn Corkrean; 816/753-
3398

MO-5

Kansas City:
Program: National Council of the Churches
of Christ in the USA/Break and Build
AmeriCorps Members: 11 full- and 8 part-
time
Description: Joining urban pastors and gang
leaders, AmeriCorps Members will work to
break the cycle of violence by offering educational alternatives to gang involvement
and support to young people already
involved in the criminal justice system.
Contact: Mr. Millus "Doc" Bass; 816/842-
7080

MO-6

Kansas City:
Program: Youth Volunteer Corps of Amer-
ica/YVCA Leadership Corps
AmeriCorps Members: 5 full- and 5 part-
time
Description: AmeriCorps Members will
develop, run, and enroll volunteers in service
projects including: summer camps, academic
enrichment programs, service-learning curricula, conflict resolution training, gang
alternative programs, and identification of
high crime areas.
Contact: Mr. William Adams; 816/561-9622

MO-7

St. Louis:
Program: National Multiple Sclerosis Soci-
ety/"Bridge to Independence"
AmeriCorps Members: 7 part-time
Description: AmeriCorps Members, many of
whom have Multiple Sclerosis, will work to
build awareness about Multiple Sclerosis
while coordinating volunteers in extensive
living assistance programs—helping disadvantaged people to make it on their own.
Contact: Ms. Pat Rettenmaier; 913/432-3926

MO-8

St. Louis:
Program: YouthBuild USA/Youth Education and Health in Soulard
AmeriCorps Members: 4 full- and 32 part-
time
Description: AmeriCorps Members will help
build affordable housing, promote positive
life styles, and promote community service
among youth, while conducting community
building exercises.
Contact: Ms. Catherine Ndgewa; 314/436-
1400

State and Local

MO-9

Cape Girardeau:
Program: Southeast Missouri State Univer-
sity/Southeast Missouri Partnership for
Community Service
AmeriCorps Members: 19 full- and 17 part-
time
Description: AmeriCorps Members will

reduce violence against children by recruiting tutors and mentors to work with high-risk youth, developing a literacy program for parents, developing after-school and summer programs, and working with juvenile authorities to develop service projects for youthful offenders.
Contact: Dr. Johnny McGaha; 314/651-5104

MO-10

Kansas City:
Program: YouthNet of Greater Kansas City/ Kansas City Urban Youth Initiative
AmeriCorps Members: 10 full- and 29 part-time
Description: AmeriCorps Members will reduce the risk of adolescent substance abuse, delinquent or criminal behavior, and distressed low-income housing by engaging youth in sports, educational, and cultural activities, and repairing and weatherizing homes.
Contact: Mr. Rick Malsick; 816/931-9900 ext. 234

MO-11

St. Joseph:
Program: Inter/Serv—Come As You Are Project
AmeriCorps Members: 21 full- and 20 part-time
Description: AmeriCorps Members will serve the St. Joseph area by developing Academic Laboratories in schools, organizing and conducting neighborhood clean-up projects and recycling programs, and working with children to establish community gardens that provide food to local food pantries.
Contact: Ms. Meg McMurray; 816/279-8903

MO-12

ST. LOUIS
Program: American Youth Foundation/ AmeriCorps Program
AmeriCorps Members: 29
Description: AmeriCorps Members will increase the capacity of schools to improve school achievement of 4th-8th graders in low-income communities by identifying and training 500 volunteers to develop service projects in literacy, care of the environment,

first aid and personal safety, and substance abuse prevention.
Contact: Mr. Robert MacArthur; 314/772-8626; 314/772-7542 (fax)

MO-13

St. Louis:
Program: Grace Hill Neighborhood Services/St. Louis Riverfront Trail Project
AmeriCorps Members: 20
Description: AmeriCorps Members will conserve the Mississippi Riverfront and increase educational success for urban youth by restoring and beautifying trails, organizing outdoor recreational and educational activities, and planning weekly summer educational events.
Contact: Ms. Sally Haywood; 314/241-2200; 314/241-8939 (fax)

MO-14

Jefferson City:
Program: Lincoln University/Success Centers
AmeriCorps Members: 16 part-time
Description: AmeriCorps Members will establish tutoring centers in three low-income neighborhoods and tutor school-age children after hours and on weekends and during the summer.
Contact: Dr. Marilyn Hoffman; 314/681-5250

MO-15

Kansas City:
Program: YMCA of Greater Kansas City/ Blue Hills Together
AmeriCorps Members: 15
Description: AmeriCorps Members will decrease crime in the Blue Hills neighborhood by teaming with police to carry out community organizing and crime prevention activities, youth activities and organization, and code enforcement.
Contact: Ms. Laurice Valentine; 816/561-9622

MO-16

St. Louis:
Program: St. Louis Partners for Service/ School Success
AmeriCorps Members: 28

Description: AmeriCorps Members will increase the capacity of schools to improve the achievement of 4th-8th graders in low-income communities, identify and train 500 volunteers to develop service projects in literacy, the environment, first aid and personal safety, and substance abuse prevention.
Contact: Ms. Kathleen Becherer; 314/772-8626

MO-17

St. Louis:
Program: St. Louis Partners for Service/Safety Service Corps
AmeriCorps Members: 43
Description: AmeriCorps Members will work to solve community problems by teaming with the St. Louis police, housing authority, and schools; teams will work to decrease crime against senior citizens and violence in housing developments.
Contact: Ms. Sally Haywood; 314/241-2200; 314/241-8939 (fax)

MONTANA

State Lead Contact:

Mary Blake, Director
Office of the Governor
State Capitol Building
Helena, MT 59620
Phone: 406/444-5547
Fax: 406/444-5529

State Commission:

Office of Community Service.

1995-96 Programs

National Service Network

MT-1

Statewide:
(Rural areas)
Program: Association of Farmworkers Opportunity Program
AmeriCorps Members: 61 Nationally
Description: AmeriCorps Members will train migrant and seasonal farmworkers on how to reduce exposure to pesticides and improve farmworkers' access to other health,

education and support services. AmeriCorps members become state-certified pesticide safety trainers and train farmworkers in pesticide safety as required by the EPA Workers Protection Standards.
Contact: Lynda Mull; 703/528-4411

MT-2

Flathead Reservation
Program: HHS Head Start/Family Serve
AmeriCorps Members: 5 full-time, 5 part-time
Description: AmeriCorps Members will work in Head Start centers educating children on the environment and safety, accompanying children to health screenings and assisting staff in nutrition planning and preparation.
Contact: Gail Collins; 202/205-8347

State and Local

MT-3

Bozeman:
Program: Montana Conservation Corps, Inc./AmeriCorps Application
AmeriCorps Members: 32 full-time, 78 part-time
Description: A program that enhances the social and natural environment of Montana by providing AmeriCorps Members with service opportunities in natural and human resource stewardship. MCC corpsmembers will work primarily on natural resource related projects such as construction and maintenance of 110 miles of trail; park improvements such as constructing shelters, making 8 playground facilities handicapped accessible, or building safe playgrounds; habitat enhancements such as stream rehabilitation and planting 1,500 trees; and a variety of community projects ranging from constructing affordable housing to repairing homes for the elderly.
Contact: Mr. Steve Nelsen; 406/587-4475; 406/487-2606 (fax)

MT-4

Browning:
Program: Blackfeet Health and Safety Corps
AmeriCorps Members: 30 full-time; 6 part-time

Description: The program will provide services, including home visits to safety and poison proof homes; one-on-one follow-up and education with victims and families involved in alcohol-related motor vehicle accidents and deaths; and work with youth and community members on conflict resolution and cultural education to prevent violence.
Contact: Colleen Williamson; 406/338-7102; 406/338-7286 (fax)

MT-5

Harlem:
Program: Fort Belknap Program
AmeriCorps Members: 20
Description: The program will accomplish two important community projects with the assistance of AmeriCorps members. The first is improvement of recreation areas through work on natural resource enhancement projects such as trail construction and maintenance; park improvements such as constructing shelters, making facilities handicapped accessible, or building safe playgrounds; and habitat enhancements such as stream rehabilitation and tree thinning. The second is the construction, program development, and operation of the first public radio communication system serving the reservation.
Contact: Ilean Hill; 406/353-2607; Barbara Stiffarm; 406/353-4803

MT-6

Missoula:
Program: Volunteer Montana!/Missoula Aging Services
AmeriCorps Members: 22 full-time
Description: Volunteer Montana! is a volunteer generator model, with AmeriCorps members recruiting and placing volunteers in community-base service organizations to provide a variety of vital services, including tutoring and mentoring at-risk children, rehabilitating homes of low-income residents, and much more.
Contact: Mr. Jim Harris; 406/728-7682; 406/728-7687 (fax)

MT-7

Helena:
Program: Learn and Serve K-12
AmeriCorps Members:
Description: Promotes practical learning programs that enrich academic learning by providing students with opportunities to learn and develop their own capabilities as they engage in service to their communities.
Contact: Linda Peterson; 406/444-5726; 406/444-3924 (fax)

MT-8

Missoula:
Program: Learn and Serve Higher Education Campus Compact
AmeriCorps Members:
Description: fourteen of Montana's universities and colleges belong to the Montana Campus compact, a program to increase campus-wide participation in community and public service and to insure that practical learning is a valued component of undergraduate work.
Contact: Ryan Tolleson Knee; 406/243-4228; 406/243-2797 (fax)

MT-9

Missoula:
Program: Montana Campus Corps
AmeriCorps Members:
Description: Program will place part-time work study college students on campuses throughout Montana. Members will make a 2-year commitment to service in community service and service-learning activities.
Contact: Ryan Tolleson Knee; 406/243-4228; 406/243-2797 (fax)

State Priorities:

Same as National Priorities

NEBRASKA

State Lead Contact:

Tom Miller
Nebraska Commission on National and Community Service
P.O. Box 98927
Lincoln, NE 68509

Phone: 402/471-6225
Fax: 402/471-6286

1995-96 Programs

National Service Network

NE-1

Statewide:
Program: USDA Rural Development Team
AmeriCorps Members: 78 in the 9 Flood States
Description: Responding to the environmental and economic damage caused by last year's flood, AmeriCorps Members will assess flood-relief needs, explain wetlands delineation to land owners and work to reduce ground water pollution.
Contact: Joel Berg; 202/720-6350

NE-2

Statewide:
Program: USDA Public Lands and Environment Team
AmeriCorps Members: 73 in the 9 Flood States
Description: AmeriCorps Members will engage a variety of flood relief work by assessing damage, restoring wetlands, and restoring flood control facilities.
Contact: Joel Berg; 202/720-6350

NE-3

Omaha:
Program: Council of Great City Schools
AmeriCorps Members: To Be Determined
Description: AmeriCorps Members will recruit teachers, develop service-learning programs, organize model service corps of volunteers working as school/classroom aides, literacy tutors, and academic mentors.
Contact: Michael Casserly; 202/393-2427

State and Local

NE-4

Lincoln:
Program: Community Action of Nebraska, Inc./Statewide Youth Violence Prevention
AmeriCorps Members: 23
Description: AmeriCorps Members will develop and implement peer mediation and conflict resolution programs for youth, age 10-15, in a multi-site, statewide youth violence prevention program. This will be a partnership between the community action agencies, Office of Dispute Resolution and the Mediation Centers.
Contact: Lorrie Benson; 402/471-3714; 402/471-3481 (fax)

NE-5

Lincoln:
Program: Lincoln Action Program/Supportive Housing Program
AmeriCorps Members: 3
Description: AmeriCorps Members will serve as case managers for homeless families to provide a holistic continuum of care. Members will assist in locating housing and link homeless families with all support services needed to promote self-sufficiency.
Contact: Brian Mathers: 402/471-4515; 402/471-4844 (fax)

NE-6

Lincoln:
Program: Indian Center, Inc./Tutoring & Mentoring Circles
AmeriCorps Members: 6
Description: AmeriCorps Members will provide tutoring to low-achieving students to reduce school dropout rates. Mentoring circles will be developed to provide encouragement and good role models. Native American cultural activities will be integrated in the educational process.
Contact: Gary Boettcher; 402/438-5231; 402/438-5236 (fax)

Priorities

(1) Youth Violence
(2) Education
(3) Human Needs
(4) Environment

NEVADA

State Lead Contact:

Christine Bundren
Nevada Department of Employment, Training, and Rehabilitation
1830 E. Sahara #314
Las Vegas, NV 89104

Phone: 702/486-7997 or 800/706-2627 (good only within Nevada yet outside Southern Nevada)
Fax: 702/486-8253

State Commission:

Nevada Commission for National and Community Service

1995-96 Programs

State and Local

NV-1

Fallon:
Program: St. Johns's Lutheran Church/ TURNABOUT Americorps Project
AmeriCorps Members: 10
Description: AmeriCorps Members will address the difficulty young, low-income parents face trying to finish school while providing quality pre-school education for their children. AmeriCorps Members are parents trained to provide quality child care for each other while earning their diploma/ GED.
Contact: Rev. Robert Porterfield; 702/423-1161

NV-2

Las Vegas:
Program: University of Nevada, Las Vegas: UNLV/Community AmeriCorps Program
AmeriCorps Members: 65 ('95-'96)
Description: Planning grant to develop a statewide program where AmeriCorps Members will link at-risk community members with appropriate service agencies, under the leadership of the Universities of Nevada at Las Vegas and Reno.
Contact: Mr. Tracy Cotton; 702/895-0638; 702/895-4786 (fax)

NV-3

Reno:
Program: Community Chest/Piñon Service Project
AmeriCorps Members: 20
Description: In concert with leaderships development activities, 20 part-time AmeriCorps Members will work in 8 community action teams throughout northern Nevada to

train community agency and school personnel in strategies for substance abuse and gang prevention, family advocacy, school readiness, and school success.
Contact: For more information, contact Nevada Commission for National and Community Service, 702/486-7998.

NV-4

Program: Athletes in Service to America
Description: AmeriCorps Members will work toward education and public safety priorities.
Contact: Matthew Williams; 702/486-7998.

State Priorities:

The Nevada Commission hosted 14 forums throughout the State, at which time the general public's ranking of priorities was as follows: (1) School Success and School Readiness; (2) Health; (3) Crime Prevention and Crime Control; (4) Home; (5) Neighborhood Environment; (6) Natural Environment

NEW HAMPSHIRE

State Lead Contact:

Molly White, Director
Executive Director
New Hampshire Job Training Council
64 Old Suncook Road
Concord, NH 03301
Phone: 603/228-9500
Fax: 603/228-8557

State Commission:

Community Service Executive Board (AAE)

1995-96 Programs

National Service Network

NH-1

Rural:
Program: USDA Public Lands and Environment Team
AmeriCorps Members: 32
Description: AmeriCorps Members will care for ecosystems supporting threatened and endangered species in addition to maintain-

ing snowmobile trail networks and campgrounds throughout the forest.
Contact: Joel Berg; 202/720-6350

State and Local

NH-2

Bedford:
Program: The Public Service Compact
AmeriCorps Members: 16
Description: The New Hampshire College and University Council will build a statewide infrastructure that facilitates the integration of service into undergraduate education at 29 affiliated institutions. Through training opportunities, subgrants, and the placement of 16 full-time AmeriCorps service-learning coordinators at various campuses, the program will enable faculty, pre-service K-12 teachers and administrators, and college students to develop high quality service-learning projects that meet identified needs within local communities and the state. In particular, the Compact will emphasize education partnerships by helping campuses link with K-12 schools to develop mentoring and tutoring programs.
Contact: Margaret J. Leahey; 603/669-3432

NH-3

Berlin:
Program: Tri-County Community Action Program, Inc./North Country Community Corps
AmeriCorps Members: 20
Description: AmeriCorps Members will work in the northern region of New Hampshire to provide tutoring, community and parent education programs; conflict resolution training; assistance to the elderly; trail building and environmental cleanup.
Contact: Ms. Pamela Dorland; 603/752-4103; 603/752-7607 (fax)

NH-4

Concord:
Program: NH Domestic and Sexual Violence Victim Assistance Program
AmeriCorps Members: 30
Description: AmeriCorps Members will earn minimum wage stipend over 10-12 months, plus an educational award for college, gradu-

ate school or student loans. Opportunity to make a significant contribution to victims of domestic and sexual violence throughout NH. The following positions are available: Crisis Center Advocate: Responsibilities include hotline crisis intervention work, one-on-one counseling, court accompaniment, work with children, and some office duties. District Court Advocate: Responsibilities include assisting victims in obtaining restraining orders and court preparation. Police Prosecutor Advocate: Responsibilities include assisting victims within the criminal justice system in an effort to successfully prosecute cases.
Contact: Aimee Deans or Kim Firth; 603/271-6804

NH-5

Gilead, ME:
Program: White Mountain National Forest
AmeriCorps Members: 32
Description: AmeriCorps Members will work in crews for 11 months and gain valuable work experience and training while working with NH State Parks and the US Forest Service in all or some of the following: outdoor conservation projects; erosion control; bridge building; environmental surveys; visitor/interpretive services; community service projects; building construction and upgrading; trail construction and maintenance; energy conservation projects; educational outreach projects; mountain patrol; recycling
Contact: Debby Hinman; 603/543-1700

NH-6

Durham:
Program: Natural Resource Conservation Service
Description: AmeriCorps Members will work on environmental and conservation projects.
Contact: Althea Weeks; 603/868-7581

NH-7

Charlestown:
Program: AmeriCorps at Bear Brook
Description: AmeriCorps Members will work on environmental projects.
Contact: Bob Coates; 603/543-1700

NEW JERSEY

State Lead Contact:

Mark Valley
Office of Innovative Programs
CN 500
Trenton, NJ 08625
Phone: 609/292-5850
Fax: 609/984-9825

1995-96 Programs

National Service Network

NJ-1

Statewide:
Program: National Association of Child Care Resource and Referral Agencies/Action for Children Today! (ACT)
AmeriCorps Members: 15 (45 Nationally)
Description: CCR&R's will educate the community about child care needs and identify critical issues. ACT will improve the quality of child care by increasing availability by 450 for infants, 1395 for school-age children and will train 1215 child care staff.
Contact: Ray Mueller; 202/393-5501; 202/393/1109 (fax)

NJ-2

Statewide:
Program: USDA Public Lands and Environment Team
AmeriCorps Members: 20
Description: AmeriCorps Members will focus their attention on three watersheds—maintaining soil, fish populations, and forest. Physical efforts will be supplemented by community education.
Contact: Carlos Henning; 908/246-1662 ext. 122; 908/246-2358 (fax)

NJ-3

Atlantic City:
Program: New York University Facility Resource Network/Safety Net—A Campaign Against Violence
AmeriCorps Members: 16 (111 Nationally)
Description: A broad coalition of colleges will support the AmeriCorps program designed to curb violence through counseling, training, and the development of solu-

tions. In Atlantic City, for instance, AmeriCorps Members will conduct after-school programs that foster safety and build self-esteem and conflict resolution skills.
Contact: Leslie Berlowitz; 212/998-2300; 212/995-4103 (fax) Beth Olsen; 609/652-4939; 609/748-5509 (fax)

NJ-4

Camden:
Program: I Have a Dream Foundation/AmeriCorps Partnership
AmeriCorps Members: 15 (114 Nationally)
Description: Members will mentor and tutor student "Dreamers" from disadvantaged areas, giving personal guidance to prevent dropouts.
Contact: Dr. J. Bruce Gristi; 609/231-9600; 609/273-9236 (fax)

NJ-5

Newark:
Program: Environmental Protection Agency/ Neighborhood Improvement Project
AmeriCorps Members: 40 Nationally
Description: AmeriCorps Members will restore the national environment of urban waterways, perform radon testing, and provide training on techniques to prevent lead poisoning.
Contact: Derek T. Winans; 201/621-1100; 210/624-7977 (fax)

NJ-6

Newark:
Program: National Multiple Sclerosis Society/"Bridge to Independence"
AmeriCorps Members: 9 (144 Nationally)
Description: AmeriCorps Members, many of whom have Multiple Sclerosis, will work to build awareness about Multiple Sclerosis while coordinating volunteers in extensive living assistance programs—helping disadvantaged people to make it on their own.
Contact: Nancy J. Holland; 212/476-0453; Frances Grant; 201/984-6667; 210/984-5658 (fax)

NJ-7

Newark:
Program: YMCA Earth Service Corps Fel-

lowship
AmeriCorps Members: 40 Nationally
Description: AmeriCorps Members will address local environmental concerns, coordinating park cleanups, urban gardening projects, and environmental symposia.
Contact: Celeste Wroblewski; 312/269-0506; Joy Fleming; 201/624-8900; 201/624-3024 (fax)

NJ-8

Urban Districts:
Program: Teach for America
AmeriCorps Members: 55 (1000 Nationally)
Description: Responding to an acute need for educators and role models in underserved urban and rural areas, AmeriCorps Members will lend their diverse perspectives on education and introduce innovative teaching methods to the classroom.
Contact: Kristin Ehrgood; 908/355-5776; 908/355-5815 (fax)

State and Local

NJ-9

Newark:
Program: Community Agencies Corporation—Newark/Essex AmeriCorps Program
AmeriCorps members: 40
Description: AmeriCorps Members will be placed in teams to provide early childhood education programs, literacy training, job development and training, support services for homeless and troubled families, and neighborhood and environmental cleanup for disadvantaged residents in the City of Newark.
Contact: Ms. Dorothy Knauer; 201/621-2273; 201/621-8120 (fax)

NJ-10

Newark:
Program: New Jersey Chapter—National Committee for Prevention of Child Abuse/ParentCorps
AmeriCorps Members: 31
Description: AmeriCorps Members will partner with existing child abuse prevention organizations to implement parent education programs, provide childcare, develop mentoring and tutoring services for teenage parents, recruit and train local volunteers and

facilitate parent support groups.
Contact: Ms. Diane Fuscaldo; 201/643-3710; 201/643-9222 (fax)

NJ-11

Paterson:
Program: New Jersey Community Development Corporation/The Community Leaders Program
AmeriCorps Members: 20
Description: AmeriCorps Members will provide independent living assistance to homeless, disabled and mentally ill individuals in four sites across the state and engage them and other volunteers in group community revitalization
Contact: Mr. Robert Guarasci; 201/225-0555; 908/225-0556 (fax)

NJ-12

Trenton:
Program: New Jersey Public Interest Research Foundation/NJ Community Water Watch
AmeriCorps Members: 20
Description: AmeriCorps Members will be placed individually and in teams to monitor, test, clean and support 16 major waterways, provide public education, identify pollution hazards, and generate volunteers in a statewide water watch program designed to address the most severe water quality problems in 9 cities.
Contact: Mr. Kenneth Ward; 609/394-8155; 609/989-9013 (fax)

NJ-13

Trenton:
Program: Urban Schools Service Corps/New Jersey's Urban Schools Service Corps
AmeriCorps Members: 250
Description: AmeriCorps Members will create community schools in 8 school districts to meet the pressing social and educational needs of urban school students by providing safe havens and educational enrichment activities, extending the school day, mentoring and tutoring and assisting parents to develop positive parenting skills.
Contact: El-Rhonda Williams Alston, Esq.; Scott Moffitt; 609/292-6290; 609/984-9825 (fax)

NJ-14

Union City:
Program: Union City Day Care AmeriCorps
Program
AmeriCorps Members: 38
Description: AmeriCorps Members who are
parents traditionally defined as aid recipients
will serve part-time as teaching assistants
within day care classes, deliver community
outreach literacy programs, assist with recycling and environmental beautification
efforts, and implement substance abuse prevention activities.
Contact: Louisa Mendez; 201/348-2754;
201/392-0833 (fax)

NJ-15

Newark:
Program: The ASPIRA Association, Inc.
AmeriCorps Members: To be determined
Description: AmeriCorps Members will
establish a comprehensive, holistic service-
delivery model for disadvantaged middle and
high school students and their parents. Members will assist Latino middle and high
school youth and their parents with language, literacy, and mathematical skills
through intensive tutoring, mentoring and
academic enrichment. Members will train
youth in conflict resolution and violence prevention, and counsel parents on coping with
adolescent behavior. AmeriCorps Members
will also link youth and parents with law
enforcement agencies and other public safety
and youth organizations inside their community.
Contact: Gloria Perez; 201/484-7554; 201/
489-0184 (fax)

NEW MEXICO

State Lead Contact:

Jeannette Miller
Executive Director
State of New Mexico
State Capitol, Suite 400
Santa Fe, NM 87503
Phone: 505/827-3042
Fax: 505/827-3015

1995-96 Programs

National Service Network

NM-1

Statewide:
Program: USDA Rural Development Team
AmeriCorps Members: 50 (Four Corners)
Description: AmeriCorps Members will help
communities protect watersheds, improve
housing, promote economic development,
boost sustainable agriculture, and respond to
disasters.
Contact: Joel Berg; 202/720-6350

NM-2

Program: Navajo Nation Youth Conservation Corps
AmeriCorps Members: 40 (120 Nationally)
Description: Building self-esteem in "at-
risk" youth takes a decidedly environmental
slant with community revitalization projects
focused on watershed and soil conservation,
using both western and traditional Navajo
technologies.
Contact: Jacques Seronda; 602/871-6592

State and Local

NM-3

Embudo:
Program: Siete del Norte Community
Development Corporation/Resolana: Learning While Serving
AmeriCorps Members: 46
Description: AmeriCorps Members, over
two summers, will work with local community organizations to educate the residents of
rural northern New Mexico of their water
rights, create a diversity of crops, tutor students, and provide home health care for the
elderly.
Contact: Dr. Tomas Atencio; 505/579-4217;
505/579-4206 (fax)

NM-4

GALLUP:
Program: National Indian Youth Leadership
Project/Gadugi Project
AmeriCorps Members:
Description: Planning grant to develop a ser-
vice program for and with Native-American

youth involving activities such as tutoring, career counseling, substance abuse prevention education, conflict resolution training, housing rehabilitation, Search and Rescue program development, and environmental hazard control.
Contact: Mr. McClellan Hall; 505/722-9176; 505/722-9794 (fax)

NEW YORK

State Lead Contact:

Ms. Nikki Smith
New York State Office of National and Community Service
State Capitol-Division of Budget
Albany, NY 12224
Phone: 518/473-8882
Fax: 518/486-1217

State Commission:

New York State Commission on National and Community Service

1995-96 Programs

National Service Network

NY-1

Statewide:
Program: HIPPY USA/The HIPPY Corps Initiative
AmeriCorps Members: 67 part-time
Description: AmeriCorps Members will work with children ages three to five in school readiness activities with their parents. Members make home visits and coordinate group meeting to facilitate interaction and learning between parents and children, working with 800 families in New York City and Rochester.
Contact: Miriam Westheimer; 212/678-3500; 212/678-4136 (fax)

NY-2

Program: USDA Public Lands and Environmental Team
AmeriCorps Members: 7
Description: AmeriCorps Members will help communities protect watersheds, improve housing, promote economic development,

boost sustainable agriculture and respond to disasters.
Contact: John Whitney; 716/652-8480; 716/652-9506 (fax)

NY-3

New York, Syracuse:
Program: National Association of Community Health Centers, Inc./Community Health-Corps
AmeriCorps Members: 16
Description: AmeriCorps Members will link families to health and social services, and through learning to practice healthy behaviors themselves, will help to increase community-based knowledge as role models and informed members of their families and peer groups throughout Brooklyn and Syracuse.
Contact: New York—Marie Morales; 718/630-0227; 718/492-5090 (fax); Syracuse—315/476-7921; 315/475-4713 (fax)

NY-4

New York:
Program: Green Corps' Neighborhood Green Corps Program
AmeriCorps Members: 60 Nationally
Description: Splitting their time between projects involving the home environment and the community environment, AmeriCorps Members will educate and then activate their communities through three projects: low income home weatherization, lead paint abatement, and urban gardening.
Contact: Chandra Egan; 212/505-5133

NY-5

New York:
Program: I Have a Dream Foundation/IHAD AmeriCorps
AmeriCorps Members: 67 part-time
Description: Members will mentor and tutor Student "Dreamers" from disadvantaged areas, giving personal guidance to prevent dropouts.
Contact: James Krauskopf; 212/229-5400 (phone & fax)

NY-6

Rochester:
Program: National Center for Family Literacy/The Family Literacy Corps

AmeriCorps Members: 8
Description: AmeriCorps Members will work with homeless and runaway youth in creative writing and poetry workshops in order to improve writing and verbal skills, while boosting self-worth.
Contact: Judy Kiley; 716/262-8326; 716/262-8330 (fax)

NY-7

New York:
Program: National Endowment for the Arts/The Writers Corps
AmeriCorps Members: 5
Description: AmeriCorps Members will work with homeless and runaway youth in creative writing and poetry workshops in order to improve writing and verbal skills, while boosting self-worth.
Contact: Geri Hayes; 718/931-9500; 718/409-6445 (fax)

NY-8

New York, Riverdale:
Program: New York University/Project Safety Net—A Campaign Against Violence
AmeriCorps Members: New York: 6 full- and 42 part-time; Riverdale: 2 full- and 35 part-time
Description: A broad coalition of colleges will support this AmeriCorps program designed to curb violence through counseling, training, and the development of solutions. AmeriCorps Members will mediate disputes and teach peacemaking to after-school students.
Contact: New York: Lee Frissell; (212) 998-5021; 212/995-4328 (fax); Riverdale: Irene King; 718/920-0142; 718/920-0483 (fax)

NY-9

New York:
Program: Public Education Fund Network/Project First
AmeriCorps Members: 26
Description: AmeriCorps Members will work with volunteers from IBM and other corporations to increase student access to computers and to integrate technology into 25 elementary and middle schools.
Contact: Gary Vazquez; (212) 645-5110; 212/645-7409

NY-10

New York:
Program: Teach for America
AmeriCorps Members: 160 (1000 Nationally)
Description: Responding to an acute need for educators and role models in underserved urban and rural areas, AmeriCorps Members will lend their diverse perspectives on education and introduce innovative teaching methods to the classroom.
Contact: Eric Weingartner; 212/228-1043; 212/982-6886

NY-11

New York:
Program: YMCA Earth Service Corps Fellowship
AmeriCorps Members: 2
Description: AmeriCorps Members will address local environmental concerns, coordinating park cleanups, urban gardening projects, and environmental symposia.
Contact: Gary Wartels; 212/630-9600; 212/630-9604 (fax)

NY-12

New York:
Program: National Organization for Victim Assistance (NOVA)/Red Hook Public Safety Corps
AmeriCorps Members: 50
Description: AmeriCorps Members will provide immediate and long-term assistance to victims of crime and violence in a model program that will establish guidelines for community restitution and provide violence prevention education.
Contact: Gregory Berman; 212/484-2744; 212/586-1144 (fax)

NY-13

Statewide:
Program: Neighborhood Reinvestment Corporation/NeighborWorks Community Corps
AmeriCorps Members: To be determined
Description: AmeriCorps Members will improve neighborhoods by bringing people together to address housing and safety issues nationwide. Members will also work with local staff in community outreach to increase

home ownership.
Contact: Ms. Marcella Williams; 202/376-3214; 202/276-3213 (fax)

NY-14

Buffalo:
Program: Northeastern University/Athletes in Service to America
AmeriCorps Members: 20
Description: AmeriCorps Members will work with Buffalo youth in four areas: conflict resolution and diversity training; academic tutoring and mentoring, and media awareness and influence.
Contact: Thomas Miller; 716/888-2130; 716/888-3190 (fax)

NY-15

Oneida:
Program: Oneida Indian Nation of NY/ AmeriCorps Youth Program
AmeriCorps Members: 25
Description: AmeriCorps Members will create neighborhood watches, construct an educational nature trail, repair elders' homes. provide afterschool care, provide meals for the homebound, and monitor and maintain a community greenhouse.
Contact: Brenda Howard; 315/361-6300; 315/361-6333 (fax)

NY-16

Oneonta:
Program: The ARC/Otsego ARC
AmeriCorps Members: 6
Description: AmeriCorps Members will help to preserve the family units of families with parents with cognitive disabilities. Members will daily work with children and parents modeling appropriate behaviors and teaching parenting skills. The four goals of this program are: consistency; safety; increased independence; and community awareness.
Contact: Patricia Knuth; 607/432-8595; 607/433-8430 (fax)

NY-17

Syracuse:
Program: US Catholic Conference/Fostering Citizenship
AmeriCorps Members: 4

Description: AmeriCorps Members will work with AmerAsian refugee population to help youth assimilate into their new environment and succeed in school; develop self-esteem in refugee women; and teach socialization, school readiness and English language skills to children.
Contact: Felicia Castricone; 315/474-7428; 315/424-6033 (fax)

NY-18

New York:
Program: US Department of Labor/Youth Fair Chance
AmeriCorps Members: 7
Description: AmeriCorps Members will serve in five areas: 1. youth literacy-identifying and tutoring children with reading difficulties; 2. community service-service learning; 3. post-secondary education-assisting with SAT's, college loans/grant applications; 4. public safety-alternate sentencing, conflict resolution, and drug prevention; and 5. home visiting-helping teen mothers with health, nutrition, and social support.
Contact: Joseph Mpa; 718/542-8333; 718/542-8444 (fax)

NY-19

New York:
Program: YouthBuild USA, Inc./Youth-Build AmeriCorps
AmeriCorps Members: To be determined
Description: AmeriCorps Members will work directly with community-based organizations to rehabilitate abandoned housing or build new housing for homeless people, people with AIDS, people with disabilities, or very low income people. Members will serve on the construction sites under the close supervision of trained trades people. In addition, members will attend an alternative school that focuses on leadership development, construction-related math education, and general vocational educational curriculum.
Contact: Yolanda Kelly; 212/860-8170; 212/860-8894 (fax)

State and Local

NY-20

Albany:
Program: New York State Council on Children and Families—AmeriCorps Family Literacy/Employment Readiness Project
AmeriCorps Members: 20
Description: AmeriCorps Members will focus on parents' literacy needs by providing individualized reading, writing, and math skills. Members will also address children's needs by conducting home visits and parenting session groups, and establishing lending libraries.
Contact: Fred Meservey; 518/473-3652; 518/473-2570 (fax)

NY-21

Bronx:
Program: Bronx Youth Conservation Corps (BYCC)/SAVE A GENERATION
AmeriCorps Members: 35
Description: AmeriCorps Members will conserve, restore and sustain the natural habitats in urban parks in the Bronx by performing road and path construction, tree planting, erosion control, statue repair, flower bed cultivation, tree trimming, and bench repairs.
Contact: Gary Bogle; 718/365-5456; 718/933-7311 (fax)

NY-22

Brooklyn:
Program: Bedford Stuyvesant Community Conference Inc./SANKOFA LINKS
AmeriCorps Members: 20
Description: AmeriCorps Members will provide community safety workshop series at local schools and community-based programs; organize and strengthen Block Associations; and act as conflict mediators and local police aides.
Contact: Ms. Margo Butts; 718/636-0003; 718/857-9057 (fax)

NY-23

New York:
Program: Health Association of Niagara County, Inc. (HANCI)/Niagara AmeriCorps
AmeriCorps Members: 20

Description: AmeriCorps Members will revitalize the neighborhood environment of Niagara falls' low income areas through neighborhood clean-up, recycling, and waste disposal projects, developing green spaces and creating neighborhood co-ops.
Contact: Dr. Irene Elia; 716/285-8224; 716/285-9689 (fax)

NY-24

New York:
Program: City Volunteer Corps Inc./The City Volunteer Corps Community Leadership Program
AmeriCorps Members: 123
Description: AmeriCorps Members will create garden sites next to elementary schools; complete recycling projects; deliver food to homebound elderly; work with pre-kindergarten centers, create safe havens for school children, and design other service projects in cooperation with the community.
Contact: Mr. Michael Bosnick; 212/475-6444; 212/475-9457 (fax)

NY-25

New York:
Program: Phoenix House Foundation, Inc.—NYIPEA/AmeriCorps Project
AmeriCorps Members: 75 full- and 10 part-time
Description: AmeriCorps Members will assist school counselors to identify, counsel and refer students to substance abuse treatment programs; work as liaisons to courts and justice agencies to provide treatment alternatives, and locate job and educational opportunities for juveniles and adult offenders.
Contact: Robert Maurer; 212/595-5810; 212/757-2208 (fax)

NY-26

New York:
Program: Aspira of New York, Inc./Project Safe and Sound
AmeriCorps Members: 81 full- and 4 part-time
Description: AmeriCorps Members will work to improve relationships between community youth and local law enforcement in the South Bronx by performing outreach,

developing public safety instructional materials, and developing crime watch programs.
Contact: Anthony Lopez; 212/564-6880; 212/564-7152 (fax)

NY-27

Plattsburgh:
Program: Clinton County Youth Bureau/ Clinton County AmeriCorps
AmeriCorps Members: 20
Description: AmeriCorps Members will train parents to choose and maintain quality day care providers, and develop after-school enrichment programs for low-income youth.
Contact: Christopher Racette; 518/565-4750; 518/565-4775 (fax)

NY-28

Rochester:
Program: Monroe Community College; Rochester AmeriCorps Program
AmeriCorps Members: 94
Description: AmeriCorps Members will serve as community police aides to increase resident access to public safety services; recreation aides to prevent crime to enhancing positive alternatives for neighborhood youth; and education aides by teaching violence prevention techniques.
Contact: Marilyn Rosché; 716/262-1778; 716/262-1733 (fax)

NY-29

Syracuse:
Program: New York State Corps Collaboration c/o Year Round Syracuse/Meeting the Challenge
AmeriCorps Members: 50
Description: AmeriCorps Members will create community gardens; work in parks; develop vacant lots; assist in emergency feeding programs; weatherize low-income homes; renovate abandoned housing; and tutor children.
Contact: Mr. Paul Winkeller; 315/473-8882; 315/486-1217 (fax)

NY-30

Syracuse:
Program: New York State Corps Collaboration c/o Year Round Syracuse/Nature and Neighborhoods: NY Corps Improving the

Environment
AmeriCorps Members: 132
Description: AmeriCorps Members will restore, improve, and maintain at least 100 miles of trails, 150 acres of park land, 5 natural habitats, and 50 other recreation facilities; and create and improve greenspace community gardens, play and recreation areas, and homes in 50 neighborhoods across the state.
Contact: Mr. Paul Winkeller; 315/473-8882; 315/486-1217 (fax)

NY-31

Corning:
Program: The Institute for Human Services, Inc./Addison Area AmeriCorps
AmeriCorps Members: 20
Description: AmeriCorps Members will construct housing, perform minor home repairs, organize "Community Clean Up Days" and provide basic home maintenance instruction to low income families in the Addison area.
Contact: Andrea J. Haradon; 607/936-3725; 607/936-1865 (fax)

NY-32

New York:
Program: New York City Police Department/NYPD National Service Police Cadet Program
AmeriCorps Members: 90
Description: AmeriCorps Members will work with police on solving the most critical problems identified by community residents, including enhancing the safety of public facilities, restoring safety to community parks, supervising "safe play streets," assisting in vehicle theft prevention, and assisting officers in investigating domestic violence complaints and assist in counseling victims of violence.
Contact: Capt. Odette Janavelle; 716/374-5377; 212/374-9233 (fax)

NY-33

Brooklyn:
Program: RF/Cuny on behalf of New York City Technical College/Tech Corps
AmeriCorps Members: 50
Description: AmeriCorps Members will organize and develop a community resource center, provide tutoring and homework assis-

tance, and provide environmental education to the Fort Green area of New York City.
Contact: Georgianna Close; 718/260-5117; 718/260-5446 (fax)

NY-34

New York:
Program: Rheedlen Centers for Children and Families
AmeriCorps Members: 65
Description: AmeriCorps Members will tutor 360 students in 6 schools in Central Harlem and 1 in Williamsburg, while helping to make schools safer for children before, during, and after the school day. Members will help create safe corridors for children walking to and from school.
Contact: Gerald Rasuli-Lewis; 212/866-0700; 212/932-2965 (fax)

NY-35

New York:
Program: YMCA of Greater New York AmeriCorps Project/YMVA AmeriCorps School Success Program
AmeriCorps Members: 20
Description: AmeriCorps Members will help 400 students in low-income communities achieve academic excellence through educational, physical fitness, health care, drug prevention and community service activities. Members will replicate a model afterschool program in Harlem and the Bronx.
Contact: Gary Wartels; 212/630-9690; 212/630-9604 (fax)

NY-36

Poughkeepsie:
Program: Youth Resource Development Corporation (YRDC)/AmeriCorps Poughkeepsie Collaboration
AmeriCorps Members: 20
Description: AmeriCorps Members will develop and implement beautification projects, organize school safety squads and conflict resolution teams, and provide escort services in the City of Poughkeepsie.
Contact: Joel Greenbaum; 914/473-5005; 914/473-5045 (fax)

State Priorities:

Address the State's critical human, educational, environmental, and public safety needs with measurable results at the community level.

NORTH CAROLINA

State Lead Contact:

Commission on National and Community Service
121 W. Jones Street
Raleigh, NC 27603-8001
Phone: 919/715-3470
Fax: 919/715-2972

State Commission:

North Carolina Commission on National and Community Service

1995-96 Programs

National Service Network

NC-1

Statewide:
Program: National Multiple Sclerosis Society/"Bridge to Independence"
AmeriCorps Members: 8 (144 Nationally)
Description: AmeriCorps Members, many of whom have Multiple Sclerosis, will work to build awareness about Multiple Sclerosis while coordinating volunteers in extensive living assistance programs—helping disadvantaged people to make it on their own.
Contact: Lori Lawler; 704/525-2955; 704/527-0406 (fax)

NC-2

Program: National Service Legal Corps
AmeriCorps Members: 6
Description: The AmeriCorps program will help work with low-income and minority communities to address the needs for affordable access to water and wastewater disposal services; decent and affordable housing; and decent jobs.
Contact: Andrew Foster; 919/856-2171

NC-3

Program: Teach for America
AmeriCorps Members: 55 (1000 Nationally)
Description: Responding to an acute need for educators and role models in underserved urban and rural areas, AmeriCorps Members will lend their diverse perspectives on education and introduce innovative teaching methods to the classroom.
Contact: Heather Harding; 919/445-4700

NC-4

Asheville:
Program: Environmental Careers Organization
AmeriCorps Members: 1
Description: Retired engineers will work with environmental organizations to reduce toxins.
Contact: Diane Mailey; 617/426-4375 ext. 132; Ginny Lindsey; 704/251-0518

NC-5

Charlotte:
Program: New York University/Faculty Resource Network/"Safety Net—A Campaign Against Violence"
AmeriCorps Members: 18
Description: A broad coalition of colleges will support this AmeriCorps program designed to curb violence through counseling, training, and problem-solving exercises. At Johnson C. Smith University, AmeriCorps Members will mediate conflicts and train students in dispute resolution.
Contact: Dr. Art Berkeley; 704/378-1188

NC-6

Charlotte/Mecklenburg:
Program: Public Education Fund Network/ Project First
AmeriCorps Members: 11
Description: AmeriCorps Members will work with volunteers from IBM and other corporations to increase student access to computers and to integrate technology into 25 elementary and middle schools.
Contact: Jessica Walter; 704/335-0100

NC-7

Durham:
Program: Public Allies
AmeriCorps Members: 20
Description: Diverse young people develop leadership skills while addressing unmet community needs.
Contact: Jason Scott; 919/687-0005

NC-8

Greensboro:
Program: New York University/Faculty Resource Network/"Safety Net—A Campaign Against Violence"
AmeriCorps Members: 25
Description: A broad coalition of colleges will support this AmeriCorps program designed to curb violence through counseling, training, and the development of solutions. At Bennett College, AmeriCorps Members will partner with youth who have been involved with the juvenile justice system and develop a mediation and restitution program for young people.
Contact: Riley Kline; 910/370-8733

NC-9

Raleigh:
Program: Summerbridge AmeriCorps Teaching Program
AmeriCorps Members: 3 locally
Description: AmeriCorps Members will recruit high school and college students to teach disadvantaged middle school students. The objective will be to improve their academic and leadership performance.
Contact: Dave Monaco, Alissa Kingsbury; 919/870-9741

State and Local

NC-10

Statewide:
Program: The University of North Carolina at Chapel Hill/The SCALE Community Literacy Initiative
AmeriCorps members: 47
Description: AmeriCorps Members will, through newly established intensive literacy programs, provide direct tutoring services and coordinate the management and training of additional student literacy volunteers.
Contact: Mr. Ed Chaney;919/962-1542; 919/ 962-1533 (fax)

NC-11

Statewide:
Program: Day Care Services Association/
T.E.A.C.H. Early Childhood Corps Project
AmeriCorps Members: 22
Description: AmeriCorps Members will
improve the quality of child care programs
by serving as substitute teachers across the
state in day care centers with demonstrated
need. While Americorps members are providing support, the day care teachers are
receiving intensive training and accreditation
which is helping raise the quality of child
care in North Carolina.
Contact: Ms. Monica Rohacek; 919/967-
3272; 919/967-7683 (fax)

NC-12

Charlotte:
Program: University of North Carolina at
Charlotte/Tutorial Connection
AmeriCorps Members: 25
Description: AmeriCorps Members will,
through a cooperative effort between the
University of North Carolina at Charlotte
and the Urban League of Charlotte, address
teenage pregnancy and parenting through
health education, parenting and career development workshops for teen parents.
Contact: Ms. Stephanie Miles; 704/379-
7744; 704/547-2616 (fax)

NC-13

Warrenton:
Program: The Leadership Academy/Warren
Service Corps
AmeriCorps Members: 34
Description: AmeriCorps Members will
work in and lead inter-generational teams
providing youth in rural communities with
homework assistance, remediation and academic enrichment through after-school,
weekend, school break, and other activities.
Contact: Ms. Berti Jones; 919/257-1134

NC-14

Statewide:
Program: The University of North Carolina
at Greensboro/North Carolina Child Care
Corps
AmeriCorps Members: 35

Description: AmeriCorps Members will
work directly with pre-kindergarten children
in child care centers and other settings,
improving staff-child ratios and increasing
children's school readiness. This program
will be part of North Carolina's statewide
Smart Start initiative.
Contact: Ms. Susan Hicks; 910/334-5328;
910/334-5926 (fax)

NC-15

Jefferson—northwest mountain region:
Program: New River Area MH, DD & SA
Programs/New River Senior Health Corps
AmeriCorps Members: 20
Description: AmeriCorps Members will
develop an inter-generational Senior Health
Corps that will work with home health programs in five counties providing personal
care needs, home management, relief from
isolation, coordination of services, exercise
therapy and other services.
Contact: Ms. Debbie Wellborn; 910/246-
4898; 910/246-2364 (fax)

NC-16

Statewide:
Program: NC Low Income Housing Coali-
tion/Service for Shelter
AmeriCorps Members: 22
Description: AmeriCorps Members will
increase accessibility to affordable housing
for North Carolina's low income citizens by
encouraging use of subsidized housing,
developing transitional rental housing for
homeless families, and rehabilitating substandard housing.
Contact: Ms. Linda Shaw; 919/881-0707;
919/881-0350 (fax)

NC-17

Statewide:
Program: North Carolina State University/
The North Carolina Support Our Students
AmeriCorps Demonstration Project
AmeriCorps Members: 60
Description: AmeriCorps Members in eight
counties will work with school-age children
in after-school programs, on teachers' work-
days, school holidays and summer vacation
providing enrichment activities and mentoring. This program will be a part of North

Carolina's Support Our Student program.
Contact: Hilary Hylces; 919/515-6387; 919/515-4241 (fax)

State Priorities:

EDUCATION
School Success

1. Literacy: increase the rate of literacy in school-aged youths, adults and families

2. Service-learning programs as well as more service/real-life learning opportunities that translate into post-high school job skills for young people.

3. More after-school opportunities for youth, as well as family support center.

School Readiness

1. Early childhood education intervention and prevention programs.

2. Mentoring and enrichment services for youth and families.

HUMAN NEEDS
Home and Rebuilding Neighborhoods

1. Community development programs which strengthen and enhance opportunities for people to come together to address problems, particularly in areas of economic need.

2. County-wide volunteer centers of clearinghouses to link volunteers with programs and available services with community need.

3. Programs which create and develop affordable housing and/or work to meet the needs of homeless individuals and families.

Health Care Issues

1. Education and prevention programs to address health care issues, particularly targeted at youth and communities of need.

2. Programs that meet the needs of senior citizens for elderly care.

3. Initiatives that involve senior citizens as resources in community-problem-solving.

PUBLIC SAFETY AND CRIME
PREVENTION
Crime Prevention
1. Peer mediation programs to combat violence in schools and neighborhoods.

2. Crime prevention programs and meaningful activities that build skills and promote self-esteem in youth.

3. Programs to help youth in punishment programs re-enter society.

4. Programs to involve community members in crime prevention and crisis management.

Crime Control

1. Community policing programs which work with local law enforcement.

2. Programs which promote judicial reform.

THE ENVIRONMENT
Neighborhood Environment

1. Develop effective recycling programs across the state.

2. Identify/meet community environmental needs by reducing environmental hazards.

The Natural Environment

1. Develop effective service programs to combat water pollution.

2. Service projects and conservation efforts that address the environmental needs of individual communities

NORTH DAKOTA

State Lead Contact:

Jody VonRueden
State Lead Agent / Liaison
Department of Human Services
State Capitol-Judicial Wing
Bismarck, ND 58505
Phone: 701/328-2310
Fax: 701/328-2359

1995-96 Programs

National Service Network

ND-1

Statewide
Program: National Multiple Sclerosis Society/"Bridge to Independence"
AmeriCorps Members: 8 (144 Nationally)
Description: AmeriCorps Members, many of

whom have Multiple Sclerosis, will work to build awareness about Multiple Sclerosis while coordinating volunteers in extensive living assistance programs—helping disadvantaged people to make it on their own.
Contact: Julie Gibson; 701/235-2678; 701/235-6358 (fax)

ND-2

Statewide:
Program: USDA Rural Development Team
AmeriCorps Members: 78 in the 9 Flood States
Description: Responding to the environmental and economic damage caused by last year's flood, AmeriCorps Members will assess flood-relief needs, explain wetlands delineation to land owners and work to reduce groundwater pollution.
Contact: Joel Berg; 202/720-6350

ND-3

Statewide:
Program: USDA Public Lands and Environment Team
AmeriCorps Members: 73 in the 9 Flood States
Description: AmeriCorps Members will engage a variety of flood relief work by assessing damage, restoring wetlands, and restoring flood control facilities.
Contact: Joel Berg; 202/720-6350

ND-4

Fort Totten:
Program: HHS—Head Start/Family Serve
AmeriCorps Members: 10
Description: AmeriCorps Members will be paired with children to help build literacy, language and social interaction skills. Field trips to schools and visiting the child's teachers will also be included to help provide for improving their school success.
Contact: Dr. David Gipp; 701/255-3258

State Priorities:

To assist groups throughout the state in applying for the funding available from the Corporation for National and Community Service for community service projects in North Dakota.

OHIO

State Lead Contact:

Kitty Burcsu, Director
5.1 North High St., Suite 481
Columbus OH 43215
Phone: 614/728-2916
Fax: 614/728-2921

Additional State Contact:

Ruth Milligan
Governor's Residence
358 N. Parkview Ave.
Columbus, OH 43209
Phone: 614/644-7644

State Commission:

Governor's Community Service Commission

1995-96 Programs

National Service Network

OH-1

Statewide:
(Rural areas)
Program: Association of Farmworkers Opportunity Program
AmeriCorps Members: 6 in Ohio
Description: AmeriCorps Members will train migrant and seasonal farmworkers on how to reduce exposure to pesticides and improve farmworkers' access to other health, education and supportive services.
Contact: Michal Urrutia; 419/354-3552; 419/354-0244 (fax)

OH-2

Cincinnati:
Program: Summerbridge AmeriCorps Teaching Program
AmeriCorps Members: 6 in Ohio
Description: AmeriCorps Members will recruit high school and college students to teach disadvantaged middle school students. The objective will be to improve their academic and leadership performance.
Contact: Ted Preston; 513/271-0963; 513/271-0841 (fax)

OH-3

Cleveland:
Program: National Council of Churches of Christ
AmeriCorps Members: 20 in Ohio
Description: AmeriCorps Members will work with the Interchurch Council of Greater Cleveland to expand the number of volunteers and projects in the School Adoption Program. Activities will include tutoring, in-class assistance, and overseeing small group activities.
Contact: Elving Otero; 216/651-2037; 216/651-4145 (fax)

OH-4

Columbus:
Program: City Year, Inc.
AmeriCorps Members: 55 (220 Nationally)
Description: Teams of AmeriCorps Members will comprehensively address interrelated community need.
Contact: Mr. Jeff Paquette; 614/224-5539; 614/224-5711 (fax)

OH-5

Columbus:
Program: University of Texas at Austin/ AmeriCorps for Math and Literacy
AmeriCorps Members: 20
Description: AmeriCorps Members will work with 1,000 young children in intercity and rural elementary schools to help students develop critical literacy and numeric skills.
Contact: Donna Roxey; 614/292-6471; 614/292-4315

OH-6

Dayton:
Program: National AIDS Fund/AmeriCorps Program
AmeriCorps Members: 8 (40 Nationally)
Description: NCAP is dedicated to supporting high-quality education and service initiatives to fight the HIV/AIDS epidemic in the United States. AmeriCorps Members will provide direct care and assistance to HIV victims and offer education for high-risk communities.
Contact: Luigi Procopio; 513/225-3058; 513/225-3074 (fax)

OH-7

Cincinnati:
Program: Notre Dame School and Community Improvement
AmeriCorps Members: To be determined
Description: AmeriCorps Members will work in the area of education. Call contact for information.
Contact: Mary Judith Tensing, SND de N; 513/381-5882; 513/281-4522 (fax)

OH-8

Cleveland:
Program: AmeriCorps College Bound
AmeriCorps Members: To be determined
Description: AmeriCorps Members will work in the area of education. Call contact for information.
Contact: Louis Niro; 216/987-4196; 216/987-4272 (fax)

OH-9

Columbus:
Program: The Community Safety Project
AmeriCorps Members: To be determined
Description: AmeriCorps Members will work in the area of public safety. Call contact for information.
Contact: Beth Hughes; 614/228-0188; 614/228-2711 (fax)

OH-10

Toledo:
Program: Urban Education Service Corps
AmeriCorps Members: To be determined
Description: AmeriCorps Members will work in the area of education. Call contact for information.
Contact: John Cryan; 419/537-2491; 419/537-7719 (fax)

State and Local

OH-11

Athens:
Program: Ohio University/Appalachian Access
AmeriCorps Members: 23
Description: AmeriCorps Members will immunize children in 21 Appalachian counties, provide support services to seniors, recruit and educate local child care provid-

ers, and improve access to area colleges through an information campaign.
Contact: Dr. Terrence Hogan; 614/593-4028; 614/593-0047 (fax)

OH-12

Cleveland:
Program: ClassMATES
AmeriCorps Members: 13 full-, 29 part-time
Description: The Neighborhood Centers Association was founded in 1963 as the first metropolitan-wide organization in the U.S. with responsibilities to plan, coordinate, and budget neighborhood center/settlement house work. Today it is the largest neighborhood center organization and voluntary social agency in the country. The Americorps Members will provide tutorial and mentoring services to middle school aged youth at six Cleveland public Middle Schools and adjoining NCA agencies.
Contact: Joyce Daniels or Howard Wolf; 216/391-4707; 216/391-4817 (fax)

OH-13

Columbus:
Program: Ohio Coalition for the Homeless/ AmeriCorps Houses for the Homeless
AmeriCorps Members: 39 full-, 10 part-time
Description: AmeriCorps Members will reduce state-wide homelessness by linking persons to social service agencies, assisting with employment skills and searches, and linking homeless persons to affordable permanent housing.
Contact: Mr. Jim Cain; 614/291-1984; 614/291-2009 (fax)

OH-14

Columbus:
Program: Ohio Department of Youth Services/Youth and Community in Partnership
AmeriCorps Members: 20
Description: AmeriCorps Members will tutor and mentor adjudicated youth, provide life skills training, and connect both youth and family members to community social services and other important community support resources.
Contact: Cheri Walter; 614/466-9343; 614/752-9078 (fax)

OH-15

Columbus:
Program: Greater Columbus Arts Council/ Children of the Future
AmeriCorps Members: 24
Description: AmeriCorps Members will address youth crime in 6 low-income communities by setting up art instruction classes in area community centers, teaching conflict resolution skills, involving area police in the creation of safe havens, and provide organized alternatives to crime and violence.
Contact: Mr. Nicholas Hill; 614/224-2606; 614/224-7461 (fax)

OH-16

Dayton:
Program: University of Dayton/SWEAT: Serve With Energy and Talent
AmeriCorps Members: 20
Description: AmeriCorps Members will tutor illiterate adults, establish community child care programs, connect low income community members to adequate & affordable housing, link former chemical dependent women to community services, and teach conflict resolution skills to residents.
Contact: Brother Ed Zamierowski; 513/229-2042; 513/229-4638 (fax)

OH-17

Newark:
Program: Center for Alternative Resources/ Community Corps
AmeriCorps Members: 27
Description: AmeriCorps Members will tutor and mentor 250 youth, connect at-risk youth to various community social service providers, provide alternatives to crime activities, and teach conflict resolution skills.
Contact: Ms. Jane Hess; 614/345-6166; 614/349-9894 (fax)

OH-18

Toledo:
Program: Toledo Area Private Industry Council/AmeriCorps Serving Northwest Ohio
AmeriCorps Members: 34
Description: AmeriCorps Members will improve low educational achievement, violence, and community health concerns by

tutoring youth, teaching conflict resolution skills, helping homeless families access quality health care, and supporting the needs of mentally retarded adults.
Contact: Gordon Kohler; 419/244-5900; 419/241-7865 (fax)

OH-19

Toledo:
Program: National Service Legal Corps
AmeriCorps Members: 5
Description: A team of lawyers and parale-gals will work to reduce homelessness in northwest Ohio, at both individual and com-munity levels. AmeriCorps Members will provide legal assistance to low income and homeless individuals to help them stay in their homes or acquire permanent housing. Members will also mobilize and assist com-munity organizations to increase the supply of affordable housing in the region.
Contact: Joyce Quinlivan; 419/255-0814; 419/259-2880 (fax)

OH-20

East Liverpool:
Program: Project W.I.T.T. (Wisdom is the Teacher)
AmeriCorps Members: 4 full-, 18 part-time
Description: AmeriCorps Members will work in the area of education. Call contact for information.
Contact: Patricia Holmes; 216/385-3580; 216/386-3715 (fax)

OH-21

Sidney:
Program: LINCS-Linking Individuals in Community Service
AmeriCorps Members: 16
Description: AmeriCorps Members will work in the area of education and human needs. Call contact for information.
Contact: Judi Overly; 513/498-4981; 513/498-7396 (fax)

OH-22

Columbus:
Program: Ohio Veterans Reintegration Project
AmeriCorps Members: 10
Description: AmeriCorps Members will

work in the area of human needs. Call con-tact for information.
Contact: To be determined--Vietnam Veter-ans of America; 614/228-0188; 614/228-2711 (fax)

OH-23

Toledo:
Program: YouthBuild USA Multi-State AmeriCorps Initiative
AmeriCorps Members: To be determined
Description: AmeriCorps Members will work in the area of human needs. Call Cor-poration for National Service for more infor-mation.
Contact: To be determined

OH-24

Youngstown:
Program: Youngstown AmeriCorps Rejuve-nation Project
AmeriCorps Members: 10
Description: AmeriCorps Members will work in the area of public safety. Call con-tact for information.
Contact: To be determined—Youngstown State University; 216/742-2371; 216/742-1527 (fax)

State Priorities:

No state-specific priorities. Local communi-ties identify critical areas of need if they fall outside the national priorities.

OKLAHOMA

State Lead Contact:

Nancy Deaver
Oklahoma Community Service Commission
1515 N. Lincoln Blvd.
Oklahoma City, OK 73104
Phone: 405/235-7278

1995-96 Programs

National Service Network

OK-1

Statewide:
(Rural areas)
Program: Association of Farmworkers

Opportunity Program
AmeriCorps Members: 61 Nationally
Description: AmeriCorps Members will
train migrant and seasonal farmworkers on
how to reduce exposure to pesticides and
improve farmworkers' access to other health,
education and supportive services.
Contact: Lynda Mull; 703/528-4141

OK-2

Tulsa:
Program: National Community AIDS Partnership (NCAP)/"Youth & HIV/AIDS Services Partnership"
AmeriCorps Members: 8 (40 Nationally)
Description: NCAP is dedicated to supporting high-quality education and service initiatives to fight the HIV/AIDS epidemic in the
United States. AmeriCorps Members will
provide direct care and assistance to HIV
victims and offer education for high-risk
communities.
Contact: Harry L. Brown; 205/458-2060

OK-3

Tulsa:
Program: Youth Volunteer Corps of Amer-
ica/YVCA Leadership Corps
AmeriCorps Members: 7 (107 Nationally)
Description: AmeriCorps Members will
develop, run, and enroll volunteers in service
projects including: summer camps, academic
enrichment programs, service-learning curricula, conflict resolution training, gang
alternative programs, and identification of
high crime areas.
Contact: David Battey; 913/432-9822

OK-4

Western:
Program: USDA Public Lands and Environ-
ment Team
AmeriCorps Members: 20
Description: AmeriCorps Members will ren-
ovate windbreaks originally planted by the
Roosevelt-era Civilian Conservation Corps
and will also carry out educational programs
on windbreak renovation and wood use.
Contact: Leroy Tull; 405/742-1207

State and Local

OK-5

Enid:
Program: Rural Health Projects, Inc./Okla-
homa PATCH
AmeriCorps Members: 23
Description: AmeriCorps Members will
improve health care in medically underserved areas by providing health care presen-
tations, promoting health care projects at
school fairs, assisting local health departments, and supporting organizations to help
community groups prioritize and address
their concerns.
Contact: Ms. Mary Jac Rauh; 405/234-6075;
405/237-3839 (fax)

OK-6

Oklahoma City:
Program: LIFE, Inc. (Love for the Independent Frail Elderly)—AmeriCorps/Ameri-
Cares
AmeriCorps Members: 25
Description: AmeriCorps Members will
increase the safety and security of older person's homes by organizing 275 volunteers to
install ramps and safety equipment, and by
cleaning and refurbishing the homes of older
people with disabilities and low-income
minority elders.
Contact: Ms. Rita Ulman; 405/235-3517;
405/235-4104 (fax)

OREGON

State Lead Contact:

Marlis Miller
PSU, 369 Neuberger Hall
P.O. Box 751
Portland, OR 97207
Phone: 503/725-5903
Fax: 503/725-8335

State Commission:

Governor's Office of Community College
Services

1995-96 Programs

National Service Network

OR-1

Statewide:
Program: USDA Rural Development Team
AmeriCorps Members: 43 (Pacific Northwest)
Description: AmeriCorps Members will help communities protect watersheds, improve housing, promote economic development, boost sustainable agriculture and respond to disasters.
Contact: Joel Berg; 202/720-6350

OR-2

Statewide:
Program: US Forest Service/Rural Conservation and Development
AmeriCorps Members: 5
Description: The Pacific Northwest will be one of 11 regions in the U.S. in which teams will serve. AmeriCorps members will facilitate project planning and development for grassroots rural development groups addressing timber and watershed issues. Members will work with existing rural development organizations to enable active local participation in all phases of activities designed to improve the livability of their communities. For example, one member will work through the auspices of the Rogue Valley Council of Governments with watershed councils to assist with identification and development of watershed enhancement activities, including grant writing, fostering community involvement and local capacity building.
Contact: Amy Wilson; 503/476-5906

OR-3

Statewide:
Program: US Catholic Conference/Fostering Citizenship
Description: Call contact for information.
Contact: Cecilia Arcivic; 503/249-5892

OR-4

Southern Oregon:
Program: USDA Public Lands and Environment Teams
AmeriCorps Members: 35
Description: Southern Oregon will be one of 32 regions in 21 states in which teams will serve. AmeriCorps members will serve in the Rogue River National Forest, replacing ten trail bridges crossing streams, maintaining 100 miles of high-elevation hiking trails, and enhancing spotted owl ecosystems at 10 locations.
Contact: Mindy Martin; 503/899-1812

OR-5

Portland:
Program: Youth Volunteer Corps of America/YVCA AmeriCorps Program
AmeriCorps Members: To be determined
Description: Call the Corporation for National Service for information.
Contact: To be determined.

OR-6

Troutdale:
Program: The Northwest Service Academy
AmeriCorps Members: 100
Description: The Northwest Service Academy was funded originally as a national demonstration project by the former U.S. Commission on National and Community Service. AmeriCorps members will serve in 10-person conservation teams. Four teams will operate from a residential site in Trout Lake, Washington, and six teams will operate from a non-residential site in Troutdale, Oregon. AmeriCorps members will focus on environmental restoration projects, such as building new salmon spawning beds, clearing forgotten trails, and rebuilding community parks.
Contact: Jon Stewart; 503/695-2292

OR-7

Statewide:
Program: Environmental Protection Agency—Green Lights
AmeriCorps Members: 10
Description: The EPA and BPA will work on an inter-agency program which will target 75 schools throughout Oregon in underserved areas. AmeriCorps members will conduct energy audits, educational workshops and installation of energy efficient lighting fixtures in the public schools. Energy efficient lighting will result in cost savings and

energy savings for the school districts.
Contact: Mark Ross; 503/230-5438

OR-8

Columbia River Basin:
Program: United States Department of
Energy—Salmon Corps
AmeriCorps Members: 24
Description: AmeriCorps Participants, most
of whom will represent the 5 Native Ameri-
can tribes in the region, will work to restore
the critical salmon habitat of the Columbia
River Basin while restoring Native American
culture.
Contact: Howlie Davis; 202/586-7970

OR-9

Portland:
Program: Green Corps' Neighborhood
Green Corps Program
AmeriCorps Members: 60 Nationally
Description: Splitting their time between
projects involving the home environment
and the community environment, Ameri-
Corps Members will educate and then activate their communities through three
projects: low income home weatherization,
lead paint abatement, and urban gardening.
Contact: Ms. Leslie Samuelrich; 617/426-
8506

OR-10

Portland:
Program: I Have a Dream Foundation/Ame-
riCorps Partnership
AmeriCorps Members: 15 (114 Nationally)
Description: Members will mentor and tutor
student "Dreamers" from disadvantaged
areas, giving personal guidance to prevent
dropouts.
Contact: Pamela Jacklin; 503/227-2439

OR-11

Tillamook:
Program: YMCA Earth Service Corps Fellowship
AmeriCorps Members: 40 Nationally
Description: AmeriCorps Members will
address local environmental concerns, coordinating park cleanups, urban gardening
projects, and environmental symposia.
Contact: Celeste Wroblewski; 312/269-0506

OR-12

Statewide:
Program: Youthbuild USA, Inc.-YouthBuild
USA Multi-State AmeriCorps Initiative
AmeriCorps Members: To be determined.
Description: Call Corporation for National
Service for information.
Contact: To be determined.

State and Local

OR-13

Bend:
Program: Central Oregon Community College Foundation/AmeriCorps Service to
Community Project
AmeriCorps Members: 40
Description: AmeriCorps Members, enrolled
in a community college, will be matched
with local agencies to coordinate volunteers
for one-on-one reading programs in 16 elementary schools; pair junior high age "at
risk" males with role models; and plan and
implement a water safety course for young
children.
Contact: Ms. Marilyn Karnopp; 503/383-
7214; 503/385-7950 (fax)

OR-14

Portland:
Program: Friends of the Children/Ameri-
Corps Friends
AmeriCorps Members: 20
Description: AmeriCorps Members will
develop one-on-one relationships with high-
risk, low-income children and their parents/
guardians, providing them with tutoring and
preventive education, increasing their
involvement in arts and cultural events, providing respite, and increasing parent involvement in schools.
Contact: Mr. Michael Forzley; 503/762-
4047

OR-15

Salem:
Program: Oregon Housing and Community
Services Department/Oregon Energy Con-
servation Corps
AmeriCorps Members: 42
Description: AmeriCorps Members will per-
form energy audits and weatherization

projects on 1800 housing units of low-income residents which will result in 15% energy cost savings to low-income service recipients. The AmeriCorps Members will be AFDC recipients participating in the Oregon JOBS program.
Contact: Mr. Alan Kramer; 503/986-2121; 503/986-2020 (fax)

OR-16

Portland:
Program: AmeriCorps Members for Neighborhood Safety
AmeriCorps Members: To be determined.
Description: Call contact for information.
Contact: Kelly Bacon; 503/248-3162

OR-17

Statewide:
Program: Oregon DHR/Reduce Adolescent Pregnancy Project
AmeriCorps Members: To be determined.
Description: Call contact for information.
Contact: Ruth Russell; 503/945-5759

OR-18

Statewide:
Program: Forest Grove High School/ "Options"—Forest Grove
AmeriCorps Members: To be determined.
Description: Call contact for information.
Contact: Dave Dorman; 503/359-2550

OR-19

Statewide:
Program: "Parents as Partners"—Springfield
AmeriCorps Members: To be determined.
Description: Call contact for information.
Contact: Charlene Renne; 503/744-6395

OR-20

Statewide:
Program: Learn and Serve Higher Education/"Community Planning—RARE Program"
AmeriCorps Members: To be determined.
Description: Call contact for information.
Contact: David Povey; 503/346-3812

OR-21

Statewide:

Program: Learn and Serve Higher Education/"Students Serving the City"
AmeriCorps Members: To be determined.
Description: Call contact for information.
Contact: Amy Driscoll; 503/725-8056

OR-22

Statewide:
Program: Learn and Serve Higher Education/"Partners in Education"/Lewis and Clark College
AmeriCorps Members: To be determined.
Description: Call contact for information.
Contact: Dale Holloway; 503/768-7175

OR-23

Statewide:
Program: Learn and Serve Higher Education/"Partners in Education"/Pacific University
AmeriCorps Members: To be determined.
Description: Call contact for information.
Contact: Ellen Hastay; 503/230-2914

State Priorities:

(Adopted March 29, 1994)
EDUCATION
School Readiness: furthering early childhood development. Examples include, but are not limited to:

Improving the quality and availability of child development programs by working in day cares, Head Start Centers, and pre-school programs.

Teaching literacy and other basic skills to parents of young children so that they can help their children learn.

Helping teen parents stay in school by providing needed services such as child care.

School Success: improving the educational achievement of school-age youth and adults who lack basic academic skills. Examples include, but are not limited to:

Working to keep students in school

Providing services in schools with high concentrations of low-income students.

Mentoring, tutoring, and providing after-school and summer learning opportunities.

95

Coordinating service-learning activities for K-12 students.

Life-long Learning: providing job and life skills to youth and adults. Examples include, but are not limited to:

Teaching life skills.

Providing job training and teaching high-wage employment skills.

Assisting with the transition from school to work.

Working to raise adult literacy.

ENVIRONMENT
Community Livability: preserving and enhancing quality of life. Examples include, but are not limited to:

Reducing waste through energy efficiency, recycling and other conservation efforts.

Revitalizing neighborhoods by removing blight, abating graffiti, and creating and maintaining recreation areas, green spaces, and community gardens.

Eliminating environmental risks through education, testing, and clean-up.

Natural Resources: conserving, restoring and sustaining natural resources. Examples include, but are not limited to:

Addressing the needs of forests, watersheds, rangelands, parks, rivers, streams, wetlands, and shorelands.

Improving air and water quality.

HUMAN
Health: providing health care. Examples include, but are not limited to:

Providing treatment for drug, alcohol and domestic abuse.

Working to curb teen pregnancy.

Promoting good health and wellness and offering preventive health services.

Housing: providing affordable housing.
Emergency Services: assisting persons in need of basic necessities. Examples include, but are not limited to:

Operating food banks and working to abate hunger,

Helping people who are homeless by providing shelter support,

Renovating and Rehabilitating low-income housing.

Employment Support: assisting persons seeking adequate employment. Examples include, but are not limited to:

Providing child care.

Providing transportation to and from work.

Providing job training services.

Supporting efforts to create jobs and develop local economies.

PUBLIC SAFETY
Crime and Violence Prevention: working to prevent crime and violence. Examples include, but are not limited to:

Providing training in mediation and dispute resolution.

Organizing neighborhood watches and other neighborhood crime prevention efforts.

Providing training in personal safety.

Broadening cultural awareness and promoting acceptance of diversity.

Providing security and organizing efforts to prevent crime in public places.

Providing alternatives and opportunities for gang members and youth at-risk of becoming gang members.

Crime Control: coping with crime and violence. Examples include, but are not limited to:

Enhancing community policing efforts.

Strengthening innovative criminal justice programs.

Providing services to victims of crime.

PENNSYLVANIA

State Lead Contact:

John W. Cosgrove, Executive Director
PennSERVE: The Governor's Office of Citizen Service

1304 Labor and Industry Building
Harrisburg, PA 17120
Phone: 717/787-1971
Fax: 717/787-9458

Commission:

State Commission on National and
Community Service

1995-96 Programs

National Service Network

PA-1

Statewide:
Program: HHS—Administration on Developmental Disabilities
AmeriCorps Members: 19 part-time
Description: AmeriCorps Members will provide personal assistance services to increase the social and economic independence of individuals with developmental disabilities.
Contact: Jane Swan; 215/204-1356

PA-2

Allegheny:
Program: National Multiple Sclerosis Society/"Bridge to Independence"
AmeriCorps Members: 8 (144 Nationally)
Description: AmeriCorps Members, many of whom have Multiple Sclerosis, will work to build awareness about Multiple Sclerosis while coordinating volunteers in extensive living assistance programs—helping disadvantaged people to make it on their own.
Contact: Anne Mageras; 412/261-6347; 412/232-1461 (fax)

PA-3

Bethlehem, Pittsburgh:
Program: Summerbridge AmeriCorps Teaching Program
AmeriCorps Members: 68 Nationally
Description: AmeriCorps Members will recruit high school and college students to teach disadvantaged middle school students. The objective will be to improve their academic and leadership performance.
Contact: Harrisburg: Jordi Comas, Eleanora Holley; 610/865-8072; Pittsburgh: Jen Huret, Steve Morris; 412/521-6744

PA-4

Harrisburg:
Program: National Multiple Sclerosis Society/ "Bridge to Independence"
AmeriCorps Members: 8 (144 Nationally)
Description: AmeriCorps Members, many of whom have Multiple Sclerosis, will work to build awareness about Multiple Sclerosis while coordinating volunteers in extensive living assistance programs—helping disadvantaged people to make it on their own.
Contact: Debra Wall; 717/652-2108; 717/652-2590 (fax)

PA-5

Philadelphia:
Program: Green Corps' Neighborhood Green Corps Program
AmeriCorps Members: 60 Nationally
Description: Splitting their time between projects involving the home environment and the community environment, AmeriCorps Members will educate and then activate their communities through three projects: low income home weatherization, lead paint abatement, and urban gardening.
Contact: Kelly Wark; 202/547-9173

PA-6

Philadelphia:
Program: Habitat for Humanity International
AmeriCorps Members: 9
Description: AmeriCorps Members will help construct 40 housing units in a project that will involve county-wide officials and community members.
Contact: Cheryl Appline; 215/765-6070

PA-7

Philadelphia:
Program: Philadelphia Bar Foundation
AmeriCorps Members: 6
Description: AmeriCorps Members will be graduating law students who have accepted jobs at large law firms, but are deferring their entry for a year during which they'll work full-time at a local legal services program. During the deferral year, the law firms will advance half of the associates' first year salary.
Contact: Eve Biskind Klother; 215/238-6347

PA-8

Pittsburgh:
Program: Youth Volunteer Corps of America/YVCA Leadership Corps
AmeriCorps Members: 3 full- and 4 part-time
Description: AmeriCorps Members will develop, run, and enroll volunteers in service projects including: summer camps, academic enrichment programs, service-learning curricula, conflict resolution training, gang alternative programs, and identification of high crime areas.
Contact: Tim McElhone; 412/682-3031

PA-9

Pittsburgh:
Program: National Institute for Literacy/Literacy AmeriCorps
AmeriCorps Members: 15 full- and 4 part-time
Description: Designed to build self-sufficiency in traditionally disadvantaged communities, AmeriCorps Members will tutor welfare mothers, provide homework assistance to children, teach ESL classes and coordinate special activities like spelling bees and read-a-thons.
Contact: Donald G. Block; 412/661-7323

State and Local

PA-10

Ebensburg:
Program: Appalachia Intermediate Unit 8—PA Mountain Service Corps/Pennsylvania Mountain Service Corps
AmeriCorps Members: 42
Description: AmeriCorps Members will work in teams to assist students with disabilities integrate into the community, provide health screening and education to the elderly and preschool children, and design watershed projects in a vast, 10 county rural area through the cooperative use of volunteers.
Contact: Edwin J. Robely; 814/472-7690; 814/472-5033 (fax)

PA-11

Harrisburg:
Program: Visions International Inc./Inner-City Youth Works

AmeriCorps Members: 24
Description: AmeriCorps Members who are economically disadvantaged 16-24 year olds will build and refurbish low-income housing and strengthen neighborhood crime watches in the Allison Hill neighborhood of Harrisburg through a residential, year-long program.
Contact: Mr. Bruce Smith; 717/233-6676; 717/567-7834 (fax)

PA-12

Harrisburg:
Program: PA Association of Colleges and Universities/Pennsylvania Service Corps
AmeriCorps Members: 50
Description: AmeriCorps Members will work individually in schools, colleges, corps and community based organizations to increase the capacity of those organizations through direct service and the recruitment of additional volunteers, with the goal of building a comprehensive system of service in Pennsylvania.
Contact: Ms. Laverna Fountain; 717/233-8577; 717/233-8576 (fax)

PA-13

Harrisburg:
Program: Pennsylvania Campus Compact/PACU/Pennsylvania Service-Scholars
AmeriCorps Members: 140
Description: AmeriCorps Members will work in local community partnerships to implement literacy programs in homeless shelters, organize town watch programs, and provide free and low cost community health care services through this new part-time program involving current college students across Pennsylvania.
Contact: Frank Newhams; 717/232-4446; 717/231-2795 (fax)

PA-14

Harrisburg:
Program: Pennsylvania Conservation Corps/AmeriCorps Projects
AmeriCorps Members: 36
Description: AmeriCorps Members will participate in a pilot initiative to form a leadership cadre within the existing conservation corps program to perform a variety of con-

servation activities across the state.
Contact: Mr. Lou Scott; 717/783-6385; 717/787-9458 (fax)

PA-15

Knox:
Program: Keystone School District/Keystone Caring for Generations with S.M.I.L.E.S.
AmeriCorps Members: 28
Description: AmeriCorps Members will implement service-learning programs, design summer education programs, create and operate a child and senior care center, monitor water quality, provide environmental cleanup and design community education programs to serve 5,500 people in the Keystone school district.
Contact: Ms. Joyce Fosdick; 814/797-5439; 814/797-5439 (fax)

PA-16

Pittsburgh:
Program: YouthBuild Pittsburgh, Inc./Intergenerational Conservation Corps
AmeriCorps Members: 30
Description: AmeriCorps Members who are economically disadvantaged 17-25 year olds, will work with volunteer professionals to rehabilitate abandoned and dilapidated, low-income housing in the East End areas of Pittsburgh, while developing life and career skills.
Contact: Ms. Jennifer Henderson-Germany; 412/242-7709; 412/243-0644 (fax)

PA-17

Selisgrove:
Program: Union-Snyder Office of Human Resources/Central Susquehanna AmeriCorps
AmeriCorps Members: 38
Description: AmeriCorps Members will provide day care assistance for special needs kids, aid to homeless and low-income families, health and nutrition education, AIDS assistance, afterschool enrichment activities and school violence prevention programs across Union and Snyder counties.
Contact: Mr. John Messer; 717/374-0181; 717/374-2330 (fax)

State Priorities:

PUBLIC SAFETY

Crime Control—improving criminal justice services, law enforcement and victim services

Crime Prevention—reducing the incidence of violence

HUMAN NEEDS

Health—providing independent living assistance and home and community-based health care

Home—rebuilding neighborhoods and helping people who are homeless or hungry

PUERTO RICO

State Lead Contact:

Gary O'Neal
State Program Office
U.S. Federal Building
150 Carlos Chardon Avenue
Suite G-49
Hato Rey, PR 00918
Phone: 809/766-5314

1995-96 Programs

State and Local

PR-1

Arecibo:
Program: Youth Service Center, Inc./AmeriCorps Program
AmeriCorps Members: 20
Description: AmeriCorps Members will provide tutoring, peer counseling, and health education for children, adolescents with low educational achievement, school dropouts, runaway and homeless youth.
Contact: Nidra Torres Martinez; 809/878-6776/6

PR-2

Cupey:
Program: Luis Munoz Marin Foundation/Un Pedacito de Tierra: A Horticulture Demonstration Program for Community
AmeriCorps Members: 24

Description: AmeriCorps Members will develop at least 60 gardens in both urban and rural settings, assist community members in planting and maintaining gardens, design education programs around the beneficial uses of community gardens, and use "square foot gardening" methods to reverse environmental decay.
Contact: Ms. Gail Peters Mignucci; 809/755-7979; 809/755-0240 (fax)

PR-3

Ponce:
Program: Centros Sor Isolina Ferre, Inc./ Museum and Communities Working Together
AmeriCorps Members: 20
Description: AmeriCorps Members will prevent juvenile delinquency and uplift community pride using the arts as a medium. Members will design and provide arts appreciation, history and education programs, train youth as peer leaders, serve as mentors, and engage parents in program development and implementation.
Contact: Dr. Delia Ramos; 809/842-0000; 809/840-5020 (fax)

RHODE ISLAND

State Lead Contact:

David Karoff Director
Rhode Island Commission of National and Community Service
P.O. Box 2822
Providence, RI 02907
401/461-6305

Additional State Contact:

Gordon Evans
RI Governor's Office
State House
Providence, RI 02903
Phone: 401/277-2080
Fax: 401/273-5301

State Commission:

Rhode Island Commission for National and Community Service

1995-96 Programs

National Service Network

RI-1

Providence:
Program: Community HealthCorps
AmeriCorps Members: 15
Description: AmeriCorps Members will provide primary and preventive health care to medically underserved populations.
Contact: Mary Jean Francis; 401/444-0411 ext. 28

RI-2

Providence:
Program: Summerbridge AmeriCorps Teaching Program
AmeriCorps Members: 68 Nationally
Description: AmeriCorps Members will recruit high school and college students to teach disadvantaged middle school students. The objective will be to improve their academic and leadership performance.
Contact: Esan Looper, Cathy Sanford; 401/521-6744

RI-3

Providence:
Program: Local Initiatives Support Corporation (LISC)
AmeriCorps Members: 5
Description: AmeriCorps Members will work on affordable housing finance and development, community outreach and neighborhood planning, home ownership development and lead paint education programs.
Contact: Rochelle Bates-Lee; 401/331-0131

State and Local

RI-4

Pawtucket:
Program: Community Partnership
AmeriCorps Members: 14 full- and 12 part-time
Description: AmeriCorps Members will provide a range of services for educationally at-risk students of all ages, including preschool assistance, tutoring for school aged youth and adults, and referral services, all to create "learning communities" in the sister cities of

Pawtucket and Central Falls.
Contact: Adriana Leon; 401/728-1130; 401/728-1550 (fax)

RI-5

Providence:
Program: City Year, Inc./Making a Difference in Rhode Island Communities
AmeriCorps Members: 77
Description: AmeriCorps Members in this diverse youth corps program will tackle the needs of Rhode Island's neediest children by tutoring and mentoring; developing conflict resolution, diversity and AIDS/HIV awareness workshops; and operating afterschool and vacation programs for urban school children.
Contact: Mr. Chad Olcott; 401/941-4004; 401/941-7017 (fax)

RI-6

Providence:
Program: The Rhode Island Children's Crusade for Higher Education/The Rhode Island Community Mentoring Coalition
AmeriCorps Members: 40
Description: AmeriCorps Members will work in pairs to create mentorship programs to support educationally at risk elementary school children succeed in school and avoid alcohol, drugs, trouble with the law and early parenthood, all with the goal of increasing the number of college and work-ready youth in the state.
Contact: Dr. Michael Jolin; 401/277-6907; 401/861-5536 (fax)

RI-7

Providence:
Program: Providence Blueprint for Education (PROBE)
AmeriCorps Members: 22 full- and 22 part-time
Description: AmeriCorps Members will develop and support parent centers in Providence Public Schools.
Contact: Dan Challene; 401/454-1050

SOUTH CAROLINA

State Lead Contact:

Jean Moore
Governor's Office on Volunteerism
Office of the Governor
1205 Pendelton St.
Columbia, SC 29201
Phone: 803/734-0398
Fax: 803/734-0505

1995-96 Programs

National Service Network

SC-1

Statewide:
Program: National Multiple Sclerosis Society/"Bridge to Independence"
AmeriCorps Members: 8 (144 Nationally)
Description: AmeriCorps Members, many of whom have Multiple Sclerosis, will work to build awareness about Multiple Sclerosis while coordinating volunteers in extensive living assistance programs—helping disadvantaged people to make it on their own.
Contact: Nancy J. Holland; 212/476-0453

SC-2

Program: USDA Rural Development Teach
AmeriCorps Members: 37
Description: AmeriCorps Members will help communities protect watersheds, improve housing, promote economic development, boost sustainable agriculture and respond to disasters.
Contact: Joel Berg; 202/720-6350

SC-3

Columbia:
Program: City Year, Inc.
AmeriCorps Members: 55 (220 Nationally)
Description: Teams of AmeriCorps Members will comprehensively address interrelated community need.
Contact: Michael Brown/Alan Khazei; 617/451-0699

SC-4

Piedmont:
Program: Youth Volunteer Corps of America/YVCA Leadership Corps

AmeriCorps Members: 9 (107 Nationally)
Description: AmeriCorps Members will develop, run, and enroll volunteers in service projects including: summer camps, academic enrichment programs, service-learning curricula, conflict resolution training, gang alternative programs, and identification of high crime areas.
Contact: David Battey; 913/432-9822

State and Local

SC-5

Columbia:
Program: South Carolina Victim Assistance Network/SCVAN-AmeriCorps
AmeriCorps Members: 39
Description: AmeriCorps Members will conduct case progress notification, organize in violent crime prevention training and education programs, and set-up and manage support groups for victims.
Contact: Mr. Kyrill Kraeff; 803/737-8122; 803/737-8001 (fax)

SC-6

Columbia:
Program: University of South Carolina; AmeriCorps Project
AmeriCorps Members: 20
Description: AmeriCorps Members planning on a career in teaching will support and enhance existing P-12 service learning projects. Members will work directly with students on local community service projects and with teachers on translating these projects into the students' academic curriculum.
Contact: Dr. H. Larry Winecoff; 803/777-3084; 803/777-3193 (fax)

SC-7

Greenwood:
Program: Lander University AmeriCorps Project
Description: AmeriCorps Members will help residents of three neighborhood centers to access social services and deal with problems.
Contact: Dr. Samendra Singh; 803/229-8965; 803/229-8998 (fax)

SC-8

Columbia:
Program: Benedict College AmeriCorps Program
AmeriCorps Members: 60
Description: AmeriCorps Members will provide tutoring to elementary, middle, and high school students.
Contact: Regina Doster; 803/253-5347; 803/253-5194 (fax)

SOUTH DAKOTA

State Lead Contact:

John Pohlman
Program Director
Governor's Office
5000 E. Dakota
Pierre, SD 57501
Phone: 605/224-5996

1995-96 Programs

National Service Network

SD-1

Statewide:
Program: National Multiple Sclerosis Society/"Bridge to Independence"
AmeriCorps Members: 8 (144 Nationally)
Description: AmeriCorps Members, many of whom have Multiple Sclerosis, will work to build awareness about Multiple Sclerosis while coordinating volunteers in extensive living assistance programs—helping disadvantaged people to make it on their own.
Contact: Nancy J. Holland; 212/476-0453

SD-2

Statewide:
Program: USDA Rural Development Team
AmeriCorps Members: 78 in the 9 Flood States
Description: Responding to the environmental and economic damage caused by last year's flood, AmeriCorps Members will assess flood-relief needs, explain wetlands delineation to land owners and work to reduce ground water pollution.
Contact: Joel Berg; 202/720 6350

SD-3

Statewide:
Program: USDA Public Lands and Environment Team
AmeriCorps Members: 73 in the 9 Flood States
Description: AmeriCorps Members will engage a variety of flood relief work by assessing damage, restoring wetlands, and restoring flood control facilities.
Contact: Joel Berg; 202/720-6350

SD-4

Rosebud:
Program: HHS/Head Start/Family Serve
AmeriCorps Members: 10
Description: AmeriCorps Members will work in Head Start centers where they will assist with lesson plans, nutrition education, field trips and bus monitoring.
Contact: Gail Collins; 202/205-8347

State and Local

SD-5

Dupree:
Program: General Convention of Sioux YMCAs/Community Volunteer Corps
AmeriCorps Members: 16
Description: AmeriCorps Members will create safe havens and after-school programs in rural communities in the Cheyenne River Indian Reservation. They will tutor, coordinate teen support groups, and conduct workshops to reduce the incidence of violence involving young children.
Contact: Mr. Robert Randall; 605/365-5232; 605/365-5232 (fax)

TENNESSEE

State Lead Contact:

Carol White
Tennessee Commission on National and Community Service
Andrew Jackson Building, Suite 1400
500 Deaderick Street
Nashville, Tennessee 37243
Phone: 615/532-9250
Fax: 615/532-2989

1995-96 Programs

National Service Network

TN-1

Statewide:
Program: USDA Rural Development Team
AmeriCorps Members: 80
Description: AmeriCorps Members will help communities protect watersheds, improve housing, promote economic development, boost sustainable agriculture and respond to disasters.
Contact: Joel Berg; 202/720-6350

State and Local

TN-2

Knoxville:
Program: Knoxville-Knox County Community Action Committee—CAD/AmeriCorps Program
AmeriCorps Members: 20
Description: AmeriCorps Members will reduce violence in inner city communities and promote non-violent conflict resolution by providing life skills training, tutoring enrollees of adult basic education classes, providing conflict resolution training, mentoring, and providing independent living assistance to senior citizens.
Contact: Ms. Barbara Kelly; 615/546-3500; 615/546-0832 (fax)

TN-3

Memphis:
Program: Exchange Club Center for the Prevention of Child Abuse of Greater Memphis/ Project TLC:-To Love a Child
AmeriCorps Members: 30
Description: AmeriCorps Members will help break the cycle of child abuse by working as parent aides in private homes, and by conducting public education programs.
Contact: Ms. Barbara King; 901/323-5479; 901/396-7777 (fax)

TN-4

Memphis:
Program: Memphis City Schools/AmeriKids Project
AmeriCorps Members: 40

Description: AmeriCorps Members will tutor and mentor individual children during the school day and provide an array of activities in an after-school setting. A service-learning component will involve children and their families in community-based service projects.
Contact: Ms. Judy Faris; 901/385-4240; 901/385-4221 (fax)

TN-5

Nashville:
Program: Nashville Healthcare Partnership/ Middle Tennessee Community Foundation/ Nashville Health Corps
AmeriCorps Members: 40
Description: AmeriCorps Members will improve the health of children and low-income families by instructing families on proper nutrition and early childhood health, assessing family health risks, and increasing their access to health education.
Contact: Ms. Joanne Pulles; 615/259-4785; 615/256-3074 (fax)

TN-6

Nashville:
Program: Student Health Coalition of Center for Health Services/Student Health Coalition on Aging
AmeriCorps Members: 20
Description: AmeriCorps Members will conduct 30 health fairs at 18 senior centers providing health screenings, physical examinations, and health education workshops free of charge.
Contact: Ms. Barbara Clinton; 615/322-4773; 615/343-0325 (fax)

TN-7

Memphis:
Program: Porter-Leath Children's Center
AmeriCorps Members: 18 full- 4 part-time
Description: AmeriCorps Members will target the educational and parenting needs of 3-5 year old children.
Contact: Ms. Jane Watkins; 901/577-2500

TN-8

Memphis:
Program: Juvenile Court of Memphis/ Shelby County

AmeriCorps Members: 50 part-time
Description: AmeriCorps Members will provide court-ordered supervision to juvenile probationers.
Contact: Tati Guzman; 901/575-8863

TN-9

Nashville:
Program: Tennessee Department of Mental Health and Mental Retardation
AmeriCorps Members: 20 part-time
Description: AmeriCorps Members will directly assist families of children with serious behavioral problems.
Contact: Matt Timm; 615/741-3711

TN-10

Clarksville:
Program: North Tennessee Private Industry Council
AmeriCorps Members: 20
Description: AmeriCorps Members will work to increase students' academic performance through mentoring, tutoring, and counseling.
Contact: Jackie Jerkines; 615/551-9110

TN-11

Nashville:
Program: NashvilleREAD
AmeriCorps Members: 21
Description: AmeriCorps Members will work to improve family literacy.
Contact: Diane Wortman; 615/255-4982

TN-12

Chattanooga:
Program: University of TN-Chattanooga
AmeriCorps Members: 20
Description: AmeriCorps Members will provide educational and support services to children at academic risk.
Contact: Jim McDonell; 615/755-4307

TN-13

Robbins:
Program: Appalachia Habitat for Humanity
AmeriCorps Members: 8
Description: AmeriCorps Members will address housing problems in Morgan and Scott counties.
Contact: Biz Ostberg; 615/627-2507

TN-14

Cookville:
Program: Upper Cumberland Community Health Agency
AmeriCorps Members: 20 part-time
Description: AmeriCorps Members will work to lower truancy rates and increase academic performance.
Contact: Betty Vaudt; 615/520-0100

State Commission:

Tennessee Commission on National and Community Service

State Priorities:

Same as National priorities

TEXAS

State Lead Contact:

Randi Shade
Governor's Office, State of Texas
201 E 14th Street, Rm. 680
Sam Houston Building
Austin, TX 78701
or
P.O. Box 12428
Austin Texas 78711
Phone: 512/463-1814
Fax: 512/463-1861

1995-96 Programs

National Service Network

TX-1

Statewide:
Program: National Association of Child Care Resource and Referral Agencies/Action for Children Today! (ACT)
AmeriCorps Members: 15 (45 Nationally)
Description: CC&R's will educate the community about child care needs and identify critical issues. ACT will improve the quality of child care by increasing availability by 450 for infants, 1395 for school-age children, and will train 1215 child care staff.
Contact: Yasmina S. Vinci; 202/393-5501

TX-2

Alamo:
Program: Department of Interior/Rio Grande Ecosystem
AmeriCorps Members: 105 (505 Nationally)
Description: AmeriCorps Members will conserve and restore failing habitat in the Rio Grande River, monitor air and water quality, and research, map and survey endangered species populations. Returning Peace Corps Volunteers and AARP members will serve as on-site partners.
Contact: Sue Kemnitzer; 202/208-4009

TX-3

Austin:
Program: National Service Legal Corps
AmeriCorps Members:
Description: Members will address critical issues such as housing preservation, child care improvements and domestic violence prevention. In addition, members will advance efforts to end homelessness, ensure equality in education, and protect the environment.
Contact: Randall Chapman; 512/477-6000

TX-4

Austin:
Program: University of Texas at Austin/ AmeriCorps for Math and Literacy
AmeriCorps Members: 20
Description: AmeriCorps Members will work with inner-city children to help improve their skills in literacy, mathematics, writing and numeracy. Members will also provide family workshops to strengthen parents ability to support their children's school success.
Contact: Jackie McCaffrey; 512/471-3285

TX-5

Colonias:
Program: USDA Rural Development Team
AmeriCorps Members: 30
Description: AmeriCorps Members will help communities protect watersheds, improve housing, promote economic development, boost sustainable agriculture and respond to disasters.
Contact: Lorraine Clements; 817/774-1306

TX-6

El Paso:
Program: UT Health Science Corps Houston/UT El Paso Americorps Health and Housing Program Fellows
AmeriCorps Members: 3
Description: AmeriCorps Members will provide health services to immigrant communities while earning their Masters in Public Health at the University of Texas–El Paso. Services will include immunizations and health education programs. Health clinics will also be able to feed undernourished homeless children.
Contact: Ms. Marilyn Farber; 915/747-6611; Debbie Kimberley; 713/792-4264

TX-7

El Paso:
Program: Environmental Protection Agency
AmeriCorps Members: 20
Description: A multi-generational group of AmeriCorps Members will assess the strained water resource in El Paso, educate the bilingual community about its options in the face of the problem, and then implement a strategy to improve water quality by controlling sources of contamination.
Contact: Helga Butler; 202/260-4179

TX-8

Fort Worth:
Program: Arc AmeriCorps
AmeriCorps Members:
Description: Members will help people with mental retardation learn independent living skills. Service activities include assisting people with mental retardation in locating jobs, linking them to existing vocational support services and helping provide them with overall independent living assistance. Members will also help service recipients become more active in community life.
Contact: Dr. Sharon Davis; 817/261-6003

TX-9

Fort Worth:
Program: I Have a Dream Foundation/AmeriCorps Partnership
AmeriCorps Members: 15 (114 Nationally)
Description: Members will mentor and tutor student "Dreamers" from disadvantaged areas, giving personal guidance to prevent dropouts.
Contact: Melissa Ashworth; 817/738-0212

TX-10

Fort Worth:
Program: Summerbridge AmeriCorps Teaching Program
AmeriCorps Members: 68 Nationally
Description: AmeriCorps Members will recruit high school and college students to teach disadvantaged middle school students. The objective will be to improve their academic and leadership performance.
Contact: Jessica Slade, Carla Brumley; 817/731-0852

TX-11

Fort Worth:
Program: The Arc
AmeriCorps Members: To Be Determined
Description: AmeriCorps Members will help people with mental retardation live independently by teaching skills such as: food shopping and preparation, locating jobs, and linking them to existing vocational support services.
Contact: Nancy Bolding; 817/261-6003

TX-12

Fort Worth:
Program: United States Department of Justice
AmeriCorps Members: 30
Description: AmeriCorps Members will enhance the neighborhood environment through teaching crime prevention to children and working with senior citizens to prevent crime.
Contact: Karl Bradley; 817/877-5161

TX-13

Galveston:
Program: Department of Navy—Seaborne
AmeriCorps Members: 133
Description: This nine-month residential program will perform direct environmental service in Galveston Bay. The participants will receive a GED and the job skills needed to work in the marine industry.
Contact: Robert Hickerson; 409/740-4796

TX-14

Galveston:
Program: USDA Public Lands and Environment Team
AmeriCorps Members: 20
Description: By building wave barriers, AmeriCorps Members will reduce shoreline erosion, allowing for more permanent vegetation and an increase in the fish population.
Contact: Joel Berg; 202/720-6350

TX-15

Hidalgo County:
Program: HHS/Head Start/Family Serve
AmeriCorps Members: 15
Description: AmeriCorps Members will work with Head Start to provide care to children of migrant farm workers. Activities will include literacy tutoring, parenting skills, and facilitating needed health and social services.
Contact: Romeo Sifuentes; 210/722-5174

TX-16

Houston:
Program: ACORN Housing Corporation
AmeriCorps Members:
Description: Members will work with local agencies and organizations to help provide affordable housing opportunities to low- and moderate-income families.
Contact: Matthew Mapron; 713/863-9002

TX-17

Houston:
Program: Department of Veterans Affairs/ National Coalition of Homeless Veterans Partnership Project
AmeriCorps Members: To Be Determined
Description: AmeriCorps Members will help in obtaining needed medical care, drug abuse prevention and treatment, and vocational training for homeless veterans.
Contact: Richard Dick and Isaac Jones (VA); 713/660-4278; Bob Gibson (Stand Down Homes); 713/334-4789

TX-18

Houston:
Program: National Institute for Literacy/Literacy AmeriCorps

AmeriCorps Members: 23 Members
Description: Designed to build self-sufficiency in traditionally disadvantaged communities, AmeriCorps Members will tutor welfare mothers, provide homework assistance to children, teach ESL classes and coordinate special activities like spelling bees and read-a-thons.
Contact: Jeannette Manzanerro; 713/845-2528

TX-19

Houston:
Program: Teach for America
AmeriCorps Members: 85 (1000 Nationally)
Description: Responding to an acute need for educators and role models in underserved urban and rural areas, AmeriCorps Members will lend their diverse perspectives on education and introduce innovative teaching methods to the classroom.
Contact: Natasha Kamrani; 713/659-4909

TX-20

Rio Grande:
Program: Department of the Interior/Rio Grande Ecosystem
AmeriCorps Members: 125 (505 Nationally)
Description: The environmental goals outlined by the North American Free Trade Agreement (NAFTA) are the basis for projects to be performed by AmeriCorps Members including habitat restoration and ecosystem surveys.
Contact: Wendy Hansen; 210/630-4636

TX-21

Rio Grande Valley:
Program: Teach for America
AmeriCorps Members: 85 (1000 Nationally)
Description: Responding to an acute need for educators and role models in underserved urban and rural areas, AmeriCorps Members will lend their diverse perspectives on education and introduce innovative teaching methods to the classroom.
Contact: Heather Stewarti; 210/630-6781

TX-22

San Antonio:
Program: United States Department of Justice

AmeriCorps Members: 30
Description: AmeriCorps Members will improve the safety of neighborhood environments through the establishment of "safe corridors" to and from school and Town Watch groups which will aid in crime prevention. Public safety will be increased through recruiting youth for after-school programs and assisting in implementing more conflict resolution and mediation programs for adults.
Contact: Carolyn Pastel; 210/207-7615

TX-23

San Antonio:
Program: Youth Volunteer Corps of America/YVCA Leadership Corps
AmeriCorps Members: 8 (107 Nationally)
Description: AmeriCorps Members will develop, run, and enroll volunteers in service projects including: summer camps, academic enrichment programs, service-learning curricula, conflict resolution training, gang alternative programs, and identification of high crime areas.
Contact: Sallie Luedke; 210/246-9622

TX-24

Houston:
Program: National Multiple Sclerosis Society/ "Bridge to Independence"
AmeriCorps Members: 8 (144 Nationally)
Description: AmeriCorps Members, many of whom have Multiple Sclerosis, will work to build awareness about Multiple Sclerosis while coordinating volunteers in extensive living assistance programs—helping disadvantaged people to make it on their own.
Contact: Sandra Thompson; 214/373-1400; 903/984-6992; 214/373-7200 (fax)

State and Local

TX-25

Arlington:
Program: Community Services Development Center, School of Social Work, University of Texas at Arlington/AmeriCorps - University of Texas at Arlington
AmeriCorps Members: 24
Description: AmeriCorps Members will increase the educational success of students in North Central Texas by helping to prepare

children in Head Start for school, providing after-school programs for students, and tutoring high school seniors for the math and English tests required for graduation.
Contact: Ms. Mary Fulbright; 817/273-2084; 817/273-2087 (fax)

TX-26

Austin:
Program: The University of Texas at Austin/ The University of Texas AmeriCorps Project
AmeriCorps Members: 150
Description: AmeriCorps Members will work to decrease the number of students who are unable to successfully pass the state-mandated achievement tests by establishing an academic-based educational intervention and support program for students in grades 6-12 in mathematics, English, health education, and community safety.
Contact: Dr. Maria Elena Reyes; 512/472-3984 or 512/475-7340; 512/495-9916 (fax)

TX-27

Austin:
Program: TX Department of Mental Health and Mental Retardation/Project Connect
AmeriCorps Members: 108
Description: AmeriCorps Members will serve people with mental illness and mental retardation by education them about the selection of services that are available, assisting such individuals to live independently, and supporting the family as the primary mainstay for persons with disabilities.
Contact: Ms. Lori Reubush; 512/206-4764; 512/206-4711 (fax)

TX-28

Austin:
Program: Middle Earth Youth Options/ Youth in Education for Service (YES)
AmeriCorps Members: 30
Description: AmeriCorps Members will serve low-income young people in high-risk situations by operating in-school student assistance centers, providing conflict resolution training, assisting public housing residents to access community resources, and reducing pollution and waste.
Contact: Mr. Charles Moody; 512/441-4225; 512/447-5943 (fax)

TX-29

Austin:
Program: American Institute for Learning/
Casa Verde Builders Program
AmeriCorps members: 64
Description: AmeriCorps members will
respond to the lack of affordable housing in
low-income areas by building 24 energy-
efficient, environmentally sensitive homes
using least toxic materials and alternative
building methods, renovating and weatherizing 24 additional homes, and achieving a
13% drop in energy costs.
Contact: Mr. Richard Halpin; 512/472-3395;
512/472-3395 (fax)

TX-30

Austin:
Program: Mental Health Association in
Texas/Parenting Education Project
AmeriCorps Members: 77
Description: AmeriCorps Members will
reduce child abuse and neglect by identifying
and referring children with developmental
delays to appropriate agencies, providing
child care for parents completing their education, and instructing families about nutrition and health.
Contact: Mr. Allen Dietz; 512/454-3706;
512/454-3725 (fax)

TX-31

College Station:
Program: Texas Agricultural Extension Ser-
vice/South Texas AmeriCorps Initiative
AmeriCorps Members: 45
Description: AmeriCorps Members will
improve the natural environment of rural
unincorporated communities by organizing
project activities that include wellhead protection risk assessment, pesticide and fertil-
izer management, composting and recycling,
and organic waste management.
Contact: B.L. Harris; 409/845-2425; 409/
847-8548 (fax)

TX-32

Dallas:
Program: Greater Dallas Community of
Churches/Making Connections for Children
and Youth

AmeriCorps Members: 50
Description: AmeriCorps Members will
serve children living in poverty by offering
nutritious food and enrichment activities at
summer food sites, tutoring and mentoring at
schools and in after-school programs, providing violence prevention/conflict resolution activities, and facilitating access to
health care.
Contact: Mr. Thomas Quigley; 214/824-
8680; 214/824-8726 (fax)

TX-33

Dallas:
Program: Dallas Youth Services Corps/Dal-
las AmeriCorps Partnership Project
AmeriCorps Members: 40
Description: AmeriCorps Members will distribute food to elderly residents, provide
minority girls and young women with science education activities, assist physically
and mentally challenged people, tutor residents of a low-income housing neighborhood, and rehabilitate homes.
Contact: Mr. Patrick McNeil; 214/824-3972;
214/828-1916 (fax)

TX-34

El Paso:
Program: The University of Texas El Paso/
Alliance for Community Development
AmeriCorps Members: 20
Description: AmeriCorps members will
meet education and public safety needs by
tutoring 400 K-12 students to achieve a 0%
drop-out rate, tutoring young parents so they
can help their children through school, providing day care while parents receive tutoring, and involving gang members in conflict
avoidance/resolution training.
Contact: Dr. William Sanders; 915/747-
5666; 915/747-5905 (fax)

TX-35

El Paso:
Program: East Central El Paso Community
Development/Project VIDA
AmeriCorps Members: 20
Description: AmeriCorps Members will
serve the low-income area of El Paso by vis-
iting homes for immunization enrollment
and health education, tutoring children at

risk of school failure, preparing non-English speakers for school, helping the elderly with repairs, reporting substandard housing, and adding housing units.
Contact: Mr. Bill Schlesinger; 915/533-7057; 915/533-7158 (fax)

TX-36

Houston:
Program: SERVE HOUSTON/SERVE HOUSTON YOUTH CORPS
AmeriCorps Members: 60
Description: AmeriCorps Members will serve Houston by administering 200 immunizations, assisting 100 residential clients yield food for those in need, renovating housing in low-income areas, providing tutoring for elementary students, and staffing a crisis helpline for parents at risk of abusing their children.
Contact: Ms. Judy Findlay; 713/666-8600; 713/666-7488 (fax)

TX-37

Killen:
Program: Central Texas Armed Services YMCA Killen/(KISSS) Kids in School on Saturday and Sunday
AmeriCorps Members: 30
Description: AmeriCorps Members will reduce juvenile crimes by establishing a five-city area safe haven for young people, collaborating with schools, youth agencies, and law enforcement to identify local needs, involving young people from the neighborhood as volunteers, and counseling and mentoring youth.
Contact: Mr. Wayne Norman; 817/634-5445; 817/634-4202 (fax)

TX-38

Pharr:
Program: Community Advocacy of South Texas, Inc./Youth Harvest Community Services Program
AmeriCorps Members: 40
Description: AmeriCorps members will increase the educational success of 300 teenage parent, school dropout, expelled, or at-risk young people by providing one-to-one computerized instruction in basic education and pre-employment and work-maturity

skills.
Contact: Mr. Francisco Briones; 210/702-8014; 210/702-9469 (fax)

TX-39

San Antonio:
Program: Children's Association for Maximum Potential (CAMP)/CAMP AmeriCorps Respite Enablers (C.A.R.E.)
AmeriCorps Members: 30
Description: AmeriCorps Members will provide respite and home-care services for children with severe developmental disabilities and their families by providing recreation, rehabilitation, and respite services as well as assisting older clients to acquire independent living skills.
Contact: Ms. Sandie Gonzalez; 210/671-5169; 210/671-3290 (fax)

UTAH

State Lead Contact:

Michael Call
Utah Commission on National and Community Services
342 S. State St., Suite 240
Salt Lake City, UT 84114
Phone: 801/538-8611
Fax: 801/538-8660

1995-96 Programs

National Service Network

UT-1

Statewide:
Program: USDA Rural Development Team
AmeriCorps Members: 50 (Four Corners)
Description: AmeriCorps Members will help communities protect watersheds, improve housing, promote economic development, boost sustainable agriculture and respond to disasters.
Contact: Joel Berg; 202/720-6350

UT-2

Statewide:
Program: Navajo Nation Youth Conservation Corps

AmeriCorps Members: 40 (120 Nationally)
Description: Building self-esteem in "at-risk" youth takes a decidedly environmental slant with community revitalization projects focused on watershed and soil conservation, using both western and traditional Navajo technologies.
Contact: Jacques Seronda; 602/871-6592

State and Local

UT-3
Moab:
Program: Grand County Council/AmeriCorps Collaborative Land Management
AmeriCorps Members: 9
Description: AmeriCorps Members will recruit and organize community volunteers to restore the threatened Moab semi-desert habitat and educate recreationists to protect the land from future degradation.
Contact: Mr. Craig Bigler; 801/259-8372

UT-4
Ogden:
Program: Ogden City Target Area
Description: AmeriCorps Members will address the increasing crime rate of the central city target area by increasing the community policing presence.
Contact: Shanna Francis

UT-5
Salt Lake City:
Program: YOUTH FORCE: The Salt Lake County Serve & Conservation Corps/Parkview -Edison - AmeriCorps Team (PEAT)
AmeriCorps Members: 7
Description: AmeriCorps members will recruit and train tutors and mentors from low-income Salt Lake City neighborhoods to improve the academic achievement of at-risk elementary school age children. AmeriCorps Members will also work with the parents of the children to improve their parenting skills.
Contact: Mr. Richard Parks; 801/468-3604; 801/468-3602 (fax)

UT-6
Salt Lake City:
Program: Association for Utah Community Health/AmeriCorps and the Medically Underserved in Utah (AMUU)
AmeriCorps Members:
Description: Planning grant that will allow a Utah health collaborative to provide much needed health services to 12 rural counties. AmeriCorps Members will address barriers to effective health care delivery for individuals facing geographic, economic, social, and cultural isolation.
Contact: Anna Lopez-Erickson; 801/974-5522; 801/974-5563 (fax)

UT-7
St. George:
Program: Dixie College of Adult Education/Southern Utah AmeriCorps Education Program
AmeriCorps Members: 9
Description: AmeriCorps Members in southern Utah will work to improve adult literacy, assist adolescent parents in achieving their GEDs, and tutor children to ensure school-readiness. AmeriCorps Members will recruit and train additional community volunteers to increase the number of people served.
Contact: Mr. Brian Cheesman; 801/673-4811; 801/628-1286 (fax)

UT-8
Statewide:
Program: Davis County Conservation Corps
AmeriCorps Members: To be determined
Description: AmeriCorps Members will respond to the environmental needs of the National Forest and State Forest systems in conserving, sustaining and restoring natural habitat.
Contact: Donna Sato; 801/451-3231

VERMONT

State Lead Contact:
Kathleen Ferguson
Office of the Governor
Vermont Commission on National and Community Service
133 State Street
Montpelier, VT 05633-4801

Phone: 802/828-4982
Fax: 802/828-4988

1995-96 Programs

National Service Network

VT-1

Statewide:
Program: USDA Rural Development Team/ Winooski River Project
AmeriCorps Members: 2 (30 New England)
Description: The Winooski River Project was a Soil Conservation Service demonstration project in 1941 to stabilize the erosion in the watershed. The goal now is to examine those practices installed at that time to see what worked, what didn't work, and how we can learn from what was done. This will be done by physically examining the sites, looking at the vegetative and mechanical protection, and by interviewing past and present landowners regarding maintenance and personal observations. This will be a "living laboratory" on bioengineering. Results will be incorporated into new engineering techniques for slope, stabilization and erosion control.
Contact: Norman Smith; 802/878-7402; 802/ 879-3920 (fax)

VT-2

Program: USDA Anti-Hunger Team
AmeriCorps Members: 40 (150 Nationally)
Description: AmeriCorps Members will reach out to several Vermont Communities, encouraging eligible citizens to utilize such resources as food stamps and to increase the awareness and availability of other anti-hunger programs.
Contact: Barri Gladstone; 802/241-2577; 802/241-2593

VT-3

Program: USDA Public Lands and Environment Team
AmeriCorps Members: 20
Description: AmeriCorps Members will enhance recreational areas and their accompanying habitats on 300 acres of forest.
Contact: Keith Hughes; 802/287-2590

State and Local

VT-4

Brattleboro:
Program: VT Association for the Blind and Visually Impaired/Independent Living Project
AmeriCorps Members: 42
Description: AmeriCorps Members will serve as rehabilitation aides for visually impaired persons by practicing daily living skills with them like sewing, cooking, using closed circuit TV, and accompanying them to public places and meetings. Members will also perform routine maintenance duties for the low-income elderly.
Contact: Ms. Carol Poole; 802/254-8761

VT-5

Lyndonville:
Program: Lyndon State College/Northeast Kingdom Initiative
AmeriCorps Members: 23
Description: AmeriCorps Members will mentor youth who are runaways, homeless, or involved in Court Diversion programs; develop and train an independent living skills project for youth who are newly on their own; and teach first-time parents reading and positive parenting skills.
Contact: Ms. Anne Brown; 802/626-6357; 802/626-9770 (fax)

VT-6

Randolph:
Program: Vermont Rural Fire Protection Project
AmeriCorps Members: 3
Description: The Purpose of the Rural Fire Protection project is to work with 40 of Vermont's rural fire departments to: 1. provide skills and technical information to help develop comprehensive fire protection plans; 2. implement fire protection plans; and 3. install improvement to enhance capabilities in reducing fire losses.
Contact: Dennis Borchardt; 802/728-9526

VIRGINIA

State Lead Contact:

Katie Noyes Campbell
Virginia Office of Volunteerism
730 East Broad Street
9th Floor
Richmond, VA 23219
Phone: 804/692-1952
Fax: 804/692-1949

1995-96 Programs

National Service Network

VA-1

Statewide:
Program: USDA Rural Development Team
AmeriCorps Members: 80 (Appalachia)
Description: AmeriCorps Members will help communities protect watersheds, improve housing, promote economic development, boost sustainable agriculture and respond to disasters.
Contact: Joel Berg; 202/720-6350

VA-2

Blue Ridge:
Program: National Multiple Sclerosis Society/"Bridge to Independence"
AmeriCorps Members: 8 (144 Nationally)
Description: AmeriCorps Members, many of whom have Multiple Sclerosis, will work to build awareness about Multiple Sclerosis while coordinating volunteers in extensive living assistance programs—helping disadvantaged people to make it on their own.
Contact: Beth Word; 804/971-8010; 804/979-4475

VA-3

Loudon County:
Program: Mid-Atlantic Network of Youth and Family Services/MANY Youth and Community Development Corps
AmeriCorps Members: 20
Description: AmeriCorps Members will facilitate a runaway youth and homeless youth service project aimed at promoting youth development through community service. This program will meet the dual needs of community assistance and self-esteem

building for the youth it involves.
Contact: Jerry Tracy; 703/771-5300

VA-4

Richmond:
Program: AmeriCorps/USDA—Public Lands & Environmental Team
AmeriCorps Members: 27
Description: The U.S Department of Agriculture works to improve farm income and develop markets for agricultural products abroad; administers rural development and conservation programs; addresses issues of poverty and grading services to safeguard and ensure standards for food quality. The Public Lands and Environment Team is one of the three AmeriCorps programs run by the United States Department of Agriculture. The public lands and environment team will run pilot projects at 32 rural and urban sites in 21 states. A diverse group of AmeriCorps Members will help solve local environmental problems, repair and upgrade community facilities, promote sustainable farming, conduct environmental education seminars, and preserve and restore national forests.
Contact: Jim Anderson; 804/287-1550; Lisa Sizemore; 804/287-1680

State and Local

VA-5

Alexandria:
Program: Northern Virginia Urban League, Inc./Service to Alexandria
AmeriCorps Members: 20
Description: AmeriCorps members will rehabilitate, revitalize and maintain public housing units in their own communities.
Contact: Deborah Brown-Anderson or Tasa Hardaway; 703/836-2858; 703/836-8948 (fax)

VA-6

Fredericksburg:
Program: Rappahannock AmeriCorps Project
AmeriCorps Members: 34 part-time, 3 full-time
Description: AmeriCorps Members will provide tutoring and mentoring services to improve the academic success of at-risk mid-

dle school and high school students.
Contact: Tony Hooper; 703/371-8233; 703/372-8758

VA-7

Norfolk:
Program: Urban League of Hampton Roads
Description: AmeriCorps Members will develop two "freedom schools" in Norfolk for youth 5-18 with low academic achievement.
Contact: Winnifred Tate; 804/627-0846; 804/847-8016 (fax)

VA-8

Richlands:
Program: Southwest Virginia Community College/SVCC AmeriCorps Tutoring Program
AmeriCorps Members: 40
Description: AmeriCorps Members will tutor elementary and middle school students in schools with high concentrations of low-income students. Members will implement tutoring services and provide afterschool and summer learning opportunities for selected students.
Contact: Ms. Karen Hudson; 703/964-7236; 703/964-9307 (fax)

VA-9

Richmond:
Program: Virginia Commonwealth University/VCU AmeriCorps
AmeriCorps Members: 36
Description: AmeriCorps members will serve as outreach workers for community based organizations providing tutoring/mentoring; parenting skills workshops; physical examinations and immunizations for at-risk preschool children; prenatal health care to pregnant teenagers; and conflict resolution training.
Contact: Ms. Sue Ann Messmer; 804/828-8418; 804/828-8172 (fax)

VA-10

Richmond:
Program: Virginia Department of Criminal Justice Service/AmeriCorps Crime Victim Assistance Program
AmeriCorps Members:

Description: Planning grant to develop a program that will increase victim/witness program volunteers. Activities include a survey of victim/witness program volunteer placements, development of a position description, and development of a practical victims' services skills development curriculum.
Contact: Ms. Mandie Patterson; 804/786-4000; 804/371-8981 (fax)

WASHINGTON

State Lead Contact:

Bill Basl
Washington Commission on National and Community Services
Insurance Building, Rm. 100
#43113
Office of the Governor
Legislative Building
Olympia, WA 98504
Phone: 360/586-8292

1995-96 Programs

National Service Network

WA-1

Statewide:
Program: USDA Public Lands and Environment Team
AmeriCorps Members: 32
Description: AmeriCorps Members will carry out a number of protective restoration projects including erosion control and planting along salmon bearing streams in addition to caring for recreation areas.
Contact: Joel Berg; 202/720-6350

WA-2

Program: USDA Rural Development Team
AmeriCorps Members: 43 (Pacific Northwest)
Description: AmeriCorps Members will help communities protect watersheds, improve housing, promote economic development, boost sustainable agriculture and respond to disasters.
Contact: Joel Berg; 202/720-6350

WA-3

Columbia River Basin:
Program: United States Department of
Energy—Salmon Corps
AmeriCorps Members: 24 Nationally
Description: AmeriCorps Participants, most
of whom will represent the 5 Native Ameri-
can tribes in the region, will work to restore
the critical salmon habitat of the Columbia
River Basin while restoring Native American
culture.
Contact: Howlie Davis; 202/586-7970

WA-4

Olympia:
Program: Department of Transportation
AmeriCorps Members: 20
Description: Independent living needs of the
elderly and disabled will be addressed
through education about public transportation between home and care facilities. AmeriCorps Members will accompany the elderly
population to theses facilities after dark.
Contact: Dave Broom; 206/438-4009

WA-5

Pierce County:
Program: Environmental Protection Agency
AmeriCorps Members: 40 Nationally
Description: AmeriCorps Members will
restore the national environment of urban
waterways, perform radon testing, and provide training on techniques to prevent lead
poisoning.
Contact: Helga Butler; 202/260-4179

WA-6

Seattle:
Program: National Council of the Churches
of Christ in the USA/Ecumenical Program
for Urban Service
AmeriCorps Members: 15
Description: AmeriCorps Members will help
homeless youth meet basic needs for food,
clothing, housing and health care while
building community awareness of homelessness and supporting after-school programs
for elementary age children.
Contact: Rev. Elaine J. Stanovsky; 206/525-
1213

WA-7

Seattle:
Program: National Institute for Literacy/Lit-
eracy AmeriCorps
AmeriCorps Members: 14
Description: Backed by a partnership
between Federal agencies and literacy
groups, AmeriCorps Members will confront
the debilitating literacy problem. In Seattle,
AmeriCorps Members will facilitate innovative ESL programs as part of a student speakers bureau.
Contact: Edith Johnson; 206/386-4661

WA-8

Seattle:
Program: Teach for America
AmeriCorps Members: 65 (1000 Nationally)
Description: Responding to an acute need
for educators and role models in underserved
urban and rural areas, AmeriCorps Members
will lend their diverse perspectives on education and introduce innovative teaching methods to the classroom.
Contact: Wendy Kopp; 212/432-1272

WA-9

Seattle:
Program: U. S. Department of Justice
AmeriCorps Members: 30
Description: AmeriCorps Members will be
placed in schools to help teach crime prevention to children through conflict resolution
techniques. Neighborhood environments will
be enhanced through empowerment strategies aimed at linking policy and neighborhood residents through law enforcement,
community policing, prevention, intervention, treatment and economic revitalization.
Contact: Dan Fleissner; 206/684-5758

WA-10

Seattle:
Program: YMCA Earth Service Corps Fellowship
AmeriCorps Members: 40 Nationally
Description: AmeriCorps Members will
address local environmental concerns, coordinating park cleanups, urban gardening
projects, and environmental symposia.
Contact: Celeste Wroblewski; 312/269-0506

WA-11

Seattle:
Program: Youth Volunteer Corps of America/YVCA Leadership Corps
AmeriCorps Members: 6 (107 Nationally)
Description: AmeriCorps Members will develop, run, and enroll volunteers in service projects including: summer camps, academic enrichment programs, service-learning curricula, conflict resolution training, gang alternative programs, and identification of high crime areas.
Contact: David Battey; 913/432-9822

WA-12

Spokane:
Program: National Multiple Sclerosis Society/"Bridge to Independence"
AmeriCorps Members: 8 (144 Nationally)
Description: AmeriCorps Members, many of whom have Multiple Sclerosis, will work to build awareness about Multiple Sclerosis while coordinating volunteers in extensive living assistance programs—helping disadvantaged people to make it on their own.
Contact: Nancy J. Holland; 212/476-0453

WA-13

Tacoma:
Program: AIDS Partnership (NCAP)/ "Youth & HIV/AIDS Services Partnership"
AmeriCorps Members: 8 (40 Nationally)
Description: NCAP is dedicated to supporting high-quality education and service initiatives to fight the HIV/AIDS epidemic in the United States. AmeriCorps Members will provide direct care and assistance to HIV victims and offer education for high-risk communities.
Contact: Harry L. Brown; 205/458-2060

State and Local

WA-14

Everett:
Program: YMCA of Snohomish County/ Snohomish County Youth Reconnection Program
AmeriCorps Members:
Description: Planning grant will enable AmeriCorps Members to tutor, mentor and counsel drop-out or expelled youth in order to reconnect them with their schools and their communities.
Contact: Ms. Maddie Metzer-Oft; 206/258-9211; 206/259-2328 (fax)

WA-15

Mountlake Terrace:
Program: Neutral Zone/Neutral Zone YouthCorp Peer Development and Education Program
AmeriCorps Members: 35
Description: AmeriCorps Members will expand to seven days a week a late night program for at-risk youth. Members will provide substance abuse counseling, conflict resolution training, and peer mentoring and tutoring. These activities will focus on helping high school drop-outs attain their high school diploma or G.E.D.
Contact: Ms. Candice Johns; 206/487-1166; 206/485-1218 (fax)

WA-16

Olympia:
Program: Community Youth Services/AmeriCorps Youth in Service
AmeriCorps Members: 37
Description: AmeriCorps Members will teach conflict resolution to and tutor "at-risk" children in 8 schools; provide front line gang intervention; implement after-school, late night and summer recreation programs to rural and Native American youth; and provide independent living support to mentally ill adults.
Contact: Ms. Paula Rauen; 206/943-0780; 206/943-0784 (fax)

WA-17

Olympia:
Program: Washington State Employment Security Department/Washington AmeriCorps
AmeriCorps Members: 300
Description: AmeriCorps Members will work in 14 agencies across the state on a wide range of service projects including developing a statewide literacy initiative for recent immigrants, providing at-risk youth with service alternatives to gang activity, and concentrating services to a needy, isolated Indian Reservation.

Contact: Mr. David Broom; 206/438-4009; 206/459-6022 (fax)

WA-18

Olympia:
Program: Department of Ecology/Washington Conservation Corps/Educational Conservation Corps
AmeriCorps Members: 100
Description: AmeriCorps Members will rehabilitate damaged watersheds and build fences to prevent further erosion, to address the problems of lower water quality, a reduced salmon population, and a threatened economic base in more than 20 Washington counties.
Contact: Mr. Robert Spath; 206/407-6936; 206/407-6902 (fax)

WA-19

Pasco:
Program: Pasco School District #1/Regional Youth Service Corps
AmeriCorps Members: 20
Description: AmeriCorps Members will provide in-class and after-school support and instruction; engage students in service-learning activities; provide emergency assistance to disabled elderly; and mobilize citizens to make physical improvements to their neighborhoods through the Adopt-A-Block program.
Contact: Mr. Stephen Harrell; 509/546-0180; 509/546-2685 (fax)

WA-20

Spokane:
Program: Educational Service District 101/ Spokane Service Team
AmeriCorps Members: 30
Description: AmeriCorps Members will rehabilitate low-income housing units; construct new housing for emergency and transitional living; restore 5 miles of rivers; restore habitats for native plants, vegetation, and wildlife; develop recreational areas of 3 state parks; and improve 10 miles of hiking/biking trails.
Contact: Ms. Anne Millane; 509/456-7660; 509/456-2999 (fax)

WEST VIRGINA

State Lead Contact:

Jean Ambrose
Program Director
One United Way Square
Charleston, WV 25301
Phone: 304/340-3627
Fax: 304/340-3629

State Commission:

West Virginia Commission on National & Community Service

1995-96 Programs

National Service Network

WV-1

Statewide:
Program: National Multiple Sclerosis Society/"Bridge to Independence"
AmeriCorps Members: 8 (144 Nationally)
Description: AmeriCorps Members, many of whom have Multiple Sclerosis, will work to build awareness about Multiple Sclerosis while coordinating volunteers in extensive living assistance programs—helping disadvantaged people to make it on their own.
Contact: Patty Snodgrass; 304/768-9775; 304/768-9776 (fax)

WV-2

Program: USDA Rural Development Team
AmeriCorps Members: 80 (Appalachia)
Description: AmeriCorps Members will help communities protect watersheds, improve housing, promote economic development, boost sustainable agriculture and respond to disasters.
Contact: Patrick Bowen; (304) 291-4152; (304) 291-4628

WV-3

Morgantown:
Program: Project HEALTH
Description: AmeriCorps Members will work to increase wellness and prevention programs in schools and, work sites, and communities.
Contact: Rudy Filek; 304/293-2895; (304)293-8764

State and Local

WV-4

Charleston:
Program: Regional Family Resource Network/West Virginia Collaborative for AmeriCorps
AmeriCorps Members: 18
Description: AmeriCorps Members will provide counseling, 24 hour hot-line services, community education, training, prevention activities, outreach and shelter-related services in the area of family violence.
Contact: Ms. Kim Barber; 304/340-3521; 304/340-3621 (fax)

WV-5

Sutton:
Program: West Virginia Coalition Against Domestic Violence/West Virginia Coalition Against Domestic Violence
AmeriCorps Members: 12
Description: AmeriCorps Members will tutor teenagers, implement family and recreation programs, develop family and youth support programs, conduct community organizing, perform outreach services, initiate environmental cleanup, among others.
Contact: Ms. Diane Reese; 304/765-2250; 304/765-5071 (fax)

WV-6

Morgantown:
Program: Energy Express AmeriCorps
Description: AmeriCorps Members participate in a six-week summer learning program focused on reading and sharing meals for school-age children in low-income and rural areas.
Contact: Ruthellen Phillips; 304/293-2694; 304/293-7599 (fax)

WV-7

Kincaid:
Program: Fayette Environmentally Safe Housing
Description: AmeriCorps Members will repair homes, distribute food, and repair and reopen a community or youth center and develop programs for the center in Fayette County.

Contact: John David or Kathryn South; 304/442-3157; 304/442-3285

State Priorities:

West Virginia intends to use the national priorities as outlined by the Corporation with the following added emphases that have been identified by citizens attending the public forums:

EDUCATION

(1) Life Skills (such as financial management, literacy, post-secondary education information); (2) Tutoring and Afterschool; (3) Job Skills (including career mentors, vocational training, job seeking skills); and (4) Child Care Programs.

ENVIRONMENT

(1) Water and Sewer (including water testing, system repair and river cleanup); (2) Natural Environment (such as trails, playgrounds and park improvement); (3) Recycling Programs.

HUMAN NEEDS

(1) Health and Wellness (including prevention, nutrition and access to clinics); (2) Housing (including renovation and repair); (3) Parenting; and (4) Elderly Care Programs.

PUBLIC SAFETY

(1) Conflict Resolution; (2) Domestic Violence programs.

WISCONSIN

State Lead Contact:

Martha Kerner
Division of Community Services
101 Wilson St., 6th Fl.
PO Box 7868
Madison, WI 53707
Phone: 608/267-2887
Fax: 608/266-7882

1995-96 Programs

National Service Network

WI-1

Statewide:
Program: USDA Rural Development Team
AmeriCorps Members: 78 in the 9 Flood States
Description: Responding to the environmental and economic damage caused by last year's flood, AmeriCorps Members will assess flood-relief needs, explain wetlands delineation to land owners and work to reduce groundwater pollution.
Contact: Joel Berg; 202/720-6350

WI-2

Program: USDA Public Lands and Environment Team
AmeriCorps Members: 73 in the 9 Flood States
Description: AmeriCorps Members will engage a variety of flood relief work by assessing damage, restoring wetlands, and restoring flood control facilities.
Contact: Joel Berg; 202/720-6350

WI-3

Madison:
Program: United States Department of Justice
AmeriCorps Members: 43 Nationally
Description: AmeriCorps Members will be placed in schools to help teach crime prevention to children through conflict resolution techniques. Neighborhood environments will be enhanced through empowerment strategies aimed at linking police and neighborhood residents through law enforcement, community policing, prevention, intervention, treatment and economic revitalization.
Contact: Bob Humke and John Olson; 608/266-6070

WI-4

Milwaukee:
Program: USDA Anti-Hunger Team
AmeriCorps Members: 40 Nationally (150 Nationally)
Description: Several local service agencies will join AmeriCorps Members in performing outreach on food assistance programs and will establish five new summer food pantries.
Contact: Joel Berg; 202/720-6350

WI-5

Milwaukee:
Program: YMCA Earth Service Corps Fellowship
AmeriCorps Members: 40 Nationally
Description: AmeriCorps Members will address local environmental concerns, coordinating park cleanups, urban gardening projects, and environmental symposia.
Contact: Celeste Wroblewski; 312/269-0506

State and Local

WI-6

Madison:
Program: Madison Urban AmeriCorps
AmeriCorps Members:
Description: AmeriCorps Members will strengthen the Madison community by providing employment opportunities, training, supervision, and volunteer opportunities to at-risk youth and by correcting building code violations for elderly home-bound individuals.
Contact: Jay Kiefer; 608/255-5044

WI-7

Kenosha:
Program: Kenosha Voluntary Action Center/Students and Neighborhoods Coming Together (SANCT)
AmeriCorps Members: 19
Description: AmeriCorps Members will recruit 220 community volunteers to work with 250 junior high students to prevent them from dropping out or falling behind. AmeriCorps Members will also provide orientation and training to these corporate, senior, college, and parent volunteers.
Contact: Gloria Ramirez; 414/657-4554; 414/657-1119 (fax)

WI-8

Madison:
Program: Operation Fresh Start, Inc./Operation Fresh Start Americorps
AmeriCorps Members: 16

Description: AmeriCorps Members, all low-income and from the 13 at-risk poverty stricken neighborhoods, will learn good work skills through carpentry, create low-cost safe homes, and improve their educational skills in this housing rehabilitation initiative.
Contact: Ms. Connie Bailey; 608/244-4721; 608/244-8162 (fax)

WI-9

Milwaukee:
Program: Open Door Community Center, Inc./Open Door AmeriCorps Project
AmeriCorps Members: 24
Description: AmeriCorps Members serving in teams will assist poor neighborhoods in Milwaukee to increase their safety through patrols and block watches, clean vacant lots, organize community gardens, operate adult literacy programs and conduct summer academic elementary programs.
Contact: Mr. Roosevelt Morgan; 414/344-2005

WI-10

Milwaukee:
Program: Milwaukee Community Service Corps/Citizenship Through Service: Milwaukee Community Service Corps
AmeriCorps Members: 15
Description: AmeriCorps members, primarily at-risk youth, will serve in teams throughout Milwaukee to build playgrounds, landscape urban vacant lots, tutor adolescents, assemble handicap-accessible picnic tables, assist recycling programs, feed the homeless, and do yard maintenance for isolated elderly.
Contact: Mr. Antonio Perez; 414/276-6272; 414/276-7330 (fax)

WI-11

Wausau:
Program: North Central Technical College/AmeriCorps Team-Marathon County
AmeriCorps Members: 15
Description: AmeriCorps Members will strengthen families through a partnership of sixteen community organizations. Activities will include support, intervention, and training in: child abuse, alcohol/drug abuse,

access to health care, domestic violence, and juvenile delinquency.
Contact: Dr. Russell Paulsen; 715/675-3331; 715/675-9824 (fax)

WI-12

LaCrosse:
Program: Youth Experiencing Success (YES)
AmeriCorps Members:
Description: AmeriCorps Members will help at-risk youth to succeed in school, explore career paths, and become more involved in the community.
Contact: Ms. Leanne Poellinger; 608/785-9936

WI-13

Superior:
Program: Superior Task Force for Community Service
AmeriCorps Members:
Description: AmeriCorps Members will develop a comprehensive program that actively engages young adults in creating responsive environments based upon trust, respect, and achievement through education, human needs and community policing activities.
Contact: Terry Hendrick; 715/394-6617

WYOMING

State Lead Contact:

Beverly J. Morrow
Wyoming Commission for National and Community Service
Herschler Building, 4th Floor East
Cheyenne, WY 82002
Phone: 307/777-5396
Fax: 307/638-8967

State Commission:

Wyoming Commission for National & Community Service

1995-96 Programs

State and Local

WY-1

Casper (Statewide):

Program: Wyoming Congress of Parents and Teachers (dba Wyoming PTA)
Volunteer Coordinating, Organizing, Recruiting for Education (V-CORE)
AmeriCorps Members: 41 Part-time
Description: AmeriCorps Members teach anger-management, substance abuse prevention and life skills programs in schools in order to reduce violence and prevent substance abuse. They also recruit and coordinate seniors, professionals, parents and older teens as volunteers in school activities. Statewide.
Contact: Mr. Bill Hambrick or Mary Hein; 307/265-2494; 307/234-4646 (fax)

WY-2

Cheyenne/Laramie:
Program: Laramie County Community College
Project UPLIFT: A Model for Community Service
AmeriCorps Members: 45 part-time
Description: AmeriCorps Members tutor and mentor a minimum of 100 at-risk elementary and secondary school students, children with disabilities, and limited-English speaking/functionally illiterate adults in ethnically diverse Laramie and Albany counties.
Contact: Mary Rusch; 307/637-2463; 307/637-2460 (fax)

WY-3

Cheyenne:
Program: AmeriCorps Victim Assistance Program
AmeriCorps Members: 20
Description: Helps to improve supportive services for victims of crime, including education about victims' rights, helping the victim through the court system, and counseling.
Contact: Michele John; 307/635-4050; 307/638-7208 (fax)

State Priorities:

Same as National.

INDEX TO PROGRAMS

This index is arranged alphabetically by program topic; the references are to codes assigned to programs, which include the state abbreviation and a numeric suffix.

MI-2
MI-4
MI-7
MI-9
MI-10
MI-13
MO-9
MT-6
NJ-4
OH-17
OR-14
OR-15
PR-1
RI-6
TN-8
TN-10
VT-5
VA-3
VA-6
WA-15
WA-17
WI-6
WI-10
WI-12

Business Development
FL-17

Child Care
AZ-6
CA-6
CA-40
CO-5
FL-10
FL-13
GA-9
GA-18
IL-10
MI-10
MN-14
MS-8
NC-11
NJ-1

NJ-10
NY-27
NV-1
OH-11
TX-1

Community and Environmental Improvement
AR-3
AZ-1
CA-10
CA-23
CA-37
CA-38
CA-39
CO-5
FL-11
FL-15
FL-16
FL-17
GA-13
IA-7
IA-8
IL-9
KS-8
KS-9
LA-12
MA-11
MA-12
MA-14
MA-20
MD-10
MI-5
MI-6
MN-10
MN-13
MO-11
MT-3
NH-3
NJ-5
NJ-9
NY-4
NY-21

NY-30
OR-1
OR-2
OR-4
PA-15
TX-13
TX-31
VA-4
WA-5
WA-10
WA-19
WI-9
WI-10
WV-7

Community Policing, Crime Prevention, Neighborhood Watches, and Anti-Violence Programs
AL-8
AR-6
A-33
CA-27
CA-32
CA-41
CA-44
CO-6
CT-11
DC-9
DE-1
FL-2
FL-10
FL-12
FL-13
FL-16
FL-17
FL-18
FL-19
FL-21
GA-15
IA-7
IA-8

HA-3
ID-1
ID-2
IL-12
IN-6
KS-7
MD-10
ME-4
MI-6
MS-4
NH-5
NJ-2
NJ-12
NM-3
OK-4
OR-4
OR-6
OR-8
PA-14
TX-2
TX-7
TX-13
TX-14
TX-20
UT-3
VA-4
WA-1
WA-3
WA-18

Construction
GA-10

Court Translators
GA-16

Creative Writing
CA-20
DC-8
NY-7

Criminal Justice
FL-18
FL-19

Developmental Disabilities
AL-1
GA-1
MI-12
MS-7
NJ-11
NY-16
OH-18
PA-1
TN-9
TX-8
TX-11
TX-27
TX-20
TX-39

Disabled Persons Assistance
AL-9
GA-18
GA-19
IN-16
KS-12
LA-12
MS-7
NJ-11
PA-10
WA-4
WI-10

Disaster Planning and Relief
AR-3
AZ-1
IA-2
IL-2
IL-3
KS-2
KS-3
KS-8
KS-10
MA-19
MN-2

MN-3
MO-2
ND-2
ND-3
NE-1
NE-2
NY-2
SD-2
SD-3
TN-1
UT-1
WA-2
WV-2
WI-1
WI-2

Domestic Violence
HA-2
IA-5
IL-13
IN-7
IN-22
LA-13
MA-9
MN-8
NH-4
WV-4
WI-11

Educational Programs (Academic and Vocational)
AZ-4
AZ-6
AZ-7
AZ-9
AZ-11
CA-11
CA-14
CA-17
CA-21
CA-23
CA-33
CA-47

Elderly and Homebound Assistance

Environmental Studies and Problem Solving

DC-2
DC-3
FL-4
GA-11
IN-3
IN-23
IN-24
MD-8
NH-6
NH-7
NJ-7
NC-4
NY-11
UT-8
VA-4
VT-1
WI-5
WV-7

Eye Care/Vision Screening and Visually Impaired Assitance
VT-4

Family Support
AK-1
AR-7
AZ-6
AZ-11
CA-36
IA-6
IA-8
MI-11
MS-6
NJ-9
WV-5

Farmworkers Assistance
AR-1
CA-1
FL-1
IA-1

IL-1
KS-1
MD-1
ME-1
MO-1
MT-1
OH-1
OK-1

First Aid Training
IL-11
KS-10

Food Assistance and Nutrition Counseling
CA-12
FL-14
MA-16
MA-19
MA-21
MD-16
MO-10
MS-5
NY-24
NY-29
PA-17
TN-5
TX-6
TX-32
TX-33
VT-2
WI-4

Gang Prevention & Resistence
AL-4
AZ-7
AZ-10
CA-40
CA-50
CO-2
CO-3
CO-6
FL-2

FL-10
IN-11
MI-2
MI-4
MI-10
MO-5
NV-3
OK-3
PA-8
SC-5
TX-23
WA-11
WA-16

Head Start and Pre-School Readiness
AZ-11
CO-4
CT-12
IN-15
MA-11
MA-17
MD-11
MD-16
MN-14
MT-2
NJ-9
NY-1
NY-24
NC-14
RI-4
SD-4
TX-15
TX-25

Health Care Counseling, Education and Delivery (including pre-natal care)
AL-2
AZ-11
CA-4.1
CA-8

MD-2
MD-12
MO-1
MO-8
MS-1
MS-2
NC-2
NC-16
NY-2
NY-13
OH-16
OH-19
OK-6
OR-1
RI-3
TN-13
TX-16
VA-5

**Immigrant
Assistance**
MN-8
TX-6
WA-17

Job Training
KS-9
MA-12
NJ-9

**Juvenile Justice and
Child Abuse
Counseling**
CA-46
FL-15
IN-7
NC-8
NJ-10
NY-25
TN-3
TX-36
WI-11

**Lead-Based Paint
and Other Poisons**
CA-10
CA-18
CN-3
DC-4
GA-5
MA-3
MI-7
MT-4
OR-9
PA-4
WA-5

Legal Assistance
CA-25
OH-19
PA-6
PA-7
TX-3

Literacy
AK-2
AR-2
CA-26
CO-4
GA-3
GA-11
GA-16
IL-13
IL-11
KY-1
LA-1
LA-3
MN-1
MO-7
MO-11
NC-10
NJ-9
NY-6
NY-18
NY-20
ND-4
OH-6

OH-16
PA-9
TX-18
UT-7
WA-7
WA-17
WI-9
WV-6
WY-2

**Migrant Workers
Assistance**
IN-18

**Multiple Sclerosis
Assistance**
CA-16
DE-2
GA-2
IN-1
MA-10
MD-9
MI-3
MN-5
MO-6
NC-1
ND-1
NJ-6
PA-2
PA-4
SC-1
SD-1
TN-11
TX-24
VA-2
WA-12
WV-1

**Native American
Communities**
AK-1
AK-3
ID-1
MN-9

WA-16

School Safety
CA-31
CA-38
CA-43
MA-20
NY-22
PA-17
TX-22
WY-1

Substance Abuse Prevention
AZ-9
CA-42
CA-44
CO-6
DE-1
FL-12
FL-13
FL-14
MA-20
MO-9
MO-11
NV-3
WA-15
WI-11
WY-1

Truancy
SR-5
LA-9
LA-14

Tutoring
AK-2
CA-37
CA-40
FL-14
FL-15
FL-21
GA-11
GA-14
GA-20

IA-4
IL-12
IL-17
IN-21
IN-25
KS-12
KY-4
KY-6
LA-9
MD-14
MI-13
MN-7
MN-8
MO-14
MT-6
NE-6
NH-2
NH-3
NJ-4
NJ-10
NJ-13
NJ-15
NY-5
NY-14
NY21
NY-33
NY-34
OH-12
OH-13
OH-18
OR-10
OR-15
PR-1
RI-4
RI-5
SC-8
TN-4
TN-10
TN-12
TN-14
TX-9
TX-26
TX-32

TX-33
TX-34
UT-5
VA-7
VA-8
VA-9
WA-14
WA-15
WA-16
WY-2

Urban Gardening
CA-10
CA-22
CN-3
DC-4
DC-5
FL-6
FL-15
IL-8
IN-4
IN-2
LA-12
MA-1
MA-3
MA-5
MA-6
MA-8
MD-3
MI-6
MN-4
MO-10
NJ-7
NY-11
NY-29
OR-9
OR-11
PA-4
PR-2
WA-10
WI-5
WI-9